THE GLOBAL CITY

THE GLOBAL CITY

NEW YORK, LONDON, TOKYO

SECOND EDITION

Saskia Sassen

PRINCETON UNIVERSITY PRESS   PRINCETON AND OXFORD

Copyright © 2001 by Princeton University Press
Published by Princeton University Press,
41 William Street, Princeton, New Jersey 08540
In the United Kingdom: Princeton University Press, 3 Market Place,
Woodstock, Oxfordshire OX20 1SY

Library of Congress Cataloging-in-Publication Data

Sassen, Saskia.
The global city : New York, London, Tokyo / Saskia Sassen.
    p.   cm.
Includes bibliographical references and index.
ISBN 0-691-07063-6(pbk.)
1. Financial services industry—New York.   2. Financial services
industry—Japan—Tokyo.   3. Financial services industry—England—
London.   4. International finance.   5. International economic
relations.   6. New York (N.Y.)—Economic conditions.   7. Tokyo
(Japan)—Economic conditions.   8. London (England)—Economic
conditions.   I. Title.
HG184.N5S27   1991
332'.042—dc20   90-23017   CIP

British Library Cataloging-in-Publication Data is available

This book has been composed in Galliard Typeface

Printed on acid-free paper. ∞

www.pup.princeton.edu

Printed in the United States of America

10 9 8 7 6 5 4 3 2
(Pbk.)

For Mara Van de Voort and Willem S. Van Elsloo
and to Suzuko Yasue and The Coalition for the
Homeless in Tokyo

Contents

List of Tables   xi

Preface to the New Edition   xvii

Acknowledgments   xxv

One
Overview   3

PART ONE: THE GEOGRAPHY AND COMPOSITION OF GLOBALIZATION   17

Two
Dispersal and New Forms of Centralization   23

Mobility and Agglomeration   24
Capital Mobility and Labor Market Formation   32
Conclusion   34

Three
New Patterns in Foreign Direct Investment   37

Major Patterns   37
International Transactions in Services   44
Conclusion   63

Four
Internationalization and Expansion of the Financial Industry   65

Conditions and Components of Growth   66
The Global Capital Market Today   74
Financial Crises   78
Conclusion   83

PART TWO: THE ECONOMIC ORDER OF THE GLOBAL CITY   85

Five
The Producer Services   90

The Category Services   92
The Spatial Organization of Finance   110
New Forms of Centrality   122
Conclusion   126

Six
Global Cities: Postindustrial Production Sites   127
   Location of Producer Services: Nation, Region, and City   130
   New Elements in the Urban Hierarchy   140
   Conclusion   167

Seven
Elements of a Global Urban System: Networks and
Hierarchies   171
   Towards Networked Systems   172
   Expansion and Concentration   175
   Leading Currencies in International Transactions   187
   The International Property Market   190
   Conclusion   195

PART THREE: THE SOCIAL ORDER OF THE
GLOBAL CITY   197

Eight
Employment and Earnings   201
   Three Cities, One Tale?   201
   Earnings   221
   Conclusion   249

Nine
Economic Restructuring as Class and Spatial Polarization   251
   Overall Effects of Leading Industries   252
   Social Geography   256
   Consumption   284
   Casual and Informal Labor Markets   289
   Race and Nationality in the Labor Market   305
   Conclusion   323

IN CONCLUSION   327

Ten
A New Urban Regime?   329

Epilogue   345
   The Global City Model   346
   The Financial Order   355
   The Producer Services   359
   Social and Spatial Polarization   361

Appendices

A   Classification of Producer Services by U.S., Japanese, and
    British SIC   367
B   Definitions of Urban Units: Tokyo, London, New York   369
C   Population of Selected Prefectures and Major
    Prefectural Cities   373
D   Tokyo's Land Market   374

Bibliography   383

Index   435

Tables

2.1 Foreign Affiliates, 1996–1998 (bn USD and percent) 28

2.2 Top Law Firms based on Percentage of Lawyers Outside of
Home Country, 2000 35

3.1 Average Annual Growth Rate of Foreign Direct Investment
from Developed to Developing Countries, 1960–1998
(percent) 39

3.2 Foreign Direct Investment Flows by Region, 1986 to 1997,
Selected Years (mn USD and percent) 39

3.3 Foreign Direct Investment Flows in Nine Industrialized
Countries, 1991–1997 (in reporting economies,
mn of USD and percent) 40

3.4A Foreign Direct Investment Flows to the United States by
Source, 1974–1997 (bn USD) 41

3.4B Foreign Direct Investment in the United States by
Source, 1994–1997 (percent) 42

3.5 Japan, United Kingdom, and United States: Foreign Direct
Investment Flows, 1991–1997 (bn of USD) 42

3.6 Japan, United Kingdom, and United States: Foreign Direct
Investment Stock, 1990–1997, Selected Years (end-period
stocks, bn USD) 44

3.7 Cross-border Mergers and Acquisitions by Region, 1997
(bn USD and percent) 44

3.8 Top 15 Buyer and Seller Countries Ranked by Value in
Global Mergers and Acquisitions, 1997 (numbers and bn
USD) 45

3.9 World Services Trade by Group and Selected Countries,
1997 (Major surplus and deficit countries reported by group)
(bn USD and percent) 50

3.10 Share in World Service Exports and Imports by Type of
Country, 1991 and 1997 (percent and bn USD) 52

3.11 United States: Share of World Trade, 1975–1997,
Selected Years (percent) 53

3.12 Japan: Exports and Imports of Services, Income and
Goods, 1991–1997 (bn of USD) 54

3.13 United States and Japan: Services to Goods Ratio Based
on Credits and Debits for Services and Exports and Imports
for Goods, 1990–1997 (bn USD) 55

3.14A U.S. Direct Investment Stock in Japan: Selected Service
Industries, 1982–1997 (bn USD, historical-cost basis)   57

3.14B Japanese Direct Investment Stock in the United States:
Selected Service Industries, 1982–1997 (bn USD, historical-
cost basis)   57

3.15 Top Eight Exporters of Services, 1996 (mn of USD and
percent)   59

3.16 United States: Foreign Direct Investment Flows in Services
Abroad, 1988, 1994 and 1997 (industry detail, bn USD)   60

3.17 United States: Business, Professional and Technical
Services Trade with Japan and the United Kingdom, 1995
and 1998 (mn USD)   61

3.18 Parent Corporations and Foreign Affiliates, by Area and
Economy, 1990–1998, Selected Years (number)   62

4.1 Financing Activity on International Capital Markets by
Type of Instrument, 1986–1996 (bn USD and percent)   73

4.2 International Capital Markets: Major Financing
Instruments, 1984–1997 (percent)   73

4.3 Borrowing on International Capital Markets by Main
Borrowers, 1984–1997 (percent and bn USD)   74

4.4 Japan, United Kingdom, and United States: Funds Raised
on International Bond Offerings, 1985–1997 (bn USD and
percent)   75

4.5 External Debt and Debt Service in Developing Countries,
1991 to 1999, Selected Years (bn USD)   75

4.6 Financial Assets of Institutional Investors, 1990–1997,
Selected Countries (bn USD)   77

4.7 Major Financial Crises of the late 1980s and 1990s   80

5.1 Number of Headquarters of the Top 500 Transnational
Firms in the World's Seventeen Largest Metropolitan Areas,
1984 and 1999   109

5.2 Growth in Backbone Capacity, 1997–1999   116

5.3 Cross-border Transactions in Bonds and Equities, 1975–
1998 (percentage of GDP)   119

6.1A United States: Growth in Total Employment and
Producer Services Employment, 1977–1996 (numbers and
percent)   131

6.1B United States and New York: Employment Changes by
Industry, 1977–1996 (percent)   132

6.2 Great Britain and London: Employment Changes by
Industry, 1981–1996 (percent change)   133

6.3 Japan and Tokyo: Employment Changes by Industry,
1975–1997 (percent change)   133

6.4 Great Britain and London, United States and New York,
Japan and Tokyo: Employment Share of Selected Producer
Services, 1980s and 1990s (percent)   134

6.5 New York and London: Share of Producer Services in
Employment, 1971 to 1999 (percent)   135

6.6 New York and London: Producer Services Location
Quotients, 1970 to 1999   135

6.7 New York, London, and Tokyo: Location Quotients for
Real Estate, 1970 to 1999   136

6.8 Manhattan, the City of London, and Tokyo's Central
Business District (CBD): Share of Selected Industries 1970s,
1980s, and 1990s (percent)   139

6.9 United Kingdom: National Employment Share of Major
Cities, 1971–1998 (percent)   141

6.10 Japan: National Employment Share of Major Cities,
1975–1995 (percent)   142

6.11 United States: National Employment Share of Major
Cities, 1977–1997 (percent)   142

6.12 United States: National Employment Share of Major
Cities in Producer Services, 1977–1997, Selected Years
(percent)   149

6.13 Location Quotients for Selected U.S. Cities, 1977 to
1997   151

6.14 New York, Los Angeles, and Chicago: Location Quotients
of Business Services and Engineering/Management Services,
1993 and 1997   152

6.15 New York, Los Angeles, Chicago, and U.S.: Changes in
Employment for Business and Engineering/Management
Services, 1993–1997 (percent)   153

6.16 Law Firms with Foreign Branches: Manhattan, Los
Angeles, and Chicago, 1988 and 2000   154

6.17 New York and Chicago: Employment in Selected
Industries, 1981–1996 (percent)   156

6.18 New York and Chicago: Employment Growth Rates in
Producer Services, 1977–1996 (percent)   156

6.19 United States, New York, Los Angeles, and Chicago:
Employment in Information Industries, 1985 and 1996
(numbers and percent)   158

6.20 United States: Location Quotients of FIRE and
Selected Services in New York, Chicago, and Los Angeles,
1985 and 1996   161

6.21 Japan: National Employment Share of Major Cities in
Selected Producer Services, 1985–1995 (percent)   162

6.22 Japan: Location Quotients of Financial and Service
Industries in Major Cities, 1981–1995   164
7.1 Capitalization in Leading Stock Markets, 1987–2000,
Selected Years (bn US)   176
7.2 Foreign Listings in Major Stock Exchanges, 1997 (number
and percent)   177
7.3 Top 10 Cities Ranked by Institutional Equity Holdings,
1998 (bn USD)   177
7.4 Institutional Investment in Equities by Region for the Top
10 Largest Cities by Holdings, 1999 (bn USD)   178
7.5 Top 12 Banking Centers Ranked by Income and Assets of
the Top 50 Commercial Banks and the Top 25 Securities
Firms, 1986 and 1997 (mn USD and number)   180
7.6 New York, London, and Tokyo: Share of World's 100
Largest Banks, 1988 and 1997 (mn USD and percent)   183
7.7 New York, London, and Tokyo: Share of World's 25
Largest Security Firms, 1988 and 1997 (mn USD and
percent)   184
7.8 United States, United Kingdom, and Japan: Foreign
Liabilities and Assets of Commercial Banks, 1992–1998 (bn
USD)   185
7.9 Top 20 Cities Ranked by Cumulated Assets of the 50
Largest Insurers, 1997 (mn USD)   186
7.10 Leading Currencies of International Debt Securities Issues,
1993–1996 (bn USD and percent)   189
7.11 Nominal and Inflation-adjusted Real Estate Prices,
1995–1998 (index, 1994 = 100)   191
7.12 London's City: Real Estate, Ownership, and Occupation,
1997 (percent)   194
7.13 London's City: Real Estate Ownership by Type and
Country, 1997 (percent)   194
8.1 New York, London, and Tokyo: Population and
Employment, 1977, 1985, and 1998 (numbers and percent)   202
8.2 New York, London, and Tokyo: Distribution of
Employment in Manufacturing and Service Industries, 1975
to 1998, Various Years (percent of total employment)   203
8.3 Manhattan: Employment Change by Industry, 1977–1997
(percent)   207
8.4 United States, New York, and Manhattan: Employment
Distribution by Industry, 1984 and 1996 (percent)   208
8.5 London: Employment Changes by Industry, 1981–1987,
1991–1999 (percent)   212

8.6 United Kingdom, London, and City of London:
Employment Distribution by Industry, 1981–1999 (percent)   213
8.7 Japan: Employment Distribution, 1975–1995 (in thousands
and percent)   220
8.8 Japan and Tokyo: Employment Distribution by Industry,
1980 and 1997 (percent)   221
8.9 Tokyo: Employment Change by Industry, 1978–1985, and
1986–1996 (percent)   222
8.10 Earnings Distributions in Selected OECD Countries,
1980 to 1992, Selected Years (percent of median and decile
ratios)   222
8.11 US, NYC, LA, and Chicago: Employment in Business
Services and Engineering/Management Services, 1993–1997
(percent)   228
8.12A New York and U.S. Growth in Earnings: Year-Round,
Full-Time Workers, 1979–1996 (percent)   229
8.12B Earnings Inequality: Year-Round, Full-Time Workers,
1979–1996 (ratio of 90th percentile earnings to 10th
percentile earnings)   230
8.13 New York City Median Hourly Wages by Occupation and
Industry, 1996–1998 (USD)   231
8.14 New York City Wage Ranges by Occupation and Selected
Industry, 1996–1998 (USD, numbers and percent)   233
8.15 London: Average Adult Full-Time Weekly Earnings,
1979–1999 (pounds)   236
8.16 Great Britain: Average Gross Weekly Earnings by Area,
1985 and 1995 (pounds)   237
8.17 Great Britain and London: Average Weekly Earnings by
Occupation and Sex, 1999 (pounds)   238
8.18 Great Britain and London: Average Weekly Earnings by
Sex, Selected Industry, and Manual/Nonmanual Occupation,
1999 (pounds)   239
8.19 Decile-based Measure of Change in Total Gross Weekly
Earnings for 1979 and 1993 (earnings revalued by median
earnings change to April 1993 values)   240
8.20 Polarization of Earnings in London and Great Britain:
1979–1995 New Earnings Survey (1979 figures are adjusted
by median income rise)   241
8.21 Japan and Tokyo: Average Monthly Earnings, 1977–1998
(yen)   242
8.22 Tokyo: Average Monthly Earnings by Industry and Sex,
1988 and 1997 (yen)   242

9.1 Unemployment, Employment & Underemployment Rates
by Sex, Age, and Race/Ethnicity: New York City, Nassau-
Suffolk, and Other Large U.S. Cities and Suburbs, 1999   307
9.2 Changes in Average Family Income in the N.Y.C. Metro
Area, by Family Income Quintiles, 1988–1990 to 1996–1998
(percent)   308
9.3 London: Population Projections in each ethnic group, 1996
to 2006 (thousands and percent)   312
9.4 Great Britain and London: Labor Force and Employment
by Ethnic Origin, 1996–1997 (thousands and percentages)   313
9.5 London: Ethnicity by Household Income, 1996
(percentiles)   313
9.6 Non-Japanese Residents in Japan by Country, 1998
(number)   315
9.7 Registered Foreigners in Japan, 1985 to 1996 (thousands
and percent)   316
9.8 Japan: Growth Rates of Foreigners by Nationality,
1990–1995 (percent)   317

Preface to the New Edition _____

I CAME at this new edition with a slash and burn attitude. My project was to strip the framework I had developed in the first edition from all the empirical materials describing the 1980s and have it confront the 1990s. As the book has become part of at least four specific types of debates, ensconced in rather distinct sets of disciplines and spreading over a large number of countries, it became simply impossible to address the issues raised by writing a few articles responding to my critics. And as the book continues to be used in classrooms all over the world and by a growing number of doctoral students all over the world, it seemed best to go through the painstaking work of sounding out the framework against the new evidence and against the astounding and rich body of critical work it has engendered or has been associated with.

The actual dynamics captured in the first edition of the book have kept on developing in often amplified and sharpened ways. Further, many researchers have explored various features of the model in many different cities in the world and thereby contributed enormously to advance the research agenda. This made the story I had tried to disentangle in the first edition come to life to growing numbers of researchers and certain sectors of the non-academic world, from activists for social justice to city mayors and financiers. To accommodate these various conditions and potentials, I have rewritten large portions of several chapters, particularly those dealing with the financial order, the emerging transnational urban system, and the growth in earnings inequality.

In this preface I briefly explicate the key features of the framework and I do this through a series of hypotheses—something I did not do in the first edition, which was in many ways a more elliptical treatment of the subject given its novelty. The framework I developed in that first edition was born of an ocean of often contradictory data and established "truths." At times it seemed an impossible endeavour. Since then the actual dynamics in these cities have given concrete contents to many of my propositions. In the first edition I was searching for the framework; in this second edition I am submitting it to new tests. When I came up with some of the terms that helped me formulate the analysis in the first edition, these were not always comfortable or persuasive. In this second edition they are a useful and by now comfortable heuristic. The work of running a global economic system, the practices of global control, the infrastructure of low wage jobs necessary to service the global economy, the emergence of a new spatial order in global cities, all these terms have now become part of the optic or the conceptual landscape through which I understand the condition of cities that are deeply articulated with the global economy.

In talking with both experts and general audiences around the world I have come to see that what the book did was to unpack the concept of "the city" and re-present it in terms of specific presences/data and dynamics. This is a partial representation, but one that captures the core. For experts, this re-presentation involved a juxtaposition of data sets and an extricating of information about the city which was not shared by nor usual for the various disciplines involved. For people at large, it was an x ray of the changes they can see on the street, but for which a new story had not been constructed. This was particularly so given the talk of the death of cities at the hand of telecommunications and the death of the local at the hands of globalization.

A New Conceptual Architecture

The globalization of economic activity entails a new type of organizational structure. To capture this theoretically and empirically requires, correspondingly, a new type of conceptual architecture. Constructs such as the global city and the global-city region are, in my reading, important elements in this new conceptual architecture. There have long been cross-border economic processs—flows of capital, labor, goods, raw materials, tourists.[1] But to a large extent these took place within empires or, over the last century especially, within the inter-state system where the key articulators were national states. The international economic system was ensconced largely in this inter-state system. This has changed rather dramatically over the last decade as a result of privatization, deregulation, digitalization, the opening up of national economies to foreign firms, and the growing participation of national economic actors in global markets.

It is in this context that we see a re-scaling of what are the strategic territories that articulate the new system. With the partial unbundling or at least weakening of the national as a spatial unit due to privatization and deregulation and the associated strengthening of globalization, come conditions for the ascendance of other spatial units or scales. Among these are the sub-national, notably cities and regions; cross-border regions encompassing two or more sub-national entities; and supra-national entities, i.e. global digitalized markets and free trade blocs. The

[1] Here Arrighi's analysis is of interest (1994) in that it posits the recurrence of certain organizational patterns in different phases of the capitalist world economy, but at higher orders of complexity and expanded scope, and timed to follow or precede particular configurations of the world economy.(See also Arrighi and Silver 1999).

dynamics and processes that get terrritorialized at these diverse scales can in principle be regional, national or global.

I locate the emergence of global cities in this context and against this range of instantiations of strategic scales and spatial units. In the case of global cities, the dynamics and processes that get territorialized are global.

The activity of naming these elements is part of the conceptual work. There are other, closely linked terms which could conceivably have been used: world cities[2], "supervilles" (Braudel 1984), informational city (Castells 1989).[3] Thus chosing how to name a configuration has its own substantive rationality. When I first chose to use global city (1984) I did so knowingly—it was an attempt to name a difference: the specificity of the global as it gets structured in the contemporary period. I did not chose the obvious alternative, world city, because it had precisely the opposite attribute: it referred to a type of city which we have seen over the centuries (e.g., Braudel 1984; Hall 1966; King 1990), and most probably also in much earlier periods in Asia than in the West (Abu-Lughod 1989; King 1990). In this regard it could be said that most of today's major global cities are also world cities, but that there may well be some global cities today that are not world cities in the full, rich sense of that term. This is partly an empirical question for me; further, as the global economy expands and incorporates additional cities into the various networks, it is quite possible that the answer to that particular question will vary. Thus the fact that Miami has developed global city functions beginning in the late 1980s does not make it a world city in that older sense of the term. (See also Abu-Lughod 1999; Short and Kim 1999; Sachar 1990.)

The Global City Model: Organizing Hypotheses

There are seven hypotheses through which I organized the data and the theorization of the global city model. I will discuss each of these briefly as a way of producing a more precise representation.

First, the geographic dispersal of economic activities that marks globalization, along with the simultaneous integration of such geographically dispersed activities, is a key factor feeding the growth and importance of

---

[2] Originally attributed to Goethe, the term was re-launched in the work of Peter Hall (1966) and more recently re-specified by John Friedmann (Friedmann and Goetz 1982). See also Stren (1996)

[3] We now know from unpublished papers and a variety of publications that by the early 1980s a number of scholars had begun to study cities in the context of globalization. I review the history of this new field of inquiry in Sassen (2001a).

central corporate functions. The more dispersed a firm's operations across different countries, the more complex and strategic its central functions—that is, the work of managing, coordinating, servicing, financing a firm's network of operations.

Second, these central functions become so complex that increasingly the headquarters of large global firms outsource them. They buy a share of their central functions from highly specialized service firms: accounting, legal, public relations, programming, telecommunications, and other such services. Thus while even ten years ago the key site for the production of these central headquarter functions was the headquarters of a firm, today there is a second key site, the specialized service firms contracted by headquarters to produce some of these central functions or components of them. This is especially the case with firms involved in global markets and non-routine operations. But increasingly the headquarters of all large firms are buying more of such inputs rather than producing them in-house.

Third, those specialized service firms engaged in the most complex and globalized markets are subject to agglomeration economies. The complexity of the services they need to produce, the uncertainty of the markets they are involved with either directly or through the headquarters for which they are producing the services, and the growing importance of speed in all these transactions, is a mix of conditions that constitutes a new agglomeration dynamic. The mix of firms, talents, and expertise from a broad range of specialized fields makes a certain type of urban environment function as an information center. Being in a city becomes synonymous with being in an extremely intense and dense information loop. This is a type of information loop that as of now still cannot be replicated fully in electronic space, and has as one of its value-added features the fact of unforeseen and unplanned mixes of information, expertise and talent, which can produce a higher order of information. This does not hold for routinized activities which are not as subject to uncertainty and non-standardized forms of complexity. Global cities are, in this regard, production sites for the leading information industries of our time.

A fourth hypothesis, derived from the preceding one, is that the more headquarters outsource their most complex, unstandardized functions particularly those subject to uncertain and changing markets and to speed, the freer they are to opt for any location because the more the work actually done in the headquarters is not subject to agglomeration economies. This further underlines that the key sector specifying the distinctive production advantages of global cities is the highly specialized and networked services sector. In developing this hypothesis I was responding to a very common notion that the number of headquarters is what specifies a global city. Empirically it may still be the case in many countries that the leading business center is also the leading concentration of headquarters, but this may well be because there is an absence of alternative locational options. But in countries with a well developed infrastructure outside the leading business center, there are likely to be multiple locational options for such headquarters.

Fifth, these specialized service firms need to provide a global service which has meant a global network of affiliates or some other form of partnership. As a result we have seen a strengthening of cross-border city-to-city transactions and networks. At the limit this may well be the beginning of the formation of transnational urban systems. The growth of global markets for finance and specialized services, the need for transnational servicing networks due to sharp increases in international investment, the reduced role of the government in the regulation of international economic activity and the corresponding ascendance of other institutional arenas, notably global markets and corporate headquarters— all these point to the existence of a series of transnational networks of cities. One implication of this, and a related hypothesis for research is that the economic fortunes of these cities become increasingly disconnected from their broader hinterlands or even their national economies. We can see here the formation, at least incipient, of transnational urban systems. To a large extent it seems to me that the major business centers in the world today draw their importance from these transnational networks. There is no such entity as a single global city—and in this sense there is a sharp contrast with the erstwhile capitals of empires.

A sixth hypothesis is that the growing numbers of high level professionals and high-profit making specialized service firms have the effect of raising the degree of spatial and socioeconomic inequality evident in these cities. The strategic role of these specialized services as inputs raises the value of top level professionals and their numbers. Further, the fact that talent can matter enormously for the quality of these strategic outputs and, given the importance of speed, proven talent becomes an added value, the structure of rewards is likely to experience rapid increases. Types of activities and of workers lacking these attributes, whether manufacturing or industrial services, are likely to get caught in the opposite cycle.

A seventh hypothesis is that the dynamics described in hypothesis six lead to the growing informalization of a range of economic activities which find their effective demand in these cities yet have profit rates that do not allow them to compete for various resources with the high-profit making firms at the top of the system. Informalizing part or all production and distribution activities, including of services, is one way of surviving under these conditions.

In the first four hypotheses, my effort was to qualify what was emerging as a dominant discourse on globalization, technology and cities which posited the end of cities as important economic units or scales. I saw a tendency in that account to take the existence of a global economic system as a given, a function of the power of transnational corporations and global communications. My counter argument was, and remains, that the capabilities for global operation, coordination and control contained in the new information technologies and in the power of transnational corporations need to be produced. By focusing on the production of these capabilities we add a neglected dimension to the familiar issue of the power of large corporations and the capacity of the new technologies to neutralize distance and place. A focus on the production of these capabilities shifts the emphasis to the *practices* that constitute what we call economic globalization and global control.

Economic globalization and telecommunications have contributed to produce a spatiality for the urban which pivots both on cross-border networks and on territorial locations with massive concentrations of resources. This is not a completely new feature. Over the centuries cities have been at the cross-roads of major, often worldwide processes. What is different today is the intensity, complexity and global span of these networks, the extent to which significant portions of economies are now dematerialized and digitalized and hence the extent to which they can travel at great speeds through some of these networks, and, thirdly, the numbers of cities that are part of cross-border networks operating at vast geographic scales.

The new urban spatiality thus produced is partial in a double sense: it accounts for only part of what happens in cities and what cities are about, and it inhabits only part of what we might think of as the space of the city, whether this be understood in terms as diverse as those of a city's administrative boundaries or in the sense of a city's public imaginary. Furthermore, some forms of this new urban spatiality operate today at a regional scale.

Structure of the Book

The structure of the book has not changed. It was my intention to stick to the framework in order to test it. But much of the detail in the first edition is replaced with new data and the discussion of the new research literatures in each of the fields involved. Further, to address the debates engenderd by each of the major parts of the book I have added several long new sections that engage these critiques both conceptually and empirically. In the first part of the book I have added sections on the meaning of the series of major financial crises we have seen since the 1987 Wall Street stock market crash; and on the features of the global capital market, including how it diverges from earlier historical global financial markets, especially at the turn of the century and in the 1930s. In the second part of the book I have added a long section on the spatial organization of the financial industry, a subject I began to develop in the first edition but which has remained under-researched even though my earlier treatment received considerable critical comment. Chapter 7 on global hierarchies has been largely rewritten to capture the emergence of a transnational urban system, with an emphasis on the intensifying of cross-border transactions among major cities. In Part Three of the book, chapter 8 on employment and earnings has also largely been rewritten. In the new epilogue I examine the major debates and critiques surrounding the first edition in the hope that this will illuminate the potentials and the problems that any new conceptual framework confronts.

This new edition could not have been written if the 1990s had not produced an explosion in the research literature on a broad range of issues I struggled with in the first edition. Many important contributions have advanced our understanding of many of the specific issues involved. I have tried to refer to this literature extensively. It covers many disciplines and originates in many countries around the world. I am deeply indebted to these scholars, including the many whom it was impossible to mention.

Acknowledgments

My single largest debt in the preparation of this new edition is to Kathleen Fernicola, a doctoral student in sociology at the University of Chicago. Without her intelligence, determination and talent, the work could have stretched over years and still not have gotten done. She worked on the massive task of updating all the tables. The work on Tokyo could not have been completed without the invaluable help from Professor Toshio Iyotani and Asato Saito; I also want to thank Professor Kamo from Osaka City University. The London team, all from the London School of Economics, included Miguel Jimenez, who was enormously helpful with the research on producer services, Francisco Mata Andrade, Shai Gross, Sarah Shousha and Maida Ahmad. I am grateful to all of them for their excellent work. Giselle Datz made all the difference helping with the analysis of the financial crises of the 1990s. No project can do without research assistants such as Harel Shapira and Lital Mehr and their determination and resourcefulness in finding particularly obscure items. At various stages, Nilesh Patel joined our efforts and I thank him for this. Ian Malcolm of Princeton University Press was very supportive throughout the various stages of this rather difficult endeavor. I doubt this second edition would exist without his efforts on its behalf. I also want to thank Bill Laznovsky, the Production Editor, for his help. Last but not least, I owe a big thank you to Lori Holland of Bytheway Publishing Services for her precision and helpfulness in producing this book. All errors are mine.

Acknowledgments

THIS BOOK is part of a project that began many years ago. There are, then, many persons and institutions to thank, many more than I could list here.

Financial support for the research and travel came from several institutions: the United Nations Centre for Regional Development in Nagoya, Japan; the Revson and Ford Foundations, for a project on the employment of immigrant women in New York that was central to my research on low-wage workers and informal labor markets; the Chicago Institute for Architecture and Urbanism, for research on social class and space; the Department of Economics of the University of Tokyo, for generous support with research assistants during my stay in Tokyo; the School for International and Public Affairs of Columbia University, for support on research on labor markets as part of a larger project funded by the Andrew and Flora Hewlett Foundation.

There are other institutions that were central to my work. The Social Science Research Council through the Committee on New York provided assistance in the preparation of a major paper on New York; the Economic Social Science Research Council of England supported an English-American team doing research on New York and London; the Department of Urban Planning at MIT set up a team of U.S. and Japanese researchers working on deindustrialization and economic restructuring; the Development and Population Unit of City College of London provided various kinds of assistance, as did the Bartlett School of Planning. Many staff members of the Greater London Council and the various units after its abolition were particularly helpful. In Tokyo, many individuals and institutions were extremely helpful and often crucial to the research: the Tokyo Metropolitan Government and several of its staff members were unusually supportive and provided much important information. I also wish to thank staff at the Ministry of Labor, Ministry of Trade and Industry, and Office of Immigration of the Ministry of Justice. I am particularly indebted to Kalabao, an organization for immigrant workers set up by daily laborers in Japan, the poorest workers helping the most vulnerable newcomers.

Many colleagues and friends, as individuals and as members of research teams, need to be thanked: Susan Fainstein and Norman Fainstein, Manuel Castells, Janet Abu-Lughod, Bennett Harrison, Michael Storper, Ann Markusen, Michael Smith, Kiriro Morita, Peter Marcuse, Ian Gordon, Michael Harloe, Nick Buck, Michael Edwards, Hidehiko Sazanami,

Toshio Iyotani, Toshio Naito, Mika Iba, Tokue Shibata, Haruhi Tono, Naoko Iyori, Mako Yoshimura, Munesuke Yamamoto, and many others.

Research assistance was a major part of this study. Michelle Gittelman and Peter Marcotullio were key persons in the research on the financial markets and the trade in services. Sako Osaka helped with preparation of materials in Japanese. Wendy Grover used her detective instincts to get at much information on the informal economy. And then there was a group of students who worked little miracles with the entering of the text and preparation of tables, and all of it under the pressure of deadlines. Jesus Sanchez, Jerry Johnson, Brian Sahd, David Silodor, Karen Hemeleski, and Julie Burros were the most supportive assistants one could have wished for. I also need to thank Ted Reinert and Barbara Hemeleski for solving many a computer crisis when all seemed lost and Jinnah Mohamed for final preparation of tables. Gail Satler often took full responsibility for ensuring that the various parts of the project functioned smoothly and managed matters while I was away. I would also like to thank the many people at Princeton University Press for their support, particularly my editor, Gail Ullman, and her assistant, Cindy Hirschfeld, and Jane Low, in charge of editorial production. The copyeditor, Lyn Grossman, took on an unusually large burden of editing and proofing; I am immensely grateful for all her work.

It is my experience that in all major projects there are one or two individuals who play a critical role, one not necessarily related to time spent on the project, but more to the strategic character and the substance of their contribution. My single largest debt is to Zhen Wu from the Department of Urban Planning at Columbia University and to Professor Kiriro Morita from the Department of Economics at Tokyo University. Zhen Wu was an exceptional researcher, whose intelligence and determination made all the difference. She did a lot of the research on the producer services in London and in New York City for chapters 5, 6, and 8. Professor Kiriro Morita made the most important contribution to my research in Tokyo. He provided me with researchers and introduced me to several key people. His generosity and interest were exceptional.

And then there are those on the family front. My husband, Richard Sennett, and my son, Hilary Koob-Sassen, were a great source of support, love, and many a fine dinner. Without them there would have been so much less laughter and enjoyment.

THE GLOBAL CITY

One

Overview

FOR CENTURIES, the world economy has shaped the life of cities. This book is about that relationship today. Beginning in the 1960s, the organization of economic activity entered a period of pronounced transformation. The changes were expressed in the altered structure of the world economy, and also assumed forms specific to particular places. Certain of these changes are by now familiar: the dismantling of once-powerful industrial centers in the United States, the United Kingdom, and more recently in Japan; the accelerated industrialization of several Third World countries; the rapid internationalization of the financial industry into a worldwide network of transactions. Each of these changes altered the relation of cities to the international economy.

In the decades after World War II, there was an international regime based on United States dominance in the world economy and the rules for global trade contained in the 1945 Bretton Woods agreement. By the early 1970s, the conditions supporting that regime were disintegrating. The breakdown created a void into which stepped, perhaps in a last burst of national dominance, the large U.S. transnational industrial firms and banks. In this period of transition, the management of the international economic order was to an inordinate extent run from the headquarters of these firms. By the early 1980s, however, the large U.S. transnational banks faced the massive Third World debt crisis, and U.S. industrial firms experienced sharp market share losses from foreign competition. Yet the international economy did not simply break into fragments. The geography and composition of the global economy changed so as to produce a complex duality: a spatially dispersed, yet globally integrated organization of economic activity.

The point of departure for the present study is that the combination of spatial dispersal and global integration has created a new strategic role for major cities. Beyond their long history as centers for international trade and banking, these cities now function in four new ways: first, as highly concentrated command points in the organization of the world economy; second, as key locations for finance and for specialized service firms, which have replaced manufacturing as the leading economic sectors; third, as sites of production, including the production of innovations, in these leading industries; and fourth, as markets for the products and innovations produced. These changes in the functioning of cities have had a massive impact upon both international economic activity and urban form: cities concentrate control over vast resources, while finance and specialized service industries have restructured the urban social and economic order. Thus a new type of city has appeared. It is the global city. Leading examples now are New York, London, Tokyo, Frankfurt, and Paris. The first three are the focus of this book.

As I shall show, these three cities have undergone massive and *parallel* changes in their economic base, spatial organization, and social structure. But this parallel development is a puzzle. How could cities with as diverse a history, culture, politics, and economy as New York, London, and Tokyo experience similar transformations concentrated in so brief a period of time? Not examined at length in my study, but important to its theoretical framework, is how transformations in cities ranging from Paris to Frankfurt to Hong Kong and São Paulo have responded to the same dynamic. To understand the puzzle of parallel change in diverse cities requires not simply a point-by-point comparison of New York, London, and Tokyo, but a situating of these cities in a set of global processes. In order to understand why major cities with different histories and cultures have undergone parallel economic and social changes, we need to examine transformations in the world economy. Yet the term *global city* may be reductive and misleading if it suggests that cities are mere outcomes of a global economic machine. They are specific places whose spaces, internal dynamics, and social structure matter; indeed, we may be able to understand the global order only by analyzing why key structures of the world economy are *necessarily* situated in cities.

How does the position of these cities in the world economy today differ from that which they have historically held as centers of banking and trade? When Max Weber analyzed the medieval cities woven together in the Hanseatic League, he conceived their trade as the exchange of surplus production; it was his view that a medieval city could withdraw from external trade and continue to support itself, albeit on a reduced scale. The modern molecule of global cities is nothing like the trade among self-sufficient places in the Hanseatic League, as Weber understood it. The first thesis advanced in this book is that the territorial dispersal of current economic activity creates a need for expanded central control and management. In other words, while in principle the territorial decentralization of economic activity in recent years could have been accompanied by a corresponding decentralization in ownership and hence in the appropriation of profits, there has been little movement in that direction. Though large firms have increased their subcontracting to smaller firms, and many national firms in the newly industrializing countries have grown rapidly, this form of growth is ultimately part of a chain.

Even industrial homeworkers in remote rural areas are now part of that chain. The transnational corporations continue to control much of the end product and to reap the profits associated with selling in the world market. The internationalization and expansion of the financial industry has brought growth to a large number of smaller financial markets, a growth which has fed the expansion of the global industry. But top-level control and management of the industry has become concentrated in a few leading financial centers, especially New York, London, Tokyo, Frankfurt, and Paris. These account for a disproportionate share of all financial transactions and one that has grown rapidly since the early 1980s. The fundamental dynamic posited here is that the more globalized the economy becomes, the higher the agglomeration of central functions in a relatively few sites, that is, the global cities.

The extremely high densities evident in the business districts of these cities are one spatial expression of this logic. The widely accepted notion that density and agglomeration will become obsolete because global telecommunications advances allow for maximum population and resource dispersal is poorly conceived. It is, I argue, precisely because of the territorial dispersal facilitated by telecommunication that agglomeration of certain centralizing activities has sharply increased. This is not a mere continuation of old patterns of agglomeration; there is a new logic for concentration. In Weberian terms, there is a new system of "coordination," one which focuses on the development of specific geographic control sites in the international economic order.

A second major theme of this book concerns the impact of this type of economic growth on the economic order within these cities. It is necessary to go beyond the Weberian notion of coordination and Bell's (1973) notion of the postindustrial society to understand this new urban order. Bell, like Weber, assumes that the further society evolves from nineteenth-century industrial capitalism, the more the apex of the social order is involved in pure managerial process, with the content of what is to be managed becoming of secondary importance. Global cities are, however, not only nodal points for the coordination of processes (Friedmann 1986); they are also particular sites of production. They are sites for (1) the production of specialized services needed by complex organizations for running a spatially dispersed network of factories, offices, and service outlets; and (2) the production of financial innovations and the making of markets, both central to the internationalization and expansion of the financial industry. To understand the structure of a global city, we have to understand it as a place where certain kinds of work can get done, which is to say that we have to get beyond the dichotomy between manufacturing and services. The "things" a global city makes are highly specialized services and financial goods.

It is true that high-level business services, from accounting to eco-nomic consulting, are not usually analyzed as a production process. Such services are usually seen as a type of output derived from high-level tech-nical knowledge. I shall challenge this view. Moreover, using new schol-arship on producer services, I shall examine the extent to which a key trait of global cities is that they are the most *advanced* production sites for creating these services.

A second way this analysis goes beyond the existing literature on cities concerns the financial industry. I shall explore how the character of a global city is shaped by the emerging organization of the financial indus-try. The accelerated production of innovations and the new importance of a large number of relatively small financial institutions led to a renewed or expanded role for the marketplace in the financial industry in the de-cade of the 1980s. The marketplace has assumed new strategic and rou-tine economic functions, in comparison to the prior phase, when the large transnational banks dominated the national and international finan-cial market. Insofar as financial "products" can be used internationally, the market has reappeared in a new form in the global economy. New York, London, and Tokyo play roles as production sites for financial in-struments and centralized marketplaces for these "products."

A key dynamic running through these various activities and organizing my analysis of the place of global cities in the world economy is their capability for producing global control. By focusing on the production of services and financial innovations, I am seeking to displace the focus of attention from the familiar issues of the power of large corporations over governments and economies, or supracorporate concentration of power through interlocking directorates or organizations, such as the IMF. I want to focus on an aspect that has received less attention, which could be referred to as the *practice* of global control: the work of producing and reproducing the organization and management of a global produc-tion system and a global marketplace for finance. My focus is not on power, but on production: the production of those inputs that constitute the capability for global control and the infrastructure of jobs involved in this production.

The power of large corporations is insufficient to explain the capability for global control. Obviously, governments also face an increasingly com-plex environment in which highly sophisticated machineries of central-ized management and control are necessary. Moreover, the high level of specialization and the growing demand for these specialized inputs have created the conditions for a freestanding industry. Now small firms can buy components of global capability, such as management consulting or international legal advice. And so can firms and governments anywhere in the world. While the large corporation is undoubtedly a key agent inducing the development of this capability and is a prime beneficiary, it is not the sole user.

Equally misleading would be an exclusive focus on transnational banks. Up to the end of the 1982 Third World debt crisis, the large transnational banks dominated the financial markets in terms of both volume and the nature of firm transactions. After 1982, this dominance was increasingly challenged by other financial institutions and the innovations they produced. This led to a transformation in the leading components of the financial industry, a proliferation of financial institutions, and the rapid internationalization of financial markets rather than just a few banks. The incorporation of a multiplicity of markets all over the world into a global system fed the growth of the industry after the 1982 debt crisis, while also creating new forms of concentration in a few leading financial centers. Hence, in the case of the financial industry, a focus on the large transnational banks would exclude precisely those sectors of the industry where much of the new growth and production of innovations has occurred; it would leave out an examination of the wide range of activities, firms, and markets that constitute the financial industry since the 1980s.

Thus, there are a number of reasons to focus a study on marketplaces and production sites rather than on the large corporations and banks. Most scholarship on the internationalization of the economy has already focused on the large corporations and transnational banks. To continue to focus on the corporations and banks would mean to limit attention to their formal power, rather than examining the wide array of economic activities, many outside the corporation, needed to produce and reproduce that power. And, in the case of finance, a focus on the large transnational banks would leave out precisely that institutional sector of the industry where the key components of the new growth have been invented and put into circulation. Finally, exclusive focus on corporations and banks leaves out a number of issues about the social, economic, and spatial impact of these activities on the cities that contain them, a major concern in this book and one I return to below.

A third major theme explored in this book concerns the consequences of these developments for the national urban system in each of these countries and for the relationship of the global city to its nation-state. While a few major cities are the sites of production for the new global control capability, a large number of other major cities have lost their role as leading export centers for industrial manufacturing, as a result of the decentralization of this form of production. Cities such as Detroit, Liverpool, Manchester, and now increasingly Nagoya and Osaka have been affected by the decentralization of their key industries at the domestic and international levels. According to the first hypothesis presented above, this same process has contributed to the growth of service industries that produce the specialized inputs to run global production processes and global markets for inputs and outputs. These industries—international legal and accounting services, management consulting, financial services—are heavily concentrated in cities such as New York, London, and Tokyo. We need to know how this growth alters the relations between the global cities and what were once the leading industrial centers in their nations. Does globalization bring about a triangulation so that New York, for example, now plays a role in the fortunes of Detroit that it did not play when that city was home to most production jobs in one of the leading industries, auto manufacturing? Or, in the case of Japan, we need to ask, for example, if there is a connection between the increasing shift of production out of Toyota City (Nagoya) to offshore locations (Thailand, South Korea, and the United States) and the development for the first time of a new headquarters for Toyota in Tokyo.

Similarly, there is a question about the relation between such major cities as Chicago, Osaka, and Manchester, once leading industrial centers in the world, and global markets generally. Both Chicago and Osaka were and continue to be important financial centers on the basis of their manufacturing industries. We would want to know if they have lost ground, relatively, in these functions as a result of their decline in the global industrial market, or instead have undergone parallel transformation toward strengthening of service functions. Chicago, for example, was at the heart of a massive agroindustrial complex, a vast regional economy. How has the decline of that regional economic system affected Chicago?

In all these questions, it is a matter of understanding what growth embedded in the international system of producer services and finance has entailed for different levels in the national urban hierarchy. The broader trends—decentralization of plants, offices, and service outlets, along with the expansion of central functions as a consequence of the need to manage such decentralized organization of firms—may well have created conditions contributing to the growth of regional subcenters, minor versions of what New York, London, and Tokyo do on a global and national scale. The extent to which the developments posited for New York, London, and Tokyo are also replicated, perhaps in less accentuated form, in smaller cities, at lower levels of the urban hierarchy, is an open, but important, question.

The new international forms of economic activity raise a problem about the relationship between nation-states and global cities. The relation between city and nation is a theme that keeps returning throughout this book; it is the political dimension of the economic changes I explore. I posit the possibility of a systemic discontinuity between what used to be thought of as national growth and the forms of growth evident in global cities since the 1980s. These cities constitute a system rather than merely competing with each other. What contributes to growth in the network of global cities may well not contribute to growth in nations. For instance, is there a systemic relation between, on the one hand, the growth in global cities and, on the other hand, the deficits of national governments and the decline of major industrial centers in each of these countries in the 1980s?

The fourth and final theme in the book concerns the impact of these new forms of, and conditions for, growth on the social order of the global city. There is a vast body of literature on the impact of a dynamic, high-growth manufacturing sector in the highly developed countries, which shows that it raised wages, reduced inequality, and contributed to the formation of a middle class. Much less is known about the sociology of a service economy. Daniel Bell's (1973) *The Coming of Post-Industrial Society* posits that such an economy will result in growth in the number of highly educated workers and a more rational relation of workers to issues of social equity. One could argue that any city representing a post-industrial economy would surely contain leading sectors such as those of New York, London, and increasingly Tokyo.

I will examine to what extent the new structure of economic activity has brought about changes in the organization of work, reflected in a shift in the job supply and polarization in the income distribution and occupational distribution of workers. Major growth industries show a greater incidence of jobs at the high- and low-paying ends of the scale than do the older industries now in decline. Almost half the jobs in the producer services are lower-income jobs, and half are in the two highest earnings classes. In contrast, a large share of manufacturing workers were in the middle-earnings jobs during the postwar period of high growth in these industries in the United States and United Kingdom.

Two other developments in global cities have also contributed to economic polarization. One is the vast supply of low-wage jobs required by high-income gentrification in both its residential and commercial settings. The increase in the numbers of expensive restaurants, luxury housing, luxury hotels, gourmet shops, boutiques, French hand laundries, and special cleaners that ornament the new urban landscape illustrates this trend. Furthermore, there is a continuing need for low-wage industrial services, even in such sectors as finance and specialized services. A second development that has reached significant proportions is what I call the downgrading of the manufacturing sector, a process in which the share of unionized shops declines and wages deteriorate while sweatshops and industrial homework proliferate. This process includes the downgrading of jobs within existing industries and the job supply patterns of some of the new industries, notably electronics assembly. It is worth noting that the growth of a downgraded manufacturing sector has been strongest in cities such as New York and London.

The expansion of low-wage jobs as a function of *growth* trends implies a reorganization of the capital-labor relation. To see this, it is important to distinguish the characteristics of jobs from their sectoral location, since highly dynamic, technologically advanced growth sectors may well contain low-wage dead-end jobs. Furthermore, the distinction between sectoral characteristics and sectoral growth patterns is crucial: Backward sectors, such as downgraded manufacturing or low-wage service occupations, can be part of major growth trends in a highly developed economy. It is often assumed that backward sectors express decline trends. Similarly, there is a tendency to assume that advanced sectors, such as finance, have mostly good, white-collar jobs. In fact, they contain a good number of low-paying jobs, from cleaner to stock clerk.

These, then, are the major themes and implications of my study.

As a further word of introduction I must sketch the reasons why producer services and finance have grown so rapidly since the 1970s and why they have high concentrations in cities such as New York, London, and Tokyo. The familiar explanation is that the decade of the 1980s was but a part of a larger economic trend, the shift to services. And the simple explanation of their high concentration in major cities is that this is because of the need for face-to-face communication in the services community. While correct, these propositions are incomplete.

We need to understand first how modern technology has not ended nineteenth-century forms of work; rather, technology has shifted a number of activities that were once part of manufacturing into the domain of services. The transfer of skills from workers to machines once epitomized by the assembly line has a present-day version in the transfer of a variety of activities from the shop floor into computers, with their attendant technical and professional personnel. Also, functional specialization within early factories finds a contemporary counterpart in today's pronounced fragmentation of the work process spatially and organizationally. This has been called the "global assembly line," the production and assembly of goods from factories and depots throughout the world, wherever labor costs and economies of scale make an international division of labor cost-effective. It is, however, this very "global assembly line" that creates the need for increased centralization and complexity of management, control, and planning. The development of the modern corporation and its massive participation in world markets and foreign countries has made planning, internal administration, product development, and research increasingly important and complex. Diversification of product lines, mergers, and transnationalization of economic activities all require highly specialized skills in top-level management (Chandler 1977). These have also "increased the dependence of the corporation on producer services, which in turn has fostered growth and development of higher levels of expertise among producer service firms" (Stanback and Novelle 1982: 15). What were once support resources for major corporations have become crucial inputs in corporate decisionmaking. A firm with a multiplicity of geographically dispersed manufacturing plants contributes to the development of new types of planning in production and distribution surrounding the firm.

The growth of international banks and the more recent diversification of the financial industry have also expanded the demand for highly specialized service inputs. In the 1960s and 1970s, there was considerable geographic dispersal in the banking industry, with many regional centers and offshore locations mostly involved in fairly traditional banking. The diversification and internationalization of finance over the last decade resulted in a strong trend toward concentrating the "management" of the global industry and the production of financial innovations in a more limited number of major locations. This dynamic is not unlike that of multisite manufacturing or service firms.

Major trends toward the development of multisite manufacturing, service, and banking have created an expanded demand for a wide range of specialized service activities to manage and control global networks of factories, service outlets, and branch offices. While to some extent these activities can be carried out in-house, a large share of them cannot. High levels of specialization, the possibility of externalizing the production of some of these services, and the growing demand by large and small firms and by governments are all conditions that have both resulted from and made possible the development of a market for freestanding service firms that produce components for what I refer to as global control capability.

The growth of advanced services for firms, a key component of producer services, along with their particular characteristics of production, helps to explain the centralization of management and servicing functions that fueled the economic boom of the mid-1980s in New York, London, and Tokyo. The face-to-face explanation needs to be refined in several ways. Advanced services are mostly producer services; unlike other types of services, they are only weakly dependent on proximity to the consumers served. Rather, such specialized firms benefit from and need to locate close to other firms who produce key inputs or whose proximity makes possible joint production of certain service offerings. The accounting firm can service its clients at a distance but the nature of its service depends on proximity to other specialists, from lawyers to programmers. Major corporate transactions today typically require simultaneous participation of several specialized firms providing legal, accounting, financial, public relations, management consulting, and other such services. Moreover, concentration arises out of the needs and expectations of the high-income workers employed in these firms. They are attracted to the amenities and lifestyles that large urban centers can offer and are likely to live in central areas rather than in suburbs.

The importance of this concentration of economic activity in New York, London, and Tokyo is heightened by the fact that advanced services and finance were the fastest-growing sectors in the economies of their countries in the 1980s. It is a common mistake to attribute high growth to the service sector as a whole. In fact, other major services, such as public and consumer services, have leveled off since the middle or late 1960s in the United States and since the 1970s in the United Kingdom and Japan. In other words, the concentration of advanced services and finance in major urban centers represents a disproportionate share of the nationwide growth in employment and GNP relative to population share.

The combination of high levels of speculation and a multiplicity of small firms as core elements of the financial and producer services complex raises a question about the durability of this model of growth. Indeed, by the mid-1990s the larger banks once again had a more central role in the financial industry, and competition and the advantages of scale had led to mergers and acquisitions of small firms. Finally, and perhaps most important, at what point do the sources of profits generated by this form of economic growth become exhausted?

Over the last twenty years, major economic growth trends have produced spatial and social arrangements considerably divergent from the configuration that characterized the preceding decades. The economic sectors, localities, and occupations that account for a large share of economic growth today differ from those central to the immediate post–World War II period. Most commonly, this process has been interpreted as the decline of old and the emergence of new industries, typically seen as two somewhat unconnected events necessary for the renewal of an economy. I shall challenge this disconnecting view; this means asserting that new growth rests, to a significant extent, on deep structural processes of decline. The question of the long-term durability of the global city that I have just posed turns on not seeing decline and growth as distinct. The "high-flying" 1980s and 1990s emerged in part out of the same dynamics that led manufacturing of the old sort to decline.

This systemic connection, I will argue, plays itself out in several economic arenas. I propose to examine this through several working hypotheses. They are the following: First, the geographic dispersal of manufacturing, which contributed to the decline of old industrial centers, created a demand for expanded central management and planning and the necessary specialized services, key components of growth in global cities. The move of large corporations into consumer services contributed to the closure and decline of many small independently owned consumer service firms. The growing complexity of governmental activity further fed the demand for specialized services and expanded central management and planning. Second, the growth of the financial industry, and especially of key sectors of that industry, benefited from policies and conditions often harmful to other industrial sectors, notably manufacturing. The overall effect again was to feed growth of specialized services located in major cities and to undermine the economic base of other types of localities. Third, the conditions and patterns subsumed under the first two working hypotheses suggest a transformation in the economic relationships among global cities, the nation-states where they are located, and the world economy. Prior to the current phase, there was high correspondence between major growth sectors and overall national growth. Today we see increased asymmetry: The conditions promoting growth in global cities contain as significant components the decline of other areas of the United States, the United Kingdom, and Japan and the accumulation of government debt and corporate debt. Fourth, the new conditions of growth have contributed to elements of a new class alignment in global cities. The occupational structure of major growth industries characterized by the locational concentration of major growth sectors in global cities in combination with the polarized occupational structure of these sectors has created and contributed to growth of a high-income stratum and a low-income stratum of workers. It has done so directly through the organization of work and occupational structure of major growth sectors. And it has done so indirectly through the jobs needed to service the new high-income workers, both at work and at home, as well as the needs of the expanded low-wage work force.

This brief introductory chapter presents the main issues and arguments the book will develop. Part One discusses the major trends in the spatial dispersion of production and the reorganization of the financial industry. The focus here is on the geography, composition, and institutions that constitute the globalization of economic activity since the 1980s. This aims to be a straightforward empirical description of the composition and direction of international investment, service transactions, and financial flows. It entailed dealing with a vast amount of evidence, disaggregating in order to capture dimensions of interest to the analysis in this book and reaggregating in order to facilitate comprehension. The many tables in these chapters serve to summarize the details. The purpose is ultimately to understand how various forms of globalizaton in economic activity generated new forms of centralization, specifically, the rapidly growing agglomeration of specialized services and finance evident in major cities.

Part Two examines the industries that form the core in these cities and the national and transnational space economy of these industries. The purpose is to arrive at an understanding of the place of global cities in the organization of these industries, and to do so through an examination of the characteristics of the industries—rather than a detailed analysis of the economic base of the cities—in the context of national urban systems as well as an elemental global hierarchy of cities. Chapter 5 examines the characteristics of the new components of centralization. They amount to a new basic industry: the production of management and control operations, of the highly specialized services needed to run the world economy, of new financial instruments. Chapters 6 and 7 discuss the role of global cities in the new organization of the world economy, examining the development of these cities into sites of production for the new basic industry and the growth of inter-city transactions.

Part Three discusses some of the key aspects in the distribution of benefits and burdens of this particular form of growth. What is the range of jobs directly and indirectly sustaining the operation of this type of economic sector? And to what extent does the occupational and income distribution of these cities' resident work forces reflect the existence of a thriving profitmaking economic core? Chapter 8 examines how these transformations in economic activity generate a new labor demand and a new income structure in these cities. Chapter 9 examines the characteristics of the backward economic sectors that appear to thrive in these cities and seeks to understand what, if any, is the articulation between these two types of growth.

The concluding chapter discusses the political implications of these developments, addressing the following three questions. What are the political implications of concentration of the benefits of economic growth in global cities and in a stratum of high-income workers alongside the decline of what were once thriving localities and sectors of the work force? How does the consolidation of the world economy and of global centers for its control and management affect the relationship between nation and city, particularly between global cities and the nation-states they supposedly belong to? The final question concerns the durability of these arrangements: What are the conditions for the reproduction of this mode of growth?

The three central questions organizing this book can be simply put as follows. What is the role of major cities in the organization and management of the world economy? In what ways has the consolidation of a world economy affected the economic base and associated social and political order in major cities? What happens to the relationship between state and city under conditions of a strong articulation between a city and the world economy? These represent only a few of all the questions one could raise in a study about major contemporary cities. But these questions are strategic for understanding such cities from the perspective of the world economy—what moment in the global accumulation process is contained by or located in major cities? And they are strategic for understanding the interaction of local and global processes—how does the historical, political, economic, and social specificity of a particular city resist, facilitate, remain untouched by incorporation into the world economy? Why has Tokyo's trajectory increasingly diverged from those of New York and London in the 1990s? In this context, the contrasts among New York, London, and Tokyo should be illuminating, given their roles as leading world financial centers and their very different histories, economies, and cultures.

Part One

THE GEOGRAPHY AND COMPOSITION OF GLOBALIZATION

A LEADING ARGUMENT in this book is that the spatial dispersion of economic activities and the reorganization of the financial industry are two processes that have contributed to new forms of centralization insofar as they have occurred under conditions of continued concentration in ownership or control. The spatial dispersion of economic activity has brought about an expansion in central functions and in the growing stratum of specialized firms servicing such functions. Reorganization in the financial industry has been characterized by sharp growth, rapid production of innovations, and a proliferation of financial firms. These conditions, I argue, shifted the point of gravity in the industry away from the large, mostly American, transnational banks that had once dominated the industry toward major *centers* of finance.

The fact that telecommunications and information technologies are essential to both processes has added yet another force for agglomeration. Finance and specialized services are major users of such technologies and need access to the most advanced facilities. These technologies, which make possible long distance management and servicing and instantaneous money transfers, require complex physical facilities, which are highly immobile. Such facilities demand major investments in fixed capital and continuous incorporation of innovations. A second and, I will argue, crucial factor giving global cities an advantage is the organizational complexity they contain which allows firms to maximize the benefits they can derive from the new technologies.

International transactions have expanded the scale and raised the complexity of these processes. However, the spatial and organizational logic at work is also evident at the national level. Whether internationalization is essential to the major outcomes, notably the acute pressure, toward agglomeration in leading cities, is difficult to establish and is perhaps a question of theory. But the requirements that global production arrangements and markets bring about are a key factor in the organization of major industries and in the significance of specialized services for firms.

Furthermore, the fact of international transactions produces a specific regulatory question: What are the conditions that make international transactions cohere? This question becomes particularly compelling in the absence of a single dominant power, as was the United States after World War II, and of a treaty containing the rules for international transactions, a treaty made persuasive by the existence of such a power. The 1980s saw the ascendance of Japan and Germany as major economic forces, the proliferation of participants, acute competition, and an increasing internationalization in the ownership or control of capital. And the 1990s saw the rise of the Eurozone. One of the questions guiding the deciphering of empirical details in chapters 3 and 4 is whether the market as marketplace—more specifically, the leading marketplaces for finance and specialized services—provided the essential organizing element beginning in the 1980s, a period of high competition, speculation, and profits.

Addressing these issues requires a detailed examination of the geography and composition of international transactions and the institutional arrangements through which such transactions take place. Much of the scholarship has focused on the geography and composition of the activities of large multinational corporations. Has the growth of finance and services brought about significant differences in the composition of international transactions and in the corresponding institutional arrangements, as compared with the 1960s and 1970s? And does a change in composition entail a change in the types of locations and forms of articulation involved in international transactions? The international mobility of capital and its growing speed contribute specific forms of articulation among different geographic areas and transformations in the role played by these areas in the world economy. Have the properties of articulation been altered by the speed and growth of electronically integrated markets? In brief, is there a transformation in the spatial expression of the logic of accumulation and in the institutional arrangements through which it takes place?

The sharp growth in the monetary value of financial transactions and its highly speculative nature raise questions about the limits of this mode of growth. Is this a particular phase in the product cycle of these industries, which will be followed by greater standardization and concentration, less competition, and less innovation? How would such a development alter the pattern that emerged in the decade of the 1980s and continues today in 2000? The accelerated production of innovations and the rapid entry of new participants in highly profitable industries once dominated by a limited number of firms raise questions about the durability of this phase in a system with strong oligopolistic tendencies and a continuing dependence on mass markets.

The documentation of these issues focuses largely on its international components, these being the major ones. The decade of the 1970s was the crucial period when some of the new forms of geographic dispersal and internationalization, in the making since the mid-1960s, became fully evident. But the conditions for the exhaustion of certain of these patterns also developed in the 1970s, thereby facilitating the formation of new patterns of geography, composition, and institutional arrangements in the 1980s. The detailed documentation of international transactions in finance and services is intent on capturing the new patterns that emerged in the 1980s and 1990s. These new patterns grew out of both the consolidation of some components of restructuring and the crisis of other components in the 1970s.

The 1990s were marked by an accelerated sequence of fluctuations which in times past might have taken several decades. We see an accentuation of some of the patterns that emerge in the 1980s. Thus, after the various financial downturns in the early 1990s there is a sharp resumption in innovations, particularly the development of new and increasingly complex derivatives, and in speculative endeavors, particularly the rapid growth of hedge funds as important actors in the financial markets. But there were also significant interruptions of some of the trends of the 1980s. Most notable is the changing role of Tokyo from a potentially major global city to a more limited role as a capital exporter, albeit a leading one. The southeast Asian crisis of 1997 followed by the Russian default of 1998 re-positioned the so-called emerging markets in global investment patterns and led to a reconsideration of some of the key policies for liberalizing cross-border capital flows. Crucial contextual conditions for this accelerated sequence of events were the instituting of free-market policies, deregulation, and privatization, in a growing number of countries which led to their integration into the global capital market and, secondly the enormous growth in the size of that market which could now overwhelm most national economies.

Of theoretical interest to the effort in this book is how the accentuation of some of these trends in the 1990s as well as the interruption or weakening of others altered some of the key issues posited in the first edition about capital mobility and new forms of centralization. A second issue is how the expansion of the global economy in the 1990s—as measured by foreign direct investment, cross-border mergers and acquisitions, networks of affiliates, and global financial flows—altered the trend I posited for the 1980s of a shift from large transnational banks to financial centers as the key configuration in the financial industry. A third issue concerns the ongoing question of what is different today from earlier phases of a global financial market, notably at the turn of the century and in the interwar period. All three of these issues were also the subject of critiques and debates about some of my theses and empirical specifications in the first edition. Particular aspects of these questions are also addressed in Part 2 of the book.

Chapter 2 elaborates the concept of capital mobility so as to capture both dispersal and agglomeration. The ensuing two chapters document these processes. The question of economic concentration is central to this examination. Given the format in which many of the data are available, the simple form of this question, at this point, is: What countries account for the vast majority of the various flows under consideration? This should then set the stage for a more detailed analysis of concentration in the leading industries of the 1980s and 1990s, specialized services for business and finance, the subject of Part Two of this book.

Two

Dispersal and New Forms of Centralization

Do CHANGES in the global flow of factors of production, commodities, and information amount to a new spatial expression of the logic of accumulation? Addressing this question entails a detailed examination of how that which we call the global economy is constituted. What are the geographic areas, industries, and institutional arrangements that are central to the current process of globalization, and how do they differ from those of earlier periods? Extracting theoretical insight from this empirical documentation requires elaborating the category of capital mobility to take it beyond the mere movement of capital across space. It must allow for the incorporation of not only the new forms of geographic dispersal, usually thought of as representing the mobility of capital, but also the new forms of centralization, which, I argue, are an integral part of the new forms of capital mobility. A theoretical elaboration of the concept of capital mobility that takes it beyond a locational dimension should also include the reorganization of sources of surplus value made possible by massive shifts of capital from one area of the world to another. Yet another aspect of the mobility of capital is the transnationalization in ownership, not only through foreign direct investment but also through mergers, acquisitions, and joint ventures, which raises anew the issue of the nationality of capital.

Key components of this process are the outflow of capital from old industrial centers (Bluestone and Harrison 1982; Massey 1982; AMPO 1987), the inflow of capital into newly industrializing countries (Fröbel, Heinrichs, and Kreye 1979), and the growth of transnational corporations (Vernon 1966; Herman 1982). These studies tend to posit the locational dimensions of capital mobility, or what Storper and Walker (1983) have termed the "locational capability" of capital. The most obvious and familiar image of the increased mobility of capital is the "runaway" shop, or the movement of manufacturing jobs from highly developed areas to less developed, low-wage areas. Perhaps as common an image is the instant transfer of money from one country to another.

But capital mobility, both as a process and as a theoretical category, incorporates a number of other components of importance to the analysis in this book. Capital mobility is constituted not only in locational terms but also in technical terms, both through the technologies that render capital mobile and through the capability for maintaining control over a vastly decentralized global production system (Sassen 1988).

Such an elaboration of the notion of capital mobility brings to the fore important questions about the broader organization and control of the economy in the current phase of the world economy. Increased capital mobility does not only bring about changes in the geographic organization of production and the network of financial markets. It also generates a demand for types of production needed to ensure the management, control, and servicing of this new organization of production and finance. These new types of production range from the development of telecommunications to that of specialized services that are key inputs for the management of a global network of factories, offices, and financial markets. And it includes the production of a broad array of innovations in these sectors. These types of production have their own locational patterns; they tend toward high degrees of agglomeration. In addition, the increased mobility of capital has reorganized the employment relationship. This subject has received attention in some aspects: the labor market dynamics leading up to and resulting from deindustrialization, and the low-wage labor enclaves of export processing zones. But other aspects of the employment relation have not been examined in the light of the increased mobility of capital: key trends in international labor migrations, notably the new unauthorized Asian immigration to Japan, and the formation of a broad stratum of medium-level workers with a global orientation in a context where school, family, and community are typically not so oriented. Here we introduce these concepts, which we return to in later sections of the book.

Mobility and Agglomeration

The implementation of global production processes by large corporations requires a certain type of international regime. The last clearly formulated such regime was the one associated with the Bretton Woods treaty, when the United States was the leading exporter of investment capital, consumer goods, and capital goods and the leading economic and military power. We can think of the 1970s as already containing the beginning of a new transnational logic in the form of multinational firms. But these were largely U.S. firms; they clearly were dominant, especially in banking; the dollar continued to function as the leading currency; and, notwithstanding the severe economic and political decline of the United States in the world, the United States was still the dominant power. By the mid-1980s the dominant banks and the leading manufacturing firms were Japanese. The examination of the specific forms assumed by capital mobility in manufacturing, services, and finance since the 1970s allows us to *begin* addressing the question of how the world economy is organized and what material practices characterize it.

The geographic dispersal of manufacturing became one of the more distinct traits in the 1980s and brought the issue of capital mobility to the fore.[1] There have been numerous plant closings in all major industrialized countries and transfers of production jobs to lower-wage domestic or foreign locations. There also have been overall declines in manufacturing employment in what were once established industrial centers, such as Detroit in the United States, or Manchester and Birmingham in the United Kingdom, and growing imports of components produced or assembled abroad and reimported for final product assembly.[2] Since the 1980s there have been similar trends in Japan, including the shift of garment production to less developed domestic and foreign areas, as well as the shift of auto parts and electronic components manufacturing to Thailand, South Korea, and Mexico. Evidence on direct foreign investment by the United States, the United Kingdom, and Japan describes shifts of manufacturing to foreign locations and the internationalization of manufacturing production in these three countries. More specifically, direct foreign investment in production for export is indicative of the existence of a global network of production sites set up by the firms of highly developed countries, insofar as this investment is geared toward production aimed not at the countries where the factories have been located but at the countries that provided the capital.[3]

---

[1] Plant closings in old industrial centers are probably the most dramatic instance. Disinvestment, shrinking, attrition, lack of maintenance—all these represent mechanisms for deindustrialization which, while not as direct as plant closings, entail a severe erosion of the old industrial complex, both in the United States and in the United Kingdom (Bluestone and Harrison 1982; Massey 1984; U.S. BLS 2001).

[2] Shutdowns are estimated to have eliminated 22 million jobs in the United States between 1969 and 1976 (Bluestone and Harrison 1982: 29). This trend continues. The most recent available data collected by the U.S. Department of Labor (2001) reports that from 1993 to 1997 7.7 million workers who had been employed for at least three years were displaced due to factory or company shutdowns and moves; the figure climbs to 17 million if all workers, regardless of length of employment, are included. In the United Kingdom, there was a 25% decline in manufacturing employment from 1978 to 1985, the period of sharpest losses. From 1990 to 1993, 600,000 manufacturing jobs were lost (Borland et al. 1998). In Japan the process began later. Mines, steel mills, and factories began being closed down in the 1980s. In 1970 there were 250,000 miners; by 1985 there were 30,000. The steel industry lost 100,000 jobs with the reduction of operations by the five leading companies. Throughout the 1990s manufacturing jobs fell by an average of 3% (Japan Institute of Labor 2001).

[3] The total value of U.S. imports under the Harmonized Tariff System (HTS) 9802 was 71.3 billion USD in 2000 (author's calculation based on aggregated data for 2000 about U.S. imports from 95 countries under this tariff system). A growing share of this investment

The decentralization of manufacturing is constituted in technical and social terms. Different kinds of processes have fed this decentralization. On the one hand, the dismantling of the old industrial centers in highly developed countries, with their strong organized labor component, was an attempt to dismantle the capital-labor relation around which production had been organized, often referred to as Fordism. On the other hand, the decentralization of production in high-tech industries was a result of the introduction of new technologies designed to separate low-wage, routine tasks from highly skilled tasks therewith maximizing locational options. Both, however, entail an organization of the capital-labor relation that tends to maximize the use of low-wage labor and to minimize the effectiveness of mechanisms that empower labor vis-à-vis capital. Thus, the term *dispersal*, while suggestive of a geographic aspect, clearly involves a complex political and technical reorganization of production as well. (For a full discussion see Sassen 1988.)

An important aspect of the mobility of capital is the transnationalization in the ownership and control of major corporations through foreign direct investment, mergers and acquisitions, and joint ventures. The United States has been one of the main objects of such investment and acquisitions. While the British and the Dutch have long been significant investors in the United States and continue to be so, the current phase has certain distinct traits. In the 1980s a range of investments and acquisitions took place that can be differentiated from traditional forms of investments and acquisitions, a subject I return to in chapter 7. One instance of this is the emergence of Southern California as the center for research and development, design, engineering, marketing, and management of the Japanese auto makers operating in the United States. The actual manufacturing tends to be concentrated in the Midwest and in the South, and now also includes twin plants in northern Mexico. Toyota illustrates this well. Cars the firm produces in its nine North American plants accounted for 30% of its total U.S. car sales in 1990 and 57% in 1995, thus surpassing imports as its main components of U.S. sales. Further, a growing share of these cars is for export to Asia, including Japan (Schnorbus and Strauss 1996). A second instance is extensive concentration of Japanese banks, securities houses, and other financial firms in New York. Japanese firms have created a large, complex, diversified base of operations in select locations of the United States. This is allowing in-

---

in the 1970s was for production or assembly of components imported from the highly developed countries and exported back after processing. A partial indicator of this is the value of goods brought into the United States under Tariff Items 806.30 and 807 (part of HTS 9802), which had a threefold increase from 1966 to 1978 (U.S. Department of Commerce, International Trade Administration 1980b, 1980c). The value of products coming from less developed countries represented only 6.3% of the total in 1966 but 44% by 1978.

creased and more direct participation in the economy, such as becoming lead managers in major real estate deals and producing cars here for export to Europe. There are many other examples. Japanese investors have bought up significant shares of major industrial firms, notably Firestone and the National Steel Corporation. By the beginning of 2000 Japanese-affiliated manufacturing plants in the U.S. numbered 2,136 (JETRO 2000). And major Arab investors acquired such legendary department stores as Harrod's in London and Saks Fifth Avenue in New York. These are huge acquisitions, with the Saks one estimated at $1.5 billion.

The Japanese case calls for a somewhat more detailed discussion, as it is less familiar and more unexpected, given a different organization of the economy. Restructuring in Japan has involved the shifting of a growing range of manufacturing to offshore locations, for example, textiles and auto parts; a shift from heavy and chemical industry to high-tech and knowledge-intensive industries; and the creation of Japanese international financial institutions. There has been a sharp increase in the number of workers employed abroad by the major Japanese manufacturers, an indication of the extent of internationalization and offshore production in such firms. From 1981 to 1987, Hitachi, a major producer of consumer goods, increased its number of employees abroad fivefold; Toshiba, threefold; Fujitsu, tenfold; and so on for a number of firms. For the three large auto manufacturers, this process only began in the 1980s, but by 1987 Toyota had 7,516 workers abroad; Nissan, over 22,000; and Honda, 6,700. These numbers represented a not insignificant share of all workers directly employed by these companies, especially in the case of auto manufacturers; Toyota's core workforce in Japan was about 28,000; Nissan's, about 70,000; and Honda's, about 34,000. With modifications this process has continued in the 1990s. For instance, Hitachi nearly doubled its overseas workforce in the 1990s while reducing its Japan-based workforce by 3%; and Matsushita doubled its overseas workforce to 134,000 while its Japan-based workforce increased only minimally to 148,000. In the 1980s, Japanese firms began setting up operations in Mexico. As Japanese manufacturers set up operations in the United States in order to avoid protectionist barriers, they developed twin plant operations[4] with Mexico, especially to supply electronic and auto compo-

---

[4] The twin plant (or in-bond) program was designated through special provisions of both Mexican and U.S. law. Mexico allows duty-free imports of machinery and equipment for manufacturing as well as components for assembly under the provision that 80% of the plant's output be exported. Mexico allows complete foreign ownership of plants. The United States in turn charges import duties only on that portion of the value of a good that was added in the process of assembly or manufacturing in Mexico of U.S.-made components that are to be reimported into the United States.

TABLE 2.1
Foreign Affiliates, 1996–1998 (bn USD)

Item	Value at Current Prices (bn USD)		
	1996	1997	1998
Sales to foreign affiliates	9,372	9,728	11,427
Gross product of foreign affiliates	2,026	2,286	2,677
Total assets of foreign affiliates	11,246	12,211	14,620
Exports of foreign affiliates	1,841	2,035	2,338
Employment of foreign affl. (thou.)	30,941	31,630	35,074

Source: UNCTAD, World Investment Report 1999: Foreign Direct Investment and the Challenge of Development, p. 9.

nents (Echeverri-Carroll 1988).[5] Japanese twin plants range from small operations employing between 25 and 50 people to very large ones employing 2,000 on several shifts. Many of these Japanese firms used to use assembly operations in Korea and Taiwan, from where the components were sent to Japanese firms in the United States or back to Japan.

One organizational form that captures these various developments is the global network of foreign affiliates of firms worldwide (see Table 2.1) which has grown sharply over the last decade reaching total assets of almost $15 trillion by 1998, and employing over 35 million workers. It now accounts for a larger volume of sales worldwide than direct exports. (See also chapter 3.)

Patterns of dispersal also are evident in the organization of office work. It is most evident in the United States and slowly emerging in the United Kingdom. It assumes a variety of forms, including the shipping or transmission of routine tasks to offices located abroad; shipping or transmission to suburban homes in the region where the head office is located; setting up offices, which are often whole divisions, in cheaper locations than that of the head office and frequently at great distance from the latter; subcontracting office work out to other firms; setting up back office operations at a short distance from the head office because the latter's location is too congested or expensive. The evidence suggests that these various forms are all increasing. Probably one of the most rapidly growing forms of office work decentralization in the United States is the use of women working out of suburban homes, a trend that began in the 1980s (Applebaum 1984; Baran and Teegarden 1983; Nelson 1984).

[5] By 1988 the Japanese had thirty-nine *maquilas* (twin plant operations) on the Mexican side of the border, of which about 70% had set up operations after 1982 (Echeverri-Carroll 1988). While the vast majority of twin plants in Mexico are U.S. owned, Japan now accounts for 3.5% of the total, having surpassed all other countries as a group, except for the United States. See the first edition for a more detailed discussion of Japanese twin plants.

There is a considerable supply of well-educated women in suburbs, where the absence of adequate child care facilities and the paucity of job choices may lead them to prefer taking work at home. Firms with large amounts of data processing, such as insurance companies, have seized on this labor market. The internationalization of this geographic dispersal of offices has been facilitated by the rather unrestricted flow and absence of tariffs on this type of data. Furthermore, the international flow of such data fits into the expanding trade of services generally. The United States government has long sought to maximize the free trade of information and has put pressure on other countries to prevent the imposition of tariffs.[6]

Transnational corporations are important in the international delivery of professional business services, in good part because they meet the need for continuous contact between the provider and the client (U.S. Congress, Office of Technology Assessment 1986). Business service firms serve foreign markets primarily through foreign affiliates. They do so in a range of ways—contractual arrangements, associated partnerships, equity participation. Statistics on large firms indicate that U.S. transnationals dominate the market for such professional services as accounting, advertising, management consulting, legal, and computer services. In some of these services, firms from France, Japan, and West Germany also have a significant share. Finally, a few less developed countries are gaining a place in the trade of certain professional services, notably computer software.

A third area that has contributed to spatial dispersion under conditions of continued economic concentration is the entry of large corporations into the retailing of consumer services. It is the possibility of obtaining economies of scale on the delivery of such services and the expanding market for such services that have led large corporations to produce for the open market consumer services that used to be produced only by small, single-site firms. This has brought about what Levitt (1976) has called the "industrialization" of services. Elsewhere (Sassen 1988) I have discussed at greater length how standardization and economies of scale in service production and delivery are predicated upon the shifting of certain components away from the establishments where actual service delivery

[6] There was great pressure from the United States to lift restrictions, long evident in Congressional debates about international trade in services already in the 1980s (U.S. Congress 1982) and in GATT (1989) negotiations aimed at ensuring and maximizing the free flow of services. Furthermore, as happened with manufacturing plants, governments of various countries are trying to draw firms to locate offshore office facilities. These governments began providing subsidies in the 1980s to draw investors, including the training of workers for the facilities (Sassen 1988). The insurance industry, for example, has argued that in order to stimulate U.S. trade and investment overseas, constraints and restrictions on the insurance delivery systems in foreign countries need to be reduced in many less developed countries, where the risks to multinational corporations are high.

takes place and onto headquarters. These come to centralize planning, development, franchising, purchasing, and other such functions.[7] The result has been a growth of large new firms, or divisions within firms, engaged in service delivery via multiple retail outlets and centralization of specialized functions. This fragmentation of the work process, parallel to that in manufacturing, is evident in hotels; restaurants; various kinds of repair services; movie theaters; car rentals; photo development; retail outlets for a broad range of consumer goods, from food to flowers; and a vast array of other service activities, which used to be largely the domain of small, local, independent entrepreneurs.

The geographic dispersal of economic activity described by the three cases above can be conceived of as a redeployment of growth poles. Thus, the development of export processing zones represents a deployment of manufacturing capacity from highly developed to less developed countries and setting up back office operations or retail outlets outside the head office entails shifting jobs from central to more peripheral locations. Dispersal of growth sites could, in principle, pose obstacles to the incorporation of such dispersed growth into processes generating surplus for the sectors of capital that concentrate much of the ownership and control in the major economies. Conceivably, the geographic dispersion of manufacturing plants and of office work could have gone along with a decentralization in the structure of ownership and profit appropriation. The market would mediate to a much larger extent than it does today between production and accumulation; that is to say, the various institutional processes we call the market would replace many of the internal transfer mechanisms of large corporations.

But such a parallel decentralization of ownership has not taken place. The large size of firms has made it possible to internalize transaction and circulation costs, thereby reducing the barriers to capital circulation and raising capital's ability to equalize the profit rate. Continued centralization of ownership poses the task of operating a worldwide production system with plants, offices and service branches in a multiplicity of foreign and domestic locations. It has brought about new requirements for the control of the vast decentralized production system and labor force.

This entails implementation of a system for the provision of such inputs as planning, top-level management, and specialized business ser-

---

[7] The globalization of markets and production together with product diversification demand the investment of greater resources in planning and marketing to reach the consumer. Advertising and consumer financing have become increasingly important components in the final product or service. The rapidly growing franchising system puts a good share of the costs and risks on the delivery outlet. (For a look from the bottom, see pp. 371–400 in Light and Bonacich 1988.) This is a form of vertical integration, I would argue, that is not in the Fordist mold.

vices. While such provision could conceivably be local, again, this has not happened. Firms with geographically dispersed plants, offices, and service outlets, as well as the firms that subsequently developed to service them, have tended to maintain considerable levels of centralized rather than localized provision of these types of inputs. As I will discuss at length in a later chapter, not only do the large industrial and trading corporations have elaborate production and contracting networks, but the specialized producer services have also developed such networks. In both cases central headquarters management, planning, and control operations expand and require additional inputs. These may be produced in-house or bought from other, specialized firms.

Several changes in the financial industry beginning in the 1980s are of significance to this discussion. Aggregate data on the industry mask the rather fundamental changes in its composition over the last two decades. In the 1970s there was a pattern of dispersal through the opening up of regional markets in many parts of the world as well as offshore banking to avoid the restrictive regulations in countries of origin. These developments were basically carried out under the aegis of the large transnational banks, the largest of which were from the United States. The form that capital mobility assumed in this industry at that time was similar to what had happened in manufacturing and services: a new, vastly expanded geography of economic activity that included a growing number of Third World locations along with the maintenance of economic control by large firms, mostly from the developed countries.

The onset of the so-called Third World debt crisis in 1982 continued to bring major changes to the industry, discussed at length later. For the purposes of this section what needs emphasizing is that its renewed concentration in and orientation toward major financial centers, beginning in the early 1980s, was not a mere geographic retrenchment but was in fact associated with new forms of capital mobility. These new forms were constituted basically through the development of a wide array of innovations, which had the effect of transforming more and more components of finance or financial assets into marketable instruments. We see an enormous increase in the liquidity of the industry and in the circulation of financial capital through the marketing of instruments rather than through lending. The central activity is now the buying and selling of instruments over and over again, thereby maximizing the circulation of financial capital. Deregulation and internationalization of major financial markets have raised the participation of investors and borrowers from all over the world. This poses the matter of control in the industry in a way parallel to that of the geographic dispersal of factories, though in a different form. Do deregulation and internationalization entail a decentralization in the ownership and control structure of the industry? I will argue that the fundamental axis for the circulation of this capital in the 1980s increasingly came to pass through New York, London, and Tokyo, rather than the regional banking centers in the Third World typical of the 1970s. In the 1990s this axis expanded into a growing worldwide network of deregulated financial centers. We see in this an instance of the new types of agglomeration associated with globalization.

Capital Mobility and Labor Market Formation

The increased mobility of capital has distinct effects on the formation of labor markets and the regulation of a global labor force. Increased capital mobility has brought about a homogenization of economic space, which conceivably could also have homogenized labor. On the one hand, there has been a worldwide standardization of consumer goods and decreasing differentiation among places in terms of the feasibility of producing a whole range of items for the world market, from apparel to electronic components. On the other hand, the dispersion of economic activity has contributed to the reproduction of structurally differentiated labor supplies and labor markets in this otherwise homogenized economic space.

The spatial and social reorganization of production associated with dispersion makes possible access to peripheralized labor markets, whether abroad or at home, without undermining that peripheral condition. Such labor markets remain peripheralized even when the jobs are in leading industries producing for the world market, for example, electronics production in Third World export processing zones. The historical tendency has been for workers employed in advanced sectors of the economy to acquire considerable economic power, that is, to become a "labor aristocracy." In different historical periods, this was the case in the auto, steel, and petrochemical industries. Under the organization of production prevalent today, even in a key industry such as electronics, labor needs can be met through a highly differentiated labor supply that corresponds to specific moments in the production process, that is, specific types of inputs. As a result, this high level of differentiation is not eroded by the incorporation of workers into an advanced sector of capital. Certain forms of the capital-labor relation can be maintained even in the most advanced and technically developed sectors of capital, such as sweatshops in the electronics industry. The geographic dispersal of economic activity can thus be seen as a tendency that ensures the reproduction of structurally differentiated labor supplies notwithstanding a context where global-sized firms have internalized the functions of the market and therewith homogenized their space of operation. Dispersion becomes a mechanism that operates against the tendency toward empowerment of workers in advanced sectors of capital and, at the limit, neutralizes the politico-economic consequences that Marx associated with the generalized increase in the capital intensity of production and that more recent analysts have associated with large, vertically integrated firms.[8] In this sense, the form of capital mobility entailed by the geographic dispersal of manufacturing is clearly yet another way in which the social compact represented by Fordism has been dismantled, even when assembly lines and mass production are retained at a transnational level.

There are also a number of economic activities that do not lend themselves to relocation. Notable among these are the large array of service jobs that need to be performed in situ: the staffing of hospitals and restaurants, the cleaning and maintenance of buildings, which cannot be moved—these need to be carried out where the offices, restaurants, and hospitals are located. Elsewhere (Sassen 1988) I have argued that the employment of immigrant workers, from highly trained personnel to unskilled laborers, may appear in this regard as a functional equivalent to the mobility of capital; but it is in fact a component of, rather than an alternative to, capital mobility insofar as (a) on the most general level, international capital mobility contributes to the formation of an international labor market and (b) more specifically, the economic restructuring associated with the current phase of capital mobility has generated a large supply of jobs and casual labor markets that facilitate the employment of disadvantaged foreign workers, and it has also generated a demand for specific high-level skills that can be met by workers from anywhere, as long as they have the required education.

The mobility of capital has contributed to new forms in the mobility of labor (Sassen 1988). The international circulation of capital has contributed to the formation of international labor markets. The major immigration flows to the United States, the United Kingdom, and now Japan are not haphazard in their origin. They are in good part rooted in the economic or political/military histories of their countries. The main countries sending immigrants to the United Kingdom were formerly part of the British Empire. The United Kingdom built "bridges" for the movement of capital, goods, and the military. But once the bridges are built, why would people not use them? Most immigrants to the United States come from countries where the United States has a strong economic or military presence. Finally, the recent formation of labor migration flows

[8] At the same time, however, the greater spatial differentiation of labor can generate rigidities for capital. Storper and Walker (1983) note that neoclassic economists and location theorists have treated labor in the same terms as those for "true" commodity inputs and outputs and therefore have underestimated its importance in location decisions. Whether highly trained personnel or low-wage unskilled laborers, labor can become one of the key locational criteria.

from several South Asian and Southeast Asian countries to Japan (discussed in chapter 9), would seem to confirm the model I developed in Sassen (1988). Through offshore production, foreign aid, investments, and the spread of markets for Japanese consumer goods, Japan has built bridges with these countries. Furthermore, the internationalization of the economies of the United States, the United Kingdom, and now Japan, associated with the development of a strong economic or political/military presence in foreign countries, also contributes to the formation of the option to employ foreign workers—a subject discussed in chapter 9. Again, this is most evident in Japan today, a country that has never considered itself an immigration country and that has a strong ideology about the importance of racial homogeneity. It seems that the internationalization of the Japanese economy has brought with it the possibility of employing foreign workers in a country where this was inconceivable a few years ago. The formation of this kind of an international labor market can also be seen as contributing to the dismantling of the conditions that made Fordism possible.

Professional workers are also increasingly moving in a cross-border labor market as their firms operate globally. Free trade agreements such as NAFTA or the GATS (General Agreement on Trade in Services) all contain specific rules for the cross-border circulation of professional service workers (Sassen 1998: chapter 2). Firms are also raising the numbers of their professional staff located overseas. This is well illustrated by the network of overseas professionals in the leading international law firms, which have rather high shares of staff overseas (see Table 2.2). Immigrant workers and professional overseas workers represent the lower and upper circuit of these forms of labor mobility, respectively.

Conclusion

In sum, central to my analysis of the mobility of capital is an elaboration that takes it beyond the notion of geographic locational capability. I seek to incorporate two additional elements. One is that the increased mobility of capital brings about new forms of locational concentration, which are as much a part of this mobility as is geographic dispersal. Furthermore, insofar as these new forms of agglomeration are associated with new forms of geographic dispersal, they do not simply represent a persistence of older forms of agglomeration, but respond to a new economic logic. This would mean that the question of why agglomeration persists in the face of global telecommunications capability is, in fact, the wrong question. This is not the persistence of old forms but the occurrence of new forms, precisely fed by the globalization and dispersal of

TABLE 2.2

Top Law Firms Based on Percentage of Lawyers Outside of Home Country, 2000

Firm	City	Lawyers Outside Home Country, %	# of Countries
Baker & McKenzie	Chicago	79.6	35
White & Case	New York	46.8	24
Clifford Chance	London	62.0	20
Linklaters	London	na	17
Allen & Overy	London	34.5	17
Freshfields	London	51.1	15
Skadden, Arps	New York	7.6	11
Sherman & Sterling	New York	25.0	9
Cleary, Gottlieb	New York	32.9	8
Sullivan & Cromwell	New York	12.6	7
Weil, Gotshal & Manges	New York	18.6	6
Slaughter and May	London	15.2	6
Davis Polk & Wardwell	New York	12.7	6

Source: Based on The Economist, "The Battle of the Atlantic: London and New York," Tables 1 and 2, 26 Feb 2000.

economic activity that such telecommunications capability makes feasible. The question should rather be at what point the cost of this agglomeration will become so high that there will be strong inducements to develop forms of agglomeration of centralized functions that are not geographically determined.

The second element I seek to incorporate into the analysis of capital mobility has to do with the transformations in the capital/labor relation that such mobility entails. Hence, beyond a changed geography of economic activity there is a constitution of new relations among the various components of a particular location. Each type of location contains a specific form of these newly constituted relations. The locations of interest to this book are major cities, specifically New York, London, and Tokyo, rather than for example, export-processing zones in Third World countries or back offices located in somewhat peripheral locations around major cities. In the case of major cities, I will argue in a later chapter that the casualization and informalization of a wide range of activities and the formation of a highly paid new professional class, are processes that can be shown to be strongly associated with the globalization of production and finance under conditions of continued economic concentration.

For the purposes of empirical analysis what needs to be extracted from the discussion here is that geographic dispersal is important to the understanding of growth in major cities today only insofar as this process has occurred under conditions of continued economic concentration. Given such conditions, the dispersal of economic activity brings about new requirements for centralized management and control. This leads to a subsequent task for empirical analysis: an examination of the actual work involved in running a highly dispersed (domestically and internationally) set of plants and offices and of the locational patterns of such work. If agglomeration economies are high, will these activities tend to be geographically concentrated, and if so, where? Major cities are obvious locations for activities geared toward the international market and transnational firms; yet there are elements in this chain of analysis that need further elucidation. Future chapters attempt this. But for now, the next two chapters examine the facts that describe the main trends discussed here.

Three

New Patterns in Foreign Direct Investment

FOREIGN DIRECT INVESTMENT (FDI) is one of several indicators of the processes of capital relocation discussed in the preceding chapter. It is a useful indicator because much of the geographic dispersion of production and of the reorganization in the financial industry is international rather than domestic. The intent here is not an exhaustive description of stocks and flows, but an identification of key patterns, magnitudes, and countries involved. The evidence discussed in this and the next chapter points to a realignment in basic trends. The massive increases in foreign direct investment by all developed countries in the 1960s and especially the 1970s have been overtaken by even more massive international financial investments in the 1980s and 1990s. Furthermore, the already high domination of investment by a limited number of countries has continued to increase. Finally, since the 1980s the flow of foreign direct investment in services has grown more rapidly than in manufacturing and extractive industries.

There has been a pronounced transformation in the composition of foreign direct investment. During the 1950s, foreign direct investment, measured in terms of stocks and flows, was largely concentrated in raw materials, other primary products, and resource-based manufacturing. In the 1980s, it was primarily in technology-intensive manufacturing and in services. By the mid-1980s, about 40% of the world's total foreign direct investment stock of about $700 billion was in services, compared to about 25% in the early 1970s and less than 20% in the early 1950s. Moreover, foreign direct investment in services became the fastest-growing component of overall foreign direct investment flows. During the 1990s, more than half of all foreign direct investment flows were in services, with about two-thirds of this in finance and trade-related activities. By 1999, over 60% of the 4.1 trillion stock in foreign direct investment was in services.

Major Patterns

The most commonly used definition of foreign direct investment is that of the International Monetary Fund. It provides international guidelines for countries in compiling balance-of-payments accounts but does not specify a minimum ownership percentage to establish foreign ownership.

In the IMF *Balance of Payments Manual*, such investment is defined as "investment that is made to acquire a lasting interest in an enterprise operating in an economy other than that of the investor, the investor's purpose being to have an effective voice in the management of the enterprise" (IMF 1977). The OECD has established a benchmark definition in order to make the data somewhat comparable. It recommends the inclusion of foreign affiliates in which a single investor controls less than 10% but has an effective voice in the management of the enterprise; it also recommends a variety of other indicators, such as participation in policymaking, exchange of managerial personnel, etc., to establish foreign ownership in marginal cases. (See also OECD 1996; 1997). The United States, through the Bureau of Economic Analysis of the Department of Commerce, has also adopted indicators that consider factors other than equity holding.

There has been a trend toward reducing the cutoff point that distinguishes foreign direct investment from other types of investments, in recognition of the fact that foreign direct investment can exist without ownership of voting shares. Large corporations may require only a small share in equity to have decisive influence in the management of an enterprise, and control may be obtained through nonequity, contractual arrangements. This is particularly important to an understanding of the place of foreign investment in services where nonequity arrangements are a common form for delivering services to a foreign location. This would be considered foreign direct investment as long as there is control over the foreign establishment. To consider zero-equity cases as foreign direct investment, does, however, create measurement problems (UN Centre for Transnational Corporations 1989c OECD 1997). The stock of foreign direct investments is a measure of equity and debt, and income from foreign direct investments is defined as a return on equity and debt investment, as distinguished from income from nonfinancial intangible assets associated with nonequity forms, which are categorized as "royalties and license fees."

The estimated world stock of foreign direct investment went from $66 billion in 1960 to $213 billion in 1972, $549 billion in 1984, $962.8 billion in 1987, and 4.1 trillion in 1998 (UNCTAD 1999: 4). Six major patterns can be extracted from the vast amount of data on foreign direct investment over the last two decades. First, all developed countries increased their foreign direct investment in the less developed countries during the 1970s, reaching an average annual growth rate of 19.4% from 1973 to 1978 (excluding petroleum). Investments in export-oriented production grew the fastest.

Since then the overall growth rate has been declining, to 1.9% on average for 1980 to 1987, and into a negative rate of −4% from 1997 to

TABLE 3.1

Average Annual Growth Rate of Foreign Direct
Investment from Developed to Developing
Countries, 1960–1998 (percent)

Period	Growth Rate
1960–1968	7.0
1968–1973	9.2
1973–1978	19.4
1980–1987	1.9
1988–1996	16.8
1997–1998	−4.0

Sources: 1960–1978: OECD, *Recent International Direct Investment Trends* (1981); 1980–1987: World Bank, *World Development* (1988); *1988–1998, OECD, Survey of OECD Work on International Investment* (1998).

1998. (See Table 3.1.) The 1990s saw an even stronger orientation of investment to the highly developed world. (See Table 3.2.)

Second, there was a sharp reversal in the position of the United States. Up to 1979, the United States had been the leading exporter of such investments. By 1981, it had become the leading recipient, and had

TABLE 3.2

Foreign Direct Investment Flows by Region, 1986 to 1997, Selected Years
(mn USD and percent)

Region	FDI Inflows			FDI Outflows		
	1986–1991 (annual avg.)	1997	% of World Totals in 1997	1986–1991 (annual avg.)	1997	% of World Totals in 1997
North Atlantic[1]	121,144	213,852	53.4	131,646	323,111	81.8
Latin America and the Caribbean[2]	9,460	56,138	14.0	1,305	9,097	2.3
South, East, and Southeast Asia[3]	15,135	82,411	20.6	8,315	50,157	12.7
Subtotal	145,739	352,401	88.0	141,266	382,365	96.7
World total	159,331	400,486		180,510	395,236	

Source: UNCTAD, *World Investment Report 1998*, Annex B, pp. 361–371.

Notes: [1]North Atlantic region includes all countries in the European Union, Iceland, Norway, Switzerland, Gibraltar, Canada, and the United States. [2]and [3]Please refer to source for detailed listing of all countries included.

fallen to second place as an exporter of capital, behind the United Kingdom, where it stayed until 1984. Since then, the levels at which the United States absorbed and exported foreign direct investment have reached historic highs. (See Table 3.3.) In the early 1970s, foreign direct investment in the United States represented less than 9% of all FDI by developed countries; by 1984, it was estimated at 60% of all FDI by developed countries, a share far higher than the 17% of the United Kingdom, the next largest recipient (U.S. Department of Commerce International Trade Administration 1984; UN Centre on Transnational Corporations 1985), and it constituted about 50% of global FDI in 1984 and in 1986 (IMF 1987b, table C14). This share fell to about 40% in the early 1990s and to 20% by the late 1990s, still leaving the U.S. far ahead of the next recipient, the UK, which received about 10% of world inflows and 16.4% of the total for the top nine countries. In 1997 alone the U.S. received $91 billion in FDI, accounting for a fifth of global inflows (UNCTAD 1999). Total FDI stock in the United States increased from U.S. $83 billion in 1980 to $328.9 billion in 1988. About 40% of this investment was accounted for by the United Kingdom and the Netherlands; Japan's share went from 6.5% in 1980 to 16.2% in 1988 (*Survey of Current Business* 1988a, 1989b). In 1997 FDI stock in the U.S. reached $1.8 trillion, jumping again in 1998 when the U.S. had record inflows of $193 b, double the level of 1997. The leading investors were the EU with

TABLE 3.3
Foreign Direct Investment Flows in Nine Industrialized Countries, 1991–1997 (in reporting economies, mn of USD and percent)

Country	Accumulated Tot. 1991–1997	% of Total for Listed Countries	% of World Total
United States	362,256	41.5	19.4
United Kingdom	143,445	16.4	7.7
France	142,296	16.3	7.6
Spain	61,483	7.0	3.3
Netherlands	57,941	6.6	3.1
Australia	45,707	5.2	2.5
Germany	27,050	3.1	1.5
Italy	24,999	2.9	1.3
Japan	8,516	1.0	0.5
Total for listed countries	873,693		
World Total	1,863,201		
Percentage of listed countries to world total	46.9		

Source: Author's calculations based on IMF, *Balance of Payments Statistics Yearbook*, vol. 49, Part 2, 1998, Table B-24, pp. 64–65.

155 b, triple their 1997 level and Japan with 9 b. German FDI investment increased fourfold and UK flows increased eightfold; together they accounted for almost 60% of U.S. FDI inflows in 1998. (See Table 3.4.)

A third pattern is Japan's rapidly growing role in global foreign direct investment. By 1985, Japan had become a leading exporter of foreign direct investment, with a gross outflow of $12.2 billion that almost tripled to $33 billion in 1987. For the first six months of 1988 it reached $22.8 billion, up 44.6% over the same period a year before (JETRO 1989: 7), with about half of this flow going to the United States. Japan had surpassed most of the leading Western European capital exporters, such as West Germany, the Netherlands, and France. But the economic crisis of the 1990s brought these levels down to $13.8 billion by 1993; it was not till 1997 that Japan's FDI rose to $26 b (see Table 3.5). What differentiates Japan from the other highly developed countries is the fact

TABLE 3.4A

Foreign Direct Investment Flows to the United States by Source, 1974–1997 (bn USD)

	1974	1987	1994	1997
Canada	5.1	24.0	41.2	64.0
Europe	16.8	186.1	294.0	425.2
Selected Countries:				
France	1.1	10.1	33.0	47.1
Germany[1]	1.5	20.3	39.6	69.7
Netherlands	4.7	49.1	66.6	84.9
United Kingdom	5.7	79.7	98.7	129.6
Latin America	—	—	24.5	35.7
Selected Countries:				
Brazil	—	—	0.6	0.7
Mexico	—	—	2.1	1.7
Asia and Pacific	—	—	113.0	148.2
Selected Countries:				
Australia	—	—	8.8	16.2
Japan	0.4	35.2	98.5	123.5
Addenda:				
European Union (12)	—	—	255.4	381.9
OPEC	2.7	4.9	4.3	4.7
Total World FDI	—	—	480.7	681.7

Source: Author's calculations based on U.S. Census Bureau, *Survey of Current Business*, various issues (Sept. 1998, pp. 82–85).

Notes: [1]For Germany before 1989, the figures refer to West Germany; —denotes that data was not in the original table.

TABLE 3.4B
Foreign Direct Investment in the United States by Source, 1994–1997 (percent)

	1994	1997
Canada	8.6	9.4
Europe	61.2	62.4
Latin America	5.1	5.2
Asia and Pacific	23.5	21.7
Total for Listed Regions	98.4	98.8
Addenda:		
European Union (12)	53.1	56.0
OPEC	0.9	0.7

Source: Author's calculations based on U.S. Census Bureau, Survey of Current Business, various issues (Sept. 1998, pp. 82–85).
Note: ¹Africa and non-OPEC countries omitted.

that it was not a significant recipient of FDI in these two decades. Such inflows had been between $250 million and $400 million since the late 1970s, compared with $400 million to $1.6 billion in West Germany, $2 billion to $3 billion in France, $1 billion to $2 billion in the Netherlands, and $2 billion to $6 billion in the United Kingdom. From 1986 to 1987, foreign direct investment inflow into Japan more than doubled, reaching a total of U.S. $2.3 billion in fiscal 1987 (though this is most probably an inflated figure, since it is based on the required notifications of intent to the Ministry of Finance, some of which may never take place) [JETRO 1989: 11]. FDI inflows dropped to about $200 million in 1996 and then rose sharply to $3.2 billion in 1997 and then again in 1998 (OECD 1999).

TABLE 3.5
Japan, United Kingdom, and United States: Foreign Direct Investment Flows, 1991–1997 (bn of USD)

	Japan			United Kingdom			United States		
Year	Outflows	Inflows	Balance	Outflows	Inflows	Balance	Outflows	Inflows	Balanc
1991	31.62	1.29	30.33	16.31	16.21	0.09	31.38	22.01	9.37
1992	17.39	2.76	14.63	18.99	16.14	2.86	42.66	17.94	24.72
1993	13.83	0.12	13.71	26.58	15.54	11.03	77.95	48.99	28.95
1994	18.09	0.91	17.18	33.80	9.19	24.62	75.21	44.59	30.62
1995	22.51	0.04	22.47	44.09	22.50	21.59	96.65	57.65	39.00
1996	23.44	0.20	23.24	35.16	25.78	9.37	81.07	77.62	3.45
1997	26.06	3.20	22.86	61.44	38.08	23.36	121.84	93.45	28.40

Source: Author's calculations based on IMF, *Balance of Payments Statistics Yearbook*, vol. 49, Part 2, 1998, Tabl B-24, pp. 64–65.

A fourth pattern is the change in the sectoral distribution of FDI. Investments in the primary sector fell by half between 1988 and 1997, and investments in the services sector rose in both developed and developing countries, raising its share in total FDI stock from 45% in 1988 to 56% in 1997. The share of manufacturing remained stable and was the highest FDI sector for developing countries. The industry with the largest share of FDI in the world is finance, followed by trade. Financial services (banks, insurance, securities, and other financial companies) have been top recipients of FDI since 1988. In developed countries finance and trade are leading recipients of FDI; in developing countries, real estate and chemicals.

A fifth pattern is the high degree of concentration in global foreign direct investment. Out of the global stock of $549 billion of foreign direct investment in 1984, the United States accounted for 42.5%, the United Kingdom accounted for 15.5%, and Japan accounted for 6.9%, or 65% of the total. By the end of 1987, the United States's share was 31.5%, the United Kingdom's was 18%, and Japan's was 10%, or 60% of the world stock of foreign direct investment. Out of the total FDI stock of 4.1 trillion in 1998, these countries accounted for 50%, with the U.S. share at 30%. In the late 1990s, the largest 10 home countries for FDI flows account for four-fifths of global FDI outflows. FDI inflows into developed countries were about $460 b (or 72% of global flows) and outflows from developed countries were about $595 b (or 92% of global outflows) in 1998 (UNCTAD 1999: p. xx). While flows to developing countries fell by 4%, flows to developed countries (coming mostly from other developed countries) increased by 68% over 1997. The EU was the largest source of FDI with US$ 386 b. in 1998, of which US$114 b. came from the UK. (See Table 3.6.) (OECD, various years a; Bank of England, various years; U.S. Department of Commerce, International Trade Administration 1980c; *Survey of Current Business* 1981b, 1988c 1999; MITI 1986 1999; IMF 1987a, 1999; JETRO 1987a, b 1999.) Multinational corporations of the developed countries accounted for 97% of recorded flows of foreign direct investment in the early 1980s (UN Centre on Transnational Corporations, 1985: 15). This has changed little today, except for the fact that there are 60,000 such corporations investing in affiliates worldwide and many of them are small and medium-sized corporations (UNCTAD 1999).

A seventh pattern, emerging in the late 1990s, is the growth of cross-border mergers and acquisitions (M&As) which now account for most FDI flows. Most of these take place among developed countries. But with privatization and deregulation in much of the developing world, there is a whole new flow of FDI directed to particular countries in Asia and in Latin America. In 1997, South, East, and Southeast Asia received US$ 40 billion or 12% of the world total FDI compared with US$ 2.8 b in 1987 (UNCTAD 1999: 24). (See Tables 3.7 and 3.8.)

TABLE 3.6

Japan, United Kingdom, and United States: Foreign Direct Investment Stock
1990–1997, Selected Years (end-period stocks, bn USD)

	1990	1993	1995	1997
Japan				
Direct investment abroad	201.44	259.8	238.45	271.9
Direct investment in	9.85	16.89	33.51	27.08
Balance	191.59	242.91	204.94	244.82
United Kingdom				
Direct investment abroad	230.82	250.38	314.29	375.43
Direct investment in	218.21	189.43	203.77	281.83
Balance	12.61	60.95	110.52	93.6
United States				
Direct investment abroad	731.76	1027.55	1307.16	1793.68
Direct investment in	539.6	768.4	1005.73	1620.54
Balance	192.16	259.15	301.43	173.14

Source: Author's calculations based on IMF, *Balance of Payments Statistics Yearbook*, vol. 49, Part 1, 1998: Japan, pp. 410–411, United Kingdom, pp. 850–851, United States, pp. 857–858.

International Transactions in Services

Overall, the service sector is oriented to a domestic and local market. Only major firms in certain service industries, particularly producer services, have a significant degree of internationalization as measured, for

TABLE 3.7

Cross-border Mergers and Acquisitions by Region, 1997 (bn USD and percent)

	Sales			Purchases		
Region	Cases	Value	Share	Cases	Value	Share
Western Europe	2350	118	35	2620	168	49
North America[1]	1305	86	25	2111	107	31
Asia	830	34	11	821	46	13
Japan, Australia, NZL	77	2	1	390	18	5
ASEAN	264	13	4	174	10	3
Other Asia[2]	489	19	6	257	18	5
South America	330	32	9	38	4	1
Central and Eastern Europe	154	5	1	6	3	0
Total	5726	341	100	5726	341	100

Notes: [1]Includes USA, Canada, and Mexico; [2]Includes Chinese Taipei, Hong Kong (China), Republic of Korea, and China.

Source: OECD, *Financial Market Trends*, no. 70, 1998, p.101, based on KMPG Corporate Finance, 1997.

TABLE 3.8

Top 15 Buyer and Seller Countries Ranked by Value in Global Mergers and Acquisitions, 1997 (numbers and bn USD)

| | Buyers | | | Sellers | |
Country	No. of Deals	Value	Country	No. of Deals	Value
United States	1655	81.8	United States	937	65.1
Switzerland	170	38.7	United Kingdom	551	55.4
United Kingdom	642	32.4	Germany	333	19.3
Canada	444	24.3	France	387	13.9
France	388	21.1	Australia	139	12.7
Netherlands	316	20.7	Brazil	131	12.6
Germany	324	16.0	Canada	298	11.0
Spain	85	13.0	China	379	9.1
Japan	313	11.7	Italy	179	8.8
Australia	80	9.9	Netherlands	131	8.0
Republic of Korea	77	6.7	Mexico	70	6.7
Sweden	133	6.2	Venezuela	21	6.4
Hong Kong (China)	127	5.5	Belgium	58	6.2
Singapore	71	4.8	Spain	142	6.2
China	28	4.6	Hong Kong (China)	71	5.9

Source: OECD, Financial Market Trends, no. 70, 1998. Based on KMPG Corporate Finance, 1997.

example, by the weight of foreign sales in total revenues of a firm. For example, despite rapid growth of the service share in the U.S. economy, the international trade in services accounts for a small share in total services output (Candilis 1988; Survey of Current Business 1999). In 1985 service industries accounted for 70% of U.S. domestic product. Service exports other than investment income accounted for only 1.4% of U.S. domestic product. U.S. private service exports other than investment income (U.S. $44.2 billion) were small relative to merchandise exports (U.S. $214.4 billion). In 1998, goods exports were $681.3 billion and service exports $285.1 billion; service exports were the equivalent of 3.2% of U.S. GDP ($8.76 trillion). Using 1998 data (Survey of Current Business 2000) for total services output and for overall service exports and imports, it can be estimated that the share of traded services is under 14%.

The characteristics of non-tradable services tend to require production and delivery in one location, which explains why foreign direct investment is at this time the main mode of international service delivery. Measurement problems with international service transactions hinder a detailed analysis of investment and trade patterns in producer services. Several special studies launched to address these problems indicate an undercount in international service trade figures, particularly intrafirm trade, and in investment figures, particularly the exclusion of nonequity arrangements from foreign direct investment measures.[1] Both the activities of transnational service firms and foreign direct investments in services have grown. The former UN Centre on Transnational Corporations, which had accumulated one of the best data sets on these developments, found that measurements based on sales and value-added of affiliates are quite consistent with the measurements of foreign direct investment.

The distinction between trade, foreign direct investment, and other modes of delivery is important for conceptual and statistical purposes. In the case of foreign direct investment, transnational corporations are an important factor, and many of the questions raised in the case of industrial transnational corporations may also emerge for the case of services (GATT various years; UN Centre on Transnational Corporations 1989b; UNCTAD 1999). The Group of Negotiations on Services for the General Agreement on Tariffs and Trade (GATT) was given the task of drafting a framework for the case of services, particularly the definitional and statistical questions, on which to base principles and rules for trade in services. The result was the 1994 General Agreement on Trade in Services (GATS) which defined such trade as the supply of a service: a) from the territory of one Member territory into the territory of another Member; b) in the territory of one Member to the service consumer of any other Member; c) by a service supplier of one Member through commercial presence in the territory of any other Member; d) by a service supplier of one Member, through presence of natural persons of a Member in the Territory of another Member. "Services" includes any service in any sector, except services supplied in the exercise of government authority.

International transactions in services can assume several forms. Services may be delivered to foreign markets directly, through the movement of people (either as providers or as consumers), through foreign affiliates in which the service provider has equity participation, licensing, or other nonequity mechanisms, and through commercial means, such as sales or representatives' offices (UN Centre on Transnational Corporations 1989c; UNCTAD 1999). In the case of nontradable services, foreign direct investment is the typical form of delivery. The two major forms of delivery are cross-border transactions and foreign direct investment.

---

[1] The data on the international trade balance are inadequate. There have been growing surpluses in "invisibles." But these cannot be fully attributed to the sales of services. On the other hand, some of the receipts of service industries are reported under the merchandise account. The data commonly used in descriptions of the service trade come from balance of payment data collected for the whole world by the Bank of International Settlement (BIS) which can then be used by governments. In the United States, these data are then prepared by the Bureau of Economic Analysis of the Department of Commerce. These data have serious inadequacies. In response to criticism, the now defunct Office of Technology Assessment of the U.S. Congress developed a more encompassing and precise measure.

The cross-border delivery of services is the only mode of delivery that has the characteristics of trade in goods, with the difference that only services embodied in goods (software or tapes, etc.) or those whose value-added can be put on paper (evaluations, drawings) can actually cross borders independently of producers.[2] Telecommunications technologies make possible and can be expected to contribute to the growth of transborder data flows, especially for information-intensive services. This technology has raised the tradability of many of the professional services. But, surprisingly, this type of transborder flow accounts for a small share of international transactions in services (UN Centre on Transnational Corporations 1989c: 3–4; OECD 1994, OECD 2000b). Telecommunications technology has raised intrafirm flows of services in transnational corporations and other corporate organizations.

The movement of persons is often a requirement for an international service transaction, either to buy or to provide the service. Travel is one of the four major services in terms of the balance of payments; it comprises various types of travel, including patients who go to a foreign country to buy medical services, tourists, and professional experts who go to a foreign country to provide a service, as is the case in many of the professional services. Providers may be unskilled construction workers, maintenance and repair workers, engineers, architects, lawyers, managers, and so on. They may be working on their own account, on behalf of a firm in the country of origin, or for a foreign company in the country of destination.

Delivery through foreign affiliates is common given the characteristics of production of many services, such as hotel, retail banking, and car rental services, computer and office equipment maintenance, accounting, and advertising. Delivery can also occur through licensing and other non-equity mechanisms, for example, franchises. In the case of professional services, such as law or accounting, arrangements often resemble foreign direct investment arrangements. Transnational firms may do business and refer clients to a particular firm in a foreign country that may or may not operate under the same name. In the case of the United States, it is clear that foreign direct investment is the most important mode of delivery of services by U.S. firms to foreign markets (UN Centre on Transnational Corporations 1989d: 8; UNCTAD 1999). Many affiliates of TNCs in manufacturing and primary industry are in services as they often begin by establishing foreign trading affiliates. Thus in 1996 63% of foreign affiliates of U.S. TNCs were in services compared to 38% of the U.S. parent

---

[2] The case of services embodied in goods raises the question of their separability. Bhagwati (1984) argues that with specialization based on economies of scale, service activities will be "splintered off" and become part of interfirm transactions, which he views as technologically progressive, unlike the reverse case, when goods are splintered off from services, which may leave behind a residue of relatively unprogressive, that is, technically static, services.

firms (U.S. Department of Commerce 1998). Similarly, 50% of foreign affiliates of Japanese TNCs in 1996 were in services, but only one-third of the parent firms (MITI 1998a: 104, 125).

Services delivered abroad by a provider are the most difficult to classify. Basically, such a transaction would be considered cross-border on the basis of four factors: (1) whether the producer's stay in the foreign country is limited; (2) whether the producer's stay is not part of a broader movement of resources, as when a transnational corporation sets up a new branch and brings over managers and other employees; (3) the nature of the service rendered (for example, architectural work, as opposed to pure labor, as with immigrants); and (4) the conduit (is it a specific service rendered to a foreign client or part of the setting up of a foreign branch by a transnational corporation and thus internal to the firm rather than provided to a client?). (Sassen 1998: 14–18)

Trade in Services

Current balance of payments guidelines do not clearly define trade or cross-border transactions in services;[3] the definition is somewhat clearer for foreign direct investment, but it is not uniformly used by all countries. Gray areas in terms of definition are transactions related to the temporary presence abroad of a provider and delivery through nonequity arrangements, offices, and agencies.

For the case of services, there are two aspects of the definition that are important. One is the cutoff point in share ownership of foreign affiliates in order to distinguish trade in services from portfolio and other types of investment. The second is the duration of operations in a foreign country in the case of movement of personnel and machinery in order to distinguish such movement from cross-border transactions. In terms of equity participation, there has been a trend toward lowering the cutoff point distinguishing other types of investment.

The evidence suggests that an early factor inducing the internationalization of producer services firms was the internationalization of manufacturing and extractive industries (U.S. Department of Commerce, International Trade Administration 1980a; Economic Consulting Services

[3] Directly traded services are largely recorded in the balance of payments, while indirectly traded services are embodied in goods trade and are part of the trade account (Sapir and Lutz 1981). The latter is typically not counted in measures of service trade and hence most of the data are an undercount. Discussion of the problem in measuring service trade by use of balance of payments data can be found in Shelp (1981) and in Tucker, Sundberg, and Seow (1983). In 1984, the ten top trading countries accounted for almost 70% of world exports and 53% of world imports; in 1997, these shares stood at, respectively, 70.6% and 66.5% of all industrial countries (see Table 3.10).

1981; UN Centre on Transnational Corporations 1985). Real growth in international trade in services was about 8% per annum from 1970 to 1980, similar to the growth in merchandise trade. After 1980, it declined to about 2.8% per annum, paralleling a decline in merchandise trade. However, by the mid-1980s the international trade in services was accelerating and surpassing the trade in merchandise, suggesting that it had become less dependent on the latter and more connected to other conditions, such as the growth of investment income flows and finance.

The overall figures on the trade in services include as key components income from investment, including debt repayments, and travel and transportation. Investment income has grown faster than all other categories. Most of the growth of this component is in industrial and non-oil-exporting developing countries. Among the factors behind the increase in investment income flow in the 1980s is the rise in real interest rates, the increased debt of the less developed countries, and the growing debt service of the United States. In 1984 exports and imports of investment income in industrial countries were about equal; by 1985, industrial countries had become net importers of capital. The trade in services for business, though small, was a growing share of overall service trade.

In the 1960s and 1970s, the international trade in services (transportation, tourism, investment income, and other services) accounted for one-fourth of total world trade; by 1984 it had increased to 29% of world trade and was worth U.S. $736.7 billion in imports. Table 3.9 shows service imports and exports in the 1990s for major surplus and deficit nations. From an overall deficit in service trade in the 1980s and much of the 1990s, the trend had reversed by 1997 to an overall surplus of $53.1 b in total service trade. This is a small surplus relative to total trade, with $1.9 trillion in exports and $1.8 trillion in imports. What is still similar is the continuing services deficit in developing countries ($46.9 b).

Table 3.10 compares developed and developing countries for 1991 and 1997. Developed countries presently dominate the trade, although their share is declining. By 1997, developed countries accounted for 66.5% of service exports, down from 71.3% in 1991, and 70.7% of imports, down from 71% in 1991 (Table 3.10). Developing countries exported more and imported about the same. Only some highly industrialized countries are net service exporters: of the countries listed in Table 3.9. this was the case for the U.S., the Netherlands, Spain, and the United Kingdom. The largest volume of trade is among developed nations, while the net direction of trade is from developed to developing countries. The non-oil-exporting developing countries have the largest deficits, mostly accounting for investment income flows, that is, debt repayments; this is especially true of Brazil and other Latin American countries.

The U.S. share of world exports of merchandise declined 3% between

TABLE 3.9
World Services Trade by Group and Selected Countries, 1997 (Major Surplus and Deficit Countries Reported by Group) (bn USD and percent)

Group/Country	Services Exports	Services Imports	Other Services Exports	Other Services Imports	Total Services Exports	Total Services Imports	Net Services	Exports % Total World Receipts	Imports % Total World Receipts
Industrial Countries	956.96	−900.29	411.60	−356.43	1,368.56	−1256.72	111.84	66.83	70.78
Selected Countries:									
United States	256.16	−166.19	99.80	−52.53	355.96	−218.73	137.23	11.63	18.41
Canada	30.02	−36.36	14.52	−16.31	44.54	−52.67	−8.13	2.80	2.30
Japan	69.30	−123.45	41.98	−57.96	111.29	−181.41	−70.13	9.65	5.76
Germany	79.90	−119.51	33.10	−25.91	113.00	−145.42	−32.42	7.73	5.84
Greece	9.29	−4.65	39.38	−49.04	48.67	−53.69	−5.02	2.86	2.52
Ireland	6.16	−15.07	2.29	−10.80	8.45	−25.87	−17.42	1.38	0.44
Netherlands	49.77	−45.20	22.45	−19.93	72.22	−65.13	7.09	3.46	3.74
Spain	43.90	−24.68	10.01	−12.63	53.92	−37.31	16.61	1.98	2.79
United Kingdom	87.24	−72.03	46.47	−19.06	133.71	−91.10	42.61	4.84	6.92
Developing Countries	397.24	−443.14	165.39	−166.44	562.63	−609.57	−46.95	32.42	29.10
Africa	20.59	−33.66	4.30	−10.58	24.89	−44.24	−19.35	2.35	1.29
Asia	206.39	−215.54	103.40	−86.34	309.79	−301.88	7.91	16.05	16.02

Selected Countries:								
People's Republic of China	24.58	−30.31	9.47	−9.65	34.06	−39.96	−5.90	2.12	1.76
Indonesia	6.94	−16.61	0.14	−8.40	7.09	−25.01	−17.93	1.33	0.37
Middle East	35.59	−63.00	17.61	−21.91	53.20	−84.91	−31.71	4.52	2.75
Selected Countries:								
Israel	8.43	−11.07	3.36	−3.02	11.78	−14.09	−2.31	0.75	0.61
Saudi Arabia	4.48	−25.48	4.48	−11.81	8.97	−37.29	−28.32	1.98	0.46
Western Hemisphere	52.29	−67.20	13.58	−21.39	65.87	−88.59	−22.72	4.71	3.41
Selected Countries:								
Argentina	3.27	−6.34	0.38	−0.67	3.65	−7.01	−3.36	0.37	0.19
Brazil	7.27	−18.46	3.73	−5.69	11.00	24.15	−13.15	1.28	0.57
Mexico	11.40	−12.62	2.21	−6.23	13.61	−18.84	−5.24	1.00	0.57
Venezuela	1.42	−5.35	0.09	−1.19	1.50	−6.54	−5.04	0.35	0.70
International Organizations	1.55	−0.95	0.71	−4.63	2.26	−5.58	−3.32	0.30	0.08
World Total	1,355.80	−1352.90	577.69	−527.51	1,933.49	−1,880.41	53.08	100.00	0.12
								100.00	100.00

Source: Author's calculations based on IMF, *Balance of Payments Statistics Yearbook*, vol. 49, Part 2, 1998, pp. 22–23, 36–37.

Notes: Services includes transportation and travel; other services includes communications, construction, insurance, financial, computer and information, royalties and license fees, other business, personal, cultural and recreational, and government n.i.e.

TABLE 3.10

Share in World Service Exports and Imports by Type of Country, 1991 and 1997 (percent and bn USD)

	Credit		Debit	
	1991	*1997*	*1991*	*1997*
Total Services				
Industrial Countries	77.5%	70.6%	71.3%	66.5%
Developing Countries	22.3%	29.3%	27.9%	32.8%
Total (bn USD)	890.9	1,355.8	934.9	1,352.9
Selected Services:				
Transportation				
Industrial Countries	76.8%	72.4%	67.0%	63.9%
Developing Countries	23.2%	27.6%	33.0%	36.1%
Total (bn USD)	227.6	308.3	278.2	379.7
Travel				
Industrial Countries	75.0%	67.3%	80.1%	71.3%
Developing Countries	24.9%	32.7%	19.9%	28.7%
Total (bn USD)	272.8	420.3	255.6	386
Other Services[1]				
Industrial Countries	79.7%	71.2%	75.2%	67.6%
Developing Countries	20.1%	28.6%	24.7%	31.5%
Total (bn USD)	340.4	577.7	323.7	527.5

Source: Author's calculations based on IMF, *Balance of Payments Statistics Yearbook*, vol. 49, Part 2, 1998, pp. 22–37.

Note: [1]Other services includes communications, construction, insurance, financial, computer and information, royalties and license fees, other business and personal, cultural, and recreational transactions. Government services (n.i.e.) have been omitted.

1975 and 1985 to 12% where it remained in the 1990s, while that of services stood around 19% throughout the 1980s and 1990s (Table 3.11).

The U.S. share of world trade in services remained at about 19% from 1975 to 1997, even as its absolute value increased sharply. Transport, travel, and other services all registered significant growth (Table 3.11). The U.S. share in goods exports fell slightly from about 15% in 1975 to 12% in 1997. On the imports side there is a similarly modest increase in goods imports and decline in services imports. Absolute values on all four variables increased markedly over the period.

In contrast to surpluses in merchandise trade, Japan's imports of services exceeded its exports throughout the 1970s and into the 1990s (see Table 3.12). Thus, in 1999, Japan had a deficit of $54 billion in its inter-

TABLE 3.11

United States: Share of World Trade, 1975–1997, Selected Years (percent)

	Credits (in percent)					
	1975	1980	1985	1991	1995	1997
Total Goods	14.82	12.20	11.33	11.88	11.42	12.38
Total Services	19.86	17.02	19.23	18.24	17.60	18.89
Selected Services:						
Transport	11.27	10.16	14.24	16.91	15.10	15.51
Travel	10.93	10.39	11.21	20.47	18.78	20.06
Other Services	—	—	—	15.47	15.77	17.28
Total Income	—	—	—	16.09	46.53	20.07
Selected Income:						
Investment Income		25.76	25.73	16.52	19.39	20.60
Direct Investment	—	—	—	73.63	63.00	56.43

	Debits (in percent)					
	1975	1980	1985	1991	1995	1997
Total Goods	13.70	13.83	17.87	7.58	15.18	16.29
Total Services	13.48	16.69	14.83	12.63	11.29	12.28
Selected Services:						
Transport	10.57	8.90	15.10	12.58	11.26	12.43
Travel	15.08	10.04	16.87	14.14	12.68	13.66
Other Services	—	—	—	8.90	9.10	9.96
Total Income	—	—	—	12.96	16.06	19.27
Selected Income:						
Investment Income	17.96	14.39	16.56	13.09	16.28	19.53
Direct Investment	—	—	—	22.62	29.57	29.10

Source: Author's calculations based on IMF, Balance of Payments Statistics Yearbook, vol. 49, Part 2, 1998, pp. 20, 22, 24, 32, 36, 38, 42, 64.

Notes: Total goods includes general merchandise f.o.b., goods for processing f.o.b., repairs on goods, goods procured in ports by carriers, and nonmonetary gold. Other services includes communications, construction, insurance, financial, computer and information, royalties and license fees, other business services, personal, cultural and recreational, and government, n.i.e. Total income includes compensation of employees, direct investment, portfolio investment, and other investment. Investment income includes direct investment as dividends and distributed branch profits and reinvested earnings and undistributed branch profits and portfolio investment as income on equity, on bonds and notes and on money market instruments and financial derivatives; — denotes that data was not in the original table.

national service trade and a surplus of $101 billion in its merchandise trade. Among the largest items in both its services trade deficit and exports were "other services" and travel. The largest overall values were for the goods trade, followed by income, which had a positive balance of $101.6 billion (Table 3.12). These figures are significantly

TABLE 3.12

Japan: Exports and Imports of Services, Income, and Goods, 1991–1997 (bn of USD)

	1991			1994			1997		
	Exports	Imports	Balance	Exports	Imports	Balance	Exports	Imports	Balance
Goods	282.31	212.08	70.23	385.70	241.51	144.19	409.24	307.64	101.60
Services	44.84	86.63	−41.79	58.30	106.36	−48.06	69.30	123.45	−54.15
Transport	17.56	26.43	−8.87	20.31	31.70	−11.39	21.82	31.11	−9.29
Travel	3.43	23.95	−20.52	3.48	30.70	−27.22	4.33	33.01	−28.68
Other	23.84	36.25	−12.41	34.51	43.95	−9.44	43.15	59.33	−16.18
Income	140.96	114.97	25.99	155.19	114.96	40.23	222.15	166.41	55.74
Direct investment	6.38	0.21	6.17	154.32	1.93	152.39	16.12	4.00	12.12
Portfolio investment	47.11	14.67	32.44	48.60	18.24	30.36	169.37	127.63	41.74
Other investment	86.93	96.94	−10.01	96.01	93.20	2.81	36.31	34.45	1.86

Source: Author's calculations based on IMF, Balance of Payments Statistics Yearbook, vol. 49, Part 1, 1998, pp. 406–408.

smaller than those for the U.S. in services trade, where imports reached $166 billion and exports about $256 billion in 1997 (see Table 3.13, Services column). However, on both the export and the import side of goods trade, Japan's absolute values were higher at over $400 billion in exports and $300 billion in imports. The differences are smaller in the more specialized imports and exports of services in the "Other Services" column (Table 3.13), a subject I return to in the discussion of producer services trade.

Among the factors contributing to a change in composition were the internationalization of Japanese business and the rise in investment income. Total service imports tripled between 1980 and 1988, and kept on growing in the 1990s by half again. Export of services, though at a much lower level, also tripled in the 1980s largely due to income on invest-

TABLE 3.13

United States and Japan: Services to Goods Ratio Based on Credits and Debits for Services and Exports and Imports for Goods, 1990–1997 (bn of USD)

	Japan (Credits)			Japan (Debits)		
	Service Credits	Goods Exports	Ratio	Service Debits	Goods Imports	Ratio
1990	41.38	282.31	0.15	−84.28	−213.02	0.40
1991	44.84	308.17	0.15	−86.63	−212.08	0.41
1992	49.07	332.56	0.15	−93.03	−207.79	0.45
1993	53.22	352.66	0.15	−96.30	−213.24	0.45
1994	58.30	385.70	0.15	−106.36	−241.51	0.44
1995	65.27	428.72	0.15	−122.63	−296.93	0.41
1996	67.72	400.28	0.17	−129.96	−316.72	0.41
1997	69.30	409.24	0.17	−123.45	−307.64	0.40

	United States (Credits)			United States (Debits)		
	Service Credits	Goods Exports	Ratio	Service Debits	Goods Imports	Ratio
1990	146.40	390.71	0.37	−117.05	−498.95	0.23
1991	162.54	418.58	0.39	−118.04	−491.40	0.24
1992	175.04	442.13	0.40	−116.49	−536.45	0.22
1993	184.35	458.73	0.40	−122.41	−589.44	0.21
1994	199.25	504.45	0.39	−132.45	−668.59	0.20
1995	217.80	577.69	0.38	−141.98	−749.57	0.19
1996	236.71	613.89	0.39	−152.00	−803.32	0.19
1997	256.16	681.27	0.38	−166.19	−877.28	0.19

Source: Author's calculations based on IMF, *Balance of Payments Statistics Yearbook*, vol. 49, Part 1, 1998, pp. 852, 405.

Note: Exports and imports of goods f.o.b. Ratio calculations based on formula ratio = credits/exports, for example and always shows the ratio of services to goods.

ment. Excluding income on investment, income from service exports in the 1990s shows growth of about 20% from 1991 to 1997, a slower rate than imports. And income on various types of investment also slows down, growing by about half from 1991 to 1997.

A comparison of the United States and Japan trade shows considerable disparity in the absolute level of service exports and some similarity in the levels of service imports. Between 1991 and 1997, service credits for the U.S. nearly doubled from $146.4 b to $256.2 b while Japanese service credits rose more modestly from $41.2 b to $69.3 b. During the 1990s the ratio of services to merchandise trade grew strongly for the U.S. on the credit side and remained stable on the debit side; for Japan the ratios remained similar to those of the 1980s. Throughout the 1980s and 1990s, notwithstanding enormous changes in the absolute value of trade in goods and services, the services to goods trade ratio remained fairly stable for both countries on both the import and the export sides, indicating the ongoing importance of trade in goods. Thus in the 1990s U.S. exports of goods went from $390 billion in 1990 to $681 billion in 1997, and in services exports from $146 billion to $256 billion. In Japan goods exports went from $282 billion in 1990 to $409 billion in 1997, and service exports from $41 b to $69 b.

Foreign Direct Investment in Services

The rapid increase of foreign direct investment in services is part of the more general internationalization of economic activity. The internationalization of industrial production through trade and foreign direct investment engendered a demand for support activities in trade, finance, accounting, law, etc. Thus, many service affiliates were, especially initially, established by industrial transnational corporations. The early 1970s saw the growth of the internationalization of service production by transnational corporations. And since then, the internationalization of service production has grown more rapidly than that of goods. Most of the services produced by transnationals are intermediate services, yet another indication that the internationalization of service production has followed industrial transnationalization. The growth of service transnationalization should not be seen as being at the cost of industrial transnationalization; they are deeply connected.

The U.S. and Japan are major investment partners. Table 3.14 shows that the major categories of services listed all experienced significant increases over the last twenty years even though initial and current levels vary sharply between the two countries. (Survey of Current Business 1998 a, b; 2000.) The strongest rates of increase happened in finance, with

TABLE 3.14A

U.S. Direct Investment Stock in Japan: Selected Service Industries, 1982–1997
(bn USD, historical-cost basis)

Year	Wholesale Trade	Depository Institutions	Finance[1]	Services	All Service Industries
1982	1.09	0.17	0.31	0.42	6.41
1988	3.47	0.26	1.26	0.21	16.87
1997	5.63	0.57	8.84	1.18	35.57
% change 1982– 1997	414.9	240.4	2733.0	180.2	455.2

Source: Author's calculations based on U.S. Census Bureau, Survey of Current Business, Oct. 1998, pp. 128–131, Sept. 1989 and Oct. 1983.

Note: [1]Also includes insurance and real estate.

U.S. FDI stock in Japan growing sharply from $0.3 billion in 1982 to $8.8 billion in 1997; and in the case of Japanese direct investment stock in the U.S., from a negative balance of $0.57 billion in 1982 to $12.3 billion in 1997. Clearly, finance is not simply a service industry—a point that is important to my analysis and to which I return in the next chapter which examines trade and investment in financial instruments. With fluctuations, real estate investments by the Japanese in the U.S. also rose sharply between 1982 and 1997, reaching their highest level in the late 1980s. The most pronounced increase in Japanese FDI in services in the U.S. in the 1980s was in real estate, which went from $0.40 billion in 1982 to $10 billion in 1988. Japanese investment stock in finance grew from $570 million in 1982 to $2.8 billion in 1988. By 1997 Japanese FDI stock in all industries in the U.S. totalled 98.5 b USD, for a 920% increase over the 1982 level. (See Table 3.14 B.)

TABLE 3.14B

Japanese Direct Investment Stock in the United States: Selected Service Industries, 1982–1997
(bn USD, historical-cost basis)

Year	Wholesale Trade	Retail Trade	Depository Institutions	Finance	Insurance	Real Estate	All Service Industries
1982	6.13	0.15	1.33	−0.57	0.17	0.40	9.68
1988	18.39	0.35	3.90	2.86	n/a	10.02	53.35
1997	35.49	1.21	5.27	12.35	0.62	9.34	98.51
% Change 1982–1997	479.3	700.7	297.5	1134.5	266.3	2257.3	918.0

Source: Author's calculations based on U.S. Census Bureau, Survey of Current Business, Sept. 1998, pp. 82–85, Sept. 1989 and Oct. 1983.

In the United States, which has vast flows of foreign direct investment, services already accounted for a third of all stock abroad in the early 1950s. During the 1970s, a major new development was the strong shift toward the growth of the service share and a change in the composition of services. U.S. foreign direct investment in transportation, communications, and public utilities declined, and finance-related and trade-related services increased (Whichard 1981: 39–56). Between 1977 and 1986, the stock of foreign direct investment in services almost doubled, climbing from $60 billion to $119 billion, with the share rising to 43%; half of the increase in U.S. foreign direct investment abroad was accounted for by services (UN Centre on Transnational Corporations 1989d: 8–21). In the 1980s the United States was the largest recipient of foreign direct investment in services, with $110 billion of inward stock in services in 1986. Between 1980 and 1985, the stock of foreign direct investment in services increased more than in any other sector, by $55 billion compared with $45 billion for all other sectors combined. Six countries accounted for over 80% of this increase in the United States, with Japan and the United Kingdom each accounting for a quarter of that 80%-plus and Canada, West Germany, the Netherlands, and Switzerland accounting for the other half. In the late 1990s a surge in M&As altered the composition of FDI inflows in the U.S. towards a sharp increase in the acquisition of manufacturing and oil companies, reducing the share of services in the 1998 inflows to under 30%. The reverse was the case in FDI outflows, where 60% was in services, especially non-bank finance and insurance.

It is in Japan that services accounted for most of the rapid growth in outward stock of foreign direct investment in the 1980s (UN Centre on Transnational Corporations 1989d: 11–14). Japan's foreign direct investment increased by $61 billion from 1977 to 1985, of which 57% was in services; in the case of developed market economies, this increase was 63%. By the mid-1980s, the share of services in Japan's total stock of foreign direct investment had reached 50%. Of the total outflow of $22.3 billion in outward foreign direct investments from Japan in 1986, 77% was in services.

International Transactions in Producer Services

A particular concern here is international trade and investment in services for firms. The data are particularly inadequate to measure this type of services because they often have mixed consumer and intermediate markets and, secondly, because the classifications used, e.g., private services, often mix producer and consumer services. Measurement problems are

TABLE 3.15

Top Eight Exporters of Services, 1996 (mn of USD and percent)

Country	Service Exports	% of OECD
United States	236,714	23.1
Germany	84,994	8.3
France	83,533	8.2
UK	81,672	8.0
Italy	70,036	6.8
Japan	67,689	6.6
Netherlands	49,659	4.8
Spain	44,333	4.3
Total OECD	1,024,796	70.1

Source: OECD, Statistics on International Transactions, 1998 Edition.

further complicated by recent redefinitions of trade and investment in services (see, e.g., Mann and Brokenbaugh 1999: 53).[4]

The top eight exporters of services in the world, including all service exports, were the U.S., Germany, France, the UK, Italy, Japan, the Netherlands, and Spain, which together accounted for 70% of the total $1 trillion of OECD countries export. (See Table 3.15.) The U.S. total at $236.7 billion accounted for almost a quarter of all OECD exports. (See also Table 3.9 Other Services, for a measure of producer services trade.)

U.S. foreign direct investment abroad in a group of services that have to do with business services very broadly defined (excluding FIRE) rose from $7 billion in 1988 to about $41 in 1997. (See Table 3.16.) Among the sharpest growth rates from 1988 to 1997 were those for computer and data processing, which went from $0.1 billion in 1988 to $11.8 billion in 1997, and in business services narrowly defined which went from $3.1 billion to $22.3 billion. Advertising grew sixfold and Management and Public Relations almost fourfold.

A narrower focus on exports and imports of business, technical, and professional services between the U.S. and, respectively, the UK and Japan, shows the enormous weight of U.S. exports. (See Table 3.17.) Total U.S. exports of these specialized services to Japan grew from $1.58 billion in 1995 to 2.3 billion in only three years and from $1.5 billion to $2.7 billion to the UK over that same short period of time. Imports from Japan barely grew, but imports from the UK almost doubled, from $0.8 billion to $1.6 billion. Certain services dominate this trade. On the ex-

[4] For a detailed discussion of measurement issues and the evidence for the 1980s, see the first edition of this book (pp. 56–62).

TABLE 3.16

United States: Foreign Direct Investment Flows in Services Abroad, 1988, 1994 and 1997 (industry detail, bn USD)

Industry	1988	1994	1997
All industries	326.9	612.9	860.7
Wholesale-trade	34.4	59.0	69.1
Depository institutions	16.1	27.4	34.4
Finance, insurance, and real estate[1]	60.6	195.9	281.0
Finance	10.4	65.0	82.8
Insurance	12.7	26.0	42.4
Real estate	2.1	1.5	1.2
Holding Companies	35.4	103.4	154.5
Services	7.1	27.0	40.9
Hotels and other lodging places	0.8	2.1	2.7
Business services:	3.1	13.9	22.3
Advertising	0.5	2.1	3.3
Equipment rental[2]	0.7	1.1	2.9
Computer and data processing	0.1	8.2	11.8
Business services, nec[3]	1.1	2.4	4.2
Automotive rental and leasing	—	2.0	4.5
Motion pictures[4]	1.0	1.3	2.6
Health	0.6	0.4	0.1
Engineering, architectural, and surveying	0.8	1.1	1.2
Management and public relations	0.7	2.1	2.7
Other[5]	0.9	4.3	4.8
Other Industries[6]	15.2	35.0	61.5
Transportation	2.1	4.6	5.6
Communication	0.1	7.6	15.2
Retail trade	5.6	10.3	12.5

Source: Author's calculations based on U.S. Census Bureau, *Survey of Current Business* (Oct. 1998), p. 15.

Notes: [1]excludes depository institutions; [2]excludes automotive and computer rentals; [3]includes services to buildings, personnel supply services, and other related services; [4]includes television tape and film; [5]includes: automotive parking, repair, and other services; misc. repair services; amusement and recreation services; legal services; educational services; accounting, auditing, and bookkeeping services; research, development and testing services; and other services provided on a commercial basis; [6]in addition to industries listed: agriculture, forestry and fishing; mining; construction; electric, gas, and sanitary services.

port side the U.S. has a clear dominance in legal services to both countries. It also does in installation and equipment repair, and in computer and data processing services. By 1998, Other Services had grown sharply, reaching $0.596 billion in exports to the UK. This group of industries includes accounting, auditing, and bookkeeping services, management of

TABLE 3.17

United States Business, Professional, and Technical Services Trade with Japan and the United Kingdom, 1995 and 1998 (mn USD)

	Japan				United Kingdom			
	Exports		Imports		Exports		Imports	
	1995	1998	1995	1998	1995	1998	1995	1998
Advertising	39	40	293	323	57	62	91	149
Computer and data processing services	83	329	3	21	107	243	6	43
Database and other info. services	105	141	20	12	141	305	68	46
Research, development, and testing	155	194	23	23	81	62	68	141
Management consulting and public relations	72	87	30	37	144	186	74	187
Legal services	328	423	59	61	330	532	106	160
Construction, engineering, architectural, and mining services	117	128	5	42	94	355	25	45
Industrial engineering	—	302	—	154	13	41	23	15
Installation, maintenance, and repair of equip	382	441	—	16	282	322	16	185
Other[1]	—	280	266	158	250	596	324	620
Total	1,588	2,365	779	846	1,499	2,704	802	1,591

Source: Survey of Current Business, October 1999, pp. 88–91.

Note: [1]Other services consist of accounting, auditing, and bookkeeping services, agricultural services, mailing, reproduction, and commercial art management of health care facilities, medical services, miscellaneous disbursements, operational leasing, personnel supply services, sports and performing arts, training services, and other business, professional, and technical services.

health care facilities, and a broad range of other professional and business services. What fed the rapid growth of imports from the UK was this group of services, which reached $0.620 billion in 1998 up from $0.3 billion in 1995; also significant was the more than doubling of U.S. imports of management and consulting services from the UK, which reached $0.187 billion by 1998.

The main vehicle for international delivery, especially in services, is international production, which in turn stimulates international trade in products and tradable services. Setting up affiliates and subcontracting are key forms of the internationalization of production. Most affiliates at this point produce services even when the parent companies are in manufacturing. The number of foreign affiliates, whether through the estab-

TABLE 3.18
Parent Corporations and Foreign Affiliates, by Area and Economy,
1990–1998, Selected Years (number)

Area/Economy	Year	Parent Corporations Based in Economy	Foreign Affiliates Located in Economy
Developed Economies		49,806	94,623
Western Europe		39,415	62,226
Selected Countries:			
Germany	1996	7,569	11,445
United Kingdom	1997	1,085	2,525
Japan	1998	4,334	3,321
United States	1996	3,382	18,711
Developing Economies		9,246	238,906
Latin America		2,594	26,577
Selected Countries:			
Brazil	1998	1,225	8,050
Mexico	1993	na	8,420

Source: UNCTAD, *World Investment Report 1999*, "Foreign Direct Investment and the Challenge of Development," p. 5.

lishment of new ones or through M&As, has increased sharply over the last decades. This brings with it an increase in activities that come under the governance of TNCs. There are several measures that allow us to understand the growth and scale of the global network of overseas affiliates. The global stock of total assets associated with international production is estimated at around $15 trillion in 1998. (See also Table 2.1.)[5] This figure excludes the asset base of international production that takes place in establishments under non-equity forms of TNC control, such as subcontracting. These non-equity forms of TNC control are known to be growing in some sectors. As a result, the TNC base of international production is far larger than the $15 trillion figure and is likely to be growing. Sales by affiliates are higher than direct exports since the early 1980s:

[5] The accumulated stock of FDI is one component of the capital base of international production. The accumulated stock of FDI is a measure that includes the value of production facilities under TNC governance, as well as other assets, financed through FDI and other channels, such as raising funds directly in domestic or international markets. It increased by 20% in 1998 to $4.1 trillion and to $5 tr in 1999. The total value of assets of foreign affiliates is 4 to 5 times the value of FDI inward stock in countries such as the U.S., Japan, and Germany. But in developing countries, this asset value is only slightly higher than FDI stock. This suggests that international production activity in developing countries relies much more on capital from parent firms than it does in the case of developed countries.

in 1998 such sales were $11 tr compared to $7 tr in direct exports. For eign affiliates of course also export. Exports by foreign affiliates, including intrafirm exports—are estimated at one-fifth of sales of foreign affiliates in the world, with enormous variations by country. Trade within TNCs accounts for a third of world trade, and trade through non-equity arrangements within TNCs for another third, making intrafirm trade about 60% of world trade (UNCTAD 1999: chap. 8). But the size of exports and the size of production by affiliates and their relative significance do not necessarily correspond because FDI can be aimed at setting up affiliates of TNCs oriented to a domestic market which are not exporting, as is the case with many foreign affiliates in the U.S., for instance. International production is closely intertwined with trade because affiliates import goods and services that are inputs for their production, and because part of affiliate production at least in some countries is for export.

By far the largest number of foreign affiliates worldwide is located in developing countries, numbering almost 240,000 compared with 94,600 in the developed economies. (See Table 3.18.) Parent corporations, on the other hand, have the reverse pattern, with a far larger number of these at almost 50,000 in developed countries compared with 9,200 in developing countries. The U.S. has one of the sharpest differences between number of parent corporations in the U.S., which numbered 3,382 in 1996, and foreign affiliates, which were over 18,700. In contrast, in a pattern that is the reverse of what characterizes most countries, Japan had a larger number of parent corporations, at 4,334 than it had of affiliates, at 3,321.

Conclusion

There has been a fundamental transformation in the geography and composition of international economic transactions. Most remarkable is the emergence of the United States as the leading recipient of foreign direct investment and of Japan as the leading net exporter of such investment. Latin America is no longer the major recipient of foreign direct investment it once was, except perhaps for Brazil, and then largely São Paulo. Southeast Asia replaced Latin America as the main location for foreign direct investment in manufacturing by highly developed countries. In terms of composition, the main developments were the rapidly growing weight of services in foreign direct investment and the immense volume reached by international financial transactions, discussed in the next chapter. Services now account for over half the global stock of foreign direct investment, a development of the 1980s that required even higher rates of increase in the flow of such investment during this period. Again, a handful of countries account for 70% of global activity in services. There is, then, a reconcentration of international transactions in the highly developed countries and a particularly high concentration of all activity accounted for by the United States, the United Kingdom, and Japan.

In terms of some of the questions organizing the inquiry in this book, several trends are of interest. First, transnational firms are central to the internationalization of services, with foreign direct investment one of the leading forms assumed by this activity. Telecommunications advances may increase the weight of transborder trade in services, but the properties of many services set limits to this mode of delivery. Second, in the case of professional services, foreign sales account for a very large share of all revenues among leading firms, reaching well over half in the case of accounting and advertising. This has reinforced the global market orientation in large cities that are key locations for such firms.

The 1980s were clearly a decade when the importance of services and finance rose sharply. The structures for international production and distribution of services and finance are in many ways quite different from those in extractive or manufacturing activities. The key production sites for the latter have often been in less developed countries; such countries are far less likely to play an important role in international transactions of professional services and finance, while such major cities as New York, London, Tokyo, Frankfurt, Paris, and others are clearly central locations for these transactions.

These patterns point to a realignment in international investment. The large-scale increases in foreign direct investment in a multiplicity of locations during the 1970s, central to the internationalization of production, were followed by a subsequent phase of large increases in financial flows in the 1980s and 1990s, on a scale that dwarfed the magnitudes of the earlier phase. The levels of concentration by country associated with this second finance-dominated phase would seem to be higher than those of the 1970s. But we also see here a realignment in the structure of concentration, a subject taken up in the next chapter.

Four

Internationalization and Expansion of the Financial Industry

SINCE THE EARLY 1980s there has been a pronounced and rapid transformation in the volume of the financial industry, in its organization, and in the supply of and demand for financial products and services. Fundamental conditions for this transformation were the opening up of national markets through deregulation; a massive influx of funds into the markets through the growing participation of major financial institutions, notably insurance companies, pension funds, and trust banks; and the rapid production of innovations that transformed a large amount of financial assets into marketable instruments. Together, these developments had the effect of raising the volume of the industry, accelerating the pace of transactions, and dramatically reducing the share of bank loans in industry volume. Bonds and equities as well as the marketing of hitherto illiquid instruments became the central components of the industry. These trends continue in the 1990s with innovation activity centered on derivatives.

The transformation was both facilitated and partly induced by constraints on the earnings capacity of the large commercial banks that had dominated the industry since World War II. Regulations prohibiting banks from entering the securities market, massive Third World loan losses, and the more traditional type of business activity characterizing commercial banking, all reduced the participation of these banks in the highly innovative and speculative phase the financial markets entered in the 1980s. There was a rapid proliferation of smaller investment banks capable of seizing the opportunities of deregulation and internationalization of the financial industry through the development of new products and new markets.

Central concerns underlying the following examination of changes in the volume and composition of the industry are the durability of this phase of growth and the space economy it engenders. This chapter examines the empirical referents of the transformation in the industry, particularly the growing importance of securities and institutional investors, the formation of an international equities market, the new role of Japanese investors in the 1980s, and major realignments in the 1990s. Deregulation and the production of innovations, two key aspects in the growth and internationalization of the industry, will be discussed in chapter 5, as part of a broader examination of the producer services.

Conditions and Components of Growth

While aggregate measures of international financial activity show high growth rates from 1972 onward, there were radically different factors creating this growth in the 1970s compared with the 1980s. From 1972 to 1985, funds raised in the international financial markets grew by 23% per year on the average, compared with an average annual growth of 13% in world trade.[1] In the 1970s the major source of capital funds was massive oil revenues generated through the increase in the price of oil, and the key financial institutions were the large U. S. transnational banks in charge of selling much of this money. Thus, developing countries were a key element in the geography of financial activity, as both producers and consumers in international finance. In the 1980s, growth was linked to massive increases in international securities transactions, which became the main mode of cross-border borrowing and lending; the key institutions were securities firms and investment banks; and almost all these funds came from and went to developed countries.

In the immediate postwar period, there was no international financial market, and governments had close regulatory control over domestic financial activity and whatever foreign operations national firms engaged in. The first instance of a significant international financial market was the Eurocurrency market that developed in the 1960s. It came about and it grew in good part as a function of the effort by transnational corporations to avoid the regulations in their domestic markets and taxes on repatriated earnings. Up to the early 1970s, the international activity of banks mostly consisted of establishing foreign branches, subsidiaries, and offices to service needs of nonbank corporations operating abroad: the financing of foreign trade, provision of credit in local currency to affiliates, and, at times, direct intermediation in local financial markets. This form of participation in international activity was linked to a direct presence abroad. The sharp increase in international banking activity in the 1970s was largely organized by the large transnational banks located in the leading financial centers. This development, along with advances in telecommunications and information technology, made the use of local branches quite unnecessary. The decision by OPEC members to channel a major

---

[1] An examination of overall capital inflows and outflows in the United States, the United Kingdom, and Japan can serve to illustrate the different magnitudes involved by comparing them with those of foreign direct investment. The global flow of foreign direct investment went from 42,254 million SDRs in 1980 to 79,205 million SDRs in 1986 (IMF 1987b: tab. C14). In contrast, the global flow of international portfolio investments reached 42,697 SDRs in assets in 1980 and increased to 153,982 SDRs in 1986 (IMF 1987b: tab. C15). Liabilities went from 2 trillion SDRs in 1980 to 2.6 trillion SDRs in 1986 (IMF 1987b; tab. B1).

share of their earnings through the transnational banks produced an immense increase in these flows compared with the preceding decade. And
OPEC price increases, along with other developments, made nations
more dependent on banking funds. The assets of the major international
banks grew by 95% from 1976 to 1980, with the U.S. banks by far the
leading ones (Daly 1987). It was in this period that offshore banking
centers and the Eurodollar market became important factors in international finance. These institutional arrangements sharply increased the
mobility of banking capital through the avoidance of regulations and
constraints typical of domestic markets. This development points to the
growing power of the major transnational banks and the disintegration of
the system for global trade contained in the Bretton Woods agreement.

The Third World debt crisis of 1982 undermined the leading position
of U.S. transnational banks, and deregulation of domestic markets undermined offshore banking centers. What had once been essential elements
of international financial activity—foreign banking branches in the 1950s
and 1960s and offshore banking centers and transnational banks in the
1970s—had by the early 1980s become far less important. The leading
financial centers in the world emerged as the key component in international finance. Banks' share of international financial activity fell sharply
for much of the 1980s, and credit passed largely through securities markets and among developed countries.

Nonbank financial firms dominated the international financial markets
in the 1980s. Among these, the most important ones were securities
firms and financial services firms that covered a wide range of activities:
stockbroking (investment portfolio management) and investment banking (underwriting, structuring of mergers and acquisitions). These institutions engaged both in traditional activity (interest spread as a source of
earnings) and in risktaking (trading positions, underwriting new issues).
There was a sharp increase in cross-border acquisitions of financial firms.
These trends continued in the 1990s along with an even stronger speculative tone and an even larger wave of M&As than that of the 1980s.

This profound transformation could not escape its own consequences.
The level of risk had grown to historic highs and had already begun to
create concern among analysts before the October 1987 crash. The level
of speculation built into this growth was extremely high; perhaps the
only way this massive increase could have occurred was through speculation, epitomized by the futures market and corporate takeovers at exorbitant prices. This is a subject I return to in chapter 5. The emergence of
growing integration at the global scale meant that the October 1987
collapse in prices in New York, the 1994–95 Mexican crisis, the 1997
East Asian crisis, and the 1998 Russian crisis, had worldwide repercus-
sions. The October 1987 crisis was perhaps the first global crisis of the

new financial era, and diverges from those that followed in that it hit hardest in the highly developed countries and their leading financial centers. The later crises brought significantly smaller losses to the major centers of the west but had a catastrophic impact on wide sectors of the economy and population in the developing countries.

Formation of International Equity Markets

The current internationalization of the equity markets is quite different from the type of international transactions in equities before 1980. In the earlier period, Swiss banks, long the recipients of much foreign capital, acquired foreign equities to complement the limited investment opportunities within Switzerland. They were the leading investors in U.S. stocks during the 1960s and 1970s. Banks and investment companies in such countries as the Netherlands, Belgium, and Luxembourg, which have long functioned as recipients of foreign deposits, also engaged in this type of transaction, and Britain has had extensive overseas portfolio investments for a long time.

But there was no international market for equity transactions, and international capital investments were relatively small and limited to a few stock markets. Most of the financial markets were oriented to domestic investors and subject to foreign exchange controls. Access to equities listed in foreign stock markets was restricted, and there was no general, globalized distribution mechanism. Competitive pressures and the growing internationalization of other financial markets contributed to the rapid growth in international equity acquisitions. In Britain there was a strong increase in investments overseas, especially in the United States and Japan after foreign exchange controls were lifted. It was not until 1986 that the Japanese began to invest on a large scale in foreign equities. After the lifting of foreign exchange controls in Japan, most investment into overseas securities had gone into bonds, especially U.S. Treasury bonds.

Since the early 1980s, there has been an extremely pronounced growth in international transactions in equities and bonds. Deregulation and the vast amount of funds introduced by large institutional investors contributed to the rapid growth in cross-border investments in equities and the formation of an international market for equities. There is now an international equity market that is highly liquid and accessible, even though the integration of the various domestic markets involved is still quite limited. The production of innovations has also been of central importance in the expansion and operation of this market across national boundaries and in making more of these markets electronically integrated, as are those of New York, London, Tokyo, and many others.

International transactions in equities may be of several types. The purpose can be to use the equity opportunities present in stock markets in other countries considered to have better price/earnings ratios or, in the case of issuers, to gain access to abundant funds and new investment opportunities. The Japanese market had both of these features until recently; but a large number of smaller markets around the world also do. Alternatively, use of the international market for equities may be a response to limitations in the availability of funds in an issuer's domestic market. For example, if an Italian corporation wants to raise a very large amount of capital by issuing stock, the use of foreign stock markets may be the only way of reaching that level. Finally, use of the international market may be a way of avoiding the limitations, restrictions, and costs of a domestic market.

The expansion of the market and the recency of this growth can be seen in various kinds of figures. Most stock markets around the world have experienced rapid increases in volumes and values, making them attractive to foreigners. Higher net returns than in the United States have occurred at various times in many markets including those of Japan, the United Kingdom, West Germany, and France. In the 1990s we see a pattern where a given stock market—usually in a so-called "emerging market"—has the highest returns in the world for a brief period, which can be as short as 6 months. This happened, among others, with Buenos Aires in the early 1990s, Istanbul in the mid-1990s, and Moscow shortly before the ruble crisis. This is often followed by a sharp decline in listed prices in those same markets. The integration of financial markets across borders, the deregulation of those markets as they become incorporated into the global network of markets, and the mobility and liquidity of financial capital, all contribute to this pattern. Massive amounts of capital can move into a market and just as easily move out. The participation of corporations in the equity markets has increased strongly over the last two decades, raising volumes.[2] In the United States, there has been an increase in the number of mergers and acquisitions and in large corporate repurchases of shares. This has meant raising vast amounts of funds to finance such acquisitions, and in the 1980s corporations chose to do much of this directly in the equity market rather than through banks.

Capitalization in stock markets grew rapidly in the 1980s, suffered declines at the turn of the decade, and accelerated in the mid-1990s and then again in the late 1990s after the various crises. In 1999, worldwide stock market capitalization stood at over $29.7 trillion, of which $13.9 trillion was in the U.S., or 49% of the world total; $2.6 trillion in the UK, or 9% of the world total; and almost $4 trillion in Japan, or 13% of

[2] In Japan the increased involvement of corporations has been through intercorporate investment in shares of customers and suppliers and by special investment trusts.

the world total. It is worth noting that even after a severe decade-long recession Japan should still occupy such a leading position, as is underlined by the fact that the aggregate for Eurozone member countries was $4.1 trillion or 14% of the total (Merril Lynch 2000). Together, the U.S., the UK, and Japan accounted for 69% of worldwide stock market capitalization. The 1999 levels represent an enormous increase over those of 1985 even considering only the largest markets at the time which were $1.1 trillion in the U.S., $528 billion in Japan, and $204 billion in the UK (Whittemore 1987: 142–43). The deregulation in the United Kingdom and the further deregulation in Japan since 1986 raised the figures of overall international investment for these countries. These figures clearly show the strong growth of Japan in the 1980s.[3] The internationalization of investment can be seen in the increasing volume of purchases of foreign equity by individual and institutional investors. From very minimal amounts, they increased steadily over the last two decades, with the most pronounced increases beginning in the 1980s.[4]

International equity issues reached $32 billion in 1986, a fivefold increase over 1983. Of these issues, a fifth of their value was represented by Euro-equity issues of European firms and almost half, or U.S. $15 billion worth, by issues of Japanese firms—a new development at that point.[5] It should be noted that many of the investors in new Japanese issues tended to be Japanese. They preferred doing this abroad in the Euromarket to avoid the regulations and the restrictions in their home markets. To put this in perspective, it is worth noting that the U.S. domestic market, long the world's largest market for new equity issues,

[3] Another type of indication of the rapid expansion of the international acquisition of equities in the 1980s is information on foreign stock purchases in individual countries. Foreign investment in Japanese stocks went from 1.1 billion yen in 1979 to 9.3 billion yen in 1985, 17 billion yen in 1986 (after the lifting of foreign exchange controls), and 23.3 billion yen in 1987 (Tokyo Stock Exchange 1988: 56). Foreign sales of Japanese equities went from 1.2 billion yen in 1979 to 10.1 billion yen in 1985, and then jumped to 20.6 billion yen in 1986 and 30.8 billion yen in 1987. On the other hand, Japanese investments in foreign equities in the Tokyo Stock Exchange in Japan went from 36 billion yen in 1979 to 1.3 trillion yen in 1985, 4.2 trillion yen in 1986, and 10.9 trillion yen in 1987. Japanese sales of foreign equities followed a parallel path, going from 44 billion yen in 1979 to 8.3 trillion yen in 1987 (Tokyo Stock Exchange 1988: 58). The 1990s saw retrenchments in many of these.

[4] Most of the foreign sales in the United States over the last few years have been the result of large corporations and shareholders wanting a larger market for their shares. This is the case with large companies, such as British Telecom and British Gas, when they became privatized and came out with huge new issues of stock.

[5] In the late 1980s the fastest growth was by Japanese Trust Banks through special accounts called "Tokkin" in which corporate funds are managed for investment on a favorable tax basis. Given the recency at the time of Japanese participation, the share of foreign equities in all holdings among Japanese investors was very small, though it grew rapidly.

offered U.S. $60 billion worth of new issues in 1986 and about U.S. $54 billion worth in 1987.[6] A development instituted in the 1980s is the organization of simultaneous coordinated distributions of shares in several national markets when dealing with a very large issue. This was originally developed for the issue of 1 billion Texaco International shares. When the large public utilities in Britain were privatized, they also used this method. British Telecom used the United States, Canada, Europe, and Japan. Most large privatizations in the world today are launched in more than one stock market.

The aggregate expansion of all equity markets, which reached $28 trillion in 1999, points to a number of trends. First, a multiplicity of countries have had expansions in their equity markets. Second, the United States share of world capitalization, which stood at 57% in 1975, has declined to 47%, though increasing in absolute value.[7] Third, besides the expansion in total volume, there has been a continuation of high concentration in a few markets. Thus, the share represented by the United States, the United Kingdom, and Japan increased from slightly over 75% in 1975 to 85% in 1988 as a result of an immense rise in Japan's share of world capitalization, from 11.6% in 1975 to 41.1% in 1988, and fell to 69% in 1999 due, this time, to Japan's severe losses.

Securitization of Finance

Direct raising of funds in the securities markets has affected the traditional role of banks as financial intermediaries. Securitization, the transformation of various types of financial assets and debts into marketable instruments, has been the vehicle for this disintermediation and for the massive expansion in the overall volume of the financial market. These are assets that were considered illiquid until recently. In the United States, where this process has been sharpest, the total value of securities

---

[6] At that time Japanese investors showed a marked preference for high-yielding bonds, and purchased mostly dollar-denominated bonds. Early in 1986 there was uncertainty as to whether Japanese investors would continue to buy dollar-denominated instruments. This uncertainty was in good part due to the fact that the main buyers, such as life insurance companies, casualty companies, and trust banks, had begun to approach the limit of 10% of their assets that they were allowed to invest in foreign securities. A slowdown in acquisitions by these institutions was offset, however, by increased purchases by Japanese institutions not subject to this limit, such as commercial banks, Japanese corporations, and leasing companies. Japanese fund managers today are mostly buyers of domestic equities and sellers of domestic bonds (Gallup Global Fund Manager Survey, March 13, 2000).

[7] In the United States the par value of outstanding publicly traded bonds and the market value of equity capital increased by five times from 1975 to 1986 (Salomon Brothers, Inc. various years). The increase in the market value of securities relative to the value of gross domestic product has continued to grow in the 1990s.

increased from $22 billion in 1980 to $269 billion in 1986 and 845 b$ in 1998 (Salomon Brothers, Inc. various years). Securitization has required a vast production of financial innovations and raised the level of competition to new heights. It also required a vastly expanded market, achieved through deregulation of domestic financial markets and internationalization.

The total volume of financial assets and transactions in the international capital market in the 1980s increased significantly; yet the commercial banks experienced a considerable decline in their market shares, while other financial institutions, such as mutual funds, raised theirs. Central to the commercial banks' loss in market share in lending was the extensive issuing of commercial paper by the big corporations, a trend that eventually spread to medium-sized corporations as well. Data on net borrowing by U.S. nonfinancial corporations show a doubling in securitized financing, from U.S. $45 billion in 1981 to U.S. $98.6 billion in 1986, almost all of it in the form of corporate bonds; in contrast, loans went from an almost similar level of U.S. $43.5 billion in 1981 to U.S. $27.1 billion in 1986 (Salomon Brothers, Inc. various years). By the late 1990s the volume of loans had risen sharply at $345.2 billion in 1996, but was still half of the value of international debt securities issues which reached 766.5 b USD in 1996 and 845 b USD in 1998 (Bank for International Settlements Annual Report 1999). Similarly, and especially in the United States, the banks' share of various kinds of consumer loans, such as auto loans, has shrunk as a result of a trend for manufacturers, notably in the auto industry, to acquire financial service firms.

Globally, as recently as 1982 when the Third World debt crisis exploded, international bank loans still accounted for a larger share of funds borrowed on international markets than did international bonds. By 1983 loans had fallen from U.S. $100 billion in 1982 to about U.S. $60 billion, a decline that continued down to U.S. $54 billion in 1985. Thus loans suffered a decline in relative and absolute terms. In 1987 there was a resurgence in the use of loans, which grew to U.S. $80 billion in that year and to U.S. $142 billion in 1988 (see Table 4.1). The resurgence of loans was in part attributable to the fact that many large corporations had been undergoing financial restructuring and there was a very large demand for funds in the capital markets and a need for immediate access when needed. Syndicated loans are a long-proven and reliable mechanism for raising money, and close working relations with a number of banks is an advantage in such a context.

Overall levels of funds raised in the international capital markets have continued to grow. The major financing instruments in the international capital markets are straight bonds, syndicated loans, and various types of Euro instruments (see Table 4.2). In 1985 these three instruments ac-

TABLE 4.1

Financing Activity on International Capital Markets by Type of Instrument, 1986–1996 (bn USD and percent)

	1986	1988	1994	1996
Securities	228.1	229.9	473.6	766.5
Loans	93.3	142.3	236.2	345.2
Other debt facilities	n/a	n/a	4.9	4.5
Non-underwritten facilities	n/a	n/a	252.9	455.4
Total	321.4	372.2	967.6	1571.6
Memorandum item:				
Year-on-year percentage change	+ 13.2	+ 18.4	+ 18.2	+ 22.4

Source: OECD, Financial Market Trends, no. 69, February 1998, p. 111.

counted for over half of the total $280.9 billion in financing in the international capital markets, a share that climbed to 80% in 1997. A breakdown by origin of borrowers (see Table 4.3) shows that the bulk of the financing went to OECD members, whose share rose from 75.8% in 1984 to 91% in 1988 and 87% in 1997. Out of the total of almost $1.7

TABLE 4.2

International Capital Markets: Major Financing Instruments, 1984–1997 (percent)

	1984	1988	1993	1997
Straight bonds	29.6	35.8	45.1	30.8
Medium-term euro-note programme[1]	—	4.3	13.9	23.2
Syndicated loans	23.2	26.7	16.7	22.1
FRNs (floating-rate loans)[2]	19.4	4.9	8.5	12.1
Euro-commercial paper programmes	—	12.6	4.7	2.7
Shares	—	1.7	5.0	4.8
Other bonds[3]	2.0	0.5	0.4	1.9
Convertible bonds	—	2.3	2.2	2.0
Bonds with equity warrants	5.5	6.3	2.5	0.2
Other debt facilities[4]	14.6	3.7	1.0	0.2
"Managed" loans[5]	5.7	1.2	n/a	n/a
Total	100	100	100	100
Memorandum item:				
Total in USD billion:	197.3	472.8	818.6	1769.3

Source: OECD, *Financial Market Trends*, no. 69, February 1998, p. 51.

Notes: [1]Including other non-underwritten facilities; [2]Including medium-term floating-rate CDs; [3]Zero bonds, deep-discount bonds, special placements, and bond offerings not included elsewhere; [4]including multiple-component facilities and other back-up facilities; [5]syndicated "new money" extended in connection with restructuring agreements.

TABLE 4.3
Borrowing on International Capital Markets by Main Borrowers, 1984–1997
(percent and bn USD)

	1984	1988	1993	1997
OECD area	75.8	91.1	88.9	87.4
Non-OECD	18.2	5.3	8.2	10.7
International development institutions	6.0	2.9	2.9	1.9
Total[1]	100.0	99.3	100.0	100.0
Total in USD bn	197.3	451.4	818.6	1769.3
of which:				
United States	33.5	61.8	124.9	447.5
Germany[2]	2.1	13.5	65.0	222.8
United Kingdom	9.0	75.4	51.3	181.2
France	12.1	28.3	58.0	84.9
Japan	21.3	60.9	85.4	79.2
Canada	8.8	21.2	38.7	42.7
Australia	9.8	19.8	27.3	38.4
Italy	6.3	14.7	31.2	30.7
U.S., U.K., and Japan (bn USD)	63.8	198.1	261.6	707.9
U.S., U.K., and Japan (percentage)	32.3	43.9	32.0	40.0

Source: OECD, Financial Market Trends, no. 69, February 1998, p. 50.
Notes: [1]1988 total not 100 due to rounding error; [2]1984 and 1988 figures for West Germany only.

trillion of financing in 1997, 57% went to five highly developed countries: 25% to the U.S., 12.6% to Germany, 10% to the UK, 4.8% to France, and 4.5% to Japan. In 1987, the U.S., the UK, and Japan had accounted for 50% of all borrowing in the international market (see Table 4.4).

A major trend in the world of international financing that strengthens in the 1990s is the growing debt by poor countries and the rapidly increasing levels of debt servicing. Net external debt of developing countries grew from $1.2 trillion in 1991 to $1.9 trillion in 1999 (see Table 4.5). Most of this debt was through private financing which saw its volume grow by 72% in that period to reach $1.16 trillion, compared with a 28% growth in official financing.

The Global Capital Market Today

The deregulation of domestic financial markets, the liberalization of international capital flows, computers and telecommunications, have all contributed to the explosive growth in financial markets described in the preceding section. Since 1980, the total stock of financial assets has in-

TABLE 4.4

Japan, United Kingdom, and United States: Funds Raised on International Bond Offerings, 1985–1997 (bn USD and percentage)

	1985	1988	1997
OECD area	229.1	372.7	716.8
of which:			
Japan	21.8	54.1	41.6
United Kingdom	20.9	62.7	52.2
United States	67.7	47.5	189.3
Non-OECD	—	—	85.9
International Development Institutions	—	—	28.9
Total	279.1	372.1	831.6
Japan, U.K., and U.S. share of OECD			
(%):	48.2	44.1	66.1
Japan	9.5	14.5	9.7
United Kingdom	9.1	16.8	12.2
United States	29.6	12.7	44.2
Japan, U.K., and U.S. share of total (%):	39.6	44.2	58.9
Japan	7.8	14.5	8.6
United Kingdom	7.5	16.9	10.9
United States	24.3	12.8	39.4

Source: Based on OECD, *Financial Market Trends*, no. 69, February 1988, p. 109.

TABLE 4.5

External Debt and Debt Service in Developing Countries, 1991 to 1999, Selected Years (bn USD)

Developing Countries[1]	1991	1995	1998	1999
External Debt	1,269.8	1,714.4	1,965.2	1,969.6
Net creditor countries	22.2	29.9	58.9	64.5
Net debtor countries	1,247.6	1,684.5	1,906.3	1,905.1
by Official financing	234.5	286.8	292.9	300.3
by Private financing	674.1	990.8	1,166.6	1,162.5
by Diversified financing	338.9	406.9	446.8	442.2
Debt-service payments	150.1	242.9	316.1	331.8
Net creditor countries	1.8	7.1	8.5	8.6
Net debtor countries	148.3	235.8	307.5	323.2
by Official financing	16.5	25.8	22.7	16.8
by Private financing	99.5	165.2	213.5	240.9
by Diversified financing	32.2	44.8	71.4	65.5

Source: World Economic Outlook and Staff Studies for the World Economic Outlook, 1992–1999, IMF.

Note: [1]Developing countries include different countries in Africa, Asia, Middle East, Eastern and Western Europe.

creased two and a half times faster than the aggregate GDP of all the rich industrial economies. And the volume of trading in currencies, bonds, and equities has increased about five times faster. Yet there is no general agreement as to whether this represents a new phase in the history of finance or even whether the structural weight of the global capital market on national economies today is larger than it was in earlier phases. The argument I developed in the first edition of this book based largely on the data for the 1980s were subjected to various critiques on both accounts. In this section I use the data for the 1980s and 1990s to examine these issues anew.

One of the marking features of the financial era that begins in the 1980s is its drive to produce innovations. The history of finance is in many ways a long history of innovations. But what is perhaps different today is the intensity of the current phase and the multiplication of instruments that lengthen the distance between the financial instrument and actual underlying asset. This is reflected, for instance, in the fact that the stock market capitalization and securitized debt in North America, the EU, and Japan amounted to $46.6 trillion in 1997, while their aggregate GDP was $21.4 and global GDP was $29 trillion; further, the value of outstanding derivatives in these same three sets of countries stood at $68 trillion, which was about 146% of the size of the underlying capital markets. (For a full description of assumptions and measures, see IMF 1999b: 47.)

In many ways the international financial market from the late 1800s to World War I was as massive as today's. This is certainly the case if we measure its volume as a share of national economies at the time and in terms of the relative size of international flows. The international capital market in that earlier period was large and dynamic, highly internationalized and backed by a healthy dose of Pax Britanica to keep order. The extent of its internationalization can be seen in the fact that in 1920, for example, Moody's rated bonds issued by about fifty governments to raise money in the American capital markets. The depression brought on a radical decline in the extent of this internationalization, and it was not till very recently that Moody's was once again rating fifty governments' bonds. Indeed, as late as 1985, only fifteen foreign governments were borrowing in the U.S. capital markets. Not until the 1980s did the international financial markets reemerge as a major factor (Sassen 1999a).

Though there is little agreement on the subject, in my reading there are important differences between today's global capital market and the period of the gold standard before WWI (Sassen 1996). One type of difference concerns the growing concentration of market power in institutions such as pension funds and insurance companies. This is the first of three developments to which I now turn.

TABLE 4.6

Financial Assets of Institutional Investors, 1990 to 1997, selected countries (bn USD)

Country	1990	1993	1996	1997
Canada	332.6	420.4	560.5	619.8
France	655.7	906.4	1278.1	1263.2
Germany	599.0	729.7	1167.9	1201.9
Japan	2427.9	3475.5	3563.6	3154.7
Netherlands	378.3	465.0	671.2	667.8
United Kingdom	1116.8	1547.3	2226.9	n/a
United States	6875.7	9612.8	13382.1	15867.5
Total OECD	13768.2	19013.9	26001.2	n/a

Source: Based on OECD, International Direct Investment Statistical Yearbook 1999, Table 8.1

Institutional investors are not new. What is different beginning in the 1980s is the diversity of types of funds and the rapid escalation of the value of their assets. In the U.S., the financial assets of institutional investors rose from $6.8 billion in 1990 to $9.6 billion in 1993 and $15.8 billion in 1997 (see Table 4.6). In the UK, such assets rose from $1.1 billion in 1990 to $2.2 billion in 1997; and in Japan, from $2.4 billion in 1990 to $3.1 billion in 1997. The total for all OECD countries doubled from $13.7 billion in 1990 to $26.0 billion in 1996, half of which is accounted for by the U.S. alone. Institutional investors today control a vast share of all assets.

Besides speculative instruments the 1990s also saw a proliferation of institutional investors with speculative investment strategies. Hedge funds are among the most speculative of these institutions; they sidestep certain disclosure and leverage regulations by having a small private clientele and, frequently, by operating offshore. While they are not new, the growth in their size and their capacity to affect the functioning of markets has certainly grown enormously in the 1990s. According to some estimates they now number 1,200 with assets of over $150 billion by mid-1998 (BIS 1999), which is more than the $122 billion in assets of the total of almost 1,500 equity funds as of October 1997 (UNCTAD 1998). Both of these types of funds need to be distinguished from asset management funds, of which the top ten are estimated to have $10 trillion under management; the level of concentration is enormously high among these funds, partly as a consequence of M&As driven by the need for firms to reach very high thresholds to be competitive in the global market today. (See also chapter 7.)

A second set of differences has to do with the properties that the new information technologies bring to the financial markets: instantaneous transmission, interconnectivity, and speed. Gross volumes have increased enormously even when net flows between countries are not relatively higher. And the speed of transactions has brought its own consequences. Trading in currencies and securities is instant thanks to vast computer networks. And the high degree of interconnectivity in combination with instantaneous transmission signals the potential for exponential growth.

A third major difference is the explosion in financial innovations, partly discussed above. Innovations have raised the supply of financial instruments that are tradable, sold on the open market. There are significant differences by country. Securitization is well advanced in the U.S., but just beginning in most of Europe. The proliferation of derivatives has furthered the linking of national markets by making it easier to exploit price differences between different financial instruments, i.e., to arbitrage.[8] The total stock of derivatives sold over the counter or traded in exchanges had risen to over $30 trillion in 1994 and to $65 trillion in 1999 (BIS Annual Report 1999).

Financial Crises

Global capital market integration which had been praised in much of the 1990s for enhancing economic growth became the problem in the East Asian financial crisis. Although the institutional structure for regulating the economy is weak in many of these countries, as has been widely documented, the fact of global capital market integration played the crucial role in the East Asian crisis as it contributed to enormous overleveraging and to a boom-bust attitude by investors, who rushed in at the beginning of the decade and rushed out when the crisis began even though the soundness of some of the economies involved did not warrant that fast a retreat. The magnitude of debt accumulation, only made possible by the availability of foreign capital, was a crucial factor: in 1996 the total bank debt of East Asia was $2.8 trillion, or 130% of GDP, nearly double that from a decade earlier. By 1996 leveraged debt for the median firm had reached 620% in South Korea, 340% in Thailand, and averaged

[8] While currency and interest-rates derivatives did not exist until the early 1980s and represent two of the major innovations of the current period, derivatives on commodities, so-called futures, have existed in some version in earlier periods. Amsterdam's stock exchange in the 17th century—when it was the financial capital of the world—was based almost entirely on trading in commodity futures.

150% to 200% across other East Asian countries. This was financed with capital inflows from other countries which quickly left in 1997.

Much of the cause for this is the new financial landscape: the declining role of commercial banks and ascendance of securities industry (with limited regulation and significant leverage), the greater technical capabilities built into the industry, and aggressive hedging activities by asset management funds. Rather than counteracting the excesses of the securities industries, banks added to this landscape by accepting the forecast of long-term growth in these economies thus also adding to the capital inflow and to the fairly generalized disregard for risk and quality of investments, and then joining the outflow. Furthermore, at the center of these financial crises were institutions whose liabilities were perceived as having an implicit government guarantee, even though as institutions they were essentially unregulated, and thus subject to so-called "moral hazard" problems, that is, the absence of market discipline. Anticipated protection from losses based on the IMF's willingness to assist in bailing out international banks and failed domestic banks in Mexico encouraged excessive risk-taking in Asia.[9] It is not the first time that financial intermediaries with substantial access to government liability guarantees pose a serious problem of moral hazard, as became evident in the U.S. savings and loan crisis (Brewer III and Evanoff 1999).

The worldwide liberalization of capital flows and the rapid increase in liquidity on international capital markets have raised the volatility of finance. Capital mobility has reduced the domestic policy autonomy of all countries, but particularly that of the developing world. The Mexican and East Asian crises show the drawbacks of excess capital inflows in a context of weak regulatory frameworks of domestic financial systems, weak corporate governance, and perhaps most importantly, enormous levels of capital that can be deployed in the international markets to the disadvantage of a particular country's currency or banking system. These crises also suggest that development of a strong domestic institutional investor base (pension funds, insurance companies, investment funds) is

---

[9] An added element here is the IMF's policy which makes it cheaper for investors to provide short-term loans protected by the IMF at the expense of other types of investments. The notion behind this capital standard is that short-term loans are generally thought to have less credit risk, and as a result the Basle capital rules weight cross border claims on banks outside the OECD system at 20% for short term loans—under one year, and at 100% if over a year. This encouraged short-term lending by banks in developing countries. Borrowers, given lower rates, took short-term loans. The result was the accumulation of a large volume of repayment coming due in any given year. Thus Basle risk weights and market risk do not interact properly as a signal. According to the Basle weight risks it was safer to lend to a Korean bank than to a Korean conglomerate as the latter would incur a 100% weight capital charge, compared to 20% for a bank. The official position was thus to extend more loans to the banks than to the conglomerates.

TABLE 4.7
Major Financial Crises of the Late 1980s and 1990s: Indicators and Consequences

1987 New York Crisis. Center of the crisis: New York
Other countries/markets affected: widespread

Major indicators/facts	Major economic and social consequences
a) INCREASE IN THE SYNDICATED LOAN MARKET: This became the single major source of international financing, growing from 25% of total recorded borrowing facilities in 1988 to 29% in 1989.	a) RAPID GROWTH IN THE PARTICIPATION OF LARGE BANKS AFTER 1987: The continuation of high levels of international financial activity after the crisis of October 1987 must be understood along with this growth in large banks' participation in the market.
b) NEW YORK STOCK EXCHANGE—WORST SINGLE-DAY DECLINE: On October 19th, 1987 the Dow Jones Industrial Average dropped 22.6%, the worst record to date; as perspective, the market crash in 1929 saw the market decline only 12.8%, while the October 1997 market crash saw the market decline only 7.2%. The rush to sell orders, a lack of processing capacity, and regulatory disruption converged on this day. In order to assure a continuing supply of credit to clearinghouse members and to prevent widespread default on marginal collections, the Fed injected large amounts of credit to preserve overall liquidity.	b) MERGERS: The late 1980s emerged as a period of massive demand for funds to finance huge takeovers and mergers, and the largest Japanese banks emerged as the leading providers of funds.
c) DECREASE IN BOND OFFERINGS: Gross issues at current exchange rates increased by 51.7% from the first quarter in 1985 to the first quarter in 1986, and again by 35% for the next year-on-period. In 1987, they declined by over 22%.	
d) EXCHANGE RATE CONTRACTION: 29% in 1987.	

1994 Mexican Crisis. Center of the crisis: Mexico
Other countries affected: Brasil, Argentina

Major indicators/facts	Major economic and social consequences
a) LOSS OF INTERNATIONAL RESERVES: The Mexican Central Bank lost US$5 bn within a few days in its attempt to defend the Mexican peso in December 1994.	a) POVERTY: 45% total increase in the population in poverty (1996—41.7 million). This was a result of the increase in inequality and the drop in GDP per capita.
b) REVERSAL IN NET PRIVATE CAPITAL FLOWS: Between 1993 and 1995, this reversal was equivalent to 13% of Mexican GDP. The short maturity of debt was identified as the main determinant of the volatility and reversals of capital flows in this crisis. NOTE: These private capital flows were mostly portfolio investments, which totalled US$23 bn in inflows in 1993, and then declined to a net outflow of US$14 bn in 1995—a turnaround of US$37 bn (13% of Mexican GDP).	b) DIMINISHED GROWTH: Real GDP growth declined to −6.2% in 1995 and averaged 2.6% from 1995–1998. Note: Mexico's economy adjusted to the crises through downward flexibility in real wages rather than through increases in unemployment.
c) BANKING SYSTEM FRAGILITY: Past-due loans had already increased sharply from 35% to 98% of total bank capital in 1994. During the period of February-March 1995, there was a further sharp rise in the stock of non-performing loans as a growing number of nonfinancial firms faced difficulties in meeting debt service obligations to banks. Similar concerns in Argentina led bank deposits to fall by 16% (more than US$7.5 bn) between mid-December 1994 and the end of March 1995.	c) UNEMPLOYMENT: Affected countries, such as Argentina, experienced an increase in unemployment of 6% in 1995.
d) OTHER FACTORS: Political instability, growing difficulties on the part of the Mexican gov-	d) THE COST OF SUPPORT TO THE BANKING SYSTEM: The fiscal cost of supporting the financial system is estimated at 14.4% of GDP for 1997, that will be amortized over 30 years during the life of the programs.

1997 Asian Crisis. Centers of the crisis: Thailand, Indonesia, Malaysia, and S. Korea
Other countries affected: Japan, Latin America (ultimately Russia)

Major indicators/facts	Major economic and social consequences
a) CURRENCY DEPRECIATION: The fall of the Thai baht on July 2, 1997 began a period of upheaval in emerging market currencies unparalleled in recent times. Three phases can be identified: (1) July-early Oct. 1997: Pressures on emerging market currencies remained restricted to Asian currencies, specifically: the Thai baht, the Malaysian ringgit, the Philippine peso, and the Indonesian rupiah; (2) October 1997: Pressure on Asian currencies intensified. The Korean won began to decline severely, with the Brazilian real and the Argentinian peso also suffering severe speculative pressures; (3) December 1997: Intensified pressure on Asian currencies. As the situation about Korea's debt and reserves became public, the pressure on the won intensified and spilled over to other currencies—which reached their lowest by January 1998.	a) POVERTY: Real per capita GDP declined throughout Asia: Indonesia: from 2.9% in 1997 to −15.1% in 1998 Malaysia: from 5.4% in 1997 to − 9.2% in 1998 S. Korea: from 4.5% in 1997 to − 6.7% in 1998 Thailand: from − 1.4 in 1997 to − 10.3 in 1998 Note: In Korea, urban poverty increased by 10% to 19.2%; in Thailand, the impact was greater in rural areas as poverty rates increased from 11.8% in 1996 to 17.2% by the third quarter of 1998.
Depreciations in Asian and related currencies from July 1997 to January 1998: Indonesian rupiah: 81% Thai baht: 56% Malaysian ringgit: 46% Philippine peso: 41% S. Korean won (October to December 1997): 55%	b) UNEMPLOYMENT: Total employment fell in Malaysia, Thailand, and S. Korea from 1997 to 1998: Indonesia: Unemployment rose from 4.4 million in 1996 to 10 m in 1998 S. Korea: from 0.4 m in 1996 to 1.5 m in 1998 Thailand: from 0.5 m in 1996 to 2 m in 1998
Note: In Brazil, market participants reported to the IMF an estimated loss of US$10 bn in reserves as pressures from Asia led to an attack by currency speculators on the Brazilian real in late October 1997.	Note: The most affected sector in the Asian economies was construction which fell from 35% to 15% of total employment. The Inactive Population increased to 9% between the second quarter of 1997 and the fourth quarter of 1998, and 75% of this increase were women. In Indonesia, around 2.5 million workers, or 3% of the total workforce, were displaced by the crisis in the first year. The manufacturing sector accounted for nearly half of all job losses, followed by construction.
b) SEVERE DECREASE IN THE SHARE PRICE INDEX FOR ASIAN STOCK MARKETS: Declines in Asian stock markets from July 1997 to February 1998: Indonesia: −81.74% S. Korea: −63.06% Malaysia: −58.41% The Philippines: −49.17% Thailand: −48.37%	
c) CAPITAL OUTFLOWS: As with the Mexican case, the crisis in Asia was also preceded by a strong capital boom, in this case, mostly bank lending flows (not portfolio investments). For the affected Asian countries, the reversal in 1997 was largely accounted for by the retrenchment of bank lending from net inflows of US$40 bn in 1996 to net outflows of over US$30 bn, a turnover of US$70 bn (equivalent to 7% of the affected Asian economies' GDP). Outflows were also severe in other affected countries. For example, Brazil registered US$8.1 bn in portfolio investments in September 1997, but finished the year at US$5.3 bn. In 1997, 77% of total investment directed to Brazil exited the country, compared to 52% in 1996; additionally, the loss in reserves totaled US$7.5 bn.	c) NONPERFORMING LOANS: Banking systems continue to face high levels of nonperforming loans. The ratio of nonperforming loans to total loans was 19.7 in 1997 and rose to 21.2 in June 1999 in Malaysia; from 16.8 to 19.2 in S. Korea.
	d) DROP IN PUBLIC SPENDING: Real government spending fell in all countries except Thailand. Although spending on health programs remained relatively unchanged, spending on education decreased relative to GDP in the wake of the financial crisis, while Thailand increased spending on education.
d) WIDESPREAD PROBLEMS IN ASIAN FINANCIAL MARKETS: In Japan, problematic bank loans totaled US$592 bn in April 1998—twice the size of Australia's economy. In contrast to other major markets, the Japanese stock market stagnated and then fell between 1997 and 1998. The Nikkei reached two-year lows in November and lost about 25% of its end-1996 value by November 1997.	e) CORPORATE DISTRESS: The percentage of firms unable to meet current debt repayments rose in all Asian countries, except Thailand. In Indonesia, defaults on bank loans rose from 12.6% in 1995 to 58.2% in 1998. In Korea, defaults rose from 8.5% in 1995 to 33.8% in 1998, and Malaysia, from 3.4% to 34.3%.

TABLE 4.7 cont.

1998 Russian Crisis. Center of the crisis: Russia

Other countries affected: Ukraine, Czech Republic, Hungary, Estonia, Latvia, Romania,
Slovak Republic, Brazil, Mexico, Chile, Venezuela, Equador, Colombia, Egypt, and S. Africa

Major indicators/facts	Major economic and social consequences
a) BUDGET DEFICIT: Approximately 50% of the government deficit (excluding off-budget funds) was in interest payments. Under Russia's new economic policy, the servicing of pre-existing debt was financed by sales of government short-term bonds, of which 30% were bought by foreign investors in 1998. In 1997, the Russian government's deficit was 5.9% of national GDP.	a) REDUCED GROWTH IN RUSSIA: Although Russia posted positive growth figures in 1997 after eight years of decline, the economy once again had negative growth between January and July 1998.
	b) DROP IN FIXED INVESTMENT IN RUSSIA: 5% lower in the first seven months of 1998 than in 1997.
b) RUBLE DEVALUATION: The ruble lost 70% of its value immediately after the Russian government defaulted on major international loans on August 17, 1998.	c) INFLATION: In Russia, consumer prices rose by 15.2% in August, compared to a 0.2% rise in July 1998.
c) PARTIAL COLLAPSE OF THE BANKING SYSTEM: The Russian government's decision to stop payments on government bonds and debt instantly made a number of major national banks insolvent. SBS-Agro-Bank, particularly active in the region for the last couple of years, was suspended. Note: For Russian banks, the losses associated with this crisis were estimated at 40% of their assets.	d) SHORTAGE OF GOODS IN RUSSIA
	e) SEVERE DECREASE IN CAPITAL FLOWS IN EMERGING MARKET ECONOMIES: After 1996, total net capital flows decreased from US$215.9 bn to US$80.5 bn in 1999. This decrease was mostly due to the drop in net investment in Africa, but also in Asia—where it fell from US$74.2 bn in 1995 to US$ – 24.6 bn in 1999.
d) LOSS IN INTERNATIONAL RESERVES: Severely affected other countries. For example, Brazil lost US$ 24 billion in international reserves between August and September 1998.	d) INCREASE IN EXTERNAL DEBTS IN EMERGING MARKET ECONOMIES BETWEEN 1994 TO 1999: (As a percentage of GDP)*
e) DECLINE IN EQUITY PRICES: Stock market declines were recorded in all 23 major emerging financial markets during August 1998 by amounts which varied from 10% or less in Hong Kong, China, India, and S. Korea to more than 25% for other affected countries.	Argentina: from 33.3% to 52.1% Brazil: from 18.2% to 39.7% Chile: from 42.2% to 49.5% Indonesia: from 57.0% to 95.5% S. Korea: from 24.1% to 33.0% Malaysia: from 38.6% to 55.3% The Philippines: from 60.4% to 68.0% Thailand: from 44.9% to 61.5%
	* Debt increases includes substantial increases in short-term debt.

Sources: Global Economic Prospects 2000, World Bank; World Economic Outlook: Financial Turbulence and the World Economy, IMF, October 1998; World Economic Outlook, IMF, April 2000; Annual Report, Brazilian Central Bank, 1997 and 1998; "What Lessons DoesThe Mexican Crisis Hold for Recovery in Asia?" Finance and Development, IMF, vol. 35, No. 2, June 1998; "The Economics and Politics of the Asian Financial Crisis of 1997–98," Council on Foreign Relations, University of California, San Diego; "The Russian Crisis of 1998," UNCTAD and UN/ECE Secretariats, UN, October 1998; "Large Capital Flows: A Survey of the Causes, Consequences, and Policy Responses," IMF Working Paper 99/17, IMF, 1999; "International Capital Markets: Developments, Prospects and Key Policy Issues," World Economic and Financial Surveys, IMF, 1998; "Tigers Adrift," The Economist, March 7, 1998; "Asia in Crisis," Financial Times Special Report, March 20, 2000; FINANCE AND DEVELOPMENT, "The Social Costs of the Asian Financial Crises," September 1998, volume 35, N. 3, Washington, D.C.: IMF; Nisid, Hajari, "Race Against Time," *Time*, January 26, 1998.

crucial since the U.S. and the EU were far less affected by the crises. As more and more countries liberalize their financial systems and capital becomes increasingly mobile, managing capital flows has become more complex.

At the international level it appears that the currency crises of East Asia and Russia did not become a systemic threat for the stability of the international financial system to the same extent as did the debt crisis of the early 1980s. But the risk of recession in the affected developing countries is high due to the abrupt adjustment process. Table 4.7 lists some of the key costs to the affected economies resulting from the major crises. Unemployment tends to remain high for long periods of time even after the financial markets begin to recover, which happened fairly soon in both Mexico in the earlier crisis and most of the Asian countries involved in the latest crisis. These crises have a stronger impact on developing economies than they do on the highly developed countries.

Conclusion

There was a pronounced transformation in the financial industry in the decade of the 1980s. International financial activity in the 1970s was dominated by large transnational banks engaged in traditional banking activities. The vast surpluses of the oil-exporting countries in the 1970s were controlled by these banks, which loaned that money to Third World countries through traditional intermediation activities. The 1980s were dominated by the transformation of often hitherto unmarketable financial instruments into securities and by financial institutions other than the transnational banks, mostly investment banks and securities houses. While the geography of the 1970s was one that included less developed countries as crucial areas, both as providers of capital and as buyers of loans, the 1980s saw sharp increases in the weight of highly developed countries as exporters and buyers of capital. In addition, the regulatory framework in the 1970s had pushed the large banks toward the creation of offshore banking centers, but the 1980s, with rapid deregulation of many key markets in the highly developed countries, saw the growing importance of major cities as financial centers and a repatriation of much of the capital held in offshore banks.

Of significance to the analysis in this book is the increased importance of the marketplace and of leading financial centers in the reorganization of the financial industry. While financial markets continue to fulfill traditional supply and demand functions, a second type of activity has grown immensely in the major financial markets. It is the often highly speculative buying and selling of instruments and the experimentation with new ones. This activity goes beyond the servicing of investors and savers traditionally fulfilled by the banks. Utility originally was attached to the actual need for what was traded; that is, a loan satisfied the need for money. Today, tradability is utility. And the more rapid the buying and selling afforded by an instrument, the greater the utility. These markets have grown in size, complexity, and scope to the point that they support a large array of specialized firms, a massive volume of trading, and a highly advanced capability for the production of more and more instruments. The greater value added in the financial industry comes from the skill- and capital-intensive activities of financial institutions: market making, underwriting, product development, mergers and acquisitions, and risk management. In this sense, describing the current situation as disinter-mediation creates a distortion; it is rather that what were historically the main intermediaries lost immense ground in the 1980s. One could say that financial centers, rather than banks, have become the key locations for intermediation functions. While banks are a simple mechanism of intermediation, the financial markets are complex, competitive, innovative, and risky. They require a vast infrastructure of financial centers with highly specialized services.

Part Two

THE ECONOMIC ORDER
OF THE GLOBAL CITY

THE CENTRAL PATTERN emerging from the discussion in the preceding chapters is the vast growth in international financial activity and service transactions. A second major pattern is the increasing concentration of this activity in highly developed countries, and particularly in the United States, the United Kingdom, and Japan. This indicates a transformation in the composition and the geography of the global economy.

Several aspects are of interest to an inquiry about the place of cities in this transformation. Producer services, financial transactions, and the complex markets both entail are a layer of activity that became central to the organization of major global processes in the 1980s. To what extent is thinking in terms of the broader category of cities as key locations for such activities—in addition to the more narrowly defined locations represented by headquarters of transnational corporations or global markets—useful to an understanding of major aspects of the organization and management of the world economy? By the 1980s, the scholarly literature had made important contributions to the analysis of the international activities of large corporations and banks. But a whole layer of activity that is part of the formation, implementation, and maintenance of global-level processes is only partly encompassed by the activities of transnational corporations and banks.

We posit that the transformation in the composition of the global economy accompanying the shift to services and finance brings about a renewed importance of major cities as sites for certain types of production, servicing, marketing, and innovation. In addition, the internationalization of mergers, acquisitions, and financial transactions makes cities "de-nationalized" centers for management and coordination, for the raising and consolidation of investment capital, and for the formation of an international property market.

The existence of such locations with a pronounced orientation to the world market raises a question about their articulation with the nation-states to which they belong. There is some literature addressing this question for the case of free trade zones and offshore banking centers, particularly since their formation involves an explicit policy of considerable autonomy from various regulations in the host state. But there is still little on cities from this international perspective. Cities are clearly a very different and a far more complex and multifaceted case. Yet it would seem important to examine cities with such a question in mind, especially cities where the dominant economic sectors are oriented to the global market and have been the object of considerable foreign investment and acquisition. These developments also raise a question about their impact on national urban systems. A new body of scholarship is beginning to address some of these questions. One distinction between earlier analyses and my recasting is the attempt to theorize the discontinuity between a region or locality and the national state to which it belongs.

Key dynamics contributing to locational patterns that favor cities are the particular combinations of increasing specialization and agglomeration economies evident in many of the producer services. We can, then, interpret the locational patterns of firms in the sector as reflecting the outcome of these dynamics. But this could not be said for finance until recently given tight regulation which limited the locational options of firms. With deregulation, however, locational patterns should reflect locational preferences of firms. The intersection of specialization and agglomeration economies is conceivably quite different in the case of financial services. The dematerialized character of the product, the growth of electronic markets, and the globalization of the industry, all suggest that it should be less subject to agglomeration economies. In fact, the available evidence shows that this is not necessarily so.

Against a background of major developments in computer and telecommunications technology and its commercial applications, these conditions promote the production of and the increasing demand for financial innovations and specialized financial services, and raise the importance of financial centers. Furthermore, these inducements and possibilities for new markets entailed a high level of internationalization in the financial markets. Some form of the internationalization of the capital market has been in place for a long time. The formation of the Europaper market, over two decades ago, represented the existence of an unregulated market in a world where the other markets were regulated. But the recent changes represent a qualitatively different development.

The evidence on the composition and growth patterns of the economies of major cities clearly points to the weight of finance and producer services, their above-average growth over the last two decades, and their disproportionate concentration in such cities. It is important to this analysis to gain a clear understanding of the nature of these industries, the conditions for their growth, the determinants of their concentration in major cities given telecommunications advances that would conceivably allow for spatial dispersal, the limits to such locational concentration, and the limits to their growth. Risk and debt have emerged as essential elements in the growth of finance. What does this tell us about the durability of this model of growth for urban economies? In addition, we need to examine the production of innovations, a key factor in the development of these industries over the last two decades. One set of questions concerns the conditions under which such production of innovations can take place and to what extent the pronounced locational concentration of these industries in major cities is linked to a particular phase in the development of industries characterized by rapid production of innovations. As standardization sets in, locational concentration is likely to weaken.

Developments in the 1990s amplified the weight of some of the trends discussed in the first edition of this book. Most importantly for the questions organizing my analysis are the domestic and global spatial organization of finance, the impact of the expanded use of information technologies in finance and the producer services on cities generally and global cities particularly, the development of electronic markets and the continuing relocation of the headquarters of major corporate firms to smaller cities and nonurban areas, and, finally, the impact of these various trends on the articulation of global cities to their regions and national economies, on the one hand, and on the formation and expansion of a cross-border network of global cities, on the other. Each of these themes was the subject of debates and critiques to the theses I developed in the first edition. I have addressed each of these through the incorporation of new empirical and conceptual materials, including whole new sections in chapters 5 and 6 and a mostly rewritten chapter 7. I have also added a whole new section in chapter 6 on Chicago as a global city based on my current research. While Chicago already played a prominent role in the first edition, it has become an even more illuminating case for some of my major hypotheses.

The focus of chapter 5 is on the development of producer services into a key input and on the development of finance not only into a key service industry but also into an industry with its own products and sphere of circulation—an industry to be distinguished from traditional banking and financial services. Chapter 6 examines the space economy of producer services. The purpose here is to understand two distinct issues. One is whether the composition of producer services varies for different types of cities in the national urban system of each of these countries. For example, is New York a different kind of location for producer services than Los Angeles or Chicago? Similar questions will be asked about the cities of the United Kingdom and Japan. The other issue of interest here is what the space economy of these leading industries reveals about the urban system in each of these countries. Chapter 7 carries these questions to the global scale, focusing in turn on two distinct issues. One is whether New York, London, and Tokyo, rather than merely competing with one another, actually constitute a sort of transnational urban system, each with somewhat distinct functions in the new leading economic sectors. The other concerns the relative position of these three leading financial and business centers compared to other major cities in the world and vis-à-vis one another, and how this has evolved since the 1980s.

Five

The Producer Services

ADVERTISING, ACCOUNTING, and business law are all producer services that were already in use in the late 1800s or early 1900s. And Taylor's time and motion studies are an early example of management consulting. How does the growth and role of these services in the current period differ from their growth and role in earlier decades? A similar question can be raised about finance, as it has long been an important industry in the major industrial economies. Does its growth over the last two decades, especially in international and nonbank finance, represent a distinct phase? The evidence to be discussed strongly suggests that there has been a major transformation in the characteristics of the producer services and of finance, and that there has, furthermore, been a major transformation in the role these industries play in the economies of major industrialized countries and in the internationalization of these economies. A thorough discussion along these lines requires a detailed examination of the characteristics of production of these industries, their role in the economy, and their markets.

Producer services can be seen as part of the supply capacity of an economy. "They influence its adjustment in response to changing economic circumstances" (Marshall et al. 1986: 16) and represent a mechanism that "organizes and adjudicates economic exchange for a fee" (Thrift 1987). They are part of a broader intermediary economy. Conceivably these activities can be internalized by firms, and many firms do so, or they can be bought on the market. Producer services cover financial, legal, and general management matters, innovation, development, design, administration, personnel, production technology, maintenance, transport, communications, wholesale distribution, advertising, cleaning services for firms, security, and storage. Central components of the producer services category are a range of industries with mixed business and consumer markets. They are insurance, banking, financial services, real estate, legal services, accounting, and professional associations. These mixed markets create measurement problems only partly overcome by the fact that the consumer and business markets in these industries often involve very different sets of firms and different types of location patterns, a subject I return to later. Given the organization of the pertinent data, it is helpful to group these services under the category of "mostly producer services," that is, services produced mostly for firms rather than individuals. I will refer to them, for convenience, as producer services.

In the initial analyses that resulted in the formulation of a distinct category of producer services (Greenfield 1966; Singelmann 1974; Singelmann and Browning 1980), the central notion was that these services supported production, whence the name *producer services*. It has now become evident that these services are also used in service organizations, both in the private and public sectors. The term *producer services* as used in this book, and increasingly by scholars on the subject, includes not only services to production firms narrowly defined but also those to all other types of organizations. The key distinguishing trait becomes the fact that they are services produced for organizations, whether private sector firms or governmental entities, rather than for final consumers; that is to say, producer services are intermediate outputs (Greenfield 1966). The relative simplicity of this definition should be placed in the context of the debates and the scholarship about services over the last twenty years, discussed later. The focus is on aspects that are critical to the analysis in this book.

Here we seek to examine the growth dynamic of these industries, their locational patterns, and the relations among agglomeration, specialization, and deregulation. There are several questions of interest. Do these services form territorial complexes with dense interfirm linkages as has been described for manufacturing plants that are small and specialized (Scott 1988; Piore and Sabel 1984)? And can we identify a distinct producer services complex in financial centers compared with industrial centers? How has the increased specialization in services intersected with advances in information and telecommunications technologies to facilitate standardization in production and expansion of the market to a global scale? And what does the potential for economies of scale and scope entail for the organization of these industries? Specifically does it strengthen tendencies toward concentration and/or vertical integration? (See Noyelle and Dutka 1988; Daniels 1985; Marshall et al. 1986.) How does the need for access to advanced telecommunications facilities shape the locational patterns of these services? Finally, what is the place of central functions in these territorial agglomerations?

The issue of deregulation plays a central role in many of the producer services, which differs in certain ways from its role in manufacturing. Several of the producer services have professional codes and governmental regulation covering the client-provider relation and the characteristics of products. This has created something akin to monopoly rights for legitimate professional practitioners, and it has affected the flow of these services, especially when more than one country is involved. In few of the major industries is the role of regulation as central as in the financial industry. The existence of a highly developed regulatory framework was a key factor shaping the spatial organization of the industry. Deregulation has brought significant changes, notably the formation of global markets. WTO negotiations on service flows and financial deregulation are two different versions of the pressure to internationalize these industries. Major players are involved: extremely powerful firms in finance and in some of the major service industries, with growing market shares and strong tendencies toward concentration.

Intimately linked with the question of deregulation in the financial industry are tendencies toward innovation and heightened risk. Innovation has served the dual purpose of circumventing regulations and of expanding the market through the sale of new products and through mechanisms for raising capital. Deregulation has further facilitated expansion through incorporation of growing numbers of financial centers into global markets. One focus for discussion is the thesis, introduced in the first edition, about the growing importance of centers compared to firms. Innovation, risk, digitization, and globalization all have raised the organizational complexity of the industry and thereby the benefits of locating in highly networked financial centers.

The first half of the chapter examines the matter of formal classification of these industries and contains a detailed analysis of their evolution into a key input for contemporary forms of economic organization, their characteristics of production, and their locational patterns. The empirical elaboration of these various aspects focuses on the cases of the United States, the United Kingdom, and Japan. In the second section of chapter 5, I particularly focus on how the locational, agglomeration, and specialization conditions discussed for the producer services generally, operate in the case of finance. We examine the broader organization of the industry in its current phase and the changing weight of the large transnational banks compared to financial centers. A more speculative aspect of this discussion is the extent to which we need to differentiate, on the one hand, between banking and financial service activities that are services properly speaking and, on the other hand, financial activities that, I will argue, are no longer usefully understood as services but are in fact more akin to commodity production, where the utility lies in the sale and resale of instruments rather than in the consumption of a service as is the case with advertising or accounting.

The Category Services

Both neoclassical and Keynesian economics long ignored any distinction between the production of goods and that of services, let alone among service industries. Studies on the service sector basically conceived of it as a residual category that was neither the primary nor the secondary sector. As late as 1940 a book by Clark (1940: 34) contained the observation that the economics of tertiary industries remained to be written, and almost three decades later, Hill (1977: 336) could deplore its continued absence. This neglect was evident in many branches of economics and was partly an outcome of key assumptions about services. It is possible that the notion that services are not tradable led to their neglect in trade theory (Corden 1985). Hill (1977: 318–19) has posited that services cannot be analyzed in terms of conventional market exchange because they cannot be physically transferred from sellers to buyers and they cannot be stored. In urban economic analysis, the prevalent proposition about manufacturing as the export or base sector, the sector with multiplier effects, may have displaced the focus away from services. And the proposition about the unproductive characteristics of services and hence their retardant effect on economic development may have led to their neglect in international development theory (Kaldor 1966; Bacon and Eltis 1978). The more important theoretical elaboration of the services category came from such social scientists as Bell (1973) in the United States and Crozier (1963) and Touraine (1969) in France, who examined the implications of the growing weight of services in highly developed economies.

Much of the recent work on producer services represents an often-unwitting neoindustrial response to the notion of a postindustrial economy.[1] The economic crisis of the mid-1970s in major industrialized economies brought about a reexamination of the role of services in the overall process of accumulation and thus in the crisis. The low productivity typical of many service industries and hence the negative impact of the service sector on accumulation were seen as key factors in the crisis by many analysts. This crisis and its analysis also contributed to an increasingly critical and negative appraisal of the postindustrial thesis and its vision of a better society based on a service economy. In subsequent work there is a considerable distancing from broader sociological perspectives concerned with the larger impact of services on the social order and a narrowing of the focus to the characteristics of these industries in terms of output, location, and employment.

In some ways Galbraith (1969) and Fuchs (1968) are among the precursors of the current neoindustrial analysis of the notion of producer services and the technical bases of management. In *The New Industrial State*, Galbraith (1969) is fundamentally concerned with the importance

---

[1] Understanding this group of industries as services for producers can be seen as entailing a neoindustrial logic and, at the limit, "an incapacity of conceiving of a development logic other than that of modern capitalist production" (Delaunay and Gadrey 1987: 124–25, my translation).

and primacy of large industrial corporations but also focuses on advanced services produced inside such corporations. These are services necessary for the organization of large firms and their marketing strategies. Furthermore, while not examining the issues central to the postindustrial thesis, Galbraith does emphasize the importance of educators and scientists for the development of the technostructure he examines. Fuchs's (1968) analysis is, in this context, a landmark study. It is a nontheoretical, empirical analysis that emphasizes the distinctiveness of the service sector and simultaneously analyzes the differences among service industries. The book analyzes growth tendencies, productivity trends, cyclical behavior, specific forms assumed by wages and salaries, profits, and revenues in service industries. It includes a critique of conventional measures and shows their failure when it comes to measuring service industries. While not in the line of analysis of the postindustrial thesis as represented by Bell, Fuchs's analysis does lead him to posit that service work is more personal and less alienating than industrial mass production. A further contribution to the specification of services can be found in Singelmann's (1974) characterization of service industries as having divergent economic behavior and social characteristics. He classifies the tertiary sector into distributive, producer, social, and personal services.[2]

In what is perhaps one of the most sophisticated and thorough treatments of the scholarship on service industries in the 1980s, Delaunay and Gadrey (1987) organize the range of studies and types of analyses that had been produced into three schools of thought, which they see as partly complementary. One is a conception that understands the growth of services as a move toward an information society (Machlup 1962; Porat 1976; Parker 1975). The second focuses on the changes in what we produce and how we produce it (Stanback 1979; Stanback et al. 1981); and the third analyzes how the industrialization of services results in a greater productivity and profitability of the sector, with a corresponding rearticulation with the process of accumulation (Aglietta 1979; Attali 1981). Some of these analyses seek to interpret recent trends in service growth from the perspective of one overarching category, such as information or regulation. Others are more empirical and descriptive. What they share is a central concern with transformations in the formal structures through which work takes place.

For the purposes of the analysis in this book there are important elements in all three bodies of scholarship. Of central interest is the transformation in the formal structures of work and how this contributes to the

---

[2] Singelmann notes the very important point that Clark's law, establishing a positive correlation between growth in tertiary employment and per capita national income, holds for certain service industries but not, or only in a minor way, for others.

expansion and demand for services. Important here is the notion that the growth in services in the 1980s is associated with the increasing demand for services as intermediate or complementary inputs, whether directly for firms, for the distribution of goods, or for human capital formation. Of importance here, also, are theories of consumption explaining the expanded demand for consumer services that contributed to the growth of the service sector in an earlier period. Today, demand expansion in services is highly segmented and linked, to a far greater extent than in the past, to organizations and to the formation of niche markets.

Secondly, the scholarship focused on changes in the mode of production points to a number of trends important to my analysis. This type of conception makes evident a complementarity between changes in services and those in goods in the sense that the consumption by firms and individuals of increasingly diversified goods entails a growing demand for increasingly complex services (Williamson 1980). Similarly, the increasing size and diversification of firms has brought about a greater need for services, either produced internally or bought on the market (Stanback and Noyelle 1982; Marshall et al. 1986; Daniels 1995). The move of large corporations into the production and sale of consumer services has made possible economies of scale and mass production and distribution of services, which in turn generated additional needs for specialized services to run such a mass production and distribution system of consumer services.

The pioneering work of scholars such as Machlup (1962), Porat (1976), and Parker (1975) on the notion of an information society is of great importance to an understanding of fundamental characteristics of contemporary society. Information technologies have raised the tradability of producer services and engendered whole new types of services. The work by Attali (1981) on information as socially dependent and Stoffaes's (1981) distinction between information that is easily available and cheap and information that is difficult to obtain and expensive are of use in understanding certain aspects of the market for producer services. So is Delaunay and Gadrey's (1987) distinction between the information per se and the service through which it is provided. The latter aspect requires an examination of the actual activities involved and hence of jobs and places.

At the core of these analyses is an emphasis on an increasingly service-intensive mode of production and on the modernization and industrialization of service technologies. These analyses differ from the more traditional conception, which sees services as nonstockable, nontransportable, and not subject to mass production or scale economies (Stanback 1979).

Castells (1989; 1996) takes these various analytical elements concerning the impact of information technologies and develops a totally new conception about their impact on urban and regional processes. Castells posits the emergence of a new mode of sociotechnical organization, the "informational mode of development," which in the context of the restructuring of capitalism provides the fundamental matrix of institutional and economic organization in the current period. (See also Graham and Marvin 1996; Graham 2000.) Information technologies have not eliminated the importance of massive concentrations of material resources but have, rather, reconfigured the interaction of capital fixity and hypermobility; the complex management of this interaction has given major cities a new competitive advantage (Sassen 2000; 2001b; 1999a).

Growth and Specialization

The elaboration of the services category and the consequent differentiation, especially between consumer and producer services, has led to a reevaluation of the traditional characteristics attributed to services (that services are not transportable, cannot be stocked or warehoused, and are not subject to accumulation or export). The subsequent scholarship on the producer services (Stanback et al. 1981; Singelmann and Browning 1980; Daniels, 1985; 1995; Wood 1987; 1999; Marshall et al. 1986) contains significant evidence that producer services are much less likely to correspond to these criteria than are typical consumer services.

Distinctions now abound. The work by Greenfield (1966) and Katouzian (1970) contributed to a differentiation among business-related services, consumer services which develop in the context of economic development, and personal services which tend to decline as economic development proceeds. Other distinctions are between the public and private provision of services and between blue-collar services and office-based, or white-collar, services (Browning and Singelmann 1978; Noyelle and Stanback 1985; Gershuny and Miles 1983; Hansen 1994). An important distinction that has emerged in the literature is between the conventional view of services as demand induced and "supply critical services" necessary for economic development (Tucker and Sundberg 1988: 23–26).

In one of the most detailed and important studies on producer services, Marshall and his colleagues (1986) document how these types of distinctions tend to neglect the extent to which services and other sectors are essentially integrated and the fact that many occupations within manufacturing are service occupations. Ultimately both services and goods are consumed together as part of final demand. The main distinction according to this study lies in the markets served. Producer services supply mainly business and government rather than individuals, but they do so in any sector, from agriculture through manufacturing to services, a fact that can be captured in the input-output tables (Sassen and Orloff 1998). Such a conception goes beyond the notion of producer services as resulting from the demand for specialized services by manufacturing firms, the latter a long tradition that posits manufacturing as the base or export sector in an economy and hence views the growth of services as dependent on manufacturing and its growth. There is here a recognition of the fact that services are needed in production processes, hence going beyond consumer services, and that such processes are present in many spheres of the economy, not just in manufacturing.[3]

There is now considerable evidence showing that beyond the demand by large manufacturing firms, there is the more general issue of the growing size, complexity, and diversification of firms in all sectors of the economy (Williamson 1978; Daniels 1995; Wood 1999; Marshall et al. 1986; Stanback et al. 1981). These conditions are now seen as central to the growth of the producer services (Illeris and Sjoholt 1994; Moulaert and Todtling 1995). The merging of highly diverse firms has further added to the complexity of management and the need for highly specialized inputs. Growing size and diversity in the components of a firm entails increasing separation of functions, often resulting in geographic dispersal. The overall result is an increase in the level of complexity at central headquarters. These are not simply centers for administration and control, but also centers for decisions about product development and expansion and mergers and acquisitions in a multiplicity of industries. Finally, central headquarters have to function as a "center for orientation of the firm within the business environment" (Daniels 1985: 160; 1995; see also Stephens and Holly 1981). This environment has become increasingly dynamic and complex in terms of legal and financial regulations and the national and international aspects of both. Governments also encounter this growing diversity and are consumers of producer services.

Product differentiation and the resultant market differentiation emerge as yet another set of specialized conditions that must be brought together at the higher levels of a corporation. Greater product differentiation expands the marketing and selling functions of a firm. The increase in the research intensity of production also creates new demands on the central headquarters of a large, diversified firm. Rapid development of innovations requires support to incorporate such innovations into the production or organizational process of a firm. New technologies generate new organizational requirements if they are to be used (Sassen 2000).

An important factor in the development of producer services industries

---

[3] This type of analysis is to be distinguished from the discussion on the export sector and the multiplier effect (Blumenfeld 1955).

was the growth of the large transnational corporations, particularly U.S. corporations. The increasingly complex and sophisticated multinational U.S. corporations, operating at both a global and national level, generated a demand for advanced intermediate service inputs. This put U.S. producer services firms in the forefront in terms of innovations and service offerings and made them operate on an international level. Manhattan became the center for advertising, new models of management, and international law firms (Noyelle and Dutka 1988), and along with London and Chicago, for financial software design. There were innovations in accounting, in business law, in advertising. Similar patterns can be seen in the producer services industries in other developed countries, though mostly less innovative and less aggressive.

In the postwar decades and into the 1960s, U.S. corporate structure was among the most advanced forms of complex organizations, and U.S. corporations generally led in the use of sophisticated intermediate inputs. These corporations represented an organizational structure rather different from that of the large trading, banking, and insurance firms of the British Empire or of other earlier empires. Many of the advanced producer services, such as international law or management consulting, were largely seen as unimportant to the functioning of the broader economy in the postwar period, and the needed inputs for large corporations oriented to domestic markets were often produced in-house.

By the late 1970s, the transformation in the organization and composition of economic activity had resulted in a sharp increase in the demand for these types of services, as all kinds of organizations—whether large transnationals or small domestic firms, whether private or public sector—began to use such intermediate inputs. Increasing specialization and increasing demand combined to induce rapid growth in the freestanding market of business service firms.

In the 1940s, accounting in Britain, for example, was mostly organized in small, single-site partnerships. Most of the business was personal and oriented to the consumer market and small private company accounts. Changes in the organization of the economy and in the regulations covering accounting and financial practices have produced a large increase in the demand for accounting services and have transformed the organization of the industry, with a sharp increase in the number of large firms and mergers and acquisitions. In 1948, the largest twenty accounting firms controlled about a third of the audits listed in the Stock Exchange Year Book. By 1979, this share had jumped to almost 70% (Briston 1979), and today five large firms control the international market.

Changes in the structure and in the scale of firms have resulted in a demand for inputs, which have become increasingly specialized and at the same time generalized, as more and more firms have these characteristics and hence this demand. Producer services can be traded in the market or within organizations, from the head office of a multisite firm to a branch or subsidiary. Whether the production of these services is internalized by a firm or bought on the market depends on a number of factors. Among these are the availability outside the firm of certain services, the degree of specialization, the strategic quality of service for a firm, the cost of alternative sources of supply of a service, and the difference in cost between producing the service in-house and buying it on the market (Greenfield 1966; Williamson 1978; Daniels 1995; Wood 1999).

In what has become a classic on the services industry, Stigler (1951) posited that the growing size of markets would increase both specialization and the realization of economies of scale in the production of such services. Stanback et al. (1981) have noted that Stigler failed to see that specialization preceded the possibility of realizing economies of scale. The increasing specialization of service functions that first arose within the large firm indicated to entrepreneurs that there was a market for these services, whence we see the development of a specialized producer-services industry. Producing certain highly specialized services inside the firm has become increasingly difficult because of the rising level of specialization and the costs of employing in-house specialists full time. Greenfield (1966) argues that specialization is the key factor pushing toward externalization. Specialized firms are in a position to sell their services to a diversity of firms and to continue developing their products and incorporating the latest innovations. Eventually, a large demand reduces the price of such producer services to small firms that otherwise would have been unable to buy such services. This in turn further expands the specialized services industry. The development of such a market entails a specialization of inputs in the production of such services and a standardization of outputs; that is, these services can be sold to a large number of firms. The specialization of inputs explains why there is a freestanding market of such services with a large number of small firms. The standardization of outputs with its corresponding expansion of the market points to the possibility that large corporations may also move into this market, as they are doing with consumer services and that they may merge with other firms in the sector. This would entail a shift of highly specialized functions to headquarters and the downgrading of what are now producer services firms to outlets for the sale of such services.

Growing complexity and an increase in the division between internally produced and externally bought specialized functions has made it possible for small highly specialized supplier firms to exist alongside the larger firms. The form through which large firms gain dominance in the leading corporate services is not vertical integration but complex networks of suppliers and contractors. Producer services firms participate in a variety of types of networks, including strategic alliances, cooperative arrangements, joint ventures, as well as less formal arrangements (Harrington 1995). These also extend to the international scale. There now is a considerable literature on the internationalization of producer services (Bagchi-Sen 1997; Warf 1991; Beaverstock, Taylor, and Smith 1999), including particular studies of accountancy (Beaverstock 1996), advertising (Leislie 1995), legal services (Dezalay and Sugarman 1995; Beaverstock et al. 1999), advertising (Daniels 1995), to name but some.

The available evidence shows that the freestanding producer services industry is growing fast and accounts for rising shares of GNP. Thus we know that a large share of these inputs are bought. Several early studies examined service employment inside firms (Miles 1985; Marshall 1979; 1982) and found that the subcontracting out of services was growing, which is certainly the case today. This subcontracting can involve routine operations, such as cleaning and transportation services, or highly specialized services. The development of certain office technologies can both favor in-house production by facilitating the work and at the same time induce subcontracting given rapid changes in technologies and machines (Miles 1985; Wood 2000; Moulaert and Djellal 1995; Bryson and Daniels 1997).

One can identify yet another phase in the growth and specialization of producer services, especially the most advanced of these. This new phase corresponds to the transformation in the geography and composition of the global economy since the 1980s. The expansion of the financial markets, securitization, the growing complexity and scale of mergers, acquisitions, and joint ventures, and the increasingly international character of these operations, all raised the demand for specialized service inputs and innovations. Producer services firms entered a phase of accelerated development of new offerings. Competition and deregulation induced both growing specialization and diversification, as well as a strong orientation toward the global market. This brought about strong pressure to build international networks and consequently pressure toward market concentration. Over the last two decades, there have been a considerable number of mergers and acquisitions among accounting firms, advertising firms, securities brokers, and financial services firms. Among the top firms, a sharp tendency toward concentration and larger market share is evident.[4] In some industries, such as accounting, the growth of transnational corporations and banks had long been inducing large size and

---

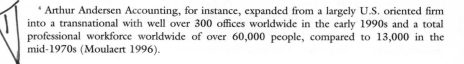

[4] Arthur Andersen Accounting, for instance, expanded from a largely U.S. oriented firm into a transnational with well over 300 offices worldwide in the early 1990s and a total professional workforce worldwide of over 60,000 people, compared to 13,000 in the mid-1970s (Moulaert 1996).

numbers of affiliates.[5] But the patterns of concentration evident by the late 1980s were on another order of magnitude.

Location and Agglomeration

A very different body of scholarship addresses the locational patterns of firms. From the perspective of classical location theory, access to transportation is one of the key variables determining a firm's locational choice; of less importance is labor availability. To these two factors Weber (1909) eventually added a third factor, agglomeration economies. From a traditional perspective, services are not subject to storage or transportation to their point of consumption, making these industrial location models inadequate for services.

At most, Christaller's (1966) central place theory can be seen as appropriate to explain consumer service location, since there is a strong correspondence between the size of the local market and the volume of service activity (Daniels 1985: 71–104). Indeed, much of the evidence we have on consumer services tends to suggest a strong correspondence between population distribution and consumer services. This is less so for cities where the diversity of the economic base affects locational choices. In Christaller's model the assumption is that suppliers of goods and services make their location decision on an isotropic plane over which a rural population with equal levels of purchasing power is uniformly distributed. This model makes it possible to establish the spatial organization of service activities in a region.[6]

In the 1980s there was not much literature on whether the growth of services had led to centralized or decentralized location patterns or on the comparative locational economies of high-value and low-value service activities or of highly innovative compared with routine services. Daniels (1985) tested several of the hypotheses on locational patterns of services using data for the European Economic Community, covering 1973–

[5] A key factor in the expansion and transformation of the accounting industry has been the change in the organization of the large client firms. Increasing size and diversification, along with geographic dispersal, generate very specific accounting requirements. Accounting services are needed at a national and international level and for a broad range of activities that are not narrowly defined as accounting, such as setting up accounting models for complex organizations and factoring-in different regulatory systems when more than one country is involved. The capability to serve different regional markets for one client has been developed largely through acquisition of regional firms, facilitated by the prevalence of small and medium-sized accounting firms, especially once the emergence of large accounting firms eroded the marketplace of independent firms (Jones 1981).

[6] Daniels (1985: 75) discusses a number of empirical studies that have confirmed the validity of the model for consumer services, especially in rural areas.

1979 (Keeble, Owens, and Thompson 1982). The evidence supported the hypotheses that consumer services are more evenly distributed than producer services and that they lack a strong contrast between central and peripheral locations. Producer services were found to be highly concentrated in central places, with gradually reduced representation in the less central places. The recent evidence also points to a strong relationship between central regions and relative specialization in producer services (Bryson and Daniels 1997). Central places are becoming increasingly specialized in producer services, while peripheral regions are increasingly specializing in consumer services. However, the evidence also shows that some of the less central regions are growing faster in terms of population and are showing higher growth rates in producer services, even though in relative terms they have underrepresentation of such services and increasing representation of consumer services (Gordon and McCann 2000). In the United States we can see similar patterns in cities, with a higher specialization in producer services in major cities, but higher growth rates, especially in the last few years, in a second tier of cities. Again, these higher growth rates do not undermine the overrepresentation of producer services in the major cities. We return to this subject in chapter 6.

In the case of producer services, then, many of the assumptions underlying the distribution of consumer services are not valid or only marginally so. Precedents to the analysis of location patterns in producer services can be found in the studies of office location concerned with understanding their concentration in urban places. Among these are studies that inferred the existence of agglomeration economies from such locational concentration (Haig 1972; Armstrong 1972); studies that analyzed communication linkages between offices (Gad 1975; Goddard 1975); more behavior-oriented studies focused on the influence of decisionmaking processes on locational outcomes (Edwards 1982); and the development of microeconomic models based on such evidence (Tauchen and Witte 1983). Generally, the locational patterns of offices are understood in terms of the higher bidding power of offices for central locations, with a resulting spatial hierarchy, in which higher-level offices tend to be more centrally located than lower-order offices (Armstrong and Milder 1984).

The literature on the relation of firms to their spatial strategies has largely focused on manufacturing. I would like to examine whether some of the key propositions are applicable to the case of producer services and to what extent the differences in tradability and delivery modes between goods and services alter the propositions generated by the discussion on manufacturing.

Much of the recent debate on vertical integration and disintegration has focused on questions of economies and diseconomies of scope, the

extent to which a firm integrates upstream or downstream. Scope economies are a major factor in the costs of organization: These are costs of
coordination, which increase as a firm integrates up- and downstream,
and transaction costs, which increase with reductions in vertical integration and the resulting growth of market exchanges. Many authors have
posited that the system of high levels of vertical integration and centralization of capital is being superseded by a variety of developments: more
disintegrated systems of industrial organization, entailing complex interfirm linkages; large firms using increasing numbers of subcontractors;
niche markets offering both innovative and traditional small firms some
protection from competition with large corporations; industrial districts
consisting of integrated networks of small firms (Dunford 1989; 1998).
Increases in the market for specialized inputs and growing advantages of
buying such inputs or subcontracting out for them rather than producing
them in-house furthered the expansion of the market for small specialized
firms. Various authors have pointed out that it is not certain that this
represents a new model of development in that flexible specialization is
often merely an adaptation to economic instabilities. And if the new types
of demand that have fueled the growth of small, innovative, flexible
firms, become more standardized and widespread, it is likely that the
conditions for industrial organization now underlying those firms will be
transformed and routinized or integrated into large firms. Furthermore,
the immense costs of research and development can eventually force
mergers and joint ventures. The propositions about a new model of development posit an increased extent and density in market relations. But
vertical disintegration and the other trends described above may result in
more interfirm planning and organization rather than in greater market
density. There have been new forms of centralization in the specialized
manufacturing districts of northern Italy, which served as one of the key
cases for the model of flexible specialization and density of market linkages. Finally, much of the small, competitive, highly innovative character
of industrial organization evident in "Silicon Valley" in the United States
or in Cambridge in the United Kingdom may be related to the early
stages of the life cycle of electronics products and the fact that entry costs
were low (Dunford 1989: 14–15; 1998). Thus, the development of small
firms is not simply a process of vertical disintegration; it will tend to be
associated with fields of technological breakthrough and innovation.[7] To-

---

[7] In the United Kingdom, small and innovative high-tech firms for very specialized products for particular high-profit niche-markets are the base of the Cambridge high-tech belt,
but there are limitations to the growth and staying power of many of these firms (Dunford
1989: 18; Gordon and McCann 2000). Often, small size is a stage in the development of
firms that is important in a period of basic technological change. Some high-tech firms are
not production oriented and need constant interaction with research centers.

day, much of electronics hardware production is determined largely by vertically integrated firms, and entry costs are enormously higher than they were in the 1960s. In the producer services, we find the three types of firm organization evident in electronics: vertically integrated firms, integrated networks of small firms, and independent small firms.

Producer services tend to require a diversified resource base and, in certain industries, considerable investment. Reaching the necessary concentration of suppliers and customers that makes this possible and feasible tends to contribute to location in urban areas of a certain size. Some early studies (Daniels 1975; Pred 1977; 1976) emphasize the centrality of information and knowledge in the operation of many services, and especially producer services. If information is central, "then the location of these services can be interpreted within the context of the demand for information, the way it circulates and who exchanges it" (Daniels 1975: 113). Since a central attribute of information is that it is spatially based (Pred 1977), proximity emerges as a key to the activity of obtaining information; that is, information will circulate through specific places and not others. One could, then, in principle, establish the differential accessibility to information offered by different types of locations (Daniels 1975: 113).

The locational concentration of producer services is in part explained by the characteristics of production of these services. These characteristics, in conjunction with the ascendance of such services in economic activity generally, both domestically and worldwide, are helpful in explaining the centralization of the management and servicing functions that have fed the economic resurgence in major cities. Producer services, unlike other types of services, are mostly not as dependent on vicinity to the buyers as consumer services. Hence, concentration of production in suitable locations and export, both domestically and abroad, are feasible. Production of these services benefits from proximity to other services, particularly when there is a wide array of specialized firms. Such firms obtain agglomeration economies when they locate close to others that are sellers of key inputs or are necessary for joint production of certain service offerings (Stanback and Noyelle 1982: 17–18). This would help explain why while New York City continued to lose corporate headquarters for two decades, the number and employment of firms servicing such headquarters kept growing rapidly (Cohen 1981; Conservation of Human Resources Project 1977; Drennan 1983; Sassen 2000). Another kind of agglomeration economy consists of the amenities and lifestyles that large urban centers can offer the high-income personnel employed in the producer services. In brief, the fact that producer services are relatively independent of proximity to the buyers, combined with the existence of agglomeration economies at the point of production, makes possible both the concentration of production in suitable locations and the export to other areas, domestically and abroad. As a result, we see the development of global centers—for example, New York and London— and of regional centers—for example, Denver and Birmingham—for the production of such services.

These general trends hold to different extents for the various branches in the producer services industries. Some industries lend themselves more readily to transborder trade and others to investment trade. (See also chapter 3.) Advertising and accounting, for example, have tended to establish a multiplicity of branch offices because of the importance of dealing directly with clients.[8] Broad networks of branches and affiliates have contributed to the importance of central functions in headquarters of service firms; these branches are more than mere service outlets and carry out important production functions. Management consulting, engineering, and architectural firms, on the other hand, have not tended to set up branches and affiliates, but, rather, have kept all functions in centralized locations. Delivery of these services can often assume the form of a good—a drawing or a disk, for example. Or it may require the specialist to go to the site. Thus both the GATS and NAFTA have specific provisions for the cross-border movement of professionals in various service industries (Sassen 1998: chap. 2).[9] These locational patterns are also affected by the existence of regulatory restrictions, especially when foreign locations or international trade is involved.

Noyelle and Dutka (1988) argue that attempts by countries to impose trade restrictions also can determine the extent to which technical developments may be fully utilized. These authors point out that advances in computerization and communications technologies are "making it in-

[8] The most significant influences on the location of service activity by transnational corporations in recent years have been regulatory changes and technical advances in transborder data flows (Dunning and Norman 1987: 47; UN Centre on Transnational Corporations 1989c; Sauvant 1986). Advances in technology may reduce the need for foreign direct investment as a mode for international movement of services; such advances may also further promote such investment by reducing the transnational costs of cross-border activities. The EU internal market, in place since 1992, includes provisions that relate to the market for services, notably rights of establishments, and the harmonization of intra-EU regulations relating, e.g., to the movement of human resources, recognition of professional and other qualifications or cross-border corporate acquisitions. One of the questions is whether there is scope for an EU-wide internal market in services to generate new patterns of location that would alter recent trends in the spatial and sectoral attributes of services markets in individual member countries.

[9] These regimes can assume different legal forms. For instance, the new immigration law in Japan allows for an increase in the number of foreign lawyers who can be admitted. In a country with an extremely closed legal system, where international law firms are still not common, employing lawyers trained in countries with which Japanese firms do international business is one way of gaining access to that expertise.

creasingly feasible to design service production procedures in the form of software and to store inputs and outputs in electronic memories" (1988: 90). The effect of such developments is to separate production from consumption, in both time and space, and allow greater centralization of production, as is the case with goods; yet the authors stress that we should not underestimate the differences between goods and services (see also UN Centre on Transnational Corporations 1989d; OECD 1994; OECD 2000b). Noyelle and Dutka (1988: 91) found a dual tendency toward centralization, resting on scale economies, and toward decentralization, resting on the computerization of routine procedures. But customization rather than mass production is the overarching organizing tendency. What this type of decentralization allows is the provision of a customized product to a client insofar as the computerization of the tasks allows for specific adaptations at a reduced cost. This trend contributes to the weight of headquarter functions but in a way that differs from the tendency toward the centralization of location.

The ability to serve clients in the home country is more and more frequently associated with the ability to serve the firm in foreign locations as well. A network arrangement can offer access to worldwide markets especially if the service is partly embodied in the professional worker who needs to be available to the client. In an increasingly complex and specialized global economic system, general expertise is not necessarily what clients want (Bryson et al. 1993). Firms can deliver highly specialized services to individual clients through network arrangements which allow a large service firm to contract specialized suppliers and consultants to produce the service. This becomes a version of just-in-time and just-in-place production/delivery made possible by the fact that the large global service firm can count on networks of specific specialized firms, including firms in specific locations if that is necessary. Bryson et al. (1993) point out that this gives the large firm enormous flexibility in taking on clients, no matter how specialized or particular the service demanded, because the large firm can mobilize its network. This represents a combination of global service delivery with highly specialized content that helps the firm maintain a competitive position in the market.

Marshall et al. (1986) found that the existence of a corporate hierarchy in the organization of firms also is one of the determinants of locational patterns for producer service firms. The high concentration of producer services in the greater London area and Southeast region "cannot be understood simply as a response of service activities to changes in the cost of sites or variations in communications costs" (p. 227). The fact that large manufacturing firms concentrate their national headquarters and many of their administrative research and technical functions in the London region while branch offices are distributed over a wider geographic territory to serve local markets may have contributed to a parallel corporate hierarchy in producer services, or in the case of single-site producer service firms, to such services being located where the headquarters and administrative functions are. The decline in central office employment in other regions of the United Kingdom during the 1970s may have been partly linked to the many takeovers in the early 1970s of the provincial firms headquartered outside the Southeast or London region (Howells and Green 1986). Insofar as these takeovers were by firms headquartered in the London region, they would have induced further locational concentration of producer services in this region, given that what were once headquarters in provincial areas had now become branch offices of firms headquartered in the London region.

In an examination of the complex interplay between in-house and external expertise and knowledge, Bryson and Daniels (1998) find that the use of external expertise and its location vary strongly between large firms and small or medium sized enterprises. Large firms are able to access specialized external expertise regardless of where they are located while SMEs are tied into local providers of a more general type of expertise. This signals the formation of a dual information economy.

These conditions and locational patterns all have the effect of further building up areas with already large concentrations of producer service firms. The need to serve clients who have decentralized their offices actually may reduce the feasibility of following clients to all their dispersed locations, and thus furthers centralization of the servicing firms. From the perspective of the decentralizing client it would seem that a central marketplace becomes important in that this is the way to find out what producer service firms are doing and with which firms to contract. Thus from both directions there is pressure on producer service firms to centralize, either following a corporate model or opting for a central location in order to obtain agglomeration economies.

There is wide ranging international evidence showing that ownership and control within producer services are increasingly concentrated in large enterprises, which are in turn increasingly transnational as a result of M&As. But concentration has been accompanied by an increasing division of labor within firms (technical specialization) as well as among firms. There is growing complexity and increase in the division between internally produced and externally bought specialized functions. As a result, alongside the larger firms and their growth there is also a large world of small highly specialized supplier firms in the service sector. Concentration here is, then, not in the form of vertical integration but, rather, of complex networks of suppliers and contractors. The focus shifts to market segments rather than products. Externalization and internalization do not necessarily represent distinct long-term organizational trends, with one replacing the other; they can coexist (O'Farrell et al. 1992; 1993). Some firms also decide to re-internalize specific functions, as externalization may weaken control over possibly sensitive information. Decisions to externalize the production of producer services deepen the social division of labor and underlie the massive growth of the sector since the 1980s.

The impact of technology on the spatial organization of the economy makes it increasingly problematic to keep on using some of the standard measures still evident in many studies on the impact of these developments on major cities. One of these standard measures is the presence of top-ranked headquarters, measured in terms of size of assets or capital, ordered by city size. These kinds of rankings provide us with information on various aspects, but they are not adequate measures to understand what makes a city a global city: it is neither city size per se, even though there are size thresholds, nor is it number of top headquarters of the largest sized firms. Each of these variables is embedded in more complex logics in the case of global cities. City size, once a fairly significant indicator, is less so when the largest cities are no longer necessarily the ones that concentrate the most important functions. Further, firm size has a different meaning today than it did in the Fordist era when the largest firms were indeed at the top of the organizational architecture of the economy and the latter was largely national. The old rankings tell us something about the spatialization of economic activities. But these three aspects need to be factored in if we want to understand what combination of elements constitutes global city functions.

Table 5.1 is emblematic of the problems with these rankings. It both captures some trends and fails to include others. Major cities such as London, New York, and Chicago have been losing top ranked headquarters for at least three decades. At the same time the concentration of Japanese headquarters in Tokyo has grown over the last two decades, partly because participation in the global economy for these firms still means going through a lot of government channels given a fairly regulated economy. Hence, location in Tokyo is crucial. The ranking for 1999 also factors in the continuing concern in Japan with firm size, now partly used as a way of making a hostile acquisition or takeover almost impossible given the size of these enterprises. Most important for the purposes of understanding what distinguishes a global city is the fact that we know from multiple measures that London and New York are the key international business centers in the global economy today, and that Frankfurt is an increasingly important center that ranks in the top five. Yet from this measure of headquarter location of the 500 largest firms in the world in the largest metropolitan areas of the world, one would not know this. I return to this subject later in this chapter and in chapter 6. (See also Sassen 2000: 71–83.)

TABLE 5.1

Number of Headquarters of the Top 500 Transnational Firms in the World's Seventeen Largest Metropolitan Areas, 1984 and 1999

	1984		1999	
	Population ('000's)	Number of Top 500 Headquarters	Population[1] ('000's)	Number of Top 500 Headquarters
Tokyo	26,200	34	27,200	63
New York	17,082	59	16,400	25
Mexico City	14,082	1	16,900	1
Osaka	15,900	15	10,600	21
São Paulo	12,700	0	16,800	2
Seoul	11,200	4	11,800	8
London	11,100	37	7,600	29
Calcutta	11,100	0	12,100	0
Buenos Aires	10,700	1	11,900	0
Los Angeles	10,519	14	12,600	2
Bombay	9,950	1	15,700	0
Paris	9,650	26	9,600	26
Beijing (Peking)	9,430	0	11,400	3
Rio De Janeiro	9,200	1	10,300	1
Cairo	8,500	0	9,900	0
Shanghai	8,500	0	13,700	0
Chicago	7,865	18	6,900	2

Sources: For 1984, based on Feagin and Smith, 1987. For 1999, author's calculations based on Fortune Magazine, Fortune Global 500, August 2, 1999 pp. F-1—F-10; UN, Dept. of Economic and Social Affairs, Population Division, Urban Agglomerations, 1996.

Notes: [1]Population figures from 1996; rankings initially based on 1984 figures and kept in order for comparison.

The space economy of technological innovation appears to follow the same pattern of dispersal and agglomeration (Moss 1986; Castells 1989). The most encompassing analysis can be found in Castells (1989). He posits that restructuring processes under way in the electronics industry produce a locational logic characterized by the strengthening—notwithstanding urban crisis and economic downturns—of centers for high-level innovation, which will command and be at the heart of a globally dispersed production system. Secondary "milieux of innovation" will continue to develop but increasingly not as a function of innovation but rather as a function of decentralization of some aspects of the process of innovation. And offshore production will continue, but with strong upgrading by the automation of routine operations and the increased offshoring of advanced manufacturing processes. Thus, a spatial division of labor will remain as a distinct trait of information technology industries (Castells 1989: ch. 2; 1996).[10]

The tendency for firms to consist of many highly diverse branches or divisions, the growing size of firms, and the tendency to be multisite, all have made the components of information to which central headquarters need access more diverse and raised the importance of precision in that information. Location thus has assumed a new importance, as some places will provide better access to information than will others. Travel as an alternative to locating in a central place loses comparative advantage in proportion to the level of spatial concentration of key resources. The marketplace, in the narrow sense of the word, assumes new importance as well—becoming a place where access to information is facilitated and where clients can gain access to a multiplicity of specialized firms. Certain urban centers emerge as servicing centers. Some are highly specialized—medical health centers, insurance centers—while others are more general, offering specialized services of all sorts, the agglomeration itself making more and more specialized firms economically feasible. This in turn contributes to increasing the importance of such cities as markets where client firms can buy any specialized service and hence an inducement to buying on the market rather than producing in-house. Foreign firms and governments can also buy in such markets. Some cities emerge as specific marketplaces for a global clientele.

The Spatial Organization of Finance

A key argument in this book is that in the 1980s the place and characteristics of the financial industry underwent a sufficiently fundamental transformation as to raise questions about the adequacy of grouping this industry with the other producer services. This argument was partly documented in chapter 4 and is further developed here. In chapter 4, I sought to show that the accelerated transformation of debt and assets into highly marketable instruments has made many of the financial markets akin to

---

[10] On the issue of new tendencies toward concentration, Ernst (1986) foresees the emergence of strategic alliances between a few major electronics systems corporations. Castells (1989) predicts that insofar as innovation is central to the industry, large firms will tend to establish networks of subcontracting in order to maintain commercial control over the innovative smaller firms without creating obstacles for them. Small, innovative firms are increasingly dependent on large corporate firms that operate worldwide. But these large firms can keep the same spatial division of labor: milieux of high innovation along with decentralized manufacturing. The difference, Castells points out, is that the spatial logic of information technology producers is being "drawn inside the organizational structure of large corporations" (Castells 1989: 125).

commodity markets, where the value of the instrument lies in its resale potential; financial markets have become less and less like service markets, where the value of the service lies in its utility to the buyer. Parallel trends are evident in certain components of the real estate market, a subject I return to in chapter 7. But there is yet another way in which the financial services industry is quite different from other producer services. This difference lies in the enormous weight of governmental regulation, much more so than in other highly regulated producer services, such as accounting and law. In these latter industries, much of the regulation is contained in professional standards. It is impossible to discuss the financial industry without discussing regulation.

One of the main aspects that emerges from an examination of the regulatory frameworks in major developed countries is that central developments in the financial industry in the 1980s did not fit well into the regulatory frameworks in place in the decade of the 1970s. At the same time, the absence of constricting regulations, as in the case of West Germany, did not necessarily lead to the type of expansion and internationalization evident after deregulation in countries such as the United States and Japan. There was clearly a more specific combination of conditions at work in those countries where finance underwent sharp growth and internationalization. This would also seem to be suggested by the fact that countries with quite diverse regulatory frameworks—the United States, the United Kingdom, and Japan—underwent regulatory changes that left them with a core of similar types of financial markets and market areas for different kinds of financial institutions even if embedded in vast domestic financial systems that remained different from each other.

The possibilities for new financial markets emerged in a context where the regulatory framework in some of the leading financial centers contained various types and levels of restriction. The regulatory apparatus in many of these countries typically led to closure in the domestic financial markets. Regulations mainly concerned interest rates on financial instruments provided by financial intermediaries; statutory distinctions among areas of business, notably between commercial banking and the securities markets, as well as a number of finer separations; and regulations, notably exchange controls, that separated domestic and international financial markets. Eventually developments in the financial markets and the characteristics of regulatory frameworks created a number of conflicts. These conflicts led to the production of various financial innovations to resolve the problem or avoid the regulation.

The internationalization of the financial markets and the production of innovations to circumvent restrictions put pressure on leading participants, such as the United States, Japan, and Western Europe to harmonize their financial regulations. At a time when the financial market consisted mostly of national markets, differences in the financial systems of various countries carried less weight than at a time of rapid internationalization.

The financial industry is an interesting industry in terms of the locational issues discussed in the first half of this chapter because regulation operated, at least in theory, as one of the key locational constraints, and secondly because this is a highly digitalized industry that produces a dematerialized output that can be hypermobile and move across conventional borders. This raises a host of locational issues that are quite specific and different from those of most other economic sectors. The large-scale deregulation of the industry in a growing number of countries since the mid-1980s brought with it a sharp increase in innovations which facilitated its expansion both geographically and institutionally, and it brought with it a heightened level of risk which in turn affected its expansion both geographically and institutionally.

The push in finance to globalize, digitalize, and liquefy hitherto illiquid assets was a key for inducing the production of innovations in the industry, but especially in financial services, and in the other specialized service industries that service finance—legal services, accounting, software design, and insurance. Questions of innovation and risk in the financial services assume meanings that go beyond what holds for the producer services generally. Innovation can amplify the spatial organization of the industry insofar as it makes possible entry into markets that would seem to be off limits. This was the case with what came to be named "emerging markets." Participation in these markets entailed development of a series of specific financial instruments and investment channels. The question of risk and how it is handled and perceived is yet another factor which has an impact on how the industry organizes itself, where it locates operations, what markets become integrated into the global capital market, and so on.

Today, after considerable deregulation in the industry, the incorporation of a growing number of centers into a global market, and the sharp use of electronic trading, the actual spatial organization of the industry can be seen as a closer indicator of its locational dynamics as driven by markets than was the case in the earlier regulatory phase. This would hold especially for the international level, but also in some cases, such as the U.S., domestically, given barriers to interstate banking—even though these are being gradually dismantled.

There are two levels for the operation of locational patterns in the financial industry, one within countries and the other international. I turn to these in the next two sections, with a particular focus on financial services and markets.

Domestic Location Patterns of Financial Services

Deregulation has made some difference in the domestic organization of financial services, depending on the specifics of a country's regulatory framework for the industry. Comparing the post-deregulation locational patterns to the earlier period is not easy because there is not much research on the locational aspects of financial services (Bennett and Graham 1998; Parr and Budd 2000; see also Tables 6.20 and 6.22 in chap. 6).

Perhaps one of the most detailed studies is that by Parr and Budd (2000) examining the spatial structure of financial services in the UK in relation to the country's urban system. They confine themselves to financial services as a type of producer service, that is, intermediate services supplied to other firms as inputs to production. Parr and Budd (2000) find a rather clearly defined locational pattern. While London has a disproportionately large share of financial services and dominates the sector, the spatial organization of the industry is complex and involves multiple locations. Further, the factors underlying this spatial organization provide important insights into the structural relations which exist within this sector. The authors posit that central place theory, one of the branches in locational theory, is helpful in accounting for the observed spatial structure of financial service activities within the UK. But central place theory is generally used to understand the location of retailing activities and shopping patterns based on these; to use the model for the financial services sector the authors introduce certain modifications.[11] For shopping, the spatial distribution of supply corresponds to the spatial distribution of demand, with the extent of the correspondence depending on the particular activity involved. This is not the case for finance. Further, in the case of financial services, input costs vary significantly over space and need to be included in the model (Parr and Budd 2000). Related to this is the fact that financial services operate across an established urban system in which costs may vary substantially within a given level and, especially, among levels.

The financial system is enormously complex, containing among others, markets, assets, and intermediaries. The organization and development of financial services have strong spatial dimensions (Sassen 1999). Parr and Budd (2000) conceptualize financial services as consisting of a multitude

[11] See Parr and Budd (1997) for a detailed discussion of these modifications. Various features of central place theory make its application to financial services difficult and hence require modification. Central place theory can only be usefully applied to a particular range of economic activities—those which face a dispersed demand and for which the pattern of supply is related to the pattern of demand. This holds for many kinds of services as well as many activities which have a locational orientation to the market (as opposed to energy, raw materials, etc.).

of flows organized around two types of end users: lenders and borrowers. Lenders can be individuals, governments, firms, and proprietary trading companies, that is, financial firms acting on their own account. Borrowers invest in real or tangible assets used in the production of goods and services—they are firms which issue stock or bonds, governments which issue bonds, and individuals who acquire financial instruments, such as mortgages. The financial system links the two types of end users; it mediates the relation between savings and investment. These various interactions can occur at different levels of the urban system, with some only taking place at the top of the system and others only at lower levels, and yet others at more than one level.

Economies of scale and scope are very important in the industry. The new phase of mergers in the 1990s involved both domestic and international partners and raised the levels of capital and assets of these financial firms (Sassen 1999a). These mergers often are aimed at diversifying the operations of the newly formed firm thereby raising the economies of scope. As changes of scale and scope allow firms to operate in different markets and to extend operations into new domains and regions, these changes also have an impact on the locational organization of the industry.

In addition, locational interdependence among firms is crucial at the top levels of the industry: their networked relation to multiple other specialized services makes financial services firms subject to localization economies (Sassen 2000).[12] This networked financial sector is one instance of the corporate services complex (Drennan 1977). Parr and Budd (2000) find that the structure of what they call "the activity complex" tends to be intricate in the case of finance, with many instances of two-way interactions rather than simply a vertical hierarchy. On the revenue side there are possibilities for cross-referral of business among firms and emergence of particular specializations within the activity, while on the cost side there are the advantages of a pool of skilled labor, other needed specialized business services, and access to high quality information, including on an informal basis.

Finally, financial services firms are also subject to urbanization economies, but localization economies are far more important. This is not generally the case for firms in a very broad range of other sectors. The Employers Survey (Feloy et al. 1997) found that financial services in the City of London stand out from other groups of respondents to the Survey in their positive evaluation of proximity to related activities and the

---

[12] In the case of manufacturing this dynamic operates typically within industrial complexes with vertical integration or with specialized divisions of labor, i.e., industrial districts and clusters (see Parr 1999; Scott and Storper 1986; Porter 1990; Gordon 1999).

specific emphasis on local intelligence as the crucial externality. Most firms in other sectors were more likely to mention urbanization economies and did not particularly emphasize localization economies. What the financial services firms in the City appear to benefit from is not generalized urbanization economies which firms might derive from proximity to or access to multiple suppliers and clients, but rather sector specific benefits—local intelligence in the financial sector, the innovative milieu in the city, the intensity of interactions with multiple types of expertise, and up-to-the-minute information not generally available or standardized (Sassen 1999).[13]

The importance of these localization economies for the financial industry is also underlined by the fact that state-of-the-art infrastructure while necessary is not sufficient. A leading financial center needs to be embedded in a significant level of organizational complexity: thus a digitalized industry such as finance might in principle locate wherever there is adequate infrastructure. The evidence on Internet backbone capacity, one indicator of connectivity, in different cities in the U.S. shows us that New York, its leading financial center, is not necessarily the one with the highest backbone capacity or the one that has consistently had the highest growth rates in this capacity. There is clearly a threshold, but this is a necessary and not a sufficient condition. Although various innovations in telecommunications may make a broad range of locations, including remote locations, technologically feasible, this is only part of the combination of elements that a financial center requires.

There is little doubt that New York City is a far more important international business center than Dallas, San Francisco, Atlanta, and Chicago. Yet in 1999 its backbone capacity for Internet transactions was below that of these cities, and its growth rate in terms of adding capacity was significantly below that of most other cities in the U.S. listed in the table. As with rankings of headquarters of the largest firms discussed earlier (see Table 5.2), a ranking of cities by backbone capacity of the Internet is a misleading measure, though one frequently used to show a city's chances for becoming an international business center. What is left out of this type of ranking is the fact that for firms to maximize, rather than simply experience, the benefits they can derive from the new digital networks they need organizational complexity: this is an intermediary condi-

---

[13] What might be economies internal to the firm may become imbricated with urbanization and localization economies in certain cases, such as that of a highly specialized complex like finance. Further, some types of urbanization economies tend to be a function of city size (Gordon 1995). Finally, in the case of activity-complex economies, Parr and Budd (2000) find that external economies tend to be related not to scope or scale but to the complexity or degree of elaboration of the activity ensemble. I have found this to be the case for global financial centers (Sassen 1999).

TABLE 5.2
Growth in Backbone Capacity, 1997–1999 (Megabits per Second)

Metro	1997	1999	Growth Rate (relative to nation)
Washington, DC	7,826	28,370	69.6
Dallas, TX	5,646	25,343	86.2
San Francisco, CA	7,506	25,297	64.7
Atlanta, GA	5,196	23,861	88.2
Chicago, IL	7,663	23,340	58.5
New York, NY	6,766	22,232	63.1
Los Angeles, CA	5,056	14,868	56.5
Kansas City, MO	1,080	13,525	240.6
Houston, TX	1,890	11,522	117.1
St. Louis, MO	1,350	10,342	147.2
Salt Lake City, UT	270	9,867	702.0
Indianapolis, IN	90	9,217	1967.3
Denver, CO	2,901	8,674	57.4
Boston, MA	1,325	8,001	116.0
Seattle, WA	1,972	7,288	71.0

Source: Moss, M.L. and A.M. Townsend. 2000. "The Internet Backbone and the American Metropolis."

tion that cannot be measured simply in terms of carrying capacity (Sassen 2001c). Furthermore, what this type of measure leaves out is the private dedicated lines used by key industries such as finance, that do not use the lines used for the public access Internet (Sassen 1998: chap. 9).

The importance of these various aspects subsumed under localization and urbanization economies is replicated partly in studies of the locational patterns of global information technology consultancy firms (ITC). Moulaert and Djellal (1995) found that the significance of the urban milieu of the top-tier cities is very high for the territorial anchorage of ITC firms. To optimize the externalities of the urban milieu (expertise, diversity of specialized professionals, universities, professional networking, high-level public authorities, conference complexes, high-tech parks in the vicinity), ITC firms organize in spatial networks. These differ from the traditional hierarchical, multidivision, or multiservice forms of organization. Instead they have built their professional and market structures according to principles of loose coupling, horizontal communication, and synergies among skills. ITC firms that specialize in the provision of general systems seem to benefit significantly from links established by their agencies in second- and sometimes third-tier cities. ITC firms that are global, on the other hand, seem to have basically networks among top-tier urban agglomerations; they tend to use collaborations with other firms when it comes to systems development.

Beyond the top level of activities, the spatial organization of the financial services industry will tend to encompass different types of activities at different levels of the urban system. In the UK urban system, Parr and Budd (2000) identify a set of activities largely concentrated in London, the top of the urban system: international portfolio services, derivatives trading, international commodity trading, international equity and bonds, and international underwriting.[14] Subsequent levels of the urban hierarchy have several centers. At the second level of activities they identify five centers (in another country it could be fewer or more) with concentrations of the following activities: UK portfolio services; foreign exchange trading; UK corporate finance; UK equity and bonds; and UK underwriting. Activities at the third level take place in nine urban centers and they are: regional portfolio services; foreign exchange intermediation; Treasury operation activities; regional corporate finance; and regional underwriting. At the lowest level there are over twenty centers and the activities are: foreign exchange agency; wholesale insurance; sub-regional equity and bond agency; equity settlement and other back-office functions. They find that intermediate financial activity, the focus here, is negligible in centers with less than 150,000 population. Yet population size is not a good indicator, since a larger city may well be lower in the hierarchy of activities; further, there could conceivably be a highly specialized center for complex yet standardized activities.

In the Digital Era: More Concentration Than Dispersal?

At the international level the issues change somewhat since it is only certain components of the organization of the industry that operate at that level (Sassen 1999; 2001b). As the case of the UK study suggests, many of the back-office activities that are also supporting the internationalized portions of the industry can locate at lower levels of the national urban system. It is markets and management functions that we see operating at the international scale.

In theory, the intensification of deregulation and the instituting of policies in various countries aimed at creating a supportive cross-border environment for financial firms could dramatically change the locational logic of the industry. This is a digitalized and globalized industry that produces

[14] Parr and Budd (2000) examine the financial services industry in the context of the UK urban system without reference to the long-term development of that system, an issue discussed in Parr (1981). The spatial structure of financial services firms is heavily influenced by the preexisting urban system. However, the importance of these services and the fact that they have a certain spatial organization is likely, in turn, to exert influence on the urban system itself, though it is not easy to tell whether in the direction of reinforcing the existing system or modifying it.

dematerialized outputs. It could be argued that the one feature that could keep this industry from having a very broad range of locational options would be regulation. With deregulation that constraint should have disappeared. Other factors such as the premium paid for location in major cities should be a deterrent to locate there and with the new developments of telecommunications there should be no need for such central locations. The first edition of this book received numerous critiques along these lines.

But empirically what stands out in the evidence about the global financial industry after a decade of deregulation and major advances in telematics is the extent of locational concentration and the premium firms are willing to pay to be in major centers. Large shares of many financial markets are disproportionately concentrated in a few financial centers, to be described in detail in chapter 7. This trend towards consolidation in a few centers also is evident within countries. What stands out is that this pattern towards the consolidation of one leading financial center in most countries is a function of rapid growth in the sector, not of decay in the losing cities.

We are seeing both consolidation in fewer major centers across and within countries *and* a sharp growth in the numbers of centers that become part of the global network as countries deregulate their economies. São Paulo and Bombay, for instance, became integrated into the global financial market after Brazil and India deregulated their financial systems, at least partly. This mode of incorporation into the global market is often at the cost of losing functions which these financial centers had when they were largely national centers. Today, leading foreign financial, accounting, and legal services firms enter their markets to handle the new cross-border operations. The incorporation of these centers into the global market typically happens without a gain in the share of the global market that they can command even though they add to the total volume of the global market and even though capitalization in their national markets can rise sharply.

One indicator of the growing importance of cross-border transactions is the value of cross-border transactions in bonds and equities as a percentage of GDP in the leading developed economies. Table 5.3 presents this information for a handful of these countries and shows the recency of this accelerated increase. Thus the value of such transactions represented 4% of GDP in 1975 in the U.S., 35% in 1985 when the new financial era is in full swing, but had quadrupled by 1995 and risen to 230% in 1998. Other countries show even sharper increases. In Germany this share grew from 5% in 1975 to 334% in 1998; in France it went from 5% in 1980 to 415% in 1998. (This entails partly escalating levels of risk and innovation driving the industry.) It is only over the last decade and a half that we see this acceleration. (See Table 5.3.)

TABLE 5.3

Cross-border Transactions in Bonds and Equities*, 1975 to 1998 (percentage of GDP)

	As a Percentage of GDP					
	1975	*1980*	*1985*	*1990*	*1995*	*1998*
United States	4	9	35	89	135	230
Japan	2	8	62	119	65	91
Germany	5	7	33	57	172	334
France	na	5	21	54	187	415
Italy	1	1	4	27	253	640
Canada	3	9	27	65	187	331

Source: Bank for International Settlements, *Annual Report 1999*, April 1998–June 1999, p. 10.
Note: *denotes gross purchases and sales of securities between residents and non-residents.

Why is it that at a time of rapid growth in the number of integrated financial centers, in overall volumes, and in electronic networks, we have such high concentration of market shares in the leading centers? Both globalization and electronic trading are about expansion and dispersal beyond what had been the confined realm of national economies and floor trading. Indeed, given globalization and electronic trading one might well ask, and many do, why financial centers matter at all.

The continuing weight of major centers is, in a way, countersensical. The rapid development of electronic exchanges, the growing digitalization of much financial activity, the fact that finance has become one of the leading sectors in a growing number of countries, and that it is a sector that produces a dematerialized, hypermobile product, all suggest that location should not matter. In fact geographic dispersal would seem to be a good option given the high cost of operating in major financial centers. Further, the last ten years have seen an increased geographic mobility of financial experts and financial services firms.

There has been, indeed, geographic decentralization of certain types of financial activities, aimed at securing business in the growing number of countries becoming integrated into the global economy. Many of the leading investment banks have operations in more countries than they had twenty years ago. The same can be said for the leading accounting and legal services and other specialized corporate services. And it can be said for some markets: for example, in the 1980s all basic wholesale foreign exchange operations were in London. Today these are distributed among London and several other centers (even though their number is far smaller than the number of countries whose currency is being traded). But these trends do not undermine the patterns of ongoing concentration described above.

There are, in my view, at least two reasons that explain the trend towards consolidation in a few centers rather than massive dispersal. I discussed some of these issue in more generic terms in the presentation of the organizational hypotheses of the global city model in the preface to this new edition.

The importance of social connectivity and central functions. First, while the new telecommunications technologies do indeed facilitate geographic dispersal of economic activities without losing system integration, they have also had the effect of strengthening the importance of central coordination and control functions for firms and for markets. Major centers have massive concentrations of state-of-the-art resources that allow them to maximize the benefits of telecommunications and to govern the new conditions for operating globally. Even electronic markets such as NASDAQ and E*Trade rely on traders and banks which are located somewhere, typically in a major financial center.

One fact that has become increasingly evident in my research is that to maximize the benefits of the new information technologies you need not only the infrastructure but a complex mix of other resources. Most of the value added that these technologies can produce for advanced service firms lies in the externalities. And this means the material and human resources—state-of-the-art office buildings, top talent, and the social networking infrastructure that maximizes connectivity.

A second fact that is emerging with greater clarity in my research concerns the meaning of "information." There are two types of information that matter to these operations. One is the datum, which may be complex but comes in the form of standardized information easily available to these firms: e.g., the details of a privatization in a particular country. The second type of information is far more difficult to obtain because it is not standardized. It requires interpretation/evaluation/judgment. It entails negotiating a series of datums and a series of interpretations of a mix of datums in the hope of producing a higher order type of information. Access to the first kind of information is now global and immediate thanks to the digital revolution. But it is the second type of information that requires a complicated mixture of elements, not only technical but also social—what we could think of as the social infrastructure for global connectivity. It is this type of social infrastructure which gives major financial centers a strategic role. In principle, the technical infrastructure for connectivity can be reproduced anywhere, but social connectivity cannot.

When the more complex forms of information needed to execute major international deals cannot be gotten from existing databases, no matter what one can pay, then one needs the social information loop and the associated de facto interpretations and inferences that come with bouncing off information among talented, informed people.[15] When this interpreting becomes "authoritative" it becomes "information" available to all. The process of making inferences/interpretations into "information" takes quite a mix of talents and resources.[16]

In brief, financial centers provide the expertise and the social connectivity which allows a firm or market to maximize the benefits of its technological connectivity.

Cross-border Networks. The global financial system has reached levels of complexity that require the existence of a cross-border network of financial centers to service the operations of global capital. But this network of financial centers will increasingly differ from earlier versions of the "international financial system." In a world of largely closed national financial systems, each country duplicated most of the necessary functions for its economy; collaborations among different national financial markets were often no more than the execution of the same set of operations in each of the countries involved, as in clearing and settlement. With few exceptions, such as the offshore markets and some of the large banks, the international system consisted of a string of closed domestic systems. The global integration of markets pushes towards the elimination of various redundant systems and makes collaboration a far more complex matter, one which has the perhaps ironic effect of raising the importance of leading financial centers.

This has brought with it a new kind of "merger" connecting financial markets across borders. The two most important forms are the consolidation of electronic networks that connect a very select number of markets and the formation of strategic alliances among financial markets. The NYSE has made a global trading alliance which includes the Toronto Stock Exchange and Euronext—though as the world's largest exchange, its strategy is to list foreign companies rather than make alliances. The National Association of Securities Dealers acquired the American Stock Exchange in June 1998. This has set off other combinations, notably the merger of the Chicago Board Options Exchange and the Pacific Exchange.

---

[15] It is the importance of this input that has given a whole new importance to credit rating agencies, for instance. Part of the rating has to do with interpreting and inferring.

[16] Risk management, for example, which has become increasingly important with globalization due to the growing complexity and uncertainty that comes with operating in multiple countries and markets, requires enormous fine tuning of central operations. We now know that many, if not most, major trading losses over the last decade have involved human error or fraud. The quality of risk management will depend heavily on the top people in a firm rather than simply on technical conditions, such as electronic surveillance. Consolidating risk management operations in one site, usually a central one for the firm, is now seen generally as more effective. We have seen this in the case of several major banks: Chase and Morgan Stanley Dean Witter in the U.S., Deutsche Bank and Credit Suisse in Europe.

NASDAQ launched Nasdaq Japan in 1999 and seeks similar links with Frankfurt and London. Perhaps most spectacular was the attempted link-up between the London Stock Exchange and Frankfurt's Deutsche Borse in the summer of 1998, with the goal of attracting the top 300 shares from all over Europe—a blue-chip European exchange. Paris reacted by setting up the Paris-led Euronext alliance with Brussels and Amsterdam.

These developments make clear a second important trend that in many ways specifies the current global era. These various centers don't just compete with each other: there is collaboration and division of labor. In the international system of the postwar decades, each country's financial center, in principle, covered the universe of necessary functions to service its national companies and markets. The world of finance was, of course, much simpler than it is today. In the initial stages of deregulation in the 1980s there was a strong tendency to see the relation among the major centers as one of straight competition, notably among New York, London, and Tokyo, the heavyweights in the system. But in my research on these three centers I found clear evidence of a division of labor already in the 1980s. In the late 1990s we are seeing this cooperation or division of functions becoming somewhat institutionalized: strategic alliances not only between firms across borders but also between markets. There is competition, strategic collaboration, and hierarchy.

New Forms of Centrality

The combination of the new capabilities for mobility along with patterns of concentration and operational features of the cutting edge sectors of advanced economies suggests that spatial concentration remains as a key feature of these sectors. But it is not simply a continuation of older patterns of spatial concentration. Today there is no longer a simple straightforward relation between centrality and such geographic entities as the downtown, or the central business district. In the past, and up to quite recently in fact, the center was synonymous with the downtown or the CBD.

Several of the organizing hypotheses in the global city model concern the conditions for the continuity of centrality in advanced economic systems in the face of major new organizational forms and technologies that maximize the possibility for geographic dispersal. Historically centrality has largely been embedded in the central city. Have the new technologies and organizational forms altered the spatial correlates of centrality?

Information technologies have had a sharp effect on the spatial organization of economic activity. But this effect is not uniform: the locational options of firms vary considerably. It is not simply a matter of reducing the weight of place. The scattered evidence for the last decade which saw the widespread use of information technologies by firms in a broad range of sectors allows us to identify three types of firms in terms of their locational patterns. First, firms with highly standardized products/services see an increase in their locational options insofar as they can maintain system integration no matter where they are located. This might also hold for firms with specialized products/services that do not require elaborate contracting and subcontracting or suppliers networks. Data entry and simple manufacturing work can be moved to wherever labor and other costs might be lowest. Headquarters can move out of large cities and to suburban locations or small towns. A second locational pattern is that represented by firms which are deeply involved in the global economy and which have increasingly complex headquarter functions. Perhaps ironically, the complexity of headquarters functions is such that they get outsourced to highly specialized service firms. This frees up the headquarter to locate anywhere so long as somewhere there is this highly networked service sector that benefits from spatial agglomeration at the point of production. The third locational pattern is evident in the highly specialized network of service firms. While their products and their top-level professionals are hypermobile, these specialized service firms are embedded in intense transactions with other such firms in kindred specializations and are subject to time pressures. Along with some of the features contributing to agglomeration advantages in financial services firms, this has the effect of rendering the network of specialized service firms more place-bound than the mobility of their products and their professionals would indicate.

The spatial correlate of the center can assume several geographic forms. It can be the CBD, as it still is largely in New York City, or it can extend into a metropolitan area in the form of a grid of nodes of intense business activity, as we see in Frankfurt and Zurich (Hitz et al. 1996). The center has been profoundly altered by telecommunications and the growth of a global economy, both inextricably linked; they have contributed to a new geography of centrality (and marginality). Simplifying I identify four forms assumed by centrality today (based on Sassen 2000: chap. 4).

First, while centrality can assume multiple spatial correlates, the CBD in major international business centers remains a strategic site for the leading industries. But it is one profoundly reconfigured by technological and economic change (Graham and Marvin 1996; Burgel and Burgel 1996; Peraldi and Perrin 1996). Further, there are often sharp differences in the patterns assumed by this reconfiguring of the central city in different parts of the world, notably the United States and Western Europe (Veltz 1996; Kunzmann 1996; Hitz et al. 1996).[17]

Second, the center can extend into a metropolitan area in the form of a grid of nodes of intense business activity. One might ask whether a spatial organization characterized by dense strategic nodes spread over a broader region does in fact constitute a new form of organizing the territory of the "center," rather than, as in the more conventional view, an instance of suburbanization or geographic dispersal.[18] Insofar as these various nodes are articulated through digital networks, they represent a new geographic correlate of the most advanced type of "center." This is a partly deterritorialized space of centrality. It is however located in an older social geography—that of the suburb or of the metropolitan region—and often confused with it. Indeed, much of the actual geographic territory within which these nodes exist falls outside the new grid of digital networks, and is in that sense partly peripheralized.

This regional grid of nodes represents, in my analysis, a reconstitution of the concept of region. Far from neutralizing geography, the regional grid is likely to be embedded in conventional forms of communication infrastructure, notably rapid rail and highways connecting to airports. Ironically perhaps, conventional infrastructure is likely to maximize the economic benefits derived from telematics. I think this is an important issue that has been lost somewhat in discussions about the neutralization of geography through telematics.

Third, we are seeing the formation of a transterritorial "center" constituted, partly in digital space, via intense economic transactions in the network of global cities. These networks of major international business centers constitute new geographies of centrality. The most powerful of these new geographies at the global level binds the major international

[17] In the United States, major cities such as New York and Chicago have large centers that have been rebuilt many times, given the brutal neglect suffered by much urban infrastructure and the imposed obsolescence so characteristic of U.S. cities. This neglect and accelerated obsolescence produce vast spaces for rebuilding the center according to the requirements of whatever regime of urban accumulation or pattern of spatial organization of the urban economy prevails at a given time. In Europe, urban centers are far more protected and they rarely contain significant stretches of abandoned space; the expansion of workplaces and the need for intelligent buildings necessarily will have to take place partly outside the old centers. One of the most extreme cases is the complex of La Defense, the massive, state-of-the-art office complex developed right outside Paris to avoid harming the built environment inside the city. This is an explicit instance of government policy and planning aimed at addressing the growing demand for central office space of prime quality. Yet another variant of this expansion of the "center" onto hitherto peripheral land can be seen in London's Docklands. Similar projects for recentralizing peripheral areas were launched in several major cities in Europe, North America, and Japan during the 1980s.

[18] Pierre Veltz's (1996) work is an important contribution to this analysis. See also Mozere et al.(1999).

financial and business centers: New York, London, Tokyo, Paris, Frankfurt, Zurich, Amsterdam, Los Angeles, Sydney, and Hong Kong, among
others. But this geography now also includes cities such as Bangkok,
Seoul, Taipei, São Paulo, and Mexico City. The intensity of transactions
among these cities, particularly through the financial markets, trade in
services, and investment has increased sharply, and so have the orders of
magnitude involved. At the same time, there has been a sharpening
inequality in the concentration of strategic resources and activities between each of these cities and others in the same country, a condition
that further underlines the extent to which this is a cross-border space
of centrality.[19]

In the case of a complex landscape such as Europe's we see in fact
several geographies of centrality, one global, others continental and regional. A central urban hierarchy connects major cities, many of which in
turn play central roles in the wider global system of cities, such as Paris,
London, Frankfurt, Amsterdam, and Zurich. These cities are also part of
a wider network of European financial/cultural/service capitals, some
with only one, others with several of these functions, which articulate the
European region and are somewhat less oriented to the global economy
than Paris, Frankfurt, or London. And then there are several geographies
of marginality: the East-West divide and the North-South divide across
Europe as well as newer divisions. In Eastern Europe, certain cities and
regions, notably Budapest, are rather attractive for purposes of investment, both European and non-European, while others will increasingly
fall behind, notably in Rumania, Yugoslavia, and Albania. We see a similar differentiation in the south of Europe: Madrid, Barcelona, and Milan
are gaining in the new European hierarchy; Naples, Rome, and Marseille
less so.

Fourth, new forms of centrality are being constituted in electronically
generated spaces. For instance, strategic components of the financial industry operate in such spaces. The relation between digital and actual
space is complex and varies among different types of economic sectors.
But it is increasingly becoming evident that the highly complex configurations for economic activity located in digital space contain points of
coordination and centralization.

---

[19] The pronounced orientation to the world markets evident in such cities raises questions
about the articulation with their nation-states, their regions, and the larger economic and
social structure in such cities. Cities have typically been deeply embedded in the economies
of their region, indeed often reflecting the characteristics of the latter; and they still do. But
cities that are strategic sites in the global economy tend, in part, to disconnect from their
region. This conflicts with a key proposition in traditional scholarship about urban systems,
namely, that these systems promote the territorial integration of regional and national
economies.

Conclusion

Producer services have become central components in the work process
of both goods- and service-producing firms. The development over the
last two decades of a broad array of new producer services is both a
response and a further inducement to this centrality. The expansion in
the use of such services as intermediate inputs is linked with the broader
technical and spatial reorganization of the economy. The introduction of
computer technology and satellite transmission of data has altered the
work process in both goods- and service-producing firms even when their
products have not changed. Transferring what were once production jobs
and blue-collar service jobs into computers and attendant technical jobs
has brought about a greater need for specialized servicing, from engineering design to data processing. The supply of such a wide array of intermediate specialized services has itself contributed to the demand for
them: It is now customary for firms and government agencies to use
outside consultants of various sorts, even when these may replicate the
work of internal staff. Finally, participation in a world market has created
a need for a range of specialized services, and these have in turn facilitated the development of a world market. In brief, what is characteristic
in the contemporary phase is the ascendance of such services as intermediate inputs and the evolution of markets where they can be bought
by foreign or domestic firms and governments.

The financial industry has functioned as one of the key producer services, with growing participation in all sectors of the economy. It has also
contributed to the development of a rapidly growing range of markets
for the circulation of its products. Deregulation, internationalization, and
innovation have been central in this development. And so have been risk-
taking and speculation.

A central concern in this chapter was the spatial organization of producer services and its articulation with cities. Specialization and agglomeration economies have contributed to making cities favored locations, especially for the most strategic and complex of these services.
Second, the growing importance of the new information technologies for
the production and distribution of these services has contributed both to
dispersal and reconcentration. Organizational complexity allows firms to
maximize the benefits they can derive from these technologies; cities are
likely to provide such complexity through dense networks of firms and
markets and intense social connectivity. Third, providing services to firms
with global operations has meant that leading producer services firms are
increasingly operating in networks of cities, a subject we return to in
chapter 7.

Six

Global Cities: Postindustrial Production Sites

How DOES the spatial and technical transformation of economic activity described in the preceding chapters play itself out in major cities? A central thesis of this chapter is that the industrial recomposition in the economic base of global cities is not simply a result of the general shift from a manufacturing to a service economy. Besides the vast set of activities that make up their economic base, many typical to all cities, these global cities have a particular component in their economic base—a component rooted in those spatial and technical changes—that gives them a specific role in the current phase of the world economy. Thus, while all cities contain a core of service industries and the leading cities of a country have long contained key banking functions, the argument here posits a more novel and specific process.

This thesis can be broken down into three parts. The first part posits that geographic dispersal of factories, offices, and service outlets and the reorganization of the financial industry over the last decade have contributed to the need for new forms of centralization for the management and regulation of the global network of production sites and financial markets. The work of management and regulation as well as the production of the needed inputs will tend to be concentrated in major cities. The second part of the thesis is that these new forms of centralization entail a shift in the locus of control and management: In addition to the large corporation and the large commercial bank, there is now also a marketplace with a multiplicity of advanced corporate service firms and non-bank financial institutions. Correspondingly, we see the increased importance of cities such as New York, London, and Tokyo, or Paris and Frankfurt, as *centers* of finance and as centers for global servicing and management. In other words, this is not merely another instance of large firms' externalization of these functions. The third part of the thesis is that the production of a wide array of innovations in services and finance has been central to the transformation of economic activity. Cities have emerged as key locations for the production of such innovations.

There is a large body of scholarly literature on urban and metropolitan regions which addresses both the conditions necessary for the particular forms of growth that major cities make possible and the recurrent processes of dispersion of those same components of growth. Much of this literature emphasizes the continued seedbed function of major cities in the context of periodic cycles of overcrowding, congestion, and emergence of agglomeration diseconomies, followed by partial resolutions through spatial dispersal. There is also a vast literature on the relation of such major cities to other cities in an urban system, the latter typically conceived of as nation based. A balanced urban system is thought to promote the diffusion of growth across the national territory and thereby to secure spatial integration.

The question for us is whether the transformation in the economy has altered the propositions about cities, their regions, and national urban systems contained in that literature.[1] The decline of manufacturing and the shift to service-dominated employment, the rapid growth of producer services, and the further service-intensification of the economy, are trends evident in all three cities. Conceptualization about the nature of the urban system or urban hierarchy in developed countries is mostly derived from a particular historical phase—one where mass production largely for the domestic market was the dominant fact in these economies. What does the sharp growth in international financial and service transactions and the growth of New York, London, and Tokyo as leading international business centers mean for the urban hierarchy and spatial integration of the national economy in each of the three countries? What happens to the diffusion of growth from the top through the urban hierarchy when the top is oriented to the global market? There is an important critical literature that never has accepted the notion of mutually beneficial exchanges in the urban hierarchy and posits that cities function as surplus-extracting and concentrating mechanisms vis-à-vis their hinterlands. Is this proposition at all altered by the rise and internationalization of producer services and finance? Do New York, London, and Tokyo function as such a surplus-extracting mechanism vis-à-vis a "transnational hinterland"?

This chapter seeks to examine these issues through a detailed analysis of the space economy of the producer services in order to specify the type of location that New York, London, and Tokyo constitute for these industries. The preceding chapters examined the conditions for and limits to the growth of finance and producer services (the major growth sectors

---

[1] Many scholars have argued that most developed economies are characterized by a rank rule city size distribution and that this represents a condition of equilibrium. Conversely, some have posited that it is the existence of an integrated space economy that produces a rank size distribution (Christaller 1965). Harvey (1973), on the other hand, argues that the appropriation and redistribution of surplus value is one of the key properties of city systems. The integration of the space economy organized along the urban hierarchy or contained in the urban system is an expression of the "process which circulates surplus value in order to concentrate more of it" (1973: 237–38).

in these three cities). This chapter provides a detailed analysis of the role of New York, London, and Tokyo as locations for the producer services and finance, and the limits to that role; the forms, if any, of integration of these new growth sectors into their larger metropolitan regions and into the general economy of the countries; and, finally, the differences, if any, between these cities and other major cities in the United States, the United Kingdom, and Japan.

The three countries under study represent considerable diversity in their urban systems. London, which accounts for 16% of the U.K. population, is as close to a primate city as one could find in a highly developed country.[2] The United States has a multiplicity of large cities, none accounting for more than 4% of the total population. Japan has a major industrial center in Osaka, and while Tokyo is clearly the dominant city, there are several other major cities, particularly Osaka, once the leading industrial center in the country. The contrast between these three countries and the presence of major industrial centers in the Japanese urban system should allow us to detect differences in the composition of producer services in finance-oriented compared with manufacturing-oriented cities. Furthermore, comparing what were once major industrial cities in the United Kingdom with those in Japan would illuminate the relation between manufacturing and producer services—specifically, whether the growth of producer services is predicated on a strong manufacturing sector. Finally, in the case of the United States today, Chicago and New York present strong contrasts, with Chicago the center of the once-leading agroindustrial complex in the country and New York emerging as the major business center in the 1980s. As a financial and business center Chicago was oriented toward its hinterland and represented a case of strong regional integration. What happens when such a regional industrial complex enters severe decline? Is this reflected in a decline and/or transformation of the producer services sector? And to what extent does the growth of the financial markets in Chicago present new conditions or seedbed functions for the growth of a different type of producer services? Los Angeles, a major recipient of foreign investment, with a strong orientation to the dynamic Pacific Rim, is considered to be the leading rival to New York's prominence as an international financial and business center. What is the position of Los Angeles vis-à-vis New York?

I will isolate the producer services to examine these questions. The

---

[2] The distribution of city sizes that is considered normal responds to a rank rule, where the second-largest city is one-half the size of the largest, the third is one-third the size of the largest, and so on. Mathematically, this is rendered through a log-normal distribution. The notion is that such a distribution will promote overall development, while urban systems with a primate city, where the largest city is inordinately larger than the rest, are not seen as conducive to development.

purpose here is not to describe the overall economic base in these cities. That will be part of the discussion of the broader socioeconomic order in Part Three of the book. The purpose here is to isolate the producer services and to carry out a comparative analysis of New York, London, and Tokyo and of their place in their national urban systems. Do New York, Tokyo, and London function as expected according to prevalent models of the urban system, diffusing growth along the hierarchy and contributing to the spatial integration of the economy?

The evidence shows clearly that in all three countries the growth rates of producer services were higher at the national level than in those cities. Moreover, the evidence shows that this higher national growth rate has not eroded the disproportionate concentration of producer services in major cities. This raises a question about the possibility of a new phase in the process of service-dominated urbanization that has been occurring for several decades now. This growth in overall services was particularly strong when manufacturing and wholesale trade were the key components in the economic base. Now that manufacturing has declined significantly as a share of employment in major cities and a new type of services, producer services, has grown rapidly and become a leading sector, there may be a different meaning to the notion of service-dominated urbanization.

The first section of this chapter is a discussion of general trends in the location of producer services, taking up where the preceding chapter left off. The second section examines producer services and finance in the context of what are often thought of as urban hierarchies. This discussion is intended to situate these cities in the space economy of the producer services in their respective countries. The next chapter will examine the place of London, New York, and Tokyo in global terms.

Location of Producer Services: Nation, Region, and City

A number of major trends are evident in the available data on the geographic distribution and composition of producer services industries in the United States, the United Kingdom, and Japan. There is no doubt that this is a significant growth sector in all three countries. The question is the specific role played by cities, especially New York, London, and Tokyo, in the organization of this sector. The main patterns described below begin with the level of the nation and conclude with that of the central business district in each of these three cities over the last decade. (For a brief comparison of classifications of producer services in these three countries, see Appendix A.)

A first trend evident in all three countries is that national employment growth in producer services was higher than total national employment and, furthermore, higher than in the leading cities (see Tables 6.1 through 6.3). This raises a question as to the composition of the producer services in different locations, specifically, the possibility that this sector is constituted quite differently in a leading city from what it is in the rest of a country.

The period of rapid growth in producer services was from the late 1970s to the mid-1990s. In the United States, while total employment increased by 15% from 1977 to 1981 and by 8% from 1981 to 1985, total employment in producer services for those same periods increased by 26% and 20%, respectively. In Japan we see, similarly, considerable disparity between the level of overall national employment growth and growth in those producer services for which there are individual data. Total national employment in Japan grew by 5% from 1977 to 1981 and by 4% from 1981 to 1985. In services, growth was 17% from 1977 to 1981 and 15% from 1981 to 1985. If we consider only the FIRE sector the growth rate was 27% during 1975–1985. In the United Kingdom, total employment fell by 5% during 1978–1985, while services employment increased by 41% and FIRE employment increased by 44%.

A second trend is that the share of producer services jobs in New York, London, and Tokyo is at least a third higher and often twice as large as the share of these industries in total national employment (see Table 6.4). But the actual shares are quite small, ranging from 4.2% in 1985 for banking, finance, and insurance in Tokyo versus 3% in Japan, to 8.8% in New York in 1997 versus 3.4% in the United States. For business services, this relation remains, but at a slightly higher level. Thus, business services accounted for 5% of all workers in Great Britain in 1984 but for 10.2% in London. In the case of Tokyo, there was no separate measure

TABLE 6.1A

United States: Growth in Total Employment and Producer Services Employment, 1977–1996 (numbers and percent)

	1977–1981	1981–1987	1987–1993	1993–1996
Total employment	74,850,402	85,483,800	94,789,444	102,198,864
Growth rate (%)	15.20	14.21	10.89	7.82
Producer Services	12,238,104	15,552,713	15,785,687	17,630,321
Growth rate (%)	25.80	27.08	1.50	11.69

Source: Author's calculations based on U.S. Census Bureau, County Business Patterns, issues for the United States, 1983, 1989, 1995, and 1998.

Note: Growth rates calculated based on previous year's reported values; for a list of SIC Codes included in Producer Services categories, see Appendix A.

TABLE 6.1B

United States and New York: Employment Changes by Industry, 1977–1996 (percent)

	1977–1985 (% change)		1993–1996 (% change)	
	New York	United States	New York	United States
All Industries	11	25	3.3	7.8
Construction	– 30	25	– 3.3	15.1
Manufacturing	– 22	– 1	– 12.9	2.1
Transportation	– 20	– 20	14.2	7.7
Wholesale Trade	14	23	– 4.0	6.5
Retail Trade	17	26	8.2	14.4
Finance, Insurance, and Real Estate (FIRE)	21	31	6.3	4.2
Banking	23	36	– 20.1	– 1.6
Insurance[1]	– 2	21	12.3	0.3
Real Estate	8	33	3.9	6.5
Services	42	53	4.2	10.8
Personal services	– 2	85	5.2	2.9
Business services	42	85	9.3	23.9
Legal services	62	75	– 2.6	– 0.3
Other[2]	44	48	25.2	16.5

Source: Author's calculations based on U.S. Census Bureau, *County Business Patterns*, issues for the United States, 1983, 1989, 1995, and 1998.

Notes: [1]Includes insurance carriers, agents, brokers, and service; [2]Includes administrative and auxiliary services.

for business services. It should be noted that both London and New York lost a considerable number of insurance jobs over this period, while they gained jobs in finance. Thus, the difference between the share of insurance jobs in the city and the nation is much smaller and, in London, increasingly so. Additionally, more disaggregated data on the producer services would reveal much higher differences for some of these industries in major cities compared with the nation. I will return to both points later in this chapter. (For a brief description of the areas covered by the data and of how Tokyo is specified, see Appendices B and C.) London and New York lost a significant number of jobs in commercial banking in the 1990s even as they gained jobs in the financial services. Banking went through a sharp restructuring through mergers and acquisitions and closures. Towards the end of the 1990s these losses stabilized.

A third observation is that a considerable number of producer services industries have very small employment shares, but together make a significant difference in the employment distribution of these cities. Besides

TABLE 6.2

Great Britain and London: Employment Changes by Industry 1981–1996 (percent change)

All Industries	1981–1991		1991–1996	
	London	Great Britain	London	Great Britain
Agriculture	36	−11	0	5
Energy and water	−37	−37	−81	−69
Manufacturing	−48	−24	−33	−21
Construction	−10	8	−24	11
Transportation and communication	−14	0	0	9
Banking, insurance, and finance	36	57	36	48
Public administration and defense	2	2	−44	−30
Education/health/other	−1	11	−4	11

Source: Author's calculations based on 1991, UK Census, *Workplace and Transport to Work Report, Table 4* and1981, UK Census, *Workplace and Transport Report,* Table 5, "LRC London Workers," p. 133; UK Employment Gazette 1991 and Annual Employment Survey 1996.

the examples discussed above, there are management consulting, advertising, engineering, and other highly specialized services. The evidence for New York and London shows that together the producer services, which include the FIRE group, accounted for about a third of all private sector workers in New York in 1981 and 27.5% in 1997, and for about 33% in London in 1984 and 31% in 1999 (see Table 6.5).

Similarly, while the actual share of national employment is small, the locational patterns of producer services employment give considerable

TABLE 6.3

Japan and Tokyo: Employment Changes by Industry 1975–1997 (percent change)

Industry	1975–1985		1985–1997	
	Tokyo	Japan	Tokyo	Japan
Agriculture/Forestry/Fishing	3	10	−19	−39
Construction	1	12	23	25
Manufacturing	−12	4	−15	5
Transport and Communication	5	15	3	18
Wholesale and retail	6	18	7	18
Finance, Insurance, and Real Estate	−3	56	28	32

Source: Author's calculations based on Government of Japan, Management and Coord. Agency, *Japan Statistical Yearbook* 1999, p. 84 and 1984; Tokyo Metropolitan Government, *Tokyo Statistical Yearbook* 1986 and 1997; Tokyo Metropolitan *Government, Plain Talk About Tokyo, 2nd ed. (1984).*
Note: For Tokyo the year range was from 1985 to 1996.

TABLE 6.4
Great Britain and London, United States and New York, Japan and Tokyo: Employment Share of
Selected Producer Services, 1980s and 1990s (percent)

		Producer Services as % of Employment				
Year	City/Country	Banking and Finance	Insurance	Real Estate	Business Services	City's Tot. Employment as a % of Total National Employment
1981	London	4.5	1.9	0.6	8.1	15.7
	Great Britain	2.1	1.1	0.3	4.3	—
1984	London	4.8	1.7	1.0	10.2	16.6
	Great Britain	2.4	1.1	0.6	5.0	—
1999	London[a]	8.4	—	2.2	—	15.4
	Great Britain	3.4	1.0	2.5	12.0	—
1981	New York	10.2	3.4	3.0	8.3	3.9
	United States	3.4	2.3	1.3	4.1	—
1985	New York	10.7	3.2	3.1	9.4	3.7
	United States	3.5	2.2	1.4	5.3	—
1997	New York	8.8	3.8	7.2	8.5	2.9
	United States	3.4	2.2	1.3	7.6	—
1980	Tokyo[b]	4.2	—	1.8	—	10.2
	Japan[c]	2.8	—	0.7	—	—
1985	Tokyo[b]	4.2	—	1.9	—	10.2
	Japan[c]	3.0	—	0.8	—	—
1997	Tokyo[b]	5.7	—	2.5	—	13.7
	Japan[c]	3.9	—	—	—	

Sources: Author's calculations based on U.K. data: *Census 1981, England and Wales; Census of Employment,*
1984, UK; *Employment Gazette,* (U.K.) 95, no.10 historical supp. No. 2, (Jan. 1987); U.K. National Statistics Office
1999 Labour Market Trends. U.S. data: U.S. Census Bureau, *County Business Patterns,* issues for the U.S. and
New York, 1981, 1985, and 1999. Japan data: Government of Japan, Management and Coordination Agency, *Japan
Statistical Yearbook* 1988 and 1999;

Notes: [a]Includes financial intermediation for insurance and pension funding; [b]Includes banking, finance, and insurance for 1980, 1985, and 1997; [c]In 1980 and 1985, Banking and finance and insurance are listed aggregately, for
1997 it also includes Real Estate.

weight to these cities in the space economy of such services. Thus, in
1985 New York accounted for 7.2% of national employment in producer
services, compared with 3.7% of all U.S. employment. London has an
extremely high degree of concentration. These differences become even
more evident if location quotients are used. Employment-based quotients, with the overall share of producer services in national employment
as the base, show a quotient of 1.9 for producer services in New York
from 1977 to 1985, falling to 1.78 in 1997, and of 2.04 for London in
1971, down to 1.72 in 1999 (see Table 6.6). Comparing a particular
industry such as real estate, for which there is separate information on
Tokyo, there is a similarly high quotient (see Table 6.7). It was 2.42 in New
York in 1977 and 2.18 in 1997; London's quotient was 2 in 1971 and
declined to 1.6 in 1999; and Tokyo's stayed at 2.0 with ups and downs.

TABLE 6.5

New York and London: Share of Producer Services in Employment, 1971 to 1999 (percent)

	Producer Services Share of Total City Employment	Producer Services Share of National Employment	City's Share of National Employ. in Producer Services
London			
1971	28.0	16.0	40.3
1981	31.0	15.7	34.1
1984	32.8	16.6	32.6
1999	30.8	4.7	25.1
New York			
1977	29.8	4.2	8.3
1981	32.9	3.9	7.8
1987	37.7	3.7	7.6
1997	27.5	2.9	15.5

Source: Author's calculations based on Employment, Earnings and Productivity Division, Office for National Statistics 1999 in *U.K. Labour Market Trends*, February 2000 T. B16; U.S. Census Bureau, *County Business Patterns*, issues for the U.S. and New York, 1977, 1981, 1987, 1998; *Census of Employment* (U.K.), issues for 1971 and 1981; *Employment Gazette* (U.K.) 95, no.10, historical supp. No. 2 (Jan. 1987).

TABLE 6.6

New York and London: Producer Services Location Quotients, 1970 to 1999

	Location Quotient
London	
1971	2.04
1981	1.85
1984	1.96
1999	1.72
New York	
1977	1.98
1981	1.99
1985	1.92
1993	1.85
1997	1.78

Source: See Table 6.5 and J. Howells and A. E. Green, "Location, Technology, and Industrial Organization in U.K. Services," *Progress in Planning 26* (1986): pt. 2.

Note: Computed with national quotient as unity.

TABLE 6.7

New York, London, and Tokyo: Location Quotients for Real
Estate, 1970 to 1999

	Location Quotients
London	
1971	2.00
1981	1.59
1984	1.75
1999	1.61
New York City	
1977	2.42
1981	2.22
1985	2.20
1997	2.18
Tokyo	
1971	2.00
1981	2.33
1984	2.28
1995	2.07

Source: Author's calculations based on Employment, Earnings and
Productivity Division, Office for National Statistics 1999 in *Labour
Markets Trends*, February 2000 T. B16; U.S. *Census Bureau, County
Business Patterns*, issues for New *York, 1977, 1981, 1995, 1997;
Japan Statistical Yearbook*, 1977, 1981, 1985, 1999; Census of Em-
ployment, 1984 (U.K.); Employment Gazette, (U.K.) 95, no. 2, histori-
cal supp. No. 2, (Jan. 1987); *Census 1971 and 1981, England and
Wales*; Tokyo Metro. Gov't., *Tokyo Statistical Yearbook 1997*.

Note: For New York City, Real Estate denotes SIC 6530, Agents
and Managers for the 5 boroughs.

Slight declines in quotients are also evident in other individual producer
services, but these declines have not made a major dent in the overrepresentation of many of these industries in New York, London, and Tokyo,
given the absolute growth of such services in these cities.

A fourth observation concerns the possibility of differences in the kinds
of producer service industries that are growing in the more central locations of a metropolitan area compared with the overall region. An important question concerning the location of producer services is their relation to and place in local labor markets. Again, when we examine
national-level data for all three countries, we see pronounced concentration and overrepresentation in key locations. What is the actual distribution within these key locations? The locational concentration of producer
services in certain regions can conceivably assume more than one pattern.

It can be geographically concentrated or dispersed within such a region. Furthermore, there may or may not be firm decentralization along with territorial dispersal within regions of high concentration. Finally, in regions of high concentration with geographically dispersed producer services, there may or may not be considerable divergence among the various locations within such a region in terms of the composition of its producer services sector.

The English case is probably the most extreme instance of high concentration of national producer services employment in one region, significant territorial dispersal within that region, and indications of different industry composition in the central and peripheral locations of that region. The London region (Greater London and the Outer Metropolitan Area) is the primary location for what are today considered successful sectors in the British economy (Gordon and McCann 2000): finance, information, general business services, luxury consumption goods and services, and health care goods. Relative to the country as a whole, the region has above national average location quotients for a broad range of sectors including printing, publishing, and reproduction of recorded media; some types of wholesaling; air, rail, and sea transport, and supporting services; finance and insurance; IT/computing; professional services; other business services; central administration and representative organizations. The concentration of these activities is sharpest in Central London and the adjoining boroughs, with secondary concentrations, notably around Heathrow airport—and extensions to Reading and Basingstoke along the M3 and M4 corridors, and a more local one, mainly for airport related activities, around Gatwick. The exceptions to these patterns are London's outer east and Thames-side in the larger OMA. (See also Dunford and Fielding 1997.)

The location of these specialized sectors varies: outside the central areas it is sectors such as IT/computing, wholesaling, and air transport that will tend to dominate while in the central areas it is money/finance, governance, or cultural services. The outer areas also tend to have a wider manufacturing base, including high-tech sectors such as electronics or pharmaceuticals in which the region as a whole has only a weak specialization (Gordon and McCann 2000; Dunford 1989). Using data from the TeCSEM group surveys of locationally sensitive sectors in several urban areas in the country at large, Gordon (1995) found Inner London locations particularly showing a distinctive set of industries and particular functions within those industries (administration and direct service provision).

In the case of New York, use of a broader regional and time frame shows that Manhattan already had a disproportionate concentration of FIRE jobs in the 1950s (Hoover and Vernon 1962) while the broader region at the time experienced declines in the finance quotient.[3] Today the broader metropolitan region for NYC consists of several counties in NY State and in New Jersey. While Manhattan remained the core of this broader region, several major new trends become evident and create an at times sharp contrast with key trends in the 1980s. In the 1990s the region added almost 200,000 jobs and generally saw strong growth rates in all its major sectors while the decline of manufacturing slowed down. There was strong growth in what are sectors with above national average location quotients: business and financial service jobs, retail and tourism, consulting, advertising, and computer services. Further strengthening Manhattan's specialization, the Wall Street securities sector grew at an annual average of over 6% from 1996 to 1998, leading the growth in FIRE employment. Since 1992, securities employment in NYC has grown by 27%. In NYC, business services increased by 8.6% in 1997 and by another 6.5% in 1998; consulting and management services firms grew by 3.9% in 1997 and by 7.9% in 1998, and legal services grew by 4.3%. As in the case of London and the Southeast, an important question concerns regional integration: Are the components of that growth articulated with other economic sectors in the region and, more specifically, with the major growth sectors in Manhattan over the last decade?

A fifth observation is that the central business and finance districts in each of these cities contains an extremely high concentration of these industries (see Table 6.8). Identification of a central business and finance district in each of these three cities poses problems in terms of definition and geographic breakdowns of the available evidence. A reasonable approximation is to use Manhattan for New York, the City for London, and the three central business district wards (Chiyoda, Chuo, Minato) in addition to Shinjuku, a new major business center, for Tokyo. London's City is a far smaller geographic area than the other two. Manhattan shows the highest concentration for finance, insurance, and real estate employment, as well as for business services, accounting for about 92% of all FIRE employment and for 83% of business services in New York in 1997. This represents an increase in concentration of FIRE, from about 86% in 1970. Business services, on the other hand, reduced their concentration in Manhattan slightly, from 88% in 1970. But both increased their share of Manhattan employment, from 17.8% in 1970 and 23.5% in 1985 to 23% in 1997 in the case of FIRE, and from 8.4% to 11 in the case of business services.

There was a decline in the concentration of total London FIRE employment in the City of London, from about 49% in 1971 to 21% in

---

[3] For a detailed discussion of the spatial organization of various sectors in the 1970s and 1980s, see the first edition of this book (pp. 136–38).

TABLE 6.8

Manhattan, the City of London, and Tokyo's Central Business District (CBD): Share of Selected Industries 1970s, 1980s, and 1990s (percent)

	FIRE		Business Services	
	% of Total FIRE Jobs in London	% of Total Jobs in City of London	% of Total Business Services Jobs in London	% of Total Jobs in City of London
The City of London				
1971	48.7	41.2	11.2	3.4
1981	44.8	37.6	20.2	19.6
1995	20.7	78.3	***	***

	FIRE		Business Services	
	% of Total FIRE Jobs in NYC	% of Total Jobs in Manhattan	% of Total Business Services in NYC	% of Total Jobs in Manhattan
Manhattan				
1970	86.0	17.8	88.1	8.4
1985	89.8	23.5	85.3	12.7
1993	90.7	22.3	81.4	10.2
1997	92.2	22.8	82.7	11.2

	FIRE		Business Services[1]	
	% of Total FIRE Jobs in Tokyo	% of Total Jobs in Tokyo's CBD	% of Total Business Services in Tokyo	% of Total Jobs in Tokyo's CBD
Tokyo CBD				
1980[2]	49.4	9.9	33.0	21.8
1997[1]	40.9	9.2	28.0	28.9

Source: Author's calculations based on U.K. Office for National Statistics, the *Annual Employment Survey*, 1995; U.S. Census Bureau, *County Business Patterns*, issues for New York 1970, 1985, 1993, 1997; Tokyo Metro. Gov't, *Survey of Tokyo Day-time Population*, 1983; Tokyo Metro. Gov't, *Tokyo Statistical Yearbook* 1997, pp. 108–111.

Note: [1]Total Services reported; Tokyo's CBD (Central Business District) includes Chiyoda-ku, Chuo-ku, and Minato-ku; [2]For 1980, Shinjuku-ku was included.

1995. There was also a decline in the share of the City's work force employed in this sector, from 41% to 38%. This may be linked to the relatively greater expansion of related sectors as well as the spread of FIRE activities into the newly developed Docklands and other adjacent areas. The relative decline in the share of FIRE in the City in the early 1980s is also partly attributable to the relocation of much insurance activity, a trend also evident in New York. The transformation of the financial sector in the City after deregulation in 1986 and especially in the 1990s is evident in the sharp increase to 78% in the share of FIRE jobs in all City jobs by 1997. In contrast the City's low share of all FIRE jobs in London is clear evidence of its minuscule share of all jobs in London and the fact that the population size of London brings with it an enormous retail financial sector. Thus we see a very different composition in the London and City economic base, because the City is highly specialized. There is a far sharper differentiation than that between Manhattan and New York. This highly specialized space in central London has now expanded outside of the city, partly to Docklands but also to surrounding boroughs. One of the key factors in this expansion is the information technology sector described later in this chapter. It is in its origins a sector driven by the development of new financial instruments and the corresponding software, London being, along with New York and Chicago, one of the places for innovation in financial software. With the further development of information technologies this sector developed into several specialized branches, with particular concentrations in a set of boroughs adjacent to the City. Business services have increased their concentration in the City from 11% in 1971 to 20% in 1981 and in the City's work force from 3.4% to 20%.

In the case of Tokyo, the available evidence is less complete at this time. While the central business district is officially defined by three wards, Chiyoda, Chuo, and Minato, the fourth added here for 1980, Shinjuku, is now widely recognized as a new major business district (see Appendix B). In 1980, these four wards accounted for over 49% of all FIRE employment in Tokyo. But FIRE accounted for only 10% of total employment in these four wards, an indication of the degree to which most tertiary activities in the whole of Tokyo are concentrated in this area. The evidence does not allow for a separate analysis of business services at the ward level. If we exclude wholesale and retail services, 33% of all Tokyo's services are concentrated in the area, and these account for 22% of all employment in these four wards.

It is evident that the producer services as a whole have grown rapidly over the last decade and that they have grown more rapidly in the countries as a whole than in these cities. But these three cities continue to account for a disproportionate share of national employment and hence of producer services.

New Elements in the Urban Hierarchy

Two important questions emerging from these trends concern the place of other major cities in the space economy of the producer services, and

TABLE 6.9

United Kingdom: National Employment Share of Major Cities, 1971–1998 (percent)

	1971	1981	1991	1998
London	16.01	15.71	14.30	15.55
City of London	1.39	1.40	1.05	1.22
Birmingham	2.14	2.21	1.99	1.97
Manchester	1.34	1.30	1.08	1.13
Liverpool	1.31	1.11	0.84	0.79
Glasgow	—	1.65	0.95	1.44
Edinburg	—	1.04	0.81	1.11
Total U.K. employment (N)	23,732,610	22,619,190	23,418,860	23,351,900

Source: Author's calculations based on U.K. Office for National Statistics, Census 1991, *Key Statistics for Local Authority and Workplace and Transport to Work Reports*; 1998, *Annual Employment Survey*.

the specific composition of these services in different types of cities. There are significant differences in the urban systems of these three countries. London's share of national employment was about 15% in the 1990s (see Table 6.9). Tokyo follows with 10% of national employment (see Table 6.10). In the United States, there are several large cities, and they account for a far smaller proportion of national employment at about 2 to 3% for the four largest (see Table 6.11). Furthermore the level of discontinuity between the largest and subsequent cities also varies considerably in the United Kingdom and Japan. In the United Kingdom, the next largest cities are far behind London in national employment share, between 2% in Birmingham to 0.8% in Edinburgh. In Japan, the next largest cities have about half Tokyo's share of national employment: 5.7% in Nagoya and its prefecture and 6.8% in Osaka and its prefecture.

One question that arises is to what extent the devastation of manufacturing in the United Kingdom may have affected the urban system by reducing the weight of cities such as Birmingham and Manchester. On the other hand, the weight of Osaka and Nagoya in Japan still reflects the phase of high industrial output, even though key sectors in basic industry are shrinking and there is a growing trend toward locating assembly plants offshore.[4] The dismantling of what were once basic industrial sectors is less pronounced in Japan, whereas in the United Kingdom and the United States it reached a peak in the 1970s. The discontinuity in the United Kingdom between London and the next largest cities is further accentuated by the acute locational concentration in London of the lead-

[4] By 1960, Tokyo, Osaka, and Nagoya were major international cities—key locations for capital, labor, and economic growth (Ishizuka 1980). Hattori et al. (1980 saw the megalopolis constituted by these three cities as the key for centralization and operation on an international scale.

TABLE 6.10

Japan: National Employment Share of Major Cities, 1975–1995 (percent)

	1980	1985	1990	1995
Tokyo (Tokyo Prefecture)	10.24	10.17	10.19	9.84
Nagoya (Aichi Prefecture)	5.47	5.58	5.70	5.75
Osaka (Osaka Prefecture)	6.84	6.86	6.87	6.81
Total Japan employment (N)	55,749,000	58,113,000	61,682,000	64,142,000

Source: Author's calculations based on Government of Japan, Management and Coordination Agency, Japan Statistical Yearbook, 1982, 1986, 1993, and 1998.

ing growth sectors in the current period, a far higher level of concentration than is the case with New York and Tokyo.

A third issue that arises is that of nonproduction employment in manufacturing. To what extent are many of the producer services jobs in industrial areas, such as Manchester, Nagoya, or Detroit, primarily linked to manufacturing, and quite distinct from the producer services jobs concentrated in cities such as New York, London, and Tokyo? Furthermore, are manufacturing-linked producer services in the latter three cities different from those in industrial cities?

In order to address some of these issues and to understand the place of New York, London, and Tokyo in their national economies, there follows a detailed examination of the locational patterns of producer services across major cities.

In the United Kingdom, the location quotients for producer services

TABLE 6.11

United States: National Employment Share of Major Cities, 1977–1997 (percent)

	1977	1985	1993	1997
New York City (5 counties)	4.2	3.7	3.0	2.9
Manhattan	2.7	2.6	1.9	1.8
Los Angeles (L.A. County)	4.1	4.2	3.7	3.4
Chicago (Cook County)	3.4	3.0	2.4	2.3
Houston (Harris County)	1.4	1.7	1.4	1.4
Detroit (Wayne County)	1.2	1.0	0.7	0.7
Boston (Suffolk County)	0.6	0.6	0.5	0.5
Total U.S. employment (N)	64,975,580	85,483,804	94,789,444	105,299,123

Source: Author's calculations based on U.S. Census Bureau, County Business Patterns, issues for the United States, 1983, 1989, 1995, and 1998.

Notes: Only private sector employment is included; New York City includes New York, Richmond, King's, Queens, and Bronx counties.

generally, and business services in particular, indicate considerable un-evenness. Notwithstanding higher growth rates in producer services out-side London and a changing composition over the last three decades, London and its region continue to account for a disproportionate share of these services (Marshall et al. 1986; Gordon and McCann 2000; Wood 1996). London's location quotient for producer services has been falling from over 2 in 1971 to 1.96 in 1984 and 1.72 in 1999 (see Table 6.6). Yet it remains considerably above the average for other cities in the coun-try. Further, its composition is likely to be very different. The most com-prehensive study for the earlier period is by Marshall et al. (1986) who find that location quotients for most cities and metropolitan areas are considerably under 1, pointing to the extreme concentration in London. Using the classification developed by Peter Wood in Marshall et al. (1986) and 1981 census data yields a total of 4.1 million jobs in pro-ducer services in Great Britain, of which 1.219 million were in London and another 329,000 were in the greater metropolitan area. The London region accounted for a third of all producer services jobs. The disaggre-gated data indicate that London accounted for 34% of nonproduction employment in manufacturing, and almost 43% of producer services in-dustry employment. The next largest concentration of producer services jobs was 10% in the Northwest.

The rapid growth of producer services for the nation as a whole has not overcome the significant overrepresentation in London, a pattern also evident in the United States and Japan. In the 1990s areas outside Lon-don had growth rates in producer services typically higher than those of London. Yet London's overrepresentation remains, even though dimin-ished. Thus London's share of national employment in producer services fell from 40% in 1971 to 34% in 1981 to 25.1% in 1999, where it remains (see Table 6.5), a share significantly higher than its share of total national employment. Furthermore, the distinctiveness of this region can also be seen in the particular industries where it is especially overrepresented, at least some of which are likely to remain concentrated in London. Finally, even when there might not be overrepresentation there is typically a dis-tinctive role that London plays in the national spatial organization of producer service industries. Specialized business services contribute to the service "regionalized mode of production" which Allen (1993) has noted increasingly distinguishes the greater Southeast from the rest of the na-tional economy (Dunford and Fielding 1997).

Most of the divergence between the Southeast and the rest of the country is attributable to the producer services industries rather than nonproduction employment in manufacturing. While most of the excess of producer services jobs in the Southeast is accounted for by the pro-ducer services industries, regions with higher concentrations of manufacturing also have relatively higher concentrations of nonproduction employment in manufacturing. These regions also have an underrepresentation of producer services industry employment. However, in what is still the most encompassing study on the subject, even though focused on the earlier period of the 1970s and 1980s, Marshall et al. (1986) found that the Southeast, a major area for producer services industries, had a higher concentration of nonproduction manufacturing workers per 1,000 workers in manufacturing than did any other region of the country. Part of this is attributable to the heavy incidence of small research and development oriented firms in the area (Hall et al. 1987; Banks et al. 1997).[5] On the other hand, areas with major concentrations of manufacturing have a lower incidence than would be expected given their manufacturing employment (Marshall et al. 1986). Thus 41% of nonproduction employment is concentrated in the greater metropolitan London area, as well as 47% of producer services industries employment. But the share that nonproduction employment in manufacturing represents of all producer services employment in this area is 18%, the lowest in the country.[6] One question raised by this difference is whether the devastating losses in manufacturing employment in Britain, which caused severe declines for Britain's largely manufacturing-based cities other than London, are associated with this pronounced underrepresentation. And to what extent is it a result of spatial reorganization in manufacturing, with the relocation of routine office work to small, low-cost urban areas, and of central functions to London?

London has significantly higher values for its location quotients than does the Southeast as a whole. This is partly because of the urbanization effect: population size resulting in greater agglomeration and the influence of centrality on all services industries, especially those with considerable intermediate inputs (insurance, banking, finance).[7]

In the UK, London concentrates the trading in derivatives, particularly derivatives related to foreign exchange and commodities, as a portfolio service or fund management activity. Portfolio services based on regional equity and bond trading are supplied from five centers, along with Lon-

---

[5] Other evidence suggests that a good number of business services firms are small, low-cost operations, such as cleaning services, and hence will prefer to locate in lower-cost areas of the city.

[6] This would suggest that, given difficulties in obtaining measures of nonproduction employment in manufacturing, considering only the producer services industry may be adequate for an examination of producer service jobs in major cities.

[7] Greater London, similarly, has lower employment-based quotients than population-based quotients, and here commuting is clearly a significant factor. Daniels (1985) argues that the commuting effect should not be exaggerated since it is likely that differences in levels of unemployment, activity rates for men and women, and the match between skills available and those in demand also have some effect.

don: Glasgow, Birmingham, Manchester, Bristol, and Newcastle (Parr and Budd 1998). The difference relates to various factors, notably the market area of the service supplied, which in the case of London is global. There are also financial service activities that appear at more than one level, signaling a hierarchy within the group of activities making up a particular financial service, e.g., foreign currency trading is concentrated in second-level financial centers while foreign exchange derivatives trading is concentrated in London.

Proximity to London can mean that a city loses certain types of financial services that would typically take place at a secondary level; they will tend to move to London (Parr and Budd 1998). Thus Birmingham does not provide UK corporate finance even though it is a type of secondary financial center where that service is usually provided. A similar case is that of centers in the Southeast, which also tend to lose their "activity-level" firms to London, again due to proximity to London. Back-office activities, such as equity settlement, are carried out increasingly as discrete activities in the Southend, Brighton, Bournemouth, and usually not in higher-level centers. This geographic dispersal results from firms' decisions to locate certain activities—routine, standardized—as discrete operations in low-cost areas. These are typically activities with no or minimal agglomeration economies.

Coe and Townsend's (1998) study of producer service concentrations in the western arc of the OMA found that what is important for generating clusters of financial, business, and computer services is the existence of common locational logics rather than any localized or even subregional linkages. In the metropolitan ring they studied, the relevant agglomeration seems to be the Greater Southeast (some 150 miles across); they also did find that formal business links were quite likely to involve business partners outside the region. At the metropolitan regional level there is little evidence for industrial complexes or strong social networks as explanations for clustering. In this regard, the London region is a rather extreme case, but important in showing that the social network model is not a precondition for the achievement of either flexibility or innovativeness.

In a study on how small and medium-sized enterprises gain access to producer services, Bryson and Daniels (1998) found that they mostly use small, independent firms.[8] Furthermore, the majority of these service firms were in the same region as their clients: 46% of external advisers

---

[8] This study is based on data from The Business Link Initiative in England, which is an attempt by the government to overcome the isolation of SMEs when it comes to access to a broad range of integrated advice, support, and information services. It was instituted at the end of 1996 in the form of a national network of independent business support centers (260 outlets from 90 partnerships).

were located within twenty miles of their clients, and 74% were located in the same region. For example, a majority of accountants employed by SMEs are local firms that are either sole practitioners or small companies with limited access to other forms of nonlocal advice. Other evidence shows that large firms search for the best advice regardless of where it is located (Bryson 1997a), while SMEs search locally because of cost and imperfect markets for identifying business services. Searches go beyond the local area if it is a very specific type of expertise not available in the region or if firms have weak-tie acquaintances outside the locality.

Local dependency on external advisers among SMEs in areas outside London range from a high of 66% in the North West to a low of 29% in the North. East Midlands and East Anglia have the lowest dependency on outside firms in the London region: 54% and 55%, respectively, explained by the relative availability of consultancy companies based in London and the SE. They are regions partially incorporated into the London information nexus. For firms located in areas where there are few business services, the picture changes again. One study of business service use by manufacturing firms in Mid Wales, an area with few such service companies, found that 61% of the service suppliers used were over 100 miles away from the largest town in the region (Hitchens et al. 1994).

This has multiple implications, beyond the possibility of searching for the best advice. Thus using the notion of weak vs. strong ties (Granovetter 1986), Bryson and Daniels (1998) posit that the multiplier effects that weak ties can bring to a business do not accrue to many of these SMEs, further putting them at a disadvantage. Among the SMEs surveyed, 64% of respondents said personal contacts, friends, and business acquaintances had helped them identify external advice and the majority of all of these contacts were based in the local area (Bryson and Daniels 1998: 271–73).

The evidence shows that the knowledge base of many of these small local consultancy companies is limited—they spend a lot of time servicing existing clients and looking for new ones (Keeble et al. 1994). This is further amplified by the presence of top-level, resource-rich consultancies in London and the Southeast. Among SMEs in London, 93% employed advisers located in the Southeast: there are significant differences in price between SE-based and London-based expertise.

Another major component of the London region is the growing information technology software sector. The city is a major driver of London's IT economy through the financial services, including especially financial software development where the city remains one of the worldwide leaders. By drawing a large pool of highly talented IT specialists the City facilitated the emergence of a broader sector in London and in the larger SE region. There is a second IT driven subeconomy concentrated in several of the boroughs immediately adjacent and known as the City Fringe regeneration area. One of the questions is whether these two are interrelated.

In terms of the value-added produced by the industry and the position of IT functions in the value chain, financial services are at the top. This is particularly so because of the development of derivatives trading and the need for complex financial software products and backup systems for effective competition. This cutting-edge aspect of software development in the financial services has attracted top talent from the whole country and from Europe. Now in turn, other cities, notably Frankfurt, are recruiting IT professionals from London. The latest available data are for 1997 and show that London accounted for 18% of the UK's IT workforce in terms of their residential patterns. Including the SE, the total comes to 46%. Considering the residential patterns of the UK Managerial and Professional workforce, this figure rises to 20% for London and together with the SE to 55% (ITNTO 1998). Most of those living in the SE actually commute to London (Corporation of London 1999a; see also Dunford and Fielding 1998).

This large supply of talent in combination with the particularly flexible work conditions of a good part of the sector has facilitated the development of other branches in the knowledge-driven IT sector. London, and especially the City, have emerged as a global IT skills center for financial and business services related software. New York and Chicago are the two other leaders, and Frankfurt is emerging fast and has indeed recruited considerable numbers of people from London. It is estimated that about 50% of Frankfurt's IT workers in Frankfurt-based banks are British contract workers. Paris and Amsterdam are also emerging as significant global IT skills centers. Several estimates posit that the City's competitive advantage over other European centers which stood at eleven years in the recent past is now down to six months (Corporation of London 1999a:20).

A second type of differentiation emerges from the composition of various subcomponents of this sector. When we exclude finance-driven IT, a tighter geography of the sector emerges, located in central western areas of London, with Hammersmith and Fulham joining Camden and Islington as key areas with a high concentration of so-called content industries, especially the multimedia sector. The difference between these subcomponents of the sector are not so much predicated on the technology per se, but rather on the particular foci and contents to which the technologies are applied. Financial software, publishing, and business services are concentrated in the inner eastern areas of the City and the City Fringe, and multimedia is centered in the Western Arc, with Soho and Central London key locations.

The spatial concentration, even within London, of the knowledge-driven IT sector is important to note as it is yet another instantiation of the importance of agglomeration effects and the more complex notion of place as crucial to the most advanced sectors of our economies.

In sum, London's overrepresentation continued, within both the country and its metropolitan area. The representation of producer services in towns and cities of London's greater metropolitan area was brought above the national level in most cases. This indicates that this broader region accounts for some of the rapid national growth in producer services. However, while the growth rate in these was markedly higher than in London for the 1971–1981 period, in absolute numbers London's dominance is overwhelming. It is worth noting again that the relative dispersal within the London metropolitan area was much more pronounced in the early 1970s, and that from 1978 onward there was a relative decline in the growth rates outside London's metropolitan area and a relative increase in London's growth rate. There is a suggestion in this evidence that the Southeast region, which experienced significant growth rates in producer services in its various territorial components—surrounding towns and cities, nonmetropolitan areas, and South and Southeast manufacturing towns—owes its growth to the presence of a larger economic complex dominated by London. If this is the case, it is in the form of a differentiated economic subsystem, one with distinct components: high-tech and local producer services in the region and internationally marketed producer services in London. This would explain why the other regions and intraregional nodes have not experienced growth but, on the contrary, have tended to experience declines in producer services. Those regions have a very different economic base and have central nodes, the once-powerful manufacturing centers, in severe decline.

There is, then, a fundamental discontinuity between London and the rest of the country, with pronounced overrepresentation in the former and pronounced underrepresentation at other levels of the urban hierarchy, except for some smaller cities in the London metropolitan area. A narrower definition of the producer services restricted to office-based services, such as insurance, financial services, banking, and so on, yields an even stronger concentration at the top and underrepresentation in the subsequent levels.

The degree of concentration represented by London is significantly higher than what we find in the United States or even Japan. In the United States there is considerable dispersion in the distribution of producer services among a number of major urban centers, especially New York, Los Angeles, and Chicago (see Table 6.12). There is clearly overrepresentation of these industries in these three cities. While there may have been declines over the last decade in some of these industries,

TABLE 6.12

United States: National Employment Share of Major Cities in Producer Services, 1977–1997, Various Years (percent)

	1977	1985	1993	1997
New York (Manhattan)	8.3	7.2	4.4	4.2
Los Angeles (L.A. County)	4.6	4.6	4.0	3.7
Chicago (Cook County)	4.2	3.5	3.2	3.1
Houston (Harris County)	1.7	1.8	1.7	1.5
Detroit (Wayne County)	1.0	0.8	0.6	0.6
Boston (Suffolk County)	1.2	1.2	0.9	0.9
Total U.S. producer services *employment (N)*	9,804,104	12,328,104	15,785,687	17,630,321

Source: Author's calculations based on U.S. Census Bureau, *County Business Patterns*, issues for the United States, 1983, 1989, 1995, and 1998.

overall the sharpest concentration is still in New York. Chicago and Los Angeles also have considerable overrepresentation, but they are a far second behind New York. In 1977 New York had 8.3% of all employment in producer services, a share that declined to 7.2% in 1985 and to 4.2% in 1997. Chicago's share similarly declined, from 4.2% in 1977 to 3.5% in 1985 and to 3.1% in 1997. Detroit, Boston, and Houston on the other hand, kept their shares of, respectively, 1%, 1.2%, and around 1.7% virtually constant over the period from 1977 to 1997. Los Angeles' share fell from 4.6% in 1977 to 3.7% in 1997. The total unemployment share of New York fell from 6% in 1970 to 4.2% in 1997.

When we disaggregate the information on growth rates and employment shares for various producer services industries, the overall patterns tend to remain, with a few major exceptions, but the levels of overrepresentation and growth tend to vary considerably among industries. Perhaps the sharpest overrepresentation for New York is its share of earnings from FIRE as a percentage of national earnings in FIRE (see Orr 2000). New York's share of these earnings went from about 14% in 1983, already a sharp overrepresentation given its 9% share of FIRE employment at the time, to 18% in early 1999. The increased level in earnings share coincides with a fall in the employment share to under 2% in early 1999. The growing gap between earnings share and employment share is partly a result of the sharp restructuring of the banking sector which reduced the employment in the sector considerably. It also indicates the enormous levels of profitability reached by the financial services firms. At the New York metropolitan scale, these trends remain though with a smaller gap between earnings share which grew from 18% in 1983 to over 20% in early 1999, and employment share which fell from 13% to 10%, respectively.

Organizing this information in terms of location quotients underlines the extent to which major cities have overrepresentation of most of these producer services, but with considerable variation in the degree of over-representation and type of industry (see Tables 6.13, 6.14, and 6.15). New York, San Francisco, and Boston have sharply higher location quo-tients for finance and banking than any of the other cities. These quo-tients have magnitudes that clearly are describing a market that extends significantly beyond an average overrepresentation and reveals a highly specialized spatial organization of an industry. The figures for Los An-geles are underestimates of the extent of concentration because they cover the whole county, which corresponds far less closely to its main city than do other counties (such as Chicago's Cook County), while leaving out key business districts. The massive industrial complex and active har-bor are central to the growth of producer services in the area, but will tend to create a demand for different types of services than those engen-dered by Los Angeles's financial activities (Cohen and Zysman 1987). The departure of major banks over the last decade clearly shows on the 0.94 location quotient the city registered in 1997.

One question we need to ask is whether there are significant differ-ences among these cities in the composition of their industries. We need to know whether Boston is as specialized in international banking and finance as New York and Los Angeles and, if so, whether it is the same type of international finance. Secondly, the absolute size of the banking sector is likely to diverge dramatically from that in New York given the much smaller employment base of Boston, under half a million, com-pared with 3 million in New York, 3 million in Los Angeles, and 2.1 million in Chicago. Detroit, once the premier manufacturing city of the country, has unexpectedly low representation in real estate, an indication of its acute manufacturing losses. Given that Detroit is still the home of major car manufacturers, it is worth noting its underrepresentation in business services, legal services, real estate, and insurance. This situation is reminiscent of the one in Britain, where what were once the major manu-facturing centers have underrepresentation of producer services. One question that needs examining is the extent to which Detroit, like those English cities, has primarily a manufacturing-oriented producer services sector. Finally, San Francisco, Boston, and New York have extremely high concentrations of legal services. To what extent is this associated with the fact that these three cities have the highest quotients in banking and finance as well? This association is discussed in chapter 5.

Focusing with more detail on the three major cities in the U.S. and

TABLE 6.13

Location Quotients for Selected U.S. Cities, 1977 to 1997

	Total Employment	Bank./Fin.	Insurance	Real Estate	Bus. Services	Legal Serv.
New York (5 counties see note)						
1977	2,714,385	2.81	1.56	2.42	2.01	2.25
1981	2,941,325	2.98	1.43	2.22	2.02	2.19
1985	3,018,000	3.04	1.45	2.20	2.20	2.31
1987	3,122,583	3.23	1.32	2.05	2.05	2.25
1993	2,876,495	2.93	1.20	2.34	1.28	2.42
1997	3,038,719	3.05	1.33	2.48	1.13	2.49
Los Angeles (L.A. County)						
1977	2,647,263	1.12	1.00	1.12	1.48	1.26
1981	3,173,460	1.16	0.93	1.33	1.41	1.29
1985	3,345,520	1.09	0.87	1.18	1.28	1.34
1987	3,546,343	1.04	0.84	1.18	1.23	1.35
1993	3,495,246	1.07	0.87	1.16	1.22	1.50
1997	3,588,831	0.94	0.86	1.12	1.22	1.34
Chicago (Cook County)						
1977	2,189,598	1.22	1.54	1.25	1.39	1.18
1981	2,247,119	1.40	1.51	1.29	1.33	1.34
1985	2,187,992	1.41	1.51	1.22	1.41	1.42
1987	2,213,434	1.39	1.50	1.27	1.20	1.47
1993	2,314,172	1.55	1.34	1.28	1.30	1.48
1997	2,395,111	1.53	1.28	1.42	1.27	1.63
San Francisco (S.F. County)						
1977	490,748	2.79	2.94	1.47	1.91	2.64
1981	508,861	2.35	1.76	1.32	1.91	2.80
1985	520,167	2.66	1.72	1.88	1.72	3.13
1987	503,859	2.54	1.69	1.69	1.69	3.56
1993	487,834	2.64	1.50	1.59	1.49	3.63
1997	516,816	3.22	1.23	1.61	1.37	3.30
Houston (Harris County)						
1977	925,257	0.92	0.84	1.43	1.83	1.01
1981	1,256,765	0.63	0.93	1.20	1.65	0.95
1985	1,215,870	1.13	0.79	1.60	1.38	1.14
1987	1,156,357	1.04	0.89	1.78	1.41	1.26
1997	1,511,905	0.88	0.81	1.30	1.43	1.26
1993	1,366,579	0.82	0.81	1.35	1.63	1.31
Detroit (Wayne County)						
1977	797,342	1.22	0.65	0.41	0.89	0.89
1981	738,866	1.02	0.71	0.51	0.82	1.12
1985	698,986	0.93	0.93	0.47	1.05	1.05
1987	730,372	0.14	0.82	0.35	0.94	0.94
1993	699,446	0.81	0.97	0.50	0.83	0.94
1997	751,145	0.69	0.95	0.55	0.87	0.86

TABLE 6.13 *cont.*

	Total Employment	Bank./Fin.	Insurance	Real Estate	Bus. Services	Legal Serv.
Boston (Suffolk County)						
1977	382,546	1.84	3.20	1.25	1.85	2.52
1981	452,189	1.81	3.12	1.25	1.74	2.62
1985	486,045	2.08	2.68	1.75	1.55	2.86
1987	498,241	2.24	2.59	1.90	1.55	2.93
1993	485,365	2.71	1.92	1.83	1.12	3.16
1997	525,783	3.50	2.01	1.53	1.12	3.30
Atlanta (Fulton County)						
1977	348,168	1.11	1.67	1.67	2.04	1.67
1981	394,565	1.13	1.89	1.70	1.70	1.70
1985	459,524	1.05	1.93	1.58	1.75	1.75
1987	487,170	1.23	1.75	1.40	1.58	1.75
1993	553,470	1.55	1.60	1.51	1.71	1.70
1997	645,595	1.55	1.40	1.50	1.84	1.76

Source: U.S. Census Bureau, *County Business Patterns*, 1997.

Notes: New York City includes 5 counties (New York, Bronx, Richmond, Queens, King's).

TABLE 6.14

NYC, LA, and Chicago: Location Quotients of Business Services and Engineering/ Management Services, 1993 and 1997

Sector Description	SIC	New York City		Los Angeles		Chicago	
		1993	1997	1993	1997	1993	1997
Advertising	7310	5.1	4.9	1.5	1.6	3.6	2.9
Credit reporting and collection	7320	0.4	0.7	1.0	0.8	2.0	2.4
Mailing, repro., stenographic	7330	2.3	2.1	1.7	1.6	2.1	2.2
Services to buildings	7340	1.5	1.1	0.8	0.8	1.5	1.6
Personnel supply services	7360	0.8	0.8	1.2	1.3	1.4	1.6
Computer and data processing	7370	0.8	0.9	1.0	0.9	1.6	1.8
Misc. business services	7380	1.5	1.4	1.5	1.5	1.9	1.8
Engineering/architecture	8710	0.8	0.7	0.9	0.8	1.2	1.3
Accounting, audit., bookkeeping	8720	2.0	1.8	2.4	2.9	1.4	1.7
Research and testing	8730	1.3	1.1	1.1	1.2	1.8	2.0
Manage. and public relations	8740	1.6	1.5	1.2	0.9	1.9	2.1

Source: Author's calculations based on U.S. Census Bureau, *County Business Patterns*, 1997.

Notes: New York City includes 5 counties (New York, Bronx, Richmond, Queens, King's); Chicago includes 3 counties (Cook, DuPage, Lake).

TABLE 6.15

NYC, LA, Chicago and US: Percentage Changes in Employment for Business and Engineering/Management Services, 1993–1997 (percent)

SIC Description	SIC Code	US	NYC	LA	Chicago
Advertising	7310	17.1	7.8	10.2	−12.2
Credit reporting and collection	7320	9.2	81.9	−23.8	25.3
Mailing, repro., stenographic	7330	23.6	3.8	6.5	18.4
Services to buildings	7340	7.5	−24.1	9.2	5.7
Personnel supply services	7360	59.7	41.8	55.6	68.2
Computer and data processing	7370	50.8	55.8	28.8	54.6
Misc. business services	7380	25.8	11.9	9.0	12.2
Engineering/architecture	8710	11.7	−10.4	−0.7	9.6
Accounting, audit., bookkeeping	8720	19.6	4.2	33.7	34.5
Research and testing	8730	13.0	−12.7	14.7	15.6
Manage. and public relations	8740	42.0	25.7	−1.7	45.3

Source: Author's calculations based on U.S. Census Bureau, County Business Patterns, 1997.
Notes: New York City includes 5 counties (New York, Bronx, Richmond, Queens, King's); Chicago includes 3 counties (Cook, DuPage, Lake).

selecting out what are particular producer services, we can see that the percent change from 1993 to 1997 varies enormously for each industry (see Table 6.15). Two sectors that had sharp growth rates in the three cities are personnel supply services and computer and data processing, ranging from about 42% in NYC to 68% in Chicago. This enormously high growth rate for Chicago indicates something about the restructuring of that city from being dominated by Fordist firms to being controlled by the specialized services sector that has grown sharply over the decade. This in turn brings with it a far more flexible and unsheltered labor market. Credit Reporting and Collection is extremely high in NYC compared to the national growth rate and to the other two cities. Beyond these sectors, one of the highest growth rates was for Management and Public Relations in Chicago, again, probably indicative of the restructuring of that city's economy. Among the producer services in these three cities, the highest location quotients for 1997 are for advertising in both NY and Chicago; notwithstanding declines since 1993, though not necessarily in absolute numbers, these quotients are well above the norm. Chicago has several extremely high location quotients in 1993 and especially in 1997, including such diverse sectors as services to buildings and research and testing. Given the high growth rates listed in personnel supply services for all three cities, it is interesting to note that the location quotients are not particularly high, except for Chicago, an indication that this is a nationwide growth sector (Table 6.14).

One question is whether New York firms differ from those of other major cities, notably Los Angeles and Chicago, in their type and level of specialization. For example, research by Mollenkopf (1984) showed that corporate legal firms in New York in the 1980s had a high level of specialization and comparative advantage in international expertise. Large firms in Los Angeles and Chicago expanded their markets and opened branches in New York and in regional growth centers. The large New York firms, on the other hand, have set up branches in other major foreign international financial centers as well as in Washington, D.C., this city being a step in the international chain of transactions. The source of growth of these services in New York has been the rise of investment banking. New York accounts for a third of U.S. corporate legal services employment and up to 50% of this sector's profits. The total number of law firms in Manhattan, Los Angeles, and Chicago increased sharply from 2,479 in 1988 to over 5,050 in 2000. And while the numbers of firms with foreign branches also increased, from 128 to 188, their share fell in NY and Los Angeles, but doubled in Chicago. In 1988 Manhattan had 78 such firms, Los Angeles had 39, and Chicago had 11 (see Table 6.16). By 2000, these numbers were, respectively, 100, 45, and 43. There are several reasons for this. First, there is growing concentration among top-level international law firms, so that the expense of opening foreign branches is not necessarily viable for many firms. Further, there are other ways in which a law firm can serve its clients in a foreign location, notably through various agreements for service delivery with local firms and through direct export of legal services (see chap. 3).

The level of specialization in many of the advanced services has increased. For example, large firms now tend to use several corporate specialized legal firms. Similarly, central to the growth of management con-

TABLE 6.16

Law Firms with Foreign Branches: Manhattan, Los Angeles, and Chicago, 1988 and 2000

| | Total Number of Law Firms | | Firms with Foreign Branches | | | |
| | | | Number | | % of Total | |
	1988	2000	1988	2000	1988	2000
Manhattan	1,147	2,425	78	100	6.8	4.1
Los Angeles	765	1,597	39	45	5.1	2.8
Chicago	567	1,028	11	43	1.9	4.2
Total	2,479	5,050	128	188		

Source: Author's calculations based on Martindale-Hubbell Law Directory, 1988 and 2000 editions.

sulting has been a high level of specialization oriented to institutional investment. Thus, while cities like Boston and Los Angeles used to have management consulting sectors that competed with New York's, the changes in the financial industry have created a specific role for New York, and one that has carried much of the industry's growth. This high level of specialization has brought about a need for and a dependence on a combination of other services and resources. There is a high level of contact among firms at the point of production. These firms can serve widely dispersed regional, national, and international markets, but at the point of production, agglomeration economies are high. New York clearly, then, emerges as a desirable location, notwithstanding higher costs of operation than in alternative cities.

Chicago, the financial, marketing, and insurance center for the once powerful agroindustrial complex in the Midwest, raises interesting questions. To what extent is the composition of Chicago's producer services quite different from that in New York or Los Angeles because it is directly related to servicing of the agroindustrial base of the region, and to what extent has the decline of this complex and the growth of the futures market reoriented Chicago to the world market through finance? New York's producer services sector caters to a world market and is heavily internationalized, servicing or making transactions at the axis between a firm and the international market. Chicago's would seem to be much less so. Chicago's large export-oriented firms typically had high levels of vertical integration and extensive internal production of the necessary services. Now we may be seeing the beginnings of a freestanding producer services industry, fed by the growth of foreign investment in the region and of the futures market (Sassen and Testa, in progress).

It is evident that these services have grown in Chicago. The proportion of producer services in Chicago probably follows a more expected pattern, somewhere between the acute overrepresentation of some producer services in New York, Los Angeles, and Boston and the marked underrepresentation in Houston and Detroit. From 1977 to 1988, average annual growth rates in several specialized services compared favorably with those of New York (see Table 6.17). The difference lies in the prevalence of certain industry groups. Table 6.18 shows that FIRE's employment share in Chicago was 6.1% in 1981 compared with 11.5% in New York; these figures increased to, respectively, 10% and 23% by 1996. One question here is whether part of the difference is explained by Chicago's sharp orientation to the agroindustrial complex now in decline and the differential impact of the global reorganization of the financial industry on each of these cities (Abu-Lughod 1999). One indication is the large concentration of foreign banks and financial firms in New York, which has increasingly outdistanced Chicago.

TABLE 6.17

New York and Chicago: Percentage Employed in Selected Industries, 1981–1996

	1981		1985		1996	
	New York	Chicago	New York	Chicago	New York	Chicago
Manufacturing	16.0	28.4	14.0	20.9	8.1	17.6
TCU[1]	6.5	5.4	6.5	5.8	6.2	7.0
FIRE[2]	11.5	6.1	12.4	7.4	23.2	10.3
Services	23.3	21.2	26.5	24.6	43.5	37.1

Source: Author's calculations based on U.S. Census Bureau, *County Business Patterns*, issues for the United States, 1983, 1989, 1995, and 1998.

Notes: [1]Transportation, communications, and utilities; [2]Finance, Insurance, and Real Estate.

To ground the comparison of the three major cities in a broader complex of industries, I added the communications group (SIC 48) to FIRE, business, and legal services (see Table 6.19). In 1985 the incidence in New York, at 31%, is significantly higher than in Los Angeles (18%) or Chicago (20%). But these levels are all above the 15% in the United

TABLE 6.18

New York and Chicago: Employment Growth Rates in Producer Services, 1977–1996 (percent)

SIC No.	Industry	1977–1985 (% growth)		1985–1987 (% growth)		1993–1996 (% growth) *	
		New York	Chicago	New York	Chicago	New York	Chicago
6000	Banking	15.4	11.9	5.6	−0.2	−20.1	−3.9
6100	Credit agencies	49.3	25.4	9.4	15.1	0.4	−7.7
6200	Security and Commodity Brokers	73.0	74.0	33.1	12.8	25.4	14.5
6300	Insurance Carriers	−9.0	−11.5	−1.6	3.9	17.1	−11.1
6400	Insurance Agents, Broker, and Service	33.5	15.0	0.1	15.8	−0.8	12.6
6500	Real Estate	7.6	3.7	3.7	14.4	3.9	6.1
6700	Holding and Other Investment Offices	−8.6	77.0	4.0	7.0	36.4	−4.8
7300	Business Services	47.0	51.3	8.3	−5.6	9.3	17.9
8100	Legal Services	58.7	67.5	14.6	17.9	−2.6	1.9
8600	Membership Organizations	4.7	4.3	8.6	3.2	−6.1	2.1
8900	Services, N.e.c.	38.6	32.9	14.4	10.4	254.5	20.3

Source: Author's calculations based on U.S. Census Bureau, *County Business Patterns*, issues for the United States, 1983, 1989, 1995, and 1998.

States as a whole. By 1996, this share had fallen to 28% in New York and risen in Los Angeles and especially in Chicago.

Chicago: A Global City?

Chicago is an interesting case to focus on in more detail because it is undergoing a rather profound transformation. For a century and more it was at the heart of an enormous agroindustrial complex and had a manufacturing-based urban economy. Even its financial markets have their origins and were centered on this complex. Both the regional and the urban economy have faced enormous declines over the last several decades in those once-dominant sectors. And the city's major financial markets are facing potentially radical transformations in terms of their once majority share in the global futures market and in terms of organizational challenges.

In her masterly new book *America's Global Cities*, the great urbanist Janet Abu-Lughod (1999) provides us with a detailed analysis of Chicago's transition from the Fordist powerhouse it once was to a city of sharp declines in most of its key sectors (see also Wievel 1988). At the height of this decline, from 1967 to 1982, the city lost 46% of its manufacturing jobs and one-quarter of all of its factories closed down (Squires et al. 1987; Sheets et al. 1984). In the 1980s a good part of the regional industrial complex closed down (Markusen and Carlson 1989).[9] And the broader metropolitan area which had seen continued growth suffered an 18% loss in manufacturing jobs and multiple factory closings (Abu-Lughod 1999:324; Betancur 1989).

Deindustrialization continued through the 1990s. Yet she finds that it is not only the widely recognized loss of manufacturing jobs and firms, but also the loss of service jobs. Between 1991 and 1992 the city lost 31,000 service jobs even as the suburbs gained 19,000 such jobs. Of this loss, almost half were in the advanced corporate services, a sector which in New York for instance had registered growth even as the city lost a significant share of its manufacturing jobs. In addition, the city's financial markets were losing employment, office vacancy rates in the center of the city had reached over 20% in the early 1990s, and nonresidential construction was down (BOMA/Chicago 1999). At its worst Manhattan's vacancy rates stood at 18.8% in a context of severe economic crisis and, in sharp contrast to Chicago, an enormous amount of overbuilding and an economic boom in the 1980s.

Abu-Lughod concludes that while Chicago's financial markets may re-

---

[9] Markusen and McCurdy (1989) find that the lack of federal defense contracts, particularly in R&D, was a key cause of the manufacturing losses.

TABLE 6.19

United States, New York City, Los Angeles, and Chicago: Employment in Information Industries, 1985 and 1996 (numbers and percent)

		Chicago (Cook County)		Los Angeles (L.A. County)		New York City[2]		United States	
SIC Code	Industry	% of total employment	N	% of total employment	N	% of total employment	N	% of total employment	N
4800	Communication[1]	1.5	31,697	1.9	61,928	2.4	71,340	1.6	1,282,616
6000	FIRE	10.2	223,501	8.0	268,379	17.3	521,402	7.4	6,004,136
7300	Business Services	7.4	162,264	6.8	226,346	9.4	283,906	5.3	4,272,200
8100	Legal Services	1.2	26,092	1.1	37,542	1.9	58,729	0.8	685,456
	Total employment in Info. Industries	20.3	443,554	17.8	594,195	31.0	935,377	15.1	12,244,408
	Total employment (all industries)		2,187,992		3,345,520		3,017,996		81,119,257

1985

TABLE 6.19 cont.

		1996							
		Chicago (Cook County)		Los Angeles (L.A. County)		New York City[2]		United States	
SIC Code	Industry	% of total employment	N	% of total employment	N	% of total employment	N	% of total employment	N
4800	Communication[1]	1.4	31,964	1.2	43,093	1.6	47,579	1.3	1,375,879
6000	FIRE	10.3	242,435	7.1	245,592	14.5	439,497	7.0	7,194,274
7300	Business Services	9.3	218,434	8.6	297,837	7.1	215,826	7.1	7,224,569
8100	Legal Services	1.5	35,498	1.3	45,239	2.1	63,078	0.9	959,809
8700	Engineering and Management Services	3.7	86,609	3.9	136,927	3.3	101,322	2.9	2,994,928
	Total employment in Info. Industries	26.1	614,940	22.2	768,688	28.5	867,302	19.3	19,749,459
	Total employment (all industries)		2,358,437		3,470,070		3,038,719		102,198,864

Source: Author's calculations based on U.S. Census Bureau, County Business Patterns, issues for the United States, 1983, 1989, 1995, and 1998.

Notes: [1]Includes telephone communication, telegraph communication, radio and television broadcasting, and communication services; [2]Includes the counties of Queens, King's, Bronx, Richmond, and New York.

main important nodes of the upper circuits of specialized financial sectors, the city may lack the critical mass to be a global city—and in that regard can function as a counterfactual in the research and theorization about global cities.

But in my reading and based on the first stages of a larger research project (Sassen and Testa, in progress; Global Chicago 2000), I find that by the late 1990s Chicago has indeed entered a new economic phase, one that is not quite evident in the aggregate data categories though one can certainly see it today by walking through the center of the city. At the same time, unemployment is high for disadvantaged sectors of the workforce, poverty is high, and so are job losses and firm closures. Further, the departure of the leading headquarters continues. It reminds me of my research on New York in the late 1970s and early 1980s when the consensus among experts and policy analysts was that the city was finished: all the aggregate indicators showed losses, the city had just gone through a fiscal crisis, and the infrastructure was in severe decay. Yet in the particular sectors that I was researching, the producer services (both the advanced services and the industrial service jobs), I found growth and began to elaborate my model of the global city.

It can be said that the end of the period examined by Abu-Lughod, the mid-1990s, represents not so much the end of that protracted phase of decline, which in many ways continues, but rather the as yet only barely detectable emergence of a new set of core economic activities (Sassen and Testa, in progress). Many of the old indicators, whether number of manufacturing jobs and factories, or certain types of service jobs, fail to capture this new economic phase. I would posit that this also holds for some of the indicators used to measure the size of the workforce in the financial markets, which merely show losses; size of this sector's workforce may no longer be as useful an indicator as it once was.

Another measure frequently used to describe the decline of the city is the share of the global futures market held by the Chicago markets. It is a less useful indicator than it once was because one of the features of the current global financial market is that it is networked and one of the ways in which leading centers actually gain strength is through the addition of new centers to the network (see chap. 5: pp. 117–21; Sassen 1999). I would posit that the actual number of transactions and value transacted are more important measures than share of the global markets because they have multiplier effects for the broader city economy. Both of these have increased sharply over the last few years. Further, I would argue that the level of transactions may be somewhat more useful as an indicator for these markets' impacts on the broader city economy than share of the global market because it represents work that needs to be done in Chicago and thereby creates additional jobs. Understanding the actual work

TABLE 6.20

United States: Location Quotients of FIRE and Selected Services in New York City, Chicago, and Los Angeles, 1985 and 1996

	1985		1996	
	FIRE	Services[1]	FIRE	Services[2]
New York City[3] to U.S.	2.334	1.783	2.055	1.146
Los Angeles (L.A.County) to U.S.	1.084	1.266	1.005	1.227
Chicago (Cook County) to U.S.	1.380	1.307	1.460	1.286

Sources: See Table 6.20.

Note: Includes business and legal services and communications (see note 1 in Table 6.20 for description); [2]Includes business, legal, engineering, and management services and communications; [3]See Table 6.20, note 2.

that needs to be executed in Chicago captures the specialized functions of the city's markets. Furthermore, actual value of total transactions suggests, though very imprecisely, the level of income of firms and professionals and is an indication of recirculation, even if very partial, in the city's economy. (For a fuller discussion, see Sassen 1999.)

There are interesting pieces of evidence about the city's transformation. For instance, Chicago has lost about half of its Fortune 500 headquarters in the last 15 years. Half of what were listed in 1980 as Chicago's 50 largest public companies have been acquired (by out-of-state firms) or moved out of state. And this process continues. From March 1998 on, takeovers have changed the ownership of major Chicago firms: Amoco, Meritech, First Chicago, Waste Management, Morton International, Inland Steel. And many other large firms (Sears, Motorola) are targets for takeovers. Nor are there many new headquarters of large firms moving in. This is a high-visibility story of losses.[10]

Yet a more detailed examination of growth and decline trends shows that Chicago's advanced corporate services have continued to grow even as their large corporate clients have moved out. They have kept serving these now out-of-town clients and they have experienced an increasing demand for their services from firms in the broader midwestern region as these have raised their participation in global export and import markets. For instance, even as all these major headquarters leave the city, Arthur Anderson's 4,000 employee Chicago-based operation has been growing by 10 to 15% a year in terms of revenues, with a growing share of this

[10] A very important point is that the recomposition of the leading sector, away from major corporate headquarters to a network of large and small corporate service firms, has major implications for a variety of conditions. Charitable and civic giving and leadership are also lost as are internal labor markets with entry-level jobs and promotion possibilities and typically better-paid supervisory and clerical work.

TABLE 6.21

Japan: National Employment Share of Major Cities in Selected Producer Services, 1985–1995, Selected Years (percentages)

	Finance and Insurance	Real Estate	Services
	City's Share (percentage)		
Tokyo (Tokyo Prefecture)			
1985	14.2	23.0	12.5
1990	14.5	22.5	12.5
1995	13.7	21.6	11.9
Nagoya (Aichi Prefecture)			
1985	4.7	4.3	4.8
1990	4.7	4.2	4.8
1995	4.9	4.5	4.9
Osaka (Osaka Prefecture)			
1985	8.2	11.3	6.6
1990	7.4	10.7	6.5
1995	7.3	10.7	6.6
	National Employment ('000s)		
1985	1,742	485	11,924
1990	1,969	693	13,887
1995	1,975	707	15,932

Source: Based on Government of Japan, Management and Coordination Agency, *Japan Statistical Yearbook*, 1986, 1993, and 1998.

work coming from out-of-town firms.[11] Similar trends are evident with a whole series of corporate service firms located in the center of the city.[12]

Tokyo

The share of national employment accounted for by major cities in Japan (see Table 6.21) follows a pattern somewhere between that of the United States and that of the United Kingdom. There is a combination of

[11] Arthur Anderson is a leading firm when it comes to expertise in derivatives, tax management, litigation, and information technology. (See also chap. 5, p. 100.)

[12] E.g., one information technology consultant firm (Whittman-Hart), founded 15 years ago has grown sharply, with a 68% increase in total revenues in 1998 alone—one measure of demand for its services; this growth took place as the departure of major headquarters was accelerating. The leading law firm for departed Continental Bank and other such corporations, Mayer Brown & Platt, has seen business grow by a third in the last decade. (For a more detailed discussion of the relation between headquarters and their corporate services firms, see Sassen 2000: 71–83; Lyons and Salmon 1995.)

medium-high shares of employment in the producer services along with a tendency toward declines in these shares. Thus Tokyo's share of finance and insurance declined from 17% in 1977 to 15% in 1981, 14% in 1985 and 13.7% in 1995. In real estate, this share declined from 26% in 1977 to 23% in 1985 and 11.9% in 1995. The overrepresentation of these industries in Tokyo notwithstanding this city's declines in national employment shares in the 1980s is evident from the fact that Tokyo accounted for about 10% of all employment in Japan in 1985. But by 1995 Tokyo accounts for almost 14% of all employment, and thus loses its overrepresentation in FIRE and RE.

In trying to understand the place of producer services in Tokyo and in the Japanese urban system one crucial fact is the ongoing importance of manufacturing both as economic activity and as the leading export sector of the country (see Table 3.12). This means that the structure of the producer services is going to be different from that of New York and London and their respective countries. A second important difference is that Tokyo is above all a center of command functions of the national economy and a less developed site for international service functions (Hill and Fujita 1995; Teranishi 1991). While it remains a leading exporter of capital and has one of the largest concentrations of assets under management of any city in the world, most of the capital and most of the assets it processes are Japanese (Kamo and Sasaki 1998). The global functions of Tokyo's financial markets during their period of global ascendance in the 1980s never developed as far as those of London and NY (Matsubara 1995). A third important difference is the extent to which the government has played a crucial role in developing Tokyo's capabilities as a global city, and, more generally, the capabilities built into the urban system. That has meant that many of the activities, which in the case of NY and London took place in the private sector, were handled by government agencies in the case of Tokyo and Japan generally (Kamo 1998; Kamo and Sasaki 1998). This includes specialized service activities necessary for global city functions. Nagoya's share of national employment in

---

[13] The centrality of Tokyo as an economic center is also suggested by its larger daytime than nighttime population, with the latter decreasing over the last few years and the former continuing to increase. Daytime population in the twenty-three central wards increased from 1975 to 1980. The population flowing into Tokyo from other preferences totaled 2.1 million in 1980, 95% of whom were commuters to places of work and schools from the three adjacent preferences (Saitama, Kanagawa, and Chiba). The flow of workers into the three central wards (Chiyoda, Chuo, and Minato), which constitute the central business district, is 2.3 million people—6.8 times the size of the 34,000 nighttime population of these three wards. For all twenty-three wards, the daytime population is 10.61 million, while the nighttime population is 8.35 million. For Tokyo as a whole, the daytime population is 13.49 million and the nighttime population is 11.6 million.

these producer services industries parallels its share of all services employ-ment, which is between 4% and 5% with a few fluctuations among the three periods under consideration. Osaka, on the other hand, shows overrepresentation in its 8% share of national employment in finance and insurance and its 12% share in real estate compared with its 6.5% share of all service employment. These levels remained practically the same during the three periods under observation, though there were changes in the absolute numbers. Finance and insurance and real estate have been cen-tral components of the rapid urbanization of the Japanese population outside of Tokyo, as well as of the rise in exports of industrial goods. It is not possible to separate the consumer market from the business one. It is quite possible that over the next few years there will be a shift in com-position and in location as the urbanization of the Japanese population subsides and a larger share of direct exports is replaced with offshore production.

Table 6.22 shows location quotients for Japan's major cities. In the mid-1980s Tokyo's quotient for finance was as high as London's at 1.82 and its Real Estate quotient at 2.28 compared with New York's. Its quo-tients for finance and for real estate fell to 1.39 and 2.20, respectively, in 1995. Compared to the other major cities in Japan, Tokyo clearly

TABLE 6.22

Japan: Location Quotients of Financial and Service Industries in Major Cities, 1981–1995, Selected Years (percentages)

	Finance and Insurance	Real Estate	Services
	Location Quotients		
Tokyo (Tokyo Prefecture)			
1981	1.49	2.33	1.23
1985	1.82	2.28	1.23
1995	1.39	2.20	1.21
Nagoya (Aichi Prefecture)			
1981	0.88	0.85	0.86
1985	1.00	0.78	0.87
1995	0.85	0.79	0.84
Osaka (Osaka Prefecture)			
1981	1.20	1.60	0.86
1985	1.56	1.66	0.96
1995	1.07	1.58	0.97

Source: Author's calculations based on Government of Japan, Management and Coordination Agency, Japan Statistical Yearbook, 1986, 1993, and 1999.

has considerable overrepresentation in these sectors while Nagoya has underrepresentation.

The second trend that emerges is that since 1977 the degree of over-representation of finance and insurance in these three cities has tended to increase, indicating locational concentration in major centers. The distri-bution of both finance and insurance and real estate follows the model of an urban hierarchy in a way that it does not in Great Britain; there is less discontinuity in Japan between Tokyo and the next major cities, even though this discontinuity has risen. A crucial question here is, again, How significant is the presence of a strong manufacturing sector in ex-plaining the strong representation of producer services industries in sev-eral major cities rather than in just one? Secondly, is there in fact a dis-continuity between Tokyo and the other two cities in terms of the composition of the overrepresented sector? To what extent is the over-representation in Osaka rooted in the existence of a very strong manufac-turing base and in that sense quite different from one of the key sources of growth in the FIRE sector in Tokyo? In that case, the structure in Japan would, indeed, be similar to that in Great Britain, with the latter appearing diverse only because the devastation of manufacturing has severely affected the growth of producer services in manufacturing-dominated cities. This would lend support to my hypothesis that key components of the financial industry today are no longer oriented toward serving production.

More detailed data show that an increasing share of Japan's national economic activity became concentrated in Tokyo. Firm relocations away from other major urban centers in Japan have accelerated since the 1980s. From 1985 to 1989, 30,000 Japanese firms moved their head offices to Tokyo according to the National Tax Administration. A survey of 1,050 large foreign firms conducted in 1986 found that 78% had lo-cated their Japanese branches or affiliates in Tokyo. The number of for-eign firms located in Tokyo rose from 997 in 1985 to 1,282 in 1995; in the three surrounding counties (Chiba, Kanagawa, and Saitama) it rose from 44 to 115 (Japan National Tax Agency, various years). An analysis by the Tokyo Metropolitan Government based on data from Japan's Management and Coordination Agency shows that in the mid-1990s one-third of Tokyo's service firms were in business services, compared with 20% in the country as a whole, and 45% of the labor force was employed in business services, compared with 30% for the country as a whole (TMG 1999).[14]

Terasaka et al. (1988: 166) point out that while the development of

---

[14] Additional indications are that 52% of Japan's corporations with over 1 billion yen capitalization were in Tokyo at the end of the 1990s.

telecommunications capability was expected to reduce the density of central offices in Tokyo, in fact during the 1980s the number of headquarters in Tokyo's central wards accelerated rapidly. In 1969, 56.5% of the headquarters listed in the main stock exchange listings were located in Tokyo and 20.3% in Osaka. In contrast, the 1981 Census of Business Establishments in Japan found that only 23.1% of all offices in the country were concentrated in Tokyo. This suggests that the overrepresentation is among certain types of firms. Almost 57% of firms with 5 billion yen or more in capital were located in Tokyo, compared with 38% of firms with capital between 100 million and 1 billion yen and almost 53% of those with 100 million to 5 billion yen.

A survey by the National Land Agency cited in Terasaka et al. (1988) found that of the companies surveyed with headquarters in Tokyo, 56.3% responded that the main reason for having headquarters in Tokyo was raising investment capital and financial investments; 45% said it was the necessity of a central location to oversee the branch offices and factories, often over a wide geographic area; 41.7% said it was access to goods and marketing; 36.4% mentioned obtaining information from business organizations; and 31.8% mentioned obtaining information from administrative agencies. Thus, one could say that besides the financial aspects of raising capital and investing it, matters that an information economy might supposedly have solved, continue to be rather important reasons for locating headquarters in Tokyo notwithstanding high prices of land, higher wages and salaries, and other costs.

The number of foreign firms also increased in Tokyo in the 1980s, both in absolute numbers and as a share of all foreign firms with offices in Japan. The Ministry of Finance found that in 1974, 279 foreign firms opened offices in Tokyo, of which 150 were nonmanufacturing firms. By 1984, the total number of foreign companies in Japan numbered 2,256; almost 63% of these had offices located in the central wards in Tokyo, and another 22% had offices located in other parts of Tokyo within the 23 ward area. Only 15.6% were located in areas other than Tokyo. The degree of concentration in Tokyo was extremely high among financial firms and banks. In 1997 foreign companies investments in Japan were 0.6% of GDP. Since then, however, a growing number of firms have made significant investments leading to a doubling of the flow of foreign investment in 1998. Among these firms are GE Capital, Merril Lynch, Cable & Wireless, Carrefour, and Renault (Sassen 1999).

Rimmer (1986) compared Tokyo, Osaka, and Nagoya along five groups of activities and measures: industrial output, wholesale output, retail sales, bank deposits, and bank advances. Osaka's share (measured at the level of the prefecture, not the city) of national industrial output fell by over a third, from 23.4% in 1960 to 16.4% in 1980, and though

Tokyo's share also fell, from 28.3% to 26.5%, it was clearly still the leading concentration. Nagoya increased its industrial output but failed to raise its share of bank deposits and bank advances, while its share of wholesaling decreased. In many ways Nagoya is an industrial city that is something of a "company town" rather than an international business center. Osaka, on the other hand, is the major economic center outside Tokyo, and according to many geographers, Tokyo and Osaka are the key points in the urban system of Japan. By the mid-1990s the orders of magnitude for each of these cities had changed. Perhaps most notable was the massive increase in the value of exports and the sharp fall in the numbers of shares traded. The overall distribution among these three cities had changed little, with Tokyo remaining by far the dominant city. The value of exports rose in all three cities, with the highest absolute value in Tokyo, twice that of Osaka and 50% higher than Nagoya. If we add Yokohama, the value of exports out of the Tokyo area doubles. We see a similar concentration on the import side. This enormous volume of trade entails a vast array of producer services to handle the work of processing exports and shipments, including legal and accounting services. Tokyo and Osaka both lost shares of key banking activities, from 13% of all bank deposits in Osaka and 38% in Tokyo in 1988 to 9% and 25%, respectively, partly as a result of the growth of urban areas throughout the country. Tokyo continues to account for most stock trading, even as its share declined from 86% in 1988 to 83% in 1997 (OPIAID 1999).

Conclusion

The space economy of producer services in the United States, the United Kingdom, and Japan contains locations of acute concentration, along with rapid growth dispersed throughout these countries. Overrepresentation in major cities continues notwithstanding growth rates that are generally higher for the nation overall. This pattern raises a number of questions. One concerns the composition of producer services in different types of locations. The evidence suggests there is a pronounced difference between New York, London, and Tokyo, which have extremely high concentrations of producer services and a strong orientation to the global market, and other cities. Other major cities in the United Kingdom tend to have underrepresentation of such services and to be somewhat marginal to the international financial industry. In Japan, Osaka has strong overrepresentation of producer services, but a more detailed analysis shows that Tokyo's concentration in all major sectors with a global market orientation—from headquarters to stock transactions and foreign firms—grew in the 1980s and 1990s. In the United States, several major cities have sharp overrepresentation in producer services and are significant locations for international finance. But, again, a more detailed examination of the composition of producer services indicates that during the 1980s New York consolidated its role as the leading international financial and business center in the United States and outdistanced Los Angeles on several counts, notwithstanding the latter's rapid growth.

The locational distribution of producer services follows, up to a point, the accepted urban hierarchy in each of these countries. The largest concentrations are in the top cities, London and Tokyo; and, in the case of the United States, where there are several leading cities, New York is clearly the leading center for producer services. While there is, then, a pattern resembling an urban hierarchy, one can also detect severe discontinuities. The most extreme case is London: It concentrates 31% of all producer services jobs in the United Kingdom, while many of the old industrial centers have underrepresentation of producer services; and it accounts for 16% of employment in the United Kingdom, while the other major cities account for under 2% each. It would seem that rather than a diffusion of growth along the urban hierarchy, there is a clear divergence in growth paths. London's disproportionate concentration of producer services and strong global market orientation has functioned as the growth engine not just for London but for the Southeast; manufacturing decline has decimated key sectors of producer services in the old industrial centers. The disproportionate concentration of the most dynamic sectors in London and its region may have altered the nature of the urban system in the United Kingdom. Similarly, in Japan, Tokyo's increasing concentration of leading sectors, headquarters, the large trading houses and banks, and the most advanced manufacturing sectors is creating a greater differential between Tokyo and the next largest city, Osaka, once the most powerful industrial center in Japan. In the United States, Chicago, once the leading city in the massive industrial complex of the Midwest, has lost considerable ground to New York and Los Angeles.

Does the orientation of leading sectors to the global market contribute to altering the nature of the urban system as it has been understood for developed economies? That understanding presumes a high degree of national integration, enough to absorb considerable unevenness in development and Schumpeter's inevitable creative destruction. The evidence discussed in this chapter indicates that growth predicated on a global market orientation induces discontinuity in the urban hierarchy. It is perhaps becoming increasingly evident that the centrality of mass production and mass consumption was a crucial factor in creating a balanced urban system and national integration in these countries. To what extent is the lesser discontinuity in Japan due to the continuing manufacturing strength of other major cities, and to what extent are tendencies now evident in the United Kingdom, and in a different way in the United States, slowly emerging in Japan? Indications of this could be the growing concentration of all major headquarters, trading houses, foreign banks, firms, and financial markets in Tokyo and the gradual decline of Osaka as the major industrial center. Osaka has also lost share in the financial markets. The growing weight of telecommunications for the organization of work may further reinforce these tendencies toward concentration of strategic functions even as routine work disperses.

Major cities tend to have overrepresentation of the main producer services industries: advertising, banking and finance, and legal services. However, cities that were once major industrial centers and are now in severe decline, notably in the United Kingdom and the United States, often have underrepresentation of these services. This would indicate that there are different producer services complexes in industrial compared with financial centers. On the other hand, much of the growth of the latter is a function of exports to the global market, as the more detailed analysis of particular producer services in chapter 5 showed. What this may be indicating is the extent to which the question of overrepresentation is bound up with major cities being appropriate production sites and marketplaces for these services, rather than with the need to service the city's economic base. To what extent is the latter form of service, central to many models of the urban economy, the mode in manufacturing-dominated urban economies?

The overall growth of producer services since the 1970s can be seen as an indication of a major transformation in the organization of work. And it is this transformation that is perhaps the essence of a service economy. The service economy has usually been identified with the massive increase in consumer services. But the growth in consumer services was strongly associated with the phase of expanded mass production and the urbanization and suburbanization of the population. Perhaps it is more appropriate to think of the growth of consumer services not as a shift to a service economy but rather as a phase of economic development based on the centrality of mass production and mass consumption.

The complexity of the economy and of regulatory frameworks has raised the need for various intermediate service inputs in many organizations of both the private and public sectors. And computerization, the development of information technologies, and telecommunication have altered the organization of work. These are developments that have occurred across industries and localities, as is made evident by the overall growth of service inputs in all types of organizations and localities. This general development constitutes the real shift to a service economy.

In this chapter we saw that New York, London, and Tokyo had outdistanced other cities in their national urban systems. What about major cities in other countries? Is there any evidence of a pattern where the growth of international financial and service flows has had parallel effects on major cities oriented to the world market? Specifically, does global market orientation create more discontinuity with national urban systems and contribute to new forms of transnational interdependence among cities? Do we see the elements of a global urban system or transnational Hanseatic League? We cannot answer all these questions here. Establishing the interdependence of cities beyond New York, London, and Tokyo is not easy, though it appears as an increasingly compelling question at a time when the nation-state is becoming a less central actor in the world (Sassen 1996; 2001b). The next chapter begins to examine these issues.

Seven

Elements of a Global Urban System: Networks and Hierarchies

NEW YORK, London, and Tokyo have long been centers for business and finance. What has changed since the late 1970s is the structure of the business and financial sectors, the magnitude of these sectors, and their networked character. In an earlier period, a limited number of large corporate headquarters and a few large commercial banks dominated a market characterized by high levels of regulation, low inflation, and moderate but predictable growth rates. High inflation in the 1970s, growing use by corporate borrowers of the Euromarkets, and the Third World debt crisis changed these conditions. Today, a large number of firms constitute the core of the business and financial sectors. These firms account for much of the office growth in the private sector and a large volume of economic transactions. The reorganization of the financial industry in the 1980s brought about fundamental changes, characterized by less regulation, more diversification, more competition, the loss of market share by the large commercial banks, and a massive increase in the volume of transactions. This chapter seeks to map the information about the financial markets presented in chapters 4 and 5 onto major cities in order to situate New York, London, and Tokyo in a broader framework. The centrality of finance in the international transactions of these cities and the immense money value of the financial industry, which dwarfs that of all other industries, invite an examination of the interactions among these and other major cities.

With rare exceptions (Walters 1985; Chase-Dunn 1985), studies of city systems assume that the nation-state is the unit of analysis and that urban systems are coterminous with nation-states. But there are cases where one nation-state may encompass several urban systems and, conversely, cases where an urban system may encompass more than one nation-state. Nor does the case described by Hall (1966) in his landmark study, *The World Cities*, quite account for the transactions binding New York, London, Tokyo, and other cities today. In addition to the central place functions performed by these cities at the global level, as posited by Hall (1966) and Friedmann and Wolff (1982), these cities relate to one another in distinct systemic ways. The interactions among New York, London, and Tokyo, particularly in terms of finance and investment, suggest the possibility that they constitute a system. These cities do not simply compete with each other for the same business. There is an economic system that rests on the three distinct types of locations these cities represent.

The international mobility of capital contributes specific forms of articulation among different geographic areas and transformations in the role played by these areas in the world economy. This brings to the fore the existence of several types of location for international transactions. The most familiar are export-processing zones and offshore banking centers; others may yet have to be specified or recognized. Our question here is the extent to which major cities are one such location, though clearly one at a very high level of complexity.

These cities contain a multiplicity of international markets, major concentrations of foreign firms, and of producer services selling to the world market, and they are the key locations for the international property market. The sharp concentrations of such activities constitute internationalized spaces at the heart of these large, basically domestic urban areas. In the preceding chapter, we examined the characteristics of these concentrations in New York, London, and Tokyo and their relation to the national urban system in each country. The first question here is, How do these three cities relate to one another and to the global market? The typical view in the 1980s was that New York, London, and Tokyo competed among themselves and would sharpen that competition by providing joint twenty-four-hour coverage of the markets. What is emerging out of the analysis of the multiplicity of financial and services markets concentrated in these cities is the possibility of a systemic connection other than competition—an urban system with global underpinnings. A second question concerns the place of New York, London, and Tokyo vis-à-vis other major cities, notably the important financial centers in Western Europe, such as Paris and Frankfurt, and other major centers in Asia, such as Hong Kong. These are all financial centers with a strong global orientation. Does a ranking emerge? Is there a global urban hierarchy?

Towards Networked Systems

In chapter two I briefly developed the thesis that capital mobility cannot be reduced simply to that which moves nor can it be reduced to the technologies that facilitate movement. Rather, multiple components of what we continue to code as capital fixity are actually components of capital mobility. The evidence on the most mobile and dematerialized of all forms of capital indicates that this thesis also holds for global finance.

In chapter 5 I introduced two sets of dynamics to explain this outcome—the importance of social connectivity for complex global operations, and the growth of crossborder networks. Let me elaborate.

The particular types of complexity created by cross-border financial operations along with the fact that one mechanism of expansion for the industry is the incorporation of growing numbers of deregulated financial centers into global markets, contribute to an emergent division of labor among financial centers. Leading centers are likely to remain a feature of the global system and, consequently, so will hierarchy. But the role of most other financial centers as facilitators for the circulation of national wealth in global circuits will entail the development of specific functions, i.e., specific financial markets, in the diverse national economies involved. This adds to the complexity of the global financial system due to a multiplication of specialized markets and to increased levels of uncertainty as the system expands and incorporates more and more countries. In this context, the network of financial centers functions as a complex organizational structure enabling each center to maximize efficiencies, transparency, and (functional) trust, even as it expands its global operations and accommodates a growing number of foreign firms. (See Sassen 2001).

The international financial centers of many countries around the world increasingly fulfill gateway functions for the inward and outward circulation of both national and foreign capital. The incorporation of a growing number of these financial centers is one form through which the global financial system expands: each of these centers is the nexus between that country's wealth and the global market and between foreign investors and that country's investment opportunities. The overall sources and destinations of investment therewith grow in number. Gateway functions are and may well continue to be their main mechanism for integration into the global financial market, rather than the production of innovations to package the capital flowing in and out. The complex operations will tend to be executed by the top investment, accounting, and legal services firms, through affiliates, branches, direct imports of those services, or some other form of transfer. Thus important innovations have indeed emerged from several of these gateway centers, e.g., Buenos Aires and Mexico, but typically these have been engineered by the leading global financial services firms and the associated legal and accounting services.

These gateways for the global market are also gateways for the dynamics of financial crises: capital can flow out as easily and quickly as it flows in. And what was once thought of as "national" capital can now as easily join the exodus: for instance, during the Mexico crisis of December 1994, we now know that the first capitals to flee the Mexican markets were national, not foreign; and in the 1998 flight of capital out of Brazil of an estimated US $1 billion a day in early September, not all of it was foreign.

In my reading of the evidence, the globally integrated financial system is not only about competition among countries. There is an increase in specialized collaborative efforts among particular sets of financial centers. The ongoing growth of London, New York, or Frankfurt is in part a function of a global network of financial centers. There is competition along certain lines but there is also an increasingly complex system of transactions and strategic alliances that cannot be subsumed under the concept of competition. In this regard, the cases of Tokyo and Hong Kong are illuminating. My argument is that there would be little if any gain for the financial markets and individual firms from crushing Tokyo or Hong Kong, until recently seen as two of the leading competitors with the major western centers.

Tokyo remains a crucial source of capital. A new phase of deregulations of the financial system has been instituted since 1996 which will lead to the "freeing up" of an estimated $13 trillion in assets that now exist in basically non-liquid form. This represents potentially a significant addition to the global financial market. The fact that since 1998 a growing number of U.S. and European financial firms have been acquiring Japanese financial sector firms in whole or in part suggests that Tokyo will become a more active participant in the global capital market than it has been since the 1991 economic crisis. Tokyo will continue to be a crucial cog in the system but increasingly through foreign intermediaries.

Since its inception, Hong Kong has been a key intersection of different worlds, forever a strategic exchange node for firms from China to the rest of the world and from the rest of the world to China, as well as among all the overseas Chinese communities. Hong Kong could only lose this historic role if all investor interest in China would cease, or if Shanghai could replicate the combination of resources represented by Hong Kong. Both of these conditions are unlikely in the near future. Today it still has one of the most sophisticated concentrations of advanced services, not far behind London, New York, Frankfurt, and Paris even though it has lost market share.

Finally, electronic networks are growing in number and in scope. But that does not necessarily mean that this will eliminate the need for financial centers. Rather, these electronic networks will intensify the transactions connecting such centers in strategic or functional alliances, most dramatically illustrated by the attempted link-up, announced in July 1998, between exchanges in Frankfurt and London, and the alliance set up in early 2000 among Paris, Madrid, Amsterdam, and Frankfurt. Such alliances may well evolve into the equivalent of the cross-border mergers and acquisitions of firms. Electronic trading will also contribute a radically new pattern whereby one market, for instance Frankfurt's Deutsche Eurex, can operate on screens in many other markets around the world, or whereby one brokerage firm, Cantor Fitzgerald, can (as of September 1998) have its prices of U.S. Treasury futures listed on screens used by traders all around the U.S.

But electronic trading does not eliminate the need for financial centers because these combine multiple resources and talents necessary for executing complex operations and servicing global firms and markets. Frankfurt's electronic futures network is actually embedded in a network of financial centers. The Nasdaq is planning for a broad presence outside the U.S., beginning with a joint venture with the Japanese conglomerate Softbank to set up Nasdaq Japan. And broker Cantor Fitzgerald has an alliance with the Board of Trade of New York to handle its computerized sale of Treasury futures. Financial centers cannot be reduced to their exchanges. They are part of a far more complex architecture and they constitute far more complex structures within that architecture.

Expansion and Concentration

Different types of evidence all tend to point to the simultaneous expansion in the number of financial centers that have become integrated into global financial markets and the continuing concentration of a disproportionate share of all assets in a still limited number of leading centers. Stock market capitalization is one indicator of both expansion in the number of stock markets that raise their level of capitalization and the ongoing concentration of a disproportionate share in the leading five or seven centers. The 1980s is the crucial decade when these new dynamics of expansion and concentration emerge which continue in the 1990s, notwithstanding several crises beginning in 1987. (See Table 7.1.)

The sharpest transformation occurred in Tokyo's stock market. At the beginning of the 1980s it was small compared to New York and basically followed New York. In the second half of the 1980s, Tokyo became the largest stock market in the world and responded less sharply to fluctuations elsewhere.[1] This shift in financial power rests in good part on the huge amount of national wealth concentrated in Japan. In 1985 Japan had national assets worth $19.4 trillion; by the end of 1989, these

[1] From 1987 onward, Tokyo's stock market was increasingly considered as a model to follow, one where the emphasis on stability differed from the model represented by New York. The Tokyo market had far less of a decline in 1987 and again in 1989 (New York: 7% decline; Tokyo: 2%). It closed in 1989 with a 31% increase over the prior year and largely without the sharp fluctuations evident in New York. However, by January 1990, the plunge in prices that took place in New York toward the end of 1989 hit the Tokyo market.

TABLE 7.1

Capitalization in Leading Stock Markets, 1987–2000, Selected Years (bn US)

	1987	1993	1997	2000
United States	2,871	5,136	11,309	15,370
Japan	2,896	3,000	2,217	4,692
United Kingdom	728	1,152	1,996	2,894
Germany[1]	255	463	825	1,447
France	185	456	674	1,442
Italy	128	136	345	702
Canada	244	327	568	763
Switzerland	165	272	575	676
Australia	132	204	697	415
Hong Kong	84	385	413	583
Subtotal for listed countries	7,688	11,531	19,619	28,984
Total for Developed Countries[2]	8,114	12,316	21,312	31,593

Sources: Author's calculations based on *Morgan Stanley Capital International Perspectives*, Jan. 1988, Jan. 2000; International Finance Corporation, *Emerging Stock Markets Factbook* 1998, p. 17.

Notes: [1]Indicates West Germany for 1987; [2]Total of listed countries will not equal listed total since some countries have been omitted; table contains year-end total market values of listed domestic companies.

had grown to $43.75 trillion. Beginning in 1984, the Nikkei 225 index of the Tokyo market outdistanced the Dow-Jones average. In 1988 the difference sharpened rapidly, and the Tokyo market came to be seen as a leader. It was also a rather stable market, with a much smaller decline after the 1987 crisis and a quicker return to the prior growth rate. It succeeded in supplying a steady pool of low-cost capital to the Japanese economy.

The number of companies listing stock on the Tokyo exchange in 1987 was 1,499, compared with 1,516 for the New York exchange and 2,101 for the London one. The number of foreign stocks listed on each was 52 in Tokyo, 59 in New, York, and—a significant difference—584 in London. Tokyo has since lost many of these listings. The degree of internationalization as measured by seats held by foreign companies varies among the leading centers with London the most international and Tokyo far less so than most of the major European centers. In 1997, London had 526 foreign companies, followed by the Nasdaq with 454, and New York with 356. These three markets accounted for 44% of the 3,032 foreign companies worldwide in the major stock exchanges. (See Table 7.2).

The concentration of assets under management while less pronounced than stock market capitalization is significant. According to Thomson

TABLE 7.2

Foreign Listings in Major Stock Exchanges, 1997 (number and percent)

	Number of Foreign Listings	Percentage Share
London	526	17.3
New York	356	11.7
Nasdaq	454	15.0
Switzerland	212	7.0
Germany	—	—
Stockholm	16	0.5
Paris	193	6.4
Brussels	140	4.6
Tokyo	60	2.0
Other	1,075	35.3
TOTAL	3,032	100.0

Source: London Stock Exchange, 1997.

Financial (1999), in 1998 about $11 trillion of the $14.9 trillion in worldwide assets under management, are concentrated in 25 cities, with $9.3 trillion in only 10 of these. (See Table 7.3.) Clearly a city can be a leading financial center without having an important exchange, if any, as is the case for instance with Boston, which in 1998 ranked third with almost $1.5 trillion under management. The geography of these invest-

TABLE 7.3

Top 10 Cities Ranked by Institutional Equity Holdings, 1998 (bn USD)

Rank	City	Total Value
1	London, England	2,177.6
2	New York, NY	2,008.4
3	Boston, MA	1,469.4
4	Tokyo, Japan	1,117.4
5	San Francisco, CA	614.9
6	Zurich, Switzerland	491.4
7	Los Angeles, CA	436.0
8	Paris, France	420.4
9	Philadelphia, PA	313.5
10	Chicago, IL	312.5
	Subtotal	9,361.5
	Total for the top 25 cities	12,116.5

Source: Based on Thomson Financial Investor Relations, 1999 International Target Cities Report, p. 3.

ments shows a sharp pattern of concentration. (See Table 7.4.) Of the assets under management in London, the leading center in 1998, the largest single concentration of non-domestic equities was European, at $372 billion, followed by the $189 billion in U.S. equities. Similarly, of the assets under management in New York, the largest single concentration of non-domestic equities was European at $112 billion. Tokyo's largest concentrations of non-domestic equities were the $81 billion in U.S. equities and the $59 billion in European equities. These three cities clearly have vast concentrations of domestic equities which represent the largest share of their total assets.

Finally, as the earlier discussion of producer services indicated, New York and London are leading producers and exporters in accounting, advertising, management consulting, international legal services, engineering services, information products and services, and other business services. They are the most important international markets for these services, with New York the world's largest source of service exports. Tokyo is emerging as an important center for the international trade in services, going beyond its initial role, which was restricted to exporting the services required by its large international trading houses.

The leading firms in advanced producer services have developed vast multinational networks containing special geographic and institutional linkages that make it advantageous for clients to use a growing array of

TABLE 7.4

Institutional Investment in Equities by Region for the Top 10 Largest Cities by Holdings, 1999 (bn USD)

City	U.S.	Latin America	Pacific Rim	Europe
London, England	189.1	—	150.5	372.2
New York, US	—	10.6	21.2	111.9
Boston, US	—	4.1	11.3	68
Tokyo, Japan	80.5	—	—	59.2
San Francisco, US	—	1.9	3.1	11.8
Zurich, Switzerland	80.8	—	19.5	217.7
Los Angeles, US	—	4.0	17.6	45.6
Paris, France	42.2	—	15.7	83.7
Philadelphia, US	—	0.6	2.3	3.4
Chicago, US	—	0.4	1.8	10.7

Source: Based on Thomson Financial Investor Relations, *1999 International Target Cities Report*, p. 3.

Note: Values listed for European cities for Europe are based on non-domestic European equities; — denotes that data was not listed in the original source.

service offerings from the same supplier. Global integration of affiliates and markets requires making use of advanced information and telecommunications technology which can come to account for a significant share of costs—not just operational costs but also, and perhaps most important, research and development costs for new products or advances on existing products. The need for scale economies explains the recent increase in mergers and acquisitions, which has consolidated the position of a few very large firms in many of these industries. These have emerged as firms that can control a significant share of the national and world markets for servicing global firms. This has been particularly evident in accounting and advertising. The top accounting firms have an immense advantage that rests on reputation: An audit by one of these accounting firms raises the status of the audited firm, inspires confidence in potential investors, and reassures government regulators. The multinational advertising firm can offer global advertising to a specific segment of potential customers worldwide.

The Japanese are more likely to gain a significant share of the world market in some producer services than in others (Rimmer 1988; Ocaji 2000; Tables 3.12, 3.14B, and 3.17 in chapter 3). Construction and engineering services are examples of the former; advertising and international law, of the latter. It is illustrative to see the development over time of Japan's international contracts. Rimmer (1987) found that as recently as 1978, the United States accounted for sixty of the top two hundred international construction contractors, and Japan, for ten. By 1985, each accounted for thirty-four of such firms. In Japan, as in South Korea, the large-scale construction programs in the oil-exporting Middle Eastern countries during the 1970s were of central importance in the internationalization of the construction industry. Together, Japan and South Korea account for fifty of the sixty-one firms listed for Asia as a whole. Also of interest here is the locational distribution of Japanese overseas contracting. In 1978, 87% of all contracts were in the Middle East and other Asian countries; no contracts were registered for the United States. By 1985, the total Asian share was down to 47%, and the North American share had reached 24%, most of it in the United States (Rimmer 1988). In 1984, the United States emerged as the main area for locating Japanese factories, offices, and banks. The growth in Japanese construction contracting in the United States is directly linked with this development. In the 1990s the pattern changed again, with Asia accounting for two-thirds of total overseas Japanese contracts (Ocaji 2000:2).

Globally, a ranking of the world's twelve largest banking centers based on cumulated assets and income of the world's top fifty commercial banks and top twenty-five securities firms in 1986 and 1997 shows once again the prominence of New York, Tokyo, and London (see Table 7.5).

TABLE 7.5

Top Twelve Banking Centers Ranked by Income and Assets of the Top 50 Commercial Banks and the Top 25 Securities Firms, 1986 and 1997 (mn USD and number)

Ranking by Income

		1986				1997	
Rank	City	Income (mn USD)	No. of firms	Rank	City	Income (mn USD)	No. of firms
1	Tokyo	6424	22	1	New York, NY	19037	14
2	New York, NY	5673	16	2	London	14363	7
3	London	2934	5	3	Paris	6936	7
4	Paris	1712	6	4	Charlotte, NC	5786	2
5	Osaka	1261	4	5	San Francisco, CA	3493	3
6	Frankfurt	1003	3	6	Amsterdam	3416	2
7	Zurich	826	2	7	Frankfurt	2846	4
8	Amsterdam	739	3	8	Beijing	1917	4
9	Basel	415	1	9	Munich	1396	3
10	Hong Kong	392	1	10	Brussels	1074	1
11	Los Angeles, CA	386	1	11	Amsterdam/Brussels	1003	1
12	Montreal	354	1	12	Utrecht	980	1
				20	Osaka	−3282	2
				21	Tokyo	−18049	15

Ranking by Assets

	1986			1997	
Rank	City	Assets (bn USD)	Rank	City	Assets (bn USD)
1	Tokyo	1801.4	1	Tokyo	3467.5
2	New York, NY	904.8	2	New York, NY	2525.3
3	Paris	659.3	3	Paris	2071.0

Rank	City		Rank	City	
4	Osaka	557.6	4	London	1650.7
5	London	390.3	5	Frankfurt	1435.6
6	Frankfurt	306.8	6	Beijing	1162.0
7	Amsterdam	193.4	7	Osaka	892.4
8	Munich	133.4	8	Amsterdam	713.8
9	Nagoya	123.9	9	Munich	667.6
10	San Francisco, CA	109.2	10	Charlotte, NC	470.3
11	Kobe	107.1	11	Duesseldorf	326.3
12	Hong Kong	90.8	12	San Francisco, CA	288.9

Ranking by Income-Asset Ratio

	1986			1997	
Rank	City	Income-Asset Ratio*	Rank	City	Income-Asset Ratio*
1	London	0.752	1	Toronto	26.628
2	New York, NY	0.627	2	Charlotte, NC	1.230
3	Los Angeles, CA	0.617	3	San Francisco, CA	1.209
4	Toronto	0.591	4	London	0.870
5	Zurich	0.524	5	St. Louis	0.768
6	Montreal	0.520	6	New York, NY	0.754
7	Basel	0.489	7	Brussels	0.529
8	Hong Kong	0.432	8	Amsterdam	0.479
9	Amsterdam	0.382	9	Utrecht	0.469
10	Tokyo	0.357	10	Amsterdam/Brussels	0.368
11	Frankfurt	0.327	11	Paris	0.335
12	Paris	0.260	12	Munich	0.209

Source: Author's calculations based on *Wall Street Journal*, "Global Finance and Investment Annual Special Report," Sept. 29, 1987, Sept. 28, 1998.

Notes: Securities firms and banks ranked by Dow Jones Indexes; most figures based on 1997 fiscal-year results. In millions of USD (unless otherwise noted) at Dec. 31 of respective reported years, exchange rates.

*denotes author's own calculations (income/assets).

By 1986 Tokyo had become the leading banking center in the world in terms of cumulated assets. It is well known that Japanese banks have operated by asset growth criteria rather than profit growth criteria. In France, especially with the nationalization of several major banks, there was a strong concentration of banking assets among a few banks at the top, in contrast, for example, to the United States, where there is relatively less concentration than in most major industrialized countries. Osaka ranked fourth, with U.S. $366.7 billion in assets in 1985 and U.S. $557.6 billion in 1986. Osaka, the major industrial city in Japan and its second-largest stock exchange, ranked fifth in 1986 but 20th in 1997. But it is clearly a very far second behind Tokyo in terms of both cumulated assets and the size of its equity market. Rankings by income for 1986 still have Tokyo at the top, followed by New York and London, and Paris and Osaka. The figures for 1997 show a significant transformation. While Tokyo remains at the top in terms of assets, followed by New York and Paris, it falls to 21st place in terms of income, with a negative income of $18 billion and 15 firms involved, compared to the 22 of 1986. This is clearly the result of the severe banking crisis in Japan. Paris ranks third in terms of income in 1997, followed by Charlotte, N.C., a newcomer to the top rankings, and San Francisco. On the income-asset ratio rankings, factors other than absolute size clearly also make a difference. Thus Toronto, Charlotte, N.C., and San Francisco outranked the top centers on the assets and income rankings.

In 1988, New York, London, and Tokyo accounted for almost half of the largest 100 banks in the world and almost all of the 25 largest securities firms; by 1997 these shares had fallen to 28 and 19, respectively. If we consider assets, capital, and income of the largest 100 banks, the fall in share is far sharper in assets, from 60% to 35% than it is in capital, from 49% to 42%, and income, from 63% to 45%. Among the more noteworthy changes is the almost doubling in the capital of the largest banks in Tokyo over this decade even as their number fell by half, and income was negative, with listed losses of $20 billion—an undercount of actual losses in these banks in an industry whose losses are estimated to have reached 600 billion.[2]

Perhaps the most striking fact in the case of securities firms is the in-

---

[2] Several recent bank mergers, such as the Sumitomo and Sakura Bank merger announced in October 1999, will further raise the capital base of Japan's top banks. The announced merger between Dai-Ichi-Kangyo Bank and Fuji Bank and Industrial Bank of Japan creates an institution that will have over 30% of the market in loans to large Japanese companies, including steelmakers, construction companies, retailers, oil companies, chemicals, cement makers—all highly protected sectors in Japan. With 9.6 trillion yen in cross-held shares, the merged bank also becomes the largest investor in the Japanese stock market—a stake of at least 10% in 103 listed companies.

TABLE 7.6

New York, London, and Tokyo: Share of World's 100 Largest Banks, 1988 and 1997 (mn USD and percent)

				1988			
	No. of Firms	Assets	% of Top 100	Capital	% of Top 100	Income	% of Top 100
Tokyo	30	4,862,509	45.64	484,759	36.51	12,420	28.94
New York	12	933,037	8.76	113,744	8.57	8,942	20.83
London	5	605,019	5.68	55,531	4.18	5,655	13.18
Subtotal	47	6,400,565	60.08	654,034	49.26	27,017	62.95
Total for Top 100	100	10,653,417		1,327,891		42,919	

				1997			
	No. of Firms	Assets	% of Top 100	Capital	% of Top 100	Income	% of Top 100
Tokyo	15	4,569,260	21.32	916,337	31.81	−20,462	n/a[2]
New York	8	1,361,993	6.36	169,022	5.87	13,654	23.09
London	5	1,505,686	7.03	130,587	4.53	12,900	21.81
Subtotal	28	7,436,939	34.70	1,215,946	42.21	24,508	44.90
Total for Top 100	100	21,429,890		2,880,772		59,137	

Source: Author's calculations based on *Wall Street Journal*, "World Business," Sept. 22, 1989; *Wall Street Journal*, Sept. 28, 1998.

Note: Ranked by assets as determined by Dow Jones Global Indexes in association with WorldScope; figures are based on each company's 1997 fiscal-year results, except data on Japanese banks, which are based on fiscal 1998 results. [1]Capital figures were available for 98 out of 100 banks; [2]Due to continuing effects of the East Asian financial crisis, figures are negative and percentages were not calculated.

crease in the absolute value of assets in New York, from $303 billion in 1988 to $1.58 trillion in 1997, only in part a function of the major mergers and acquisitions that took place over the decade. A second inter- esting fact is that notwithstanding the severe recession in the Japanese economy, assets of the top securities firms grew by 70% even as they accounted for less than 12% of all assets among the largest 25 firms worldwide.

Comparing the growth in assets in the top banks in New York with the growth in assets in the top security firms shows us the extent to which New York is a crucial financial services center with a large number of very powerful firms; these firms accounted for almost 80% of capital and earn- ings among the top 25 securities firms in the world. And comparing the growth of assets in the top banks in London with that of its top securities firms shows us the extent to which London is a banking center and has a large number of financial services firms that are not among the largest. Perhaps most striking is that even as the number of top securities firms in these three cities fell from 24 to 19, they continued to account for well over 90% of assets and capital.

TABLE 7.7

New York, London, and Tokyo: Share of World's 25 Largest Security Firms, 1988 and 1997 (mn USD and percent)

	1988				
	No. of Firms	Assets	% of Top 25	Capital	% of Top 25
Tokyo	8	153,587	29.65	40,825	42.91
New York	12	303,479	58.58	47,543	49.98
London	4	57,321	11.07	4,622	4.86
Subtotal	24	514,387	99.30	92,990	97.75
Total for Top 25	25	518,017	100	95,130	100
	1997				
	No. of Firms	Assets	% of Top 25	Capital	% of Top 25
Tokyo	6	236,712	11.86	36,827	14.10
New York	11	1,586,737	79.50	200,615	76.81
London	2	41,396	2.07	9,501	3.64
Subtotal	19	1,864,845	93.44	246,943	94.55
Total for Top 25	25	1,995,782	100	261,180	100

Source: Author's calculations based on Wall Street Journal, "World Business," Sept. 22, 1989; Wall Street Journal, Sept. 28, 1998.

Note: Ranked by capital as determined by Dow Jones Global Indexes; figures based on 1997 fiscal- year results.

TABLE 7.8

United States, United Kingdom, and Japan: Foreign Liabilities and Assets of
Commercial Banks, 1992–1998 (bn USD)

	1992	1995	1998
United States			
Liabilities	247.3	302.2	380.7
Assets	125.4	34.1	242.1
United Kingdom			
Liabilities	475.2	713.1	1122.6
Assets	460.6	686.9	1145.4
Japan[1]			
Liabilities	713.4	734.2	693.6
Assets	625.3	1069.7	943.5

Source: Author's calculations based on IMF, International Financial Statistics, June 1999, pp. 418, 774, 780.

Note: Based on items 21 and 26c, foreign assets and foreign liabilities.

When we compare the figures for deposits from and loans to foreigners through deposit banks, it becomes evident that by far the most pronounced change has occurred in Japan on both counts and in the United States regarding liabilities (see Table 7.9). In the 1980s the U.S. saw a sharp increase in the total value of foreign liabilities, going from $254 billion in 1982 to almost $700 billion by 1989; while strong, the increase was far less pronounced on the assets side. These levels fell sharply in the 1990s. Japan's increase in foreign liabilities and assets were the sharpest, going from $100 billion in 1982 to over $845 billion in 1989, with a similar increase in absolute values on the assets side. In the 1990s, liabilities fell to about $700 billion while assets grew further to almost $1 trillion. London's role as a key international banking center comes to the fore in the high volume of liabilities and assets, each at well over 1.1 trillion by 1998.

Table 7.9 shows the top twenty cities ranked by assets of the 50 largest insurers in the world. One of the striking features is the high value of assets in Japan, at $1.4 trillion compared with $1.6 trillion in the U.S., the latter a far larger economy. Tokyo accounted for $896 billion in assets compared to $544 in New York. London, with $707 billion in assets accounted for over two-thirds of the total value of assets in the U.K. Osaka, with $504 billion and Munich and Paris, each with just over $400 billion, are the other major concentrations of these types of assets. Insurance companies being far less innovative and speculative than financial services, bring to the fore a range of cities that is far broader and diverse

TABLE 7.9
Top 20 Cities Ranked by Cumulated Assets of the 50 Largest Insurers, 1997
(mn USD)

City (listed by country)	Rank	Total Assets
United States		1,609,468
New York, NY	2	543,740
Newark, NJ	7	259,482
Hartford, CT	9	228,275
Boston, MA	13	107,827
Philadelphia, PA	14	106,411
Bloomington, IN	15	103,600
Cleveland, OH	16	96,001
Columbus, OH	19	83,214
Northbrook, IL	20	80,918
Japan		1,400,603
Tokyo	1	895,659
Osaka	4	504,944
United Kingdom		707,370
London	3	527,929
Edinburgh	17	92,888
Norwich	18	86,553
Other Countries		
Munich	5	409,762
Paris	6	407,930
Zurich	8	238,924
Trieste	10	40,742
The Hague	11	134,618
Amsterdam	12	120,849

Source: Author's calculations based on Wall Street Journal "World Business," Sept. 22, 1989; Wall Street Journal, Sep. 28, 1998.

Note: Ranked by assets as determined by Dow Jones Global Indexes: figures based on 1997 fiscal-year results.

than that evident in the rankings for financial services firms and equities management.

In several ways, New York, London, and Tokyo are rather different types of leading business and financial centers. Tokyo has, perhaps, been the most distinct one. This has become even clearer in the 1990s when its influence over the broader Asian region declined, even as its weight as a capital exporter remains enormous.

There are several distinct phases in the geography and composition of

Tokyo's area of transnational control. Tokyo's main area of control in the 1970s and early 1980s was over goods and commercial transactions in South and East Asia (Rimmer and Black 1982), where it was and remains the central power. However, in the 1980s, its links became strongest with the United States, in terms of volume of transactions, joint ventures, and acquisitions and, secondarily, with Western Europe. By the end of the 1980s, Tokyo had begun to strengthen its financial ties and investments in Southeast Asia through its securities houses, and Japan proposed massive investments in Eastern Europe with Tokyo's banks the key players. The economic recession of the 1990s has profoundly altered the pattern of influence of Tokyo over a broader geography. What it represents above all else today in the global economy is a massive concentration of resources, many of which will soon become far more liquid as deregulation proceeds. The period of the 1980s remains the one where Tokyo's active entrance into the world markets was most evident and sharpest.

In the 1980s Tokyo signaled to the world that it was on its way to becoming a major international financial center. But it never quite deregulated the economy along the lines of New York and London and thereby kept foreign firms from attaining the levels of profitability they might have hoped for. In the mid-1990s the Japanese government launched a series of new deregulations but they did not internationalize Tokyo any further. Thus, the number of foreign-owned firms did not change much, going from 1,093 in 1988 to 1,187 in 1996 and 925 in 1999. The numbers of employees in these firms went from 25,066 in 1988 to 32,406 in 1996 and 30,681 in 1999. A breakdown by industrial sector shows clearly that a good share of the foreign firms and about half of the employees were in finance, and that this sector did experience an increase in the 1990s, going from 184 firms and 10,493 employees in 1988 to 241 firms and 18,336 employees in 1999. Most of the losses were in the service sector (TMG 2000).

Leading Currencies in International Transactions

There are advantages in being the key international currency. First, the country does not need to earn foreign exchange to pay for imports. Hence the balance of trade matters less and domestic economic policy can more easily accommodate a negative balance of trade. Secondly, the country is less sensitive to exchange fluctuations because trade and capital transactions are largely denominated in the country's currency. Finally, the country's role as a leading financial international center is facilitated, although this role also varies according to whether there is a high or low level of internationalization in the capital markets. But there are also costs associated with this status of primary currency. Providing the rest of the world with liquidity often entails running a deficit on the current account or long-term capital account. Yet this deficit cannot exceed certain thresholds because this would undermine the role of key currency, a threat not only to the country itself but also to the global economic system. The need to maintain stability and balance in the exchange rate system also means that monetary policy is not free from the constraints associated with trying to keep such stability. Finally, being the key currency in a period of high internationalization in the financial markets means that large holdings can be amassed by foreign entities and hence make domestic monetary control somewhat less effective.

The costs associated with being the key currency require a country to have a strong economy and a strong place in world trade as well as world finance at a time of internationalization of the capital markets. The dollar today is still the key currency, even though other currencies, notably the yen, the German mark, and the Swiss franc, began to gain share in the 1980s, a time when the U.S. was increasingly incapable of maintaining a strong economy given the high budget and trade deficits. The rapid devaluation of the dollar after 1985 was testimony to that. The early 1990s saw the beginning of a strong recovery.

As a currency, the U.S. dollar still plays the major role in the international financial system. But this role has declined. By 1984, the dollar's share was down to 65%, the German mark's share was up to 12%, and the yen's share was up to 5%. In 1985, 61% of the total issues of international bonds were still denominated in U.S. dollars. Even though the dismantling of the Bretton Woods agreement made possible the implementation of a multireserve currency system to replace the dollar standard system, the dollar is still the key international currency. The expectation that other currencies, such as the German mark, would be used more widely in world trade and finance has only partly been met. Now it is expected that the Euro will play a much larger role.

Japan, with its increasingly strong position in world trade and growing participation in the international financial market, emerged as a key second currency in the 1980s. However, Japan's economy is highly sensitive to global forces, such as a decline in foreign demand for its products or an increase in the price of oil. Japan's economy is also highly sensitive to changes in foreign exchange rates and in financial markets. Its leading trading partner in the 1980s, the United States, had also become its leading investment recipient. From 1975 to 1986, the U.S. share of Japanese exports increased from 20% to 36%, and the U.S. share of Japan's foreign

investment increased from 28% to 45%. Most Japanese portfolio investments are in dollar-denominated instruments.

The use of the yen in the international marketplace increased as a result of deregulation in Japan and the implementation of the Euroyen
market. Japan's large current account surplus, the magnitude of available
funds in Japan through domestic savings and private sector earnings, and
the low value of the yen were all factors that helped increase the use of
the yen in the international capital market. In 1985, about $7 billion
worth of issues in yen were made by non-Japanese corporations in Japan;
Japanese banks extended $14 billion of credit in yen to foreign bor-
rowers; and there were $8 billion worth of Euroyen bond issues. In only
five years, the yen had gone from a very minor role to being the second
or third key currency in the world capital market.

In the area of current transactions, the yen's role is still very minor
compared with that of the U.S. dollar and the German mark.

Considering, for instance, the leading currencies in which international
debt securities have been issued it is clear that the dollar leads. (See Table
7.10.) Of the stock of such debt ($4.3 trillion at the end of 1998), al-
most half is in dollars, well over 20% is in euro currencies, and about 12%

TABLE 7.10
Leading Currencies of International Debt Securities Issues, 1993–1996 (bn USD and percent)

	bn USD						% change	Stocks at
	1993	1994	1955	1996	1997	1998	1993–1998	end-1998
US dollar	28.6	66.5	69.0	261.7	332.0	411.1	1337.4%	1,971.9
Yen	29.3	86.0	81.3	85.3	34.6	−29.3	−200.0%	487.5
Euro area currencies	82.6	80.2	84.3	135.8	139.0	220.3	166.7%	1,173.8
Other currencies	48.3	20.9	28.5	54.4	67.8	75.5	56.3%	682.9
Total for listed currencies	188.8	253.6	263.1	537.2	573.4	677.6		

	Percent							
	1993	1994	1995	1996	1997	1998		
US dollar	15.1	26.2	26.2	48.7	57.9	60.7		
Yen	15.5	33.9	30.9	15.9	6.0	na		
Euro area currencies	43.8	31.6	32.0	25.3	24.2	32.5		
Other currencies	25.6	8.2	10.8	10.1	11.8	11.1		

Source: Author's calculations based on the bank for International Settlements, Annual Report 1999, April 1998–
June 1999, p. 8.

is in yen. Just taking the 1998 issues, which reached a record high of $678 billion, the prominence of the dollar is even higher, at almost two-thirds of the total, compared with a share of under one-sixth in 1993, equal to that of the yen at that time. Even as it grew in absolute levels for most of these years, the yen lost share.

The International Property Market

The sharp increases in prices of central urban property we see beginning in the 1980s in cities such as New York, London, and Tokyo capture the new phase in the spatial organization of the economy and the role of cities within it. As the network of financial and business centers expands we see similarly sharp increases in a growing number of cities worldwide. Excess speculative building contributed to amplify the recession of the turn of the decade. But overall much of the price increase of the 1980s is sustained by sharp new growth, with fluctuations in the 1990s in New York and London. There is a whole new set of cities going through sharp price increases of central land as they become incorporated in the global network of financial and business centers. The most notable cases among those listed on Table 7.11 are Dublin, Stockholm, and Madrid. But such increases also happen in cities such as São Paulo, Buenos Aires, and Bombay. Over the 1990s, commercial property prices in many but not all major cities grew significantly. Using the 1994 price in a city as its index, it is clear that prices have grown for many of these cities, stabilized for the older centers, and kept on falling for Tokyo after exorbitant increases for 1980–1991 (see Table 7.11).

The rapid growth in the number of financial firms, services firms, and high-income workers concentrated in major cities has contributed to rapid growth of a high-price real estate market. The concentration of major firms and markets in New York and London, in particular, has raised the importance of locating in these cities and has been a key factor in the development of massive construction projects. The active participation of foreign firms as investors and as buyers and users of real estate in these cities contributed to the formation of an international property market in the 1980s, which expanded as the network of cities grew.

One distinct aspect of this process has been that the price of land in the 1980s in central New York and London appeared to be increasingly unrelated to the conditions of the overall national economy. Furthermore, the bidding for space was confined to specific locations, and did not necessarily spread to all available space in these cities. High, often foreign, bidders were clearly willing to pay an extremely high premium for a central location and had no interest whatsoever in a less central

TABLE 7.11

Nominal and Inflation-adjusted Real Estate Prices, 1995–1998 (index 1994 = 100)

	Nominal Prices				Real Prices			
	1995	1996	1997	1998	1995	1996	1997	1998
New York	100	109	125	150	97	103	115	136
Tokyo[1]	83	72	66	59	83	72	65	58
Frankfurt	97	97	97	105	95	94	92	98
Paris	89	83	88	102	88	80	83	96
Milan	100	91	88	111	95	84	79	98
London	107	112	128	132	103	106	118	117
Toronto[2]	91	84	87	100	89	81	83	94
Madrid	100	118	128	183	95	109	116	162
Amsterdam	109	118	128	156	107	114	121	144
Sydney	102	106	113	118	97	99	105	109
Zurich	99	90	87	84	97	88	84	81
Brussels	100	106	109	109	99	102	104	103
Stockhom	129	137	163	185	126	133	158	179
Copenhagen	107	107	119	124	105	103	111	115
Oslo	108	115	131	119	105	111	123	110
Helsinki	105	107	111	121	104	105	108	116
Dublin	112	134	169	241	109	128	160	222

Source: Bank for International Settlements Annual Report 1999, April 1998–June 1999, p. 10.
Notes: [1]Land prices; [2]Price index for offices in Ontario.

location. This led to a process of "rehabilitation" of what had been considered marginal areas and their reconstruction into "central" areas: the western side of midtown Manhattan and the old docks in London were made into prime office land. Only a few years earlier, these areas had been defined as undesirable, derelict, unworkable parts of these cities. The proposals for massive reconstruction of Times Square and its environs were central to this rehabilitation for corporate office uses. And so was using a stunning array of internationally known architects to make once "derelict" areas into glittering offices. The concentration of high-income workers, including employees of foreign firms, also brought about an expansion in the demand for space and a parallel rehabilitation of developed urban land for new residential uses. This was a process with a multiplicity of minor locations throughout these cities and several radical transformations of whole neighborhoods: the old warehouse district in Manhattan, which became fashionable as Soho, is probably the most accomplished of these transformations, with its concentration of famous and/or wealthy residents, luxury shops, and art galleries, with enough not-so-famous and even poor artists to ensure its "bohemian" aura.

While there were strong spread effects throughout the office and housing markets in these cities, there also were, perhaps less noted, discontinuities. The prices commanded by central locations and by the "right address" for offices or residences were extremely high. And while there was an overall increase throughout the metropolitan regions of these cities, there was considerable disparity between central locations and the rest. The notion of a gradual decline with distance from the center is inadequate to describe the land price gradient. After the crises of the early 1990s we see a resumption of these trends in New York and London; and their inception in other cities. There were and remain locations at the heart of each city close to the center that have been devalued, a long-term process that began with suburbanization in the interwar period in London and in the postwar period in Tokyo and New York. We return to this in greater detail in chapter 9. There is considerable discontinuity in the functioning of the land market. This would also help explain the coexistence of abandoned empty spaces and extreme density, particularly in New York.

The central areas of a growing number of cities have become part of an international property market; and conversely, these central areas account for much of the international property market that has developed since the 1980s. The entry of institutional investors into the financial markets has been a significant fact in the expansion of this market. Institutional investors have sought to internationalize their holdings generally. Corporations that operate internationally have expanded their holdings in a growing number of leading centers.

But it would seem that other conditions had to come together for an international property market to come about. It is the existence of a multiplicity of other markets, and particularly leading markets, that raises the value of land in the leading financial centers. It is the highly international character of these markets and of the bidders that differentiates this property market and differentiates these cities from other major cities with desirable building stock. They become the arena for major architectural projects, with architects from various countries building in all three cities, further enhancing the value, international visibility, and difference of these cities. This, in turn, emerges as a formula for signaling that a city is ready to enter the global system and assume global city functions. There is now a growing research literature documenting the combination of processes it takes (Huybrechts 2001; Ciccolella and Mignaqui 2001; Schiffer 2001; Parnreiter 2001).

One important feature of this new international property market is the extent to which the financial industry is both an owner and a financer of real estate development in city centers. This strengthens the cyclical tendencies in the property market. These dynamics of ownership and occupation can be observed in what is the most concentrated and specialized instance of an international property market, London's City. Structurally, one of the features of the City's property market is the high incidence of financial services firms which are also owners of the buildings they occupy (Lizzieri 1999). This further strengthens the already strong connection between the two sectors, and amplifies the fluctuations both sectors are subject to (Fainstein 2001). In 1997, the financial services sector owned over 27% of real estate in the heart of the City and accounted for 50% of all occupiers. Only the property and construction sector had a higher incidence of ownership of the buildings it occupied, but it represented a very small proportion of all occupiers, thereby weakening the impact of its ownership on the City's property market—the opposite of the financial services (Table 7.12). Ownership by country makes it clear that well over a third of owners are not from the UK, both in absolute numbers and in terms of shares in various sectors (Table 7.13). Thus 52% of the buildings used by financial services are UK owned. Property firms and insurance and pension funds had a higher incidence of UK ownership. Firms from Germany, Japan, and the U.S. were among the major foreign owners.[3]

The highest returns are to be found in the leading international centers. While much attention has gone into the acquisition of New York real estate by Japanese investors, firms from many countries have bought up property in all three cities. They have emerged as transnational places where major architects from the world over will be found building one or more major buildings. New types of transactions have further strengthened and developed this market, notably new types of institutional investment, such as property unit trusts, new forms of finance, such as property leasing, and the emergence of a growing secondary mortgage market handled by investment banks and brokers that trade mortgages (Daly 1987; Feagin 1988; Fainstein 2001). Buildings become commodities, which can be bought, sold, and resold as commodities, in a market that is autonomous from broader conditions in a national economy. The case of Tokyo is somewhat different and remains so notwithstanding new legislation, because of acute concentration in ownership, state regulation, and the common practice of intracorporate property deals.

The traditional strong cyclical trends in the real estate industry were sharply accentuated by the financial speculation in the 1980s, especially

---

[3] The highest incidence of foreign ownership was Japan's share of 65% of buildings occupied by firms in sectors other than those listed in the table; this was followed by the 34% share of U.S. ownership of financial services occupied buildings, and the 15% of property companies owned by Germans.

TABLE 7.12

London's City: Real Estate, Ownership and Occupation by Sector, 1997 (percent)

Owner	Occupier						
	Financial Services	Insurance	Property & Construction	Bus. & Prof. Services	Public & Charitable	Other	TOTAL OWNEL
Financial Services	20.2	2.4	0.2	3.4	0.4	1.0	27.5
Insurance	5.3	1.6	0.3	4.8	0.2	1.6	13.8
Property & Construction	19.2	3.2	0.5	10.4	1.0	3.2	37.7
Bus. & Prof. Services	0.1	0.2	0.0	2.4	0.0	0.3	3.0
Public to Charitable	3.7	0.8	0.2	4.5	2.2	1.2	12.7
Other	1.4	1.1	0.0	1.4	0.0	1.3	5.2
TOTAL OCCUPIERS	49.9	9.4	1.3	26.9	3.8	8.6	100.0

Source: Baum, A. and C. Lizieri, 1999, "Who Owns the City? Office Ownership and Overseas Investment in the City ot London," *Real Estate Finance*, 16(1): 87–100.

in major cities. The English firm Richard Ellis reported that in the mid-1980s, when these financial centers were experiencing sharp expansion, net rents in centrally located offices of prime quality reached £33 per square meter in London's City, £38.75 in midtown Manhattan, £27.17 in downtown Manhattan, and £37.10 in central Tokyo (Ellis 1985). After 1985 prices rose further, with Tokyo's prices jumping to unheard-of heights, notably $210,000 a square yard in late 1989 for top commercial space (see Appendix D for detailed information on 1985, when the steep rise began, to 1987). In 2000, a sq. ft. was $110 in Midtown Manhattan, £58 in London's City, and 41,000 yen in central Tokyo (Ellis 2000).

TABLE 7.13

London's City: Real Estate Ownership by Type and Country, 1997 (percent)

	Insurance & Pension Fund	Property Company	Financial Services	Other Firms	Public & Charitable
UK	85%	70%	52%	12%	100%
Germany	1%	15%	7%	0%	00%
Japan	4%	12%	0%	65%	0%
USA	4%	0%	34%	0%	0%
Other European	0%	0%	3%	0%	0%
Other	7%	3%	4%	23%	0%

Source: Baum, A. and C. Lizieri, 1999, "Who Owns the City? Office Ownership and Overseas Investment in the City of London," Real Estate Finance, 16(1): 67–100.

The major construction projects of the 1980s in these three cities are vast, represent massive investments, and involve a multiplicity of top-level financial, engineering, architectural, and other professional firms. New York's Battery Park City, built on a 92-acre landfill in lower Manhattan, comprises 6 million square feet of commercial space and 14,000 residential units. Part of the complex is the World Financial Center. The Times Square redevelopment project covers a 13-acre area and includes massive office towers, a theater district, and shops. Like Battery Park City, the Times Square development implants a luxury complex in what had been a devalued area of the city.

London has two of the largest urban redevelopment projects in Europe. Canary Wharf, a 71-acre site on the historic Isle of Dogs, within the London docklands, is a vast luxury complex of offices and residences with highly designed public spaces and parks, and about 10 million square feet of commercial space, primarily to meet the needs of London's financial sector. The second major project in London is the redevelopment of the old railroad yards at King's Cross. This is at this point the largest inner-city redevelopment project in the whole of England and Europe. It involves a 125-acre site located on unused railway land on the northern fringes of London's West End. Smaller scale rehabilitations have multiplied in the 1990s.

About forty major projects were launched in Tokyo in the 1980s. Among the largest was the Tokyo Waterfront Development, now renamed Rainbow City, expected to provide residences for 42,000 people and offices for 70,000 when completed in 2016. The project, a city within the city, is located on 442 hectares of reclaimed land (TMG 2001).

Conclusion

There is a growing concentration of foreign service and financial firms in New York, London, and, with ups and downs, Tokyo, handling business on behalf of both host country firms and co-national firms operating in the host country. In this sense we can think of New York, London, and, to some extent, Tokyo, as transnational centers for financial and service activity. While the governments involved are important participants in the approval and legitimacy of these arrangements, it is also the case that the lifting of restrictions on foreign direct investment in the United States, the UK, and increasingly in Japan and the deregulation of the financial markets have created a whole arena of economic activity where governments participate only minimally, and in this sense we can think of these cities as containing transnational economic spaces for the operation of both domestic and foreign firms.

In the 1980s New York, London, and Tokyo became the key locations for a variety of other transnational activities. Illustrative of these are the formation of an international property market and the growing transnationalization of corporate ownership and control. In the 1990s these have assumed characteristics that point to a distinct form of the internationalization of economic activity, one beyond customary types of direct foreign investment and acquisition. This is partly because of the scale of acquisitions and investments and partly because of the growing institutionalization of cross-border transactions.

One might raise the question as to whether these acquisitions are not akin to U.S. investments and acquisitions in Latin America in the 1950s and 1960s. But I would argue that the latter differ from what we are examining here because they took place in a context of marked political inequality, where the United States was clearly dominant and the U.S. government was a central element in economic transactions. The transnationalization of ownership and acquisitions, which is particularly evident in the United States, is a rather different process, one where the states involved are increasingly not participating and where the question of the nationality of capital assumes new meanings—as for example, when Japanese auto makers put twin plants in northern Mexico to make cheap auto parts for their plants in the United States, where those exported to Europe are also produced. In an earlier book (Sassen 1988) I posited that the United States emerged as a sort of international zone for manufacturing in the 1980s. Today New York in particular has become an international zone for the financial transactions and legal transactions that are part of these and other arrangements.

The massive expansion of international financial transactions, the integration of stock markets into a global network, and the growth of international markets for producer services have become part of the economic base of many major cities. But cities such as New York, London, Tokyo, Paris, Frankfurt, or Hong Kong concentrate a disproportionate share of these, transactions and markets. We also see a change in use in these central areas with a growing share of residential and hotel space. They contain the largest concentrations of leading producer services firms and the largest concentrations of a variety of commodity and currency markets. These types of cities handle a disproportionate share of international financial transactions. London handled nearly 20% of the global total in 1998 for cross-border international bank lending and 36% of the global total for over-the-counter derivatives. New York City's stock exchanges today account for 59% of worldwide equity market capitalization; in 1998 the securities industry raised $2.5 trillion USD for national and foreign businesses. The cross-border network of the growing number of global cities constitutes a key component of the organizational structure of the global economy.

Part Three

THE SOCIAL ORDER OF THE GLOBAL CITY

THE NEXT two chapters address the social order associated with this particular form of growth, which, according to standard economic criteria, is very successful, makes use of our most advanced technologies, and utilizes a large proportion of highly educated workers. Conceivably, this core of leading industries in the premier cities of the world economy could have the overall effect of raising the quality of life and the quality of jobs for large segments of both the workforce and the rest of the population in these cities. And, conceivably, the profits and tax revenues these sectors have generated, even if we were to consider only tax revenues based on the prices of developed land, could have made it possible for the governments of these cities to help support those in the population who could not share in this new economic order. Such conditions should further the overall well-being of workers and other people in these global centers of finance and business services. Finally, the expansion of the stratum of highly educated professional and service workers could represent, in principle, the growth of an enlightened type of workforce.

There is, clearly, no simple way of establishing this. There are only indications, such as income and occupational distribution, changes in the prevalence of poverty and incidence of impoverishment, the effects of this type of growth on other sectors of the economy, and the range of jobs sustaining the operation of the corporate and financial service economy, from high-salaried to low-wage occupations and from white-collar to blue-collar services.

The advanced sectors of the economies of these cities are indeed central and of great weight; but they do not account for all firms and jobs in these cities. One question concerns the relationship between advanced and less advanced sectors. Conceivably, growth in leading sectors of a city's economy could (1) be neutral regarding employment and wages in less advanced sectors of the economy; (2) promote growth in the other sectors under existing or enhanced wage and employment levels; (3) promote growth in other sectors but under conditions that represent a deterioration of employment and wage levels; or (4) constrain, block, or reduce growth in other sectors. Precise measures of these various outcomes either are impossible or would demand a whole treatise by themselves. Furthermore, there will tend to be multiple factors contributing to those outcomes; growth sectors may increase or reduce the weight of various factors, but it is unlikely that they would be the sole cause for a particular outcome. An analysis of forward and backward linkages or input-output tables would not overcome these problems or provide a satisfactory measure either. This, then, raises the matter of the validity of an inquiry about the effects of high-growth sectors an the rest of a city's economy and population.

The question, I would argue, can be addressed in a general way and still provide a meaningful answer. Does the success of the postindustrial core tend to reduce poverty and marginality for significant numbers of the population? Is there less poverty and marginality in today's major global centers for finance and services than there was two decades ago, a less "advanced" period of economic development, one where manufacturing still accounted for a third of all jobs and the telecommunications revolution had not quite taken hold in the economy?

The 1990s saw both an accentuation and a weakening of various trends I used to develop my interpretation of the broader socio-spatial configuration in global cities in the first edition of the book. Some of these trends either reversed or did not continue. Most important to my argument is the strengthening of dynamics that fragment urban space and their impact on the possibility of a new spatial order in global cities, the continuing growth of producer services in cities generally and the associated expansion in high-income professional workers in all these cities, the continuing growth of informal economies in global cities, the weight of finance and advanced producer services in the overall earnings distribution of global cities, the impact of global city status on the lower percentile of the earnings distribution, and the ongoing role of immigration.

Large cities have historically been places with significant concentrations of wealth and poverty, long-established households as well as transients, immigrants, and casual laborers. Have these conditions been affected by the transformation in the economic base of global cities? Did the presence of a thriving postindustrial economic core, which generated vast amounts of profit for a large number of firms and large revenues for the governments of these cities, manifest itself in a reduction of the poverty and transiency we expect to find in very large cities? What is the social dynamic whereby people become articulated with this growth? Does this growth circulate and incorporate large numbers of workers and firms, and under what conditions? We know that the growth of manufacturing after World War II had strong multiplier effects on other sectors, thereby promoting overall growth in manufacturing localities. Does today's postindustrial growth have the same effect? In brief, does a thriving postindustrial urban economy reduce the number of poor people, the unemployed, casual laborers, and the working poor? Does it represent social and economic development in the sense of incorporating a growing share of people into reasonably good working conditions?

Eight

Employment and Earnings

THE ADMITTEDLY PROVOCATIVE inquiry set out for Part Three of the book begins, in this chapter, with a straightforward description of the overall economic base of each of these cities. The focus is particularly on the employment and earnings distribution in each city. These are far broader than the particular global city component in each of these cities. The purpose is to understand the changes in these distributions and to infer how the new sectors and occupations fit into the broader city structure. Further, a good part of the change is a function of larger processes of restructuring affecting all three cities and their national economies which may have little to do with globalization directly. This chapter seeks to establish whether the occupational and income distribution of the city's resident work force reflects the existence of a thriving high-profit economic core.

This is very much an analysis of the official data on employment and an analysis anchored in the formal labor market. The next chapter addresses the more difficult question of what the official data may not be counting or activities not encompassed by the formal labor market.

Three Cities, One Tale?

All three cities have experienced changes in their industry and occupational structure over the last two decades. Alongside the growth in the producer services and finance, discussed in chapter 6, there were pronounced losses during the 1970s in overall job levels in New York and London and in manufacturing in all three cities. Both New York and Tokyo had severe fiscal crises in the mid-1970s, which forced their governments to take strict measures, notably cuts in government jobs and services. In London the fiscal crisis assumed the form of a more protracted shrinkage in government jobs and services. Let me illustrate with a few figures, to be developed in greater detail below.

Table 8.1 shows employment levels in New York, London, and Tokyo for 1977, 1985, and 1998; Table 8.2 shows the manufacturing and service shares for those years. The aggregate data for New York from 1970 to 1980 show a decline in the absolute level of employment, from 3.7 million to 3 million; a 35% loss in manufacturing jobs; a 41% loss of

TABLE 8.1

New York, London, and Tokyo: Population and Employment, 1977, 1985, and 1998 (numbers and percent)

	1977	1985	1998
New York			
Population	5,618,000	5,748,000	7,380,906
Employment	3,056,000	3,225,000	3,004,200
Employment as % of pop.	54.4	56.0	40.7
London			
Population	7,012,000	6,767,500	7,122,000
Employment	3,652,600	3,476,000	3,489,000
Employment as % of pop.	52.1	51.4	49.0
Tokyo			
Population	11,663,000	11,828,000	11,794,000
Employment	5,620,000	5,910,000	6,310,000
Employment as % of pop.	48.2	50.0	53.5

Sources: Based on New York State, *Statistical Yearbook*, 1998, 23rd edition; UK Office of National Statistics, Government Actuary's Department, *Focus on London 99*, p. 20; Management and Coordination Agency, Gov't. of Japan, *Japan Statistical Yearbook 1999*.

headquarters' office jobs; a 15% overall decline in office jobs; and the departure of a significant number of corporate headquarters. To this should be added the decay in much of the city's infrastructure and a severe fiscal crisis in 1975–1976.

Employment in London also fell, from 4.3 million in 1961 to 3.5 million in 1985 and in 1998. There was a tenfold increase in unemployment from 40,000 in the mid-1960s to 400,000 in 1985, a figure that would rise if we included unregistered unemployment. Much of this unemployment was due to large cuts in public sector jobs, beginning in the late 1970s. And, as in New York, there has been a significant decline in manufacturing jobs, from 1.4 million in 1961 to 572,000 in 1985, less than a fifth of all jobs; further losses put its share at 9% in 1996.

Employment in Tokyo remained fairly constant in the decade of the 1970s and rose to 5.9 million in 1985 and 6.3 million in 1998. Though absolute losses were on a much smaller scale than in London and New York, the share of manufacturing employment also fell in Tokyo, from 30% in 1970 to 22% in 1985 and 17% in 1998. The actual components of this decline, however, are somewhat different from those in New York and London. Besides the decline of the old traditional manufacturing districts, there was a government-directed dispersal of highly polluting factories, notably chemical plants. Perhaps less known is the fact that

TABLE 8.2

New York, London, and Tokyo: Distribution of Employment in Manufacturing and Service Industries, 1975 to 1998, Various Years (percent of total employment)

New York	1977	1985	1996
Manufacturing	21.9	15.4	9.0
Tertiary Industry	63.7	73.8	80.3
(selected sectors):			
Wholesale/retail	19.4	20.2	19.3
FIRE	15.9	17.3	17.0
Services	28.4	36.3	44.1

London	1977	1985	1996
Manufacturing	22.0	16.0	8.4
Tertiary Industry	73.0	78.5	88.5
(selected sectors):			
Wholesale/retail	13.5	20.5	15.4
FIRE	9.9	18.2	11.7
Services	49.6	39.8	61.4

Tokyo	1975	1985	1998
Manufacturing	25.1	22.0	16.9
Tertiary Industry	54.5	59.8	62.8
(selected sectors):			
Wholesale/retail	27.5	28.4	26.1
FIRE	6.4	6.1	6.7
Services	20.6	25.3	30.0

Sources: U.S. Census Bureau, County Business Patterns, issues for New York, 1977, 1985, and 1996; Greater London Council, Labour Market Report, Spring 1987; id., London Labour Market Review, 1980/1981 (1981); European Union, Regional Trends 1997; UK, Annual Employment Survey, 1996 Office for National Statistics; 1980 Population Census of Japan; Government of Japan, Management and Coordination Agency, Japan Statistical Yearbook, 1986 and 1999.

Note: Percentages do not total 100 because the following industries are excluded: agriculture, forestry, mining, construction, electricity, gas, water, and heat supply, transport and communication, and government.

Tokyo's deficit reached 101 billion yen in the mid-1970s, a record high for the Tokyo Metropolitan Government. In 1979, Tokyo's governor set up a committee to address and work out the financial crisis.[1]

[1] The ratio of current expenses to total revenues had been increasing for many years and had already reached deficit levels in 1975. After the severe deficit of 1978, Tokyo's government set up a commission, whose recommendations led to the implementation of a plan for financial rehabilitation by bringing down expenses to 90% of revenues by the end of 1982. The recommendations were as follows: (1) reductions in staffing ceilings of the Tokyo Metropolitan Government and revision of the wage scale; (2) review of projects of the

It is against this background of fiscal crisis and government job cuts in all three cities in addition to absolute employment declines in New York and London that we need to place the high growth rates in select industries discussed in the preceding chapter. An examination of the overall economic base in these cities shows a pattern of pronounced declines and equally pronounced growth, especially in the case of New York and London and to a lesser extent in Tokyo.

New York

Several major facts dominate the economic history of New York since 1960. First, there was a massive decline in manufacturing, with a loss of over half a million jobs. Second, there was a massive loss of headquarters and hence of office jobs. Third, there was a rapidly deteriorating fiscal situation, culminating in an officially declared crisis in 1975–1976. Fourth, amidst the overall decline in the period after the fiscal crisis, there was rapid growth of finance and producer services, concentrated in Manhattan, beginning in 1977, and accelerating in the early 1980s.

New York's employment was stable at about 3.5 million in 1950 and 1960, increasing to 3.8 million in the late 1960s. After 1969, there was a relentless decline, with overall employment reaching its lowest level in 1977, after the fiscal crisis, at 3 million (including government jobs). Since then two major trends are evident. One is the continuing decline of manufacturing, notwithstanding small increases in particular branches and periods. The other is the rapid growth in the producer services, which accelerated at the turn of the decade and into the 1980s. By 1987 employment stood at 3.6 million, a significant recovery based on producer services growth. But New York's was clearly a transformed economy, with a severely reduced manufacturing sector, a thriving finance and

---

Tokyo Metropolitan Government and promotion of reasonable cost-sharing by the beneficiaries; (3) reasonable sharing of administrative responsibilities and fiscal burden between the Tokyo Metropolitan Government and the wards of other municipalities; and (4) improvement of various taxation and fiscal systems through increase and expansion of taxable sources in large cities such as Tokyo, through the reform of the financial resources allocation adjustment system, and through promotion of the national government's financial assistance to maintain Tokyo's police. The Tokyo Metropolitan Government, like New York's government, concentrated much of its effort on the first, reducing staff by 9,255 employees, in addition to a cut in services, imposition of fees on consumer services, and a reduction or abolition of subsidies. A first reduction in the deficit was reached in 1979, and a surplus by 1981, the first time in twenty years that the Tokyo Metropolitan Government did not have a deficit. Thus, Tokyo's financial rehabilitation was completed a year before the scheduled date of 1982. It went from a 101 billion-yen deficit in 1979 to a 31 billion-yen surplus in real terms in 1981.

producer services complex, and 0.2 million fewer jobs than at its peak in 1969.

Manufacturing accounted for 1 million jobs in 1950, 0.9 million in 1960, 0.8 million in 1970, half a million in 1980, and 387,000 in 1987. Between 1969 and 1987, New York lost half of its manufacturing jobs and more than half of its office jobs in manufacturing headquarters. It also had severe losses in related wholesale and distribution jobs. While New York was never as important a manufacturing center as London was in the United Kingdom, the manufacturing sector was once central to the city's economy. Thus, in their landmark study, Hoover and Vernon (1962) predicted an actual increase from 1956 to 1985 in the absolute number of manufacturing jobs. Instead of the predicted increase of 0.8 million manufacturing jobs for the region, there were losses of 0.6 million in the region and of 0.5 million in the city. New York's was a diversified manufacturing sector, which included important concentrations of electrical engineering and machine goods manufacturing, in addition to the more traditional consumer industries of furniture and apparel. Beyond the city, the broader New York metropolitan region extending into New Jersey contained a vast industrial complex which included chemical and instruments manufacturing and a broad range of factories producing components for military suppliers. New York's harbor and distribution facilities were an important element in the growth of this industrial complex and made it a key location for headquarters.

While it is true that average wages in production in New York were never among the highest in the country because of the absence of such key industries as steel, auto, and aerospace, it is also true that average wages were increasing and reached their highest relative level as recently as 1970—101.2% of the national average hourly wage in production. One indicator of the extent of change in manufacturing is the decline of that wage level, which had fallen to 87.6% of the national average by 1982. (A similar relative decline can be seen in Los Angeles, whose manufacturing sector is radically different from New York's, being dominated by aerospace and electronics; nonetheless, hourly production wages fell from 108% of the national average in 1970 to 100.7% in 1982. As in New York, that wage level would be significantly lower if sweatshops and industrial homework were included.)

The losses in manufacturing were not simply due to closing or departing factories but also due to the departure of manufacturing headquarters, particularly those of the so-called Fortune 500 companies, the largest industrial firms in the country. In 1965 New York had 128 of these headquarters; in 1976 there were 84, and in 1986, 53 (Drennan 1987: 25). In 1917, before there was a Fortune 500 list, data compiled from Moody's Industrials and annual reports indicate that 150 of the 500 larg-

est industrial corporations were headquartered in New York (Conservation of Human Resources Project 1977: 38–40). These losses represent
departures to suburban locations and outside the region, acquisitions by
other corporations, and corporations no longer on the list because of
reclassification or changed size. The change is further underlined by the
fact that there were also 28 gains: mostly companies that moved their
headquarters into New York or were added to the list because of size or
reclassification (Conservation of Human Resources Project 1977: 40). It
is evident that the headquarters of industrial corporations became more
mobile toward the 1970s. Data for the ten largest old metropolitan areas
of the Northeast and North Central states show that together they accounted for 302 of the Fortune 500 headquarters in 1957, a level they
had maintained since 1917 according to the data from Moody's Industrials, when they had 316 such headquarters. But by 1974, seven of the
ten metropolitan areas had losses, leaving a total of 237 headquarters
(Conservation of Human Resources Project 1977: 38).

Some of the reasons that led to the decline in manufacturing in New
York are the same as in London: inadequate amount and kinds of space
at a time of growing needs by industry; the development of an interstate
highway system, which further contributed to the declining relative advantage of a central city location and contributed to the movement of
manufacturing, wholesale trade, trucking, and warehousing outside the
city; the weaknesses in certain branches, which reduced their competitiveness for land and resources with other sectors of the economy. In
addition there are the general factors that affected all old industrial
areas—growing international competition; inadequate investments for
modernization of plants, leading to lower productivity; and the development of technologies that made possible locating production and assembly facilities in low-wage countries or low-wage regions of the United
States. In brief, the combination of factors that led to the large concentration of plants and headquarters in cities such as London and New York
came to lose its relevance and importance in the late 1960s because of
changes in international, political, economic, and technical conditions.

In contrast, services, excluding FIRE, increased from half a million in
1950 to over 1 million in 1987, and FIRE went from 0.3 million to over
half a million—a figure that incorporates sharp losses of insurance jobs
over this period. A more refined analysis of the city's economy shows that
the producer services and finance reached over 1 million jobs in 1987, in
a perfect reversal of the manufacturing trajectory. None of the other major industry groups had such pronounced changes. Thus wholesale and
retail trade declined from 0.7 million to 0.6 million, and transportation
and utilities declined from 0.3 million to 0.2 million. After a fall to
77,000 jobs in 1980, construction, not surprisingly, regained much of its

loss, almost reaching its 1950 level of 0.12 million jobs by 1987. Government jobs overall increased from 0.37 million in 1950 to 0.6 million in 1987.

In the years following the 1975–1976 fiscal crisis, when overall employment continued to decline, several industries had pronounced growth rates. The overall 17% increase in white-collar industries from 1977 to 1980 was even higher in some industries, with rates of over 50% (computer services) and others hovering around 20% to 30% (management consulting and public relations, engineering and architecture, accounting, protective services, securities, etc.) (U.S. Department of Labor, Bureau of Labor Statistics various years). In this period employment increased by 7.7% in finance, insurance, and real estate, by 9.4% in communications and media, and by 24.7% in business services. Also, employment expanded by 8.9% in educational services and research institutions, by 7.4% in entertainment, culture, and tourism, and by 3.9% in social services (U.S. Department of Labor, Bureau of Labor Statistics, various years). (See Table 8.3 for related data.)

A comparison of the industry distribution in the private sector (U.S. Department of Commerce, Bureau of the Census, 1984–1996) for Manhattan, New York, and the United States as a whole (see Table 8.4) shows that the single sharpest difference is in the FIRE sector. Both in the 1980s and in the 1990s, 23% of all workers in Manhattan are employed in FIRE; this share falls to 17% for the city as a whole and to 7%

TABLE 8.3
Manhattan: Employment Change by Industry, 1977–1997 (percent)

	1977–1985 (% change)	1993–1997 (% change)
Legal services	62	−2
Business services	42	17
Banking	23	−13
Retail	17	16
Wholesale	14	−1
Real estate	6	6
Transportation	−20	−4
Manufacturing	−22	−18
Construction	−30	5
Insurance	−2	10

Source: Based on U.S. Census Bureau, *County Business Patterns*, issues for New York Metropolitan Area, 1977, 1985, 1993, and 1997.

Notes: Banking includes depository and nondepository institutions; Insurance includes carriers and agents.

TABLE 8.4
United States, New York, and Manhattan: Employment Distribution by Industry, 1984 and 1996 (percent)

	United States		New York		Manhattan	
	1984	1996	1984	1996	1984	1996
Construction	5.3	5.1	3.7	2.8	2.0	1.3
Manufacturing	24.8	18.2	16.4	9.0	14.6	8.1
Transport[1]	6.0	5.9	8.1	7.7	6.9	6.2
Wholesale	6.7	6.5	7.6	6.7	8.0	6.8
Retail	20.6	21.0	12.5	22.3	9.9	10.8
FIRE	7.4	7.0	17.4	17.0	23.6	23.2
Total Services	26.0	35.0	33.4	44.1	33.9	43.5
Business Services	4.9	7.1	8.9	8.3	11.6	10.8
Legal Services	0.8	0.9	1.9	2.3	2.6	3.4
Personal Services	1.3	1.3	1.0	0.9	0.7	0.7
Health Services	7.9	10.8	8.1	13.9	4.9	8.2
Educational Services	1.9	2.1	3.2	4.2	3.1	4.3
Other Services[2]	9.2	12.9	10.3	14.4	11.0	16.2

Source: U.S. Census Bureau, County Business Patterns, issues for the United States and New York, 1984 and 1996.

Note: Percentages do not total 100 because other categories are not listed. Such categories include: agricultural, forestry, fisheries, mining, and nonclassifiable establishments; [1]Includes communication and utilities; [2]Other services include: hotels and other lodging, auto repair and garages, social services, misc. repair services, motion pictures, amusement and recreation services, museums, botanical and zoological gardens, and miscellaneous services; New York includes the 5 boroughs: NYC/Manhattan, King's, Queens, Bronx, and Richmond.

for the United States as a whole. A second set of differences between the occupational distribution for the city and that for the country as a whole is in manufacturing and in retail. In 1984 24.8% of all workers in the United States were in manufacturing, compared to 16.4% for New York and 14.6% for Manhattan, with a good number of these in the offices of manufacturing firms. By 1996 these shares had fallen to 18%, 9%, and 8%, respectively. In an interesting reversal also evident in other major cities, a larger share of workers in Manhattan were in apparel than in the country as a whole. Only 10.8% of workers in Manhattan were in retail in 1996, compared with over 20% in each New York and the country as a whole. Clearly, this does not point to inadequate retail facilities in Manhattan, but rather to the marked overrepresentation of other sectors, such as FIRE. Also of interest to this inquiry is the fact that while less than 1% of workers in the United States were in legal services, the share was more than three times higher in Manhattan; business services showed a shrinking differential, accounting for 7% of all workers in the United

States in 1996 compared with about 11% in Manhattan. The group of "Other Services" (a mix of sectors such as hotels, museums, and recreation services) raised its share in Manhattan from 11% in 1984 to 16% in 1996.

While New York is according to many criteria a single labor market, there are pronounced differences among the various boroughs and especially between Manhattan and the other four boroughs. One could argue that for certain industries we are dealing with separate markets or, certainly, separate submarkets. The distribution of economic activity by borough points to a number of trends. First, there is a disproportionate concentration (60%) of all activities in Manhattan. This disproportion becomes even more accentuated when we consider certain types of activities. Most pronounced is the greater concentration of FIRE and business services in Manhattan, totaling 35% of all the borough's workers compared with about 10% in each of the other boroughs. A second difference is the much larger share of retail activity in the four outer boroughs, where it reached about 17% of employment in 1985, while in Manhattan it was 10%. These trends together with the decline in offices and manufacturing jobs point to a recomposition in the city's economy. In 1950, manufacturing supplied almost one job in three while services supplied one in seven. By 1980, these figures were reversed. There was a parallel loss of office jobs, particularly headquarters' office jobs, which declined by 41% between 1969 (highest employment) and 1980 (Ehrenhalt 1981: 46). The producer services also had a decline in employment of 9.4% from 1970 to 1977. But over the ensuing five years, from 1977 to 1982, they grew by 19%. By 1996, over a third of New York employment was in these industries, while the share of manufacturing had been further reduced from 22% in 1977 to 9% in 1996.

As of 1998, NYC has had the largest absolute employment growth among all the sections of the broader NY-NJ region, accounting for nearly half of the region's job growth. This reverses the pattern of the 1970s and 1980s, when the broader NY-NJ region had much higher growth than NYC. The city has contributed nearly half the region's new services jobs growth since 1992. In a second reversal of past trends, all three components of the region grew at a similar rate from 1991 to 1998 while for much of the preceding two decades NYC had lagged behind the suburban areas.

London

Three facts dominate London's economic history since 1960: first, the loss of 800,000 manufacturing jobs by 1985 in a city that was once an important center for light manufacturing; second, a rather stagnant economy for about twenty years, with steady losses in employment and population; and third, a new phase of rapid growth based on finance and producer services, beginning in 1984, with employment in these industries overtaking that in manufacturing in 1985. That was the year when net employment gains replaced net losses in London, after twenty-five years of losses. The equivalent event took place in New York in 1984. In only fifteen years, there had been a pronounced shift from manufacturing to services. In 1971, 27% of all London jobs were in manufacturing, and 68.6% were in services. By 1986, these shares had changed to 15% and 80%, respectively. In a period of two decades, there had been a pronounced transformation in the employment distribution of London, pointing to a restructuring of the economic base.

London's employment fell from 4.3 million in 1961 to 3.9 million in 1971 and to 3 million in 1998 (U.K. Office of Population and Surveys 1963, 1983; UK Office of National Statistics 1999).[2] It fell to its lowest level of the postwar period in 1983 at 3.4 million, and began to increase again after 1985 (Department of Employment estimates). As in New York, this fall in employment was dominated by the loss of manufacturing jobs, which fell from 1.4 million in 1961 to 680,000 in 1981 and about half a million in 1985. A further loss of 100,000 jobs occurred from 1985 to 1988. This parallels trends in the rest of the country, where manufacturing has declined from 10.7 million in 1961, to 5.8 million in 1982 and 5.3 million in 1985. But it is a relatively larger loss. In the two decades after World War II, about a third of London's population was in manufacturing. In their detailed study of the London economy, Buck, Gordon, and Young (1986) established that in the postwar decades the city's manufacturing sector was, with a few exceptions, structurally sound, paying relatively good wages overall, with considerable inputs of skilled and craft work, and relatively high levels of specialization. London accounted for significant output shares in several industries.

As with any large manufacturing sector, the reasons for the decline of London's are complex. There are general reasons shared by most old industrial countries in the West: growing international competition, declining productivity as a result of insufficient investment in modernizing plants, and, in some cases and at certain times, foreign exchange rates that did not favor manufacturing exports. In addition, there are specific conditions (primarily inadequate space and high land prices) in large, older cities, such as London and New York and to some extent Tokyo, that toward the late 1960s began to exercise constraints on many indus-

[2] The figures for 1961 are adjusted to be comparable with a Census of Employment basis. See Buck, Gordon, and Young (1986).

tries. Fothergill and Gudgin (1982) argue that the decline of manufacturing in London was in part related to the constraints on expansion at a time of greater needs for large-scale spaces in industrial production, an argument also advanced by analysts of New York's manufacturing decline. This would seem to explain partly the finding of Buck, Gordon, and Young (1986) that job losses in London were negatively related to national changes in manufacturing. After controlling for changes expected on the basis of the national rate of change, they found that London lost relatively more jobs in nonrecession periods and relatively fewer during national recessions. This suggests that the losses in London were in part a result of constraints on growth specific to London. It is worth noting that much of London's manufacturing loss was not due to shifts of jobs out of London; it is estimated that about 200,000 job losses can be attributed to factory closures (Greater London Council 1986: 46–47) and that first-time locations outside of London, notably in the Southeast region, have also contributed to the manufacturing loss in London. In the same line of analysis, Buck, Gordon, and Young (1986) found that some of the weaker manufacturing branches in London were increasingly unable to compete under the conditions of higher prices for inputs in London, again a trend parallel to the case of several industries in New York. London, like New York, experienced a rapid loss of low-wage manufacturing jobs in the 1960s and 1970s, especially in the apparel and furniture branches. My fieldwork in London points to a very minor expansion in some of these industries in London in the last few years, notably clothing and leather accessories. Though on a much smaller and restricted scale, it parallels New York. In the late 1970s, New York began to experience a renewed expansion in some of these branches, though under different conditions from the pre-1970 period.

Finally, as in New York, London today has several fairly strong manufacturing industries notwithstanding continuing overall losses. They are high-wage, high value-added industries, such as printing (tied to London's leading industries: finance and producer services), the high-tech sector based in the M4 corridor, and the communications industries. Average wages for full-time manual workers in the larger London area are higher than the national average.

A comparison of employment changes in various industries for London and Britain shows how deep the losses were for the country as a whole since the late 1970s. From 1978 to 1985 there was an absolute decline in total employment of 5% in Britain and 4% in London. The country as a whole had a 24% decline in manufacturing jobs. London lost 10% of public service jobs compared with 3% for Britain as a whole. In addition to manufacturing and public services, other major sectors lost jobs in London during the 1970s: construction, utilities, transport and communications, and the distributive trades. From 1973 to 1983 these sectors lost 218,000 jobs. As in New York, public sector services employment fell during the 1970s after decades of growth. Public services had continued to grow up to 1976 and since then have been cut back. Local authority and central government employment both suffered severe cuts. Construction, on the other hand, declined by 21% in London, compared with 24% for Britain.

The total of service jobs has remained more or less constant at 2.6 million jobs in London and has increased in the rest of Britain from 13.1 million to 13.6 million jobs. Behind constant levels for service jobs in London, there are declines in some industries, notably transport and communications, and increases in banking, insurance, and finance jobs. From 1987 to 1997 there were decreases in some of these once high-growth sectors: thus finance fell by 5% and so did air transport and other transport in Greater London. The highest growth in this decade was in other business services at 38%; information technology services, research and development, and telecommunications also had significant growth at 14%. However, the growth rates for these two groups of industries were even higher in the Southeast at 53% and 39%, respectively, and in the country at 46% and 34%, respectively (Gordon 1999).

A more detailed analysis of trends in recent years shows extremely pronounced changes in certain industries during the 1980s (see Table 8.5). From 1981 to 1987, business services increased by 30%, personal services by 20%, and banking and finance by 13%. In contrast, several key manu-

TABLE 8.5
London: Employment Changes by Industry 1981–1987; 1991–1999 (percent)

	1981–1987 (% change)	1991–1999 (% change)
Business services	30	95
Personal services	20	26
Banking and finance	13	5
Insurance	0	e
Wholesale	−8	57
Construction	−21	−24
Electrical engineering	−22	n/a
Footwear and clothing	−30	n/a
Mechanical engineering and vehicles	−37	n/a

Source: Author's calculations based on Greater London Council: Labour Market Report, Spring 1987; London Labour Market Review, 1980/81 (1981); Employment Gazette, Feb. 1991, Table 1.4. UK Office for National Statistics, Labour Market Trends, Feb. 2000, T. B.16.

Notes: Some information was not available due to the change in reporting structure from 1981 to 1999; ᵉInsurance is included in banking and finance.

TABLE 8.6

United Kingdom, London, and City of London: Employment Distribution by Industry, 1981–1999 (percent)

	United Kingdom		London		City of London[1]	
	1981	1999	1981	1999	1981	1999
Agriculture, forestry, fishing	2.2	1.3	0.0	0.1	0.0	0.0
Energy and water supply	3.1	0.6	1.6	0.2	0.9	0.0
Manufacturing	27.0	16.7	19.2	7.4	10.9	2.2
Construction	7.0	4.5	4.5	2.9	0.8	0.9
All Services	60.5	76.4	74.6	89.3	87.3	96.6
of which (detailed listing of Services):						
Wholesale and retail	19.2	16.9	19.2	15.9	8.4	3.2
Transport and communications	6.5	6.0	10.4	8.5	—	4.4
Banking, insurance, finance, and real estate[2]	7.8	18.7	15.9	32.2	71.7	82.7
Financial intermediation	—	4.2	—	8.7	—	53.3
Business services	—	14.6	—	23.5	—	25.0
Other services[3]	27.0	0.7	29.1	6.6	7.2	10.8

Source: UK National Statistics Office, *Labour Market Trends 2000*.

Notes: [1]Data for the City of London are from 1995, the latest available year; [2]For 1981 Business Services and Real Estate are not disaggregated and are included in banking, insurance, finance, and real estate; [3]Other services includes (partial list, see source for complete list: activities of professional organizations, trade unions; news agency activities; fair and amusement parks, radio and televison; artistic and literary creation, interpretation.

facturing industries had severe declines.[3] These trends continued in 1991–1999, but at sharply higher rates for business services and wholesale trade (after losses in the earlier period) and sharply lower rates for banking and finance.

When we compare the employment distribution by industry for the United Kingdom, London, and the City of London, the most pronounced difference is in the category of banking, insurance, and finance, with, respectively, 7.8%, 15.9%, and 71.7% of all workers in 1981 and 18.7%, 32% and 82.7% in 1999 (see Table 8.6). Correspondingly, the United Kingdom had a high share of all its workers in manufacturing. Another pronounced difference emerges in retail and wholesale, with about 16% of all jobs in both the United Kingdom and London but only 3.2% in the City. Finally, a very sharp differential is evident in the other services category, with over 27% of all jobs in the United Kingdom in 1981 and down to 0.7% in 1999, but rising to 10.8% in the City. In the

[3] See Massey (1984) for an examination of the complex context in which these figures need to be placed.

case of retail, wholesale, and other services key factors shaping these levels are the disproportionate concentration of finance and related jobs in the City, which would contribute to bringing down the share of other sectors, and the relative absence of such services as health and education, which tend to account for significant shares of jobs nationally.

Spatial dispersion has also affected service industries, and only partly as a result of technical developments. London's share of the nation's insurance jobs and its share of banking fell quite sharply in the 1970s and early 1980s. Except for top-level functions, which have tended to remain in London, large components of headquarter offices have relocated (U.K. Department of Employment 1986, 1987a; Greater London Council 1986), reminiscent of what happened in New York.

There are several reasons for these changes, some specific to London and others generally found in major urban centers. Transformations in the organization of work, especially the growth of mass production and scale economies, contributed to the suburbanization of part of the production process. Some of the conditions are familiar: the search for cheaper and better housing, cheaper land for firms and fewer land use regulations, lower wages and less unionized labor. The loss of population and of jobs was a development that stretched with fluctuations over a period of time and contained a number of distinct processes. During the 1970s, the Southeast region emerged as a new area for growth and had population and job increases (excluding London) while London had losses. From 1971 to 1981, the Southeast gained 346,000 jobs and London lost 414,000 jobs. Though the Southeast lost jobs in many manufacturing branches, it gained manufacturing jobs in electrical engineering and the brick industry. This region also gained jobs in most of the other economic sectors, often at higher growth rates than in London's growth sectors (U.K. Department of Employment 1986, 1987b).

From 1987 to 1997 there are some sharp differences in the pattern of employment change in the Southeast, Greater London, and Britain. In some sectors the Southeast region was closer to the national norm than to London; for instance, retail gained, respectively, 16% in the Southeast and 18% in the country compared to 5% in Greater London. This was also the case of air transport, finance, professional services, and other business services. Overall the Southeast gained 5% employment as did Britain, while Greater London lost 1%. (See Gordon 1999.)

Tokyo

A crucial fact shaping Tokyo's economic history over the last three decades is the strong role played by the government in facilitating and promoting the urban restructuring of the 1980s (Saito 1999; Kamo and Sasaki 1998). In terms of Tokyo's evolution into a global city, the key policy switch was from a strategy of multi-polar, autonomous and sustainable development that would promote dispersal of activities out of Tokyo (Third Comprehensive Development Plan) to one of selective concentration of global economic functions such as finance, information services, and media in Tokyo (Fourth Plan) (Saito 1999).

After the massive employment and population growth of the postwar decades, Tokyo's job levels remained rather constant from 1970 onward. Manufacturing losses were far less pronounced than in New York and London, and the FIRE sector did not quite have the sharp growth it did in those two cities. It is not easy to establish to what extent this is a function of timing and to what extent of a different economic base. The rapid growth of finance and producer services began in the late 1970s in New York and in the early 1980s in London. Perhaps in Tokyo this process only began after the mid-1980s and has many years to go before it is the overwhelming presence that it is now in London and New York.

Yet by the mid-1980s a profound transformation had taken place in Tokyo, not captured in aggregate employment figures. The dismantling and disintegration of many old industrial districts in central areas of the city occurred along with the rapid construction of high-rise buildings in the central business district. But these two distinct processes, which in New York and London dominate economic transformation, in the case of Tokyo are embedded in a massive economic base serving a vast region with services, trade, and clerical work. Tokyo's labor force of 5.9 million is far larger than those of London and New York. And the region for which Tokyo is the central hub contains 17 million people. While this compares with the 18 million of the New York metropolitan area or the 12 million of London's metropolitan area, the difference is the centrality of Tokyo to the whole region, evidenced by the fact that it receives 2.4 million commuters a day, most of whom are workers. The profound transformation evident in the central areas of the city is lost in the numbers describing the broader economic base.[4]

Over a period of thirty years, Tokyo's labor force more than doubled,

[4] Tokyo's population growth rate began to decline in the mid-1960s. By then, migration out of Tokyo had begun to surpass in-migration. Much of the population loss was due to residential suburbanization rather than actual departure from the region; consequently, the number of commuters increased. But there was also an actual decline in the number of jobs during the 1970s because of the fiscal crisis and overall economic decline in Tokyo. After 1967, when net migration began to be negative as a result of suburbanization, there was a continuing influx of people from outside the metropolitan region. Suburbanization of Tokyo's population and in-migration from outside the region have contributed to a strong increase in the metropolitan population, from a total of 7.4 million in 1955, or 8.1% of the national population, to 18 million, or 15% of the national population, in the early 1980s.

reaching 5.6 million in 1950. It then fell to 4.5 million in 1960, rose to 5.6 million in 1970, and, after a decline in the mid-seventies, rose to 5.9 million in 1985 and 6.3 million in 1998. There were significant transformations in the occupational and industrial distribution. Of Tokyo's 5.6 million workers in 1970, 30.2% were in manufacturing, 26.3% were in wholesale and retail industries, 5.4% were in finance, insurance, and real estate industries, and 21.3% were in service industries. By 1980 these shares had changed most markedly in manufacturing, falling to 23.5%, and in services narrowly defined, climbing to 22.7%. Most other sectors showed little growth, partly an indication of Tokyo's fiscal crisis. By 1985, we see the consolidation of the finance and producer services complex (Tokyo Metropolitan Government 1987a).

The high growth years between 1985 and 1990 saw a sharp increase of 720,000 in the number of workers; in contrast, from 1990 to 1995 the number of workers rose by only 130,000. Tokyo's occupational structure showed a consistent increase from 1975 to 1995 of professionals, both in actual numbers and in labor force share (Machimura 1998), though at a declining growth rate. The highest growth rate of professionals was at 55% from 1975 to 1985, after which it fell to 17.5% from 1985 to 1990, and to 8% from 1990 to 1995, when managerial and services jobs saw rapid increases. Manual labor saw the sharpest decline in numbers from 1975 to 1995, largely due to their decline in the manufacturing sector.

Behind the minor changes in aggregate figures for manufacturing lies a significant recomposition of the sector. On the one hand, there is the disintegration of the old manufacturing districts alluded to above, as well as the government-directed relocation of many of the large factories in the chemical and steel complex located on the south of Tokyo, a process that began in the 1960s. On the other hand, two types of growth trends have emerged over the last decade in manufacturing. There has been the resurgence of craft-based, small-batch factories in the old industrial districts and other parts of central Tokyo, especially in industries linked to fashion and designer markets, from apparel to furniture. The second type of growth consists of specialized, high-tech industries. Many of these firms used to be subcontractors for a particular company: they have now become more autonomous and sell in a highly specialized market where large enterprises buy components and research and development they cannot provide in-house. There are also firms, mostly in electronics-related industries, that develop new products for what are basically old lines of production. The core of Tokyo's high-tech manufacturing is in the development of new products and technology for simple mass production lines. It is an important center for product development and testing. Many of these products are eventually mass produced, but increasingly

Tokyo factories are also accepting contracts for small batches of highly customized production. Let me elaborate on these aspects.

The overall decline of manufacturing is in part due to the reduction in heavy industry and chemical factories. These sectors reached their highest level of growth in the 1950s. During this period, large-scale chemical factories developed along Tokyo Bay, becoming a crucial element in the economic base of the area. Since then the Tokyo government has restricted and basically made it impossible for this type of factory to be built. In the 1950s the Japanese government sought to restrict and redirect industrial development in Tokyo and Osaka through the Promotion of Replacement of Industry Act of 1952 and the Restriction of Industry and Others Act of 1959.

Before World War II the main location of factories was in the lowlands of the eastern part of Tokyo, the old shitamachi district, since its origins a working-class district. These are areas containing small factories and workshops as well as workers' residences, often combined in two- to four-story buildings. At the time, this area lay outside Tokyo's central business district and hence meant cheaper and more available land. The area was well served through rivers and canals. The southwest area had similar characteristics and offered easy access to sea transport on Tokyo Bay, close to the ports of Tokyo and Yokohama. It became the site of the massive new industrial complex that eventually made Kawasaki, an area that lies between Tokyo and Yokohama, the largest industrial complex in Japan. After World War II new factories and industrial districts were developed in the eastern and northern region of the capital region, outside Tokyo proper. Relocation of factories to the less populated areas on the west, in the mostly undeveloped Tama district, had already begun before World War II, but most of the growth is recent.[5] Some of this relocating led to the formation of new industrial suburbs.

Although manufacturing reached its peak in Tokyo in 1961 and has since declined, to 17% of all jobs in 1998, the larger Tokyo region, not unlike the Los Angeles area in the United States, contains a massive industrial complex. As cost pressures on manufacturing grow sharply with the urban restructuring of the 1980s, land use increasingly shifts to high-level services (Kamo and Sasaki 1998). The whole Kanto industrial area dominated by Tokyo had well over 5 million manufacturing workers in the 1980s, a third of the nation's total, and 36.2% of all factories in

---

[5] Among the industrial cities in the Tama district are Musashimurayama, Inagi, Akishima, Ome, and Hinto. The Tama district also contains predominantly white-collar cities, such as Tama and Kyose, and those lining what is the busiest commuter rail line in suburban Tokyo, Kunatachi, Koganei, Kokubunji, and Musachino.

Japan.[6] It contains advanced high-technology industries, and is well connected to key areas of the country. About half of the industries in Tokyo are in metal processing and machine goods. The southern area of Tokyo and the Tama district area along the Tama river contain a large share of Japan's most important enterprises. Most factories in the southern part of Tokyo are small or medium-size because of government restrictions. But most of the small and medium-sized factories use advanced technologies of production. Three types of industries are to be found among the small and medium-sized enterprises in the area: (1) specialized high-tech processing industries; (2) old-style processing industries that are not incorporating new technologies or are doing so only minimally; and (3) mostly electronics-related industries that are developing new products for older industries.[7]

According to Murata (1980, 1988), Tokyo has a distinct role as a center for innovation and new product development. Tokyo's manufacturing industries faced two problems. First, the massive concentration of economic and political functions in addition to the management of large manufacturing enterprises created immense strains on land use and prices. Murata (1988) posited that Japan would have to strengthen an alternative center for its manufacturing industries, with Osaka, once the main manufacturing center in the country, a leading candidate for development of the support infrastructure that would be required. Second, the growing expansion of high-rise residential and office buildings in the old industrial districts of the inner city, which still house many factories, is creating growing strains between these two very different land uses and the different sectors of the population involved. High land prices and densities,[8] along with growing numbers of high bidders, put constraints on manufacturing. The productivity of industrial land use is far lower than that of commercial uses; however, Tokyo's industrial land is twice as productive as Osaka's and seven times more productive than that of many smaller areas. Yet, as in New York and London, manufacturing industries cannot compete with other land uses.

Against this background, it is interesting to note the recent growth of printing and publishing associated with the growth of finance and pro-

---

[6] The Kanto area, dominated by Tokyo, contains one-third of Japan's professional and technical workers, managers and officials, and clerical workers. The corresponding figures for the Kansai area, dominated by Osaka, range from 15% to 23%. It is interesting to note that the Kanto area has a significantly larger concentration of production workers than does the Kansai area: 28%, compared to Kansai's 14.5%.

[7] Tokyo's electronics industry accounts for an overall small share of Japan's total electronics production: 30% of the country's computer manufacturing, 13% of its integrated circuits manufacturing, and 10% of its robotics industry.

[8] Average density in Tokyo is 14,000 people per square kilometer, compared with 9,000 for New York.

ducer services and the recent growth of the apparel industry linked to fashion and associated with the existence of a critical mass of high-income, mostly rather young workers with distinct consumption patterns as well as a growing export market for Japanese designers. In the 1970s printing and publishing, textiles, and apparel declined (Ide and Takeuchi 1980). Textiles and some components of printing and publishing were moved offshore. Apparel was moved to low-wage areas in Japan and offshore. The rapid growth over the last few years in the printing and publishing industry parallels developments in New York and London. I will elaborate briefly on the apparel industry because the evidence is not generally available given the recency of this development.

Unpublished data of the Tokyo Metropolitan Government show the distribution for apparel and accessories by industry branch and describe the spatial organization of the industry. One particular area in Tokyo (Sumida) is the key location for development, design, and testing. These are mostly large and medium-sized firms and are in some ways the equivalent of the so-called "manufacturers" in New York—large firms that "produce" label clothing but increasingly subcontract production to small firms. Harajuku and Aoyama are the information and design centers of the industry, also locations with large concentrations of fashionable boutiques and fashion shows. This part of the industry consists of a range of firm sizes, from large to small. Wholesale activity is concentrated in Nihonbashi. These are all very central areas of the city. The large firms now have offshore production, especially in the newly industrializing countries (NICs) and in Oceania. Smaller firms tend to have production facilities in Tokyo and in the less developed areas in Japan, such as Hokaido, where apparel production has grown sharply. A broad range of fashion-linked apparel and accessories, however, are produced in Tokyo proper. Unpublished data show clearly that the largest single concentration of factories is in eastern and northern Tokyo, areas that contain many of the traditional manufacturing districts. Eastern Tokyo alone (Katsushika, Edogawa, Sumida, Kouto, Adachi) contains over 8,000 firms, comprising manufacturers of coats, knit goods, ornaments, bags and luggage, and decorative accessories and other linked industries. Farther to the north in Tokyo are another 4,000 factories in the industrial wards of Taito and Arakawa. Several wards in the west and south of Tokyo also have concentrations of firms in these industries. In brief, as in New York and London, fashion-linked apparel manufacturing grew in the 1980s at the heart of the postindustrial core in these cities.

Overall the category of producer services increased by 71% in Tokyo from 1977 to 1985 (Japan Ministry of Labor 1986a). It reached extremely high growth rates for certain industries (see Table 8.8), notably increases of 134% in information, research and development, and adver-

TABLE 8.7

Japan: Employment Distribution, 1975–1995 (in thousands and percent)

	1975		1985		1995	
	N ('000s)	National	N ('000s)	National	N ('000s)	Nationa
Agriculture and Forestry	7,354	13.9	5,418	9.3	3,512	5.5
All non-agriculture total	45,619	86.1	52,695	90.7	59,889	93.4
Mining	132	0.2	95	0.2	61	0.1
Construction	4,729	8.9	5,300	9.1	6,631	10.3
Manufacturing	13,245	25.0	13,811	23.8	13,556	21.1
Energy, transport, and communication[1]	3,686	7.0	3,870	6.7	4,254	6.6
Wholesale and retail trade[2]	11,372	21.5	13,453	23.1	14,618	22.8
Finance and insurance	1,383	2.6	1,742	3.0	1,975	3.1
Real estate	372	0.7	485	0.8	707	1.1
Services	8,741	16.5	11,924	20.5	15,932	24.8
Government	1,959	3.7	2,015	3.5	2,155	3.4
All industries	52,973	100.0	58,113	100.0	64,142	98.8

Source: Government of Japan, Management and Coordination Agency, *Japan Statistical Yearbook*, 1986 an
1999 eds.

Notes: [1]Includes electricity, gas, heat supply, and water; [2]Includes eating and drinking places; Percent columns d
not always equal 100.0 due to rounding.

tising; 124% in real estate; 30.7% in legal services; 43.1% in accounting; over 93% in other corporate services; and over 99% in other professional services. From 1986 to 1996 FIRE grew by over 25%.

The extent to which Tokyo is a service center can be inferred from the fact that this sector accounts for over 60% of all employed people in Tokyo in the late 1990s. The percentage of workers in Tokyo in clerical, administrative, technical, retail, and services is significantly higher than in the nation as a whole, with a tendency toward further increase (Tokyo Metropolitan Government 1987b, 1999; Japan Economic Planning Agency 1988). The industry distribution of the national labor force (see Table 8.7) shows that of the total of 58 million workers in 1985, about one-quarter each were in manufacturing and in wholesale and retail, with only 3.8% in FIRE. The largest differences between Tokyo and the country are in agriculture, in wholesale and retail, in FIRE, and in services. These differences become more pronounced when we compare Tokyo's central business district with the country as a whole (see Table 8.8).

In 1997, almost 32% of jobs in the CBD were in wholesale and retail compared with about 23% for the country and 26% for Tokyo; and 11.5% of jobs in the CBD were in FIRE, compared with 4.9% and 6.7%, respec-

TABLE 8.8

Japan and Tokyo: Employment Distribution by Industry, 1980 and 1997 (percent)

	1980			1997		
	Japan	Tokyo	CBD	Japan	Tokyo	CBD
Agriculture and forestry	9.6	0.6	0.0	5.5	0.5	0.0
Mining	0.2	0.0	0.1	0.1	0.0	0.1
Construction	9.9	8.3	6.1	10.3	8.7	5.8
Manufacturing	24.7	23.5	19.1	21.1	16.9	10.6
Energy and water supply, transportation and communication	6.9	6.7	8.2	6.6	6.5	6.5
Total services	47.6	60.5	66.1	51.8	62.8	77.0
Wholesale and retail	22.5	28.5	29.6	22.8	26.1	31.9
FIRE	3.4	6.0	9.9	4.9	6.7	11.5
Services	18.1	22.7	21.8	24.8	30.0	29.9
Public services	3.6	3.3	4.8	3.4	5.6	3.7

Sources: Author's calculations based on Tokyo Metropolitan Gov't. *Plain Talk About Tokyo*, 2nd ed. (1984); Government of Japan, *Management and Coordination Agency, Japan Statistical Yearbook*, 1999; Tokyo Metro. Gov't., *Tokyo Statistical Yearbook 1997* pp. 108–111.

Note: The Central Business District includes Chiyoda-ku, Chuo-ku, Minato-ku, and Shinjuku-ku.

tively. While 21% of jobs in the country were in manufacturing, it was 10.6% in the CBD, and then mostly in administration rather than production. By the late 1990s, over 77% of all jobs in Tokyo's CBD were in services, signaling the transformation of Tokyo from a manufacturing to a service city.

The 77% of overall service jobs in the CBD consists of a far higher share of specialized, world market oriented service industries than that for the country as a whole or larger Tokyo. The service sector in Shinju-ku is largely domestic and heavily retail oriented, while Chiyoda-ku is dominated by headquarters and major international operations.

Earnings

Existing information on earnings varies considerably among the three cities under study and is rarely exhaustive. This poses problems that basically cannot be solved if the objective is a rigorous comparison of detailed characteristics of the earnings distribution in New York, London, and Tokyo. After a careful examination of the available information it became clear that for the purposes of this study greater insight could be derived from a descriptive account of earnings in each city than from standardized measures, which though facilitating comparison, would do so at the price of losing all detail and specificity. This seems particularly

TABLE 8.9

Tokyo: Employment Change by Industry, 1978–1985, and 1986–1996 (percent)

	% change 1978–1985	% change 1986–1996
Agriculture	−39.3	−36.2
Mining	−9.4	−35.4
Construction	−3.0	16.2
Manufacturing	−6.7	−12.9
Electricity and Other Utilities	0.9	6.4
Transportation and Communication	1.4	14.8
Wholesale	16.4	8.9
Finance and Insurance	7.1	25.7
Real Estate	24.8	29.5
Services	33.7	37.2
Government	−2.1	6.9
Total Employ. Change for all Industries	11.0	12.9

Source: Author's calculations based on Tokyo Metropolitan Government, pp. 108–111, 1997.

TABLE 8.10

Earnings Distributions in Selected OECD Countries, 1980 to 1992, Selected Years (percentage of median and decile ratios[a])

Country/Year	Full-Year, Full-Time Workers[b]				All Workers[c]			
	P10	P90	P90/P10	P80/P20	P10	P90	P90/P10	P80/P20
Males								
Australia (1989)	56.8	160.6	2.8	1.9	54.0	161.6	3.0	1.9
Canada (1987)	38.0	174.9	4.6	2.3	36.3	176.0	4.7	2.6
The Netherlands (1987)	71.5	172.8	2.4	1.4	69.3	168.7	2.4	1.7
United Kingdom (1986)	61.4	188.1	3.1	2.1	60.7	186.3	3.1	2.1
United States (1991)	33.6	193.1	5.7	3.0	28.1	203.7	7.2	3.5
Females								
Australia (1989)	49.2	156.3	3.2	1.9	23.2	183.0	5.7	3.4
Canada (1987)	34.7	179.1	5.2	2.6	27.9	181.8	6.5	3.2
The Netherlands (1987)	72.6	173.5	2.4	1.7	29.9	185.1	6.2	3.1
United Kingdom (1986)	64.9	181.0	2.8	2.0	34.6	223.0	6.4	3.5
United States (1991)	40.0	190.0	4.8	2.5	17.7	206.0	11.6	4.0

Source: Gottschalk and Smeeding (1997), based on Luxembourg Income Study database.

Notes: [a]Persons aged 25 to 54, living in households with zero self-employment income. Wages are net of employer contributions to social insurance (payroll taxes), but gross of employee payroll taxes; [b]Full-Year: 50 full-time weeks or more a year; Full-Time: 35 or more working hours a week; [c]All workers with non-zero wage and salary income.

appropriate because the primary emphasis is on differentials within each city and country rather than among the three cities. For this same reason, I decided to keep earnings in the original currency; keep the information in the original format of each country and city; and include types of information not necessarily available for all three cities.

The aim is to understand the trajectory of wages and salaries in different industries and occupations during a period of pronounced transformation in the economic base of these cities, as described in the previous section. Central to this trajectory is the relative change in pay levels by occupation and industry. Wages and salaries are embedded in a set of broad economic and political processes that cannot be done full justice here; I will only briefly discuss this more general context in which to place the detailed information on earnings presented later.

Today there is a fairly solid consensus about the fact of growing earnings inequality in most highly developed countries. Notwithstanding diverse starting points and evolutions, earnings inequality increased in most but not all OECD countries. The level of inequality growth was not found to be associated with initial levels of inequality, which signals the presence of a new dynamic. A few countries, such as the UK, experienced at least as large an increase in inequality as the U.S.[9] The U.S. also showed an absolute decline in earnings at the bottom of the distribution. This did not happen in the other countries, though there were relative declines in Japan and the UK (OECD 1993: Table 5.2). The U.S. and the UK had the sharpest increases in the top earnings groups of all the countries considered.

In their cross-national Earnings and Income Inequality study, Gottschalk and Smeeding (1997) find that almost all highly developed economies experienced some increase in wage inequality among prime-aged males during the 1980s, except for Germany and Italy. Germany has long had a centralized corporate wage-setting and bargaining arrangement, and Italy is characterized by a proliferation of small, high-quality, medium-sized firms, by large-scale unionized factories and by sheltered public sector employment. They found the sharpest level of inequality in the U.S. and the UK, with increases in earnings inequality sharper than in household inequality.

Experts in the U.S. today agree on the fact of an increase in earnings inequality, though there is some disagreement as to the reasons (Howell

[9] A second group saw substantial increases though not as high as those of the U.S: among these are Canada, Australia, and Israel. Relatively small increases in inequality were evident in Japan, France, the Netherlands, Sweden, and Finland, though sharper increases became evident towards the end of the 1980s. The initial measure of inequality was very low in many of the Nordic countries so that even increases put them on a totally different level from that of the U.S.

2000). In the 1980s there was an intense debate in the U.S. around the preliminary evidence on increased inequality with many analysts disputing the findings. Today the debate centers on the causes, an issue I return to below. Levy and Murnane (1992) review the literature documenting substantial earnings inequality in the U.S. in the 1980s both in terms of wage rates and annual earnings. Further, there is a consensus that this earnings inequality is an important factor explaining family income inequality (Danziger and Gottshalk 1995; Blank 1994).

Table 8.10 presents a summary measure of the earnings distribution in five countries.[10] Earnings at selected percentile points are measured as a proportion of earnings at the median; there are two additional measures, one of these captures the relation of the top percentile to the bottom percentile, and the second the relation of the eightieth to the twentieth percentile. These relations are a measure of overall earnings inequality.

The U.S. and Canada have the most unequal distributions of earnings for both men and women measured by their 90/10 and 80/20 ratios. However, it should be noted that Canada still has a far more developed set of non-earned forms of income for its population, notably through its public health service. For men especially, the earnings inequality was largely a consequence of considerably lower earnings at the bottom of the distribution; for women, of unusually low and high earnings at each end. The countries with the most equal distribution of earnings are Germany and the Netherlands, though this may be changing as key institutional changes are being implemented in both of these countries, notably the partial deregulation of the labor market.

The sharpest increase in earnings inequality among all the countries covered has taken place in the U.S., also the country with the highest level of initial inequality measured at the beginning of the 1980s. Between 1975 and 1992 the P75 ratio for hourly earnings of full-time males in the U.S. increased by 10% and the P90 ratio by 14%; the P10 and P25 ratios fell by 3.2 and 5.1 percent, respectively. The earnings of persons at the lowest percentile in the U.S. are lower relative to the median than in any of the other nine countries covered in the study, and they are the lowest in absolute terms using dollars and purchasing power parities across these countries. Earnings in the lowest percentile measured in U.S. dollars are higher in all the other countries considered.[11]

[10] In the original work on which this table is based, Gottschalk and Smeeding (1997) present the evidence on nine countries for which the LIS (Luxembourg Income Study) database provides consistent data on annual before-tax earnings for men and women aged 25 to 54. Workers from households with self-employment income have been excluded. The LIS uses national statistical sources and applies consistent measures and concepts across countries.

[11] A worker at the P10 in Germany in the mid-1980s (before current deregulations)

Where there is disagreement is in the explanation of this growing inequality. There is now a large number of studies which control for various conditions in order to understand changes in the earnings distribution. (For a critical review, see Howell 2000). These studies use a range of variables to explain part of the increased inequality without arriving at a conclusive causal explanation. Part of the change has been explained in terms of the higher return to education, which for college graduates reached 43% in 1989, controlling for hours worked; since college graduates tend to have full-time year-round jobs, the increase is actually 54% (Gottschalk and Smeeding 1997: 645). The UK, U.S., and Japan all experienced increased returns to education. However, the data also show wage dispersion within skill groups (Macurdy and Mroz 1995), so that for a given level of education those in the top of the earnings distribution had growth in earnings while those at the bottom had declines. All countries considered experienced increased inequality within skill groups.

If there is one causal factor that has the most agreement as to its impact on producing inequality it is technology (but for a critique, see Howell 2000). Yet even the technology-induced skill demand explanation which is the only one that analysts have claimed explains the widespread presence of such earnings dispersion in different sectors and in different skill groups, and within sectors and within skill groups, cannot explain the whole story. Further, this explanation has been found to have serious problems, including measurement and interpretation problems in the standard literature that holds this explanation. In his detailed review of the expert literature on this issue, Howell (2000) shows what the main problems are, including importantly time-line issues, since most of the impact of technological change on earnings is measured for the 1970s not the 1980s, while the growth in earnings inequality is measured for the latter decade (Howell 2000).

What is more difficult to establish through this type of research is the impact of structural changes in the economy, industrial composition, increased cross-border trade and investment, deregulation, and the decline in unions and minimum wage standards (Danziger and Gottschalk 1995). Several studies estimate that the decline in the latter two accounts for 30% of the increase in earnings dispersion (Fortin and Lemieux

---

earned 51% of the U.S. median compared with 34% for the U.S. worker. At the other end, workers in the 90th percentile in the U.S. have the highest earnings of all the countries covered. The greater inequality in the U.S. has meant that its bottom tier actually winds up with lower living standards than the bottom tier in the other 14 countries with a lower median than that of the U.S. (See Gottschalk and Smeeding 1997). Even countries whose median is only about 70% of the U.S. median, have a better standard of living in the bottom percentile than does the U.S. And at the top percentile, the U.S. average at the P90 was half again as high as that of all the other countries considered.

1997). According to Gordon (1996: 206) the most important factor has to do with management's decisions and practices.

There is considerable disagreement about the reasons for the increase in low-wage jobs. The most extensive debates have taken place in the United States, long a country where the middle class is supposed to be an expanding stratum. In the United States, several analyses of the 1980s maintain that the increase in inequality in the earnings distribution is a function of demographic shifts, notably the growing participation of women in the labor force and the large number of young workers as the baby boom generation has come of age. Women and youth are two types of workers who have traditionally earned less than white adult males (Lawrence 1984; Levy 1987). Harrison and Bluestone (1988: chap. 5) analyzed the data, controlling for various demographic factors as well as the shift to services; they found that these demographic variables did not explain away the increased inequality in the earnings distribution. Rather, they found that within each group (white women, young workers, white adult men, and so on) there has been an increase in earnings inequality. They found that the sectoral shift accounted for one-fifth of the increase in inequality, but most of the rest of the growth in inequality occurred within industries so that, as with demographic groups, there has been a growth in inequality in the earnings distribution within industries (see their app. tab. A.2 for eighteen demographic, sectoral, and regional factors). They explain the increased inequality in the earnings distribution in terms of the restructuring of wages and work hours (chaps. 2 and 3). Though a parallel study does not exist for either the United Kingdom or Japan, it would seem that at least some of these outcomes are also present there. There has been an increase in the labor force participation of women in the United Kingdom and in Japan. But, as in the United States, this demographic shift cannot be the only source of growth in low-wage jobs when there are declines in what were once leading industries and the major growth industries of the 1980s have above- or below-average wage levels.

A second major trend is that some of the fastest-growing service industries are characterized by larger than average concentrations of lowly and of highly paid jobs, a subject examined at length later. This is most clear in New York and London. It is more difficult to establish in Tokyo. The technological transformation of the work process, in part underlying the above trends, has further added to earnings polarization by either upgrading or downgrading a vast array of middle-income jobs. Mechanization and computerization have transferred skills to machines and have shifted certain operations from the shop floor to the engineering office; many middle-level management jobs have been eliminated through computerization, and many secretarial jobs have been downgraded into routinized word processing. If one were to add the increase in the numbers of workers who are not employed full time and year round, then the inequality becomes even more pronounced. This is also a subject examined at greater length in a later section.

What matters for the purposes of the analysis here is the erosion of the broader institutional framework characterized by the social compact between labor and employers in the leading industries. This compact rested on mass consumption: Workers' wages were part of the production equation because they represented a key factor in profit realization. In the case of industries geared to the export market, as are the producer services in New York and London, such a compact is unlikely. The decline of this broader institutional framework has taken place in a context of rapid growth in several service industries. In all three countries the growth industries of the 1980s—FIRE, trade, business services—show significant shares of low-wage jobs, weak, if any, unions, and higher percentages of part-time and of female workers. Estimates of the impact of unions put it at 20% of the increase in male earnings inequality, but for little in that of women (Freeman 1994; Fortin and Lemieux 1997). Countries with union coverage and centralized wage-setting were able to limit the growth in inequality (Freeman and Katz 1993; Fortin and Limieux 1997). This is the case for Germany, Italy, and the Nordic countries (OECD 1994b). Unionization rates declined in the U.S. and wage bargaining became less centralized in the UK. In many OECD countries a large share of workers is covered by collective bargaining and centralized wage-setting. This explains part of the difference in the degree of inequality increases.[12] (See also Katz, Loveman, Blanchflower 1995 on the case of Japan.)

Given the enormous differences in institutional settings among the OECD countries, it is difficult to establish to what extent these institutions, even if weakened, prevented inequality from reaching much higher levels or there was a growth in inequality because these institutions weakened (Gottschalk and Smeeding 1997: 656–57). But it is clear that the existence of such institutions which limit the impact of market forces has meant that none of these countries has the high levels of inequality that the U.S. and the UK have today. Good evidence for this also comes from

---

[12] Union membership does not necessarily represent the full spectrum of centralized wage-setting. In France, 85% of the workforce was covered by collective agreements in 1980, but only 17.5% belonged to unions (OECD 1994c: Table 5.8). Bargaining is decentralized but there is a tightly controlled minimum level of wages. In Japan there is low union membership and the unions are mostly company unions, but wage setting is centrally coordinated through a nationwide Shunto which sets the guidelines that are the basis for company-level bargaining (see first edition of this book for a detailed examination). Many countries with strong centralized wage-setting or high union coverage saw these institutions weaken in the 1980s.

comparing declines at the bottom and increases at the top in terms of growing inequality. Thus in France, where the institutional constraint is strong to keep the bottom decile from falling, we see the bottom hold even as there were greater increases at the top: the P90 grew faster than the median and the P10. Also Germany, Finland, and other countries with floors under the P10 saw similar results. Where such floors do not exist we see that inequality is both raised by increases in the P90 and declines in the P10, as was the case in the U.S.

A major trend feeding the growth of low-wage jobs is the high incidence of part-time jobs in growth sectors. In the U.S., 40% of sales jobs, 30% of service jobs, and 17% of FIRE jobs were found to be part-time; more generally, industries with a greater proportion of part-time workers had a higher overall employment growth rate from 1983 to 1993, a trend not present before the 1980s (Fallick 1999). Fallick (1999) found a similar pattern in other highly developed countries. In Japan, part-time employment rose by 80% from 1982 to 1992 especially in agriculture, sales, services, and manufacturing (Houseman and Osawa 1995). These trends have held and by 1998, 30% of sales jobs, 24% of service jobs, and 18.7% of FIRE jobs were part-time; women are a growing share of the part-time labor force, and, further, the share of part-time women workers grew from 19% of all women workers in 1980 to 36.5% in 1998 (Management and Coordination Agency 1998).

Yet another set of structural factors emerges from a classification of economic sectors by whether they contain mostly high- or low-skilled jobs and the incidence of these sectors in the economy, allowing for the fact that each sector will tend to contain a range of occupations in terms of skill. Using the case of urban economies, Table 8.11 shows that in NYC low-skilled sectors grew by 23% from 1993 to 1997 compared with 11.7% for mostly high-skilled sectors (see also Table 8.14); Chicago's

TABLE 8.11

US, NYC, LA and Chicago: Employment in Business Services and Engineering/ Management Services, 1993 to 1997 (percent)

	U.S.	New York City	Los Angeles	Chicago
Non-professionalized occupations (SIC: 7320, 7330, 7340, 7360, 7380)	25.2	23.1	11.3	26.0
Professionalized occupations (SIC: 7310, 7370, 8710–40)	25.7	11.7	14.2	24.6

Source: Based on author's calculations, U.S. Census Bureau, *County Business Patterns*, 1997.
Note: New York City includes 5 counties (New York, Bronx, Richmond, Queens, Kings); Chicago includes 3 counties (Cook, DuPage, Lake).

growth rates were about 25% in each of these sectors, while Los Angeles had lower growth rates of about 11% in the mostly low-skill and 14% in the mostly high-skill occupations. One inference is that each of the three leading U.S. global cities showed significant growth in both types of sectors, with NYC concentrating the sharpest conditions for inequality.

The next three sections presenting detailed information on earnings in New York, London, and Tokyo, should be read against this broader context.

New York

The growth in earnings inequality measured at the national level is fully evident in the New York area. (See Tables 8.12A and 8.12.B.) From 1979 to 1996 earnings inequality in the NY-NJ region grew by more than 50%, notwithstanding strong economic growth beginning in the mid-1990s (Federal Reserve Bank of NY 1998). The degree of growth in inequality is similar to that of the country. But in the 1990s it grew markedly sharper in NYC. Using the top and bottom percentiles among year-round full-time workers, both men and women, earnings inequality grew by 50%, a consequence of the different trends in earnings growth at each of the ends.

Full-time year-round male workers aged 25 to 64, in the 90th percentile saw a 26% increase in real earnings from 1979 to 1996 (from $63,700 to $80,000), while those at the 10th percentile fell by 21% (from

ABLE 8.12a

Iew York and U.S. Percentage Growth in Earnings: Year-Round, Full-Time Workers (percent), 979–1996, Selected Years

	Men			Women		
	1979– 1996	1979– 1989	1989– 1996	1979– 1996	1979– 1989	1989– 1996
Inited States						
0th percentile	10.1	9.4	0.6	27.7	17.8	8.4
Oth percentile	−20.6	−13.9	−7.8	−13.6	−11.6	−2.3
Iew York–New Jersey region						
Oth percentile	25.7	19.2	5.4	37.5	32.1	4.1
Oth percentile	−21.0	−6.7	−15.3	−7.0	0.4	−7.4

Source: Federal Reserve Bank of New York, *Earnings and Inequality: New York–New Jersey Region*, "Current ssues in Economics and Finance," vol. 4, no. 9, July 1998.

Note: a denotes the metro area as New York City and Westchester, Rockland, Putnam, Nassau, and Suffolk ounties.

TABLE 8.12b

Earnings Inequality: Year-Round, Full-Time Workers, 1979–1996
(ratio of 90th percentile earnings to 10th percentile earnings)

	Men			Women		
	1979	1989	1996	1979	1989	1996
United States	3.6	4.6	5.0	2.9	3.9	4.3
New York–New Jersey region[a]	3.4	4.3	5.3	3.0	3.9	4.4
New York City Metro. Area	3.7	4.6	6.8	3.0	4.0	4.8
New York State[b]	3.3	3.6	4.3	2.5	3.5	3.6

Source: Federal Reserve Bank of New York, *Earnings and Inequality: New York–New Jersey Region*, "Current Issues in Economics and Finance," vol. 4, no. 9, July 1998.

Notes: [a]denotes the metro area as New York City and Westchester, Rockland, Putnam, Nassau, and Suffolk counties; [b]excludes the NYC metro area.

$19,000 to $15,000). The trend was similar for women, with a gain from $39,300 to $54,000 at the top and a loss from $13,200 to $12,300. These gains at the 90th percentile were sharper than the 10% gain in the country overall; the fall at the bottom was similar to the 21% for the country overall. During the 1980s, the fall in the bottom percentile was actually milder in the NY-NJ region than in the country as a whole. This would confirm some of the detailed analyses of earnings for metropolitan areas based on 1990 census data which found workers and families at the lower ends of the income distribution fared better in global cities than in industrial centers or cities further down the urban hierarchy (Elliott 1999; Drennan et al. 1999). In the 1990s this appears to have reversed, with the earnings dispersion becoming sharper in the region than in the country as a whole, notwithstanding the strong growth beginning in the mid-1990s. Between 1989 and 1996 total declines in earnings for full-time male workers at the 10th percentile were nearly double the country's, while those at the top grew much faster than the country's.

The New York metropolitan area has been the greatest source of this inequality in the region. The 90/10th percentile ratio for year-round full-time male workers rose from 3.7 to 6.8 from 1979 to 1996, that is to say the top percentile workers earned almost four times as much as the lowest percentile workers in 1979, and 7 times as much in 1996 (Table 8.12.A) while that of the rest of the region was at the national level. The higher degree of inequality in the NYC area is due largely to the financial services industry. It pushed earnings in the top percentile higher. From 1989 to 1996 earnings at the 90th percentile grew by 8% compared to 0.6% in the country as a whole. In that same period, earnings at the 10th percentile fell by 27% in the NYC region compared to 7.8% for the country as a whole. (See Brauer 1998; Orr, Rosen and DeMott 1998.) Man-

TABLE 8.13
New York City Median Hourly Wages by Occupation and Industry, 1996–1998 (USD)

Occupation	Occup. Code	Manufacturing (selected industries)					Services (selected industries)		
		SIC 23	SIC 25	SIC 27	SIC 35	SIC 37	SIC 72	SIC 73	SIC 87
Managerial & Administrative	100003	36.69	32.64	40.49	41.17	38.93	18.09	38.77	45.27
Professional/Paraprofessional & Technical	200003	26.09	18.65	21.39	23.09	22.43	11.69	24.07	21.89
Sales & Related	400003	27.86	18.86	19.06	22.53	21.35	8.29	17.76	14.78
Clerical & Admin. Support	500003	12.20	9.72	12.82	14.08	12.22	9.32	11.48	14.39
Service	600003	8.87	7.80	8.88	8.88	9.41	6.96	8.59	11.59
Product/Construct/Operate-Maintenance/ Material Handing	800003	7.29	10.35	11.94	12.01	12.79	7.14	9.42	13.73

Occupation	Occup. Code	Finance, Insurance, and Real Estate						
		SIC 60	SIC 61	SIC 62	SIC 63	SIC 64	SIC 65	SIC 67
Managerial & Administrative	100003	44.03	50.14	55.99	40.99	45.80	30.88	40.42
Professional/Paraprofessional & Technical	200003	26.24	21.04	27.79	26.16	24.75	19.56	25.75
Sales & Related	400003	20.64	15.94	25.92	15.59	19.57	21.53	26.22
Clerical & Admin. Support	500003	12.21	13.45	16.47	14.84	15.52	13.96	16.18
Service	600003	11.72	14.80	14.27	13.57	21.08	14.50	13.61
Product/Contruct/Operate—Maintenance/ Material Handling	800003	13.03	14.98	16.54	14.18	15.79	15.22	15.66

Source: Author's calculations based on New York State Bureau of Labor Statistics, 1996/7/8 OES Survey.

Notes: SIC Codes and Descriptions listed: SIC23 Apparel and Other Textile Products; SIC25 Furniture and Fixtures; SIC 27 Printing and Publishing; SIC35 Industrial Machinery and Equipment; SIC 37 Transportation Equipment; SIC 60 Depository Institutions; SIC 61 Nondepository Institutions; SIC 62 Security and Commodity Brokers; SIC 63 Insurance Carriers; SIC 64 Insurance Agents, Brokers, & Service; SIC 65 Real Estate; SIC 67 Holding and Other Investment Services; SIC 72 Personal Services; SIC 73 Business Services; SIC 87 Engineering and Management Services.

hattan remains as the region's core: it is the source of about 42% of regional wages and 73% of the wages in the top paying FIRE sector (NY and NJ State Departments of Labor 2000).

Private sector wages in the region overall advanced 7.4% in 1996 and 7.7% in 1997 (NY and NJ State Departments of Labor 2000). Business and financial service jobs, retail and tourism, consulting, advertising, and computer services all grew strongly. FIRE's growth provided the region with its highest earning jobs, overcoming the losses and declines of the early 1990s; according to data from the NY and from the NJ Departments of Labor, FIRE jobs had the highest growth rates in earnings among all major sectors from 1994 on. The Wall Street securities sector grew at an annual average of over 6% from 1996 to 1998, leading the growth in FIRE employment. Since 1992, securities employment in NYC has grown by 27%. Today, unlike what was the case in the 1980s, Wall Street is regarded as a key engine of growth for the city and the region.

Private sector wages in NYC increased 8.4% in 1997 and 8.8% in 1996. The average wage per job in NYC rose by 5.5% to $43,500 in 1997, for the third consecutive year of 5% or more such growth. The average wage per job in Manhattan is almost $63,000. Manhattan has increased its distance from the next highest counties compared to 1992. It has the region's highest paying jobs, with the highest average compensation on Wall Street at $175,300. There was an increase of 17.5% in total wages paid in the securities industry in 1997 (NY and NJ State Departments of Labor 2000); this industry also contains some of the lower paying jobs (see Tables 8.13 and 8.14).

A comparison of median hourly wages for major occupational groups in manufacturing compared to finance shows a significantly higher pay in the latter, most pronounced among managerial and administrative occupations in the commodities and securities brokerage sectors, followed by non-depository institutions (Table 8.13). This was the only occupation/industry niche to surpass the $50 hourly pay for the 1996–1998 period. We know that at the top these are undercounts since they exclude a whole range of non-salary forms of compensations which amount to much larger amounts than in other occupations lower down the pay scale. The differences in pay levels between manufacturing and finance disappear for professional and technical occupations, sales, and clerical occupations. Service occupations and blue-collar service jobs grouped under construction and operational occupations all tend to pay higher wages in finance than in manufacturing, a trend that reverses some of the findings in the earlier period discussed in the first edition of the book. Among service industries, except for engineering and management services (SIC 87) pay resembles the lower levels of manufacturing. This is particularly noticeable

TABLE 8.14

New York City Wage Ranges by Occupation and Selected Industry, 1996–1998 (USD, numbers and percent)

Selected SIC	Mean Wage ($)	Median Wage ($)	Breakdown by Wage Ranges						Total Occ. Listed
			$50 above	$40–$50	$30–$40	$20–$30	$10–$20	$10 below	
SIC 23—Apparel & Other Textile Products (total)	12.34	8.22							
General Managers & Top Exec. (highest hr. wage)	44.55	*****							
Other Textile & Related (lowest hr. wage)	7.40	5.74	3	1	14	11	51	43	123
			2.4%	0.8%	11.4%	8.9%	41.5%	35.0%	
SIC 62—Security and Commodity Brokers (total)	28.68	23.20							
Managerial & Admin. (highest hr. wage)	46.02	55.99							
Switchboard Operators (lowest hr. wage)	10.18	8.29	7	2	16	35	82	11	153
			4.6%	1.3%	10.5%	22.9%	53.6%	7.2%	
SIC 72—Personal Services (total)	10.38	7.81							
Other Computer Scientists & Rel. (highest hr. wage)	38.71	42.08							
All Other Trans. & Rel. Workers (lowest hr. wage)	5.40	5.57	0	1	4	9	39	54	107
			0.0%	0.9%	3.7%	8.4%	36.4%	50.5%	
SIC 73—Business Services (total)	17.65	13.59							
General Managers & Top Exec. (highest hr. wage)	44.96	55.04							
Sewing Machine Operators, Garment (lowest hr. wage)	6.75	5.95	2	3	17	43	88	61	214
			0.9%	1.4%	7.9%	20.1%	41.1%	28.5%	
SIC 87—Eng. and Management Services (total)	24.40	20.06							
Financial managers (highest hr. wage)	47.96	*****							
News, St. Vendors & Phone Solicitors (lowest hr. wage)	7.26	6.53	4	3	11	57	96	15	186
			2.2%	1.6%	5.9%	30.6%	51.6%	8.1%	

Source: Author's calculations based on New York State Bureau of Labor Statistics, 1996/7/8 OES Survey.

Note: *****denotes value greater than $60. The first line of each SIC is the average wage within the sector among all occupations listed by the NY State Bureau of Labor Statistics. The second line is the occupation under the SIC with the highest mean wage; the third line is the occupation with the lowest mean wage. Wage ranges list the number and percentage of occupations within the SIC that fall above or on the listed range.

for business services (SIC 73). Personal services (SIC 72) have sharply lower pay at all levels compared to any of the other industry groups.

Table 8.14 examines some of these earnings trends in greater detail. Taking the highest and lowest paying occupations for select industries we can see that the mean hourly pay level for managers and executives in apparel (SIC 23) was over $44 compared to $7.40 for the lowest paid occupations; median wage is not available for highest paid occupation in this industry sector. While the median wage in the security and commodity brokers group is $23.20, the highest wage is well over $50 and the lowest, for switchboard operators, is $8.29. Mean wages give slightly higher results. In the personal services group the median wage is $7.81, the highest, for computer scientists, is over $40, and the lowest, for transport and related workers, is $5.57. In business services, the median wage is $13.59, and, in what is the sharpest differential of the industry groups in Table 8.14, the highest paid are managers and executives at $55, and the lowest, sewing machine operators at just under $6.

Further, by breaking down the numbers of occupational groups by wage ranges we can see the composition of the sector. For instance, commodity and security brokers clearly have the largest concentration of occupations listed in the $10 to $20 hourly wage range and secondly in the $20 to $30 wage range. The number of occupations in a sector does not necessarily tell us how many individuals are employed in each of these occupational/earnings niches. In business services the largest concentrations of occupations are the 88 in the $10 to $20 range, and the 61 in the below $10 wage range. These two groups of occupations in two high-growth sectors in NY, commodity and security brokers and business services, clearly have a high concentration of low-paying occupations.

In sum, detailed data on earnings by occupation, industry, and job location in the city as well as by occupation and type of institution of employment all point to significant divisions between manufacturing and nonmanufacturing, between Manhattan and the other boroughs, and between corporate services and other service industries.

London

In the United Kingdom, the evidence from the New Earnings Survey (U.K. Department of Employment 1985, 1985c 1999) also points to greater income inequality in some of the most dynamic sectors, notably financial and professional services, than is the case in traditional manufacturing. The evidence also points to higher pay levels in these sectors in London than in Britain as a whole, and to a male-female differential.

Since the concern is with differentials we have kept the following pay levels in English pounds as presented in the original data.[9] Using information from the *New Earnings Survey* for various years, Table 8.15 provides data on average adult full-time weekly earnings from 1979 to 1999 controlling for sex and manual vs. non-manual occupations. The differentials between men and women and between manual and non-manual workers held for much of this period, even though there is a trend towards relative increases among non-manual women compared to all the other groups. If we add a geographic variable, it becomes clear that both for manual and non-manual workers and for women and men, the City of London had the highest average pay levels, followed fairly closely by the city of Westminster (see Table 8.16).

Table 8.17 shows 1999 earnings by occupation and sex in London and Britain. Most pronounced is the significantly higher than average earnings between London and the country overall for all major occupational levels, and between professional and manual occupations in both London and the country overall. Earnings levels in the professional and related supporting management and administrative occupations in London are the highest single cell.

Further, for all occupational groups and both sexes London's average earnings were higher in both 1986 and 1999 than those for Britain as a whole. Among occupational groups, the top-ranked professional and related management occupations have the highest earnings for men in both London and Great Britain and for both years under consideration, 1986 and 1999 (see Table 8.17). Overall this holds for women as well with one exception, the second ranked professional category which includes education and welfare related professions, gave women higher average earnings in 1999 than did the top-ranked professional category. The single lowest occupational group for both years, sexes, and regions, is catering, cleaning, hairdressing, and other personal services, which gave its workers significantly lower earnings than the rest of the occupational groups, with women significantly more disadvantaged than men.

The sharpest differential that emerges across the major groups is that of men in professional and kindred occupations in the City of London with earnings of 821 pounds a week compared to women in Great Britain overall in the catering and cleaning group, earning 213 pounds a week in 1999. This differential is significantly higher in 1999 than it was in 1986. Among the smallest differentials between men and women for both years within each region is that of security and protective services, which tend to be fairly regulated occupations.

The evidence for earnings by sex, region, and industry group show that the highest earnings in 1999 are all for men in non-manual occupations

TABLE 8.15
London: Average Adult Full-Time Weekly Earnings, 1979–1999 (pounds)

	Manual		Nonmanual		All Occupations	
	Men	*Women*	*Men*	*Women*	*Men*	*Women*
1979	97.9	60.5	129.0	76.3	115.5	73.3
1985	183.8	118.3	264.7	160.0	233.2	154.4
1990	270.6	175.3	440.6	270.7	383.1	258.9
1997	351.0	232.6	614.0	402.7	541.3	386.3
1999	366.7	242.1	645.9	420.1	58.4	422.8

Source: Based on Inner London Education Authority, *London Labour Market Trends—Facts and Figures* (July 1987); U.K. Office for National Statistics, *New Earnings Survey 1990* Part E: Analysis by Region, Table 108–113; *New Earnings Survey 1995* Part E: Analysis by *Region, Table 108–113*; *New Earnings Survey 1997* Part E: Analysis by region table 1–4. Part A: streamlined Analysis, Table 22–23; *New Earnings Survey* 1999 Part E Table A22, A 23, E1, E2, E3 and E4.

Note: Average excludes those whose pay was affected by absence.

in, first, FIRE and business services in London, at 932 pounds, an earnings level that stands sharply above the next highest cell, which is this same industry group for Britain as a whole at 686 pounds, followed by transport and telecommunications in London at 662 pounds (see Table 8.18). The single highest earnings cell among women is non-manual occupations in the London FIRE sector at 516 pounds, followed by miscellaneous services in London at 471.9 pounds. Average earnings for women in Britain as a whole are well below 400 pounds a week in all these industry sectors. Since these figures include London, the actual levels for Britain excluding London, are lower. Juxtaposing Tables 8.17 and 8.18 makes it clear that the differentials between London and Britain for both men and women are significant even within a given industry group and occupational group. Perhaps the industry sector that makes this clearest is FIRE and the occupational group that makes this clearest is the professional and related managerial group.

A few additional trends also indicate the existence of differentials between London and the country overall. Male employees are more likely to work in part-time jobs in London than in the UK overall while the opposite holds for women. But in both cases there is a distinction between London and the country overall. Another important factor in understanding the earnings distribution in London is the age of the workforce since youth tend to have lower paid jobs. From 1988 to 1998 the proportion of workers in the London labor force aged between 25 and 34 rose by 5% while that aged between 16 and 24 fell by 9%.

Hamnett and Cross (1998) using General Household Survey data and

TABLE 8.16

Great Britain: Average Gross Weekly Earnings by Area, 1985 and 1995 (pounds)

	Men			
	1985		1995	
	Manual	Nonmanual	Manual	Nonmanual
London	197.1	291.3	376.9	664.6
City London	248.7	340.0	387.6	880.9
City of Westminster	185.8	306.4	342.2	808.8
Remainder of Southeast Region	175.8	247.2	—	—
Total Southeast Region	184.7	270.0	347.1	546.5
Total England and Wales	174.6	245.5	335.4	528.9
Total Great Britain	174.4	244.9	335.0	525.5

	Women			
	1985		1995	
	Manual	Nonmanual	Manual	Nonmanual
London	—	175.8	261.2	439.1
City of London	—	204.6	—	535.8
City of Westminster	—	185.4	254.3	482.4
Remainder of Southeast Region	—	145.0	—	—
Total Southeast Region	—	160.8	235.7	359.4
Total England and Wales	—	146.4	222.5	349.4
Total Great Britain	—	145.7	221.9	346.9

Source: U.K. Department of Employment, "Part E: Analysis by Region and Age Group," New Earnings Survey 1987; U.K. Office for National Statistics, *New Earnings Survey* 1995, Part E: Analysis by Region, Table 108–113.

Note: Dash indicates that figures were not available; Average excludes those whose pay was affected by absence.

New Earnings Survey data from 1979 to 1993 find that there has been a considerable degree of earnings inequality growth in both Britain and London (see Tables 8.19 and 8.20). They find that most earnings groups have had increases in real terms but that the gains in the top earnings groups have been significantly higher than for the rest. Thus the percentile distribution of earnings in London has grown sharply more unequal, even though the bottom percentile saw an increase in its earnings. A similar trend is evident for New York in the 1980s (Elliott 1999; Drennan et al. 1998) but not for the 1990s when the bottom percentile actually lost ground (see Table 8.12.B).

Hamnett and Cross (1998) interpret these findings as showing that while there has been a growth in earnings inequality, it cannot be said that there has been an increase in social polarization because all groups

TABLE 8.17

Great Britain and London: Average Weekly Earnings by Occupation and Sex, 1999 (pounds)

	1986				1999			
	London		Great Britain		London		Great Britain	
Occupational Group	Men	Women	Men	Women	Men	Women	Men	Women
Professional and related supporting mgt. and admin.	399.8	281.3	328.2	237.7	821.2	564.6	657.3	461.4
Professional and related in education, welfare, and health	293.6	204.5	261.2	183.6	692.7	557.3	584.3	477.2
Literary, artistic, and sports	357.8	243.8	283.7	213.0	—	527.5	—	408.8
Professional and related in science, eng., tech., and similar fields	304.2	214.7	267.0	178.1	550.0	479.1	461.1	397.1
Managerial (excluding general management)	315.6	222.1	265.5	176.1	499.1	373.3	432.6	307.9
Clerical and related	209.2	168.6	181.4	137.0	335.4	336.1	299.1	267.3
Selling	229.2	145.7	200.8	114.2	385.5	290.6	353.0	245.2
Security, protective service	263.5	—	239.0	211.0	461.1	431.7	424.1	404.8
Catering, cleaning, hairdressing, and other personal service	169.0	131.9	147.0	108.2	306.8	255.1	259.4	213.5
Materials processing (excluding metals)	201.6	—	190.2	119.2	370.4	—	319.5	—
Making and repairing (excluding metals and electrical)	232.6	—	193.5	111.3	484.4	—	411.6	347.7
Processing, making, repairing, and related (metals and electrical)	229.6	—	539.0	130.3	367.8	—	334.9	216.7
Printing, repetitive assembling, inspecting, packaging, and related	200.3	127.5	179.3	122.2	395.9	245.5	341.6	234.6
All full-time workers	255.0	169.3	207.5	137.2	584.4	422.8	422.4	326.5

Source: U.K., *New Earnings Survey*, 1999, Office for National Statistics; U.K. Department of Employment, *New Earnings Survey*, 1986.

have gained in real terms. This interpretation is predicated on a particular type of definition of polarization, one where both the top and the bottom have to grow in order to have a condition of polarization.

The gap in mean earnings between London and the rest of the Southeast and the rest of Britain actually widened from 1979 to 1995. Mean gross weekly earnings for male full-time workers rose by 35% in Britain, 39% in ROSE, and 57% in Greater London. Percentage increases for women, even though in absolute terms they remain lower than those of men, were actually higher, at 56% for Britain, 59% in ROSE, and 73% in London. This also holds for part-time female workers, whose earnings increased more rapidly in London and by 1995 were 25% above those for part-time female workers in Britain as a whole. For all categories, mean pay increased more rapidly in London, so that by 1995 the pay gap with

TABLE 8.18

Great Britain and London: Average Weekly Earnings by Sex, Selected Industry, and Manual/Nonmanual Occupation, 1999 (pounds)

	London				Great Britain			
	Men		Women		Men		Women	
	Manual	Nonmanual	Manual	Nonmanual	Manual	Nonmanual	Manual	Nonmanual
Electrical engineering	....	....	....	....	....	603.5	....	366.4
Food, drink, and tobacco manufacturing	n.a.	n.a.	n.a.	n.a.	n.a.	n.a.	n.a.	n.a.
Construction	435.6	574.4	....	....	354.6	508.5	....	306.5
Wholesale, dist., and commission agents	314.2	512.7	228.8	332.3	299.4	444.7	215.3	276.5
Hotel and Catering	254.7	....	....	....	230.5	404.5	180.5	278.6
Retail, dist., vehicle repairs, and cons. goods	n.a.	n.a.	n.a.	n.a.	n.a.	n.a.	n.a.	n.a.
Transport and telecommunications	424.3	662.6	393.4	453.3	359.6	530.0	311.5	352
Banking, finance, ins., leasing, and bus., services	....	932.1	....	516.3	377.9	686.1	....	378.0
Professional and scientific services**	337.0	545.5	252.8	448.8	285.2	485.3	223.0	386.3
Miscellaneous services	366.1	621.6	....	471.9	300.8	497.2	197.4	359.7
All manufacturing industries	413.8	665.5	237.1	462.1	354.6	541.6	231.7	341.5
All nonmanufacturing services	360.4	660.2	264.4	436.9	313.0	518.5	215.7	347.6
All industries	376.9	664.6	261.2	493.1	335.0	525.5	221.9	346.9

Source: U.K. Office for National Statistics, New Earnings Survey 1999.

Notes: **refers to Education sector in 1999 New Earnings Survey; n.a. = not available; .... = not in the sample.

TABLE 8.19

Decile-based Measure of Change in Total Gross Weekly Earnings for 1979 and 1993 (earnings revalued by median earnings change to April 1993 values)

Decile	Gross Weekly Individual Earnings in 1979 (pounds)	Size of Group 1979		Size of Group 1993		Percentage Point change in Size of Group 1979–1993	
Greater London							
1	66.41	10	10	12.9	12.9	2.9	2.9
2	116.50	10		7.7		−2.3	
3	159.11	10		7.7		−2.3	
4	188.65	10		5.8		−4.2	
5	216.93	10	80	6.4	64.1	−3.6	−15.9
6	243.08	10		6.9		−3.1	
7	280.04	10		7.2		−2.8	
8	320.38	10		8.6		−1.4	
9	397.39	10		13.8		3.8	
10		10	10	23.0	23.0	13.0	13.0
Great Britain							
1	49.51	10	10	13.5	13.5	3.5	3.5
2	87.38	10		10.2		0.2	
3	128.15	10		9.3		−0.7	
4	161.30	10		8.9		−1.1	
5	192.23	10	80	8.1	68.6	−1.9	−11.4
6	222.64	10		8.0		−2.0	
7	255.40	10		7.7		−2.3	
8	296.70	10		7.0		−3.0	
9	364.10	10		9.4		−0.6	
10		10	10	17.9	17.9	7.9	7.9

Source: Hamnett, C. and M. Cross. "Social polarisation and inequality in London: the earnings evidence, 1979-95," p. 667.

the rest of the country had widened. The same holds for median earnings.

Tokyo

There was a slight tendency for Tokyo to have a lower level of real wages than that for Japan as a whole. Since 1980, however, the opposite is the case with the absolute differential in average earnings for full-time workers becoming quite pronounced. The evidence on average earnings for the period from 1977 to 1998 shows that the differential increased by about 25% in the 1990s (see Table 8.21). Still, compared to the differen-

TABLE 8.20

Polarization of Earnings in London and Great Britain: 1979–1995 New Earnings
Survey (1979 figures are adjusted by median income rise)

Earnings	Greater London			Great Britain		
	1979	1995	% change	1979	1995	% change
Male full-time workers						
Bottom decile	10.0	12.5	2.5	10.0	18.0	8.0
Bottom quartile	25.0	24.1	−0.9	25.0	31.8	6.8
Middle 50%	50.0	36.8	−13.2	50.0	36.7	−13.3
Top quartile	25.0	39.1	14.1	25.0	31.5	6.5
Top decile	10.0	22.5	12.5	10.0	16.9	6.9
Female full-time workers						
Bottom decile	10.0	10.6	0.6	10.0	19.1	9.1
Bottom quartile	25.0	21.5	−3.5	25.0	31.6	6.6
Middle 50%	50.0	36.3	−13.7	50.0	35.6	−14.4
Top quartile	25.0	42.2	17.2	25.0	32.8	7.8
Top decile	10.0	21.8	11.8	10.0	18.1	8.1

Source: Hamnett, C. and D. Cross. "Social polarisation and inequality in London: the earnings evidence, 1979–95," p. 669.

tials discussed for London and New York relative to their countries, To-kyo's is significantly smaller. However, it should be noted that unemployment in Japan reached an all-time postwar high of 4.9% in early 2000, or almost 3.5 million unemployed; furthermore, manual labor fell by 213,000 from 1999 to 2000, which shows both industrial and occupational restructuring and hence the possibility that Japan may begin to resemble Western countries in some of these patterns.

Average monthly earnings by industry group and sex make it clear that men in finance and insurance had the highest earnings in both 1988, a period of enormous growth, and 1997, when the economy was in recession. The next highest paying industry groups for men are manufacturing, energy, and real estate. As was the case for women in New York and London, women in Tokyo are also paid significantly less across industry groups compared to men. The industries paying women the lowest average monthly wages are agriculture, construction, and manufacturing. The industries paying women the highest wages in 1997 are services and finance and insurance. The differential between men and women did not change much from 1988 to 1997 in FIRE; it changed most markedly to the advantage of women in retail and wholesale. (See Table 8.22.)

Income per capita in Tokyo has tended to be about 1.4 to 1.5 times higher than the country average. From 1985 to 1991 this gap increased further but after 1991 with the onset of the recession it fell back to prior

TABLE 8.21
Japan and Tokyo: Average Monthly Earnings 1977–1998 (yen)

	Tokyo	Japan
1977	260,821	219,620
1981	330,622	279,096
1987	468,137	390,114
1995	513,369	409,000
1998[1]	542,742	416,000

Source: Tokyo Metropolitan Gov't., *Trends of Labor and Wages in Tokyo-to* (monthly report), Apr. 1977, Apr. 1981, Apr. 1987; id., *Statistics Profile for Tokyo*, 1984 (1985); Tokyo Metropolitan Government, Tokyo Statistical Yearbook, 1997 p. 342; Government of Japan, Management and Coordination Agency, Japan Statistical Yearbook 1999.

Note: [1]Earnings for Tokyo is from 1997.

values. In Tokyo, the increase in property prices is understood to be an especially important factor in raising the gap as owners sold at inflated prices to large corporations assembling small lots to create larger scale buildings. Average property prices doubled between 1983 and 1987 and far more sharply in certain areas of Tokyo. Most increases and investments were concentrated in the central-west wards of the city. This meant that whoever owned an even small plot of land in valued areas of the city, including some farmland areas, multiplied the income differential with those who did not own land. (See also Appendix here for a detailed examination of the land price boom in the 1980s.)

TABLE 8.22
Tokyo: Average Monthly Earnings by Industry and Sex, 1988 and 1997 (yen)

	All Workers		Men		Women		W/M ratio	
	1988	1997	1988	1997	1988	1997	1988	1997
Agriculture	318,889	678,789	355,208	—	167,815	—	0.47	—
Construction	323,946	598,261	347,987	437,000	173,481	246,400	0.50	0.56
Manufacturing	302,359	550,923	347,559	436,300	164,246	256,100	0.47	0.59
Energy[1]	397,359	674,041	436,376	—	211,401	—	0.48	—
Transport and Communication	323,546	527,292	335,569	—	215,859	—	0.64	—
Retail and wholesale[2]	283,216	510,441	341,060	400,700	170,519	258,400	0.50	0.64
Finance and insurance	365,605	651,289	459,421	527,400	251,163	280,400	0.55	0.53
Real Estate	358,933	500,122	406,613	456,300	216,222	258,900	0.53	0.57
Services	288,326	519,529	335,069	425,600	193,964	294,400	0.58	0.69
All industries (average)	311,132	542,742	356,686	431,000	199,183	273,700	0.56	0.64

Source: Tokyo Metro. Gov't., *Trends of Labor and Wages in Tokyo-to* (monthly report), Apr. 1988 and *Tokyo Statistical Yearbook*, 1997.

Notes: [1]Energy includes electricity, gas, heat supply, and water; [2]Retail and wholesale includes eating and drinking places; — denotes that data was not available for these industries disaggregated by gender.

Machimura's detailed analysis shows considerable differentials inside Tokyo (see Machimura 1999). The highest per capita income was in Chiyoda-ku and the lowest in Adachi-ku. The relative position of these two wards, one at the top and the other at the bottom of the income distribution, did not change over the period but there were some sharp changes in absolute levels. In 1975 income per capita in Chiyoda was 2.3 times higher than in Adachi-ku, a differential that had increased to 3.13 times by 1991. Further, while the level of income of Adachi-ku showed little change in this high growth period in relation to the median in Tokyo, Chiyoda's rose markedly over the median.

The main wards with sharp increases from 1985 to 1990 and decreases after 1991 are the CBD wards (Chiyoda, Chuo, and Minato), the new so-called sub-centers Shinjuku and Shibuya, and the high-quality residential areas Setagaya and Meguro.

Machimura (1999) specifies three more types of wards in terms of the trajectory of income from 1975 to 1995. A second type of ward was stable at a high level: higher per capita income than the average which, unlike the first group of wards, underwent changes similar to those of the average: the central area ward Bunkyo and two residential areas (Suginami and Musashino). A third type of ward showed stable income at the middle level, the average for Tokyo: this was the case of the western inner Tokyo suburbs. Finally, a fourth type of ward also remained stable throughout this period but at low income levels. The north and east of Tokyo represent this fourth group: at the peak of the high growth years in the second half of the 1980s their average income actually lost ground against the median for Tokyo.

Household income in percentiles for Tokyo shows that the lowest percentile received 3.5% of income and the highest percentile 23% in 1979. It changed to 3.1% and 25%, respectively, in 1989. Middle to lower percentiles lost share while middle to higher percentiles gained share. The gap between the top and the bottom was 6.6 in 1979 and 8 in 1989. While going in the same direction overall, these changes are far less pronounced than in New York or London. After 1991 the degree of inequality began to decrease, falling to 7.3 times by 1994, thus still above the 1979 level.

According to Machimura's analysis (1999), some of the factors feeding or underlying the growth of inequality are the increase in professional occupations due largely to industrial structural change rather than occupational transformation within sectors. A second trend is the increase of manual jobs in non-manufacturing sectors which could be adding to the expansion of low-income workers also in growth sectors.

For the 1975–95 period he finds an increase in both low-skill and high-skill jobs. There was a decline in the share of clerical workers in the post-1991 period and an increase in service workers. The occupations that showed increases in the 1990s were the professional, sales, services, and low-skill manual groups. Machimura (1999) concludes that the growth in the professional occupations is a long-term trend, regardless of whether the economy is undergoing the hypergrowth of the 1980s or the recession of the 1990s. In this Tokyo resembles New York and London. During the 1980s high-growth period, both white-collar and blue-collar jobs increased. (See also Tachabanaki and Yagi 1995; Bauer and Mason 1992.)

EARNINGS AND INEQUALITY

Today we have a large number of detailed studies about trends in earnings and household income inequality in major cities. These types of studies did not quite exist in the 1980s when I wrote the first edition of this book. The decennial census in each the U.S. and UK provided enormously important information on some of these trends and allows us to clarify some of the key questions in the debate evinced by my hypothesis of growing inequality in global cities.

This section examines two types of issues that came out in the debate. One, internal to global cities, concerns the question of inequality and polarization. The other concerns the incidence of inequality in global cities compared with other cities in each of these countries. The available data do not allow us to include the case of Japan in this second issue nor does it allow us to go much beyond the detailed analysis by Machimura (1999) on Tokyo already discussed in the preceding section. Some of the material of the preceding sections in this chapter on inequality in each of these three cities is also relevant and should be considered as part of the following discussion.

Several authors have made a point of distinguishing earnings inequality and polarization, arguing that one may be present without the other. In the first edition of this book I distinguished between earnings and income inequality on the one hand and polarization on the other. I emphasized that it was not just a matter of growing inequality but also a qualitative transformation in the social forms emerging out of the increased distance between the world of work and home of the new professional strata at the top and the world of work and home of those at the bottom. My concern was precisely to distinguish the fact of the numbers on earnings and income distributions from the more complex and sociological reality that they shape. The high-level professional workforce in global cities is characterized by work and lifestyles that distinguish it from earlier forms of a small elite of urban rich or the broader middle class. Their numbers are large enough in many of these cities and their preference for urban living is high enough that they have, as a stratum, re-inscribed a good part of the urban landscape, a subject I return to in chapter 9. Similarly, the lower income strata are also partly reconstituted as a distinct social form. I was less concerned with whether the size of the middle class had shrunk at the expense of the ends of the spectrum, though I was persuaded by the evidence that there was a significant recomposition in the occupational and earnings distribution within that middle sector, with its upper strata raising their earnings and the lower strata losing ground. This recomposition could go along with a basically unaltered size in the whole middle sector. Again, my concern was with the possibility of newly emerging social forms. In brief, I did not use both variables to interpret the same earnings and income distribution.

There are other ways of specifying the distinctions. Perhaps one of the clearest and most useful formulations can be found in Klosterman (1996). His is a straightforward concern with establishing a literal definition of polarization, that is, whether the top and the bottom of the earnings and income distribution have actually grown at the expense of the middle sectors. Following OECD usage, Klosterman (1996) distinguishes between inequality as referring to the extent of dispersion between levels of earnings or income, and polarization as referring to the changes in the absolute and relative size of the groups in different income or earnings brackets over time. This still leaves open the question as to how we measure the size of each earnings or income group over time. Kloosterman (1996) divides the distribution into the 25% lowest earnings level, the 50% share of the middle and the 25% of the highest earnings group; these earnings levels then get transferred, adjusting for inflation, to subsequent years. Polarization would be taking place if the proportion of earners in the middle group shrinks in size and the two other groups increase. Harrison and Bluestone (1988: 121–23) divided the earnings distribution into three main categories, one with incomes at least twice the median, one with incomes less than half the median, and a middle group with everyone fitting between the two other cutoff points; polarization would take place if the earnings differential between the top and the bottom share increases.

Hamnet and Cross (1998) use Klosterman's model in their study on London but make significant adjustments and find that the only group that grew in size, and did so by 25%, is the top quarter of the earnings distribution. The middle 50% group shrank by 21% and the lower group by 4%. In their interpretation this does not qualify as polarization; it is merely an increase in earnings dispersion. Using other measures they find an even stronger growth at the top 10th decile and in the 9th decile, along with a fall in the lowest decile, which I would interpret as support for the polarization thesis. But Hamnet and Cross (1998) do not consider this an instance of polarisation because the increased size of the top is 15 times greater than the bottom group; in other words, even though the bottom grew in size, it did not grow enough to allow us to interpret this as polarization. It would also have had to grow by about 15 times as did the top stratum.

A second type of issue is how the earnings distribution and polarization in global cities compare with the situation in other cities in a country. The best studies at this time have been done for the U.S. In a major study on cities and inequality in the U.S. based on 1990 census data, Drennan et al. (1998) find that cities with high growth resulting from dynamic economies, particularly producer services growth, had increases in the average income of low-income people. These cities saw increases in the incomes of all sectors of the population and as a result also in the median. This positive effect also held for blacks, including blacks in New York whose median income rose. The largest increases were found in the leading cities, particularly New York. In contrast, cities centered on manufacturing had declining median incomes and stagnant economies. Among the worst in this regard were cities such as Detroit and Cleveland, which saw falls in the income level of the lowest decile generally, and falls in the median income of blacks.

An important finding coming out of the 1990 census and relevant to the global city model is that in the 1980s for the first time in decades there was divergence in per capita income among regions of the U.S. This followed many decades of growing convergence. From 1979 to 1989, seven of the nine census regions showed divergence while none did in the prior period.

One interesting aspect here is that market-based models would predict convergence, especially within a country. This has certainly been the case in the U.S. for a long period of time. But in the 1980s this strong and persistent trend reverses.[13] Several researchers have noted this (see especially the analysis of the 1980s by Garnick 1990). Some have explained it as a shock of the economic transition that will eventually even out (Carlino 1992). Garnick (1990) disagrees and argues that standard explanations predicting regional convergence are no longer valid. Drennan et al. (1998) produce an explanation as to why divergence has set in and the standard market models no longer work which is centered on urban specialization and the importance of traded goods and services. They find that the shift to producer services explains some of the divergence, and since these services are primarily an urban specialization, they focus on cities and find that those cities most specialized in producer services had

---

[13] An important trend in the U.S. evident already in the 1970s and continuing in the 1980s is the dispersal of manufacturing and the closing down of many factories in areas that had been major manufacturing concentrations. In contrast, producer services did not particularly disperse; rather, they registered high growth rates in cities in the country overall.

the best income growth in the 1980s. Further, the rate of income growth for the black population was also greatest in those cities.

Drennan et al. (1998) find that median family income also diverged across regions in the 1980s, after decades of a trend towards convergence. The authors focus on manufacturing and producer services to get at the growth of median family income by region. The top three regions in terms of median family income growth were also the top three regions in terms of producer services share in the gross regional product for both 1979 and 1989. They find that greater specialization in producer services in a region was more conducive to growth in real median family income than greater specialization in manufacturing for the period 1979–1989. Every 1% point share of GRP in producer services in 1979 added 2.8% to growth of the region's real median income from 1979 to 1989. The effect was also positive for manufacturing, but minor at 0.5%.

Because producer services are concentrated in cities, the authors analyzed the growth of median household income in the 51 largest cities over the 1980s for all households and for black households. They find that cities more specialized in producer services at the beginning of the decade had much better income growth than cities more specialized in manufacturing. The results for black households were very similar to those for households overall. In a more detailed ranking of 20 cities, the results show that the growth in real median household income from 1979 to 1989 was highest in Boston and in NY for all households and for black households. The range among the ranked cities is enormous, including an increase of 39% in Boston and a decline of 20% in Detroit. Growth for black households shows the same wide range. NY ranked second with an increase of 33.7% in median family income from 1979 to 1989. Producer services earnings as a percentage of all earnings in 1979, were 27% in Boston and 35.6% in New York, the highest of the 20 cities listed. In 1989, these shares had risen to 48.4% in New York, 37% in Boston and 26% in Chicago. In contrast, producer services earnings as a share of all earnings in 1989 were 13.5% in Detroit and 14% in Cleveland.

The study concludes that regional specialization in producer services contributed to upward divergence in family income for regions with above-average income. This leads them to refute the hypothesis that a manufacturing based economy creates a better earnings distribution and better conditions for large sectors of the low-income population. But this contradicts their finding that an increase in a city's share of earnings from manufacturing would add more to real household income than the equivalent increase in producer services earnings share. As there were no cities with such a growth in the manufacturing earnings share, producer services actually added more even though the level of earnings increase was lower than it would have been had manufacturing had a similar increase in its share of a city's earnings. This also meant that a given percentage loss of earnings from manufacturing required a greater increase in earnings share by producer services to offset the decline in median income from the loss of manufacturing.

Not unrelated, yet distinct, is the issue of location in the urban hierarchy, particularly, whether that location has an impact on earnings and income inequality. Compared to other variables, this is not one that has received much study with a few exceptions (see, e.g., Sheets et al. 1987; Nelson and Lorence 1985 which I discussed in the first edition of the book). In a recent study, Elliott (1999) examines the effect of urban position and the role of the urban system in shaping these outcomes, including a control for individual characteristics. This allows him to establish not only which cities actually had the highest rates of low-income employment but also to what extent differences within the urban hierarchy have persisted over time, and the extent to which these differences remain systematically ordered among distinct social groups. He uses Public Use Microdata Samples (PUMS) from 1950 to 1990 and Noyelle and Stanback's (1989) urban typology that allows identification of manufacturing or service orientation of an urban area rather than simply size. He identifies the position of 105 metropolitan labor markets that can be tracked from 1950 to 1990.[14] The 1990 census data show that there was a 35% increase in the numbers of employed workers in metropolitan labor markets whose earnings were below the individual poverty line over what had been their share in 1970. From 1970 to 1990 all types of metropolitan areas experienced increases in low-income employment rates, but the highest were in production centers and the lowest in resort areas and in global cities. Controlling for race and gender produces the same results. The four centers he classifies as global cities—New York, Chicago, Los Angeles, and San Francisco—show consistently smaller low-income employment rates than metropolitan centers lower down the urban hierarchy. The sectors that made the largest absolute contribution to the increase of low-income employment were retail trade, which added the most to low-income employment in every type of metropolitan area from 1970 to 1990, followed by health and educational services, producer services, and consumer services. Finally, and very briefly, in terms of individual characteristics the data show that overall regardless of race and gender an individual's chances of low-income employment are the smallest at the top of the hierarchy.

---

[14] Elliott uses an indicator of metropolitan underemployment developed by Nord and Sheets (1987): the inability of an employed worker (who worked at least 1 week during the reference year) to earn wages and salaries above 1.25 times the individual poverty level ($8,064 in 1990). He relies on an absolute earnings threshold that does not change across time or space, except to account for national changes in the Consumer Price Index. The data he uses are all for years that coincide with the peak of the business cycles; thus low-income employment rates are likely to be at a low.

He concludes that these findings show that being at the top of the hierarchy, as is the case with global cities, is related to a lower incidence of low-income employment, and he sees in this finding a refutation of my thesis that the new forms of economic growth promote greater inequality. Yet, one important issue would seem to be the composition of low-income employment in each of these types of cities: in peripheral manufacturing centers with stagnant economies, economic growth is not a significant variable and hence the increase in low-income employment is almost by default likely to be a result of economic decline. The point about global cities is that they are the site for enormously dynamic sectors and that in many of the growth sectors we see an increase of low-income jobs. The fact that the largest relative increase in low-income employment took place in stagnant economies does not in itself constitute a refutation of the thesis that high-growth sectors produce more low-income jobs than erstwhile growth sectors at a time when they were growing. Further, the growth of low-income jobs in a city such as New York which experienced an enormous increase in average family income and had highly dynamic growth sectors, is clearly a different combination of elements from that of a peripheral stagnant economy. Finally, using the national individual poverty line to establish low-income employment in such diverse places makes comparisons problematic since the cost of living index is known to be much higher in a city like New York and hence the cutoff point should probably be raised. Yet, even if the share of workers winding up in low-income jobs in global cities is found to be smaller than that of peripheral urban economies when we control for local cost of living, this outcome can still coincide with growing inequality inside global cities.

Nonetheless, this study is enormously illuminating on a whole set of issues, many of which I could not touch on here. Perhaps most important is the fact that compared to other cities, global city status does not necessarily represent the disadvantage for the bottom stratum that I had postulated in the first edition. It adds a broader context for interpreting what takes place in global cities. What Elliott (1999) and Drennan et al. (1998) show is that being in a global city may not be all that bad for low-income workers compared to being in other types of cities. The dynamic character of these economies has some positive impacts on such workers even if the distance between them and the top has increased sharply inside global cities.

Conclusion

Data on earnings and employment are typically highly problematic, and they may be even more so in the case of cities since often the best data sets are at the national rather than the urban level. The object in this chapter was not a direct comparison of these three cities, a task that would be quite precarious given the differences in the types and availability of data, but rather to capture major trends in employment and earnings as well as transformations in the relative positions of industries, occupations, earnings, and sex within each city.

New York, London, and Tokyo show parallel employment and earnings trends. All three experienced losses of manufacturing jobs and above-average growth in producer services, though the timing and magnitude varied. Finance paid the highest average salaries in all three cities, but the gap between men and women is enormous. Among the fastest-growing jobs are professional and service occupations, the former paying some of the highest salaries and the lattter paying increasingly lower salaries. In all three cities, part-time jobs have increased especially in growth industries; they are disproportionately held by women; the available evidence shows that part-time jobs tend to be more lowly paid than full-time jobs.

Several of the trends identified in the 1980s have become sharper in New York and London, and, though to a lesser extent, in Tokyo. For the first time in many decades job growth was higher in New York than in its suburbs and the larger metropolitan region, with the financial sector leading growth. This sector also registered a far sharper increase in earnings than the rest of the city's and region's economy. In London we see similar patterns with higher job growth than in the rest of the country and an increased earnings differential which by 1998 stood at 28.7% higher average weekly earning in London than in Britain as a whole. Tokyo, while experiencing far less dynamic growth, continued to show sharp earnings differentials with the rest of the country. Second, earnings inequality also increased inside New York and London, though not in Tokyo. More detailed data show a trend towards increases in the bottom quintiles of the earnings distribution even as inequality between the top and the bottom of the distribution also increased. This suggests that the dynamics of global cities could conceivably create more opportunities for low-income groups even as they also enrich the upper levels of the income distribution.

When we compare the leading growth sectors of the post–World War II period with today's, we can see pronounced differences in their occupational and earnings distributions. Today's leading sectors generate a higher share of high-income jobs and of low-wage jobs. The growth in inequality is further fed by the erosion of workers' gains in manufacturing and the high incidence of layoffs and plant closures involving unionized and well-paying jobs, especially in the United States and the United Kingdom, but now also in Japan. Finally, the general shift to a service economy entails a much larger share of low-wage jobs than is the case with a strong manufacturing-based economy. The overall result is an increased income polarization.

Nine

Economic Restructuring as Class and Spatial Polarization

EMPLOYMENT AND EARNINGS statistics, such as those discussed in the previous chapter, provide only a partial description of the socioeconomic conditions in New York, London, and Tokyo under the current economic regime, one characterized by the dominance of producer services and finance. They leave out components of the economic and social order that are not captured through these kinds of figures and especially undercount, or do not count at all, employment in informal and casual labor markets as well as industrial homework. Nor do these statistics describe the specific labor markets in which employment and earnings are embedded. Finally, employment and earnings statistics do not convey the concrete conditions of life in these cities for the population at large.

I propose to address these broader questions through an examination of the specific forms assumed by socioeconomic conditions in New York, London, and Tokyo. Running through this analysis is a concern with the articulation of the leading growth sectors to other components of the economic base of these cities. The attempt is to identify key elements in the dynamics that contribute to constituting and reconstituting—whether in part or in full—the social order in these cities, beyond what is happening in the leading sectors, as discussed in the preceding chapters, but continuously raising the question of the articulation of this order.

The first section discusses the consequences of such a new economic core of advanced, high-growth industries for the organization of other economic sectors in these cities. Specifically, does the existence of a high-growth sector feed the expansion of what appear to be declining or backward economic sectors, sectors that do not conform to our image of a postindustrial economy? To what extent do the most sophisticated white-collar industries that characterize the new economic core need easy access to a broad range of industrial services, a land use that is not competitive in such cities? The second section discusses how the greater income polarization in the leading industries, as described in the preceding chapter, is constituted socially; that is to say, is it merely a change in the income distribution, or are there new social forms associated with an increase of high-income and of low-income workers? What is the social geography emerging from this transformation?

The third section examines the evidence of the growth of casual and informal labor markets. Are there conditions in the global city that stimulate the expansion of casual and informal work, or, on the contrary, do these forms of work shrink as a result of the presence of a thriving postindustrial core? Is the sphere of casual and informal work a somewhat autonomous one, not affected by conditions in the leading economic sectors, basically a remnant from an earlier economic period or, in the case of New York and London, perhaps associated with immigration from the Third World?

The facts of immigration, ethnicity, and race need to be incorporated for an adequate understanding of labor market questions, most particularly in New York, but to some extent also in London. The fourth section discusses the available evidence on immigrant and black workers in New York and London and on the new unauthorized immigration in Tokyo. It examines the place of the new Third World immigration phase beginning in the 1970s in New York, the earlier Asian and Caribbean immigration in London, and the recent immigration of Asian workers into Tokyo. Is theirs a circumstantial arrival? Do they inhabit a world of work basically unconnected to the social and economic order of the global city? Or, on the contrary, are significant components of their employment articulated by economic polarization?

Overall Effects of Leading Industries

We can identify at least three major bodies of theoretical work that address the question of the articulation of leading economic sectors with the rest of the economy and, more generally, the socioeconomic conditions in cities under the current regime of advanced services. One is general economic development theory; another, the model of the economic base or export sector in urban economies and its multiplier effects; and the third, the sociological model of the postindustrial economy.

According to general economic development theory, as economic development progresses it will bring about a generalization of the market and market relations to an increasing number of institutional spheres in a society. In the case of the labor market, this entails a growing incorporation of workers, and people of working age generally, into formal work relations. This process is part of the broader expansion of the regulatory capability and intent of the state. The period of rapid growth after World War II was, indeed, characterized by the attainment of high levels of economic development in major industrialized countries and the growing incorporation of workers into the formal labor market. A series of regulatory aspects ensured that a majority of workers had full-time, year-round jobs, often with unemployment and retirement benefits. Unions were central in this expansion of formal work relations. Fordism is the most institutionalized version of this model of the labor market. This process was to continue as development proceeded to higher stages. One would, according to this thesis, expect that the leading cities in the most advanced countries would certainly be characterized by a strong expansion in the share of workers incorporated in highly developed and encompassing formal labor markets. The growth of casual work would be interpreted as a development lag or as exogenous to the advanced sectors of the economy; for example, informal labor markets could be viewed as imported through Third World immigration.

The model of basic versus nonbasic industries addresses the issue of city-building economic activities (Mayer 1969; Alexander 1954). City-building industries are those that generate more than is consumed internally and hence produce for "export" as well. It is this export activity (including domestic and international) that becomes a vehicle for multiplier effects in that it contributes to the expansion of the other sectors in the economy that service the basic industries. Exports provide an exogenous source of additional income for the city and induce a demand for additional support services beyond those required by the resident population. Expansion in the nonbasic sectors of the economy is basically reproductive; it cannot generate new growth. Much debate has centered on whether manufacturing, always held to be a basic sector, is indeed so in the current era. Classic arguments on services as the basic sector were developed by Blumenfeld (1955) and by Tiebout (1957); a notion of services as the basic sector seems particularly appropriate for the case of major cities that are leading centers in the production and export of producer services. This thesis would suggest that the high level of exports and the extremely high value of these exports in the three cities under consideration, should have a rather high multiplier effect and the benefits should be evident over a wide range of industries in these cities.

In its original and richest formulation, the postindustrial model posits a major transformation, one where the expansion of the highly educated workforce and the centrality of knowledge industries will lead to an overall increase in the quality of life and a greater concern with social rather than narrowly economic objectives. It is impossible to recapitulate the full thesis, and unnecessary given the widespread familiarity with Bell's (1973) text. For the purposes of this discussion what matters is Bell's notion of a hierarchy in the growth of services, the first type of services developed being those linked to industry, notably transportation and distribution, and the later ones being those linked to a higher quality of life. For Bell, this latter stage in the development of services will be characterized by a more collective or communal nature, given the type of needs they respond to and the public character of provision for many of these services. Furthermore, the preeminence of theoretical and technical knowledge with a scientific base makes postindustrial society one resting on knowledge. The central problem of society is no longer that of capital or the organization of industrial work but that of the organization of scientific knowledge. This means that the class of professionals and technicians not only expands greatly but becomes the vital center of postindustrial society. This is a heterogeneous and stratified class, ranging from teachers and health workers to engineers and scientists. But at its core are the latter, engineers and scientists. It is an enlightened elite, whose politics can play a significant role in changing the social order. The transformation of work is also evident in the organization of firms and power. The preeminence of services is expected to entail a growth of smaller-sized firms, where professional knowledge is more important, contributing to making firms and the organization of work more humane and social. This represents the transition from an economic to a more sociological mode of thought in the management of firms and of society.

Several elements in this model have certainly taken place. If we consider the producer services and finance as knowledge industries, then it is evident that there has been rapid growth of such industries and that they have become the dominant sectors in advanced economies. Furthermore, as the preceding chapter indicated, there has been an expansion of highly paid professional-level jobs and a growth in the high-income stratum of workers. Finally, high-income gentrification as we see it in these three cities does in many ways represent a higher quality of life for those that benefit from it. Important questions that arise are first, whether the increase in low-wage jobs and the increase in informal and casual work are or are not articulated with these advanced, higher forms of growth. Second, does the rapid increase in the number of small firms in the advanced services alter the nature of concentration in these economies? The evidence presented in preceding chapters suggests that high levels of economic concentration continue, though often in different forms from that represented by the large manufacturing-oriented multinational corporations and the large transnational banks that dominated economic activity in the 1960s and well into the 1970s. Alongside these types of corporations, there is now a vast number of comparatively small firms, which together exercise immense control over investment and economic activity, especially in these cities. And finally, how is the vast proliferation of small firms with marginal returns and mostly low-wage jobs we see in these cities articulated with the advanced sectors of the economy?

A central question in light of the evidence presented in all the preceding chapters is to what extent these models are ultimately derived from a historical period that has come to an end, a period characterized by strong tendencies toward growth in the middle sectors of the economy. There was sharp growth in consumer and capital goods industries, construction, and other industries associated with the suburbanization of the population in the United States after World War II and in the United Kingdom beginning in the interwar period and with rapid urbanization of the population in Japan. In both the United States and the United Kingdom, growth in the economy was centered on a range of industries servicing the needs of the population. Japan's accelerated industrial growth after World War II was in basic industry and eventually consumer goods for export; however, the equally accelerated urbanization of the population—one of the fastest in the world—meant that notwithstanding a low standard of living, the construction and furnishing of housing and the provision of public services and goods were also central in Japan. What is distinct about the current period is a pronounced discontinuity in this pattern, with growth centered on finance and the production of services for firms.

Different types of economic growth promote different types of social forms. In the post–World War II era, growth was characterized by the vast expansion of a middle class and formal labor markets. This middle class was not as well off in the United Kingdom and Japan as in the United States, but it was not, ultimately, a fundamentally different process. The historical forms assumed by this expansion, notably capital intensity, standardization, and suburbanization, promoted the generalization of formal labor market relations and acted against the casualization of work. Large, vertically integrated firms in manufacturing as well as in insurance and banking, offered elaborate internal labor markets with possibilities for advancement, considerable job security, and various fringe benefits (Edwards 1979). The lifetime job security in Japan rested not only on culture, as has often been asserted, but on conditions akin to elaborate internal markets that offered possibilities for shifting workers to different jobs if necessary. The social forms accompanying this process, particularly as they shaped the structures of everyday life, reproduced and further induced a middle-class culture. A major inference that can be drawn from this is that a large middle class contributes to patterns of consumption that promote standardization in production and hence, under certain conditions, are conducive to greater levels of unionization or other forms of worker entitlement that can be derived from large plants or large offices—an entitlement which is, in turn, conducive to middle-income jobs. Many of the patterns evident today work in the opposite direction, promoting small scales, less standardization, an increasingly casualized employment relation.

The consolidation of an economic core of top-level management and servicing activities needs to be viewed alongside the general move to a service economy and the decline of manufacturing. New economic sectors are reshaping the job supply. However, so are new ways of organizing work in both new and old sectors of the economy. Components of the work process that twenty years ago took place on the shop floor and were classified as production jobs today have been replaced by a combination of machine/service or worker/computer/engineer. Activities that were once all consolidated in a single service retail establishment have now been divided between a service delivery outlet and central headquarters. Finally, a large array of activities that were being carried out in large-scale, vertically integrated firms in the postwar decades are today increasingly characterized by small-scale, flexible specialization and subcontracting. In brief, the changes in the job supply evident in major cities are a function both of new sectors and of the reorganization of work in both new and old sectors.

These trends assume distinct forms in (1) the spatial organization of cities, (2) consumption and more generally the structures for social reproduction, and (3) the organization of the labor market. I will discuss each of these.

Social Geography

The theoretical models briefly cited above tend to correspond to prevailing notions about the spatial configuration of major cities in highly developed countries. One key element is the suburbanization of the population associated with the expansion of a middle class and understood as an increase in the quality of life associated with economic development. A second element is the continued suburbanization of jobs: in an earlier phase, suburbanization of factories as central cities became obsolete locations for large, mechanized plants, and more recently, the suburbanization of office jobs made possible by modern telecommunications. At the same time, the inner city became an increasingly powerful image in Western cities to describe central areas where low-income residents, unable to afford a house in the suburbs, were left behind. In the case of New York and London, the inner city increasingly also contained concentrations of public housing inhabited by minority residents. The continuing existence of a sizable middle class in large cities was overshadowed by the growth of suburbanization and the inner city. Generally, older cities lost population in the 1960s and 1970s. Demographic, economic, and technological factors all contributed to strengthen this image of the sociospatial configuration of major cities, one to a large extent rooted in postwar developments that continued into the 1960s.

The following discussion of sociospatial patterns in these cities aims at detecting major changes and the underpinnings of new conceptions of space.[1] An emerging body of scholarship is producing new knowledge about these issues (Marcuse and van Kempen 2000; Allen 1999; Gregory and Urry 1985; Soja 1989; Massey 1984; Scott et al. 2000), also discussed in several preceding chapters. In addition, an important reexamination of the impact of technology on the spatial organization of the economy is now under way (Castells 1989; 1996; Graham and Marvin 1996; 2000; Garcia 2001).

Have the various transformations discussed throughout this book engendered a new social geography, or have they been absorbed by the existing spatial patterning of social forms? Spatial differentiation based on social and economic characteristics is a basic trait of cities, often expressed by changes in land use. The focus here is on changes associated with the economic transformation of the last two decades, specifically the sociospatial forms through which the changes in the industrial, occupational, and earnings distribution are made concrete. These sociospatial forms are one expression of the relation between space, in this case urban space, and the economy in major cities dominated by the new leading industries. This expression is not necessarily captured by a detailed description of the spatial distribution of various types of firms and households. The built-in rigidities of physical structures limit the spatial transformation. And the vastness of these urban economies limits the overall impact of leading industries. Thus the attempt here is to capture ruptures, instances where the leading growth trends have altered existing arrangements or where massive declines have made possible totally new land uses or sociospatial forms. Distinct sociospatial forms arising out of these processes are high-income residential and commercial gentrification, the massive construction projects described in chapter 7, and sharp increases in spatially concentrated poverty and physical decay. One question for us is whether we are seeing the formation of a new territorial complex at the level of the spatial and institutional arrangements in cities dominated by corporate services and finance: a complex of luxury offices and housing, massive construction projects, and appropriation of urban areas that previously had gone to middle- and low-income households and to moderately profitable firms.

It has been several decades since these cities experienced such massive transformations. Notwithstanding different political systems and planning traditions, all three cities underwent large-scale, state-directed spatial reorganization in the past (Fainstein and Fainstein 1983; Savitch 1988; Ishizuka and Ishida 1988). Though under different forms and with differ-

---

[1] My analytic strategy for treating these issues is to distinguish between "topographic" representations *of* a city and spatializations of global dynamics *in* a city.

ent players, New York, like London, went through a period of state-directed redevelopment (Fainstein and Fainstein 1983; 1985).[2] Under its master planner, Robert Moses, there was a rapid modernization and development of highways and bridges, there were slum clearance programs that eliminated whole neighborhoods, and there were public housing construction programs that benefited significant numbers and sectors of the working and middle classes even though they hurt and displaced others.

In London, there was massive development of the outer area in the interwar period through housing construction and location of manufacturing firms; public (authority) housing was built largely in inner London and contributed to concentrations of low-income households, as in New York. Inner London eventually received much of the Asian and Caribbean immigration of the postwar period. This was a period when London was seen as overcongested and overpopulated; its expansion was seen as threatening the balanced development of the outer areas. One response was the Green Belt, introduced in 1934. Abercrombie's Greater London Plan of 1944 sought to strengthen the Green Belt by concentrating development in so-called New Towns within the region and controlling the development of rural land. The interwar and postwar periods were major planning eras for London and its surrounding areas, marked by the departure of people and jobs from London, the Green Belt, the New Towns, and, increasingly, the physical and economic decay of inner London.

In Tokyo, the central element in urban planning and management policy from the late 1950s had been the attempt to regulate the concentration of the commuting population and of industry in Tokyo through the development of a green belt. The decentralization of industry called for in the 1963 National Capital Region Development Plan further sought to regulate Tokyo's growth. But a much higher than expected concentration of population and manufacturing, forcing a vast expansion of Tokyo, led to the abolishment of the green belt concept. In the 1968 Plan, this

---

[2] Fainstein and Fainstein (1983) distinguished three types of local regimes and three stages in the postwar politics of urban development in the United States. From the mid-1940s to 1965, there was an emphasis on large-scale development projects, initially sponsored by governments. This was a period characterized by strong government participation and little popular opposition. It was followed by "concessionary regimes," a phase that lasted up to about the mid-1970s. This phase was dominated by the necessity to make concessions in addressing the urban struggles of the late 1960s and early 1970s led by minority groups and community organizations. The final period, which can be seen as including the present, is dominated by business interests and characterized by a stress on fiscal stability, along with the maintenance of some of the institutions and programs stemming from the preceding concessionary regime. According to Fainstein and Fainstein (1983), New York City entered the directive period earlier than did most other cities in the United States but otherwise followed this pattern.

concept was replaced by that of suburban development. The decentralization of population and manufacturing to the suburbs continued to be promoted during the 1960s and 1970s with massive construction of suburban housing and transportation systems.

In all three cities, attempts to stem population growth through decentralization were replaced by alarm at the rapid decline of central areas due to population and job losses. In all three cities, though at slightly different periods, a prevalent conception in the postwar era had been that left unattended, they would grow excessively. Planning was aimed at regulating this growth by decentralizing population and jobs. This conception prevailed even as the population in central areas was beginning to decline (see Buck, Gordon, and Young [1986: chaps. 2–3] for a good account of this process in the case of London).

Important to the transformation of New York was the massive outflow of white residents to the suburbs and a massive influx of Southern blacks and Puerto Ricans in the 1950s and 1960s; later, in the 1970s and continuing today, these flows were replaced by a large new immigration from South America, the Caribbean Basin, and Asia. The radical transformation in the city's demographic composition altered the meaning of public housing. White voters withdrew their support for what they saw as mostly housing benefiting blacks (Fainstein and Fainstein 1983). Segregation in the city increased immensely. The urban renewal programs ultimately resulted in greater segregation because they destroyed the various smaller black neighborhoods in a larger number of areas to make room for highways, large-scale public housing, or middle-class housing. Greater residential segregation also accelerated white flight to the suburbs, further increasing residential segregation. In 1940, 94% of the city's population was white. In 1985, the proportion was down to 49%.

In London, the interwar period was one of growing homeownership among workers and manufacturing expansion in the outer areas. As is the case with many old cities, inner London had long contained above-average unemployment and a considerable incidence of casual employment. Suburban growth of population and jobs at best left these conditions in inner London unchanged and at worst contributed to the decay by draining better-off people and better jobs. Furthermore, in the postwar period, the City of London was continuing to decline, a process that had begun in the interwar period. The City had increasingly become financial rather than trade oriented. The further decline of the British Empire and the collapse of the international financial system caused the City to decline. It became far less important to the London economy than it had been before the war, when international trade and banking were central to the British economy.

In Tokyo, the continuing outmigration of young people from the central wards to the suburbs led to a change in urban policy during the 1980s: The three wards that constitute the central business district— Chiyoda, Chuo and Minato—sought to encourage migration, especially of young people, into their wards through the construction of new housing at a time of extremely rapid increases in the price of land due to the large-scale construction of high-rise office buildings (Nakabayashi 1987). This points to a strong element in the government's conception of the central city: The notion that areas of the city should become completely deserted by night as a result of the lack of a critical mass of residents was strongly resisted, unlike what was the case in the United States after World War II, where the emphasis was on the suburbanization of the population and the continuing perception of central cities as undesirable places for family life. In this regard, then, Japan is closer to the European conception of the central city.

The loss of manufacturing jobs and the associated loss of people have further eroded the base of local services and commerce in central Tokyo, in turn further inducing outmigration. There is very strong concern in local ward governments with promoting a stable residential base that includes young people of working age, residential buildings, neighborhood commerce, and consumer services. There is an understanding that population loss will affect the mix of activities and lead to a quick deterioration of these areas. There is, in addition, a political loss of power associated with a declining population for the local governments of these wards.

In the 1980s, the central areas of London, New York, and Tokyo increased their specialization as high-priced locations for firms and residences on a scale and with traits that diverged markedly from earlier periods. Crucial to all three cities has been the development of large-scale, high-cost luxury office and residential complexes, as was discussed in chapter 7 in the context of the international property market and the expansion of new growth industries. But along with these developments, there has been a continuation and consolidation of concentrated poverty and extreme physical decay in the inner cities. The appropriation of a growing area of the city for high-priced rehabilitation and redevelopment has also contributed to a sharp increase in homelessness, especially in New York, but also in London and, on a much smaller scale, in Tokyo. All three cities have long had a significant concentration of high-income residents—but not quite on this scale or quite so evident and not quite producing a complex of consumption practices and lifestyles that others could buy into, wholly or in part, depending on their incomes: the boutiques, the fine restaurants, the renovated housing or new condominiums in the city. And all three cities have long had a significant concentration of poor people. But the extent of the segmentation and spatial unevenness has reached dimensions not typical of earlier decades.

One process that articulates these various outcomes is gentrification. Gentrification was initially understood as rehabilitation of decaying or low-income housing by middle-class outsiders in central cities. In the late 1970s, a broader conceptualization of the process began to emerge, and by the early 1980s, new scholarship had developed a far broader meaning of gentrification, linking it with processes of spatial, economic, and social restructuring (Hamnett 1984; Holcomb and Beauregard 1981; Smith, N. 1982). Smith and Williams (1986) note that up to the late 1970s, the notion of gentrification as residential rehabilitation may have been an adequate understanding of the process, but by the early 1980s, it was becoming evident that residential rehabilitation was only one facet of a far broader process linked to the profound transformation in advanced capitalism: the shift to services and the associated transformation of the class structure and the shift toward the privatization of consumption and service provision. Gentrification emerged as a visible spatial component of this transformation. It was evident in the redevelopment of waterfronts, the rise of hotel and convention complexes in central cities, large-scale luxury office and residential developments, and fashionable, high-priced shopping districts.

When homes are also considered places of work—either unpaid housework or paid industrial homework—then the industrial geography of the city assumes new meanings. As Harris (1988) put it, there is a geography of unpaid work—and, I would add, a geography of informal work (Sassen 1988).[3] Insofar as different socioeconomic, ethnic, and racial households are embedded in different sets of relationships there may be distinct patterns by class and race. High-income households will tend to be locations for paid rather than unpaid housework, and so will the new two-career city-based households. Low-income immigrant households are often workplaces for paid industrial homework and mostly unpaid housework. Middle-class suburban and urban households may increasingly become places for a growing portion of paid housework (day nannies and cleaning women who come once a week) and for paid work (word processing, freelance professional work, etc.). This brings up a series of questions about standard descriptions and definitions of labor market areas. It suggests also that for low-income immigrants and middle-class suburban women engaged in clerical homework, the "labor market" may be a rather different entity than that contained in standard definitions (Sassen 1995). Increasingly segregated residential areas for blacks in New York

[3] Harris (1988) has pointed out that, while there are many studies about the impact of job location on place of residence and, more generally, determinants of residential change, for example, gentrification (Hoover and Vernon 1962; Ley 1986), little attention has been given to the way in which the social geography of the city affects the location of work.

and the small number of black suburban commuters also may be altering the geography of the labor market.

A full account of the social geography of each city would require a whole book in itself. The following discussion emphasizes particular processes in each of these cities. The focus will be on particular aspects. In the case of New York, much has been written about suburban growth, so we will limit the discussion largely to an examination of the reorganization of space in Manhattan, a key location for some of the most pronounced changes, and focus somewhat less on the rest of the city and the suburbs. In the case of London, the key dynamic continues to be the relationship of London to the rest of the Southeast; the concern for us will be the extent to which the transformations in the economic base of London and the sharp rise in the importance of finance have weakened that relation or have created new forms of incorporation of the Southeast. In the case of Tokyo, much has been said about its vast suburban sprawl, its bedroom communities, and its masses of commuters to central Tokyo. This monotony of outward suburban expansion has been sharply broken by two developments: One is the massive construction projects discussed in chapter 7 and the second is the growth of an inner city. Here, we will focus on this unexpected and little-known growth of an inner city, reminiscent of what we see in Western cities.

New York

Manhattan's specialized role as a place for office jobs increased over the three decades between 1950 and 1980. But it also became too expensive for the vast majority of office workers to reside in. Using census data, Harris (1988) found that between 1950 and 1980 the location quotient for managerial and professional jobs in Manhattan rose from 102 to 120, and that for clerical jobs rose from 114 to 128. The massive job losses in the 1970s become evident, however, when we compare 1970 and 1980. The overrepresentation of clerical jobs in Manhattan declined from 141 in 1970 to 128 in 1980, a function of the departure of large offices and headquarters and the growing concentrations of clerical jobs in the suburbs.[4] It also declined in the rest of New York and increased in outlying areas, especially in the inner suburban ring, where it went from 88 to 96. According to some analysts (Moss and Dunau 1986), the relative decline in Manhattan's overrepresentation of clerical jobs was expected to continue. Indeed, one could have expected that the suburbanization of the

---

[4] Decentralization of clerical jobs has involved moving jobs not only to suburbs, but also a short distance to the areas surrounding the central business district or to distant locations (Armstrong and Milder 1985; Roberts 1987).

population and of many firms and the resultant need in the suburbs for various types of businesses, and for professional and clerical workers, would have led to a more pronounced reduction in the locational concentration of such jobs in Manhattan and a higher increase in the suburban quotient. But as of 1988, clerical jobs, as well as managerial and professional jobs, remained underrepresented in all areas of the region except Manhattan. Indeed, the location quotient for these jobs in the region had hardly changed over the previous decades, notwithstanding large increases in absolute numbers. In stark contrast, in 1988 Manhattan had underrepresentation of all other occupational categories (sales, crafts, operators and laborers, and service workers), while these were all overrepresented in the rest of the city and in the inner and outer suburban rings (for a more detailed account, see Harris 1988).

In the 1990s Manhattan remains as the region's core with sharp overrepresentation of several industries. In 1999 it was the source of about 42% of regional wages and 73% of the wages in the top paying FIRE sector (New York and New Jersey Port Authority 2000). Manhattan's core of business and financial service jobs, retail and tourism, consulting, advertising, and computer services all grew strongly. New York had the region's largest absolute employment growth in the late 1990s, accounting for nearly half of the region's growth in jobs, and surpassing the employment growth rate of the country overall. The city has generated over half of the state's earnings over the last several years (Orr and Rosen 2000: 1–3). This growth has fed the expansion of the high price office and residential areas in the city and has continued to sustain the expansion of high price auxiliary services on a scale that has overtaken the developments that began in the 1980s in terms of the actual size of the space it occupies.

In terms of residential patterns, Manhattan has overrepresentation of managers, professionals, and service workers. The sharpest increase has been for professionals. The weight for service workers, on the other hand, had been declining for the previous thirty years. Its continuing representation as of 1980 is clearly a function of the high share of minority and immigrant workers who reside in Manhattan. The preference for urban living among the new high-income professionals was a key element in the gentrification of large sectors of the city. The available evidence for the 1990s indicates that this trend for urban living among professionals has become even stronger, especially among women, even though their absolute numbers are smaller. A far larger share of female than of male managers and professionals working in Manhattan live in Manhattan (location quotient of 168 compared with 115 for men). Women managers are more likely to be single or part of two-career households, while male managers are still more likely to have a traditional household situation, with the woman working in a nonprofessional job. Susser (1988) has shown in her work the extent to which the urban household depends on hired houseworkers, also mostly women.[5] In this context, it would seem, then, that women are a key factor in the process of gentrification in New York (Rose 1984: 62; Smith, N. 1987: 158; Sassen 1995), a process that is today largely a corporate enterprise rather than the urban pioneering of an earlier era (Smith 1996).

A more disaggregated analysis of professionals points to significant differentiation. Evidence on upper-level professionals living in New York provides information on a central element in the restructuring of consumption and rapid gentrification in Manhattan and certain areas in Brooklyn. It should also provide information on the extent to which this sector of the population is linked to various institutional complexes. Clearly, the overall group of upper-level professionals actually working in New York is far larger given a considerable number of commuters.

Brint (1988) classified professionals and managers into four categories based on New York census data: upper professionals, rank-and-file professionals, smaller employers, and marginal professionals. In Brint's analysis the first group is characterized by highly valued intellectual resources, employment in powerful organizations, and involvement with the cosmopolitan side of the economic and cultural life of the city. It includes many corporate lawyers, professionals in the leading accounting, advertising, engineering and other such firms, leading artists and designers, television executives, and researchers in leading scientific and civic institutions. The other three categories do not quite fit the model of the new professional: they are teachers, social workers, engineers, government lawyers, and professionals in small, locally oriented firms. Among the small employers group, there are now significant numbers of upper professionals, but as a group, the vast majority of small employers are not upper professionals. In his examination of the upper professionals group, Brint disaggregates the census information in terms of the type of organization they are employed in. Brint (1988) found that the highest-paid segment of professionals were those employed in the corporate headquarters and producer services and living in Manhattan.[6] They were also most likely to be white and young, 90% of them being non-Hispanic whites,

---

[5] There is considerable evidence on the extent to which owner-occupied houses, especially in suburban areas, contain a lot of unpaid work (Ehrenreich 1984). On the subject of unpaid work in households beyond a narrow definition of *household work*, see Gershuny and Miles's (1983) analysis of the shift of furniture, toy, and tool assembling from the factory or retailer to the household. See also Pahl (1984).

[6] Brint (1988) used a 5% sample from the 1980 Census data for New York. The demographic and employment information contained in this sample makes it possible to identify the differences among professionals in terms of the institutional sectors of employment.

and over half of them under 45 years of age. The other categories of professionals living in New York had far lower average earnings, were far more likely to live in the outer boroughs of the city and to be black and/ or women. Indeed, blacks and Asians were a presence only in the human capital services complex. Hispanic professionals in 1980 were employed only in very small numbers. While it needs updating, the classification and some of its key features would seem to be appropriate for the 1980s as well (see Brint 1997).

If we consider the high growth sectors of the 1990s in New York we can detect two distinct sectors for professionals which correspond to the distinctions proposed by Brint (1988; 1997): on the one hand, the securities industry, with its extremely highly paid professionals with overall salary earnings (excluding the far larger earnings through bonuses) of $32 billion in 1998, and on the other the health and social services sector, with overall salary earnings of $14.8 billion and a far larger number of professionals.

Much of the social geography of New York is a mosaic of groups and neighborhoods that have been constituted as ethnically and racially distinct components of the city. Using 1990 census data Logan (2000) finds that while segregation levels among older ethnic groups (English, German, and Irish) are low, they are generally higher for more recent (e.g., new Italian immigrants) and newer white ethnics (e.g., Russians). Segregation is also higher between white ethnics and the non-European groups. Segregation of blacks and whites has actually increased over the decades, reaching an all-time high in 1990, the latest year for which data were available. The segregation of Hispanics has also kept increasing. Further, the various minority groups also have high segregation levels among themselves. Thus all Asian groups are highly segregated from blacks, but so are blacks and Dominicans, for instance. Logan also found significant segregation within the major groups: African-Americans and Afro-Caribbeans have high levels of inter-group segregation and so do Dominicans and Puerto Ricans. (See also Alba et al. 1997.) These patterns of segregation also correspond to a hierarchy of spaces in terms of household income. The widest gap is between whites and blacks. But as with residential segregation, the difference cannot be reduced to a white-black divide (Logan 2000: 180–82; see also Massey and Denton 1993).

The 1980s launches a crucial period when multiple conditions come together and reconfigure the social geography of New York. Alongside the sharp growth in high earnings on Wall Street there is a sharp rise in the number of poor working families in NYC, by 80% in the 1990s alone (Center on Budget and Policy Priorities 1999: chapter 2; Freitas 2000). The latest poverty estimates indicate that nearly one in every four residents in NYC (or 1.8 million people) lived below the federal poverty income level, which stood at U.S.$16,665 for a family of four) in 1998. This is twice the national poverty rate (Community Service Society 1999). Sharply rising rents have forced an estimated 10% of the city's poor families with young children into homeless shelters for at least some period of time each year (Burt and Aran 2000).

Overall, the outer boroughs have had sharp declines in household income. In the 1950s and 1960s, they contained a vast middle class and a prosperous working class. They now have less than their share of managerial and professional households, notwithstanding gentrification in certain areas of Brooklyn, which if excluded would bring this quotient down even further. And they have an overrepresentation of clerical and service workers, operatives, and laborers. The income distribution in the outer boroughs has a strong concentration at the lower end: In 1987 half of the households with annual incomes less than U.S. $5,000 were concentrated in the outer boroughs, compared to only 14% of those with incomes over U.S. $50,000 (Stegman 1988).

Manhattan's location quotient of blue-collar jobs (crafts, operatives, laborers) has reached an all-time low, while the location quotient of such jobs has tended to increase in the outer boroughs and neighboring New Jersey's Hudson county, places that have long had significant concentrations of blue-collar workers.[7] In 1980, the residences of these workers were severely underrepresented in Manhattan and overrepresented in the rest of the core; residences of craft workers were overrepresented in the suburbs as well. These trends have held since then. The location quotients of both the jobs and the residences of service workers have mostly decreased, except for the outer boroughs.

The expansion in the numbers of professionals, especially in the high-income segment working and living in Manhattan, has been a central fact in the gentrification of several parts of the city. It is evident in Manhattan and certain areas in Brooklyn where once poor and middle-income neighborhoods now contain highly priced commercial and residential buildings: parts of Greenwich Village, the area South of Houston Street (referred to as Soho), parts of the Lower East Side (now referred to as the East Village), large portions of the Upper West Side in Manhattan, and the vast office and residential complex named Battery Park City at the southern edge of Manhattan. Gentrification also transformed Brooklyn Heights, Park Slope, and a few other neighborhoods in Brooklyn in the 1980s (DeGiovanni 1984; Zukin 1982; Chall 1984).

This gentrification entailed a growth in ownership by high-income res-

---

[7] The location quotient for blue-collar jobs in the outer boroughs and Hudson county increased for craftsworkers from 108 in 1950 to 119 in 1980, for operatives and laborers from 107 to 132, and for service workers from 91 to 121 (Harris 1988).

idents and displacement of the poor. The New York Housing and Vacancy Survey carried out every three years provides some detailed data in this regard. Contrary to national trends, home ownership in New York rose from 27.4% in 1978 to 30.3% in 1987. Between 1981 and 1987, the period of sharpest increase, the proportion of households that owned their homes increased by 5.9% in Manhattan compared to 2.5% for the city as a whole. Most of the increase in ownership occurred through the conversion of existing rental units into condominiums or cooperatives, both typically requiring a significant amount of money.[8] The evidence shows that those who bought units in this period had a median income of $36,000, compared with a median income of $16,000 among tenant households (Stegman 1988: 100, 185). The households that bought converted units were 77% white and 78% had no children. Given these trends in addition to the displacement of low-income households associated with conversion, household incomes in Manhattan have risen more rapidly than in any other borough, increasing by 18.3% from 1983 to 1986 (Stegman 1988: 100, 182, 185).

Yet Manhattan also contains areas that have experienced sharp declines in household incomes: northern Manhattan, containing Harlem and East Harlem, has high unemployment, sharp increases in poverty, and sharp increases in crime and delinquency rates. There is a ring of poverty that runs through northern Manhattan, the South Bronx, and much of northern Brooklyn (Tobier 1985). In 1980 New York contained a larger number of census tracts with higher levels of poor households than in 1970.

The low-rent housing market suffered a massive decline in the 1980s that, along with the stagnation and decline in household incomes at the lower end, created a situation that led to severe overcrowding and homelessness. From 1978 to 1987 there was an absolute decline in the number of rental units, whether occupied or vacant, of over 57,000, along with a sharp increase in owner-occupied units. In addition to the absolute decrease in rental units, the share of rental units lacking protection from eviction or inordinate rent increases rose from 25% to 31% of all units, or 522,000 units. Finally, there was a sharp decline of 26% in the share of low-cost rental units and a sharp increase of 26% in the share of high-cost rental units, with an even sharper increase of 30% for very expensive units.[9]

[8] From 1981 (the first year these data became available) to 1987, over 93,000 housing units in New York were converted from rental to co-op or condominium tenure (Stegman 1988: 175). Of these, 49% were located in Manhattan, where the ownership rate rose by a sharp 5.9% from 1981 to 1987 alone.

[9] A category of housing units that is important for low-income people and that does not quite exist in London or Tokyo is the stock of in-rem housing held by the city's government as a result of abandonment by or tax delinquency of the owners. About half of the in-

Several conditions produced the sharp increase of homelessness that began in the 1980s: the growth in low-income households, the sharp reduction in government subsidies for housing due to conversions, and high-income gentrification. While the combination of deinstitutionalization of mental patients with a shrinking in the low-priced housing supply and in subsidies may have produced much of the homelessness in the 1970s, other conditions were the major generators of homelessness in the 1980s. The sharp increase in homeless families was the clearest evidence of the transformation. By 1988, there were over 5,000 registered homeless families in city shelters, a quintupling of the estimate for 1980. And there were over 10,000 registered homeless individuals. Furthermore, for the first time, a large share of the homeless were women and children. In addition, there is an uncounted population of homeless individuals and childless families who avoid the shelters and live on the streets, in train stations, in parks, and beneath highways. There are no precise figures, but it is estimated that up to 100,000 single room occupancy units (SROs) disappeared in the 1980s as a result of conversion or demolition of these units, particularly in central Manhattan (Tobier 1990: 311). Homelessness has continued to grow. The National Coalition for the Homeless estimates that 100,000 people in NYC experienced homelessness at some time during 1999; 23,000 of these, including 9,000 children, slept in NYC shelters on any given night.

Deinstitutionalization began in the 1950s, but the availability of single room occupancy units and, eventually, housing subsidies deterred homelessness.[10] It was in the 1980s that the sharp increase in the demand for housing made a precarious situation into a crisis. Second, the supply of low-priced housing began to shrink, mostly through urban renewal and abandonment by landlords, in the late 1960s. But it was only in the 1980s that the dimensions of this shrinkage reached a new scale and produced massive homelessness of families. Third, public assistance payments began to level off in the 1970s, but it was in combination with the

---

rem units are occupied by blacks and about a third by Hispanics; whites and others occupy the rest. Another important source of housing for low-income people is single room occupancy units. These are one-room rental units that lack complete plumbing and kitchen facilities for the exclusive use of the occupant(s). There were over 51,000 such units in 1987, a significant decline from earlier periods falling to 11,000 in 1999 (U.S. Bureau of the Census 1999: Series IA-Table 15; Series IIA-Table 15).

[10] Passage of the Community Mental Health Care Act in 1963 provided federal funds for community-based mental health facilities, setting the stage for large-scale deinstitutionalization. From 1965 to 1975, the number of patients in New York State psychiatric hospitals fell by 62%, from 85,000 to 33,000, and by the late 1980s, it was down to 19,000 (Tobier 1990: 310). Single room occupancy units were cheap and abundant and disability allowances covered the cost.

shrinking supply of low-priced housing and massive job losses in the 1980s that the full impact of this became evident in the form of homelessness.

New York's property tax subsidy, extended in 1976 to stimulate a languishing real estate industry, contributed to raising the profitability of rehabilitating old structures and converting low-income housing into high-priced units. In the 1960s there had been few alternative uses for many such properties. The growing demand in the 1980s for centrally located housing by high-income households contributed to the accelerated replacement of SROs by high-cost housing. In a short period of time, the profitability of the market for affordable housing had been acutely outdistanced by that of the booming market for high-priced housing. This only added to the rapid shrinkage in the supply of low-priced housing.[11]

While the luxury housing sector is a small proportion of all housing it represents much of new construction since the 1980s. This sector is also part of the international property market and can command prices that leave most of the residents in the city out of the bidding. Again, while New York, London, and Tokyo have long had a luxury housing sector, the scale emerging in the 1980s represents a new development in that it generated a sharp expansion in the supply of such housing and hence absorbed areas of these cities that only a decade earlier were considered marginal or worse. Moreover, the sharp competition and the high prices of the 1980s in central locations altered the terms defining profitability in the industry and induced significant increases along the price chain. While there was an increase in high-income workers and high-income households, it is also true that, with the probable exception of the top-income level, households had to allocate larger shares of income to housing than had been customary, and there were more two-earner households. Thus it would seem that the industry managed to extract a higher

---

[11] A fruitful area for future research would be quantification of the relationship between a concentration of high-income households and the infrastructure of service jobs associated with it. Although not directly applicable to this discussion of New York, it is interesting to note that such an analysis of London and Britain was developed by Lee (1984) and then replicated by Thrift and Williams (1987). Using the ratio between the population of an area and service employment in that area, they obtained what could be read as a service provision ratio. This is clearly a very crude measure, and not too much can be read into it. But the findings are interesting. They found the ratio to be 3,058.95 per 10,000 population in the Southeast compared with an average for Britain as a whole of 2,466.21. Isolating specific service industries, they found this service provision ratio to be 575.96 per 10,000 population for the Southeast compared with 362 for Britain as a whole in banking, finance, insurance, and business services. Wales, with 198.77, had the lowest ratio for this industry group.

level of prices from households than had been the norm in preceding decades.

The distribution of household income in New York reflects these developments. Based on a state-by-state analysis of Census Bureau data by the Center for Budget and Policy Priorities and the Economic Policy Institute (2000), New York has the worst income inequality in the U.S. The average annual income, adjusted for inflation, of the richest one-fifth of NY families rose to a level 20 times above the income of the bottom fifth of families in the 1996–98 period, more than double this gap in the late 1970s. The city's middle class also lost ground to the richer fifth, with the median income of the top quintile of families rising to a level four times that of the middle fifth of families. Notwithstanding income inequality, it might be the case that all incomes rose, only more slowly than those of the top quintile. The evidence shows that the average family income of the top fifth rose 18% since 1980 while the average incomes of the remaining four-fifths actually fell, by 12% for the middle fifth and by 13% for the lowest fifth. It is well known that high-income families have multiple sources of income that are not included in standard family income counts, thereby producing underestimates of the actual difference between the top quintiles and the lower ones. The triannual survey on housing and vacancies, the most detailed source for intercensal periods, indicates that the lowest quintile lost 15% of income between 1977 and 1986, while all other quintiles gained in income (Stegman 1988). The highest gain in real income (deflated by the Consumer Price Index) was in the top quintile, at 28%; the next to the highest gained 23.5%. The share of income going to the lowest quintile decreased from 4.9% in 1977 to 3.9% in 1986, equivalent to a 20% decline, while the top quintile raised its share from 45.2% to 47.3%, a small increase but still the largest gain in share of all five groups.

For minority groups there is the added burden of above average unemployment rates (Massey and Denton 1993). New York has a higher unemployment rate than that of the central cities of the 20 largest metropolitan areas in the U.S. even though it has declined in the 1990s. All major racial/ethnic groups in the city have lower employment to population ratios than do their counterparts in the other 20 cities studied.

London and the Region

Central London has long specialized in office jobs. But the number of these jobs has risen immensely since the 1980s. By the late 1990s we see a strong overrepresentation of finance, banking, and insurance: two-thirds of all London jobs in FIRE compared with a third of all employment in London, and half of all London jobs in professional and business services. Manufacturing, on the other hand, is overrepresented in outer London, an area that accounts for well over three-fifths of such jobs compared with somewhat over a third of all London employment.

The most central areas of London have undergone a transformation that broadly parallels Manhattan's, though the concrete details are diverse. We see a parallel increase in the stratum of what Brint (1988) described as upper professionals, a group largely employed in the corporate services, including finance. The sharp growth in the concentration of mostly young, new high-income professionals and managers employed in central London represents a significant change from a decade ago.[12]

The internationalization of the city itself inevitably brought greater pressures toward earning levels comparable to those in other major international financial centers. It was not till the 1980s that salaries of professionals and managers in London's City began to reach such levels. Furthermore, the accelerated growth in the magnitude of operations brought about an increase in the demand for workers and a tight labor market in certain occupations, especially those involving specialized skills. The movement of foreign firms into London further accelerated these trends putting great upward pressure on salary levels. Deregulation, by opening up the market, raised the demand for certain types of specialized skills and experience and generally reduced the feasibility for many firms of simply using their old workforce.

While the expansion in the number of jobs directly and indirectly associated with the growth of London as an international financial and producer services center affected a broad range of occupations, from unskilled service workers to highly specialized personnel, the upward pressure on salaries did not similarly affect all these occupations. As in New York, the overall outcome of these various trends has been the expansion of both a high-income stratum and a low-income stratum of workers. And there has been an increase in high-income residents in central areas of London, along with a growing concentration of poor in inner London (Townsend, Corrigan, and Kowarzik 1987; U.K. Office for National Statistics 1999).

Research on the new segment of the professional and managerial stratum (Thrift and Williams 1987) shows that two categories of workers account for most of the increase in the number of high-paying jobs in the

---

[12] There has been a greater demand for highly trained workers, and more university graduates are going into business occupations. By 1985 over 18% of all graduates in Britain were going into finance, many of these in the City (O'Leary 1986). Alongside the increase in numbers of highly trained workers with advanced degrees, there has been a greater specialization associated with the greater complexity and multiplicity of innovations in the financial industry and in the specialized services generally.

1980s: a group composed of top-level managers and dealers and a group of mostly young graduates whose advancement or promotion lines lead to high-paying jobs over a fairly short period of time. This, again, parallels trends in Manhattan in the 1980s. Thrift and Williams (1987) found that for the first group, the whole period surrounding the 1986 deregulation saw a very large increase in the demand for their expertise. In 1985, there were only sixty-seven such employees in fourteen companies in the City who earned more than £100,000; two years later there were about 2,000 (Thrift and Williams 1987). In 1999 the average gross weekly earnings of City workers were 78% above Great Britain's average and 37% above the London average (Corporation of London 2000). To these earnings should be added a whole range of other types of income associated with such jobs. We see here a process of cultural and social capital formation (e.g., Low 1999) and an unequal distribution of that capital (Fernandez Kelly 1995).

It is in the 1980s that this new socioeconomic alignment is produced. Thrift and Williams (1987) note that this stratum of workers should be distinguished from the top of the corporate hierarchy, the directors and partners of the City's firms. These have received extremely high salaries for a long time, and the developments of the 1980s raised their salaries, but lacked the dramatic impact on these salary levels and their numbers that they have had among the group of top managers and dealers described above.[13] Among the second group, the well-paid recent graduates, Thrift and Williams (1987) found that there was an across-the-board increase in salaries and frequently a highly accelerated rate of salary growth. This is also the group where there are at times labor shortages in certain specialties, another factor that raises salaries. A key example is that of computer experts. Young graduates make up a large share of this category. In her research on hiring practices in the City, McDowell (1997) found that credentialism and merit have become increasingly important since financial deregulation. She found this to be particularly significant for women in that it opened opportunities not available when old-boys networks were more prominent.

As in New York, a distinct lifestyle has emerged, and there is a suffi-

[13] The continuing weight of the class system in English economic and social life is evident in the extent to which top-level executives in City firms come from upper-class backgrounds, which is not necessarily the case among the new professionals. Using various sources, Thrift and Williams (1987) estimated that about three-quarters of top executives in merchant banks, clearing banks, accountancy firms, and insurance companies; stockbrokers; and insurance brokers went to a private school. Among stockbrokers, this figure rises to 96% (cited in Thrift 1987). Furthermore, 68% of top City executives went to one of two universities: Oxford or Cambridge. To this concentration should be added that of the considerable presence of members of the aristocracy and, in the 1990s, the growing numbers of foreign executives.

ciently critical mass of young, high-income workers engaged in high levels of consumption that it makes itself felt in certain parts of London and its region. New, elegant shops and restaurants—and sharp increases in the prices of housing—manifest the new lifestyle. There has also been high-income gentrification of several parts of London, including areas of inner London once inhabited by lower-income people, especially minorities. For example, in my 1987 fieldwork in Hackney, one of the poorest areas in London, I found a number of renovated townhouses and warehouses and factories converted to living lofts, a trend that has gone along with growing numbers of minority residents in the 1990s (London Research Centre 1997). Similarly, in the area called Little Venice, once rather grand townhouses that had decayed and been subdivided into dense tenements for immigrants in the 1950s and 1960s were being "rehabilitated" at immense speed and in large numbers in the mid-1980s. Walking through those streets in the summer of 1987 offered what is probably one of the most stunning instances of how landlords will let row after row of what had been elegant cream-colored facades fall into dark gray disrepair for decades, only to be quickly restored to their old splendor in a few months when the market calls. In the early 1990s, Clerkenwell, one of the oldest parts of London, began to gentrify. Its industrial structures have been transformed into some of the most sought-after luxury residential lofts and its street-level craft-based workshops into designer spaces.

The evidence shows that household income has increased faster in London and in the Southeast region as a whole than in the rest of the country (U.K. Department of Employment, 1987a, 1987b, 1987c; UK Office for National Statistics 1999). The Southeast has a disproportionate concentration of earnings, national income, investment income, and accumulated assets. This has contributed to an expansion in the consumption of goods and services and in home acquisitions. The average level of household expenditures is far higher than in other regions. The prices of houses have increased enormously and been at least 25% higher than in the rest of the country since the late 1970s. The Family Expenditure Survey (U.K. Department of Employment, various years) reports that the Southeast region has higher household expenditures than does any other region of the country.

This is well illustrated by the distribution of the IT workforce in the UK. The latest available data are for 1997 and show that London accounted for 18% of the UK's IT workforce in terms of their residential patterns. Including the SE, the total comes to 46%. Just considering UK Managerial and Professional workforce residential patterns this figure rises to 20% for London and together with the SE to 55% (ITNTO 1998). On the other hand, a different picture emerges in terms of workplace distribution as many of these professionals commute to London. The wage differential of IT support staff between the City and the rest of London and the South East is estimated at 66%, and significantly higher at top levels of the occupational structure in the sector. For instance, financial services IT specialists can earn up to four times the going rate compared to other subsectors (Corporation of London 1999:16–18).

However, while this region contains a disproportionate concentration of high-income households, the region as a whole does not contain a disproportionate concentration of high-income jobs. This parallels the New York region, with its large numbers of high-income workers residing in the suburban ring and commuting to high-paying jobs in Manhattan. It is London rather than the rest of the Southeast that has a disproportionate concentration of high-paying jobs. The key point here is that the Southeast excluding London, while representing a large concentration of high-income households, high levels of household expenditure, and highly priced houses, is not a location with a disproportionately larger concentration of high-income jobs compared with Britain as a whole. This further suggests that the concentration of wealth and high-income households in this region is partly maintained and reproduced by the accelerated growth and high incomes generated by London's expanded role as a financial and specialized service center.

Finally, the Southeast can be seen as a location for the generation of a range of jobs that service the needs of the high-income households, directly and indirectly. As in New York, areas with large concentrations of high-income households generate an infrastructure of often low-wage jobs, notably the overrepresentation of sales jobs in the suburban ring. Ethnographic materials of various kinds can be used to describe and illustrate the range of services that are purchased by high-income households, from various kinds of cleaning and maintenance work through governesses, masseuses and beauty care, to more elaborate and specialized work, such as accountants, lawyers, and trust managers. The decentralization of offices has contributed clerical jobs. Interestingly, the Southeast is also a location for secondary servicing or production for firms in London. Some of these jobs may be high-income jobs but a large share are likely to be low-wage.

Yet another key component in the spatial organization of the region is the geography of London's knowledge-driven IT sub-economy. It makes clear to what extent these high value-added industries can generate fine-grained spatial and socioeconomic inequalities inside the city. The IT sector is centered in the City, and the London boroughs of Camden, Westminster, Islington and Tower Hamlets, the latter including Canary Wharf and Docklands. There is an important second layer of activity which includes the Western Arc boroughs (excluding Hillingdon), Hackney directly to the north of the City, and Croydon and Southwark to the south. On the other side, further strengthening the socio-spatial differentiation are a group of boroughs which are not developing in this direction and increasingly have more in common with the less prosperous northern regions of Britain rather than with the more advanced areas of London. A third of London's local authorities lag behind the national average employment profile for the knowledge-driven information economy. These are mostly, but not exclusively, concentrated in the Northeast and East of London. Thus while London as a whole is above the national average, there is often sharp differentiation within the city.

The considerable concentration of IT jobs in London and within London, its disproportionate location in the City and several adjacent boroughs signals the further expansion of the urban glamour zone, of firms and households with high money making capabilities. IT is thus contributing to an expansion of the high-value-added area of the city. And so is the growth in the share of City jobs in finance and business services, up from 53% in 1981 to 78% in 1997 (Corporation of London 2000). Business services grew by 31% from 1991 to 1997 and Other Services by 24%, two sectors with both low- and high-income jobs. This development also contributes to an expansion in low-wage servicing jobs for both the firms and the households, and state-of-the-art ancillary services, from designer shops to designer restaurants and hotels.

The number of clerical and blue-collar service jobs has also increased significantly in London. But these workers have not experienced a parallel growth in their wages and salaries. It is important to repeat that, as in New York and Tokyo, these kinds of jobs account for a large share of all workers in the new economic sectors. They constitute a significant share of the work force necessary to keep the so-called new economy going. Since as yet many of these jobs have not been relocated to lower-cost areas, these workers have to compete for housing with the expanding higher-income sectors. Not only have their incomes typically not increased; their conditions of life have often declined, given the privatization of public housing and the higher prices in gentrified commercial areas. Another trend that has accentuated this tension is the increased representation in this group of part-time and temporary workers, who are mostly women. Furthermore, much clerical work is becoming deskilled and routinized, which is gradually leading to lower average salaries at the same time that most higher-level occupations are becoming more specialized and leading to higher average salaries.

A third major component of the social geography of London is the consolidation of areas of concentrated poverty and other multiple disadvantages. Violent confrontations in 1976 in Notting Hill and in 1977 in East London's Lewisham brought out in full force the facts of severe decay, high unemployment, and poverty in many places in Britain's major cities, and especially London.[14] These areas became known as "the inner city." Blacks and Asians were disproportionately concentrated in the inner city, especially in London, which had the largest share of this population. The 1974–1975 recession and the continuing loss of manufacturing and low-level warehousing and distribution jobs in combination with discrimination in employment and in housing against Asians and blacks all contributed to their high unemployment. Unemployment also rose sharply among whites, especially among working-class youths, low-wage workers, the unemployed, and the elderly (Friend and Metcalf 1982). The sharp rise of unemployment in the 1980s and the continuing loss of manufacturing jobs extended these problems to areas beyond the inner city.

Between 1971 and 1981, over 20% of whites left London for the suburbs or elsewhere compared with 10% of minorities; among Afro-Caribbeans four out of five stayed in the inner city between 1971 and 1981, while half of inner-city Indians moved out, mostly to the suburbs. The Bengali population, however, was still highly concentrated in East London and heavily involved in the garment industry, thus resembling the first generation of many immigrant groups in the United States and the United Kingdom. In the late 1990s many of these differences persist (see Tables 9.4 and 9.5).

It is increasingly evident that there are two major areas of minority concentration in London: the inner-city boroughs of Hackney, Haringey, Lambeth, Lewisham, and Wandsworth and the outer-city boroughs of Brent, Ealing, Hounslow, and Waltham Forest. These two areas of concentration are increasingly diverse in terms of the predominant population, with the former mostly Afro-Caribbean and the latter mostly Asian. The exceptions are Tower Hamlets and Brent, which have fairly mixed populations and are among the poorest (Townsend, Corrigan, and Kowarzik 1987; London Research Centre 1997).

As the evidence discussed in chapter 8 showed, the UK along with the U.S. were the two countries among those examined which had the highest growth in inequality. Privatization and deregulation have contributed

---

[14] The great worry for the government was that urban uprisings on the scale of those in the United States in the 1960s were going to take place in London and other British cities (Friend and Metcalf 1982). There were many violent clashes; the National Front grew and became very violent in its racism, and the police made hundreds of arrests. In September 1976, the Secretary of State for the Environment announced that the government was beginning a major review to address urban decay. Development resources were switched from outer areas and New Towns to inner-city areas; the special urban aid program, started in the 1960s, was expanded; and special efforts to help small businesses in the cities were implemented.

to cut a large number of jobs that used to be in the government and enjoyed the full range of benefits by relocating them to the private sector. Some of these jobs became part-time or temporary and some of those that remained full-time lost protections and benefits and even had lower levels of pay. (Low Pay Unit 1988b; see also Hamnett and Cross 1998; Logan and Taylor-Gooby 1993.)

Using a deprivation index for 1984, Townsend, Corrigan, and Kowarzik (1987) found that in the most deprived boroughs, a majority of households had incomes under £6000 per year.[15] The five most deprived boroughs reported in the 1984 data were Hackney, Tower Hamlets, Islington, Lambeth, and Newham. Working from government statistics, they estimated that in 1985–1986 there were 1.8 million people in London living in poverty or on the margins of poverty, a doubling of the 1960 figure.[16] Other kinds of evidence point to additional growth in poverty: Increases in dependency, in early retirement, and in the number of people over seventy-five years old all feed the expansion of a low-income population. So does high unemployment among minority residents. The number of homeless people is rapidly growing in London, and was estimated at 100,000 in 1999; London also accounts for a disproportionate share of Britain's 167,000 homeless households (NHA 2000).

The distribution of income clearly reflects these conditions. The New Earnings Survey for various years shows that relative to the median income, top earnings increased in the early and mid-1980s and bottom earnings decreased. When we add to this the increase in resources at the top and the reduction in various types of benefits at the bottom, then the gap is even larger than the earnings figures indicate. Tax changes have favored those with higher incomes. Thus if we were to measure the gap in posttax income, it would be even wider. In the 1980s, the average company director's income increased by 43%; the average income for households with an unemployed head fell by 12%. There was a growth in unearned income, a growth in the earnings gap, and a growth in households headed by single persons, the aged, and the unemployed.

In a detailed examination of London and the Southeast compared with

---

[15] The deprivation index is a standardized measure based on the share of a borough's population constituted by residents who are unemployed, are overcrowded, lack basic amenities, or are single parents, one-person pensioner households, black immigrants, or unskilled working class.

[16] This study was a representative sample survey of the population of Greater London in 1985–1986 based on available evidence on deprivation and mortality in the 755 wards of the city. Compared to Townsend's (1979) earlier study, Townsend, Corrigan, and Kowarzik's (1987) found more poverty and far more severe poverty, with people living far below the poverty threshold, and in the most extreme cases becoming homeless.

the rest of the country, Dunford and Fielding (1997) find clear evidence of growing differentials. In the 1980s and continuing in the 1990s London and the Southeast gained share of GDP, of employment, including professional workers, and had continued overrepresentation in logistical functions of transport, storage, and communications. Higher labor force participation rates and higher incidence of highly paid types of occupations also characterized London and the Southeast. Financial and business services are overrepresented at almost a third of GDP in Greater London and a fifth in the ROSE. Almost a third of the UK's output in financial and business services is produced in Greater London and between 39% and 58% of all the UK's professional jobs in the producer services are located in Greater London. (See also Corporation of London 1999a.) In the Southeast this overrepresentation, though present, was much lower, partly because it is to a large extent a residential area for many of these top-level professional workers who commute to London. The overrepresentation of professional jobs in the ROSE was particularly concentrated in research and development activities. They also find that even as London and the Southeast appeared to be thriving, the rest of the UK experienced a number of negative conditions. (See also Benko and Lipietz 1992 on these types of disjunctures.)

Tokyo

In the 1980s globalization promoted massive growth and capital accumulation in Tokyo. In the 1990s it did not. There was, nonetheless, a continuing increase in the concentration of economic, social, and political activities in Tokyo and its wider metropolitan region (Hill and Fujita 1995; Saito 1999). Here Tokyo diverges from London and New York in two regards. One is that globalization continued to promote massive growth in these two cities during the 1990s and the other that the concentration of the types of activities that continue to locate and relocate to Tokyo did not happen in New York and London. Further, the role of the government also differentiates Tokyo's trajectory as a global city from New York and London. In four of its major plans for the Tokyo Metropolitan Region over the last two decades, the government of the region launched a series of initiatives that contained important measures positioning Tokyo in the global system (Saito 1999; Teranishi 1991). The First Plan's focus on the restructuring of capital and space led to the closure and relocation of heavy manufacturing, expansion of service industries in urban areas, and the concentration of globally linked economic functions in Tokyo. By the time of the Fourth Plan, the globalization of Japanese capital produced a counterreaction in the 1980s from other governments which pressured Japan into a reorientation away from just exports and towards expanding internal consumption. At the urban level it fueled the Minkatsu policy of getting private investors to fund redevelopment projects, as these also generate large multiplier effects for other sectors of the economy. Saito (1999) notes that these policy agendas shaped much of Tokyo's economic history in the 1980s and 1990s. When the new governor of the TMG is elected in 1995 he drops mention of Tokyo as a world city and reorients policy towards the city's internal agendas.

One consequence of the government's strong role is that the social geography of Tokyo exhibits far less differentiation than that of London and New York. Tokyo's expansion took place in a brief period and was influenced by a different cultural and political conception guiding the allocation of resources, one which gave strong priority to the development of industry rather than to increasing the standard of living. The vast size of Tokyo's population and the rapidity of urbanization have produced a landscape dominated by the modest dwellings of the enormous numbers of middle- and lower-income workers who commute to central Tokyo every day. Nonetheless, there are in central Tokyo areas, such as Minato and generally the hilly western side called the Yamanote, that have long contained the residences of the wealthy and now are also inhabited by many of the new top corporate officials, including foreigners. The central business district has, like central areas in Manhattan and in London, evolved into a highly specialized place for offices, while Shinjuku has become a second major commercial center. High-income gentrification in several older areas of central Tokyo and new luxury developments grew rapidly in the 1980s. The elements of an expensive lifestyle centered around fashion, designer stores, and elegant restaurants are also evident, for example, in the Roppongi area of Minato. Indeed, the 1980s saw a sharp increase in imports of luxury goods, including German cars and Italian designer clothes.[17]

[17] An interesting question concerns the impact on consumption of the revaluation of the yen after 1985, which the Japanese refer to as "endaka." Using the OECD model for calculating multilateral purchasing power parities, Japan's Economic Planning Agency found that Japan's parity had increased during the strong increase in the value of the yen from October 1985 to March 1987 compared with other currencies. Purchasing power parities are comparative figures for each country's own currency with which the same amount of a particular consumer good or service can be bought in each country. This is clearly complicated by differences in lifestyle and consumption patterns, the lack of comparability on many consumer items, and great variations in standards and quality. During that eighteen-month period the yen/dollar rate was changing more rapidly than were the purchasing power parities. This was partly because the purchasing power of the yen includes land and services, which are not traded and hence do not reflect changes in currency value. It also takes longer for changes in currency values and prices of imported goods to be reflected in the purchasing power parities. Therefore, the Japanese did not feel that the

As in New York and London, the growth in corporate and financial services since the 1980s raised the demand for professional workers. This has particularly been the case in finance, information research and development, advertising, accounting, architecture, and engineering services. Between 1975 and 1985, the number of professional workers in Tokyo rose by 200,000 in service industries; these workers were mostly between twenty-four and thirty-four years of age (Japan Management and Coordination Agency 1988). This figure excludes a growing category of highly trained professional women workers who are being hired as part-time workers in these occupations (Japan Ministry of Labor 1989). The growing need for professional workers and their strategic location in leading industries put strong upward pressure on salaries. This, along with the rapid increase in domestic and foreign corporate staff generally, fed the expansion of the high-priced housing market in central Tokyo. The growth of the luxury housing market and the demand for office space further induced sharp rises in the cost of housing. There is now a large number of young Japanese professionals and employees of foreign firms who are likely to reside in central Tokyo and have the consumption and lifestyle patterns evident among such workers in London and Tokyo. Areas such as Roppongi, Aoyama, and Akasaka resemble equivalent areas in New York and London. Tokyo has long had elegant restaurants and shopping districts for wealthy Japanese and foreigners and corporate elites. Now there is an expansion of a less exclusive version of such districts, where a fashion-oriented lifestyle, or fragments of it, can be bought. There also has been a growth in new luxury residential and office complexes, such as Ark Hill, which, like Trump Tower in New York, are sites for the new corporate elite.

The city also contains a growing number of jobs in new and old industries that pay rather low wages. For these workers, access to housing in Tokyo is increasingly difficult. There has been a vast growth in personal

---

purchasing power inside Japan had increased much, notwithstanding huge increases in the value of the yen (Japan Economic Planning Agency 1988). The increase in the yen in 1985 had an effect on luxury imports (Japan Economic Planning Agency 1988: 38). Imports from France and Italy, which are mostly expensive or luxury clothing items, also increased. Automobile imports increased by 98.5% over 1985; imports of arts and antiques, by 68.4%. Imports from South Korea, China, and Taiwan had been growing throughout the 1980s; but in 1986 they grew by 40%, to 50% over the 1985 level. Imports from South Korea and Taiwan of toys and play equipment, which formerly had been exports from Japan, increased by 79.6% in 1986. According to the Japan External Trade Organization (JETRO), in 1986 about forty import consumer items grew by more than 50% over 1985. JETRO found a new trend toward imports of certain expensive consumer goods, especially luxury cars, paintings, calligraphic works, other art objects, antiques, and tropical fruits, all items not formerly imported. A survey of consumers (Japan Economic Planning Agency 1988: 43) found that 66.8% did not care whether an item was imported or domestic as long as the quality and price were satisfactory; only 21.3% reported that they tended to choose domestic products.

services, with many new types of services being sold. Jobs in these industries are mostly low-wage and held by women. Many of the professional jobs in high demand are being filled by part-time workers, often women. Another growth occupation, clerical work, employs an increasing number of part-time workers. Seventy percent of women part-time workers are in clerical jobs. Furthermore, the gap between full-time and part-time women has increased: In 1977 part-time workers' earnings stood at 80% of those of full-time workers; by 1987 they stood at 65%. Between 1987 and 1997 the share of part-time jobs rose, and so did the gap between Tokyo's female part-time clerical workers and male full-time professional workers, two growing categories.

For the mass of workers in Tokyo, affordable housing increasingly entails a two-hour trip to work. The rate of homeownership began to decline in the 1980s, and the average size of new apartments shrunk after increasing in the 1970s. The average floor space of newly built apartments fell to 46 square meters in 1987, from 57 square meters in 1980 (*Economist*, August 31, 1987). Commuting distances have kept growing, and prices of housing even in distant locations have made ownership increasingly impossible, to the point that ninety-nine-year mortgages are now available. In 1995, the average price of a condominium of 75 sq. meters was equivalent to over 7 times the average yearly household income (Japan Statistical Yearbook 2001: 159). There has been an almost tripling in the numbers of homeless since 1995, reaching 5,700 in August 2000 (TMG 2001). While still mostly men, the numbers of women are growing.

These divergent trends parallel conditions in New York and London, and, as in these cities, assume concrete forms in the spatial organization of the city. Gentrification articulates both the expansion of a housing supply for high-income households (either through renovation of old structures or their demolition and construction of new ones) and the displacement of low-income households (either through direct physical displacement or through their elimination from the bidding and from effective demand). The familiar outcomes are increasingly evident in Tokyo as well: the emergence of fashionable residential and commercial districts along with growing poverty, including homelessness, particularly among older residents displaced by gentrification.

But perhaps the most important process of change in the social geography of Tokyo is, at this point, the emergence of an inner city. It deserves some detailed discussion.

TOKYO'S INNER CITY

There has been some discussion as to whether the decline of manufacturing in central Tokyo and the outmigration of working-age residents from these areas may have contributed to the development of what in the West is often referred to as an inner-city problem (Okimura 1980; Kimijima 1980; Narita 1980; Sakiyama 1981; Komori 1983; KUPI 1981). The very rapid growth of the economy in Tokyo, extensive construction of public and private sector projects, the decline in the young population in central Tokyo, and the loss of many traditional manufacturing firms could conceivably contribute to a decline in the employment base and in the physical conditions of older areas in central Tokyo that have not been incorporated into the new types of growth evident in the city, especially in the 1980s.

The most detailed empirical study of this issue is by the geographer Nakabayashi (1987), who addressed this question through an examination of government data on thirty-two variables for each of Tokyo's twenty-three wards in 1986. These range from basic demographic variables to employment, land prices, environmental conditions, and the presence of minority populations. Data on these variables were organized into four indices of socioeconomic conditions. The degree to which these conditions were present and their degree of geographic concentration allowed the author to establish the extent to which there are in Tokyo social, economic, and physical conditions resembling the inner-city problem in cities such as New York and London, and the extent to which such conditions, if present, are concentrated in Tokyo's inner areas. The four indices are neighborhood social decline; local economic decline; physical and housing decline; and presence of disadvantaged minorities, including immigrants. Nakabayashi's findings are as follows (for the sake of clarity and because there is much reason to believe the trends still hold, I have set these forth in the present tense).

In terms of the first index, there is a rather clear pattern of social decline in old downtown areas of wards characterized by mixed commercial, residential, and traditional manufacturing uses. These, especially Taito and Sumida Wards, are the most problematic, having clearly suffered from a severe loss of jobs and young people. A second tier of problematic areas are to be found in both the traditional manufacturing districts, such as Arakawa and in the central business district wards of Chiyoda and Chuo. All of these areas are characterized by extreme declines in the resident population and a sharp relative increase in the share of old people in the resident population. A good share of those who have outmigrated are people who lived and worked in these areas for at least twenty years; thus the outmigration has not been confined to the young. In the evaluation of the author, these communities "are dying as social units" (Nakabayashi 1987: 122).

In terms of economic decline, the most affected areas are those where manufacturing was once a thriving economic base supporting a whole array of other commercial and service activities as well as a significant residential and commuting workforce. Most severely affected are the wards of Arakawa, Sumida, Kita, Koto, and Ota. These areas thus offer a sharp contrast to others in Tokyo where there has been a massive increase in the level of economic activity and in the numbers of commuting workers. But clearly this growth involves very different economic sectors.

In terms of decline in physical and housing conditions, the most severe cases are Toshima and Kita wards, which have a high density of both poor housing and poor people. These areas have a high proportion of tenement housing with no private bathrooms or kitchens. It is worth noting that poor housing conditions and blight were also found in two of the wards in the central business district, Chuo and Minato, where land fetches the highest prices and the most elegant homes, hotels, office towers, and shops are located. This is not unlike Manhattan, which contains both some of the poorest and some of the most expensive housing. Other areas with poor housing and blight are located in the wards immediately surrounding the central business district; they are areas characterized by significant concentrations of small houses for rent, factories, shops, and offices, with continuing high population density notwithstanding a gradual decline in absolute numbers. In the central business district wards there is simultaneously a very high density of buildings, contributing to the deterioration of living conditions, and a growing number of unoccupied rental housing (one of the results of the increase in residential land prices). The dominant fact in these three wards is the rapid expansion of the highly dynamic business center and the rapid decline of the residential population.

In terms of the fourth element, the association between social disadvantage and minority residents, the types of data available make it difficult to establish such an association. However, there is little doubt that the presence of minority residents has not been a significant factor in the development of an inner-city area of economic and social decline. Furthermore, this factor plays itself out quite differently in Tokyo than in New York or London, where the evidence clearly indicates the higher prevalence of poverty, unemployment, poor housing conditions, and residence in blighted areas among immigrants and blacks than among native-born whites.

Given common conceptions of a totally homogenous society held both by many Japanese and by many commentators abroad, it is important to point out that there is a growing Southeast Asian immigrant population (discussed in greater detail later in this chapter). Nakabayashi (1987) expanded the research on the spatial distribution of socially disadvantaged and ethnic minorities, including foreign residents. The most disadvantaged locations were found in the Taito and Arakawa wards and, to a lesser extent in the Sumida, Kita, Toshima, Shinjuku, and Shibuya wards. These are all areas that are part of inner Tokyo, immediately surrounding the three central business district wards. The wards of Shinjuku, Shibuya, and Toshima comprise the major subcenter of Tokyo, and Shinjuku, of course, is the new seat of the Tokyo Metropolitan Government and a major area for new business development. Shinjuku and Shibuya contain a significant Korean community and most of the foreign Asian women recruited as "entertainers," who live there, as do many of the new illegal male immigrants from South and Southeast Asia. These are wards where I found extremely dense concentrations of very poor housing and small restaurants catering to these legal and illegal immigrants who are clearly in a condition of severe social, economic, and political disadvantage.

When all four of Nakabayashi's sets of characteristics are considered, the areas with the strongest incidence of these various conditions are the Arakawa, Taito, and Sumida wards, all immediately adjacent to the central business district. The loss of traditional manufacturing lies at the heart of the social, economic, and physical decline of Arakawa and Sumida. Taito has long had high concentrations of poor and low-income households. It now also has a high incidence of crime. Taito ward contains the largest concentration of daily laborers; it is one of the four major hiring camps for such workers in Japan, heavily controlled by gangsters. Arakawa and Taito now also have socially disadvantaged minority and immigrant populations.

In brief, the greatest social, economic, and physical decline is not in the central business district but in the areas immediately surrounding it, which were once centers for manufacturing and trading. While they are losing population they continue to have very high residential density and deteriorating housing conditions. There is a high incidence of poverty, illness, and crime in the worst areas, such as Taito, but also in Toshima and Kita. According to Nakabayashi (1987), the key factor in the social, economic, and physical decline of inner areas in Tokyo has been the decline of traditional manufacturing and trading, which in turn affects the viability of a whole range of secondary local activities. Nakabayashi also sees this decline as linked to some of the factors associated with the rapid growth evident in central Tokyo, notably the high price of land.

Consumption

Economic inequality in major cities has assumed distinct forms in the consumption structure, which in turn has a feedback effect on the organization of work and the types of jobs being created. There is an indirect creation of low-wage jobs induced by the presence of a highly dynamic sector with a polarized income distribution. It takes place in the sphere of consumption (or social reproduction). The expansion of the high-income workforce, in conjunction with the emergence of new cultural forms in everyday living, has led to a process of high-income gentrification, which rests, in the last analysis, on the availability of a vast supply of low-wage workers. As I have argued at greater length elsewhere (Sassen 1988), high-income gentrification is labor intensive, in contrast to the typical middle-class suburb, which represents a capital-intensive process—tract housing, road and highway construction, dependence on private automobile or commuter trains, heavy reliance on appliances and household equipment of all sorts, and, in the United States, large shopping malls with self-service operations. High-income gentrification in a city, on the other hand, is labor intensive: Renovation of townhouses and storefronts and designer furniture and woodwork all require workers, directly and indirectly. Behind the gourmet food stores and specialty boutiques lies an organization of the work process that differs from that of the self-service supermarket and department store. High-income urban residences in luxury apartment buildings depend to a much larger extent on hired maintenance staff than do the less urban homes of middle-level-income workers, epitomized by the middle-class suburban home in the United States with its heavy input of family labor and of machinery, from household appliances to lawn mowers.

The differences in the organization of the work process are evident in both the retail and the production phase (Sassen 1988). High-income gentrification generates a demand for goods and services that are typically not mass produced or sold through mass outlets. Customized production and limited runs of production will tend to be associated with labor-intensive methods of production and sold through small, full-service outlets. Subcontracting part of this production to low-cost operations, including sweatshops and households, is not uncommon. The over-all outcome is an increase in low-wage jobs and in small firms for production and retailing. The large department stores and supermarkets, on the other hand, need large quantities and standardized products; they will tend to buy from mass producers, often located in other regions and involving large-scale transportation and distribution. Mass production, standardization, and mass distribution facilitate unionization. Customized production, limited runs, and small retail outlets can promote the informalization and casualization of work.

Professionals and managers have long been important occupational groups in large cities such as New York, London, and Tokyo. But two traits distinguish the current period from earlier times. One is the extent to which these occupational groups have grown. For instance, census data show salaried professionals and managers represented under 5% of

New York residents in the nineteenth century and early twentieth century; today they constitute 30%. The second is the extent to which they, along with other high-income workers, have become a very visible part of city life through distinct consumption patterns, lifestyles, and high-income gentrification.

It is the magnitude in the expansion of high-income workers, their concentration in cities, and their high levels of spending that contribute to this outcome. New York, London, and Tokyo, like all major cities, have long had a core of wealthy residents and commuters. And while this core has probably been expanded by a large influx of wealthy foreigners, especially in New York and London, and now increasingly in Tokyo, by itself it could not have created the large-scale residential and commercial gentrification recently evident in these cities, discussed in the preceding section. As a stratum, the new high-income workers are to be distinguished from this core of wealth, or upper class. Their disposable income is usually not enough to make them into important investors. Furthermore, their level of disposable income is also a function of lifestyle— spending rather than saving—and demographic patterns, such as postponing having children and setting up two-career households. The critical point here is that this disposable income reached a level sufficient for a significant expansion in the demand for highly priced goods and services—that is to say, sufficient to ensure the economic viability of the producers and providers of such goods and services. The extent to which this dynamic operates is reflected in the losses registered by restaurants, designer shops, and certain kinds of service providers in New York beginning in 1988, when the financial industry began to lay off significant numbers of employees. By late 1989 similar effects were becoming evident in London. This indicates that this relatively very small segment of consumption of highly priced goods and services is intimately connected to the new economic core in these cities and is distinct from older forms of elite consumption.

Thus, the existence of major growth sectors, notably the producer services, generates low-wage jobs directly, through the structure of the work process, and indirectly, through the structure of the high-income lifestyles of those therein employed and through the consumption needs of the low-wage workforce. Even a technically advanced service industry, such as finance, generates a significant share of low-wage jobs with few educational requirements. High-income residential and commercial gentrification is labor intensive and raises the demand for maintenance, cleaning, delivery, and other types of low-wage workers. And the massive array of low-cost service and goods-producing firms selling to the expanded low-wage workforce further contributes to the growth of low-wage jobs.

Beyond this impact of the new economic core, there have been broader transformations in the forms of organizing production, with a growing presence of small-batch production, small scales, high product differentiation, and rapid changes in output. These have promoted subcontracting and the use of flexible ways of organizing production. Today many industrial branches need to accommodate rapid changes in output levels and in product characteristics. There has been an overall decline in the production of basic goods and consumer durables, the leading growth industries in manufacturing in the postwar period. The most rapidly growing sectors within manufacturing in the 1980s and 1990s were the high-technology complex and craft-based production, which also grew in traditional branches, such as furniture, footwear, and apparel. Flexible forms of production can range from highly sophisticated to very primitive and can be found in advanced or in backward industries.

Such ways of organizing production assume distinct forms in the labor market, in the components of labor demand, and in the conditions under which labor is employed. Indications of these changes are the decline of unions in manufacturing, the loss of various contractual protections, and the increase of part-time and temporary work or other forms of contingent labor. An extreme indication of this downgrading is the growth of sweatshops and industrial homework. The expansion of a downgraded manufacturing sector partly involves the same industries that used to have largely organized plants and reasonably well-paid jobs but replaces these with different forms of production and organization of the work process, such as piecework and industrial homework. But it also involves new kinds of activity associated with the new major growth trends. The possibility for manufacturers to develop alternatives to the organized factory becomes particularly significant in growth sectors. The consolidation of a downgraded manufacturing sector, whether through social or through technical transformation, can be seen as a politicoeconomic response to a need for expanded production in a situation of growing average wages and militancy, as was the case in the 1960s and early 1970s, and intense competition for land and markets, as was the case in the late 1970s and 1980s.

The expansion in the low-wage workforce has also contributed to the proliferation of small operations and the move away from large-scale standardized factories and stores. The decline in wages has reached the point where sweatshop production in New York or London has become price competitive with cheap imports from Asia. The consumption needs of this workforce are met in good part by production and retail establishments that are small, often fail to meet safety and health standards, and frequently rely on family labor—that is, work situations that further expand the low-wage workforce. The growth of sweatshop production of garments in New York and London, for example, has meant that some of it can replace cheap Asian imports in meeting the demand for low-cost products.

It is my hypothesis that this form of economic polarization brought about by growth trends contains conditions that promote the informalization and casualization of work in a wide range of activities (Sassen 1998: chap. 8). Linking the informalization and casualization of work to growth trends takes the analysis beyond the notion that the emergence of informal "sectors" in such cities as New York and London is due to the large presence of immigrants and their supposed propensity to replicate survival strategies typical of Third World countries. It suggests, rather, that basic traits of advanced capitalism may promote conditions for informalization. The presence of large immigrant communities then can be seen as mediating in the process of informalization rather than directly generating it: The demand side of the process of informalization is therewith brought to the fore. The same argument holds for women and the growth of part-time jobs: The fact of inadequate child care support may make them more likely to seek part-time work, but the growth of part-time jobs is rooted in economic conditions. These are subjects I examine in the next section.

All these trends are operating in major cities, in many cases with greater intensity than national average data describe. This greater intensity is rooted in at least three conditions. First, there is locational concentration of major growth sectors with highly polarized income distributions in major cities. The evidence on different occupational and earnings distributions for various industries in combination with the locational patterns of such industries indicates that major cities, and especially New York and London, have a high proportion of industries with considerable income and occupational polarization. Second, there is a proliferation of small, low-cost service operations, made possible by the massive concentration of people in such cities, in addition to a large daily inflow of nonresident workers and tourists. The ratio between the number of these service operations and resident population is most probably significantly higher than in an average city or town. Furthermore, the large concentration of people in major cities will tend to create intense inducements to open up such operations, as well as intense competition and very marginal returns. Under such conditions, the cost of labor is crucial—hence the likelihood of a high concentration of low-wage jobs. Third, for these same reasons, together with other components of demand, the number of small, labor-intensive, low-wage manufacturing firms would tend to be larger in London, New York, or Tokyo than in average-sized cities. Indeed, in many cities such a downgraded manufacturing sector is not a significant factor if present at all.

Casual and Informal Labor Markets

There has been a pronounced increase in casual employment and in the informalization of work in both New York and London. This trend is also emerging, under different form, in Tokyo where the increase in the number of casual workers, particularly "daily laborers" and part-time workers has led the government to express alarm publicly. The increase in various types of casual work is often thought of as a function of the increased participation of women in the labor force. Indeed, part-time, temporary, and seasonal jobs are more common among women than among men in all three cities. However, all the evidence points to significant increases of such jobs among men over the last decade. More generally, the industry/occupational mix prevalent among such jobs indicates that they account for a significant share of new jobs created in these economies. In addition, jobs that were once full-time ones are now being made into part-time or temporary jobs, pointing to a transformation in the employment relation. While so-called flexible work arrangements may be a development of advanced economies associated with a higher quality of life, the vast majority of casual jobs hardly fits this category. A majority are low-wage jobs, with no fringe benefits and no returns to seniority—a way of organizing work that reduces costs for employers. However, there is a new trend that I consider significant in this study: High-income professional and managerial employees in many of the new specialized service and financial firms are more vulnerable to dismissal and have fewer claims on their employers than was the case with their equivalents in the large commercial banks and insurance houses. This greater "flexibility" in the employment relation is another way of saying that these jobs have become casualized as well. I will return to this subject, which has received little attention in the pertinent literature.

The growth of service jobs is crucial to the expansion of part-time jobs. The pressures to reduce labor costs in industries with limited profit margins, such as catering, retail, and cleaning, assumes added weight when these account for a growing share of jobs. In addition, many service industries require work at night, on weekends, and on holidays, which would entail costly overtime payments for full-time workers. And since many of these jobs do not require many skills or training, they can be downgraded into part-time, more lowly paid jobs. As these service industries have grown, the gap between the work week in such industries as retail, reaching seventy hours a week with multiple work-shifts, and the forty-hour full-time work week has grown in weight. Part-time jobs can recruit women more easily, create greater flexibility in filling various shifts, and reduce labor costs by avoiding various benefits and overtime payments required by full-time workers. In its review of part-time employment trends in advanced industrialized countries, the OECD (1983; 1999) finds that the shift to services was a major factor and that much of the growth involved female workers. Eurostat (2000:6) finds that in the European Union, 2% of men and 24% of women had part-time jobs in 1996; in the UK these shares were, respectively, 3% and 34%. In its analysis of the retailing industry, the National Economic Development Office (NEDO 1985) in Britain found a substitution of full-time jobs for part-time ones and that much of the employment growth in the industry was actually a function of this substitution.

There is also evidence pointing to an expansion of the underground economy. Of interest to the analysis here is one particular component of the underground economy, informal work.[18] This encompasses work that is basically licit but takes place outside the regulatory apparatus covering zoning, taxes, health and safety, minimum wage laws, and other types of standards.[19] In other words, this is work that could be done in the formal economy, unlike the criminal activities that are also part of the underground economy. Government regulations play a particularly important role in the rise of informal production because of the costs that they impose on formal businesses through their various licensing fees, taxes, and restrictions. Labor costs also have an effect on the formation and expansion of the informal economy: directly, in terms of the wage paid, and indirectly, in terms of various contributions demanded by law. One question is whether the importance of these inducements to informalization varies by industry and location.

The specification of this particular component, the informal economy, has implications for theories on the nature of advanced capitalism and the postindustrial society. While criminal activities and underreporting of income are recognized to be present in advanced industrialized economies, informal sectors are not. The literature on the informal sector has mostly

---

[18] We can distinguish at least three very different components of the underground economy: (1) criminal activities, which by their very nature could not be carried out aboveground; (2) tax evasion on licit forms of income (all governments confront this and have implemented mechanisms to detect and control tax evasion); and (3) the informal economy.

[19] The concept of an informal economy describes a process of income-generating activity characterized by lack of regulation in a context where similar activities are regulated (Castells and Portes 1989). The term *regulation* here refers to the institutionalized intervention of the state in the process of income-generating activity. Thus, while particular instances of informal work in highly developed countries may resemble those of an earlier period, they are actually a new development in the organization of work, given decades of institutionalized regulation that have led to a pronounced reduction and in many sectors virtual elimination of unregulated income-generating activity. Because the particular characteristics of informal work are derived from the existence of a context where such work is regulated, the informal economy can be understood only in its relation to the formal economy.

focused on Third World countries and has, wittingly or not, assumed that as a social type such sectors are not to be expected in advanced industrialized countries. And the literature on industrialization has assumed that as development progresses, so will the standardization of production and generalization of the "formal" organization of work. Since much of the expansion of the informal economy in developed countries has been located in immigrant communities, this has led to an explanation of its expansion as being due to the large influx of Third World immigrants and their assumed propensities to replicate survival strategies typical of their home countries. Related to this view is the notion that backward sectors of the economy are kept backward, or even kept alive, because of the availability of a large supply of cheap immigrant workers. Both of these views posit or imply that if there is an informal sector in advanced industrialized countries, the sources are to be found in Third World immigration and in the backward sectors of the economy—a Third World import or a remnant from an earlier phase of industrialization.

A central question for theory and policy is whether the formation and expansion of informal and casual labor markets in advanced industrialized countries is the result of conditions created by advanced capitalism. Rather than assume that Third World immigration is causing informalization and the entry of mothers into the labor force is causing the casualization of work, what we need is a critical examination of the conditions that may be inducing these processes. Immigrants, insofar as they tend to form communities, may be in a favorable position to seize the opportunities represented by informalization. And women, insofar as they have children and inadequate access to child care, may be interested in part time or temporary job opportunities. But the opportunities are not necessarily created by immigrants and women. They may well be a structured outcome of current trends in the advanced industrialized economies. Similarly, what are perceived as backward sectors of the economy may or may not be remnants from an earlier phase of industrialization; they may well represent a downgrading of work connected to the dynamics of growth in leading sectors of the economy.

There is a strong tendency for the service sector overall to produce or make possible more part-time jobs than does manufacturing. This tendency is clearly embedded in a number of basic institutional arrangements and in specific historical conditions. The institutionalization of the family wage was closely interlinked with the rise of powerful manufacturing-based unions and a male-dominated "labor aristocracy." The family wage is—or, rather, was—the institutionalized principle that a man's wage should be high enough to support his family. Thus, it contributed to establishing the gender-based occupational work structure characteristic of industrialized economies (Hartmann 1981). "The perpetuation of the family wage system has depended on two things, one a fact, the other an assumption. The fact is that men, on the average, earn more than women. The assumption is that men use their higher wages to support women, and hence that most women are at least partly supported by men" (Ehrenreich 1984: 8).

The shift in the economy toward a prevalence of service industries contains what one could think of as a structurally induced erosion of the—albeit limited—institutional bases for the family wage. The growth of part-time work, the growth in the numbers of female-headed households, the decline of manufacturing-based unions, and the large-scale displacement of male workers—all these conditions have contributed to an erosion of the institution of the family wage, limited as its implementation was, especially in the United States, and to an erosion of the ideology of the family wage. One important question is whether the current conditions—a sort of disarray compared with the ideal type presupposed in the family wage—represent a transition to less gender-based structures of work or are yet another step in the formation of a supply of cheap and powerless workers.

The overall effect is the casualization and informalization of the employment relation. The differences among these three cities stem partly from the distinct institutional arrangements through which work is organized. In the United Kingdom, the government has until recently played a rather fundamental role as supplier of a vast range of services and goods, from housing to health services, which in the United States are largely delivered through the private market. The net effect was to incorporate a vast number of workers who were employed by the government or public authorities. This carried with it a considerable degree of government regulation over large sectors of the labor market. The implemented withdrawal of the government from these various markets through the privatization of services and goods has created a situation that has facilitated the transformation of many of these jobs from regular full-time, year-round jobs with the requisite fringe benefits into various kinds of part-time temporary jobs, as well as the subcontracting of work. The historical obligation assumed by a government to enforce its own regulations covers a shrinking share of the workforce and an increasingly restricted set of labor markets. The recency of this transformation in the government's role in the economy and the rapidity of the process of privatization has provided the conditions for a pronounced spread of part-time and temporary work, while the growth of service industries further facilitates the expansion of these types of work.

In the United States, the governments role in the economy, while strong, has not been centered on the labor market or oriented toward the provision of housing and health services on a national scale. The mere absence of a national health system entails a much less encompassing role for government in shaping the characteristics of jobs. Economic conditions in the postwar era—the dominance of consumer-oriented industry, large unions, the expansion of a middle class, the growth of standardized production—all promoted the expansion of a large number of jobs that respected the regulatory framework. Thus, the outcome was similar to that in Britain in the postwar era, but was effected through different channels. The key vehicle in the expansion of part-time work over the last decade was the combination of a shift to services and the dismantling of the manufacturing-based unions, which had the power to impose work standards on broad sectors of the economy.

Beyond the trend toward an increase in part-time work arising from these various conditions, we see the expansion of informal work arrangements, at times resembling an informal sector with a fairly elaborate set of relations of production, distribution, and markets for labor and inputs—that is to say, informal arrangements that do not simply consist of a few individuals working off the books. In the case of the United States there has not been such rapid wide-scale privatization of the production and delivery of various public goods and services as in Britain, partly because so much was already private. But there has been a somewhat similar development in terms of the shift of a growing number of jobs from highly regulated formal labor markets to semiregulated, unregulated, or casual labor markets. Work in the informal economy does not have to be casual strictly speaking in that it is part of a well-organized chain of production and involves full-time, year-round work. But much of it is casual, this flexibility being precisely the key advantage of informal work for employers or contractors.

In Japan, rapid industrialization, immensely rapid urbanization, and culture have created very specific conditions. The securing of a reliable industrial workforce under conditions of extremely rapid growth and different cultural preferences and expectations from those in the West has contributed to the development of the so-called lifelong job security system. This system now accounts for only a fifth of all workers, having also suffered from the shift to and rapid growth of service industries. The growing participation of women in the labor force has assumed the form of a rapid growth in part-time and temporary jobs. However, the growth of the category of daily laborers and the rapid erosion of the institutional arrangements that are supposed to cover daily laborers, are reminiscent of the casualization and informalization of work evident in Britain and the United States but in many ways worse.

While present in all three cities under study, these developments assume rather specific forms and operate through distinct social arrangements. The available evidence suggests that the most pronounced form over the last decade in London was the growth of part-time work; in Tokyo it was the expansion of daily labor; in New York, the growth of informal work. The following sections discuss each of these instances of the casualization of the employment relation.

Informalization in New York

A small but growing body of evidence points to the expansion of informal work in major cities of the United States beginning in the 1980s (Tabak 2001; Fernandez-Kelly and Garcia 1989; Stepick 1989; Sassen-Koob 1984, 1989; *Yale Law Journal* 1994). These studies are based mostly on ethnographic research. They are to be distinguished from studies that aim at overall estimates of the underground economy based on aggregate figures for the supply and circulation of money (Gutman 1979; Spitznas 1981; Tanzi 1982). As categories for analysis, the underground economy and the informal economy overlap only partly. Studies on the underground economy have sought to measure all income not registered in official figures, including income derived from illicit activities, such as drug dealing. Studies on the informal economy focus on the production and sale of goods and services that are licit but produced and/or sold outside the regulatory apparatus covering zoning, taxes, health and safety, minimum wage laws, and other types of standards.

The difference in focus has major consequences for the kind of information produced and issues raised. General measures of unregistered income make the underground economy into a homogeneous category; the distinction between underground income derived from criminal activities (e.g., drug sales) and underground income derived from such activities as an unregistered, non-taxpaying shop cannot be applied to these aggregate monetary measures. Studies on the informal economy based on fieldwork document the existence of a diverse group of activities in need of diverse policy responses.

Grover and I investigated these activities from 1986 to 1989 (Sassen-Koob and Grover 1986; Columbia University 1987; Sassen-Koob 1989). The concern was to specify a relationship between the growth of informal activities in New York and overall conditions in the economy and the existing regulatory environment. In this context, one can think of informalization as an emergent, or developing, "opportunity" structure that avoids or compensates for various types of constraints, from regulations to market prices for inputs. This type of inquiry requires an analytical differentiation of immigration, informalization, and the characteristics of the current phase of advanced industrialized economies in order to establish the differential impact of (1) immigration and (2) conditions in the economy at large on the formation and expansion of the informal economy. The theoretical and policy implications associated with the primacy of one or the other will vary. For theory, the primacy of economic structure would point to the need for further theoretical elaboration on the current understanding of the nature of advanced capitalism. For policy, the primacy of immigration would suggest, at its crudest, that controlling immigrant activity in the informal economy would eradicate the latter; it would, then, also reinforce standard theories on advanced industrialization or the postindustrial society, which allow no room for such developments as an informal economy.

The industries covered were construction; garments; footwear; furniture; retail activity; and electronics. We did field visits in all the boroughs of New York (for a detailed account, see Sassen-Koob 1989). On the basis of our fieldwork, interviews, and secondary data analysis, we found the following profile of the informal economy in the New York area: (1) A rather wide range of industrial sectors use informal work—apparel, general construction contractors, special trade contractors, footwear, toys and sporting goods, electronic components, and accessories. (2) Informal work is also present in lesser measure in particular kinds of activities, such as packaging notions, making lampshades, making artificial flowers, jewelry making, distribution activities, photoengraving, manufacturing of explosives, etc. (3) There is a strong tendency for informal work to be located in densely populated areas with very high shares of immigrants. (4) There is an emergent tendency for "traditional" sweatshop activity (notably in garments) to be displaced from areas undergoing partial residential and commercial gentrification; such areas engender new forms of unregistered work, catering to the new clientele.

There are several patterns in the organization of the informal economy in New York that are of interest to an examination of its articulation with leading growth trends. One pattern is the concentration of informal activities in immigrant communities, where some activities meet a demand from the communities and others meet a demand that comes from the larger economy. A second pattern is the concentration of informal activities in areas undergoing rapid socioeconomic change, notably gentrification. A third is the concentration of informal activities in areas that emerge as a type of manufacturing and industrial servicing area in a context where both regulations and market forces do not support such activities; while these are frequently located in immigrant communities, they cater to the larger economy. There follows a more detailed description of each.

The first pattern contains what are possibly two very different components of the informal economy. One is the use of immigrant workers and communities to lower the costs of production and raise the organizational flexibility of formal sector industries. The garment industry is the clearest example. Certain components of the construction industry, footwear industry, and industrial services also illustrate this pattern. Immigrant communities can be seen as collections of resources that facilitate informal production or distribution of certain activities (Sassen-Koob 1989). These resources consist of cheap, willing, and flexible labor supplies; entrepreneurial resources in the form of individuals willing to engage in the long hours and often low returns involved and the availability of family labor; various informal credit arrangements that make possible small-scale capital formation; and a supply of low-cost space available for a multiplicity of uses, some of them in violation of regulated uses. The issue of space may be far more important for firms using informal operations than is usually recognized. The sharp competition for land by high bidders, regulations that do not support manufacturing or industrial services, and the need for such activities to be easily accessible may make the availability of informal workspaces, whether sweatshops, basements, or homes, as important as the low cost of labor.

The other component of the informal sector in immigrant communities represents a type of neighborhood subeconomy. It consists of a variety of activities that meet the demand for goods and services inside the community, including immigrants residing in other neighborhoods that may lack commercial facilities. These goods and services may be of a kind not provided by the larger economy, or provided at too high a price, or provided in locations that entail a long or cumbersome trip. Certain aspects of the informal transportation system are illustrative, notably "gypsy" cabs servicing low-income or immigrant areas not serviced by the regular cabs. Also illustrative are certain aspects of the construction industry, especially renovations and small-store alteration or construction. A wide array of personal services are informally provided, frequently in the home of the buyer or provider. Certain types of manufacturing, including production of garments and footwear, and, at least in a few cases, furniture, are carried out in the community and meet local demand. Such a local economic base may well represent a mechanism for maximizing the returns on whatever resources are available in the communities involved. In this regard, these activities may help stabilize low-income areas by providing jobs, entrepreneurship opportunities, and enough diversification to maximize the recirculation of wages spent on goods and services inside the community where the jobs are located and the goods and services produced.

A second pattern is characterized by the concentration of informal activities in areas undergoing high-income residential and commercial gentrification. The leading industrial sectors involved are construction and various forms of woodwork, including furniture making. Also involved in this process are various industries supplying the goods and services sold by the new commercial facilities associated with high-income gentrification—clothing boutiques, gourmet food shops selling prepared dishes, shops selling customized household items. But unlike construction and customized woodwork, many of the latter activities are not necessarily located in the area undergoing gentrification. While immigrant workers often were found to provide the requisite labor, including highly skilled craftswork, the demand for the goods and services clearly stems from the larger economy.

The third pattern we can discern is the concentration of manufacturing and industrial services in certain areas, which emerge as a type of manufacturing district or service market. For example, in one particular location in the New York borough of Queens we found shops doing glasswork for buildings and vehicles; shops doing refinishing of restaurant equipment; auto repair shops; garment shops; carpentry shops that make frames for furniture and then send them to other locations for finishing; cabinetmakers. All these shops are operating in violation of various codes, and they are located in an area not zoned for manufacturing. This area has emerged as an informal manufacturing district. The city government is well aware of its existence but has, it seems, opted for disregarding the violations, probably because of the scarce supply of manufacturing space in Manhattan and the city's interest in retaining small businesses. The concentration of manufacturing shops in this area of Queens has brought about a whole array of related service shops as well as contributing to the development of a zone where new industrial uses are occurring. One implication in this case is that what may initially be a small cluster of manufacturing shops operating informally may, under certain conditions, develop into an industrial district with agglomeration economies that will draw an increasing number of industrial users. This becomes a de facto manufacturing zone. We found significant clusters of auto repair shops in several areas of the city. The number of shops and cars involved was large enough to point to a service being sold beyond the neighborhood. It is a development that goes against prevailing notions of the economic base in "post-industrial" cities, and points to an ongoing need for manufacturing firms and industrial services.

In sum, we can identify different types of locations in the spatial organization of the informal economy. Immigrant communities are a key location for informal activities meeting both internal and external demand for goods and services. Gentrifying areas are a second important location; these areas contain a large array of informal activities in renovation, alteration, small-scale new construction, woodwork, and installations. A third location can be characterized as informal manufacturing and industrial service areas serving a citywide market.

An examination of what engenders the demand for informal production and distribution indicates several sources: (1) One of these is competitive pressures in certain industries, notably apparel, to reduce labor costs to meet massive competition from low-wage Third World countries. Informal work in this instance represents an acute example of exploitation. (2) Another source is a rapid increase in the volume of renovations, alterations, and small-scale new construction associated with the transformation of many areas of the city from low-income, often dilapidated neighborhoods into higher-income commercial and residential areas. What in many other cities in the United States would have involved a massive program of new construction was mostly a process of rehabilitation of old structures in the case of New York. The volume of work, its small scale, its labor-intensiveness and high skill content, and the short-term nature of each project all were conducive to a heavy proportion of informal work. (3) A third source is inadequate provision of services and goods by the formal sector. This inadequacy may consist of excessively high prices, inaccessible or difficult-to-reach location of formal provision, or actual lack of provision. It would seem that this inadequacy of formal provision involves mostly low-income individuals or areas. (4) The existence of a cluster of informal shops can eventually generate agglomeration economies that induce additional entrepreneurs to move in. (5) The existence of a rather diversified informal economy making use of a variety of labor supplies may lower entry costs for entrepreneurs and hence function as a factor inducing the expansion of the informal economy. This can be construed as a type of supply-side factor.

We can distinguish different types of firms in the informal economy, particularly in terms of the locational constraints to which firms are subject. For some firms, access to cheap labor is the determining inducement for a New York location. While access to the city's final or intermediate markets (or the city's sheer size, which facilitates informalization) may also be significant, it is ultimately access to cheap labor, specifically low-wage immigrant workers, that determines location. because it allows these firms to compete with Third World factories. Many of these shops could be located in a diversity of areas with cheap labor. Certain segments of the garment industry are illustrative.[20] In contrast, many of the

---

[20] Interviews with homeworkers confirmed what is generally accepted, that hourly or piece rate wages are extremely low. However, we also found a new trend toward an upgraded version of homework. One pattern we found was for designers (typically free-lance or independent designers) to have immigrant workers come into their homes (typically large converted lofts in lower Manhattan) and work off the books. The other pattern was for middle-class women to take in very expensive cloth and clothes to do finishing work at home or do highly specialized knitting on special machines purchased by the workers themselves; the cases we studied all involved Chinese or Korean households in middle-class

shops engaged in customized production or operating on subcontracts evince a whole host of locational dependencies on New York. These firms are bound to the city (or to any large city they might be located in that is undergoing the kinds of socioeconomic transformations we identified for New York) for some or all of the following reasons: (1) localized demand, typically involving specific clients or customers; (2) proximity to design and specialized services; (3) brief turnover time between completion of design and production; (4) demand predicated on the existence of a highly dynamic overall economic situation that generates a critical volume of demand and spending capability on the part of buyers; and/or (5) the existence of immigrant communities, which have some of the traits associated with enclave economies.

Finally, we can distinguish differences in the types of jobs we found in the informal economy. Many of the jobs are unskilled, with no training opportunities, involving repetitive tasks. Another type of job demands high skills or acquisition of a skill. The growth of informalization in the construction and furniture industries can be seen as bringing about a certain reskilling of the labor force. In the case of highly skilled work for which there is a considerable demand, for example, stonecutters and woodworkers for architect-designed buildings, informalization served as the vehicle for making use of undocumented immigrants with such skills.

It would seem from our study that important sources of the informalization of various activities are to be found in characteristics of the larger economy of the city. Among these are the demand for products and services that lend themselves to small scales of production, or are associated with rapid transformations brought about by commercial and residential gentrification, or are not satisfactorily provided by the formal sector. This would suggest that a good share of the informal economy is not the result of immigrant survival strategies, but rather an outcome of structural patterns or transformations in the larger economy of a city such as New York. Workers and firms respond to the opportunities contained in these patterns and transformations. However, in order to respond, workers and firms need to be positioned in distinct ways. Immigrant communities represent what could be described as a "favored" structural location

---

residential neighborhoods in the city. The overall evidence from our ongoing research points to the existence of a very dynamic and growing high-price market where production has been organized so as to incorporate sweatshops and homes (of poor and middle-class immigrants and of designers) as key workplaces. Finally, a distinct pattern of ethnic ownership characterizes the informal sector in this industry beginning in the 1980s. The new Hispanic immigrants, especially Dominicans and Colombians, have replaced Puerto Ricans as the leading group of owners in the Latino population; the Chinese have increased their number of shops immensely over the last ten years; and the Koreans are emerging as the fastest-growing new ethnic group setting up sweatshops and homework arrangements.

to seize the opportunities for entrepreneurship as well as the more and less desirable jobs being generated by informalization.

The Casualization of Work in London

The 1980s saw a great increase in part-time, casual, and sweated labor in construction, clothing, catering, retailing, tourism, cleaning, and even printing in London and in the United Kingdom generally. This continued in the 1990s. The growth of unorganized and low-paid labor can drag down the pay and working conditions of the better-paid, organized workers. This is contributing to a further erosion of the socioeconomic conditions of low-income workers. While the vast majority of part-time workers in the United Kingdom, as well as in most developed countries, are women, the share of men has grown. In the early 1970s, men accounted for a small share of part-time workers. By 1981, 19% of all part-time workers in the United Kingdom were men. Not only is part-time work increasing, part-time contracts are becoming shorter (see chapter 8).

Studies by the former Greater London Council and the Low Pay Unit estimated that over 20% of workers in the hotel and catering sectors are on temporary contracts. There is a job center for casual employment, with lines forming every morning at six and waiting until the center opens at eight. The regular use of casual labor has also increased in this industry, not simply as a response to seasonal demand in hotel and catering, but largely as a way to cut costs and avoid addressing poor working conditions and low pay. There has also been an increase of these practices in the construction industry. Every morning there is a hiring hall in certain areas and a scramble for jobs. These jobs carry no benefits, and workers are often classified as self-employed in order to exempt the employer from taxes and other responsibilities. Again we see here parallels with what is occurring in New York.

These practices, however, are not confined to the more traditional industries. In such specialized service industries as architectural and engineering services and banking there has also been an increase of workers paid by the hour and a reduction in part-time workers with the same rights as full-time workers. These workers, mostly women, have no sick pay, no overtime pay, no holiday pay, and no job security. Yet they work as much as a regular worker. As in the garment or construction industries, these workers are also classified as self-employed by their employers to avoid regulations. These practices contribute to the income polarization evident in the advanced services sector.

The growth of part-time jobs is not only a function of the increase in service jobs or a tight labor market and hence the need to accommodate married women with child care responsibilities. Part-time jobs allow for wage cuts, greater flexibility in workforce size and in a firm's response to fluctuations in demand, use of workers on night and weekend shifts or overtime without added cost, the replacement of men by women, no unions, no overhead. Employers are exempt from paying various taxes and fringe benefits.

Homework and sweated work have also increased. The clearest case is apparel. To be able to use the cheapest workers, ethnic minorities and women, smaller textile and clothing firms now tend to be concentrated in London and other cities. The London clothing industry consists of about 3,000 firms, a few of which employ over 100 workers. London has lost all its large factories, as many of the large manufacturers no longer do production: They subcontract to overseas or domestic producers. And in the 1960s the big retailers began subcontracting as well, initially to Hong Kong and Taiwan and now also to domestic firms. As a result, the number of firms and workers has increased, especially "fly-by-night" factories. The majority of the workers are from ethnic minorities and up to a third are homeworkers. Many are part-time or temporary workers, employed in the busy season. The vast majority of homeworkers and part-time workers in clothing are women. It has been estimated that the number of homeworkers and other unregistered workers in women's light wear increased by 17,000 between 1978 and 1982 (Mitter 1986). As in New York and Tokyo, the whole new emphasis on fashion and luxury— or simulated luxury—has also led to a new need for quick turnover from design to finished product and hence for producers close by. The estimate is that 30% to 50% of all East End and northeast London garment production is through homework and that at least half of these homeworkers are Bangladeshi or Pakistani women; of the rest, a large number of women in garment work are from Cyprus. And in fieldwork in 1989, I found a significant presence of recently arrived Turkish entrepreneurs and workers. Homework is taking place not only in clothing but also in other lines of production, including the making of lampshades, electrical goods, painted toys, and zippers. Indeed, even excluding the unregistered activities, London has overrepresentation in several traditional low-paid industries, such as footwear, clothing, and textiles (Dunford and Fielding 1997: 252), a condition also evident in New York.

The levels of unemployment and its duration changed markedly over the two decades between 1965 and 1985 (Greater London Council. Intelligence Unit 1988). Total unemployment levels went from about 25,000 for men and almost 6,000 for women in the late 1960s to 277,524 and 124,722, respectively, in 1985, or a total of 400,000 unemployed in a workforce of 3.4 million. Furthermore, registered unemployment figures are known to be underestimates in periods of high unemployment, because they exclude workers who have used up their allowance and discouraged workers, including those who decided not to enter the labor force. Yet another strong trend emerges when we control for duration of unemployment. The number of unemployed men with two weeks or less of registered unemployment went from 7,000 in 1965 to 17,375 in 1985; those with two but no more than eight weeks went from 6,800 to 32,500; and those with eight weeks or more went to 227,672. For women, the total levels were much smaller in each of the categories, but the trends were similar. Thus a vast majority of the increase in unemployment was among those unemployed for eight weeks or more, a group that was in 1985 twenty-one times larger than in 1965 for men and sixty times larger for women.

Reviewing the evidence for Britain, Hurstfield (1987) found that by far the greatest savings to employers derived from using part-time employees seem to be on National Insurance contributions, by keeping part-time workers' earnings below the threshold (Hart 1986). This was further suggested by another study, which found that in Britain the threshold was twice as high as in Germany, thus facilitating the creation of part-time jobs with wages below the National Insurance threshold, especially in industries with low average pay (Schoer 1987; Dunford and Fielding 1997).

As in the United States, the government has passed legislation that further weakens the position of part-time workers, creates additional incentives for employers to use part-time workers, and legitimizes the use of part-time workers. Compared with other European countries, Britain has lost significant ground in terms of the protection of workers, though it is probably still more generous than the United States. At present, part-time workers employed at least sixteen hours a week in continuous employment are entitled to various rights. Below this threshold, the employer has few if any obligations to the workers. In a recent White Paper entitled "Building Businesses . . . Not Barriers," there are proposals for raising this threshold to twenty hours. About 95% of the workers affected by these changes would be women.

Tokyo's Daily Laborers

Daily laborers, especially in construction, construction-related industries, and longshoring—all major industries in Japan—are supposedly registered and entitled to unemployment compensation and other benefits according to their work records. They have work carnets in which are registered the days worked every week and month—necessary to establish the amount of unemployment compensation a worker is entitled to.

There are specific locations where jobs are listed and allocated by government employees, who staff the various desks or counters, give workers their job slips, and write the information in the workers' carnets. These workers supposedly also can write themselves into a waiting list for housing and have access to other services. There was a time when their numbers were smaller, fairly well-paying jobs in longshoring were their main occupation, and daily laborers generally were better incorporated in mainstream society.

The massive expansion of this category of workers in the 1980s has meant that a minority of them are actually covered by these regulations. Daily labor has increasingly become a residual category, formed by those who were fired from other jobs, including white-collar workers, elderly men who no longer can work in the jobs they once held, and young men unable to get any other job. In my fieldwork in Yokohama's daily laborers' camp, I found university graduates, including one who had been a political militant at the University of Tokyo and had subsequently been blacklisted. Daily labor has also become a key employment form for new unauthorized immigrants from several Asian countries. In my fieldwork I found that a number of these immigrants had actually attended university in their home countries.

There are four major hiring halls for daily laborers in the country, two in the Tokyo-Yokohama area and one each in Nagoya and Osaka. The largest of these hiring halls is in the Taito ward in Tokyo. It has a reputation for being a rather dangerous place. While the Japanese version of Western-style gangsters or Mafia, the "yakusa," are known to control all four of the large hiring halls in the country, Taito's is supposed to be the worst. As I discussed above in describing Tokyo's inner city, Taito is one of the most deprived wards in the city, with growing rates of criminality, poverty, and unemployment. There is clearly a massive breakdown of the system that was supposed to protect daily laborers and low-income residents generally. The hiring halls are also frequently places for homeless men.

On my first visit to one of these halls, Kotobuki-cho in Yokohama, we walked over at five in the morning. It was still dark. There was a gray concrete structure, the equivalent of four stories, with wide-open platforms at street level and one at the equivalent of two stories up, covered by a flat, slablike roof. It was a square structure with about 50 meters per side. Both on the street level and on the second-story platform on one of the enclosed sides were what looked like train station ticket counters, with long lines of men at each one. Through the ticket window I could see lists of jobs, with wages listed. At the other end of the platform were large groups of men, lying on the ground or just rising, clearly homeless, covered with tattered clothes, lying on dirty blankets, unshaven, unhealthy. An image of absolute misery. There were also young, neat men, among them many immigrants, and many older men standing in line. Amongst this vast and varied sea of men walked about twenty flashy, flamboyant men, arrogant and aggressive looking, with dark sunglasses notwithstanding the predawn darkness. They were the yakusas. They acted in rather threatening ways toward me, circling me. But I knew I was safe for a complicated set of reasons, not the least being that murder is still extremely rare even in the absolute bottom of the Japanese social structure. At about 8 A.M., the contractors have left with their hired laborers, and the large numbers that stay behind have nothing much to look forward to. They sit at the edges of the streets and talk, play various games. There is no place beneath this place.

I visited some of the living quarters of those who had been left behind. You enter an old, minute version of a New York tenement: a long, very dark and narrow hallway, with an extremely low ceiling. There is an endless row of roughly made wooden doors. Behind each door is a cubicle the size of a narrow double bed and, at least in the ones I saw, a small window. Some of the quarters I visited were extremely neat, the occupant clearly intent on salvaging as much as he could of his dignity. Some of the daily laborers are extremely clean and neat in appearance; they make use of the public showers, for which they are willing to pay. They have not been morally broken. At least not yet; they may still have the hope of a better job.

The meager evidence we have and the fate of the older, less employable daily laborers suggest that increasing hardship and demoralization lie ahead for the mass of daily laborers. One can still see amidst the misery and the darkness and the dankness the behavior of individuals who consider themselves integrated in a wider society; there is in fact no exit for most of them. The distance between the world of the daily laborer and the rest of society, the world of regular, full-time jobs, has grown immensely in only a few years. So has the distance between the world of the daily laborer and the society of men and women and families and children. This is a world exclusively of men. I had been warned that many of the older men had probably not seen women, live and up close, for many years, that they would come up to me and stare and try to touch me, innocently, with no mean intent. They did. This is a world far removed from the Japan we think of in the West. It is neither the old, foreign culture nor the new, modern Japan. It is a place of no name, with no image to call it forth.

A group of daily laborers have sought to organize the union of daily laborers. This would represent a threat to the place and source of money of the yakusa. The top leader of the newly born "Union of Daily Workers" was murdered, an event which received considerable attention because it was viewed as truly unusual and stepping beyond all boundaries. The second in command was supposed to be on the death list and was keeping a low profile. My reading is that it is a quid pro quo: you keep a low profile and we stay away from you. I was at a large meeting of daily laborers where this organizer attended briefly, gave a speech, and left. It was being described as an act of extreme courage, but I do believe that the key context is one that is quite different from, for example, the drug business in the United States in that murder is not as common an occurrence yet among the Japanese. Most of the labor-related murders have thus far been of illegal immigrants, including women in the sex industry.

Daily labor in Japan is, perhaps, the sharpest instance of casualization in the employment relation. Along with female part-time work, it represents a growing stratum of the labor force.

Race and Nationality in the Labor Market

It is impossible to disregard the facts of race and nationality in an examination of social and economic processes in New York. To a lesser extent this is also the case with London. Tokyo, on the other hand, is rather different, since Japan has lacked a history of immigration as we understand it in the West. The very recent new illegal immigration of the last few years does raise a number of questions about the future. Thus, while Tokyo is indeed to be distinguished from New York and London, it would seem important to present the available information on the new immigration insofar as it may signal the beginning of a new process of labor force formation in the context of the internationalization of the Japanese economy.

While there are complex reasons that explain the patterning and the directionality of international migration flows (Sassen 1988; 1999b) this still leaves unanswered a number of questions about the place of Third World immigrants in the leading economic centers of the world. The argument that New York keeps receiving immigrants because it has always been a city of immigrants emerges as clearly inadequate given the formation of a completely new illegal immigration into Japan and Tokyo in the 1980s and continuing today. In London, we see the continuation over two generations of Asian and Afro-Caribbean populations highly concentrated in London and with employment patterns quite distinct from those of the majority population. It raises questions about (a) the conditions in these cities that bring about the highest number of immigrant entries ever in the history of New York; (b) a continuing differentiation of Asians and Afro-Caribbeans in London, as well as a new illegal immigration into that city after a long period of little or no immigration;

and (c) a first-time immigration into Tokyo, a city in a country that has never before had a major immigration and has firmly resisted the notion.

If immigrant and native minority workers had the same earnings and occupational distributions as native workers and similar residential patterns, then there would be less purpose in examining these populations here. But they do not. Notwithstanding great differences in the three cities and among the multiplicity of nationalities involved, immigrants are still, in the end, disproportionately concentrated in large, central cities and in low-wage jobs and casual labor markets. The following sections emphasize the specificity of each of these processes and the concrete details characterizing each city.

New York City's Minority and Immigrant Workforce

Alongside the increase in high-income jobs, there has been a second, perhaps less noted growth trend in New York's labor force since 1980. Blacks and Hispanics increased their share of all jobs, while whites lost share. Half of all resident workers in New York are now minority. The evidence also shows that blacks and Hispanics are far less likely than whites to hold the new high-income jobs and far more likely than whites to hold the new low-wage jobs. Thus, one can infer a trend toward replacement of whites in existing lower-income jobs by blacks and Hispanics as well as these minorities' entry into new lower-income jobs. A third trend that is expected to become more pronounced over the next few years is the growing share of jobs held by women from all groups. The share of women in New York's resident workforce increased from 39% in 1970 to 45% in 1986 and 56% in 1990. Several projections show that this trend will continue and even more resident workers will be women than men.

Minority workers continue to be underrepresented in higher-level jobs (U.S. Department of Labor, Bureau of Labor Statistics 1988; 2000). In 1986, still the phase of high growth, 16% of all Hispanics and 21% of all employed blacks and other races held managerial, professional, and technical support jobs as compared to 36% of whites. These occupational groups represent the major sector of employment growth for New York. From 1983 to 1986, a period of sharp job growth, 213,000 resident workers, or three-fourths of net employment growth, were in these occupational groups. Hispanics and blacks in these occupations tend to be concentrated in social and health services, sectors with relatively lower earnings. The figures for whites are underestimates in that they exclude commuters, 90% of whom are white and many of whom have higher-level jobs. Among Hispanics there continues to be overrepresentation in manufacturing compared with their share in the labor force.

Table 9.1 presents information on employment, unemployment, and underemployment controlling for various individual attributes and location for 1999. The unemployment rate for Blacks in NYC is the single highest rate for any of the other groups and locations, excluding teenagers. This rate is even higher than that of other large cities, the second highest level. Unemployment rates for Spanish origin persons are the next highest, generally surpassing the rate for women. The underemployment rate is at 18.2% for Blacks in NYC and at 16% in large cities, and it is 14.2% for Spanish origin persons, again the three highest levels presented in the table. The unemployment and underemployment rates among foreign workers are significantly lower at 5.7% and 11%, respectively, in NYC. Again the city has the highest levels of all other locations. These rates are significantly lower for all three groups of workers in the

TABLE 9.1

Unemployment, Employment & Underemployment Rates by Sex, Age, and Race/Ethnicity: New York City, Nassau-Suffolk, and Other Large U.S. Cities and Suburbs, 1999

	All Ages 16 & Up	Males	Females	White, Non-Spanish	Black, Non-Spanish	Spanish Origin	Teens, 16–19	Foreign Born
				Unemployment Rate				
NYC	6.1	6.2	5.8	2.8	10.6	7.7	14.0	5.7
Big Cities	5.4	5.2	5.5	3.5	9.6	5.2	18.7	4.4
Nassau/ Suffolk	3.2	3.3	3.0	2.8	3.2	6.2	6.8	5.4
Suburbs	3.2	3.2	3.2	2.7	5.1	5.3	11.2	3.9
				Percentage of Population Employed				
NYC	54.2	63.1	46.4	58.1	54.4	49.9	19.0	58.6
Big Cities	64.2	70.6	58.4	67.3	58.2	65.7	36.2	63.2
Nassau/ Suffolk	63.9	72.7	56.1	63.0	65.4	74.0	46.0	63.3
Suburbs	66.8	74.5	59.5	66.6	69.1	66.2	44.2	65.2
				Underemployment Rate				
NYC	10.9	10.6	11.3	5.7	18.2	14.2	31.5	11.0
Big Cities	9.7	9.5	9.9	6.4	16.0	10.3	29.4	9.5
Nassau/ Suffolk	6.0	6.5	5.4	5.3	5.6	11.5	14.2	10.0
Suburbs	6.0	5.7	6.3	5.0	8.9	10.6	18.4	7.9

Source: G. DeFreitas, 2000, "The Boom Breaks Records but So Does Inequality," Regional Labor Review, p. 7.

Notes: The "underemployment rate" is here measured as the total officially counted as "unemployed," plus those "marginally attached" to the labor force who are discouraged workers plus persons employed part time for economic reasons, expressed as a percent of the sum of the official labor force plus those counted as marginally attached. The "big cities" category consists of the subsample of center-city residents in the 20 largest metropolitan areas, excluding New York City.

TABLE 9.2

Changes in Average Family Income in the NYC Metro
Area, by Family Income Quintiles, 1988/90 to 1996/98

	1988/90 to 1996/98
Top Fifth	18%
4th Fifth	−5%
Middle Fifth	−12%
2nd Fifth	−16%
Lowest Fifth	−13%

Source: G. DeFreitas, 2000, "The Boom Breaks Records but So
Does Inequality," *Regional Labor Review*, p. 8.
Note: Adjusted for inflation.

suburbs of NYC. Activity rates for Blacks and for Foreign Born workers
tend to be similar to those of whites or higher in NYC, and for all three
groups in the broader metropolitan region of the city.

An important question, particularly from the perspective of major cities
with large concentrations of immigrant workers, is whether the expansion
of low-wage jobs is a function of the large new Third World immigrant
influx. DeFreitas (1991) analyzed the sector and skill distribution of
workers in the United States by country of birth and found a rather similar concentration of native-born Anglos and foreign-born Hispanics in his
grouping of "immigrant intensive industries" (industries where at least
one-fifth of the workforce are immigrants). This would suggest that it is
the economy rather than the immigrants which is producing low-wage
jobs. (See Table 9.2.) Race and nationality segment the labor force and
contribute to the formation of a supply of low-wage workers.

London's Black and Asian Workforce

During the period of high immigration in the 1950s, almost half of the
Afro-Caribbean and Asian entrants settled in London, and most of the
rest settled in other large cities. They doubled their share in Britain's
labor force from 1971 to 1981, accounting for 5% and 1.1 million of all
British workers in 1981. By 1981, they numbered 945,000, or 14.6% of
London's total population and 19.4% of inner London's population. This
share rose to about a third of the population in three inner London boroughs (Hackney, Haringey, and Brent) and about a fourth in several
other London boroughs (Lambeth, Newham, Ealing). The average concentration was below 5% in the rest of London. The largest groups were

and remain Asians, followed by Afro-Caribbeans (West Indians and Guyanese), also referred to as blacks. In inner and outer London, 29% and 22%, respectively, of residents are from ethnic minorities in 2000 (Stuart 1989; London Research Centre 1997; UK Office of Statistics 2000). While those of Caribbean origin remain overwhelmingly concentrated in inner London, a good number of Asians have moved to the suburbs. The evidence shows that Afro-Caribbeans are less likely to move out of the inner city than Asians and the general population. In 1998–99, one in four Londoners belonged to an ethnic minority.

Originally, Commonwealth citizens had been encouraged to come to Britain to meet shortages of unskilled labor in several industries. But by 1962 the first of a series of immigration laws restricting their entry was implemented.[21] Furthermore, in 1979 temporary work permits were eliminated. The tourist and catering industry had used temporary work permits to recruit workers mostly from non-Commonwealth countries: Turkey, Spain, Greece, the Philippines, and Colombia.[22] Now work permits can be issued on a temporary basis to employers who apply for them. They have mostly been issued to white professionals. In 1984, of all the permits issued, 5,480 went to North Americans and 30 to Bangladeshi, and in 1999/2000, 35,000 went to the former and 7,000 to those from the Sub-continent (Jackson and McGregor 2000).

There is also an increasing number of "illegal" migrant workers in low-wage service jobs. For temporary workers, dismissal is equivalent to deportation, so they are forced to keep the jobs they have and to accept low wages. Most migrants with temporary work permits come from outside the New Commonwealth. A very high proportion of these temporary workers are women. Although work permits for unskilled and semiskilled workers were abolished in 1970, in fact many of these workers continue to be employed illegally, because they have overstayed their visas, because their pre-1980 permits have run out, or because they are women who have married and separated without obtaining U.K. citizenship (Greater

---

[21] An even stricter law was introduced in 1968. By the early 1970s, no new workers were being allowed to enter for permanent settlement; only close relatives of those already in Britain were allowed to enter on a permanent basis, but even this was not easy, and many applications were rejected. Finally, the Nationality Act of 1981 redefined the status of certain British passport holders so that they no longer had automatic rights of entry or citizenship. One result was an increase in deportations. Other revisions followed (Sassen 1999).

[22] From the late 1960s until 1979, when temporary work permits no longer were issued, there was an inflow of workers from Turkey, Greece, Spain, the Philippines, Malaysia, Latin America (especially Colombia), and elsewhere, whose status was highly vulnerable and who lacked the right to settle. These migrant workers were used by the London tourist industry, among others, and were subjected to frequent raids by the police and immigration authorities (Greater London Council 1986).

London Council 1986; Sassen 1999). They work in tourism, catering, domestic service, and the public health service and as homeworkers. Migrant workers are generally the most vulnerable and desperate of all minority workers in Britain.

Controlling for industry, the 1981 Labor Force Survey found that black workers were much more concentrated in manufacturing than white workers. Manufacturing accounted for 25% of Asian workers and 27% of black ones, compared with 12% of white male workers. According to the 1981 Survey, black workers have strong concentrations in industries such as engineering and vehicles, food, and textiles. They are absent from industries that tend to involve more skilled work or have strong unions, such as gas, water, electricity, printing, dock work, and property development industries. Most blacks work in production-related activities, such as packing, and, to a lesser extent, in service and maintenance activities in manufacturing. Asians and blacks are overrepresented in industries that have been most affected by decline. Pakistanis and Bangladeshis are particularly concentrated in clothing, textiles, and leather, especially in East London, and also in the furniture trades. There are few Asians in the construction industry. Other ethnic groups, such as Greeks, Cypriots, and Italians, are also found in textiles and clothing.

The 1991 census shows sharp overrepresentation and underrepresentation patterns among most of the non-white ethnic minority groups. Among whites, representation ranges from 1.12 in agricultural and farming work to 0.92 in unskilled manual work. In contrast, the range for most ethnic groups is far sharper, particularly among Black Caribbeans and Irish born, with, respectively, a 1.67 and 2.17 level of overrepresentation in personal services and semi-skilled manual work, to underrepresentation of, respectively, 0.26 and 0.76 in professional work. Sub-continent Asians have high overrepresentation in unskilled manual work, with the sharpest level at 3.5 among Bangladeshi. In contrast the highest overrepresentation among Chinese is as professional workers (2.25). The sharpest underrepresentation of any group for any occupation is among Black Caribbeans as professional workers (0.26) and among Chinese as unskilled manual workers (0.25) (London Research Centre 1994). The evidence for the 1990s suggests these trends have held.

A more detailed occupational analysis shows that Black Caribbean and Bangladeshi men have the lowest representation among corporate managers; Black Africans and Pakistani men have the highest unemployment rates among men in this occupation, at about 17% in 1991, compared to 6% among whites and 5% among Chinese. Information on level of education/qualification for the London population showed that 30% of Chinese and 25% of Black Africans compared to 17% of whites had high qualifications. In 31 of the 33 boroughs minority qualified workers had a higher chance to be unemployed than whites. The concentration in the health services explains why in Britain as a whole 40% of black women are in the professional and scientific category compared with 25% of white women and 16% of Asian women. There are interesting parallels with the United States, where Caribbean women are also highly represented in the health services, particularly nursing and various forms of home care delivery. Among Asian women, 14% work in the distributive trades, compared with 8% of Caribbean women. This is partly explained by the high number of Asian shopowners. But these figures are still much lower than the 27% for white women. Black men and women have considerable concentrations in public service and vehicle maintenance. As a result they have been severely affected by government cutbacks and by privatization.

The sharpest differentials are at the top of the occupational distribution for whites and Black Caribbeans, at, respectively, 19% employers and managers and 6.4% professionals among whites compared to 8.4% and 1.7%. The differential is minor or nonexistent between whites and workers from India, Pakistan, Bangladesh, and Other Asian countries of origin. The composition of the professional and the employers/manager categories is quite different for Whites than for the other groups. A second differential is evident in the personal services and semi-skilled occupations, with 11% of whites compared to 18.8% of Black Caribbeans, 18% of Chinese, and 41% of Bangladeshi. The other ethnic groups all hover around 15 to 17%.

Out of London's total population of almost 7 million in 1996, over 5.3 million were whites and 1.6 million were non-white (see Table 9.3). The largest single nationality groups were the almost 400,000 Indian population, followed by the 331,000 Black Caribbean population. The Chinese and other Asian population is significantly smaller at 166,000. Black Caribbean and Black Africans together account for almost 600,000 while the total population from the Indian subcontinent was over 600,000. If we add the Chinese and Other Asian populations, then Asia is the main region of origin in the nonwhite population of the city. The highest growth rates are projected for the Black African and Black Other populations, followed by Bangladeshi and Pakistani. London's ethnic population is expected to grow by 17% between 1996 and 2006 while the white population is expected to decline by 3.6%, leaving an overall positive balance (London Research Centre 1997; UK Office of Statistics 2000). As was the case in New York in the 1980s and 1990s, it is the minority population that compensates for the losses of the city's white population.

London is the main place of work for the Black Caribbean labor force in the UK, and for under half of the workforce from the Indian subconti-

TABLE 9.3

London: Population Projections in Each Ethnic Group, 1996 to 2006 (thousands and percent)

	1996	2006	% change '96–'06
White	5,358	5,163	−3.6
Black Carribean	331	371	12.1
Black African	240	313	30.4
Black Other	108	143	32.4
Indian	398	443	11.3
Pakistani	110	136	23.6
Bangladeshi	107	133	24.3
Chinese	66	74	12.1
Other Asian	132	147	11.4
Other	144	162	12.5
Total non-white ethnic minorities	1,636	1,921	17.4
TOTAL	6,994	7,084	1.3

Source: Cosmopolitan London: Past, Present and Future, London Research Centre, 1997.

nent (see Table 9.4). Out of a total labor force of almost half a million in the UK, 320,000 Blacks were in London, two-thirds of whom were in Inner London. This contrasted with the Indian subcontinent population: of the 665,000 Indian, Pakistani, and Bangladeshi workers, about 250,000 were in London. Each of these major nonwhite ethnic groups represented about 2% of the labor force of Britain. Together they accounted for 20% of the Inner London labor force. They also represented a disproportionate share of all the unemployed in London (see Table 9.4). Using the more encompassing ILO unemployment measure shows a very high incidence among Blacks in Inner London: while they were 15% of the population of Inner London, they were 28% of the unemployed. Similarly, while they were 5% of the workforce in Outer London, they were 12% of the unemployed. The incidence of unemployment is also considerably above their share of the population for Indians, Pakistani, and Bangladeshi as a group, but not quite as marked as for Blacks.

Income data for 1997 by ethnic origin, excluding pensioneers, shows a rather clear higher incidence of low incomes among non-whites. In the lowest percentile, 67% were white and 33% were nonwhite while in the highest percentile 81% were white and 19% were non-white. The sharpest difference is in the second highest percentile, probably one characterized by highly competitive professional markets where discrimination or lack of membership in certain types of exclusive networks has a stronger ef-

TABLE 9.4

Great Britain and London: Labor Force and Employment[1] By Ethnic Origin, 1996–1997[2]
(thousands and percentages)

	Thousands			Percentages		
	Inner London	Outer London	Great Britain	Inner London	Outer London	Great Britain
Economically active						
White	979	1818	26623	74	83	95
Black	205	116	470	15	5	2
Indian/Pakistani/						
Bangladeshi	71	181	665	5	8	2
Other	70	87	302	5	4	1
All origins[3]	1326	2202	28066	100	100	100
ILO unemployed						
White	105	131	1900	57	70	88
Black	52	21	99	28	12	5
Indian/Pakistani/						
Bangladeshi	14	23	107	7	13	5
Other	14	10	42	8	5	2
All origins[3]	185	186	2150	100	100	100

Source: Focus on London 99, UK Office of National Statistics and London Research Centre 1999.
Notes: [1]ILO definition; [2]Four quarter average from Summer 1996 to Spring 1997; [3]Includes those who did not state their origin, but percentages based on totals which exclude them.

fect: thus whites were 91% in this percentile compared to 9 percent of non-whites.

A breakdown for this evidence for each of the major ethnic origin groups shows that except for the 86% of Bangladeshi concentrated in the two lowest percentiles, most other groups have fairly even distributions

TABLE 9.5

London: Ethnicity by Household Income, 1996 (percentiles)

Percentile	Bangladeshi	Pakistani	Black African	Black Carribean	Black Other	Chinese	Other Indian	All non-White	White
1 (lowest)	76	36	35	30	31	27	18	28	13
2	10	24	20	20	18	14	23	20	14
3	10	20	23	23	21	16	26	23	20
4	1	13	15	20	21	23	22	19	26
5 (highest)	2	7	7	7	10	20	11	10	27

Source: Contrasting London Incomes: A Social and Spatial Analysis, Harriet Anderson and John Flateley London Research Centre 1997.

across the five percentiles (see Table 9.5). About half of Black Africans, Caribbean Blacks, and Other Blacks are in the two lowest percentiles and about 40% are in the third and fourth percentiles. Chinese have the highest concentrations in the higher percentiles of all major ethnic groups, with over 50% in the two highest percentiles.

The New Illegal Immigration in Japan

In Japan massive rural migrations to a few major urban areas provided the needed labor supply during the 1950s and 1960s, a period of accelerated industrialization in a country closed to foreign immigration but with massive labor reserves in the countryside. It was also a period of large-scale construction of public and private infrastructure in order to accommodate the industrialization of the economy and the urbanization of the people. In brief, the demand for labor was immense. It was the kind of period in which countries such as the United States or those of Western Europe have relied on foreign workers. In Japan, rural migration to the cities took the place of immigration. The scale and the speed of rural outmigration reached historic dimensions. Whole villages were reported to have voted to abandon their settlements together, rather than leave a few members behind (Douglass 1987: 11). From 1955 to 1965, the height of this migration, more than half of the nation's forty-six provinces experienced an absolute decline in population, and fourteen others had annual growth rates of less than 1%. Tokyo, Osaka, and Nagoya, the three largest metropolitan areas, were the main destinations of this massive migration. From 1960 to 1970, these three areas raised their populations by 10 million and came to account for 40% of the national population. The Greater Tokyo Metropolitan Area increased by 10 million between 1950 and 1970, reaching 17.7 million people. In 1950, almost 50% of Japan's labor force was in agriculture; by 1970 this figure was down to 19%.

Elsewhere (Sassen 1988) I have posited that one of the properties of an immigrant workforce is its condition as a mobilized workforce. Once uprooted, such workers will accept options that settled members of a community would not. They will take jobs, accept hours and wages, and travel distances to their workplaces that "native" workers would not. Japan's vast workforce, formed through massive rural outmigration, is such a mobilized workforce. This condition may have contributed, along with culture, to the well-established qualities of Japanese workers in this period: hard work, willingness to travel long distances to jobs, endurance of extremely uncomfortable and harsh living conditions.

The immigration of Asian workers in the 1980s began in a completely different phase of the Japanese economy. The second native, urban-born generation was fully grown and in the labor force; there was a large demand for workers at all occupational levels; and it had become increasingly clear that there were labor shortages in very arduous jobs (for example, ocean fishing), and in a growing percentage of low-wage jobs. Though fragmentary, the evidence clearly points to a rapid increase in the 1980s and 1990s in the number of foreigners working illegally in Japan, mostly in the Tokyo metropolitan area, Nagoya, and Osaka. Typically, they have entered the country with tourist visas and overstayed their officially permitted time. The estimate is that by mid-1988 there were 200,000 illegal male workers in Japan in manual work, from construction to restaurant kitchens. Almost all of these were from Asia. The estimate for the 1990s is a continuing presence of undocumented immigrants though possibly at lower levels given the economic recession (Iyotani 2000).

The 1.5 million non-Japanese residents in 1998 consisted largely of three nationality groups. By far the largest group is South and North Korean, numbering about 639,000, followed by the Chinese numbering 272,000 (see Table 9.6). It is important to know that many of these are actually second- and third-generation residents in Japan who still have not been granted or have chosen not to take the Japanese nationality. However, there is also a new immigration of Koreans and Chinese, including an undocumented flow. The next largest groups are from Brazil, probably almost exclusively of Japanese origin and therefore entitled to enter Japan without restrictions up till the third generation.

The number of non-Japanese residents has increased by over 30% since

TABLE 9.6

Non-Japanese Residents in Japan by Country, 1998 (numbers)

Country	Persons
S. and N. Korea[a]	638,828
China[a]	272,230
Brazil	222,217
Philippines	105,308
United States	42,774
Peru	41,317
Other Countries	189,442
Total	1,512,116

Source: Japan Ministry of Justice, Statistics on Foreign Residents, Immigration Bureau, http://www.jinjapan.org.

Notes: [a]Includes second- and third-generation residents.

TABLE 9.7
Registered Foreigners in Japan, 1985 to 1996 (thousands and percent)

Year	Total	Korea	China	Brazil	Philippines	United States	Peru
1985	851	683	75	2	12	29	0
1990	1075	688	150	56	49	38	10
1995	1362	666	223	176	74	43	36
1996	1415	657	234	202	85	44	37
% change							
1990–1996	31.6	−4.5	56.0	260.7	73.5	15.8	270.0

Source: Japan Ministry of Justice, Statistics on Foreign Residents, Immigration Bureau, http://www.
jinjapan.org.

1990, with the two highest rates of increase among those from Brazil and
Peru, almost all descendants of Japanese (see Table 9.7). Filipinos increased by 73% and Chinese by 56%. This population includes a broad
variety of types of residents and reasons for being in Japan.

The case of immigrants of Japanese descent is a very special one. In
what is one of the best studies on this population, Tsuda (1999) shows
how these men and women are increasingly caught in a situation where
they are likely to stay in Japan even if they intended to just come for a
few years. Among the pressures are the impossibility of actually securing
enough savings through a few years of work in Japan to start a business
when returning home, and their children's growing attachment to Japan
and identification with the country.

However, the sharpest rate of increase of registered foreigners is
among nationality groups that count small numbers (see Table 9.8). A
group of diverse countries saw increases of over 300% from 1990 to
1995: Bolivia (mostly Japanese descent); Iran; Peru (mostly Japanese descent); and Myanmar. Controlling for sex some interesting differences
emerge: Colombians also are among the fastest growing nationalities
among men and Bangladeshi among women.[23]

The vast majority of the legal foreign population reside in the large
metropolitan areas, particularly Tokyo, Osaka, and Nagoya. Over 20% of
the Koreans, 60% of the Chinese, and 40% of Filipinos reside in the Tokyo region and about 30% of Koreans, 35% of Chinese, and less than 10%
of Filipinos in the Osaka region. Rural areas have become quite dependent on access to foreign workers—and to foreign wives.

There was considerable debate within the Japanese government about

---

[23] For an analysis and explanation of some of these immigration flows, see Sassen 1998:
chap. 4).

TABLE 9.8

Japan: Growth Rates of Foreigners by Nationality, 1990–1995 (percent)

	Total		Male		Female	
Rank	Nationality	Increase (%)	Nationality	Increase (%)	Nationality	Increase (%)
1	Bolivia	461.4	Bolivia	604.7	Peru	506.5
2	Iran	397.8	Iran	454.3	Myanmar	384.5
3	Peru	338.6	Colombia	380.2	Bangladesh	327.6
4	Myanmar	338.3	Myanmar	316.7	Bolivia	323.9
5	Nepal	239.5	Peru	264.8	Nepal	274.2

Source: Japan Ministry of Justice, Statistics on Foreign Residents, Immigration Bureau, http://www.jinjapan.org.

what to do regarding the new illegal immigration. The centrality that this issue assumed for the Japanese government in the late 1980s is evident from the fact that all the major ministries were asked to set up working parties to study and consult on the issue, and most came up with position papers. Among these were the Ministry of International and Foreign Affairs, the Ministry of Justice, the Ministry of International Trade and Industry, the Ministry of Labor, and, not unexpectedly, the Ministries of Construction, Fisheries, and Transportation, three industries that hire foreign workers. A review of the main positions asserted by each of the ministries points to the complexity the issue assumed and also to the fact that the growing employment of illegal foreign workers was recognized as a given.[24] An official paper issued in 2000 further confirmed this (Iyotani 2001).

[24] A survey of 266 small to medium-sized manufacturing firms in Tokyo in 1989 carried out by Iyotani (1989) found that three out of every five firms interviewed could not find enough employees, particularly young male workers, to fill the available positions. The reasons given were as follows: Many respondents said that young Japanese tend to want better, higher-paying jobs; almost 60% said that young men did not want to work in skilled manual labor; and 20% said they lacked training in manual skilled work. In order to cope with this labor shortage, firms were considering improvements in automation; almost 15% were considering employing foreign workers; 14% were considering bringing in rural young men and women; and some were considering several other types of adjustments. Over 11% of the firms interviewed said that they were employing foreign workers, and almost 13% said that they had hired foreign workers even if currently they had none on the payroll. Thus, about a quarter of all the firms interviewed had at one point or another hired foreign workers. The largest single concentration, 26.8%, of foreign workers in the survey was in metal-related factories; another 21% were in printing and publishing, and about 16% were in electric and electronic goods. Over 15% of the firms asserted that they would not hire foreign workers. In terms of the treatment of foreign workers, 3% of firms believed that foreign workers should be treated exactly like Japanese workers. Over 34% believed that foreign students should be allowed to work without restrictions. And well over a quarter believed that professional foreign personnel should be increased. Well over half of all the

   The Ministry of Labor had initially proposed formation of a guest-worker program, giving foreign workers short-term contracts for specific jobs. It proposed opening the Japanese job market to foreigners by implementing a law that would require them to obtain a full-time employment status permit from the Ministry. But the Ministry of Justice held that such a law would further complicate an already complicated immigration process and that it would create a competitive disadvantage for Japanese workers. The added opposition of several sectors of the economy to the employment permit proposal led the Ministry of Labor to postpone its proposal.

   The Ministry of Justice proposed its own immigration law, which contained provisions on permanent residency, sanctions against employers who hire illegal workers, and a number of other issues concerning foreign workers. Key aspects of the proposed law were (1) expansion of the eighteen categories of professional workers whom the Japanese government already allows prolonged stays for work to include other categories, notably technicians, software engineers, teachers, professors, employees of foreign firms, lawyers, public health professionals, doctors, students, and refugees; (2) a permit entitling the holder to accept employment with a Japanese firm if the foreign worker is the most suitable person for the job; and (3) heavy penalties for employers who knowingly hire illegal foreign workers. The Ministry of Justice is intent on protecting Japanese workers, and it maintains that supply and demand in the labor market should be examined carefully from the perspective of firms. In this context, the Ministry of Labor is assuming a rather different stance, main-

---

firms interviewed asserted that they had no objections to the hiring of foreign workers, while a third said that they would rather not do so in order to avoid problems with foreigners who do not speak Japanese and do not understand the culture.

A 1988 survey of the general public by the Agency of Management and Coordination found that 45% of the 10,000 respondents believed in accepting unskilled foreign workers, but with certain conditions. Asked what they thought about foreign workers doing a job that Japanese did not want to take, almost 35% responded that it was all right if the foreign workers did not object. But over one-third said that it was indecent to offer foreign workers jobs that Japanese would not accept. A fourth said that it was not a good idea, but that if that was the only option for the foreign workers and they were willing to take these jobs, then that was all right. The law preceding the 1990 changes in the immigration law already forbade the entry of unskilled foreign workers for employment. The younger age groups among respondents showed far more flexibility toward accepting unskilled foreign workers. And only one-fourth of all respondents said that unskilled foreign workers should not be allowed to enter and work in Japan. But well over half said that skilled and highly educated workers should be allowed to enter. Almost half said that they could understand why foreign workers came to Japan and worked illegally; and over 60% said that it was understandable because they had to support their families back in their home countries.

taining that in the long run what will be needed is a system of support for what is de facto a foreign workforce and one that is expanding rapidly. Furthermore, the Ministry of Labor maintains that its own proposals for facilitating employment and legalization of foreign workers will be insufficient to control the problem of foreign workers, given the rapid growth in their numbers.

The position taken by the Ministry of Foreign Affairs is that it is important for Japan to accept its new place in the world and that the government should handle the foreign labor question from the perspective of Japan's new power. The Ministry of Foreign Affairs maintains that the government should control the numbers of foreign workers in order to protect the Japanese labor market, but recognizing that Japan's protectionist era is over and the country must assume its role as one of the economic leaders in a "global economy." Finally, it has urged the Ministry of Justice to reconsider its position on foreign workers and stressed that the key to the issue is to support economic development in countries with high emigration to Japan.

A rather different set of positions has emerged from ministries that are clearly representing sectors of the economy that need a supply of workers willing to take very low-paying or dangerous jobs. Thus, the Ministry of Fisheries, in conjunction with private sector organizations, produced a report asserting its need and willingness to hire foreign unskilled laborers, especially for ships operating in international waters and on long-distance expeditions. This is extremely hard and dangerous work, and Japanese fishermen are, according to this report, hesitant to take these jobs. The position of the fishing industry is that Taiwan and South Korea have a growing advantage because their workers are far cheaper than Japanese fishermen. In sum, the Ministry of Fisheries would like to see the Japanese labor market opened to foreign workers, even if on a limited scale. Another type of situation is exemplified by the Ministry of Transportation. The transportation industry hires large numbers of foreign sailors even though there is no shortage of Japanese sailors. The hiring of foreign sailors cuts the cost of wages sharply for the large companies who own the international shipping industry. Limited hiring of foreign transportation workers is already permitted, but the ministry has asserted that the market should be further opened to foreign workers and has denied that foreign workers are taking jobs away from Japanese ones or reducing wages. The Ministry of Construction, representing an industry that is probably a large employer of illegal foreign workers, has maintained strong opposition to the entry of unskilled laborers. It asserts that the presence of foreign unskilled illegal workers is bringing down wage levels and hence creating increasingly unattractive conditions for native Japanese youth; health insurance is minimal among foreign workers and is further being eroded by their presence, as are the general conditions of work.

The Japanese Parliament eventually approved several amendments in 1990 to the immigration law that sought to control immigration. On the one hand, the amendments expand the number of job categories for which the country will accept foreign workers to twenty-eight. These are mostly for professional workers, ranging from lawyers, investment bankers, and accountants with international expertise to medical personnel. On the other hand, the amendments restrict and control the inflow of unskilled and semiskilled workers. Moreover, for the first time, the amendments provide sanctions against employers employing illegal workers. Japan is, then, in many ways replicating the efforts of the United States to control who can come into the country. It will be interesting to observe whether it succeeds in view of the growing internationalization of its economy (Sassen 1988; 1998: chap 4). According to Iyotani (2001) there is a shift from the backdoor policy for handling the need for unskilled workers to a "sidedoor" policy of accepting them as "trainees." There is today also a special visa for IT workers and for nurses, just as is the case in the U.S. and in the UK.

I spent many hours speaking with illegal immigrants in Tokyo and in Yokohama in an attempt to learn how and why they decided to migrate to Japan, given its reputation as a closed society. It is impossible to do full justice to their answers here, but the main points were as follows: First, they were individuals who had, in one way or another, become mobilized into labor migrations before coming; second, Japan's growing presence in their countries, together with the consequent availability of information about Japan, had created linkages and made Japan emerge in their minds as an option for emigration. One interesting question here is, To what extent are we witnessing the emergence of alternative "lands of opportunity" to the United States? The new law will undoubtedly deter some employers; but cases as diverse as the United States, Western Europe, and the Middle Eastern oil-exporting countries have all sought to control immigration and not quite succeeded in the intended way.

My hypothesis is that the segmentation and casualization of the labor market now increasingly evident in Japan have facilitated the labor market incorporation of the new illegal immigration. Casualization opens up the hiring process, reduces the regulatory constraints on employers, and lowers the indirect and typically also direct costs of labor. The relative decline of manufacturing and the growth of services have contributed to a critical mass of small, freestanding firms not incorporated in the large economic groupings into which much of the Japanese economy is still organized—yet another form of casualization. The overall effect may well be to undermine the efficacy of regulatory enforcement, including the new immigration regulations.

Immigration in Economic Restructuring and Social Geography

What is the place of immigration in the economic recomposition process in such cities as New York and London? A common view in the literature is that the bulk of the immigrants provide low-wage labor to declining, backward sectors of capital. This is correct in part, but incomplete. I see two additional roles for immigration, both pertaining to the recomposition process.

First, immigration can be seen as providing labor for the low-wage service and manufacturing jobs that service both the expanding, highly specialized service sector and the high-income lifestyles of those employed in the specialized, expanding service sector (Sassen-Koob, 1982). Some of these jobs held by immigrants may routinely be classified as belonging to declining sectors of the economy. But in fact, insofar as they service the most dynamic sector of the city's economy, we need to make a distinction between "backward jobs"—which they often are—and declining sectors of the economy, which they are not necessarily.

Second, immigration is a factor in the occupation of areas both in New York in the 1970s and in London in the 1960s that would otherwise have had a high proportion of abandoned housing and closed stores. Through the immigrant community, immigrants become agents actively engaged in rehabilitating both spatial and economic sectors of the city. The immigrant community can be seen as representing a small-scale investment of direct labor (through neighborhood upgrading) and of capital (through neighborhood commerce) in a city's economy. Another way of putting it is that the immigrant community is a structure or vehicle that maximizes the benefits of individual investments of direct labor and money for the community, by concentrating such investments spatially, a concentration effected by residential segregation. Thus, home repairs by multiple households become neighborhood upgrading; differences of language and food preferences create a captive market for ethnic shopkeepers.

Elsewhere (Sassen 1988), I have argued at length that the large influx of immigrants into the United States from low-wage countries over the last fifteen years, which reached massive levels in the 1980s, cannot be understood separately from this restructuring. The expansion in the supply of low-wage jobs generated by major growth sectors is one of the key factors in the continuation of ever-higher levels of the current immigration. The magnitude, timing, and destination of the current migration to the United States becomes more understandable when juxtaposed with these developments. While changes in United States immigration legislation in 1965 and the existence of prior immigrant communities are important factors explaining immigration over the subsequent decades, they are not sufficient to explain the continuation of this flow at ever-higher levels, even in the late 1970s and early 1980s, a time of growing unemployment in the United States and rather high employment growth in the immigrants' countries of origin (see Sassen 1988). Nor are they sufficient to explain the disproportionate concentration of immigrants in major urban areas, a trend that continued in the 1990s. Parallel conditions hold in London and other major European cities, each with its own specific immigration history and legislation (Sassen 1999).

There is clearly a structural process at work here as well. Global cities are a key site for the incorporation of large numbers of immigrants in activities that service the strategic sectors. The mode of incorporation is one that renders these workers invisible, therewith breaking the nexus between being workers in leading industries and the opportunity to become—as had been historically the case in industrialized economies—a "labor aristocracy" or its contemporary equivalent. In this sense "women and immigrants" emerge as the systemic equivalent of the offshore proletariat.[25] Further, the demands placed on the top-level professional and managerial workforce in global cities are such that the usual modes of handling household tasks and lifestyle are inadequate. This is a type of household that could be described as the "professional household without a 'wife'" regardless of the demography, i.e., sex composition, of that household, if both members are in demanding jobs. As a consequence we are seeing the return of the so-called "serving classes" in all the global cities around the world, made up largely of immigrant men and women. Finally, the growth of an informal economy in all these cities is a mechanism that raises the level of flexibility in a broad range of activities, from housing rehabilitations to designer clothing and furniture, which are in high demand in global cities. For reasons discussed earlier, immigrants are in a position that renders them a likely workforce and entrepreneurial class in the informal economy.

The expansion in the supply of low-wage jobs, particularly pronounced in major cities, can thus be seen as creating objective employment opportunities for immigrants even as middle-income blue- and white-collar na-

---

[25] In my account "women and immigrants" as a category comes to replace "women and children." One could see the first as a post-Fordist (the flexibilized, casual unvalued service worker) and the second as a Fordist (cf. the family wage earned by the male worker and the unpaid household work of the woman as wife and mother) category of the invisible/unrecognized worker. It is, in my reading, a new topos which replaces the Fordist-family wage topos of women and children. (Sassen 1998: chap. 1).

tive workers are experiencing high unemployment because their jobs are being either downgraded or expelled from the production process.

Conclusion

The central question in this chapter was whether the increase in various types of inequality has brought about new social forms. There is now greater inequality in earnings distribution and in household income, a greater prevalence of poverty, and a massive increase in foreign and domestic investment in luxury commercial and residential construction. Do these merely represent changes in magnitude along an upward or downward gradient, or are they ruptures and discontinuities in the social fabric of these cities?

Gentrification is not a new process. But what is different from earlier episodes is the scale on which it has taken place in all three cities and the extent to which it has created a commercial infrastructure that anyone can buy into, fully or in part. It has engendered an ideology of consumption that is different from that of the mass consumption of the middle classes in the postwar period, which was centered around the construction and furnishing of new suburban housing and the associated infrastructure. Style, high prices, and an ultraurban context characterize the new ideology and practice of consumption, rather than functionality, low prices, and suburban settings. This is not merely an extension of elite consumption, which has always existed and continues to exist in large cities. It is quite different in that it is a sort of new mass consumption of style, more restricted than mass consumption per se because of its cost and its emphasis on design and fashion. There are distinct areas in all three cities where this new commercial culture is dominant and where one finds not only high-income professionals for whom it is a full-time world, but also "transients," from students to low-income secretaries, who may participate in it for as little as one hour. Poverty is not new either. What is new is its severity, leading in the extreme to homelessness on a scale not seen in a long time in highly developed countries.

Similarly, these cities have long been key centers for international business and finance. But the enormity of major central city projects in all three cities, discussed in chapter 7, constitutes yet another instance of a transformation of urban areas that is not simply a continuation of old trends but, rather, represents a massive appropriation of public resources and urban space.

The second major subject of concern in this chapter was the transformation of the employment relation. Transient and casual employment is likely to be part of any large city, but developments over the last decade in New York, London, and Tokyo point to the institutionalization of casual labor markets. These have become a growing and central part of the employment relation in these service-dominated economies. The increase in various types of part-time work is the most general and largest trend. But the dynamics of casualization assume specific forms in each of these cities, and it is important to capture this distinctiveness.

I decided to focus on forms of casual employment somewhat distinct to each city. In New York, one of the more unexpected and dynamic forms of the growth of casual labor markets has been the emergence of an informal economy. This informal economy has had the overall effect not only of cheapening production and servicing costs for firms in both growth industries and declining ones, but also of increasing flexibility in their organization. Such flexibility is particularly important in a city where leading sectors can easily outbid all other sectors for space, but at the same time need to have access to these other industries. The informal economy can thus be seen as providing a flexible arrangement to accommodate firms that are necessary for the operation of leading sectors but could not compete in the open market. Similarly, it reduces the costs of reproduction for low-wage workers, who are in demand in the new economy but would find it difficult to compete for all goods, services, and housing in the open market. In London, perhaps the most dramatic form of the casualization of employment has resulted from the privatization of many of the services once provided by the state. Jobs that used to be full-time and carry a full array of fringe benefits, have now been thrown into the open market, where they have been transformed into part-time, subcontracted jobs at even lower wages. The key here is that even though many of these jobs have long been rather low-paid ones, now they have become part of a growing casual labor market, institutionally a far more vulnerable employment condition. Finally, in Japan what used to be a flexible but protected labor force, "daily laborers," is now a rapidly growing and increasingly heterogeneous stratum of workers, with a sharp erosion in regulatory protection and wage levels.

A third issue discussed in this chapter is that of race and nationality in the economy of these cities. If blacks, Asians, and other immigrants had employment and earnings distributions basically similar to those of whites and/or natives, then this would not be an issue. But they do not. Blacks and Third World immigrants in New York are disproportionately concentrated in lower-paying, more traditional service industries, notably health and social services and in the low-paying jobs of the producer services. In London, notwithstanding the closing of immigration, there has been a continuing influx of illegal or semilegal immigrants, who tend to hold low-wage jobs. And there is now a second and a third generation, descendants of Caribbean and Asian immigrants, who continue to have distinct labor market positions, with high rates of unemployment and, especially among blacks, a disproportionate concentration in public housing and inner-city areas in severe economic and physical decay. As in New York, blacks and Asians in professional occupations tend to hold the lower-paying jobs in both growth and declining industries and to be disproportionately concentrated in the central city. And in both we also see the emergence of persistent and concentrated poverty among these populations and a growing share of young adults who have never held a regular job. We see a dual tendency toward the growing isolation and economic irrelevance of a growing share of these workers and households on the one hand, and on the other hand, the full incorporation of others in the form of a casual, highly flexible, low-cost labor force. Even in Tokyo, a new illegal immigrant workforce similarly occupies low-wage jobs in manufacturing and services, while a growing number of legal immigrants provides necessary technical and professional skills.

The new illegal immigration to Tokyo raises a number of important questions, especially in view of Japan's strong anti-immigration stance and historical absence of immigration. I posit that this new immigration is one outcome of the intersection of two basic processes in these advanced countries: first, the rapid internationalization of the economy, notably the growth in direct foreign investment, foreign aid, and offshore manufacturing facilities in those countries that have been the main sources of the new illegal immigration; and second, the growing presence of casual labor markets and generally a growing casualization of the employment relation, which has facilitated the absorption of the new illegal immigrants.

This suggests that a similar dynamic may be partly underlying some of the new immigration to New York and the United States generally. The notion that New York keeps receiving immigrants because it has always been a city of immigrants is simply insufficient. Migrations are produced, and this requires specific conditions (Sassen 1988; 1999b). Along with the continuation of older immigrations, we may be seeing a set of new conditions producing the increased immigration to the United States and to major cities, which received half of all the immigrants in the 1980s and 1990s. The case of Japan suggests the formation of a new social process, rather than merely the continuation of an old pattern. It would seem that two of the basic processes identified in this book—the internationalization of the economies of these countries, particularly centered in their premier cities, and the casualization of the employment relation—contribute both to producing new migrations and facilitating their absorption.

IN CONCLUSION

Ten

A New Urban Regime?

DO THE CHANGES described in this book amount to a significant transformation in the place of New York, London, and Tokyo in their respective nation-states and in the world economy, and secondly, have those changes brought about a significant realignment in the social and economic structure of these cities? Are we seeing a new type of city, the global city? And if so, how does this affect the urban hierarchy? Is there a new type of urban hierarchy, a new urban system, as a consequence of the global role of major cities, or is this transformation just affecting these cities themselves? Finally, what happens to city politics when the leading economic forces are oriented to the world market?

A central proposition organizing the inquiry was that in order to understand the pronounced social and economic changes in major cities today, we need to examine fundamental aspects of the new world economy. Such changes cannot be adequately explained merely in terms of the shift from manufacturing to services in developed economies. The first part of the book analyzed and documented key trends in the world economy: the growth of the global financial market, the expansion of the international trade in services, and the repatterning of foreign direct investment. Next, it examined the form of this internationalization, one characterized by an increasingly global network of factories, service outlets, and financial markets, along with continued economic concentration. A limited number of countries account for most of the flows and international transactions; very large firms dominate some of the flows; a few cities emerge as leading centers for international transactions.

The most pronounced development is the massive increase in the volume of transactions of the financial industry, by far the most significant international industry. While in the 1950s and 1960s foreign direct investment in primary activities was the main type of international flow, by the late 1970s and especially in the 1990s financial transactions dwarfed the former. In foreign direct investment, a new pattern emerged, with most of the growth directed to two major areas, the United States and Southeast Asia. In contrast, Latin America, which had been among the major recipients in the 1950s and 1960s, became less significant in the 1980s. By far the largest importer of capital in the 1980s was the United

States; and Japan became the leading net exporter of capital. Most foreign direct investment is now in services.

Having confirmed the growth of international transactions in the economy and the central place of a limited number of countries, notably the
United States, the United Kingdom, and Japan, in these transactions, the
question then was how cities fit into this globalization of economic activity—particularly the major cities for international business and finance,
among which, New York, London, and Tokyo. A central thesis organizing this discussion is that increased globalization along with continued
concentration in economic control has given major cities a key role in the
management and control of such a global network.

Many of these patterns in the development of a global economy express themselves in terms of territory. Within this context, the territory of
major cities as a site for world economic activity was explored. We were
concerned with understanding why the extremely rapid growth of finance
and business services took place and why their location patterns were
characterized by such high concentration in major cities. There are two
hypotheses that we explored. One is that the spatial dispersion of production and the reorganization of the financial industry over the last decade
have created new forms of centralization in order to manage and regulate
the global network of production sites and financial markets. The second
is that these new forms of centralization entail a shift in the locus of
control and management: In addition to the large corporation and the
large commercial bank there is now also a marketplace with a multiplicity
of advanced corporate service firms and nonbank financial institutions.
Correspondingly, we see the increased importance of such cities as New
York, London, and Tokyo as *centers* of finance and as *centers* for global
servicing and management.

The spatial dispersion of production, including its internationalization,
has contributed to the growth of centralized service nodes for the management and regulation of the new space economy. Major cities, such as
New York, London, and Tokyo, have greatly expanded their role as key
locations for top-level management and coordination. And the reorganization of the financial industry has led to rapid increases in the already
significant concentration of financial activities in major cities. The pronounced expansion in the volume of financial transactions has magnified
the impact of these trends. Finally, the reconcentration of a considerable
component of foreign investment activity and the formation of an international property market in these major cities has further fed this economic core of high-level control and servicing functions. In brief,
alongside well-known decentralization tendencies, there are less known
centralization tendencies.

Different locations manifest different aspects of these developments. To a considerable extent, the weight of economic activity since the 1980s years has shifted from production places, such as Detroit and Manchester, to centers of finance and highly specialized services. While the dispersion of plants speeds the decline in old manufacturing centers, the associated need for centralized management and control feeds growth in servicing centers. Similarly, the ascendance of the advanced services in economic activity generally has shifted tasks out of the shop floor and into the design room and has changed management from what was once an activity focused on production to one that is finance focused today.

Key questions for investigation concerned the actual work involved in such management and control and what exactly is the work that takes place in major cities. This examination was the subject of Part Two of the book. The organizing concept is that of the *practice* of global control— the activities involved in producing and reproducing the organization and management of the global production system and the global labor force. The argument organizing the discussion was that the maintenance of centralized control and management over a geographically dispersed array of plants, offices and service outlets cannot be taken for granted or seen as an inevitable outcome of a "world system." The possibility of such centralized control needs to be produced. Central to its development is the production of a vast range of highly specialized services and of top-level management and control functions.

The focus on "production" serves several purposes. First, it provides an empirical referent for identifying specific modes of integration of global cities in the world economy. Besides being nodal points in a vast communications and market system, these cities are also sites for the production of global control capability. Second, a focus on production introduces the categories of labor and work process into the analysis. If we look only at power issues, the tendency is to think of, for example, financial factors in terms of highly specialized financial outputs rather than the wide range of jobs, not all of which have to do with highly specialized financial know-how, involved in *producing* such outputs. Third, a focus on production does not have as its unit of analysis the powerful actors, be they multinational corporations or governments, but the site of production—in this case, major cities. Thus, even though global control capability is a basic mechanism that allows large corporations to operate a widely dispersed domestic and global production system, this should not necessarily be taken to mean that the production of this capability can be contained within the corporation. If we look at the production of this capability, we can incorporate in the analysis a rapidly expanding market of freestanding specialized service firms. Such firms, an important growth sector in New York, London, and Tokyo, would be left out if the focus were on the power of large firms. Fourth, a focus on production and production sites brings to the fore the role of a few key cities in the current phase of the world economy as well as the differences among major cities in the highly industrialized countries.

This second part of the book established that the whole array of activities that make up or facilitate the various internationalization processes discussed in Part One has indeed grown over the last fifteen years, is heavily concentrated in major cities, particularly New York, London, and Tokyo, and is a significant factor in the economies of these cities. There is a complex of industries, such as advertising, accounting, legal services, business services, certain types of banking, engineering, and architectural services, etc., which assist, facilitate, complement, and in many cases make possible, the work of large and small firms and of governments. A central and growing component of this complex of industries is linked to the servicing of firms engaged in international transactions and with a farflung domestic and/or international network of service outlets, factories, and markets. In the case of finance, part of the industry fulfills this servicing function. But in the 1980s, a growing sector of the industry, the book argues, became akin to a commodity sector, where the buying and selling of instruments has its own sphere of circulation and does not function as a service industry in the narrow sense of the word. New York, London, and Tokyo are the leading marketplaces for this sector of the industry, as well as functioning as a single, transterritorial marketplace.

This part of the book also examined other major cities in these countries to specify what, if anything, is distinct about New York, London, and Tokyo. The salient difference is the extent of concentration of the producer services and finance. But many cities have growing producer services sectors, as do these countries as a whole. Part of this growth is clearly related to the overall transformation in the composition and organization of the economy, beyond the mere growth in services. There is a greater proportion of services in many industries and more service inputs in many kinds of work. Furthermore, the development of regional and national markets and networks of service outlets and factories also has created the same pressures toward expanded central functions for regional or national-level firms. And we see, indeed, that trends similar to those evident in New York, London, and Tokyo are also emerging in other major cities, though on a lower order of magnitude and based on regional- rather than global-level processes. The proliferation of producer services firms has itself created a demand for more service inputs bought on the market rather than produced in-house. And the growing complexity faced by governments has also created a demand for more specialized services bought in the market. There is, then, a fundamental relationship between the growth of these kinds of service industries catering to the needs of complex organizations and various aspects of economic restructuring in the last two decades. I argue that it is these transformations that constitute the shift to a service-dominated economy, rather than the mere fact of a shift in employment from manufacturing to services, a process usually centered on the growth of consumer services. On the contrary, I posit that the period of massive growth of consumer services is associated with the expansion of mass production in manufacturing.

A third issue addressed in this part of the book is the question of urban hierarchies: How has the globalization of economic activity affected the whole notion of urban hierarchies, or urban systems, which the specialized literature typically sees as nationally based? Are New York, London, and Tokyo actually part of two distinct hierarchies, one nation-based and the other involving a global network of cities? Each of these three cities is the preeminent urban center in its country, though none quite to the extreme that London is in the United Kingdom. And unlike London and Tokyo, New York is part of a tier of major cities that includes Los Angeles, Chicago, Boston, San Francisco, and, because it is the national capital, Washington, D.C. Yet the evidence made it clear that New York remains the leading international financial and business center in the United States, with the other cities a far second.

Through finance more than through other international flows, a global network of cities has emerged, with New York, London, and Tokyo and today also Frankfurt and Paris the leading cities fulfilling coordinating roles and functioning as international marketplaces for the buying and selling of capital and expertise. Stock markets from a large number of countries are now linked with one another through this network of cities. In the era of global telecommunications, we have what is reminiscent of the role of an old-fashioned marketplace in each city, which serves as a connecting and contact point for a wide diversity of often distant companies, brokers, and individuals.

Furthermore, the book sought to show that in many regards New York, London, and Tokyo function as one transterritorial marketplace. Each market is in an increasingly institutionalized network of such marketplaces. These three cities do not simply compete with each other for the same business. They also fulfill distinct roles and function as a triad. Briefly, in the 1980s Tokyo emerged as the main center for the export of capital; London as the main center for the processing of capital, largely through its vast international banking network linking London to most countries in the world and through the Euromarkets; and New York as the main receiver of capital, the center for investment decisions and for the production of innovations that can maximize profitability. Beyond the often-mentioned need to cover the time zones, there is an operational aspect that suggests a distinct transterritorial economy for a specific set of functions.

The management and servicing of a global network of factories, service outlets, and financial markets imposes specific forms on the spatial organization in these cities. The vastness of the operation and the complexity of the transactions, which require a vast array of specialized services, lead to extremely high densities and, at least for a period, extremely high agglomeration economies, as suggested by the rapid building of one high-rise office complex after another in all three cities, extremely high land prices, and sharp competition for land. This process of rapid and acute agglomeration represents a specific phase in the formation and expansion of an industrial complex dominated by command functions and finance.

There are two questions at this point. One concerns the durability of an economic system dominated by such management, servicing, and financial activities; the second one concerns the durability of the spatial form associated with the formation and expansion of this industrial complex in the 1980s.

Regarding the first, there is considerable debate as to whether a service-dominated economy can grow, or keep on growing, without a strong manufacturing sector. This point can be argued from different perspectives. Simplifying, some argue that manufacturing is actually a key factor in service growth. For example, Cohen and Zysman (1987) found that a third of producer service sector output in the United States was linked to manufacturing and that it is precisely the most important and dynamic service industries that have this characteristic. Others argued, more specifically for the United States, that the only way to overcome a severe budget deficit—and by implication this would hold for any major country with a budget deficit—was to develop a strong manufacturing sector and engage in exports. Such a manufacturing sector, in this view, should be one with good, well-paying jobs, to avoid becoming an economy with a high percentage of low-wage jobs and a low standard of living (Thurow 1989). These are analyses that are oriented toward nations.

What comes out of this book is that the globalization of manufacturing activity and of key service industries has been a crucial factor in the growth of the new industrial complex dominated by finance and producer services. Yes, manufacturing matters, but from the perspective of finance and producer services, it does not have to be national. This is precisely, as this book sought to show, one of the discontinuities (between major cities and nations) in the operation of the economy today compared with two decades ago, the period when mass production of consumer goods was the leading growth engine. One of the key points developed in this book is that much of the new growth rests on the decline of what were once significant sectors of the national economy, notably key branches of manufacturing that were the leading force in the national economy and promoted the formation and expansion of strong middle class.

Furthermore, the new industrial complex has contributed to a transformation in the social structure of major cities where it is concentrated. This transformation assumes the form of increased social and economic polarization. While some of this may not affect the functioning and expansion of the new industrial complex, some of it does. The growing inequality in the bidding power of firms has meant that a whole array of firms that produce goods and services that indirectly or directly service the firms in the new industrial core have growing difficulty surviving in these cities. They must either resort to various mechanisms for reducing costs of production—notably subcontracting, employing undocumented immigrants at below-average wage levels and in below-standard work conditions—or have to raise their prices to the point where it begins to affect the costs of operation of the core sector and eventually makes these cities less attractive locations, with a changing trade-off between agglomeration economies and locations costs. Finally, the growing inequality in the bidding power for space, housing, and consumption services means that the expanding low-wage workforce that is employed directly and indirectly by the core sector has increasing difficulty living in these cities. This may reduce the *effective* supply of such workers and lead to a deeper impoverishment of significant sectors of the population, something that has indeed happened over the last decade in all three cities. At what point do these tensions become unbearable? At what point is the fact of homelessness a cost also for the leading growth sectors? How many times do high-income executives have to step over the bodies of homeless people till this becomes an unacceptable fact or discomfort? At what point does the increasing poverty of large numbers of workers begin to interfere with the performance of the core industries either directly or indirectly? It is perhaps the social involution that this mode of growth brings about in significant sectors of a national economy that may be more devastating to its own growth than the decline of manufacturing at the national level, since there is significant manufacturing growth globally, and in that sense there is grist for the mill of the producer services complex.

Another major tension derives from the fact that much of the new growth rests on a weakening of the national state. For instance, the national budget deficits in the United States and in Japan were a crucial source of growth for the financial industry and specialized service industries in the 1980s. Much recent policy has favored internationalization and finance, with the corresponding decline of significant manufacturing sectors in the United States and in the United Kingdom (and now increasingly in Japan) contributing to large trade deficits. How will this tension between the conditions for growth of leading industries in major cities and the decline of significant national economic sectors be managed? Will there be a point when national decline will exercise downward pressure on the economy of these cities?

Regarding the durability of the spatial form associated with this mode of economic growth, a critical question concerns the development of telecommunications technologies for centralizing functions. Up till now the major outcome of the development of telecommunications capability has been to expand the spatial dispersion of the economy. But this dispersion has required the expansion of central functions. At what point will telecommunications be applied to centralizing functions and the complex of professional, managerial, and executive functions at the top? The urban form that has developed in the last two decades associated with this spatial reorganization of economic activity has clearly been one of growing densities and extreme locational concentration of central functions and of the production of innovations. In 1990 I asked whether we were reaching the limit of this urban form, notwithstanding the massive high-rise office complexes under construction in London and Tokyo, with a few more planned for New York. New York suggested to me that we had partly because of an increasingly disadvantageous trade-off between the benefits and costs of this agglomeration. Yet the late 1990s launched a whole new building phase in London and New York (and other emergent global cities) which is further expanding the space of the high-priced center.

An important factor that needs to be considered is the massive infrastructural investments required by telecommunications systems and the organizational complexity that allows firms to maximize the benefits they can derive from such systems (see chapter 5). This effectively creates barriers to entry. While in principle any city could consider developing telecommunications capability of the first order and hence compete for a number of functions now concentrated in leading cities, in practice entry costs are so high, in addition to the costs of continuous incorporation of the newest technology, that for the foreseeable future, major cities, have an almost absolute advantage. And most cities lack the mix of resources which creates organizational complexity in leading cities. We are entering a whole new phase in the development of urban economic systems.

In this context, the Japanese case is of interest. In the 1980s the Japanese aimed at building the most advanced form of office complexes and telecommunications infrastructure—"intelligent buildings," the teleport city being built on land extracted from Tokyo Bay, and especially the proposals to rearrange the capital city and its crucial functions in more "rational" ways. One of these proposals would link Tokyo, Osaka, and

Nagoya by means of a high-speed train of the most advanced type and through telecommunications. The effect would be that of the structure of a single agglomeration in the form of a line—not what is conventionally represented as an agglomeration. A rational allocation of functions along this line would make maximum use of the comparative advantages of each point along this line. This is a very different conception of urban form from that of the concentric or axial pattern characterizing the market-led, often haphazard development of major cities today. It would link everything to a single axis, a fact that would matter for the movement of certain elements in the economy—notably workers, goods, and certain type of services—but not for those aspects subject to telecommunication. It would, arguably, be a design that would recognize that we are not a purely informational economy, that a lot of components still have very much a physical dimension, and that the juxtaposition of an ideology of telecommunications and a reality that is only partly subject to the latter or reducible to information results in massive tensions and congestions embedded in the spatial structure of large cities today. What the arrangement of crucial functions along a line would mean for politics and society is a different type of question.

The third part of the book addresses the impact of this new industrial complex on the economic and social structure of the city. We know that manufacturing, as epitomized by the two decades after World War II in the United States, had a strong multiplier effect and contributed to the expansion of a strong middle class. In the period when manufacturing based on mass consumption and large scales of production was the leading economic sector, there was a pronounced orientation in the general economy toward the production of housing, roads, shopping centers, new schools, and all the other components of the suburbanization process that dominated economy and society. The decline of Fordism entailed a change in the economic and political place of unions and mass production as well as the demise of a broader institutional framework sustained by that model of production, one with significant shadow effects for larger sectors of the economy.

The historical forms assumed by economic growth in the post–World War II era—notably capital intensity, standardization of production, and suburbanization-led growth—contributed to the vast expansion of a middle class. And so did the cultural forms accompanying these processes, particularly as they shaped the structures of everyday life insofar as a large middle class contributes to mass consumption and thus to standardization. At the same time, suburbanization also left behind a mass of poor and disadvantaged people in the older central areas in all three cities, which eventually became a factor in the formation of so-called inner cities. Nevertheless, overall, these various trends were conducive to greater levels of unionization or other forms of workers' empowerment that can be derived from large scales in production and the centrality of mass production and mass consumption in national economic growth and profits. In the case of Britain, there was, in addition, a massive expansion in public services, which entailed a corresponding growth in full-time, year-round jobs with the requisite fringe benefits, the state being the employer. It is in that postwar period extending into the late 1960s and early 1970s when the incorporation of workers into formal labor market relations reached its highest level in all three countries.

This combination of processes was important for the expansion of a middle class and generally rising wages. In the post–World War II period and into the early 1970s, a growing proportion of firms in all three countries organized their labor force in terms of full-time jobs and internal labor markets with training and career opportunities. During this period, unions in the United States and the United Kingdom gained legitimacy and were central to the employment relation in the leading industries. Economic growth in this period was based largely on providing a critical mass of people with houses, roads, cars, furniture, and appliances. This was particularly strong in the United States. In the case of the United Kingdom, there was less of a process of suburbanization than in the United States and more of a process of social provisioning along with the infrastructure and organizations required for this; most notable was the development of a national public health system and of public housing. In Japan, the choice was toward massive reinvestment to expand the infrastructure for production rather than that for social reproduction, as in the United States. The delay in investment in infrastructure to house and service the population led to a significantly lower standard of living in Japan. Considerable suburbanization occurred as a sheer consequence of the need to house a vastly expanded urban population, swollen by extremely rapid and large-scale rural-to-urban migrations in the 1950s and into the 1960s. However, by far the leading growth factor in the economy was the expansion of the production apparatus, Japan in that period being, after all, far behind the United States and United Kingdom as an industrial power. One common thread was the formation and expansion of a vast middle class, though a much poorer one in Japan than in the United States. The decline of the centrality of production for mass consumption in national growth and the shift to services as the leading economic sector contributed to the demise of this broader set of arrangements. This has been the case especially in the United States and the United Kingdom, but is now also becoming evident in Japan.

As discussed in the third part of the book, today growth is based on an industrial complex that leads not to the expansion of a middle class but to increasing dispersion in the income structure and in the bidding power of firms and households. There is social and economic polarization, particularly strong in major cities which concentrate a large proportion of the new growth industries and create a vast direct and indirect demand for low-profit services and low-wage jobs.

Furthermore, growth in the new industrial complex is based less on the expansion of final consumption by a growing middle class than on exports to the international market and on intermediate consumption by firms and governments or, more generally, consumption by organizations rather than individuals. The key, though not necessarily the largest, markets are not the consumer markets but the global markets for capital and services. These are the markets that shape society and economy.

Does this make a difference? The evidence presented in this book suggests that it makes a large difference. The book argues that there has been pronounced transformation, characterized by major class realignments and major changes in the institutional framework within which the employment relation takes place. There has been a generalized dismantling of a system that provided a measure of job security, health benefits, and other components of a social wage to a critical mass of workers. This compact rested ultimately on an economic necessity: the fact that the consumption capacity of a critical mass of workers was of central importance to profit realization for the leading industries in the economy. But out of this economic necessity grew a series of social and political arrangements that went beyond the specific economic relation. These arrangements were supported by a series of other processes. While much has been said about the household becoming a secondary and unimportant arena in society in this period compared with the farm household, a genuinely productive unit, it is also true that the household is the key unit of consumption, and in an economy based on final consumption, this mattered immensely. Confinement of women to housework created full-time workers for the organization and management of the consumption of goods and services by the household. The notion of a family wage and the responsibility of the whole economic and political system toward maintaining and supporting the institution of the family (understood as the nuclear family) was probably nowhere as developed as in the United States. This is not surprising given that it was also here that mass production reached its highest level of development, and that suburbanization— the key mechanism to stimulate massive consumption—was nowhere as developed. Today the institution of the family wage and the social compact between labor and employers has been severely eroded in the United States and the United Kingdom and is beginning to erode in

Japan. There now are more part-time workers, temporary workers, and workers without pension and health benefits, fewer workers with seniority rights, and, in the case of Japan, a pronounced shrinking in the category of workers with "life-long job security," along with an increase in "daily" workers. There are also many more women in the labor force, and, in the case of the United States, many more minority and immigrant workers.

This development raises a number of questions about the intersection of economics and politics and about the "natural" tendencies of capitalist economies. Was the social compact of the postwar period the result of the weight of local politics in a phase of economic development that gave local claims unusual powers? And is what we are seeing today—increased economic and social polarization—the "natural" outcome of the operation of the economic system when political claims carry little weight? A central question for politics is what happens to accountability when the leading economic sectors are oriented to a world market and to firms rather than to individuals. The uncomfortable question is whether the sudden growth in homelessness, especially in New York and in London but also beginning in Tokyo in the late 1980s, the growth of poverty generally, the growth of low-wage employment without any fringe benefits, and the growth of sweatshops and industrial homework are all linked to the growth of an industrial complex oriented to the world market and significantly less dependent on local factors than, for example, household durables manufacturers in the 1950s. To this should be added the growth of what amounts to an ideology of globalism, whereby localities are seen as powerless in an era of global economic forces.

There is clearly one class of workers who benefited from this new industrial complex. They are the new professionals, managers, brokers of all types, whose numbers increased dramatically in these three cities, and to some extent in all cities. How do they fit into the economic and political system of the city? The evidence in this book suggests that it is important to distinguish this new class of high-income workers from the wealthy, also a significant presence in leading cities. This is definitely a class of high-income workers, who, unlike top-level executives and managers, have no significant control or ownership in the large corporations and investment banks for which they work. They are not really part of C. Wright Mills's "power elite." They are ultimately a stratum of extremely hard-working people whose alliance to the system leads them to produce far more profit than they get back in their admittedly very high salaries and bonuses. In some ways it could be argued that they engage in self-exploitation insofar as they work extremely hard, put in very long hours, and ultimately make significantly less money than the stratum of top-level managers and executives, who earn ten to twenty times as much. The

1987 crisis in the stock market, which eventually led to the dismissal of significant numbers of these workers, especially in New York, laid bare the extent to which they have no claim on the system or their employers, unlike top-level managers who, when displaced by mergers, can claim large sums of compensation or "golden parachutes." This book also suggests that high-income gentrification and the type of conspicuous consumption associated with it serves a strong ideological function of securing the alliance of these workers to a system for which they produce immense profits in exchange for relatively low returns and few claims.

The new high-income workers are the carriers of a consumption capacity and consumption choices that distinguish them from the traditional middle class of the 1950s and 1960s. While their earned income is too little to be investment capital, it is too much for the basically thrifty, savings-oriented middle class. These new high-income earners emerge as primary candidates for new types of intermediate investments: stock, arts, antiques, and luxury consumption. The conjunction of excess earnings and the new cosmopolitan work culture creates a compelling space for new lifestyles and new kinds of economic activities. It is against this background that we need to examine the expansion of the art market and of luxury consumption on a scale that has made them qualitatively different from what they were even fifteen years ago—a privilege of elites. The growth of a stratum of very high income workers has produced not only a physical upgrading of expanding portions of global cities, but also a reorganization of the consumption structure.

The high income of the new workers is not sufficient to explain the transformation. Less tangible factors are considerable. The new work culture is a cosmopolitan one, for the objective conditions of work are world oriented, being embedded in a context of growing internationalization in the economies of these cities. The growing number of young professional women has further contributed to an urbanization of the professional class rather than the suburbanization typical of an earlier period. Concomitantly, we see what amounts to a new social aesthetic in everyday living, where previously the functional criteria of the middle class ruled. An examination of this transformation reveals a dynamic whereby an economic potential—the consumption capacity represented by high disposable income—is realized through the emergence of a new vision of the good life. Hence the importance not just of food but of *cuisine*, not just of clothes but of designer labels, not just of decoration but of authentic objets d'art. This transformation is captured in the rise of the ever more abundant boutique and art gallery. Similarly, the ideal residence is no longer a "home" in suburbia, but a converted former warehouse in ultra-urban downtown. Consequent to this new social aesthetic is, of course, a whole line of profitmaking possibilities, from "nouveaux" restaurants to a thriving art market. What is notable is the extent to which a numerically small class of workers imposed such a visible transformation—of the nature of commerce and consumption—on key areas of these extremely large cities. This is, I argue, connected to questions of the social reproduction of a strategic yet not very powerful class of workers.

Immigrants in New York and London, in turn, have produced a low-cost equivalent of gentrification. Areas of New York once filled with shut-up storefronts and abandoned buildings are now thriving commercial and residential neighborhoods. On a smaller scale, the same process has occurred in London. The growing size and complexity of immigrant communities has generated a demand and supply for a wide range of goods, services, and workers. On both the demand and supply sides, the residential and social separateness of the immigrant community becomes a vehicle to maximize the potential it contains. Small investments of money and direct labor in homes and shops by individuals become neighborhood upgrading because of the residential concentration of immigrants. This upgrading does not fit the conventional notions of upgrading, notions rooted in the middle-class experience. Its shapes, colors, and sounds are novel. They, like the cosmopolitan work culture of the new professionals, are yet another form of the internationalization of global cities.

The changes in the economic base and the new income structure in global cities cannot explain this configuration fully. For a number of reasons we have seen the ascendancy of the arts as an arena containing elements central to the quotidian, that is, the structures of everyday life. One reason for this ascendancy can be found in the practices of artists that became prevalent in the 1960s. These practices in turn were generated by economic and other constraints on artists. For example, artists moved into what were at the time undesirable areas of large cities, such as the warehouse district in New York, in part because it was impossible to afford studio space in better areas. Once this move happened, however, it generated its own possibilities for new types of artistic practices and strategies for economic survival of artists. Eventually, artists came to imbue the environment in old warehouse districts with "value," notably aesthetic value. That these elements soon were translated into an arrangement highly desirable for nonartists, does not, however, necessarily flow from the fact that the artists imbued their "neighborhood" with aesthetic and existential value. But the vision, the capacity, the talent, the faith, the obsession that these residents could muster—often unwittingly—to give it that value acquire weight given other conditions.

These other conditions bring us back to the sphere of the economy, particularly the new consumption capacity represented by the large increase in high-income earners. For example, real estate developers picked up on the "value-giving power" of artists and made it into a profitmaking tactic. In the early 1980s, one firm bought a set of buildings on the

Lower East Side of New York, at a time when it was not yet fashionable but merely a very run-down section of Manhattan, and turned them into artists' residences and studios for rent. The rationale, as the real estate developer put it, was as follows: If artists move in, we accomplish two things with one stroke; we can charge higher rents than those of the present residents, and we upgrade the area and make it desirable for much higher income people. This model-setting power attributed to artists as a group is, clearly, not inherent to the condition of being an artist. We know from past epochs that artists were mostly regarded as fundamentally undesirable types by the bourgeoisie and certainly by the new rich. In the current economic situation, this model-setting power becomes a vehicle for crystallizing new profitmaking opportunities, ranging from real estate development to luxury consumption.

There are political implications in this implementation of a new vision of the good life for those with the money to but it. The workers holding the good jobs translate their incomes into lifestyles that clash with traditional middle-class values. There is, then, not only an economic schism, in that the elimination of middle-income jobs from the production process is one of the conditions for the new high-income jobs; there is also a cultural-ideological distancing that captures this schism on another level. Is politics far behind?

In brief, the third part of the book examined the local consequences of the globalization of economic activity, and asked whether the transformations evident in the social and economic structure of each city amount to a new urban regime. By focusing on production processes in the new industrial complex, the analysis makes it possible to see in relation to one another the full range of jobs, firms, and households involved in each city, from the top to the bottom, from those that are quintessentially postindustrial to those that look as though they belong to an earlier industrial era but are necessary to the operations of the new industrial complex. In this perspective, such developments as the growth of an informal economy and the casualization of the labor market—evident in all three cities—emerge not as anomalous or exogenous to these advanced urban economies, but as in fact part of them. A new class alignment is being shaped, and global cities have emerged as one of the main arenas for this development: They contain both the most vigorous economic sectors and the sharpest income polarization. The concrete expression of this new class alignment in the structures of everyday life is well captured in the massive expansion of a new high-income stratum alongside growing urban poverty.

This book has examined the consequences for cities of a global economy. Beyond their sometimes long history as centers for world trade and finance, some cities now function as command points in the organization of the world economy, as sites for the production of innovations in finance and advanced services for firms, and as key marketplaces for capital. In the literature of both urbanism and political economy, there are important gaps in our knowledge of the regulation, management, and servicing of spatially dispersed but globally integrated economic activities. This book sought to fill these gaps in current knowledge by showing how certain cities function in concert to fulfill such tasks.

These cities play, then, a strategic role in the new form of accumulation based on finance and on the globalization of manufacturing. The clearest representation, if one were to abstract a simplifying image from the complexity of this reality, is that the global city replaced the industrial/regional complex centered on the auto industry as the key engine for economic growth and social patterning. This is not to say that finance was unimportant then and manufacturing is unimportant today. Nor is it simply that the financial industry has replaced the auto industry as the leading economic force. It is to emphasize that a whole new arrangement has emerged for accumulation around the centrality of finance in economic growth. The sociopolitical forms through which this new economic regime is implemented and constituted amount to a new class alignment, a new norm of consumption where the provision of public goods and the welfare state are no longer as central as they were in the period dominated by mass manufacturing. A focus on the actual work processes involved in these various activities reveals that it has contributed to pronounced transformations in the social structure, directly through the work process in these industries—finance, producer services, and the range of industrial services they require—and indirectly through the sphere of social reproduction, the maintenance of the high-income and low-income workers it employs. It is this combination of a new industrial complex that dominates economic growth and the sociopolitical forms through which it is constituted and reproduced that is centered in major cities and contains the elements of a new type of city, the global city.

Epilogue

GLOBALIZATION has brought with it a change in the scales at which strategic economic and political processes territorialize. Global cities have emerged as major new scales in this dynamic of territorialization. Key features of this rescaling entail an overriding of older categories for analysis and older hierarchies of scale. This has brought with it the need for theoretical and methodological innovations and hence, inevitably, a lively debate. The decade of the 1990s saw a multiplication of debates and a launch of a whole new research agenda around questions of cities and the variety of substantive issues they encompass. Globalization in turn also generated a whole new research literature, some of it focused on cities, also a new departure.

In this epilogue to the new edition I focus on several of these debates and how they stand up to the new data presented in this edition of the book. And I focus on the numerous critiques addressed to the first edition and examine how the data for the 1990s stands up against these critiques. This is one way of illuminating the multiple issues that this new type of conceptual architecture evokes. Hopefully, it also is a way of addressing the many queries I have received from all over the world from researchers and those struggling to advance the theorization of these issues. The debate has also been nurtured by a large number of studies done by scholars in many disciplins and countries who have contributed to strengthen the global city model. I allude to some of these contributions. Finally, it is an occasion for me to address some of the critiques that set up a straw man or rested on an understanding of the global city model which was faulty, partial or completely wrong. I could have taken the high road and disregarded this last bit; but I could not resist doing the low road as well.

Generally, my interpretation of the data for the 1990s show an amplification of the trends I first detected, often dimly, in the 1980s. These trends are now much clearer, partly because we know what we are looking for. When I was working on these issues in the 1980s, there was no clear picture, no formulated trends that could aid me in seeing what was taking place. I remember often being in doubt or puzzled by the multiple stories that the data were telling. It took some courage or lack of prudence to formulate some of the trends in such forceful language. It was bound to get me into trouble. And it did. It was both worrisome and exciting to study the 1990s and to try to understand how my analysis remained useful. I have discussed the major issues in each of the chapters, including completely new sections warranted by the developments of the 1990s.

Throughout this new edition I have mentioned some of the critical literature, both the negative and the constructive one. But this critical literature is enormous and it is in many languages and in many different disciplines. It would be impossible for me to cite the English language and those foreign languages I know, let alone pieces in languages I do not know. In this epilogue I wanted to avoid singling out a few and leaving out the majority of scholars; whenever possible I have not listed names.

There are six sets of debates. One concerns the construct or the model of the global city, its validity, its explanatory power, its "ontological" status, and the questions of measurement it generates. A second set of debates concerns the financial industry, its weight in global cities, its spatial organization, notably the extent to which the increasingly digitalized markets are articulated at all with global cities. A third concerns producer services, particularly their role as indicators of global city status, their articulation with or dependence on manufacturing, and their spatial organization. A fourth set of debates concerns the relations among cities, including the question of competition, hierarchies, and networks. A fifth set of debates concerns the question of inequality in global cities, including earnings inequality and spatial forms of polarization. A sixth set of debates concerns the question as to whether we see in global cities the emergence of a new spatial order. I have grouped the discussion of these debates into four sections to which I now turn.

The Global City Model

The debate around the validity and nature of the construct itself raised a number of conceptual, methodological and empirical questions. Some of these questions directly or indirectly intersect with the more specific issues I present in subsequent sections. Several types of criticism are based on a conception of the global city model that is faulty and even flat wrong, while others are, in my reading, correct and yet others are constructive in the sense that they have added questions or actual empirical and theoretical elements to the research literature on the subject.

a) Globalization and homogenization.

A first group of critiques of the concept centered on questions linked to globalization and the associated homogeneization it is supposed to bring about. One version of this critique is the assertion that in the global city model globalization is conceived of as a force coming from outside and homogenizing cities. This type of critique is fundamentally flawed in that the global city model is precisely an analytic strategy to correct the common assumption in economic approaches to globalization that the global is that which crosses borders, as in international trade and investment.

The global city represents a strategic space where global processes materialize in national territories and global dynamics run through national institutional arrangements. In this sense the model overrides the zero-sum notion about the global economy and the national economy as mutually exclusive. A key purpose of the model is to conceive of economic globalization not just as capital flows, but as the work of coordinating, managing and servicing these flows and the work of servicing the multiple activities of firms and markets operating in more than one country. This means also that globalization is not simply something that is exogenous. It comes partly from the inside of national corporate structures and elites, a dynamic I conceive of as a process of incipient de-nationalization. There are sites where global processes are indeed experienced as an invasion, as coming from the outside, but the global city is precisely the site where global processes can get activated inside a country with the participation of some of its national actors. The global city represents the endogenizing of key dynamics and conditionalities of the global economy.

Methodologically this means that globalization can also be studied through detailed sociological and anthropological examinations of these processes as they take place in cities. For me this has meant going all the way from the top levels to the bottom levels in an effort to capture the variety of work processes, work cultures, infrastructures, and so on, that are part of the global control capacity concentrated in cities, a capacity that is one of the features of the global economic system.

Furthermore, I unpack the "global economy" into a variety of highly specialized cross-border circuits corresponding to specific industries, more precisely, those components of industries which are operating across borders. Among these are a variety of financial sub-sectors, accounting, legal, advertising, construction, engineering, architecture, telecommunication services, and others. Each of these may have its own specific geography of networks, even though there will tend to be strong overlap in the case of some of these, notably finance and its sister industries.

This also means that these networks may run through distinct sets of global cities. The global circuits for gold will be different from those for oil, and those for the futures markets may be different from the major currency trading networks. Some cities which are part of these circuits may have highly specialized global city functions and be located on specialized networks that connect them with the leading global cities even though they themselves are not necessarily global cities. Kuala Lumpur is significant as a futures market and Singapore is significant for currency trading, which gives each of these cities specific global city functions; it also puts each of these cities on a different global specialized circuit. The leading global cities in the world tend to have a very large range of these specialized circuits running through them, but even these cities do not involve all specialized components of the global economy. Even the leading global cities will tend to be highly specialised for the servicing of a particular set of global markets and global firms.

The above conditions signal that there is no such entity as a single global city. This is one important difference with the capitals of earlier empires or particular world cities in earlier periods. The global city is a function of a cross border network of strategic sites. In my reading there is no fixed number of global cities, because it depends on countries deregulating their economies, privatizing public sectors (to have something to offer to international investors), and the extent to which national and foreign firms and markets make a particular city (usually an established business center of sorts) a basing point for their operations. What we have seen since the early 1990s is a growing number of countries opting or being pressured into the new rules of the game and hence a rapid expansion of the network of cities that either are global cities or have global city functions—a somewhat fuzzy distinction that I find useful in my research. The global city network is the operational scaffolding of that other fuzzy notion, the global economy.

A common critique asserts that the global city model posits convergence and homogenization among these cities. The development of global city functions in different cities across the world does indeed signal convergence of something. But this is a highly specialized, institutionally differentiated process. It is a very different process from the kind of homogenization/convergence we see in consumer markets and the global entertainment industry.

As I argued already in the first edition of this book, there is a division of functions among the major global cities rather than simply competition as was and is commonly asserted. This was certainly the case in their financial sectors. But this is not a division of labor à la Ricardo, with the ideal of mutually exclusive specializations. That was a model of comparative national advantage. This is a model of cross-border systems, each by necessity installed in multiple different national locations.

Methodologically this underlines the difference between studying a set of cities from a classical comparative approach and from a global approach. The issue of comparability in the latter is not standardizing in order to compare. It is, rather, tracking a given system or dynamic (e.g. a particular type of financial market) and its distinct incarnations (operations, institutional setting, accommodation with national laws and regulations, etc.) in different countries. Though there is some overlap, this entails different analytic categories, research techniques and interpretation standards from that of classical comparative methods. There is work to be done on the methods front, an effort that I am currently engaged in.

Further, many of the critiques along the homogenization notion are centered on an incorrect understanding of the type of convergence the model specifies. The content given to this notion is often that, according to the global city model, the various global cities around the world will become alike, and particularly, that they will resemble New York City. Put that way, I would agree with the critique: why should Paris and Tokyo become like New York. The weight of their institutional, political, cultural histories, the inertia of the built environment, the different roles played by the state in each city will diverge and have its own rich specific history. But that is not the point of convergence in the global city model: it is the development and partial importation of a set of specialized functions and the direct and indirect effects this may have on the larger city.

2) A second major set of issues comes out of the existence of several similar concepts. Most notably the "world city" concept, both its older meaning and the more current one formulated by John Friedmann and Goetz (1982). As mentioned briefly in the introduction to this new edition, the difference between the classic concept of the world city and the global city model is one of level of generality and historical specificity. The world city concept has a certain kind of timelessness attached to it where the global city model marks a specific socio-spatial historical phase. A key differentiating element between Friedmann and Goetz's formulation and mine is my emphasis on the "production" of the global economic system. It is not simply a matter of global coordination but one of the production of global control capacities.

A focus on the *work* behind command functions, on the actual *production process* in the finance and services complex, and on global market*places* has the effect of incorporating the material facilities underlying globalization and the whole infrastructure of jobs typically not marked as belonging to the corporate sector of the economy. What emerges from such an analysis is an economic configuration that differs sharply from that suggested by the concept information economy. We recover the material conditions, production sites, and place-boundedness that are also part of globalization and the information economy.

Another differentiation is with Castell's (1996) argument about the space of flows and the notion that the global city is not a place but a network. While I already argued in the first edition that the global city is a function of a network, I insisted that it is also a place. I briefly touch on my conception of the global city as a network in the above discussion on the unpacking of the global economy in terms of multiple specialized

circuits. In chapter 5 there is a more developed presentation which focuses, among other aspects, on the network of transactions among global
cities conceived of as a space of centrality that is partly deterritorialized
and takes place largely in digital networks but is also partly deeply territorialized in the set of cities that constitute the network.

The place-ness of the global city is a crucial theoretical and methodological issue in my work. Theoretically it captures Harvey's notion of
capital fixity as necessary for hypermobility. A key issue for me has been
to introduce into our notions of globalization the fact that capital even if
dematerialized is not simply hypermobile or that trade and investment
and information flows are not only about flows. Further, place-ness also
signals an embeddedness in what has been constructed as the "national,"
as in national economy and national territory. This brings with it a consideration of political issues and theorizations about the role of the state
in the global economy which are excluded in more conventional accounts
about the global economy. Part of the place-ness of the global city is that
it is a function of a network—a condition particularly evident in certain
sectors. One could say that I do not agree with the opposition space of
flows vs. place. Global cities are places but they are so in terms of their
functions in specific, often highly specialized networks. Finally, of the
four different types of spatial correlates for spaces of centrality that I discussed in chapter 5, it is the transterritorial networks of global cities
which best capture the way in which global cities are functions of
networks.

A third concept is that of global city-region. As categories for analysis,
these two concepts share key propositions about economic globalization
but overlap only partly in the features they each capture. The focus on a
region introduces a set of different variables. I find this an enormously
useful concept precisely because of these different variables and hence
will return below to a more detailed discussion of this specific concept.

A different kind of distinction is that between the global city construct
and the city in general. Quite a few of the negative but also positive
critiques fail to understand that I make a distinction between what is
encompassed by the global city model and the larger urban entity called
New York, Paris or Tokyo. This confusion may partly be a function of the
fact that in Part Three of the book I examine the larger city. What may
not have been stated with adequate clarity in the first edition is that the
effort in Part Three was to understand the impact of the global city function on the larger city, to see whether this impact is beneficial for a large
sector of the population or not. My assumption was not that all of the
empirical conditions described are necessarily part of the global city function. Every city has its own larger materiality, polity, sociality, each often
part of old lineages. The development of global city functions, the endo-

EPILOGUE **351**

genising of the dynamics and conditionalities of economic globalization in the space of the city is a strategic but not all-encompassing event. An important methodological implication is that one can actually study the global city function without having to study the whole city. One methodological issue raised by this way of conceiving matters, is the boundary question, to which I also return below.

Another distinction is my use of the notion of global city functions to identify a particular case, that of a city which fulfilled a fairly limited and highly specialized set of functions in the management and servicing of the global economy, rather than the multiplicity of functions evident in major global cities. I used the case of Miami as an example as it has emerged with a growing role for European, North American and Asian firms which have operations in Latin America and the Caribbean. This is not necessarily a static condition: it may disappear in a way that would be much less likely for London or New York, or it may evolve into the more complex and multifaceted condition of a global city. A certain level of complexity in global city functions has its own impact on these functions; it can ratchet them upwards into top-level capabilities. For instance, the sophistication of domestic investors in the U.S. pushed the U.S. financial services firms into becoming a state of the art sector which in turn gave it its advantage in global markets.

Finally, there is the distinction between international cities, such as Florence or Venice, and global cities. I agree completely with this differentiation and find it useful. It helps to strengthen the case for a tighter analytic conception of the global city.

3) The concept of the global city-region adds a whole new dimension to questions of territory and globalization. Here I want to confine myself to examining the differences between the two concepts. A first difference concerns the question of scale. The territorial scale of the region is far more likely to include a cross-section of a country's economic activities than the scale of the city. It is likely, for instance, to include as key variables manufacturing and basic infrastructure. This, in turn, brings with it a more benign focus on globalization. The concept of the global city introduces a far stronger emphasis on strategic components of the global economy, and hence on questions of power. Secondly, the concept of the global city will tend to have a stronger emphasis on the networked economy because of the nature of the industries that tend to be located there: finance and specialized services. And, thirdly, it will tend to have more of an emphasis on economic and spatial polarization because of the disproportionate concentration of very high and very low income jobs in the city compared with what would be the case for the region.

Overall, I would say, the concept of the global city is more attuned to questions of power and inequality. The concept of the global city-region is more attuned to questions about the nature and specifics of broad urbanization patterns, a more encompassing economic base, more middle sectors of both households and firms, and hence to the possibility of having a more even distribution of economic benefits under globalization. In this regard, it could be said that the concept of the global city-region allows us to see the possibilities for a more distributed kind of growth, a wider spread of the benefits associated with the growth dynamics of globalization.

Both concepts have a problem with boundaries of at least two sorts, the boundary of the territorial scale as such and the boundary of the spread of globalization in the organizational structure of industries, institutional orders, places, and so on. In the case of the global city I have opted for an analytic strategy that emphasizes core dynamics rather than the unit of the city as a container—the latter being one that requires territorial boundary specification. Emphasizing core dynamics and their spatialization (in both actual and digital space) does not completely solve the boundary problem, but it does allow for a fairly clear trade-off between emphasizing the core or center of these dynamics and their spread institutionally and spatially. In my work I have sought to deal with both sides of this trade-off: by emphasizing, on the one side of the trade-off the most advanced and globalized industries, such as finance, and, on the other side, how the informal economy in major global cities is articulated with some of the leading industries. In the case of the global city-region, it is not clear to me how Scott et al. (2001) specify the boundary question both in its territorial sense and in terms of its organization and spread.

A second difference is the emphasis on competition and competitiveness, much stronger in the global city-region construct. In my reading, the nature itself of the leading industries in global cities strengthens the importance of cross-border networks and specialized division of functions among cities in different countries and/or regions rather than international competition per se. In the case of global finance and the leading specialized services catering to global firms and markets—law, accounting, credit rating, telecommunications—it is clear that we are dealing with a cross-border system, one that is embedded in a series of cities, each possibly part of a different country. It is a de-facto global system.

The industries that are likely to dominate global city-regions, on the other hand, are less likely to be networked in this way. For instance, in the case of large manufacturing complexes, the identification with the national is stronger and the often stronger orientation to consumer markets brings to the fore the question of quality, prices and the possibility of substitution. Hence competition and competitiveness are likely to be far more prominent. Further, even when there is significant off-shoring of production and in this regard an international division of production, as in the auto industry, for instance, this type of internationalization tends to be in the form of the chain of production of a given firm. Insofar as most firms still have their central headquarters associated with a specific region and country, the competition question is likely to be prominent and, very importantly, sited—i.e., it is the U.S. versus the Japanese auto manufacturers.

Finally, the question of the competitiveness of a region is deeply centered in its infrastructure. To some extent this is also a crucial variable in the case of global cities, but it is, probably, a far more specialized type of infrastructure. The regional scale brings to the fore questions of public transport, highway construction, and kindred aspects in a way that the focus on global cities does not. Again, it reveals to what extent a focus on the region allows for a more benevolont appreciation of competitiveness in a global economy. In contrast, a focus on the global city will tend to bring to the fore the growing inequalities between highly provisioned and profoundly disadvantaged sectors and spaces of the city, and hence questions of power and inequality. A focus on the regional infrastructure is far more likely to include strong consideration of middle class needs in this regard.

A third difference, connected to the preceding one, is that a focus on networked cross-border dynamics among global cities also allows us to capture more readily the growing intensity of such transactions in other domains—political, cultural, social, criminal. We now have evidence of greater cross-border transactions among immigrant communities and communities of origin and a greater intensity in the use of these networks once they become established, including for economic activities that had been unlikely until now. We also have evidence of greater cross-border networks for cultural purposes, as in the growth of international markets for art and a transnational class of curators; and for non-formal political purposes, as in the growth of transnational networks of activists around environmental causes, human rights, and so on. These are largely city-to-city cross-border networks, or, at least, it appears at this time to be simpler to capture the existence and modalities of these networks at the city level. The same can be said for the new cross-border criminal networks. Dealing with the regional scale does not necessarily facilitate recognizing the existence of such networks from one region to the other. It is far more likely to be from one specific community in a region to another specific community in another region, thereby neutralizing the meaning of the region as such.

4) Perhaps deserving separate treatment although it is yet another instance of differentiation, is the assertion that using the notion of global city to describe cities such as London is unwarranted since they were far

more international in an earlier era than they are today. At its most extreme this type of critique rejects the specificity of the concept, either arguing that there is no such entity as a global city or that nothing is new, that London and New York have been international centers for a long time and, if anything, are less international today than they were in the past.

The clearest case of this is London which can indeed be represented as having much less global influence in the 1990s than it had in the era of British empire. My response to this critique is to emphasize the intervening period, when the national state gained ascendance and cross-border economic flows took place within the framework of the inter-state system. It is against this phase of variable length for different types of countries, that the emergence of global cities needs to be understood. I do not argue that this is the first time or the most acute instance of this development of intense cross-border networks among cities. My point is rather, that the formation of a global economic system after a phase of national and interstate governance of economies needs to be specified theoretically and empirically and cannot be seen simply as a renewal of older forms. The global city network is one of the marking features of the organizational architecture of the current phase.

5) Identification and measurement.

When it comes to identification and measurement of the variables we can use to specify or understand what makes a city a global city, we enter a somewhat fuzzy domain. This is partly due to the fact that existing categories, data sets, and research techniques tend to be based on certain notions of closure and scale. The city is a difficult scale at which to have precise empirical measures. The best data sets are at the national scale.[1] Further, closure is a key feature of many data sets, including those at the urban scale. Thus attempting to measure a unit that is characterized by lack of closure brings additional problems, and when this is at the urban scale the problems escalate. One result has been a series of rather problematic indicators of global city status.

Global city functions are a specific set of processes taking place in a city. But they are not the whole urban economy, even though they have large shadow effects. Nor can these functions simply be reduced to the whole producer services sector of a city. This is a recurrent confusion when it comes to measures. I discuss these issues in greater detail in the section on producer services below.

Finally, a confusion in some of the literature is the failure to distinguish

---

[1] In recognition of this fact and given the increasing importance of cities for a broad range of socio-scientific issues, the U.S. National Academy of Sciences has launched a major initiative to study ways of raising the quality of urban-level data.

between the particular role that a global city or a city with global city functions may have in the global economy and the impact of that role on the city itself. The former may be very significant without the latter being so. The reverse case is rare. The key point regarding the research literature is that an urban economy might be largely domestic—most urban economies probably are—yet play a strategic role in multiple specialized circuits of the global economy. There tends to be a threshold effect whereby global city functions tend to reach a certain level before a city is particularly significant in the global economy. But this is to some extent an empirical question. We need more studies to specify this.

The outcomes that we capture in the concept of the global city are a result of multiple processes. Different time periods, different contents, different scales, each shape the various processes involved. All of these variables in turn feed the distinction between the significance of global city functions to a particular city's economy and to the organization of the global economy itself.

The Financial Order

The analysis of the financial sector in the first edition brought a number of issues on the table that had not been part of the standard accounts and representations. One of the most important of these was my insistence on emphasizing financial centers rather than financial markets and individual financial institutions. This was a crucial part of my global city model in that it underlined the embeddedness of financial flows in complex organizational structures. A second one was an emphasis on division of functions rather than competition.

1) Centers vs. firms and markets.

A focus on centers introduces a broad range of conditions and inputs that are excluded from consideration if we focus on firms or markets. Most important perhaps was the fact that this type of interpretation was my response to what I considered an overemphasis on the dematerialized and hence hypermobile outputs of the industry and its increasingly digitalized markets. This was then also partly a response to the notion that the industry can locate anywhere. I argued that a financial center cannot be reduced to its exchange(s). Since then a small but growing number of scholars have begun to do ethnographies about financial markets and firms, and shown to what extent these are embedded in a variety of conditions that are usually not taken into account when we focus on markets or firms, for instance, systems of trust (e.g., Zaloom 2001). More generally, introducing the notion of financial centers rather than simply firms and markets, allows us to understand the existence of a space within which a new subculture could be created and enacted. I consider this new subculture important in facilitating the successful circulation of innovations evident in the 1980s and 1990s, many of which went against the older conventional forms of banking that had dominated the sector.

In retrospect I would say that my emphasis on financial centers rather than markets and institutions was a good distinction to make at a time when this was not evident. In my current research I have added yet another variable to explain the importance of centers and their distinct role. It is the fact that organizational complexity is an important condition for firms and markets to be able to maximize the benefits they can derive from the new digital technologies. I develop this in chapter 5 of this new edition.

The vast new economic topography that is being implemented through electronic space is one moment, one fragment, of an even vaster economic chain that is in good part embedded in non-electronic spaces. There is no fully dematerialized firm or industry. Even the most advanced information industries, such as finance, are installed only partly in electronic space. And so are industries that produce digital products, such as software designs. The growing digitalization of economic activities has not eliminated the need for major international business and financial centers and all the material resources they concentrate, from state of the art telematics infrastructure to brain talent. The new strategic alliances among financial markets in different cities or the project of the New York Exchange of going global are enhanced by the fact that they take place through a network of specific financial centers with distinct advantages. The project is not to eliminate these diverse financial centers but, on the contrary, to maximize the advantages of a network of centers each with specific strengths and weaknesses.

The emphasis on centers also intersects with the renewed interest in the 1990s in activity clusters and, generally, localised spatial growth evident in a broad range of disciplines. The coincidence between spatial industrial clustering and regional specialisation which underlies the proposition of increasing returns to scale in urban and regional economic analysis, may also be at work in the dynamics of financial centers. But what is straightforward in the case of the manufacturing and standardized services sectors which are the focus of these studies, is much more complex and requires making endogenous a series of new variables in the case of highly specialized services and finance. This is especially so for firms geared to the world markets given added complexity and pressures of speed in these industries. The particular interpretation of financial centers developed in the first edition and discussed at greater length in new sections in chapters 5 and 7, can be seen as yet another instance of such activity clusters, only at a higher level of complexity.

2) Competition vs. division of functions.

A second major theme was my argument that global cities, particularly their financial centers, do not simply compete with each other, a subject I already discussed in the section on the concept of the global city. There is, besides competition, also a division of functions. I already saw that in the relationship among New York, London and Tokyo in the late 1980s. It has become even more evident over the last few years. In developing and underlining this feature I was responding to the notions of competition and hierarchy that prevailed at the time and continue to dominate the analysis of financial centers. Thinking in terms of competition leads to an emphasis on position and hence an interpretation of gain or loss depending on that position. It also entails an ongoing state-centric perspective on a sector that is increasingly not embedded in the inter-state system, certainly not in the ways it used to be. As I already discussed in the preceding section, emphasizing competition at the international scale brings with it the optic of conventional comparative studies. My effort was not to deny the validity of this optic for certain purposes, but to add a different optic.

Thinking in terms of a division of functions introduces other variables into the analysis. For one, emphasizing such features as networks of affiliates or the flows of financial instruments among specific sets of financial centers, brings to the fore the networked nature of much of the global economy. This is quite different from the earlier competition among towns for drawing a particular manufacturing plant—a condition that resembled a zero-sum situation. Secondly, it brings to the fore that global firms and global markets need to operate out of a set of cities and hence do not necessarily operate as if these cities were competing with each other, but rather as forming a cross-border network for their operations. Such firms and markets need to ensure state of the art infrastructure and resources in a network of cities, not in a single city. The issues I discussed in the preceding section on the multiple specialized circuits that constitute the global economic system are also pertinent here. I would say that the competition is predominantly among firms rather than among cities. The recent proliferation of strategic alliances among financial markets in different cities, discussed in chapters 5 and 7, is a good illustration.

Introducing the notion of a division of functions among financial centers also recasts the question of the spatial organization of the industry. Focusing on a cross-border network of financial centers and conceiving of it as an integrated system rather than a series of individual centers in competition with each other, radically alters our representation of the spatial organization of the industry. The key locational features of the global financial sector are, in my reading, a cross-border division of func-

tions, and the embeddedness of firms, markets and operations in tight
territorial concentrations combined with global digital networks and
electronic markets. With a few rare exceptions, which I discuss in chapters 5 and 7, there still is not much research on the spatial organization
of the global financial industry. The state of the art image is that the
globalization of the industry entails its digitalization and the shift to electronic markets thereby reducing if not eliminating the role of financial
centers. There is no doubt that the role and functions of financial centers
have changed profoundly, but they have gained a whole new strategic
importance as crucial sites in complex networks.

3) Global finance and the state.

A third major theme that has since become central to my work but
remained underdeveloped in the first edition was the question about the
influence of finance and the global capital market on the state. This was
one of the forms assumed by the more general critique about the absence
of politics in the global city model. I have to agree fully with both the
particular formulation about global finance and the more general one
about the role of the state. Indeed it led me to start a major new multi-
year project on the role of the state in globalization and the impact of the
latter in altering the logic explaining whose claims become legitimate
(1996; In Progress). This new edition still does not do justice to this
important set of issues. It is such a complex matter that it seemed quite
difficult to insert into the organization of the book which is still shaped
by the first edition. My response would be that the role of the state in the
case of global cities and finance is introduced indirectly through the domain of policy touched upon in chapter 4. But this is clearly an insufficient treatment of the issues.

4) The substantive nature of the industry.

There is a whole range of issues concerning the financial industry and
financial firms coming out of my proposition that finance is not simply a
service industry. One of the impacts of globalization has been to develop
and strengthen those features of the industry that are precisely not confined to servicing other sectors. The formation of new markets and the
numbers and types of innovations produced in the 1980s and 1990s increasingly delinked finance from its role as servicing the "real" economy.
This is not the first time this happens in recent Western history. Clearly
the financial markets of the turn of the century and the 1930s shared
many features with the current phase. But in my reading there are dis-
tinctive features that differentiate the current phase from earlier phases.
This was the object of many a criticism. In chapter 4 I elaborate on what
I had presented in the first edition. This is also a response to critiques
that assert that there is nothing new in today's market.

The Producer Services

The key issues in the debates around this subject have centered on questions of measurement and use of indicators. Many authors consider the share of producer services employment as an indicator of global city status; so a small share or a declining share or a share that is growing faster in other, usually smaller cities gets interpreted as an indicator of global city status decline. Often the decline or a low share of producer services is interpreted as signaling that the city in question is not a global city. A variant on this indicator is the share a city has of national employment in producer services and whether it has grown or fallen. The notion here is that if a city such as New York or London loses share of national employment in producer services, it loses power. Even more problematic is the case of authors who use the measure of total service employment and its growth as an indicator of global city status. None of these measures in themselves are an indicator of global city status. It requires a far more detailed and disaggregated analysis of producer services.

The key indicator of global city status is whether a city contains the capabilities for servicing, managing, and financing the global operations of firms and markets. In order to establish whether the variety of producer services likely to be present in any major city include this capability, we need a far more disaggregated analysis of the producer services sector and, to a variable degree, we also need qualitative information. This can be operationalized in a variety of ways: do the firms in the various specialized producer services have global networks of affiliates, does the city in question have significant exports of producer services, are foreign firms locating significant headquarter functions in the city in question, does the city have institutions that can finance cross-border operations, does it have global markets, is it part of the global property market. The producer services are a crucial factor in all of these variables but they cannot simply be used in toto.

This then brings me to the next misunderstanding, one very common in the literature. It is largely a question of interpretation. The fact that cities that are not global are registering higher growth rates of producer services is interpreted as signaling the decline of the global city(s) in question. I developed a different interpretation, one which addresses the issue of the spatial organization of these services: the high growth rates of producer services in smaller cities as compared with global cities is not necessarily a function of relocations from global cities to better priced locations, as a microeconomic explanation would have it. It is a function of the growing demand by firms in all sectors for producer services. When these services are for global firms and markets their complexity is such that global cities are the best production sites. But when the demand is for fairly routine producer services, cities at various levels of the urban system can be adequate production sites. The current spatial organization of the producer services reflects this spreading demand across economic sectors rather than the loss of advantage and share of global cities.

In my analysis, what is specific about the shift to services is not merely the growth in service jobs but, most importantly, the growing service intensity in the organization of advanced economies: firms in all industries, from mining to wholesale buy more accounting, legal, advertising, financial, economic forecasting services, and so on, today than they did twenty years ago. Whether at the global or regional level, urban centers—central cities, edge cities—are adequate and often the best production sites for such specialized services. When it comes to the production of services for the leading globalized sectors, the advantages of location in cities are particularly strong. The rapid growth and disproportionate concentration of such services in cities signals that the latter have re-emerged as significant "production" sites after losing this role in the period when mass manufacturing was the dominant sector of the economy. Under mass manufacturing and fordism, the strategic spaces of the economy were the large-scale integrated factory and the government through its Fordist/Keynesian functions.

This in turn carries major implications for urban economic growth. Cities emerge as important production sites for what are key inputs for firms in all industries. I posit that this represents yet another phase in the evolution of cities as economic spaces: with the ascendance of Fordism they lost key production functions; with the ascendance of finance and specialized services they gained new types of production functions.

Another kind of criticism has centered on measures of domestic oriented versus global oriented employment. Thus showing that London's jobs are primarily oriented to the domestic economy is then interpreted as a sign that London's status as a global city has been exaggerated. This raises two types of issues in terms of my analysis. One is parallel to the arguments made above for the producer services, particularly that it is not necessary for a city to have a majority of internationally-oriented jobs to be a global city. It is rather a matter of a city having the bundle of specialized services and professionals that can handle the needs of global firms and markets. This may not necessarily be a very high share of the city's workforce. Further, some internationally oriented jobs may not have much to do with global city functions and some domestically oriented jobs may be part of the infrastructure for such functions. This latter case brings up a second issue here, and that is that there is a range of jobs which are not typically coded as being part of the global city function but are in fact part of it. Generally, I would posit that measuring value of the global city sector by employment is increasingly inadequate given the orders of magnitude that can be produced and mobilized by a very small number of professionals.

There are a whole series of critiques concerning the weight of different economic sectors as measured by employment. In large cities such as Paris or Tokyo finance and specialized producer services account for a relatively small share of total employment. This is then used as proof that these are not global cities. Again, this misses the point of the model. The question is whether coordination and specialized servicing of global firms and markets is taking place. And in both cities it is, though mostly for their national firms operating abroad. Yet this has brought with it a growing number of top level firms, especially from the U.S. and UK, to handle the specialized servicing. This is in turn making it easier for foreign firms to move into these countries, therewith ratcheting the whole specialized services complex upwards. The critique is correct for the extreme case: if there is no financial and producer services sector in a city, chances are it is not a global city. One caveat here is that high-tech centers such as Silicon Valley and cultural centers such as Berlin, may well be akin to global cities in their own specialized domains even though they do not have financial sectors.

A final debate concerned the relation between the producer services and manufacturing. Several authors argue that the producer services sector needs manufacturing in order to grow. I agree with this but argue that the location of manufacturing activity is somewhat irrelevant as long as it is part of a corporate firm in that these are likely to use a significant range of producer services. Thus Detroit's factories may relocate to Mexico and elsewhere but this does not preclude that many, and indeed a growing share, of the specialized servicing of auto manufacturing firms continue to be produced in New York City.

Social and Spatial Polarization

The critiques here centered on questions of earnings inequality and spatial polarization. Many of these criticisms represented my position as one that asserted that the middle class was disappearing, that the city's spatial order had become dualized, and that all of this was due to globalization. This is partly a misrepresentation, but only partly. My central point in the polarization argument is not that inequality is new, that the middle class has disappeared and that it is all due to globalization. The point is rather that specific consequences of globalization have the effect not of contributing to the expansion of a middle class, as we saw with Fordism, but that the pressure is towards increasingly valuing top level professional workers mostly in the corporate sector—it is not just a matter of being a lawyer, but where it is that you are applying these skills—and the devaluing of other types of economic activities and workers. It is difficult to measure these trends, but in my reading there is evidence to show a growth in advantage of top sectors and of disadvantage at the bottom in all of these cities. This does not mean that the middle disappears; not at all. Only that the basic thrust of the growth dynamic is not towards expanding the middle. Whether the middle class will continue to be a significant sector even under conditions of little growth is likely to depend on a range of issues, notably state policy.

My treatment of these issues warranted further elaboration, which I have done in a whole new section in chapter 8 about earnings dispersion and inequality. Earnings inequality received little interest in the U.S. and other highly developed economies in the post war decades, partly because it was assumed to be a constant, "like watching grass grow," as one observer put it. But it became an issue in the U.S. in the 1980s and eventually in Europe in the 1990s when it became evident that there was growing inequality. Today we have a rich literature and considerable consensus on the fact of growing earnings dispersion in most developed economies.

Another critique centered on my focus on low-wage service jobs, rather than unemployment, as a source of poverty in global cities. It is true that most of my concern was with the types of jobs that growth sectors generate, which meant excluding or at least neglecting such conditions as unemployment. I think and I argue this in the current edition, that both are important sources of low-income status. Yet I continue to privilege theoretically low-wage employment rather than unemployment, since part of the model posits precisely that new growth sectors are one factor promoting a trend towards growth of high and low income jobs.

While globalization has its own specific impacts in producing these outcomes, I would agree with my critics—and said so myself—that it is not the sole cause and that it is very difficult to establish for how much it accounts. The impact of globalization will also vary across different cities and countries, in good part because of the different role of the state. Yet we can dissect some of its impacts through a detailed examination of a variety of markets and their impacts on social and spatial features of cities. This is my effort in chapters 8 and 9. These expand the focus beyond the narrowly defined cluster of global city functions discussed in the rest of the book. In these last two chapters I explore the broader impacts, the larger shadow effects of global city functions.

It is also this material which has created a confusion in being understood by some researchers as signaling that a city's overall employment and sectoral structure is an indicator of global city status. Or led to assertions that Paris and Tokyo are not like New York because the criminality, decay, poverty, social exclusion we see in the latter is not present in the former, and hence these cannot be global cities. I would agree that these are enormously different cities—how can one not—but add that this does not prove anything about the global city status of these cities nor does it prove the absence of dualization tendencies—as described above—in cities such as Paris and Tokyo. An additional assertion is that the pressures towards these sharper forms of polarization or differentiation are absent in many of the cities considered global and hence that this characterization is unwarranted. I would respond that it is partly an act of interpretation to assert that the pressures are or are not there. In my reading they are, and they are so in a range of very different cities, such as Paris and Sao Paulo, and in an expanding number of cities, notably Dublin and Helsinki.

There is also an issue of interpretation when it comes to the results of studies documenting growing inequality and spatial differentiation in cities. What I would interpret as signaling the emergence of new spatial dynamics, for instance, is frequently interpreted in far more prudent terms—as a mere accentuation of one or another feature or the development of a new layering. I do interpret the data I studied both for the earlier and this edition as signaling that there is a new spatial dynamic at work in global cities, even though this does not mean that everything has changed. How could it, with the inertia of built environments and socio-spatial segregations that characterize cities. As a social scientist I think it is important to attempt to dissect what appears as a mere incremental transformation and dare to theorize it as the possible emergence of a new dynamic. I am persuaded by the evidence I have gathered and by the enormously rich scholarship in this domain that we are seeing a new spatial order in global cities, albeit one that inhabits only parts of the city and is constituted as a partial, yet strategic new spatiality. One of the ways, though perhaps a minor one, in which social science advances is by some of us being willing to go out on a theoretical limb in order to gain a different perspective. Epochs of transition such as the one we live in demand taking theoretical risks. It is then up to the less risk-prone to bring us back via painstaking empirical documentation to a more comfortable place.

APPENDICES

A

Classification of Producer Services by U.S., Japanese, and British SIC

United States		Japan		United Kingdom	
80	Banking	J	Financial and Insurance Services	65	Financial Intermediation, Except Insurance and Pension Funding
61	Credit	K	Real Estate	65.12/1	Banks
62	Commodity Brokers	69	Insurance	65.2	Other Financial Intermediaries
63	Insurance Carriers	82	Information Services and Research	66	Insurance and Pension Funding, Except Compulsory Social Security
64	Insurance Agents	83	Advertisement	67	Activities Auxilliary to Financial Intermediaries
65	Real Estate	84	Specialized Services	71	Renting of Machinery and Equipment without Operator and of Personal and Household Goods
67	Holding and Other Investment Offices	841	Legal and Patent Offices	74	Other Business Activities
73	Business Services	842	Notary Publics, Judicial Scriveners	74.1	Legal, accounting, book-keeping, and auditing activities; tax consultancy; market-research and public opinion polling; business and management consultancy; holdings
81	Legal Services	85	Cooperative Unions	74.2	Architectural and engineering activities and related technical consultancy
86	Membership Organizations	86	Other Services to Businesses	74.4	Advertising
899	Services, not elsewhere Classified	93	Religion	91	Activities of Membership Organizations not elsewhere Classified
		94	Political, Economic, and Cultural Organizations	91.1	Activities of Business, Employers, and Professional Organizations
		95	Other Services	91.2	Activities of Trade Unions

United States: Minor changes have occurred in the original SIC listings – (66) "Combined Real Estate and Insurance" has been dropped; (67) has been reworded from "Holding, Investment Offices" to "Holding and Other Investment Offices"; (89) has been changed from "Miscellaneous Business Services" to (899) "Services, not elsewhere Classified." SIC codes and definitions can be found at http://www.osha.gov/oshstats/sicser.html. Additionally, the North American Industry Classification system is scheduled to gradually replace the SIC by 2004. Information about these changes can be found at http://www.ntis.gov/naics.

Japan: Shifts in numbering have occurred: (69) "Insurance" replaces (67); (84) "Information Services, Research and Advertisement" has been separated into (82) "Information Services and Research," (83) "Advertisement," (84) "Specialized Services," (86) "Other Services to Businesses"; (861) has been changed to (841); (862) has been changed to (842); (83) has been changed to (85); (90) has been changed to (93). The main source is *The Establishment and Enterprise Census, 1999*, Statistics Bureau and Centre, Ministry of Public Management, Home Affairs, Post and Telecommunication, Japan.

United Kingdom: There have been marked changes from the UK SIC definitions from 1980 to 1992: (814) "Banking" has been changed to (65.12/1) and (815) to (65.2); (82) "Insurance" has been changed to (66) "Insurance and Pension Funding, Except Compulsory Social Security"; (834) "House and Estate Agents" has been dropped; (839) "Business Services" and (81) "Legal Services" fall under the major category of (74) "Other Business Services" as (74.1) while (831/2) "Aux. Services to Bank/Insurance" and (837/8) "Professional Technical Services and Advertising" have been recategorized into (74.1), (74.2) and (74.4); (9631) "Trade Unions, Business and Professional Associates" has been changed to (91) "Activities of Membership Organizations not elsewhere Classified", with subcategories (91.1) and (91.2). UK SIC 1992 codes and definitions can be found at: http://www.statistics.gov.uk/themes/compendia—reference/articles/sic.asp.

Definitions of Urban Units: Tokyo, London, New York

WHEN THE TERM *Tokyo* is used, it refers to the Tokyo Metropolis consisting of twenty-three central wards, the Tama district, and the Islands. The heart of Tokyo's economy, Tokyo's business district, consists of about one-tenth of the central ward area. Probably a better unit to use is central Tokyo, consisting of the twenty-three central wards and in some ways akin to the region represented by Manhattan and the four outer boroughs. For example, if one were to go from one of the three central business district wards to Setagaya, one of the outer ring wards, often referred to as bedroom communities because the inhabitants mostly commute to Tokyo, one would first have to take the subway to one of the train stations and then spend about thirty minutes on a train, for a total commute that could take anywhere from forty minutes to one hour. This is not unlike what it would take to get from midtown Manhattan to some of the more distant areas in the other boroughs of New York City.

The twenty-three central wards have 8.35 million people, or 71% of Tokyo's population, and they cover a total of 598 square kilometers. Population density is 14,000 per square kilometer, compared with New York City's density of 9,000 per square kilometer. The Tama area is inhabited by 3.4 million people, and covers 1,160 square kilometers. The Islands cover 400 square kilometers and have 30,000 people. It should be noted that some of the Islands are located 1,000 or more kilometers from the mainland. These are clearly part of an administrative rather than a labor market area. Overall Tokyo covers an area of 2,162 square kilometers, or 0.6% of Japan's area. Overall density is 5,471 per square kilometer. This area contains 11.93 million people, or 9.8% of Japan's total population.

Tokyo's central twenty-three wards, often referred to as central Tokyo, contain considerable diversity. They are not a central business district, but rather more the equivalent of New York City's five boroughs. The equivalent of Manhattan's midtown and Wall Street areas or central London and the City is to be found in a core of what until recently comprised three wards; two or three more wards are rapidly being added to this core. The Tokyo Metropolitan Government has designated an official central business district consisting of the three wards of Chiyoda, Chuo, and Minato. These are, indeed, locations in which governmental offices, corporate headquarters, banks, and now a growing number of foreign firms, are centralized. The area contains the government district, the financial district, and the corporate district for firms with national and international markets. It contains elegant shopping and residential districts, foreign embassies, restaurants, and nightclubs. The rapid growth of Tokyo has, however, incorporated other wards into an expanding central business district. Most notable is Shinjuku, whose growing importance as a location for business has been anchored by the decision of the Tokyo Metropolitan Government to move all of its offices to a massive new complex in that ward, completed in March 1991.[1]

A considerable share of central Tokyo consists mostly of residential areas, not unlike many parts of New York City or London. There is an extreme concentration of workplaces in four or five of these wards and much commuting by workers from a very broad geographic area. This is not very different from New York City. Except for the growing density in its City and the immediately adjacent areas, London has a somewhat more dispersed set of workplace locations.

Much of what is called the Tokyo Metropolis consists of areas, including a number of islands, that are not viable as residential areas for people working in Tokyo; thus, they constitute separate geographic labor market areas. Many of these are very sparsely inhabited, even though the outer ring of the commuting belt has been pushed further and further out. The Tokyo Metropolitan Government is planning to develop a good share of the western part of the Tokyo Metropolis in the so-called Tama district as a group of economic subcenters in an attempt to stem growing agglomeration of economic activities in Tokyo. The Tama district accounts for one-third of Tokyo's land area but a fourth of its population.

The Tokyo Metropolitan Region, distinct from the Tokyo Metropolis, includes, besides the latter, the three prefectures ("*ken*") of Chiba, Saitama, and Kanagawa. There are areas in these three prefectures that are closer to Tokyo's central business district than are the more outlying western areas of the central twenty-three wards. In many ways, these three prefectures are more articulated with the central Tokyo economic

---

[1] The six city subcenters that are being developed or already have been developed are Shinjuku, Shibuya, Ikebukuro, Ueno and Asakusa, Kinshicho, and Kameido. The Tokyo Metropolitan Government has added a 442 ha. site to the Tokyo Bay reclamation project to make it into a sophisticated central telecommunications center and office and residential complex linking the city's business operations with the rest of the world, and including "intelligent buildings," which would operate twenty-four hours a day. The Tokyo Metropolitan Government would also provide touring, recreation, etc. There are to be joint private and public development projects, such as those for the Takeshiba dock area of Tokyo and expected for the Shibaura and Hinode districts on Tokyo Bay.

base than are many areas of the Tokyo Metropolis. The Tokyo Metropolitan Region contains 25% of the nation's population.

Finally a third entity is the National Capital Region. This, the largest of the three units, is so spread out that it hardly functions as an economic unit. This is truly an administrative region, clearly dominated by Tokyo but containing many minor economic subcenters.

In many ways, London is an aggregation of communities governed by local councils. For a long time it lacked a unifying organ such as New York City's powerful Office of the Mayor. This changed in the late 1990s, with the decision to reinstate the office of the mayor. London consists of 32 boroughs divided into 755 wards and the City. These form the Greater London Conurbation, which in this book is simply referred to as London. The Metropolitan Green Belt surrounds the conurbation, and beyond it lies the Outer Metropolitan Area, a widespread region with freestanding villages and towns. It consists of Bedfordshire, Hertfordshire, Essex, Kent, Surrey, West Sussex, Hampshire, Berkshire, and Buckinghamshire. As in the case of New York's outer metropolitan region, this is the area where most of the growth took place in the postwar period until the massive central city construction projects of the 1980s. In 1998 London had a population of 7.2 million, and including the Outer Metropolitan Area, the London region has a population of 15 million.

The creation of the Greater London Council (GLC) in 1965 gave London an overall planning authority. As in New York, the relation of the region to the city was not clearly resolved at the political and regulatory level (Herbert 1960). It is far clearer in Tokyo, where there is a Tokyo Metropolitan Government with a Governor. In 1985 the Thatcher government abolished the GLC, which had become a vehicle for interests antithetical to those of the national government, and transferred greater power to local development corporations, which are far more responsive to business interests. Probably the most notorious of these is the Docklands Development Corporation, which launched the largest construction project of any European city. Local borough councils have also lost power and resources. The central political forces in London in the late 1980s were the development corporations and the national government.

New York City consists of five boroughs: Manhattan, Brooklyn, Queens, the Bronx, and Staten Island (respectively, New York, King's, Queens, Bronx, and Richmond Counties). This is the unit we will refer to simply as New York in the book. The city is divided into areas under the jurisdiction of community planning boards. Its metropolitan region includes twelve counties in addition to the five listed above: Westchester, Rockland, Suffolk, Nassau, Bergen, Passaic, Morris, Essex, Hudson, Union, Somerset, and Middlesex. In 1998, the population of the city was 7.4 million, and that of the metropolitan region reached about 18 million. New York City has a municipal government headed by a mayor who is by far the most powerful officer in the city's government. Each of the boroughs has a borough president. A major revision of the city charter implemented in 1989–1990 altered the distribution of power somewhat, giving the city council, community planning boards, and the City Planning Commission more power. In addition, an institution that was a key venue for borough presidents, the Board of Estimates, was declared illegal by the U.S. Supreme Court and eliminated, thus enhancing the power of the mayor and the other bodies listed above.

The State of New York is responsible for the legislation within which the City operates; it also has specific duties to oversee the city's finances. More recently, the State of New York has devolved a number of powers and the responsibility for funding them to the City. Two-thirds of the finance for New York City's local self-government comes from local taxation on sales, property, income, and business. New York City is unusual for the U.S. insofar as it has a metropolitan-wide government; the more common pattern for a large metropolitan area is a far higher level of administrative fragmentation.

C

Population of Selected Prefectures and Major Prefectural Cities

Prefecture	Total Population	Major City Population	Major City Population as % of Prefecture Population
		Tokyo	
Tokyo	11,618,281 (1982)	8,351,983 (1982)	72 (1982)
	12,059,237 (2000)	8,130,408 (2000)	67 (2000)
		Nagoya	
Aichi	6,221,638 (1982)	2,087,902 (1982)	34 (1982)
	7,043,235 (2000)	2,171,378 (2000)	31 (2000)
		Osaka	
Osaka	8,473,446 (1982)	2,648,180 (1982)	31 (1982)
	8,804,806 (2000)	2,598,859 (2000)	30 (2000)

Number of Cities, Towns, and Villages in Selected Prefectures by Size

Prefecture	Total	Total Cities[a]	Number with Population ('000s) of:					
			Over 500	300–500	200–300	100–200	50–100	Under 50
Tokyo	42	27	1	1	1	10	11	18
Aichi	96	30	1	1	4	5	23	62
Osaka	44	31	3	4	3	9	12	13

Sources: Japan Statistical Yearbook, 1982, Management and Coordination Agency, 2000 Census of Estimates as of 1 October 2000.

Notes: From these 1982 data, one can infer that for the 1970–1987 period under study the city of Tokyo is reasonably represented by Tokyo Prefecture, as in 1982 it was the only major city exceeding 500,000 people in the prefecture and it had 72% of the total prefecture population. Nagoya was also the only major city in Aichi Prefecture, but its share of the prefecture's population was only 34%. Osaka had the lowest prefecture population share of these three major cities. Osaka Prefecture has three cities with more than 500,000 people, making the city of Osaka less dominant than Tokyo or Nagoya within their respective prefectures.

[a]Settlements with populations less than 50,000 are not "cities."

D

Tokyo's Land Market

THE RAPID economic transformation in Tokyo in the 1980s probably expressed itself most clearly in the land market. From 1986 to 1987, prices for residential land increased by 95% and those for commercial land increased by 79%. The most pronounced relative increases occurred in areas as yet quite undeveloped but primed for development. Thus, the Tama district, where the Tokyo Metropolitan Government's ambitious master plan called for massive investment and development by the government, experienced some of the highest increases. If we compare the actual price levels of land per square meter in the Tama district with those in more central locations, it becomes evident that the actual sale prices were quite low and that the high rates of increase were in good part a function of very low past price levels. Yet one can also see in the extremely high increases a dynamic at play that goes beyond what one would expect as average price increases. Indeed, the figures for earlier years show mostly mild increases of a few percentage points, compared to the 8% in the Tama district in 1987. What we saw, even in this very distant area, was an extension of the highly speculative and immensely profitable land market of Tokyo. High liquidity made investment in land a most desirable form of investment and thereby brought about extremely high increases in prices of land.

A brief review of actual transactions in central locations shows that the price per square meter in central Tokyo was far above that in other major cities, notably New York and London. In the central business district, the average price of a square meter in Chiyoda went from $33,480 in 1986 to $46,256 in 1987. (These values are based on the 1987 rate for the dollar.)

Another extremely high average price of $43,040 per square meter was paid in 1987 for land in Minato, in the Akasaka area, one in high demand. In the commercial market, the prices were double and triple those in the residential market. It is worth noting that land prices in Shinjuku were among the highest. Shinjuku is not one of the three central business district wards, but it is where the Tokyo Metropolitan Government developed its massive new headquarters and where a vast number of luxury high-rise office buildings have been built over the last two decades.

In 1987, a square meter of developed space fetched an average of

$136,564 in Shinjuku and $140,969 in Chuo. The difference is that while Chuo has long been one of the three wards forming the central business district, Shinjuku was until recently largely a working-class district. One still sees block after block of working-class houses and shops there. Out of this vast low-rise sea of small, low-income houses and shops rises a complex of tall luxury office buildings, several over 100 stories high, with vast designer plazas, a homogeneous space that one could find in any major city in the West. In their shadow, if one happens to take a wrong turn, one can find short, narrow, almost invisible streets lined with small, very old houses with flowerpots in front and vegetable patches.

There have been changes in planning legislation to address the distortions arising out of the high growth and highly speculative functioning of the land market in the 1980s. In 1991, the government tightened the conditions on how farm land owners can dispose of their land; for taxation purposes they must commit to either a farming or a non-farming use for the ensuing thirty years, thereby reducing the speculation on farmland. The government also further deregulated brown field site development in Tokyo in the 1990s. And a revision of the original Urban Planning Act of 1968 was passed in May 2000 by the national government giving local governments more autonomy on decisions regarding land use and zoning.

The evidence for the 1990s underlines the extreme character of the patterns of the 1980s. In the Tokyo metropolitan region, using the highest average price level of the 1980s and 1990s as the index (March 1991), the price at March 1985 was about 40% of the March 1991 price and so was that of March 2000. One difference was that in the latter period there was more divergence among different types of land than there was in 1985 or 1991, with commercial land showing the sharpest decline, to about 30%, and residential land the least decline at about 58% of the March 1991 value. While the highest values were reached in March 1991, the sharpest increases happened from 1986 to 1987, and especially during 1987. Both the increases in the 1980s and the fall in the 1990s were not as sharp nationwide or in Nagoya as in Tokyo. Osaka showed the extreme increases and sharp falls evident in Tokyo.

For the entire Tokyo Metropolis, the average increases in land prices for the two periods 1985 to 1986 and 1986 to 1987 were, respectively, 18.8% and 93% for residential land; 34.4% and 79% for commercial land; 16% and 80.7% for mixed-use land; and 10.7% and 71.6% for industrial land. There were thus across-the-board increases. Furthermore, there were significant increases, though at much lower prices, in the more peripheral regions that are undergoing massive development, initially by the government and now by the private sector as well (see Table D.1 for a breakdown of residential land prices by district). Except for the Islands,

TABLE D.1
Tokyo: Residential Land Price by District, 1986–1987 (dollars)

District	Average Residential Land Price per Square Meter	
	1986	1987
Central	10,359.03	21,745.81
Surburban	3,342.73	6,944.93
Surrounding	1,833.48	3,711.01
Central, surburban and surrounding	2,851.54	5,877.53
North Tama	1,173.13	2,646.26
South Tama	789.87	1,438.77
West Tama	544.05	722.03
Tama	981.50	2,049.34
Island	41.41	41.85
Total area	1,897.36	3,922.03

Source: Tokyo Metropolitan Gov't, "Land Value Shift December 1986–December 1987" (in Japanese) (unpublished report, 1988).

no area in Tokyo seemed to escape the dynamics of a real estate market that was generating immense profits through vast increases in the price of land.

Tokyo's expanded and new functions as an international financial center put immense pressure on the prices of land. The 1987 Fourth Comprehensive National Development Plan contained proposals for the dispersion of central government offices to reduce the concentration of administrative functions in Tokyo, a proposal to impose a new tax system that discourages businesses from maintaining their offices in Tokyo, and other such proposals aimed at dispersal in order to reduce the pressure on the price of land and the congestion in central Tokyo. The overall recommendation of the plan was to implement a multipolar urban system, with several subcenters and core cities. Land and taxation were crucial priorities for the government. One example was the Tokyo Metropolitan Government's enforcement of a regulation requiring reports of land transactions in areas designated by the governor; another was the July 1987 instruction by the Ministry of Finance requesting financial institutes to curb loans for land transactions.

When studies for the Fourth Plan began in September 1984, it was decided for the first time ever that the plan should include land-related measures. The National Land Agency's interim report of the Fourth Comprehensive National Development Plan, issued in December 1986, was intended to guide land use up to the year 2000. It envisioned even greater concentration of facilities and functions in Tokyo and surrounding prefectures and recommended further development of Tokyo as an international financial and information center. Immense protests against this plan led to its revision. The draft of the Fourth Plan, presented on May 28, 1987, deemphasized Tokyo's role and called for a multipolar, dispersed pattern of national land development. Much of the plan focused on the development of large-scale projects, such as road construction, building up of industries and information services in each region, and urban redevelopment, which local governments had been requesting. It is doubtful, according to some experts, that the measures contained in the plan will alleviate the excessive concentration in Tokyo.[1]

In central Tokyo, land prices in the late 1980s reached 30 million yen per square meter and more. The government faced immense costs if it wanted to build infrastructure, from housing to roads. A much cited case is a 1.3-kilometer section of a road in central Tokyo that cost 500 billion yen, with construction per se amounting to only about 2 or 3 billion yen and the rest going for land. As land prices rise, the effectiveness of funds allocated for social capital declines, and selling land to real estate developers becomes the most profitable through tax revenues. Furthermore, it leads to distortions in the development of social infrastructure when so much of the economy is concentrated in one region. For example, the construction of new subways can contribute to rather than alleviate congestion, since new housing will be developed around the new lines and stations and bring in more people to the city; the same is true of the proposed bridge over Tokyo Bay, which will open new areas for urban development, and the 10,000 hectares of land to be reclaimed from Tokyo Bay.[2]

According to some, the only solution to the accelerating rise in prices was to reduce land demand in Tokyo and the only way of doing this was to reverse the concentration of facilities and functions in Tokyo. There have been proposals for a corridor or megalopolis linking Tokyo and Osaka. A magnetically levitated train (Maglev) capable of 500 kilometers per hour, would take one hour between Osaka and Tokyo, making it one

[1] Estimates of latent demand for buildings in central Tokyo ranged from ninety to a hundred buildings the size of the Kasumigaseki Building, the first skyscraper completed in Japan, in 1968, which has thirty-six floors aboveground and is 147 meters high. If one assumes 10,000 square meters of land per building, this is a total land requirement of up to 2 million square feet, or a minimum of 900,000 square meters of land. The Tokyo Bay area that is being redeveloped is about 3,000 hectares, and only four kilometers from the center of Tokyo.

[2] With current technologies, land can be reclaimed at a rate of 500 hectares a year at most.

"city." Intelligent buildings (fully computerized facilities) would be built alongside train stations in Nagoya and Kofu. Together with the Kasumigaseki-Marunouchi district in Tokyo, these three special sectors, each 100 to 300 hectares in area and wired to permit application of the latest telecommunication and data processing technology, would become the nerve centers of a megalopolis that would serve as Japan's new economic capital. The central government's twelve ministries and eight agencies headed by state ministers, currently concentrated in Tokyo's Kasumigaseki district, would be dispersed across the 500-kilometer corridor, with three or four of them relocated in each of the three districts.

The question of land-related constraints on economic development had already surfaced at the end of the high growth period. In 1972 there was a strong increase in the price of land, linked to Prime Minister Tanaka's plan to remodel or modernize the whole Japanese archipelago. The major difference between the 1972 increase in prices and the 1980s one is that the 1972 increase affected the whole country while the later one was limited largely to Tokyo's commercial districts and adjacent residential areas. At that time, the boom caused by the so-called remodeling dramatically pushed up all prices, not only those of land. Eventually land prices stabilized as a result of the tight credit policy, and land-related constraints began receiving less attention. In the 1980s, excess liquidity stemming from various conditions, including a series of cuts in interest rates as the yen rose, again induced land prices to rise rapidly. While land prices in several areas of Japan rose relative to Tokyo's prices (see Table D.2), they declined in overall relative terms. (See also Table D.3 for related data.) It was, in the words of Tatsuo Izumi, "an era of bipolar land prices" (in his book *Chika o Yomu* [Reading the Land Prices]). Others saw it as a transition period, after which land prices would rise sharply throughout the country. It is quite possible that land prices would have risen all over Japan if easy credit had prevailed for long. It is unlikely, however, that the money supply would have been allowed to grow at an annual rate of more than 20%, as it did before the massive inflation rise in the early 1970s. Given the pressures on land in central Tokyo, overall measures designed to increase the general supply of land through conversion of rural areas in the urban metropolitan area to commercial uses would not have affected land prices in central Tokyo, though they would have stabilized land prices in Japan as a whole.[3] A tight credit policy helped stabilize land prices in the 1970s, when the price of everything else rose. But this would be less effective with polarized land prices.

---

[3] In Tokyo, farmland helps compensate for the absence of green zones. Currently, Tokyo's green zone ratio is two square meters per person, which is one-tenth that of New York City and one-fifteenth that of London.

TABLE D.2

Japanese Prefectural Cities: Average Residential Land Prices Relative to Tokyo, 1985–1986

	1985 Index (Tokyo = 100)	1986 Index (Tokyo = 100)	Change 1985–1986[a]
Tokyo	100.0	100.0	0.0
Sapporo	15.6	12.5	−3.1
Aomori	16.1	12.8	−3.3
Morioka	18.8	15.1	−3.6
Sendai	19.5	15.8	−3.7
Akita	14.2	11.3	−2.9
Yamagata	17.5	13.7	−3.8
Fukushima	15.6	12.4	−3.2
Mito	16.4	13.1	−3.3
Utsunomiya	16.0	13.1	−2.9
Maebashi	19.2	15.2	−4.0
Urawa	50.4	39.9	−10.5
Chiba	33.3	26.5	−6.7
Yokohama	47.2	38.3	−9.0
Niigata	21.0	16.4	−4.6
Toyama	18.7	15.0	−3.6
Kanazawa	24.8	19.7	−5.2
Fukui	24.0	19.2	−4.8
Kobe	20.3	16.6	−3.7
Nagano	20.4	16.5	−3.9
Gifu	24.6	20.4	−4.2
Shizuoka	34.1	27.5	−6.6
Nagoya	36.9	29.7	−7.2
Tsu	13.5	11.5	−1.9
Ohtsu	26.6	21.7	−4.9
Kyoto	56.8	46.5	−10.2
Osaka	61.6	51.0	−10.6
Kobe	46.1	36.3	−9.8
Nara	31.8	25.4	−6.4
Wakayama	28.2	22.5	−5.7
Tottori	19.6	15.1	−4.4
Matsue	16.8	13.5	−3.4
Okayama	16.1	13.0	−3.1
Hiroshima	33.1	26.3	−6.8
Yamaguchi	11.5	9.3	−2.1
Tokushima	26.3	20.9	−5.5
Takamatsu	25.8	22.0	−3.7

TABLE D.2 (cont.)

	1985 Index (Tokyo = 100)	1986 Index (Tokyo = 100)	Change 1985–1986[a]
Matsuyama	22.7	18.0	−4.6
Ko Chi	29.8	23.6	−6.2
Fukuoka	25.0	20.0	−5.0
Saga	14.7	11.7	−3.0
Nagasaki	21.5	10.8	−10.7
Kagoshima	25.0	19.6	−5.4
Naha	33.0	27.5	−5.5

Source: Same as in Table D.1

[a]Indicates change in price relative to Tokyo's change in price.

The bipolarization in land prices suggest that attention should be paid to how land is used rather than the mere availability of land. It is not just a matter of the land supply. In the competition for creating an international center for finance and business, the infrastructure and the availability of excellent locations is more important than the extent of available land. Agglomeration economies are high for these kinds of economic activities.

Japan's national government addressed the land price issue in the 1980s by selling off national land to the highest bidder. The Tokyo Metropolitan Government did not agree with this policy.[4] In the case of national land in Tokyo, this only intensifies the pressure on prices. National land sold to private developers is exempt from the restrictions placed on the sale of privately held land. One site in Chiyoda Ward was auctioned

---

[4] In September 1986 the Tokyo Metropolitan Government passed an ordinance empowering the Governor to require prior notification of transactions involving 500 square meters or more in designated districts. The National Land Use Planning Act, older than the Tokyo ordinance, is designed to keep land prices in check by requiring that the prefectural governments (including the Tokyo Metropolitan government) be notified in advance of any real estate transaction involving 2,000 square meters or more. If the asking price is significantly higher than the value at which the National Land Agency has appraised it, the Governor can formally recommend that the price be renegotiated. There are penalties for failure to notify, but the Governor's recommendations have no binding force. It is expected that the fact that the price will become public knowledge should have some deterrent effect. Tokyo passed the subsequent ordinance because most transactions involve less than 2,000 square meters, and there was no way to control such deals. The National Land Use Planning Act was amended on June 2, 1987, to incorporate most of the restrictions of real estate transactions included in the 1986 ordinance. When the new law took effect in August 1987, Tokyo eliminated its ordinance.

TABLE D.3

Japan: Land Prices in Major Cities, 1985 (yen per square meter)

	Residential	Proposed Residential	Residential Land in UCAs	Commercial	Industrial
Tokyo	196,500	48,700	36,200	1,299,400	92,500
Osaka	168,900	47,300	45,400	822,200	124,900
Nagoya	97,100	30,100	38,300	332,700	58,500
Cities with over 500,000 pop.	74,200	26,900	23,400	394,800	51,900
Cities with over 300,000 pop.	71,600	29,800	25,900	344,300	40,000
Others	54,000	24,200	19,900	213,000	30,700

Source: OECD, Urban Policies in Japan (1986).
Note: UCA (undeveloped central areas).

off for 8.5 million yen per square meter in 1986. The Ministry of Transportation's intended sale of 163 hectares of Japanese National Railways lands in Tokyo by competitive bidding led to immense increases in prices of adjacent land, even before the site was bought. (Japanese National Railways had land slated for sale throughout Japan.)[5] The Tokyo Metropolitan Government asked Japanese National Railways to sell its Tokyo land to Tokyo, as it was setting up a land trust; the purpose of this trust was to avoid selling land at high profits but still obtain a return so as to avoid feeding the price spiral.[6]

[5] One concern was that one key Japanese National Railways land piece in Minato ward (Shidome, in the Shimbashi area), if sold to the private sector, would be used for a large concentration of high-rises, becoming, in Governor Suzuki's words, "a disorderly thicket of skyscrapers like Manhattan's urban jungle" (Reference Reading Series 19, Foreign Press Center, Land price program: 16). In the case of the Shidome plot, Governor Suzuki proposed that the Tokyo Metropolitan Government acquire the land, put in roads and the other infrastructure, and then sell off some plots and put others in land trust. This is what the Tokyo Metropolitan Government did in the Shinjuku subcenter, built on the site of a water purification plant. It set aside 45% of the area for parks and roads, "something that would never have happened if the land had simply been sold to the highest bidder" (ibid.).

[6] Cf. the Singapore model: a freeze on land prices and governmental planning; most housing is government owned and so is most land.

Bibliography

Abu-Lughod, J. L. 1989. *Before European hegemony: the world system A. D. 1250–1350*. New York: Oxford University Press.

———. 1999. *New York, Los Angeles, Chicago: America's Global Cities*. Minneapolis: University of Minnesota Press.

Abu-Lughod, Janet L. 1980. *Rabat: Urban Apartheid in Morocco*. Princeton, N.J.: Princeton University Press.

Aglietta, Michael. 1979. *A Theory of Capitalist Regulation: The U.S. Experience*. Norfolk, Great Britain: Lowe and Brybone Printers.

Agnew, J. 1994. "The territorial trap: the geographical assumptions of international relations theory." *Review of International Political Economy* 1: 53–80.

Alba, R. D., Logan, J. R., and Crowder, K. 1997. "White neighborhoods and assimilation: the Greater New York Region, 1980–1990." *Social Forces*, 75: 883–909.

Aldrich, A. et al. 1981. "Business Development and Self-segregation: Asian Enterprise in Three British Cities." In C. Peach, V. Robinson, and S. Smith, eds., *Ethnic Segregation in Cities*. London: Croom Helm.

Alexander, I. 1979. *Office Location and Public Policy*. London: Longmans.

Alexander, J. 1954. "The Basic-Nonbasic Concept of Urban Economic Functions." *Economic Geography* 30(3): 246–61.

Allen, J. 1992. "Service and the UK space economy: regionalization and economic dislocation." *Transactions, Institute of British Geographers* 17:292–305.

Allinson, Gary D. 1979. *Suburban Tokyo: A Comparative Study in Politics and Social Change*. Berkeley: University of California Press.

Altschul, James S. 1984. "Japan's Elite Law Firms." *International Financial Law Review* 3(6) 6–12.

American Banker. 1982. "500 Largest Banks in the World." *American Banker*, July 28, 145–47.

———. 1986. "The Top 300 Commercial Banks in the United States." *American Banker*, March 18, 57–58.

Amin, A. and J. Thrift. 1994. *Globalisation, Institutions and Regional Development in Europe*. Oxford: Oxford University Press.

AMPO. 1986. *The Challenge Facing Japanese Women*. Special issue of *Japan-Asia Quarterly Review* 18 (2, 3).

———. 1987. *Japanese Industry Moves Out: Expansion Abroad, Depression at Home*. Special issue of *Japan-Asia Quarterly Review* 19(1).

———. 1988. *Japan's Human Imports: As Capital Flows Out, Foreign Labor Flows In*. Special issue of *Japan-Asia Quarterly Review* 19(4).

Anderson, H. and J. Flateley. 1997. *Contrasting London Incomes: A Social and Spatial Analysis*. A Report published by the London Research Centre, July 1997. Website address: *http://www.londonresearch.gov.uk/et/Etincom.htm*.

Appelbaum, Eileen. 1984. *Technology and the Redesign of Work in the Insurance Industry*. Project report, Stanford University, Institute of Research on Educational Finance and Governance.

Armstrong, Regina. 1972. *The Office Industry*. New York: Regional Plan Association.

——. 1988. *New York and the Forces of Immigration*. New York: Citizens Budget Commission.

Armstrong, Regina, and D. Milder. 1985. "Employment in the Manhattan CBD and Back-Office Location Decisions." *City Almanac* 18:1–2, 4–18.

Aronson, Jonathan David, and Peter F. Cowhey. 1984. *Trade in Services: A Case for Open Markets*. Washington and London: American Enterprise Institute.

Arrighi, G. 1994. *The long twentieth century: money, power, and the origins of our times*. London; New York: Verso.

Arrighi, G. and Beverly J. Silver with Iftikhar Ahmad et al. 1999. *Chaos and Governance in the Modern World System*. Contradictions of Modernity Series; v. 10. Minneapolis: University of Minnesota Press.

Ascher, Francois. 1995. *Metapolis ou L'Avenir des Villes*. Paris: Editions Odile Jacob.

Asian Development Bank. Various years. *Yearbook of National Accounts*. New York: United Nations.

Asian Women's Association. 1988. *Women from Across the Seas: Migrant Workers in Japan*. Tokyo: Asian Women's Association.

ATKearney. April 2000. *Globalization Ledger*. Global Business Policy Council.

Attali, Jacques. 1981. *Les Trois Mondes*. Paris: Fayard.

Bach, C. L. 1987. "U.S. International Transactions, Fourth Quarter and Year 1986." *Survey of Current Business* 67(3): 32–64.

Bacon, Robert, and Walter Eltis. 1976. *Britain's Economic Problems: Too Few Producers*. London: Macmillan.

Bagchi-Sen, S. and Sen J. 1997. "The Current State of Knowledge in International Business Producer Services." *Environment and Planning* A 29: 1153–1174.

Baker, James C. 1978. *International Bank Regulation*. New York: Praeger.

Baker, James C., and M. Gerald Bradford. 1974. *American Banks Abroad: Edge Act Companies and Multinational Banking*. New York: Praeger.

Balmori, Diana. 1983. "Hispanic Immigrants in the Construction Industry: New York City, 1962–1982." Occasional Papers, no. 38, Center for Latin American and Caribbean Studies, New York University.

Bank for International Settlements. 1986. *Recent Innovations in International Banking*. Basel: BIS, Monetary and Economic Department.

——. 1987. *International Banking Developments*. Basel: BIS Monetary and Economic Department.

——. 1998. *Annual Report for 1997/98*.

——. 1999. *Annual Report for 1998/99*.

——. 1999. *Annual Report* (April 1998–June 1999).

Bank of England. Various years. *Quarterly Bulletin*. London: Bank of England.

Bank of Japan. 1986. *Kokusai hikaku tokei* (Comparative International Statistics). Tokyo: Bank of Japan.

———. 1988. *Economic Statistics Annual 1987*. Tokyo: Bank of Japan, Research and Statistics Department.

Bankers Monthly. 1981. "21st Annual Financial Industry Survey." *Bankers Monthly*, May 15, 14–21.

Baran, Barbara, and Suzanne Teegarden. 1983. "Women's Labor in the Office of the Future." Paper presented at Berkeley Roundtable on the International Economy, University of California, Berkeley.

Bartlett, A. 2001. "Politics Remade: Modernization and the New Political Culture in England." (Unpublished thesis, Department of Sociology, University of Chicago.)

Basche, James R. 1986. *Eliminating Barriers to International Trade and Investment in Services*. Economic and Policy Analysis Program, Research Bulletin no. 200. New York: The Conference Board.

Bauer, J. and Mason, A. 1992. "The Distribution of Income and Wealth in Japan." *Review of Income and Wealth*, December, vol. 38, no. 4: 589–632.

Baum, A. and C. Lizieri. 1999. "Who Owns the City? Office Ownership and Overseas Investment in the City of London." *Real Estate Finance*, 16(1): 87–100.

Baum, Scott. 1997. "Sydney, Australia: A Global City? Testing the Social Polarisation Thesis." *Urban Studies* 34 (11): 1881–1901.

Bavishi, V., and H. E. Wyman. 1983. *Who Audits the World: Trends in the Worldwide Accounting Profession*. Storrs, Conn.: University of Connecticut, Center for Transnational Accounting and Financial Research.

Beaverstock, J. V., R. G. Smith, P. J. Taylor, D.R.F. Walker, and H. Lorimer. 2000. "Globalization and world cities: some measurement methodologies." *Applied Geography* 20: 43–63.

Beaverstock, J. V., P. J. Taylor, and R. G. Smith. 1999. "The long arm of the law: London's law firms in a globalising world economy." *Environment and Planning A* 31: 1857–1876.

Beaverstock, Jonathan V. and Joanne Smith. 1996. "Lending jobs to global cities: skilled international labour migration, investment banking and the City of London." *Urban Studies* 33 (8): 1377–1394.

Bell, D. 1999. *The Coming of Post-Industrial Society: A Venture in Social Forecasting*. Special anniversary ed. with a new foreword by the author. New York: Basic Books.

———. 1973. *The Coming of Post-Industrial Society: A Venture in Social Forecasting*. New York: Basic Books.

Bell, Linda, and Richard B. Freeman. 1987. "The Facts about Rising Industrial Wage Dispersion in the U. S." *Proceedings*, Industrial Relations Research Association, May.

Beneria, Lourdes. 1989. "Subcontracting and Employment Dynamics in Mexico City." In A. Portes et al., eds., *The Informal Economy: Studies in Advanced and Less Developed Countries*. Baltimore: Johns Hopkins University Press.

Benko, G. and Lipietz, A. 1992. *Les Regions qui Gagnent: Districts et Reseaux: Les Nouveaux Paradigmes de la Geographie Economique*. Paris: Universite de Paris.

Bennett, R. J. and Graham, D. J. 1998. "Explaining size differentiation of business service centers." *Urban Studies*. 35, no. 9: 1457–1480.

Benston, George J. 1983. "Federal Regulation of Banking: Analysis and Policy Recommendations." *Journal of Bank Research* (Winter): 216–44.
———. 1984. "Financial Disclosure and Bank Failure." *Economic Review* (March). Atlanta: Federal Reserve Bank of Atlanta.
Berger, Suzanne, Michael L. Dertouzos, Richard K. Lester, Robert M. Solow, and Lester C. Thurow. 1989. "Toward a New Industrial America." *Scientific America* 260(6): 39–47.
Bergsten, C. Fred. 1987. "The U.S.-Japan Economic Problem: Next Steps." In H. Patrick and R. Tachi, eds., *Japan and the United States Today: Exchange Rates, Macroeconomic Policies, and Financial Market Innovations.* New York: Columbia University Press.
Berry, Brian J. L. 1961. "City Size Distributions and Economic Development." *Economic Development and Cultural Change* 9(4): 573–88.
———. 1971. "City Size and Economic Development." In L. Jakobson and V. Prakash, eds., *Urbanization and National Development.* Beverly Hills, Calif.: Sage.
Bessant, J. and H. Rush. 1995. "Building bridges for innovation: the role of consultants in technology transfer." *Research Policy* 24: 97–114.
Bestor, Theodore. 1989. *Neighborhood Tokyo.* Stanford, Calif.: Stanford University Press.
Betancur, J. J., Teresa Cordova, and Maria de los Angeles Torres. 1993. "Economic Restructuring and the Process of Incorporation of Latinos Into the Chicago Economy." In Rebecca Morales and Frank Bonilla, eds., *Latinos in a changing U.S. economy: comparative perspectives on growing inequality.* Sage Series on Race and Ethnic Relations, vol. 7, Newbury Park, Calif.: Sage Publications.
Bhagwati, J. N. 1984. "Splintering and Disembodiment of Services and Developing Nations." *World Economy* 7(2): 133–43.
Blank, R. 1994. "The Employment Strategy: Public Policies to Increase Work and Earnings," In S. Danziger, Gary Sandefur, and Daniel Weinberg, eds., *Confronting Poverty: Prescriptions for Change,* Cambridge, Mass.: Harvard University Press.
Bleeke, Joel, and James Goodrich. 1981. *Capitalizing on Opportunities Created by Deregulation of the Banking Industry.* Chicago: McKinsey and Co.
BLS. See U.S. Department of Labor, Bureau of Labor Statistics.
Bluestone, Barry, and Bennett Harrison. 1982. *The Deindustrialization of America.* New York: Basic Books.
Bluestone, Barry, Bennett Harrison, and Lucy Gorham. 1984. *Storm Clouds on the Horizon: Labor Market Crisis and Industrial Policy.* Boston: Economic Education Project.
Blumberg, P. 1981. *Inequality in an Age of Decline.* New York: Oxford University Press.
Blumenfeld, H. 1955. "The Economic Base of the Metropolis." *Journal of the American Institute of Planners* 21 (Fall): 114–32.
Blunden, George. 1975. "The Supervision of the U. K. Banking System." *Bank of England Quarterly Bulletin,* June: 188–89.
Boreland, J., P. Gregg, G. Knight, and J. Wadsworth. 1997. "Worker Displace-

ment in Australia and Britain." International Displaced Workers Workshop, Canadian International Labour Network (CILN) (October).

Boulding, Kenneth. 1978. "The City as an Element in the International System." In L. S. Bourne and J. W. Simmons, eds., *Systems of Cities*. New York: Oxford University Press.

Bowles, S., David Gordon, and Thomas Weisskopf. 1984. *Beyond the Wasteland*. N.Y.: Doubleday Publishing.

Bowles, S., David M. Gordon, and Thomas E. Weisskopf. 1990. *After the Wasteland: A Democratic Economics for the Year 2000*. Armonk, N.Y.: M. E. Sharpe, Inc.

Boyer, Christine. 1983. *Dreaming the Rational City*. Cambridge, Mass.: MIT Press.

Boyer, Robert, ed. 1986. *La flexibilité du travail en Europe*. Paris: La Decouverte.

Braudel, Fernand. 1984. *The Perspective of The World*—Vol. III. London: Collins.

————. 1992. *The Perspective of the World: Civilization and Capitalism 15th–18th Century*. Berkeley: University of California Press.

Brazilian Central Bank. 1997. *Annual Report*. Brazilian Central Bank website: *http://www.bacen.gov.br/ingles/banual97/hiie3100.htm*.

————. 1998. *Annual Report*. Brazilian Central Bank website: http://www.bacen.gov.br/ingles/banual98/banual.shtm.

Breheny, Michael J., and Ronald W. McQuaid. 1985. "The M4 Corridor: Patterns and Causes of Growth in High Technology Industries." In *Geographical Papers*, University of Reading, Department of Geography.

Brett, E. A. 1983. *International Money and Capitalist Crisis: The Anatomy of Global Disintegration*. London: Westview Press.

Brewer III, and Douglas Evanoff. 1999. "Global Financial Crises: Implications for Banking and Regulation." *Federal Reserve Bank of Chicago, Chicago Fed Letter*, August, no. 144A.

Brint, S. 1997. *Professionals and the "Knowledge Economy:" Rethinking the Theory of Postindustrial Society*. Paper presented at the annual meeting of the American Sociological Association, Toronto, August, 1997.

Brint, Steven. 1988. "The Upper Professionals of the 'Dual City': A High Command of Commerce, Culture, and Civic Regulation." Paper prepared for the Dual City Working Group. New York: Committee on New York City, Social Science Research Council, November 11–12.

Briston, R. J. 1979. "The U.K. Accountancy Profession: The Move Towards Monopoly Power." *Accountants' Magazine*, November: 458–60.

Brosnan, P., and F. Wilkinson. 1987. *Cheap Labour: Britain's False Economy*. London: Low Pay Unit.

Brown, C. 1984. *Black and White Britain*. London: Heinemann.

Browne, L. E. 1983. "High Technology and Business Services." *New England Economic Review*, July–August: 5–16.

Browning, H. L., and J. Singelmann. 1978. "The Transformation of the U.S. Labor Force: The Interaction of Industry and Occupation." *Politics and Society* 8 (3 and 4): 481–509.

Bryson, J. R. 1997. "Business Service Firms, Service Space and Management of Change." *Entrepreneurship and Regional Development*, vol. 5, pp. 265–77.

Bryson, J. R. and P. W. Daniels. 1998. "Business links, strong ties, and the walls of silence: small and medium-sized enterprises and external business-service expertise." *Environment and Planning C* (16): 265–280.

Bryson, J. R., D. Keeble, and P. Wood. 1993. "The Creation, Location and Growth of Small Business Service Firms in the United Kingdom." *Services Industries Journal*, vol. 14, no. 3: 451–81.

Buck, N., I. Gordon, and K. Young. 1986. *The London Employment Problem*. Oxford: Clarendon Press.

Buckley, John W., and Peter R. O'Sullivan. 1981. "International Economics and Multinational Accounting Firms." In John C. Burton, ed., *The International World of Accounting: Challenges and Opportunities*. Proceedings of the Arthur Young Professors' Roundtable held at Reston, Va., 1980.

Budd, Leslie. 1995. "Globalization, territory and strategic alliances in different financial centers." *Urban Studies* 32 (2): 345–360.

Bungei Shunju. 1986. "Kokutetsu vochi kyoso nyusatsu ni igi ari" (Opposition to competition in bidding for Government railroad land). *Bungei Shunju*, December: 176–82.

Bureau of National Affairs. 1982. *Layoffs, Plant Closures, and Concession Bargaining*. Washington, D.C.: Bureau of National Affairs.

Burgel, G. and Burgel G. 1996. "Global Trends and City Politics: Friends or Foes of Urban Development?" In Cohen, M. A., Ruble, Blair A., Tulchin, Joseph S., and Allison M. Garland, eds. 1996. *Preparing for the Urban Future: Global Pressure and Local Forces*. Washington, D.C.: Woodrow Wilson Center Press.

Burt, M. and Aran, L. 2000. *America's Homeless II: Populations and Services*. Washington, D.C.: Urban Institute.

Burton, John C., ed. 1981. *The International World of Accounting: Challenges and Opportunities*. Proceedings of the Arthur Young Professors' Roundtable held at Reston, Va., 1980.

Business Week. 1977. "Annual Survey of Bank Performance." *Business Week*, April 18.

———. 1986. "Annual Survey of Bank Performance." *Business Week*, April 6.

Candilis, Wray O., ed. 1988. *United States Service Industries Handbook*. New York and London: Praeger.

Cargill, Thomas F. 1981. "The Impact of Deregulation on the Financial System." *Issues in Bank Regulation*, Winter: 10–14.

———. 1986. *Money, the Financial System and Monetary Policy*. Englewood Cliffs, N.J.: Prentice Hall.

Cargill, Thomas F., and Gillian G. Garcia. 1985. *Financial Reform in the 1980s*. Stanford, Calif.: Hoover Institution Press.

Casey, B. 1987. "The Extent and Nature of Temporary Employment in Great Britain." *Policy Studies* 8(1): 64–75.

Castells, Manuel. 1977. *The Urban Question: A Marxist Approach*. Cambridge, Mass.: MIT Press.

———. 1989. *The Informational City: Information Technology, Economic Restructuring, and the Urban-Regional Process*. London: Blackwell.

———. 1996. *The Rise of the Network Society*. Oxford: Blackwell.

Castells, Manuel and Alejandro Portes. 1989. "World Underneath: The Origins, Dynamics, and Effects of the Informal Economy." In A. Portes et al., eds., *The*

Informal Economy: Studies in Advanced and Less Developed Countries. Baltimore: Johns Hopkins University Press.

Cave, M. and L. Waverman. "The Future of International Settlements." *Telecommunications Policy*, vol. 22, no. 11: 883–898.

Caves, R. E. 1976. "International Corporations: The Industrial Economics of Foreign Investment." *Economica*, new ser., 38(149): 1–27.

———. 1980. "Industrial Organization, Corporate Strategy and Structure." *Journal of Economic Literature* 28(1): 64–92.

Central Bank of Germany. Various years. *Monatsbericht der Deutsche Bundesbank.* Frankfurt.

Centre for Economics and Business Research Ltd. and Observatoire de l'Economie et des Institutions Locales. 1997. *Two Great Cities: A Comparison of the Economies of London and Paris.* August 1997.

Chall, Daniel. 1984. "Neighborhood Changes in New York City during the 1970s. Are the Gentry Returning?" *Federal Reserve Bank of New York Quarterly Bulletin*, Winter 1983–1984: 38–48.

Chandler, Alfred. 1977. *The Visible Hand: The Manager in American Business.* Cambridge, Mass.: Harvard University Press.

Chaney, Elsa and Constance Sutton eds. 1979. "Caribbean Migration to New York." Special issue of *International Migration Review* 13 (Summer).

Chase-Dunn, C. 1984. "Urbanization in the World System: New Directions for Research." In M. P. Smith, ed., *Cities in Transformation.* Beverly Hills, Calif.: Sage.

———. 1985. "The System of World Cities, A.D. 800–1975." In M. Timberlake, ed., *Urbanization in the World-Economy.* New York: Academic Press.

Chen, Xiangming. 1995. "Chicago as a Global City." *Chicago Office* 5: 15–20.

Cheshire, P. C. and Gordon, I. R., eds. 1995. *Territorial Competition in an Integrating Europe.* Aldershot: Avebury, UK.

Christaller, Walter 1966. *Central Places in Southern Germany.* Englewood Cliffs, N.J.: Prentice Hall.

Church, A. and P. Reid. 1996. "Urban Power, International Networks and Competition: The Example of Cross-border Cooperation." *Urban Studies*, vol. 33, no. 8: 1297–1318.

Ciccolella, Pablo and Iliana, Mignaqui. 2000. "Buenos Aires." In Sassen, S., ed. *Cities and Their Crossborder Networks.* New York and London: Routledge.

———. 2001. "Buenos Aires: Socio-Spatial Impacts of the Development of Global City Functions." In Sassen, S. ed., *Global Networks/City Links.* New York and London: Routledge.

City of Nagoya. 1988. *Statistical Sketch of Nagoya 1987.* Nagoya, Japan.

City of New York. 1985. *Atlas of the Census.* New York: Department of City Planning.

Clairmonte, Frederick F., and John H. Cavanagh. 1984. "Transnational Corporations and Services: The Final Frontier." *Trade and Development: An UNCTAD Review* 5: 215–73.

Clark, Colin. 1940. *The Conditions of Economic Progress.* London: Macmillan.

Clark, G. L. 1993. "Global Interdependence and Regional Development: Business Linkages and Corporate Governance in a World of Financial Risk." *Transactions of the Institute of British Geographers* 18: 309–25.

Clark, Gordon L. 1981. "The Employment Relation and Spatial Division of Labor: A Hypothesis." *Annals of the American Association of Geographers*: 412–24.

———. 1983. *Interregional Migration, National Policy, and Social Justice*. Totowa, N.J.: Rowman and Allenheld.

Clark, Terry Nichols and Hoffman-Martinot, Vincent, ed., 1998. *The New Public Culture* Oxford: Westview Press.

Coe, N., and Townsend, A. 1998. "Debunking the myth of localized agglomerations: The development of a regionalized service economy in South-East England." *Transactions* 23, no. 3: 385–405.

Cohen, M. A., Ruble, Blair A., Tulchin, Joseph S., and Allison M. Garland, eds., 1996. *Preparing for the Urban Future: Global Pressure and Local Forces*, Washington, D.C.: Woodrow Wilson Center Press.

Cohen, R. 1987. *The New Helots: Migrants in the International Division of Labour*. London: Avebury.

Cohen, R. B. 1981. "The New International Division of Labor, Multinational Corporations and Urban Hierarchy." In Michael A. Dear and Allen J. Scott, eds., *Urbanization and Urban Planning in Capitalist Society*. London and New York: Methuen.

Cohen, Robert. 1981. "The New International Division of Labor, Multinational Corporations and Urban Hierarchy." In Michael Dear and Allen J. Scott, eds., *Urbanization and Urban Planning in Capitalist Society*. New York: Methuen.

Cohen, Stephen S., and John Zysman. 1987. *Manufacturing Matters—The Myth of the Post-Industrial Economy*. New York: Basic Books.

Columbia University. 1987. "The Informal Economy in Low-Income Communities in New York City." New York: Columbia University, Program in Urban Planning.

Conference Board. 1983. "International Trade in Services: A Growing Force in the World Economy." *World Business Perspectives*, no. 75 (October). New York: Conference Board.

Congdon, T. 1988. *The Debt Threat: The Dangers of High Real Interest Rates for the World Economy*. Oxford: Basil Blackwell.

Conservation of Human Resources Project. 1977. *The Corporate Headquarters Complex in New York City*. New York: Columbia University. Conservation of Human Resources Project.

Conzen, M. P. 1975. "Capital flows and the developing urban hierarchy: state bank capital in Wisconsin, 1854–1895." *Economic Geography*, 51: 321–328.

Cooke, P., F. Moulaert, E. Swyngedouw, O. Weinstein, and P. Wells. 1992. *Towards Global Localization*. London: University College Press.

Coombes, M. G., J. S. Dixon, J. B. Goddard, S. Openshaw, and P. J. Taylor. 1982. "Functional Regions for the Population Centres of Great Britain." In D. T. Herbert and R. J. Johnston, eds., *Geography and the Urban Environment*. Vol. 5. Chichester: John Wiley.

Cooper, Kery, and Donald R. Fraser. 1984. *Banking Deregulation and the New Competition in Financial Services*. Cambridge, Mass.: Ballinger.

Corbridge, S., Nigel Thrift, and Ron Martin, eds. 1994. *Money, Power and Space*. Oxford, England and Cambridge, Mass.: Blackwell.

Corden, W. Maxwell. 1985. *Inflation, Exchange Rates, and the World Economy.* Oxford: Oxford University Press.

Corporation of London. June 2000. "London-New York Study: The economies of two great cities at the millenium." Executive Summary, website: *www.cityoflondon.gov.uk.*

———. May 2000. "The Role of the City in London's Knowledge-Driven Information Economy." Report presented by The Local Future Group. See *www.lfg.co.uk.*

———. 2000. *London's Contribution to the U.K. Economy.* Annual Report. London: Corporation of London, Centre for Economic and Business Research.

Council on Foreign Relations. 1999. "The Economics and Politics of the Asian Financial Crises of 1997–1998," University of California, San Diego.

County Business Patterns. *See* U.S. Department of Commerce, Bureau of the Census, 1977–1987.

Cox, Gabrielle. 1988. *The Pay Divide.* Low Pay Briefing Papers, no. 10. Manchester, England: Greater Manchester Low Pay Unit.

Crabb, Kelly C. 1983. "Providing Legal Services in Foreign Countries: Making Room for the American Attorney." *Columbia Law Review* 83(7): 1767–1823.

Cross, M. 1988. "Ethnic Minority Youth in a Collapsing Labour Market: The U.K. Experience." In C. Wilpert, ed., *Entering the Working World.* London: Grower.

Crouch, Colin, ed. 1979. *State and Economy in Contemporary Capitalism.* London: Croom Helm.

Crozier, Michel. 1963. *Le Phénomène bureaucratique.* Paris: Le Seuil.

Cybriwsky, Roman. 1998. *Tokyo.* New York: John Wiley and Sons.

Daly, M. T. 1994. "The Road to the Twenty-First Century: the Myths and Miracles of Asian Manufacturing." In Corbridge, Stuart, Nigel Thrift, and Ron Martin, eds. 1994. *Money, Power and Space.* Oxford, England and Cambridge, Mass.: Blackwell, 1994.

Daly, Maurice. 1987. "Rationalization of International Banking and the Implications for the Pacific Rim." In J. Friedman, ed., *International Capital and Urbanization of the Pacific Rim.* Proceedings of conference held at the Center for Pacific Rim Studies, UCLA, March 26–28.

Daniels, Peter W. 1975. *Office Location.* London: Bell.

———. 1985. *Services Industries: A Geographical Appraisal.* London and New York: Methuen.

Daniels, Peter, Andrew Leyshon, and Nigel Thrift. 1986. "U.K. Producer Services: The International Dimension." Working Paper, St. David's University College, Lampter and University of Liverpool, August.

———. 1995. "The EU Internal Market Programme and the Spatial Development of Producer Services in Great Britain." *European Urban and Regional Studies* 2(4): 299–316.

Daniels, P. W. and William F. Lever, eds. 1996. *The Global Economy in Transition.* Harlow: Longman.

Danziger, S. and Peter Gottschalk. 1995. *America Unequal.* Cambridge: Harvard University Press.

Davies, L. 1996. "Four World Cities: a Comparative Study of London, Paris, New York and Tokyo," Paper presented at UCL Bartlett School of Planning.

Davis, Mike. 1985. "Urban Renaissance and the Spirit of Postmodernism." *New Left Review* 151:113.

DeFreitas, Gregory. 1991. Inequality at Work: Hispanics in the U.S. Labor Force. New York: Oxford University Press.

———. 2000. "The Boom Breaks Records but So Does Inequality: Recent Trends in Job Growth, Unemployment, and Wages." *Regional Labor Review* 2: 3–11.

DeGiovanni, F. 1984. "Neighborhood Revitalization in Fort Greene and Clinton Hill." *New York Affairs* 8(2): 86–104.

Delaunay, Jean Claude, and Jean Gadrey. 1987. *Les Enjeux de la Société de Service*. Paris: Presses de la Fondation des Sciences Politiques.

Dezalay, Y. and D. Sugarman, eds. 1995. *Professional Competition and Professional Power: Lawyers and Accountants and the Social Construction of Markets*. London: Routledge.

Denison, Edward. 1979. *Accounting for Slower Economic Growth: The U.S. in the 1970s*. Washington, D.C.: Brookings Institution.

Deutermann, Jr., W. V., and S. C. Brown. 1978. "Voluntary Part-Time Workers: A Growing Part of the Labor Force." *Monthly Labor Review*, June: 101(6): 3–10.

deVries, Rimmer. 1987. "International Imbalances and the Search for Exchange-Rate Stability." In H. Patrick and R. Tachi, eds., *Japan and the United States Today: Exchange Rates, Macroeconomic Policies, and Financial Market Innovations*. New York: Columbia University Press.

Dicken, P. 1994. "Global-local tensions: firms and states in the global space-economy." *Economic Geography* 70(2): 101–28.

DiLullo, Anthony J. 1981. "Service Transactions in the U.S. International Accounts, 1970–1980." *Survey of Current Business* (November): 29–46.

Dore, Ronald P. 1958. *City Life in Japan: A Study of a Tokyo Ward*. Berkeley: University of California Press.

Douglass, Mike. 1987. "Transnational Capital and Urbanization in Japan." In J. Friedman, ed., *International Capital and Urbanization of the Pacific Rim*. Proceedings of conference held at the Center for Pacific Rim Studies, UCLA, March 26–28.

Drennan, Matthew P. 1983. "Local Economy and Local Revenues." In R. Horton and C. Brecher, eds., *Setting Municipal Priorities 1984*. New York and London: New York University Press.

———. 1997. "The Performance of Metropolitan Area Industries." Federal Reserve Bank of New York, *Economic Policy Review*, Feb. 1997.

———, E. Tobier, and J. Lewis. 1996. "The Interruption of Income Convergence and Income Growth in Large Cities in the 1980s." *Urban Studies*, vol. 33, no. 1, pp. 63–82.

Dunford, Mick. 1989. "Industrial Paradigms and Social Structures in Areas of New Industrial Growth." Typescript. School of European Studies, University of Sussex.

———. 1998. "Economies in space and time: economic geographies of development and underdevelopment and historical geographies of modernization." In

Brian Graham, ed., *Modern Europe: Place, Culture and Identity*. London: Arnold.

―――. 1998. "Regions and economic development," pp. 89–107 in Le Galès, P. and Lequesne, Christian, eds., *Regions in Europe*. London: Routledge.

Dunford, M. and Fielding, A. 1997. "Greater London, The South-East region and the Wider Britain: Metropolitan Polarization, Uneven Development and Inter-Regional Migration." Chapter 13 in Blotevogel, Hans H. and Anthony Fielding, eds., *People, Jobs and Mobility in the New Europe*. Chichester, New York: John Wiley.

Dunning, J. H., and G. Norman. 1987. "The Location Choice of Offices of International Companies." *Environment and Planning A* 19: 613–31.

Eade, J., ed. 1996. *Living the Global City: Globalization as a Local Process*. London: Routledge.

Echeverri-Carroll, Elsie. 1988. *Economic Impacts and Foreign Investment Opportunities: Japanese Maquilas—A Special Case*. Austin, Texas: University of Texas, Graduate School of Business, Bureau of Business Research.

Economic Consulting Services. 1981. *The International Operations U.S. Service Industries: Current Data Collection and Analysis*. Washington, D.C.: Economic Consulting Services, Inc.

Economic Intelligence Unit. 1984. *Multinational Business Quarterly*, no. 1. London: Economic Intelligence Unit.

Economic Planning Agency, Japan, 1980. *Standard Revised National Economic Accounting*. Tokyo: Japan Government.

―――. 1983. *National Economic Accounting*.

―――. 1985. *White Paper on the Global Economy, 1985*.

―――. 1986. *Outline of the Economy, 1985*.

―――. 1987. *Economic Survey of Japan, 1986–1987*.

―――. Various years a. *Indices of External Economic Trends*.

―――. Various years b. *Report on Revised National Accounts*.

Economist, The. 1986a. "Investment Management Survey." *Economist*, November 8.

―――. 1986b. "Global Investment Management." *Economist*. November 8.

―――. 1998. "Tigers Adrift." March 7, 1998.

―――. 2000. "The Battle of the Atlantic: London and New York." February 26, 2000.

Edel, Matthew. 1981. "Capitalism, Accumulation and the Explanation of Urban Phenomena." In Michael Dear and Allen J. Scott, eds., *Urbanization and Urban Planning in Capitalist Society*. New York: Methuen.

Edwards, Franklin R. 1987. "The Dark Side of Financial Innovation." In H. Patrick and R. Tachi, eds., *Japan and the United States Today: Exchange Rates Macroeconomic Policies, and Financial Market Innovations*. New York: Columbia University Press.

Edwards, L. E. 1982. "Intra-Urban Office Location: A Decision-Making Approach." Ph. D. diss., University of Liverpool.

Edwards, Richard. 1979. *Contested Terrain: The Transformation of the Workplace in the Twentieth Century*. New York: Basic Books.

Ehrenhalt, Samuel M. 1981. "Some Perspectives on the Outlook for the New

York City Labor Market." In *Challenges of the Changing Economy of New York City*. New York: The New York City Council on Economic Education.

——. 1988. "New York City in the New Economic Environment: New Risks and a Changing Outlook." New York: U.S. Bureau of Labor Statistics, Mid-Atlantic Regional Office.

Ehrenreich, Barbara. 1984. *The Hearts of Men: American Dreams and the Flight from Commitment*. Garden City, N.Y.: Anchor Books.

Eisenbeis, Robert A. 1981. "Regulation and Deregulation of Banking." *Banking Magazine*, March–April: 25–33.

Elliot, James R. 1999. "Putting 'Global Cities' in their Place: Urban Hierarchy and Low-income Employment during the post-war Era." *Urban Geography*. 20 (2): 95–115.

El-Shakhs, Salah. 1972. "Development, Primacy and Systems of Cities." *Journal of Developing Areas* 7 (October): 11–36.

Ernst, Dieter. 1986. "U.S.-Japanese Competition and the Worldwide Restructuring of the Electronics Industry—a European View." Paper prepared for the Pacific-Atlantic Interrelations Conference held at the Institute of International Relations, University of California, Berkeley, April 24.

Euromoney. 1983. "Foreign Banks in America." *Euromoney*, August, supplement no. 6.

——. 1987. "The Euromoney/InterSec 250: The Largest Investors outside the U.S.; the 75 Largest U.S. Investors." *Euromoney* September: 365–80.

European Economic Community. 1984. *Study on International Trade in Services*. Document I/420/84-EN. Brussels.

European Union. 1997. *Regional Trends 1997*. Brussels.

Fainstein, N. I. 1987. "The Underclass/Mismatch Hypothesis as an Explanation for Black Economic Deprivation." *Politics and Society* 15(4): 403–51.

Fainstein, Susan. 2001 (2nd ed). *The City Builders: Property, Politics, and Planning in London and New York*. Lawrence, Kans.: Kansas University Press.

——, I. Gordon, and M. Harloe. 1993. *Divided Cities: Economic Restructuring and Social Change in London and New York*. London: Blackwell. Forthcoming.

——, N. Fainstein, R. C. Hill, D. R. Judd, and M. P. Smith. 1983. *Restructuring the City*. New York: Longman.

—— and Norman I. Fainstein. 1983. "Regime Strategies, Communal Resistance, and Economic Forces." In Susan S. Fainstein et al., eds., *Restructuring the City*. New York: Longmans.

——. 1985. "Citizen Participation in Local Government." In D. R. Judd, ed., *Public Policy across States and Communities*. Greenwich, Conn.: JAI Press.

Fallick, B. 1999. "Part-time Work and Industry Growth." *Monthly Labor Review* (March): 22–29.

Feagin, J. R. 1987. "The Secondary Circuit of Capital." *International Journal of Urban and Regional Research* 11: 171–92.

——. 1988. *Houston Boomtown*. New Brunswick, N.J.: Rutgers University Press.

—— and Michael P. Smith. 1987. "Cities and the New International Division of Labor: An Overview." In M. P. Smith and J. R. Feagin, eds., *The Capitalist City: Global Restructuring and Community Politics*. Oxford: Blackwell.

Federal Reserve Bank of Atlanta. 1983. "Signals from the Future: The Emerging Financial Services Industry." *Economic Review*, September: 20–32.

Federal Reserve Bank of New York. 1998. "Earnings and Inequality: New York, New Jersey Region," *Current Issues in Economics and Finance*, vol. 4, no. 9, July.

Feige, E. L. 1979. "How Big Is the Irregular Economy?" *Challenge*, November– December: 14–17.

Fernandez-Kelly, M. Patricia. 1995. "Slums, Ghettos, and Other Conundrums in the Anthropology of Lower Income Urban Enclaves." *Annals of the New York Academy of Sciences* 749: 219–235.

———— and A. M. Garcia. 1989. "Informalization at the Core: Hispanic Women, Homework, and the Advanced Capitalist State." In A. Portes et al., eds., *The Informal Economy: Studies in Advanced and Less Developed Countries*. Baltimore: Johns Hopkins University Press.

Filed, Peter. 1981a. "M & A: The Transatlantic Battle." *Euromoney* (January): 82–97.

————. 1981b. "Regulation and Financial Innovation: Implications for Financial Structure and Competition among Depository and Nondepository Institutions." *Issues in Bank Regulation*, Winter: 15–23.

Finance and Development. "The Social Costs of the Asian Crisis." Sept. 1998, Vol. 35. No. 3. Washington, D.C.: IMF.

Financial Times. 2000. "Asia in Crisis." *Special Report*. March 20.

Ford, William F. 1982. "Banking's New Competition: Myths and Realities." *Economic Review*, January: 3–11. Published by Federal Reserve Bank of Atlanta.

Fincher, R. and Jane M. Jacobs, eds., 1998. *Cities of Difference*. New York: Guilford Press.

Findlay, A.M., F.L.N.Li, A.J. Jowett and R. Skeldon. 1996. "Skilled international migration and the global city: A study of expatriates in Hong Kong." *Transactions of the Institute of British Geographers* 21 (1): 49–61.

Foreign Press Center. 1987. *Facts and Figures of Japan*. Tokyo: Foreign Press Center of Japan.

Fortin, N. M. and T. Lemieux. 1997. "Institutional Changes and Rising Wage Inequality: Is there a Linkage?" *Journal of Economic Perspectives*, vol. 11, no. 2: 75–96.

Fortune Magazine. 1999. *Fortune Global 500*, August 2.

Fothergill, S., and G. Gudgin. 1982. *Unequal Growth: Urban and Regional Employment Change in the UK*. London: Heinemann.

Freeman, R., ed. 1994. *Working under different rules*. New York: Russell Sage Foundation.

———— and L. Katz, eds. 1995. *Differences and changes in wage structures*. Chicago: University of Chicago Press.

Freeman, Richard. 1984. *Aspects of Recent Japanese Financial Markets Liberalization*. Washington, D.C.: Board of Governors of the Federal Reserve System.

Frenkel, Jeffrey A. 1984. "The Yen-Dollar Agreement: Liberalizing Japanese Capital Markets." In *Policy Analysis in International Economics*, publication no. 9. Washington, D.C.: Institute for International Economics.

Friedman, David. 1988. *The Misunderstood Miracle: Industrial Development and Political Change in Japan*. Ithaca, N.Y.: Cornell University Press.

Friedmann, John. 1964. "Cities in Social Transformation." In J. Friedmann and W. Alonso, eds., *Regional Development and Planning*. Cambridge, Mass.: MIT Press.

———. 1986. "The World City Hypothesis." *Development and Change* 17: 69–84.

——— and Goetz Wolff. 1982. "World City Formation: An Agenda for Research and Action." *International Journal of Urban and Regional Research* 6(3): 309–44.

Friend, A. and A. Metcalf. 1982. *Slump City: The Politics of Mass Unemployment*. London: Pluto Press.

Fröbel, Folker, Jurgen Heinrichs, and Otto Kreye. 1980. *The New International Division of Labor*. London: Cambridge University Press.

Fuchs, Victor. 1968. *The Service Economy*. New York: National Bureau of Economic Research and Columbia University Press.

Fujita, Kuniko. 1988. "The Technopolis: High Technology and Regional Development in Japan." *International Journal of Urban and Regional Research* 2(4): 566–94.

——— and Richard Child Hill. 1987. *Toyota's City: Corporation and Community in Japan*. Sociology Working Paper no. 5, Department of Sociology, Michigan State University.

Fukuhara, Masahiro. 1981. *Keizai seicho to ginko tempo* (Economic growth and banking outlets). Tokyo: Kokon Sho-in.

Gad, G. 1975. *Central Toronto Offices: Observations on Location Patterns and Linkages*. Toronto: City of Toronto Planning Board.

———. 1979. "Face-to-Face Linkages and Office Decentralization Potentials: A Study of Toronto." In P. W. Daniels, ed., *Spatial Patterns of Office Growth and Location*. London: Wiley.

Gaebe, W., S. Stambach, P. A. Wood, and F. Moulaert. 1993. *Employment in Business-Related Services: An Inter-country Comparison of Germany, the United Kingdom, and France*. Brussels: European Commission.

Galbraith, J. K. 1969. *The New Industrial State*. London: Hamish Hamilton.

Gans, Herbert. 1984. "American Urban Theory and Urban Areas." In Ivan Szelenyi, ed., *Cities in Recession*. Beverly Hills, Calif.: Sage.

Garcia, L. 2001. "The Architecture of Global Networking Technologies." In Sassen, S. ed. *Global Networks/City Links*. New York and London: Routledge.

Garcia, Soledad. 1996. "Cities and Citizenship." *International Journal of Urban and Regional Research* 20 (1): 7–21.

Garnick, D.H. 1990. "Accounting for Regional Difference in Per Capita Personal Income Growth: an updated extension." *Survey of Current Business* 70: 29–40.

GATT (General Agreement on Tariffs and Trade). Various years. *International Trade*. Geneva: GATT.

GATT (General Agreement on Tariffs and Trade). Various years. "International Trade" Geneva: GATT.

Gelb, Joyce. 1991. "Japanese Women: The Search for Equal Opportunity." *Kaleidoscope*. Forthcoming.

———. 1991. "Tradition and Change: The Case of the Equal Employment Opportunity Law." *US/Japan Women's Journal* July: 48–75.

———. 2000. "The Equal Employment Opportunity Law: A Decade of Change for Japanese Women? " *Law and Policy* October, 22, 3–4: 385–408.

Gershuny, Jonathan. 1978. *After Industrial Society? The Emerging Self-Service Economy.* London: Macmillan.

——— and Ian Miles. 1983. *The New Service Economy: The Transformation of Employment in Industrial Societies.* New York: Praeger.

Giarini, Orio, ed. 1987. *The Emerging Service Economy.* Oxford and New York: Pergamon Press.

Gilbert, A. 1996. *The Mega-city in Latin America.* Tokyo: United Nations University Press.

Gillespie, A. E. and A. E. Green. 1987. "The Changing Geography of Producer Services Employment in Britain." *Regional Studies* 21(5): 397–412.

Ginzberg, Eli and George J. Vojta. 1981. "The Service Sector of the U. S. Economy." *Scientific American* 244 (March): 48–55.

Glasmeier, A., Howland, M. 1995. *From Combines to Computers: Rural Development in the Information Age.* Albany, New York: State University of New York Press.

Glickman, N.J. 1979. *The Growth and Management of the Japanese Urban System.* New York: Academic Press.

———. 1987. "Cities and the International Division of Labor," pp. 66–85. In Michael P. Smith and Joe R. Feagin, eds., *The Capitalist City.* Oxford and New York: Blackwell.

Goddard, J. B. 1973. "Office Linkages and Location: A Study of Communications and Spatial Patterns in Central London." *Progress in Planning* 1: 109–232.

———. 1975. *Office Location in Urban and Regional Development.* Oxford: Oxford University Press.

Goddard, J. B., and R. Pye. 1977. "Telecommunications and Office Location." *Regional Studies* 11: 19–30.

Gordon, D. 1990. "Who Bosses Whom? The intensity of supervision and the discipline of labor." *American Economic Review* 80(2): 28–32.

Gordon, D., ed. 1990. *Green Cities: Ecologically Sound Approaches to Urban Space.* Montreal: Black Rose.

Gordon, I. R. 1995. " 'London: World City': political and organizational constraints on territorial competition." In Cheshire, Paul C. and I. R. Gordon, eds., *Territorial Competition in an Integrating Europe.* Aldershot: Avebury, UK.

———. 1996. "The Role of Internationalization in Economic change in London over the past 25 years," paper presented to the World Cities Group, CUNY Graduate School, New York.

———. 1999. "London and the South East." In M.J. Breheny, ed. *The People: Where Will They Work?* London: Town and Country Planning Association.

——— and McCann, P. 2000. "Industrial Clusters: Complexes, Agglomeration and/or Social Networks?" *Urban studies* 37, Part 3: 513–532.

Gottdiener, M. 1985. *The Social Production of Urban Space.* Austin, Tex.: University of Texas Press.

Gottschalk, P. and Smeedig, T. 1997. "Cross-National Comparisons of Earnings and Income Inequality." *Journal of Economic Literature*, vol. XXXV: 633–687.

Graham, Daniel and Nigel Spence. 1997. "Competition for metropolitan resources: 'the crowding out' of London's manufacturing industry?" *Environment and Planning A* 29 (3): 459–484.

Graham, Stephen and Simon Marvin. 1996. *Telecommunications and the City: Electronic Spaces, Urban Places.* London: Routledge.

———. 2000. *Splintering Urbanism: Technology, Globalization and the Networked Metropolis.* London: Routledge.

Granovetter, M. 1983. "The strength of weak ties: a network theory revisited." *Sociological Theory,* 1: 201–233.

Greater London Council. 1986. *The London Labour Plan.* London: Greater London Council.

———. 1987. *Labour Market Report,* Spring 1987.

———. Industry and Employment Branch. 1985. *Ethnic Minority Retailing.*

———. Industry and Employment Branch. 1986. *Textiles and Clothing: Sunset Industries.*

———. Intelligence Unit. 1988. *Annual Abstract of Greater London Statistics, 1986–1987.* Vol. 19.

———. London Manpower Committees. 1981. *London Labor Market Review 1980/1981.*

———. London Regional Manpower Intelligence Unit. Various years. *Labor Market Report.*

Gravesteijn, S.G.E., S. van Griensven, and M.C. de Smidt, eds., 1998. *Timing Global Cities. Nederlandse Geografische Studies* 241. Utrecht.

Greenbaum, Stuart I., and Charles F. Haywood. 1981. "Secular Change in the Financial Services Industry." *Journal of Money, Credit and Banking,* May: 571–89.

Greenfield, H. I. 1966. *Manpower and the Growth of Producer Services.* New York: Columbia University Press.

Greenwood, M. 1980. "Metropolitan Growth and the Intra-Metropolitan Location of Employment, Housing and the Labor Force." *Review of Economics and Statistics* 62: 491–501.

Gregory, Derek and John Urry, eds. 1985. *Social Relations and Spatial Structures.* London: Macmillan.

Gurr, T. and D. S. King. 1987. *The State and the City.* Chicago: University of Chicago Press.

Guth, Wilfried. 1986. "Bank Strategy in an Age of Rapid Change." *Banker* 136 (722): 36–45.

Gutmann, P. M. 1979. "Statistical Illusions, Mistaken Policies." *Challenge,* November–December: 14–17.

Gyooten, Toyoo. 1987. "Internationalization of the Yen: Its Implications for the U.S.-Japan Relationship." In H. Patrick and R. Tachi, eds., *Japan and the United States Today: Exchange Rates, Macroeconomic Policies, and Financial Market Innovations.* New York: Columbia University Press.

Haig, R. M. 1927. *Major Economic Factors in Metropolitan Growth and Arrangement.* New York: Committee on Regional Plan for New York and Its Environs.

Hajari, Nisid. 1998. "Race Against Time." *Time* January 26th.

Hall, Peter. 1963. *London 2000.* London: Faber and Faber.

————. 1964. "Industrial London: A General View." In T. Coppock and H. Prince, eds., *Greater London*. London: Faber and Faber.

————. 1966. *The World Cities*. New York: McGraw-Hill.

Hall, Peter, M. Breheny, R. McQuaid, and D Hart. 1987. *Western Sunrise*. London: Allen and Unwin.

Halliday, J. 1975. *A Political History of Japanese Capitalism*. New York: Pantheon Books.

Hamnett, C. 1984. "Gentrification and Residential Location Theory: A Review and Assessment." In D. Herbert and R. Johnston, eds., *Geography and the Urban Environment, Progress in Research and Application*. Chichester: Wiley.

———— and D. Cross. 1998. "Social Polarisation and Inequality in London: the earnings evidence, 1979–95." *Environment and Planning C: Government & policy* 16, no. 6: 659–681.

———— and Bill Randolph. 1986. "Tenurial Transformation and the Flat Break-Up Market in London: The British Condo Experience." In Neil Smith and Peter Williams, eds., *Gentrification of the City*. London, Sydney, and Boston: Allen Unwin.

————, L. McDowell, and P. Sarre. 1989. *The Changing Social Structure*. London: Sage.

Hansen, N. 1994. "The Strategic Role of Producer Services in Regional Development." *International Regional Science Review* 16(1–2): 187–95.

Haringey Women's Unemployment Project. 1984. *Survey of Women's Unemployment in Haringey*. London: Haringey Women's Unemployment Project.

Harrington, J. W. 1995. "Empirical research on producer service growth and regional development: international comparisons." *The Professional Geographer* 47(1): 66–69.

Harris, Nigel and I. Fabricius, eds., 1996. *Cities and Structural Adjustment*. London: University College London.

Harris, Richard. 1988. "Home and Work in New York since 1950." Paper prepared for a meeting of the Dual City Working Group held in New York City, February 26–27. New York: Committee on New York City, Social Science Research Council.

Harrison, Bennett, and Barry Bluestone. 1988. *The Great U-Turn*. New York: Basic Books.

Hart, P. E., ed. 1986. *Unemployment and Labour Market Policies*. London: Gower.

Hartman, Chester. 1984. *The Transformation of San Francisco*. Totowa, N.J.: Rowman and Allanheld.

Hartmann, Heidi. 1981. "The Unhappy Marriage of Marxism and Feminism. Towards a More Progressive Union." In Lydia Sargent, ed., *Women and Revolution*. Boston: South End Press.

Harvey, David. 1973. *Social Justice and the City*. Baltimore, Md.: Johns Hopkins University Press.

————. 1985. *The Urbanization of Capital*. Oxford: Blackwell.

Hattori, Kenjiro, Nobuji Sugimura, and Setsuo Higuchi. 1980. "Urbanization and Commercial Zones." In Association of Japanese Geographers, eds., *Geography of Japan*. Tokyo: Teikoku-Shoin, United Nations University.

Haussermann, Hartmut, and Walter Siebel. 1987. *Neue Urbanität*. Frankfurt: Suhrkamp Verlag.

Heller, Robert H. 1987. "Future Directions in the Financial Services Industry: International Markets." *World of Banking* 6(3): 18–21.

Henderson, Jeff. 1986. "The New International Division of Labour and American Semiconductor Production in South-East Asia." In D. Watts, C. Dixon, and D. Drakakis-Smith, eds., *Multinational Companies and the Third World*. London: Croom Helm.

Henderson, Jeff, and Manuel Castells, eds. 1987. *Global Restructuring and Territorial Development*. London: Sage.

Herbert, Sir E. 1960. *Report for the Royal Commission on Local Government in Greater London 1957–1960*. Cmnd. 1164 (HMSO).

Herman, Edward. 1982. *Corporate Control, Corporate Power*. New York: Cambridge University Press.

Hermelin, B. 1998. "Location of Professional Business Services: Conceptual Discussion and a Swedish Case-study." *European Urban and Regional Studies*, vol. 5, no. 3: 263–275.

Hicks, D. A. 1983. "Urban and Economic Adjustment to the Postindustrial Era." In D. A. Hicks and N. J. Glickman, eds., *Transition to the 21st Century: Prospects and Policies for Economic and Urban-Regional Transformation*. Greenwich, Conn.: JAI Press.

Hill, R. C. and Fujita, K. 1995. "Osaka's Tokyo Problem." *International Journal of Urban and Regional Research*, vol. 19, no. 2: 181–91.

Hill, Richard C. and J. R. Feagin. 1984. "Detroit and Houston: Two cities in global perspective." Presented at the 79th Meeting of the ASA, San Antonio, Texas, 29 August.

Hill, Richard Child. 1987. "Global Factory and Company Town: The Changing Division of Labour in the International Automobile Industry." In J. Henderson and M. Castells, eds., *Global Restructuring and Territorial Development*. London: Sage.

Hill, T. P. 1977. "On Goods and Services." *Review of Income and Wealth* 23(4): 315–38.

Hino, Masateru. 1984. "The Location of Head and Branch Offices of Large Enterprises in Japan." *Science Reports of Tohoku University (Sendai Japan), Geography Series* 34(2).

Hinojosa, R. A., and R. Morales. 1986. "International Restructuring and Labor Market Interdependence: The Automobile Industry in Mexico and the United States." Paper presented at the Conference on Labor Market Interdependence held at El Colegio de Méjico; Mexico, September 25–27.

Hirasawa, Sadaaki. 1988. "Role of Japanese Banks in the Internationalization Process." *Business Japan* 33(1): 37–39.

Hiroshi, Tanaka. 1987. "Foreign Workers and Their Rights." In *The Problem of Foreign Workers*. Report of Japan Ministry of Justice.

Hitchens, D.M.W.N., O'Farrell., P. N., and Conway, C. 1994. "Business service use by manufacturing firms in mid-Wales." *Environment and Planning A*, vol. 26: 95–106.

Hitz, Keil, Lehrer, Ronnenberger, Schmid, Wolff, eds. 1995. *Capitales Fatales:*

Urbanisierung und Politik in den Finanzmetropolen Frankfurt und Zürich. Zurich: Rotpunkt Verlag.

Hoffman, Dieter H. 1971. "German Banks as Financial Department Stores." *Federal Reserve Bank of St. Louis Review.* November: 8–13.

Holcomb, H. B., and R. A. Beauregard. 1981. *Revitalizing Cities.* Washington, D.C.: Association of American Geographers.

Holleman, Leon. 1982. "Japan's New Banking Laws." *Banker,* January: 37–39.

Hoover. Edgar M., and Raymond Vernon. 1962. *Anatomy of a Metropolis.* New York: Anchor.

Hoppe, John C., and Zachary Snow. 1974. "International Legal Practice—Restrictions on the Migrant Attorney." *Harvard International Law Journal* 15(2): 298–332.

Horvitz, Paul M. 1983. "Reorganization of the Federal Regulatory Agencies." *Journal of Bank Research* (Winter): 245–63.

Hoselitz, Bert. 1955. "Generative and Parasitic Cities." *Economic Development and Cultural Change* 3 (April): 278–94.

Howell, D. R. 1999. "Theory-Driven Facts and the Growth in Earnings Inequality." *The Review of Radical Political Economics,* vol. 31, no. 1: 54–86.

———. 2000. "Increasing Earnings Inequality and Unemployment in Developed Countries: A Critical Assessment of the "Unified Theory." Center for Economic Policy Analysis (CEPA) the New School for Social Research, Working Paper Series I—Globalization, Labor Markets and Social Policy, No. 22, Feb. *www.newschool.edu/cepa.*

Howells, J., and A. E. Green, 1986. "Location, Technology and Industrial Organization in U.K. Services." *Progress in Planning* 26 (pt. 2): 85–185.

Hurstfield, Jennifer. 1978. *The Part-Time Trap.* Low Pay Pamphlet, no. 9. London: Low Pay Unit.

———. 1987. *Part-timers: Under Pressure.* London: Low Pay Unit.

Hymer, Stephen. 1971. "The Multinational Corporation and the Law of Uneven Development." In J. W. Bhagwati, ed., *Economics and World Order.* New York: Macmillan.

Ide, Sakuo, and Akio Takeuchi. 1980. "Jiba Sangyo: Localized Industry." In Association of Japanese Geographers, eds., *Geography of Japan.* Tokyo: Teikoku-Shoin, United Nations University.

Illeris, S. and Sjoholt, P. 1995. "The Nordic Countries: High Quality Service in a Low Density Environment." *Progress in Planning.* 43, no. 2/3: 205.

IMF, *see* International Monetary Fund.

———. 1987. *London Labour Market Trends—Facts and Figures.* (July).

———. 1987. "Facts and Figures," *London Labour Market Trends,* (July).

———. 1987a. *London Labour Market Trends—Facts and Figures.* London: Inner London Education Authority.

———. 1987b. *The London Labour Market: Facts and Figures.* London: Inner London Education Authority.

International Financial Corporation. 1998. Emerging Stock Markets Factbook 1998. Washington, D.C.: IFC.

International Labor Office (ILO). 1981. *Employment of Multinational Enterprises in Developing Countries.* Geneva: ILO.

International Labor Office (ILO). 1985. *Women Workers in Multinational Enterprises in Developing Countries.* Geneva: ILO.

International Monetary Fund (IMF). 1988c. *Balance of Payments Statistics Yearbook.* Vol. 39, pt. 2.

——. *Direction of Trade Statistics Yearbook.*

——. 1977. *Balance of Payments Manual.* 4th ed. Washington, D.C.: IMF

——. 1982. *Balance of Payments Statistics Yearbook.* Vol. 33, pt. 2.

——. 1987a. *Direction of Trade Statistics, October 1987.*

——. 1987b. *Balance of Payments Statistics Yearbook.* Vol. 38, pts. 1 and 2.

——. 1988a. *World Economic Outlook*, April.

——. 1988b. *International Financial Statistics* 41(8).

——. 1988d. *Balance of Payments Statistics Supplement.* Vol. 39, supplement.

——. 1989. *Balance of Payments Statistics Yearbook.* Vol. 40, pts. 1 and 2.

——. 1990. *International Financial Statistics* 43(2).

——. 1998. "Financial Turbulence and the World Economy." *World Economic Outlook*, October.

——. 1998. "International Capital Markets: Developments, Prospects and Key Policy Issues." *World Economic and Financial Surveys.*

——. 1998. *Balance of Payment Statistics Yearbook*, vol. 49, pts. 1 and 2. Washington, D.C.: IMF.

——. 1999a. "Large Capital Flows: A Survey of the Causes, Consequences, and Policy Responses." *IMF Working Paper 99/17.*

——. 1999b. *International Financial Statistics,* June 1999.

——. 2000. World Economic Outlook. April 2000.

——. 1998. "What Lessons Does the Mexican Financial Crisis Hold for Recovery in Asia?" *Finance and Development*, vol. 35, no. 2, June.

InterSec Research Corp. 1988. *Foreign Investment of Private Sector Pension Funds 1980–1990.* Stamford, Conn.: InterSec Research Corp.

Isard, Walter. 1956. *Location and Space-Economy: A General Theory Relating to Industrial Location, Market Areas, Land Use, Trade, and Urban Structure.* New York: Wiley.

Ishizuka, Hiromichi. 1980. "Methodological Introduction to the History of the City of Tokyo." Project on Technology Transfer, Transformation and Development: The Japanese Experience. HSDRJE-2/UNUP-85. Tokyo: Teikoku-Shoin. United Nations University.

Ishizuka, Hiromichi, and Yorifusa Ishida. 1988. *Tokyo: Urban Growth and Planning: 1968–1988.* Center for Urban Studies, Tokyo Metropolitan University.

ITNTO. 1998. *UK Trends in IS Employment.* London: ITNTO. (July).

Ito, Tatsuo, and Masafumi Tanifuji. 1982. "The Role of Small and Intermediate Cities in National Development in Japan." In O. P. Mathur, ed., *Small Cities and National Development.* Nagoya: UNCRD.

Iyotani, Toshio. 1989. "The New Immigrant Workers in Tokyo." Typescript. Tokyo University of Foreign Studies.

——. 1995. "Japan's Policy towards Foreign Workers and the Case of Kawasaki City in Regional Development Dialogue." United Nations Centre for Regional Development, Nagoya. Vol. 16, no. 1, Spring.

————. 1998. "Globalization and Immigrant Workers in Japan" Tokyo: National Institute for Research Advancement (winter).

————. "Globalization and Culture." *The Japan Foundation Newsletter* 23(3).

————. 2001. *Gender and Globalization.* Tokyo: Akashi-Shoten.

Jackson, K. and R. McGregor. 2000. "Control of Immigration: Statistics UK." Home Office, Immigration Research and Statistics Service.

Jacobson, Louis S. 1978. "Earning Losses of Workers Displaced from Manufacturing Industries." In W. C. DeWald, ed., *The Impact of International Trade and Investment on Unemployment.* Washington, D.C.: GPO.

Japan Daily Labor Union Meeting Report. 1988. *The Solutions to Foreign Labor Problem.* May 30. Tokyo: Japan Daily Labor Union.

Japan Development Bank. 1988. *Growing Foreign Investors' Activities and the Future of Internationalization.* Tokyo: The Japan Development Bank.

Japan Economic Planning Agency. 1987. *Economic Survey of Japan, 1986–1987.* Tokyo: Economic Planning Agency. *See* Economic Planning Agency, Government of Japan.

————. 1988. *Annual Report on the National Life for Fiscal 1987.*

————. 1989. *Annual Report on the National Life for Fiscal 1988.*

Japan External Trade Organization (JETRO), see JETRO.

Japan, Management and Coordination Agency (1999, 1998, 1993, 1988, 1986, 1982, and 1984) *Japan Statistical Yearbook.* Tokyo, Japan Statistical Association.

Japan Management and Coordination Agency. 1981. *Japan Statistical Yearbook.* Tokyo: Management and Coordination Agency Statistics Bureau.

————. 1982. *1980 Population Census of Japan.* Tokyo: Management and Coordination Agency Statistics Bureau.

————. 1984. *Japan Statistical Yearbook.*

————. 1985. *Japan Statistical Yearbook.*

————. 1986. *Japan Statistical Yearbook.*

————. 1986. *Japan Statistical Yearbook.*

————. 1987a. *Labor Force Survey.* Tokyo: Management and Coordination Agency Statistics Bureau.

————. 1987b. "Japanese Statistics, 1986." In *Facts and Figures of Japan.* Japan: Foreign Press Center.

————. 1988. *Japan Statistical Yearbook.*

————. 1993. *Japan Statistical Yearbook.*

————. 1997. *Japan Statistical Yearbook.*

————. 1999. *Japan Statistical Yearbook.*

Japan Ministry of Construction. 1987. *1987 Tokyo's Average Land Price Listings,* September 30: 1–6.

————. 1988a. *1987: Direct Investments to Foreign Markets and Domestic Market,* May 31.

————. 1988b. *The Situation of Increasing Unskilled, Illegal Aliens.*

————. 1988c. *White Paper on Construction.*

————. 1988d. *A Report to Prevent Illegal Aliens Getting a Job in Construction Firms.* November 10.

————. 2000. *Establishment and Enterprise Census.* Tokyo: Japan Management and Coordination Agency.

Japan Ministry of Foreign Affairs. 1986. *Kaigai zairyu hojinsu chosa tokei* (Survey of Japanese living overseas). Tokyo: Ministry of Foreign Affairs.

———. 1987. *Statistical Survey of Japan Economy.*

———. 1988. *Statistics on Japan.*

———. Various years. *Foreign Trade Statistics.*

Japan Ministry of Justice. 2000. *Statistics on Foreign Residents*, Immigration Bureau, *http://www.jinjapan.org.*

———. 2000. *Symposium on The International Movement of People and Immigration Policy toward the 21ˢᵗ Century.* Tokyo: Ministry of Justice (Novemeber, 29).

———. Immigration Office. 1985. *Annual Report on Entries and Departures.* Tokyo: Ministry of Justice.

Japan Ministry of Labor. 1984. *Monthly Labour Statistics and Research Bulletin.* Tokyo: Ministry of Labor.

———. 1986a. *Rodo hakusho* (White Paper on Labor). Tokyo: Ministry of Labor.

———. 1986b. *Rodo tokei yoran* (Labor statistics manual).

———. 1987. *Monthly Labour Statistics and Research Bulletin.*

———. 1988. *Rodo hakusho* (White Paper on Labor).

———. 1989. *Labor Conditions of Women 1988.*

Japan Ministry of Public Management. 1999. *The Establishment and Enterprise Census.* Tokyo: Ministry of Public Management, Statistics Bureau and Centre.

Japan National Land Agency. 1985. Capital Restructuring Plan. Tokyo: National Land Agency.

———. 1986. *"Price Index Report": Average Price Index of Residential Land Prices In Prefectural Cities.*

Japan National Tax Agency. 2000. "The Number of Foreign Owned Firms in Japan and Tokyo Region." Tokyo: Annual Statistics, National Tax Agency.

Japan Office of the Prime Minister. 1987. *New National Plan of Action Towards the Year 2000.* Tokyo: Headquarters for the Planning and Promoting of Policies Relating to Women, May.

Japan Statistical Yearbook. See Japan Management and Coordination Agency.

———. 2001.

Japan Tariff Association. Various years. *Summary Report, Trade of Japan.* Tokyo: Japan Tariff Association.

Jensen-Butler, C., A. Shachar, and J. van Weesep, eds., 1997. *European Cities in Competition.* Aldershot: Avebury.

Jessen, Johann et al. 1987. "The Informal Work of Industrial Workers." Paper presented at the 6th Urban Change and Conflict Conference held at University of Kent at Canterbury, United Kingdom, September 20–23.

Jessop, Robert. 1999. "Reflections on Globalization and its Illogics." In Olds, Kris, et al. eds., *Globalization and the Asian Pacific: Contested Territories.* London: Routledge.

JETRO (Japan External Trade Organization). 1981. *Japan Manufacturing Operations in the United States.* Tokyo: JETRO.

———. 1987a. *The World and Japanese Direct Foreign Investment 1986.* Tokyo: JETRO.

———. 1987b. *Japan's Overseas Investment Entering a New Phase with the Yen's Appreciation.* White Paper on World and Japanese Overseas Direct Investment.

————. 1989. *New Phase in Foreign Direct Investments and Strategic Alliances.* White Paper on World Direct Investments.

————. 2000. *Nippon 2000.* Tokyo: JETRO (June).

Jimenez, M., 2001. "Global Change and Economic Restructuring in Mexico City." (Unpublished dissertation, Department of Urban and Public Planning, London School of Economics).

Jimenez, M. Bo-Sin Tang, Murat Yalcintan and Ertan Zibel. 2001. "The Global-City Hypothesis for the Periphery: A Comparative Case Study of Mexico City, Istanbul and Guangzhou." In Thornley, A. and Yvonne Rydin, eds., *Planning in a Globalised World.* London: Ashgate.

Johnson, Chalmers. 1982. *MITI and the Japanese Miracle: The Growth of Industrial Policy, 1925–1975.* Stanford, Calif.: Stanford University Press.

Johnson, G. 1997. "Changes in Earnings Inequality: The role of demand shifts." Journal of Economic Perspectives, vol. 11, no. 2, 41–54.

Johnson, Manuel H. 1987. "The Yen-Dollar Relationship: A Recent Historical Perspective." In H. Patrick and R. Tachi, eds., *Japan and the United States Today: Exchange Rates, Macroeconomic Policies, and Financial Market Innovations.* New York: Columbia University Press.

Jones, E. 1981. *Accountancy and the British Economy 1840–1980: The Evolution of Ernst and Whitney.* London: Batsford.

Jones, Randall S. 1985. *Japan's High Savings Rate: An Overview.* Report no. 46A. Washington, D.C.: Japan Economic Institute.

Jones, T. 1982. "Small Business Development and the Asian Community in Britain." *New Community* 9(3): 467–77.

Judd, D. R., and M. Parkinson 1989. "Urban Revitalization in America and the U.K.: The Politics of Uneven Development." In M. Parkinson, B. Foley, and D. R. Judd, eds., *Regenerating the Cities: The U.K. Crisis and the U.S. Experience.* Manchester: Manchester University Press.

Kakabadse, Mario A. 1987. "International Trade in Services: Prospects for Liberalization in the 1990s." In *Atlantic Paper*, no. 64. The Atlantic Institute for International Affairs. London, New York, and Sydney: Croom Helm.

Kakumoto, Ryohei. 1978. "Metropolis and Megalopolis—A General Survey of the Tokaido Region from the Standpoint of Transportation." *Waiseda Business and Economic Studies* 14: 65–98.

Kaldor, Nicholas. 1966. *Causes of the Slow Rate of Economic Growth of the United Kingdom.* Cambridge: Cambridge University Press.

Kamo, T. 1995. "The Change of Tokyo's Economic Functionings as a Global City." *Hogaku Zasshi* (The Journal of Law) 41, No. 4.

————. 1997. "Time for Reform?: Fifty Years of the Postwar Japanese Local Self-Government System." In Foreign Press Center, Japan, ed., *Japan: Eyes on the Country.* Tokyo: Foreign Press Center.

————. 1998. "An Aftermath of Globalization? East Asian Economic Turmoil and Japanese Cities Adrift." (Unpublished paper from Osaka City University.)

Kamo, T. and Sasaki, M. 1996. "The political economy of 'the global city Tokyo': its emergence and uncertain future." Unpublished paper.

Kane, Edward J. 1987. "Competitive Financial Regulation: An International Perspective." In R. Portes and A. Swoboda, eds., *Threats to International Financial Stability.* Cambridge: Cambridge University Press.

Kantor, P., and D. Stephen. 1988. *The Dependent City: The Changing Political Economy of Urban America*. Glenview, Ill.: Scott Foresman.

Kasarda, J. D. 1985. "Urban Change and Minority Opportunities." In P. Peterson, ed., *The New Urban Reality*. Washington D.C.: Brookings Institution.

———. 1988. "Economic Restructuring and America's Urban Dilemma." In *The Metropolitan Era*, vol. 1, *A World of Giant Cities*, M. Dogan and J. D. Kasarda, eds., Newbury Park, Calif.: Sage.

Katouzian, Homa. 1970. "The Development of the Service Sector: A New Approach." *Oxford Economic Papers* 22: 362–82.

Keeble, D. and Bryson, J. R. 1996. "Small-firm creation and growth, regional development, and the North-South divide in Britain." *Environment and Planning A* 28: 909–934.

——— and P. A. Wood. 1991. "Small firms, business service growth and regional development in the U.K.: some empirical findings." *Regional Studies* 25: 439–458.

Keeble, D. E., P. L. Owens, and C. Thompson. 1982. *Centrality, Peripherality and EEC Regional Development*. London: HMSO.

Kellerman, A. 1997. "Fusions of information types, media and operators, and continued American leadership in telecommunications." *Telecommunications Policy*, vol. 21, no. 6: 553–564.

Kennedy, H. Patrick. 1982. "The Role of Foreign Banks in a Changing U.S. Banking System." *Banker* (February): 101–03.

Kenney, Martin, and Richard Florida. 1988. "Beyond Mass Production: Production and Labor Process in Japan." *Politics and Society* 16(1): 121–58.

Khoury, Srakis J. 1980. *Dynamics of International Banking*. New York: Praeger.

Kimijima, T. 1980. "Inner-City Problems of Kawasaki City." *Jutaku: A Monthly of Housing* 29(7): 55–61. Tokyo: Japan Housing Association.

Kindleberger, C. P. 1974. "The Formation of Financial Centers: A Study in Comparative Economic History." In *Princeton Studies in International Finance*, no. 36.

King, A. D. 1986. "Margins, Peripheries and Divisions of Labor: U.K. Urbanism and the World Economy." In Dennis Hardy, ed., *On the Margins: Marginal Space and Marginal Economies*. Middlesex Polytechnic Geography and Planning Paper no. 17.

———. 1990. *Global Cities: Post-Imperialism and the Internationalization of London*. London: Routledge.

———. 1990. *Urbanism, Colonialism, and the World Economy: Culture and Spatial Foundations of the World Urban System*. London and New York: Routledge.

Kloosterman, R. C. 1996. "Polarization trends in Amsterdam and Rotterdam after 1980." *Regional Studies* 30(5): 467–476.

Kobayashi, Noritake. 1981. "The Present and Future of Japanese Multi-National Enterprises: A Comparative Analysis of the Japanese and U.S.–European Multi-National Management." *Wheel Extended* 9(3): 10–18.

Komlosy, Andrea, Christof Parnreiter, Irene Stacher, Susan Zimmermann, eds., 1997. *Ungeregelt und Unterbezahlt. Der Informelle Sektor in der Weltwirtschaft*. Frankfurt: Brandes & Apsel/Sudwind.

Komori, S. 1983. "Inner City in Japanese Context." *City Planning Review* 125: 11–17.

Kostinsky, Grigory. 1997. "Globalisation de l'economie et notions urbanistiques." In P. Claval and A.-L. Sanguin, eds. *Metropolisation et Politique*. Paris: L'Harmattan.

Krieger, Joel. 1986. *Reagan, Thatcher and the Politics of Decline*. New York: Oxford University Press.

Krueger, R. C. 1988. "U.S. International Transactions, First Quarter 1988." *Survey of Current Business* 68(6): 28–69.

Krugman, Paul. 1986. "Is the Strong Dollar Sustainable?." Working Paper no. 1644. Washington, D.C.: National Bureau of Economic Research.

Kunzmann, K. R. 1995. "Berlin im Zentrum europaeischer Staedtnetze." In Werner Suss, ed., *Hauptstadt Berlin*. Berlin: Berlin Verlag.

————. 1996. "Euro-megalopolis or Themepark Europe? Scenarios for European spatial development." *International Planning Studies*, vol. 1: 143–63.

KUPI. 1981. *Policy for Revitalization of Inner City*. Kobe: Kobe Urban Problems Institute.

Landrieu, Josee, Nicole May, Therse Spector, and Pierre Veltz, eds., 1998. *La Ville Eclatee*. La Tour d'Aigues: Editiones de l'Aube.

Lash, Scott, and John Urry. 1987. *The End of Organized Capitalism*. Cambridge: Polity Press.

Law, C. M. 1988. *The Uncertain Future of the Urban Core*. London: Routledge.

Lawrence, Robert Z. 1984. "Sectoral Shifts and the Size of the Middle Class." *Brookings Review* 3(1): 3–11.

Leborgne, D., and A. Lipietz. 1988. "L'après-fordisme et son espace." *Les Temps Modernes* 43(601): 75–114.

Lee, C. H. 1984. "The Service Sector, Regional Specialization, and Economic Growth in the Victorian Economy." *Journal of Historical Geography* 10: 139–56.

Lee, Chung H., and Seiji Naya, eds. 1988. *Trade and Investment in Services in the Asia-Pacific Region*. Center for International Studies, Inha University, Korea.

Lee, F. 1981. "Ethnic Minority and Small Firms: Problems Faced by Black Firms—Lambeth Case Study." In *Planning Studies*, no. 14. London: Polytechnic of Central London.

Leipert, Christian. 1985. "Social Costs of Economic Growth as a Growth Stimulus." Paper presented at the Conference for a New Economics, The Other Economic Summit, held at Bedford College, London, April 16–19.

Leontieff, W., and F. Duchin. 1985. *The Future Impact of Automation on Workers*. New York: Oxford University Press.

Leopold, Ellen. 1987. *Inequality at Work in London's Small Firms*. London: London Strategic Policy Unit.

Levich, M. 1988. "Financial Innovations in International Financial Markets." In M. Feldstein, ed., *United States in the World Economy*. Chicago: University of Chicago Press.

Levitt, Theodore. 1976. "The Industrialization of Services." *Harvard Business Review* 54:63–74.

Levy, F. and Murane, R. 1992. "U.S. Earnings Level and Earnings Inequality: A Review of Recent Trends and Proposed Explanations." *Journal of Economic Literature*. September, vol. 30, no. 3: 1333–1381.

Levy, Frank. 1987. *Dollars and Dreams: The Changing American Income Distribution*. New York: Russell Sage Foundation.

Ley, D. 1986. "Alternative Explanations for Inner-City Gentrification. A Canadian Assessment." *Annals of the Association of American Geographers* 76(4): 521–35.

Leyshon, Andrew. 1994. "Under Pressure: Finance, Geo-economic competition and the Rise and Fall of Japan's Postwar Growth Economy." In Corbridge et al., op cit.

———, Peter Daniels, and Nigel Thrift. 1987. "Large Accountancy Firms in the U.K.: Spatial Development." Working Paper, St. David's University College, Lampter, U.K., and University of Liverpool.

Light, Ivan. 1972. *Ethnic Enterprises in America*. Berkeley: University of California Press.

———. 1979. "Disadvantaged Minorities in Self-Employment." *International Journal of Comparative Sociology* 20: 31–45.

———. 1983. *Cities in World Perspective*. New York: Macmillan.

——— and Edna Bonacich. 1988. *Immigrant Entrepreneurs: Koreans in Los Angeles 1965–1982*. Berkeley. University of California Press.

Lipietz, Alain. 1986. "New Tendencies in the International Division of Labor: Regimes of Accumulation and Modes of Regulations." In Allen J. Scott and Michael Storper, eds., *Production, Work, Territory*. Boston: Allen and Unwin.

———. 1987. *Mirages and Miracles: The Crises of Global Fordism*. London: Verso.

Lislie, D.A. 1995. "Global Scan: The Globalisation of Advertising Agencies, Concept and Campaigns." *Economic Geography* 71 (4): 402–426.

Lo, Fu-chen and Yue-man Yeung eds., 1996. *Emerging World Cities in Pacific Asia*. Tokyo: United Nations University

Logan, John. 1978. "Growth, Politics, and the Stratification of Places." *American Journal of Sociology* 84(2): 404–15.

———. 2000. "Still a Global City: The Racial and Ethnic Segregation of New York." In Marcuse, P. and van Kempen, R., eds., *Globalizing Cities*. Oxford: Blackwell.

——— and M. Molotch. 1987. *Urban Fortunes: Making Place in the City*, Berkeley: University of California Press.

——— and P. Taylor-Gooby. n.d. "New Patterns of Inequality in London and New York." In S. Fainstein, I. Gordon, and M. Harloe, eds., *Divided Cities: Economic Restructuring and Social Change in London and New York*. London: Basil Blackwell. Forthcoming.

———, Taylor-Gooby, and M. Reuter. 1993. "Poverty and income inequality." In S. Fainstein, I. Gordon, and H. Harloe, eds., *Divided Cities: New York and London in the Contemporary World*. Oxford: Blackwell.

Lomnitz, Larissa. 1978. "Mechanisms of Articulation between Shantytown Settlers and the Urban System." *Urban Anthropology* 7: 185–205.

London Labour Market Review 1981.

London Research Centre. 1997. *Cosmopolitan London: Past, Present and Future.* London: London Research centre.

———. 1988. *Annual Abstract of Greater London Statistics, 1986–1987.* Vol. 19. London: London Research Centre.

———, Office for National Statistics. 1999. "Focus on London '99." London: London Research Centre.

London Stock Exchange. *Key Statistics 1998.* Website address: www.londonstock-exchange.com/market.

London Strategic Policy Unit. 1986. *Black Workers.* The London Labour Plan.

Losch, August. 1965. "The Nature of Economic Regions." In J. Friedmann and W. Alonso, eds., *Regional Development and Planning.* Cambridge, Mass.: MIT Press.

Low Pay Unit. 1987. *Cheap Labour: Britain's False Economy.* Prepared by Peter Brosnan and Frank Wilkinson. London: Low Pay Unit.

———. 1988a. "Poverty: Is the Government Being 'Statistical with the Truth'?" *Low Pay Review* 34 (Summer): 8–13.

———. 1988b. *The Great Pay Robbery.* Prepared by Chris Pond. London: Low Pay Unit.

Low, S., ed. 1999. *Theorizing the City.* New Brunswick: Rutgers University Press.

Lyons, D. and Salmon, S. 1995. "World cities, multinational corporations, and urban hierarchy: the case of the United States." Chapter 6 in Paul Knox and Peter Taylor, eds., *World Cities in a World System.* Cambridge: Cambridge University Press.

Machimura, Takashi. 1988. "Mechanism of the World Urbanization—New International Distribution and a System of Urbanization Movement." Paper presented at the Japan Urban Sociology Conference held at Tsukuba University, Tsukuba, August.

———. 1998. "Symbolic use of globalization in urban politics in Tokyo." *International Journal of Urban and Regional Research* 22 (2): 183–194.

———. 1999. "A Study of social-polarisation in post 'Bubble' metropolis." Unpublished paper.

Machlup, F. 1962. *The Production and Distribution of Knowledge in the United States.* Princeton, N.J.: Princeton University Press.

Macurdy, T. and Mroz, T. 1995. "Measuring Macroeconomic Shifts in Wages from Cohort Specifications." Presented at the NBER Labor Markets conference in August 1989. Mimeo, Department of Economics, Stanford University.

Marcuse, Peter. 1986. "Abandonment, Gentrification, and Displacement: The Linkages in New York City." In Neil Smith and Peter Williams, eds., *Gentrification of the City.* Boston: Allen and Unwin.

——— and R. van Kempen, eds. 2000. *Globalizing Cities: A New Spatial Order?* Oxford; Malden, Mass.: Blackwell.

Markusen, A. 1981. "City Spatial Structure, Women's Household Work, and National Urban Policy." In C. Stimpson, E. Dexler, M. J. Nelson, and K. B. Yatrakis, eds., *Women and the American City.* Chicago: University of Chicago Press.

———. 1985. *Profit Cycles, Oligopoly, and Regional Development.* Cambridge, Mass.: MIT Press.

Markusen, A. 1996. "Sticky places in slippery space: a typology of industrial districts." *Economic Geography*, 72: 293–313.

——— and V. Carlson. 1989. "De-industrialization in the American Midwest: Causes and Responses." In L. Rodwin and H. Sazanami, eds., *De-industrialization and Regional Economic Transformation: The Experience of the United States and Japan*. Winchester, Mass.: Unwin Hyman.

——— and McCurdy, K. 1989. "Chicago's Defense-Based High Technology: A Case Study of the 'Seedbeds of Innovation' Hypothesis," *Economic Development Quarterly*, vol. 3, February: 15–31.

Marlier, E. and S. Ponthieux. 2000. "Low-wage Employees in EU Countries." Luxembourg: EUROSTAT.

Marquand, J. 1979. *The Service Sector and Regional Policy in the United Kingdom*. Research Series no. 29. London: Centre for Environmental Studies.

Marshall, J. N. 1979. "Corporate Organisation and Regional Office Employment. *Environment and Planning A* 11: 553–64.

———. 1982. "Linkages between Manufacturing and Business Services." *Environment and Planning A*. 14: 1523–40.

———. 1983. "Business Service Activities in British Provincial Conurbations." *Environment and Planning* 15: 1343–59.

Marshall, J. N. et al. 1986. *Uneven Development in the Service Economy: Understanding the Location and Role of Producer Services*. Report of the Producer Services Working Party, Institute of British Geographers and the ESRC, August.

Marshall, J.N. and P.A. Wood. 1995. *Services and Space*. London: Longman.

Martin, J. E. 1966. *Greater London: An Industrial Geography*. London: C. Bell and Sons.

Martin, R. 1988. "Industrial Capitalism in Transition: The Contemporary Reorganization of the British Space Economy." In D. Massey and J. Allen, eds., *Uneven Re-Development: Cities and Regions in Transition*. London: Hodder and Stoughton.

Martindale-Hubbell Corporate Law Directory. 1998, 1999 and 2000. New Providence, N.J.

Massey, D. and Nancy Denton. 1993. *American Apartheid: Segregation and the Making of the Underclass*. Cambridge: Harvard University Press.

Massey, Doreen. 1984. *Spatial Divisions of Labour: Social Structures and the Geography of Production*. London: Macmillan.

Mastropasqua, Salvatore. 1978. *The Banking System in the Countries of the EEC: Institutional and Structural Aspects*. Germantown, Md.: Sijthoff and Noordhoff.

Mayer, H. 1969. "Making a living in Cities: The Urban Economic Base." *Journal of Geography* 18(2): 70–87.

McCall, L. 1998. "Spatial routes to gender wage (in)equality: regional restructuring and wage differentials by gender and education." *Economic Geography*, vol. 74(4): 397–404.

McCann, P. 1995. "Rethinking the Economies of Location and Agglomeration." *Urban Studies*, 32: 563–577.

McDowell, Linda. 1997. *Capital Culture*. Oxford: Blackwell.

Menahem, G. 2000. "Jews, Arabs, Russians and Foreigners in an Israeli City:

Ethnic Divisions and the Restructuring Economy of Tel Aviv, 1983–96." *International Journal of Urban and Regional Research.* 24 (2): 634–653.

Merrill Lynch. Gallup Global Fund Manager Survey, March 13, 2000.

Meyer, D. 1986. "The world system of cities: relations between international financial metropolises and South American cities." *Social Forces,* 64 (3): 553–581.

Meyer, David. 2001. "Hong Kong." In Sassen, S., ed., *Global Networks/Citylinks.* New York and London: Routledge.

———. 2001. "Synergy Between Hong Kong's Global Networks of Capital and Its Telematics." In Sassen, S., ed., *Global Networks/City Links.* London: Routledge.

Michigan State, City of Detroit. 1983. *Annual Overall Economic Development Program Report and Program Projection.* Detroit: Planning Department.

Miles, I. 1985. *The Service Economy and Socioeconomic Development.* Paper prepared for UNCTAD Science Policy Research Unit, University of Sussex.

Mineo, Imai. 1988. "Foreign Employment I: Special Report, No More 'Pure-Blood Principle,' the Age of Internal Internationalism." *Toyo Keizai Weekly Magazine,* March 12: 5–10.

Mitchell, M. and Saskia Sassen. 1996. "Can cities like New York bet on manufacturing?" in *Manufacturing Cities: Competitive Advantage and the Urban Industrial Community.* Conference sponsored by the Harvard University Graduate School of Design and The Loeb Fellowship. Cambridge, Mass. March 8, 1996.

Mitchelson, R. L. and J. O. Wheeler. 1994. "The Flow of Information in a Global Economy: The Role of the American Urban System in 1990." *Annals of the Association of American Geographers* 84 (1): 87–107.

MITI (Japan Ministry of International Trade and Industry). 1974. *Foreign Trade of Japan, 1974.* Tokyo: MITI.

———. 1985a. *Statistics on Japanese Industries, 1985.*

———. 1985b. *White Paper on Economic Cooperation, 1985.*

———. 1985c. *White Paper on International Trade, 1985.*

———. 1986. *White Paper on International Trade, 1986.*

———. 1987. *White Paper on Small and Medium Enterprises in Japan, 1987.*

Mitter, S. 1986. "Industrial Restructuring and Manufacturing Homework: Immigrant Women in the U.K. Clothing Industry." *Capital and Class,* no. 27: 37–80.

Miyakawa, Yasuo. 1983. "Metamorphosis of the Capital and Evolution of the Urban System in Japan." *Ekistics* 50: 110–22.

Miyamoto, Ken'ichi, Yokota Shigeru, Nakamure Kojiro, 1990. *The Regional Economy.* Tokyo: Yichikaku.

Miyazaki, Isamu et al. 1987. *Opinions on Japan's Economic Restructuring.* Reference Reading Series 18. Tokyo: Foreign Press Center.

Mollenkopf, John. 1984. *The Corporate Legal Services Industry.* A Report to New York City's Office of Economic Development.

——— and Manuel Castells, eds. 1991. *Dual City: The Restructuring of New York.* New York: Russell Sage Foundation.

Moody's Investors Service. 1984. *Moody's Bank and Finance Manual.* New York: Moody's Investors Service.

Morales, R. 1994. *Flexible Production: Restructuring of the International Automobile Industry.* Cambridge, UK: Polity Press.

Morgan Guarantee Trust. Various years. *World Financial Markets,* various issues New York: Morgan Guarantee Trust.

Morgan Stanley. 1987. *Morgan Stanley Capital International Perspectives,* October. New York: Morgan Stanley.

———. 1988a. *Morgan Stanley Capital International Perspectives,* January.

———. 1988b. *Morgan Stanley Capital International Perspectives,* October.

———. 1990. *Morgan Stanley Capital International Perspectives,* January.

———. 1998. *Morgan Stanley Capital International Perspectives.* January.

———. 2000. *Morgan Stanley Capital International Perspectives,* January.

Morris, J. L. 1988. "Producer Services and the Regions: the case of large accountancy firms." *Environment and Planning,* vol. 20: 741–759.

Moss, Mitchell L. 1986. "Telecommunications and the Future of Cities." *Land Development Studies* 3: 33–34.

———. 1988. "Telecommunications and International Financial Centers." *Information and Behavior* 3: 239–52.

Moss, Mitchell L., and A. Dunau. 1986. "Office, Information Technology, and Locational Trends." In R. Lipper, A. Sugarman, and R. Cushman, eds., *Teleports and the Intelligent City.* New York: Dow-Jones-Irwin.

Moss, M. L. and A. M. Townsend. 2000. "The Internet Backbone and the American Metropolis." *The Information Society Journal,* 16(1): 35–47.

———. 1999a. "How Telecommunications Systems are Transforming Urban Spaces." In J. Wheeler et al., eds., op cit.

Moulaert, F. 1994. "Arthur Andersen: from national accounting to international management consulting firm." In J. E. Nilsson, P. Dicken, and J. Peck, eds., *Transnational Corporations in Europe: Functional and Spatial Divisions of Labour.* London: Chapman.

——— and F. Djellal. 1995. "Information technology consultancy firms: economies of agglomeration from a wide area perspective." *Urban Studies,* vol. 32, no. 1: 105–122.

——— and Allen J. Scott, eds. 1997. *Cities, Enterprises and Societies on the Eve of the 21st. Century.* London: Pinter.

——— and F. Tödtling. 1995. "The geography of advanced producer services in Europe: conclusion and prospects." *Progress in Planning,* vol. 43, parts 2–3: 261–274.

Mozere, L., Peraldi, M., and Henri Rey, eds. 1999. *Intelligence Des Banlieues.* La Tour d'Aigues: Editiones de l'Aube.

Multinational Monitor. 1983. *Focus: Women and Multinationals.* Special issue of *Multinational Monitor* 4(8): (August).

Murakami, Yasuske, and Yukata Kosai, eds. 1986. *Japan in the Global Community: Its Role and Contribution on the Eve of the 21st Century.* Tokyo: University of Tokyo Press.

Murata, Kiyoji. 1980. *An Industrial Geography of Japan.* New York: St. Martin's Press.

———. 1988. *Tokyo no Sangyokozo no Henbo* (Industry Restructuring in Tokyo). Typescript, Chuo University.

Murie, A. and S. Musterd. 1996. "Social Segregation, Housing Tenure and Social Change in Dutch Cities in the late 1980s." *Urban Studies* 33 (3): 495–516.

Nakabayashi, Itsuki. 1987. "Social-Economic and Living Conditions of Tokyo's Inner City." Reprinted from *Geographical Reports of Tokyo Metropolitan University*, no. 22.

Nakamura, Hachiro. 1985. *Development of Chonaikai in Prewar Days of Tokyo.* Special issue of *Tsukuba Journal of Sociology* 9 (1 and 2). English reprint available from University of Tsukuba, Tsukuba, Japan.

———. 1986. *Tokyo in the Last Few Decades,* Special issue of *Tsukuba Journal of Sociology* 10. English reprint available from University of Tsukuba, Tsukuba, Japan.

———. 1988. *Urban Growth in Prewar Days of Modern Japan.* Special issue of *Tsukuba Journal of Sociology* 13. English reprint available from University of Tsukuba, Tsukuba, Japan.

Nariai, Osamu. 1988. *Progress of Japan's Economic Restructuring and Future Taxes.* Reference Reading Series no. 20. Tokyo: Foreign Press Center, Japan.

Narita, K. 1980. "Inner-City Problems in European and American Cities." *Jutaku: A Monthly of Housing* 29(7): 21–27. Tokyo: Japan Housing Association.

Nash, June, and M. P. Fernandez-Kelly, eds. 1983. *Women, Men and the International Division of Labor.* New York: State University of New York Press.

National Economic Development Office, see NEDO.

National Homeless Alliance. 2000. *Homelessness—the Facts.* London: NHA.

Nederlandse Bank. 1988. *Survey of Current Business.* Quarterly statistics. Amsterdam: Nederland.

NEDO (National Economic Development Office). 1985. *Employment Perspectives and the Distributive Trades.* London: NEDO.

Nelson, Daniel. 1975. *Managers and Workers: Origins of the New Factory System in the United States, 1880–1920.* Madison: University of Wisconsin Press.

Nelson, Joel I., and Jon Lorence. 1985. "Employment in Service Activities and Inequality in Metropolitan Areas." *Urban Affairs Quarterly* 21(11): 106–25.

Nelson, Kristin 1984. *Back Office and Female Labor Markets: Office Suburbanization in the San Francisco Bay Area.* Ph.D. diss., University of California, Berkeley.

Netzer, Dick. 1974. "The Cloudy Prospects for the City's Economy." *New York Affairs* 1(4): 22–35.

Newman, K. 1989. *Falling from Grace.* New York: Vintage Books.

Newsam, P. 1986. *Annual Report of the Commission for Racial Equality, 1985.* London: Commission for Racial Equality.

New York State Bureau of Labor Statistics. 1996, 1997, 1998. OES Survey.

———. 1998. *Statistical Yearbook 23rd edition.*

New York State Department of Labor. 1982a. *Report to the Governor and the Legislature on the Garment Manufacturing Industry and Industrial Homework.* Albany.

———. 1982. *Study of State-Federal Employment Standards for Industrial Homework in New York City.*

———. 1986. *Occupational Employment in Finance, Insurance and Real Estate, New York State.*

New York State Department of Labor. 1989. *Occupational Needs, 1988–1990, New York City.* New York: Division of Research and Statistics.

——. Various years. Employment Review.

New York State Department of Taxation and Finance. 1986. *The Task Force on the Underground Economy: Preliminary Report.* Albany.

New York State Office of Management and Budget and Office of Economic Development. 1982. *Report on Economic Conditions in New York City: July–December 1981.* Albany: Office of Management and Budget and Office of Economic Development.

——. 1986. *Report on Economic Conditions in New York City: January–April 1986.*

——. 1989. *Report on Economic Conditions in News York City: July–December 1988.*

Nijman, J. 1996. "Breaking the rules: Miami in the urban hierarchy." *Urban Geography* 17 (1): 5–22.

Nomura Sogo Kenkyujo. 1982. *Bunsankei kezai shakai o mezashita kotsu. Tsushintai ni kansuru chosa II—kokusai kotsu yuso kiban no seiritsu joken kiso chosa.* (Investigation of the Transport and Communication Structure with the Emphasis on a Dispersion Model of Economic Society—Fundamental Research into the Conditions for Establishing an International Base in Transport and Communications). Tokyo: Nomura Sogo Kenkyujo.

Noyelle, Thierry. 1984. *The Coming of Age of Management Consulting: Implications for New York City.* Report to New York City's Office of Economic Development.

——. 1986. *New York City and the Emergence of Global Financial Markets.* Report to the Regional Plan Association, New York, November.

—— and A. B. Dutka. 1988. *International Trade in Business Services: Accounting, Advertising, Law and Management Consulting.* Cambridge, Mass.: Ballinger Publishing.

—— and T. M. Stanback 1985. *The Economic Transformation of American Cities.* Totowa, N.J.: Rowman and Allanheld.

Nusbaumer, Jacques, ed. 1987. *Services in the Global Market.* Boston, Dordrecht, and Lancaster: Kluwer Academic Publishers.

O'Connor, David C. 1983. "Changing Patterns of International Production in the Semiconductor Industry: The Role of Transnational Corporations." Mimeo.

Odaka, Konosuke. 1985. "Is the Division of Labor Limited by the Extent of the Market? A Study of Automobile Parts Production in East and Southeast Asia." In K. Ohkawa and G. Ranis, eds., *Japan and the Developing Countries: A Comparative Analysis.* London: Basil Blackwell.

OECD, *see* Organization for Economic Cooperation and Development.

O'Farrell P. N. et al. 1992. "The competitiveness of business service firms in Scotland and the South East of England: an analysis of matched pairs." *Regional Studies*, vol. 26: 519–533.

——. 1993. "The competitiveness of business service firms in Scotland and the South East of England." *Urban Studies*, vol. 30, no. 1: 629–652.

O'Farrell, P. N. and P. A. Wood. 1994. "International market selection by business service firms: key conceptual and methodological issues." *International Business Review*, Vol. 3: 243–261.

————. 1998. "Internationalisation by business service firms: towards a new regionally based conceptual framework." *Environment and Planning A*, vol. 30: 109–128.

———— and J. Zheng. 1996. "Internationalisation by business services: an interregional analysis." *Regional Studies*, vol. 30, no. 2: 101–118.

Office of Management and Budget (1997). North American Industry Classification, Economic Classification Policy Committee. http://www.ntis.gov/naics (March 2, 2001).

Office of the U.S. Trade Representative. *See* United States Department of Commerce, Office of the U.S. Trade Representative.

Ogilvie, Nigel. 1980. "Foreign Banks in the U.S. and Geographic Restrictions on Banking." *Journal of Bank Research*, Summer: 72–79.

Okimura, T. 1980 "Inner Area Problems and Housing." *Jutaku: A Monthly of Housing* 29(7): 13–20. Tokyo: Japan Housing Association.

Olson, Margarethe H. 1983. *Overview of Work-at-Home Trends in the United States*. New York: New York University Graduate School of Business Administration.

Organization for Economic Cooperation and Development (OECD). 1978. *Investing in Developing Countries*. Paris OECD.

————. 1981. *International Investment and Multinational Enterprises: Recent International Direct Investment Trends*.

————. 1983. *OECD Employment Outlook*.

————. 1985. *OECD Employment Outlook*.

————. 1986a. *Main Economic Indicators, September 1986*. Department of Economics and Statistics.

————. 1986b. *Urban Policies in Japan*.

————. 1988a. *Financial Market Trends*, no. 40 (May).

————. 1988b. *Financial Statistics Monthly: International Markets*, April.

————. 1989a. *Financial Market Trends*, no. 43 (May).

————. 1989b. *Financial Statistics Monthly: International Markets*, June.

————. 1981. *Recent International Direct Investment Trends*.

————. 1988. *Financial Market Trends*, no. 69, February 1988.

————. 1993. *Main Economic Indicators*, September 1993.

————. 1994. *The Economic Dimension of Electronic Data Interchange*. Paris: OECD. ICCP Committee.

————. 1998. *Survey of OECD Work on International Investment, 1988–1998*.

————. 1998. *Financial Market Trends*, no. 70.

————. 1998. *Statistics on International Transactions*.

————. 1999. *Financial Market Trends*, no. 73.

————. 1999. *Statistics on International Transactions, 1987–1996*, 1998 Edition. Paris: OECD.

————. 2000. *International direct investment statistics yearbook 1999*. Paris: OECD.

————. 2000a. *Transborder Data Flow Contracts in the Wider Framework Mechanisms for Privacy Protection on Global Networks*. Paris: OECD. Directorate for

Sciences, Technology and Industry; Committee for Information, Computer and Communication Policy." (September 22).

———. 2001. *Labour Market and Social Policy: trends in working hours in OECD countries*, paper no. 45. Paris: OECD.

———. Various years a. *Economic Outlook*, various issues.

———. Various years b. *Monthly Statistics of Foreign Trade*, various issues.

———. Various years c. *Recent International Direct Investment Trends*, various issues.

———. Various years d. *Statistics on Foreign Trade*.

Oriental Economist. 1983. *Japan Economic Yearbook*, 1981–1982.

Orr, J. 2000. "The Evolving New York Regional Economy." Paper presented at the Regional Plan Association's Tenth Regional Assembly, May 3.

——— and Rae Rosen. 2000. "New York-New Jersey Job Expansion to Continue in 2000." Federal Reserve Bank of New York: *Current Issues in Economics and Finance*, vol. 6, no. 5, April.

Osaka Municipal Government. 1987. *Brief Sketch of Osaka*. Osaka, Japan.

———. 1988. *Economic Profile of Osaka City*.

Pahl, R. 1984. *Divisions of Labor*. London: Oxford University Press.

———. 1988. "Some Remarks on Informal Work, Social Polarization and the Social Structure." *International Journal of Urban and Regional Research* 12(2): 247–67.

Palumbo-Liu, David. 1999. *Asian / American*. Stanford: Stanford University Press.

Parker, A. J. 1975. "Hypermarkets: The Changing Pattern of Retailing." *Geography* 60: 120–24.

Parnreiter, C. 2001. "Mexico: The Making of a Global City." In Sassen S., ed., *Global Networks/City Links*. New York and London: Routledge.

Parr, J. 1981. "Temporal change in a central place system." In *Environment and Planning A*, vol. 13: 97–118.

——— and L. Budd. 2000. "Financial Services and the Urban System: An Exploration" *Urban Studies*, vol. 37, no. 3: 593–610.

Parrott, J., A. Meaker, and Z. Nowakowski. 1999. "The State of Working New York, The Illusion of Prosperity: New York in the New Economy." The Fiscal Policy Institute, Sept.

Patrick, Hugh T., and Ryuichiro Tachi, eds. 1987. *Japan and the United States Today: Exchange Rates, Macroeconomic Policies, and Financial Market Innovations*. New York: Columbia University Press.

Peraldi, M. and Evelyne Perrin, eds. 1996. *Reseaux Productifs et Territoires Urbains*. Toulouse: Presses Universitaires du Mirail.

Perrin, Evelyne et Nicole Rousier, eds. 2000. *Ville et Emploi: Le Territoire au coeur des nouvelles formes du travail*. La Tour d'Aigues: Editions de l'Aube.

Persky, J. and W. Wievel. 1994. "The Growing Localness of the Global City." *Economic Geography* 70 (2): 129–143.

Pigott, Charles. 1983. "Financial Report on Japan." *Economic Review* (Federal Reserve Bank of San Francisco), Winter: 25–45.

Piore, M., and C. F. Sabel. 1984. *The Second Industrial Divide: Possibilities for Prosperity*. New York: Basic Books.

Policy Studies Institute. 1984. *Black and White Britain*. London: Policy Studies Institute.

Pollert, Anna. 1988. "The 'Flexible Firm': Fixation or Fact?" *Work, Employment and Society* 2(3): 281–316.

Pond, Chris. 1988. *The Great Pay Robbery*. London: Low Pay Unit.

Porat, Marc U. 1976. *The Information Economy*. Ph.D. diss., Stanford University. 2 vol.

Porter, M. E. 1990. *The Competitive Advantage of Nations*. New York: Free Press.

Porter, Richard D., Thomas D. Simpson, and Eileen Mauskopf. 1979. "Financial Innovation and the Monetary Aggregates." In *Brookings Papers on Economic Activity*: 213–29.

Portes, Alejandro. 1983. "The Informal Sector: Definition, Controversy, and Relation to National Development." *Review* 7 (Summer): 151–74.

——— and John Walton. 1981. *Labor, Class and the International System*. New York: Academic Press.

———, Manual Castells, and Lauren Benton, eds. 1989. *The Informal Economy: Studies in Advanced and Less Developed Countries*. Baltimore: Johns Hopkins University Press.

Porzecanski, Arturo C. 1981. "The International Financial Role of U.S. Commercial Banks: Past and Future." *Journal of Banking and Finance* 5 (December): 5–16.

Powell, W. W. and Laurel Smith-Doerr. 1994. "Networks and Economic Life." In *The Handbook of Economic Sociology*, Smelser, Neil J. and Richard Swedberg, eds. Princeton: Princeton University Press; New York: Russell Sage Foundation.

——— and Paul J. DiMaggio, eds. 1991. *The New institutionalism in organizational analysis*. Chicago: University of Chicago Press.

Pred, A. R. 1976. "The Interurban Transmission of Growth in Advanced Economies: Empirical Findings versus Regional Planning Assumptions. *Regional Studies* 10:151–71.

———. 1977. *City Systems in Advanced Economies*. London: Hutchinson.

——— and P. J. Coppock. 1978. *The United Kingdom Economy*. London: Weidenfeld and Nicholson.

Preteceille, E. 1986. "Collective Consumption, Urban Segregation, and Social Classes." *Environment and Planning D: Society and Space* 4: 145–54.

Quinn, James Brian. 1987. "The Impacts of Technology in the Service Sector." In B. R. Guile and Harvey Brooks, eds., *Technology and Global Industry: Companies and Nations in the Third World Economy*. Washington, D.C.: National Academy Press.

Rakodi, C., ed. 1997. *The Urban Challenge in Africa: growth and management of its large cities*. Tokyo: United Nations University Press.

Razin, E. and I. Light. 1998. "Ethnic Entrepreneurs in America's Largest Metropolitan Areas." *Urban Affairs Review*, vol. 33, no. 3: 332–360.

Regional Plan Association of New York. 1987. *New York in the Global Economy: Studying the Facts and the Issues*. Research Document. New York: Regional Plan Association.

Renooy, P. H. 1984. *Twilight Economy: A Survey of the Informal Economy in the Netherlands*. Research Report, Faculty of Economic Sciences, University of Amsterdam.

Revell, Jack. 1973. *The British Financial System*. London: Macmillan.

Richard Ellis International Property Consultants. 1985. *World Rental Levels*. London: Richard Ellis, Inc.

————. 2001. *World Office Rents*. England: Richard Ellis Inc.

Riddle, Dorothy L. 1985. "Stimulating Economic Development via the Service Sector." Paper prepared for meeting on Services and Development held at UNCTAD, Geneva, December 2–4.

Rimmer, P. J. 1986. "Japan's World Cities: Tokyo, Osaka, Nagoya or Tokaido Megalopolis?" *Development and Change* 17(1): 121–58.

————. 1988. "Japanese Construction Contractors and the Australian States: Another Round of Interstate Rivalry." *International Journal of Urban and Regional Research* 12(3): 404–24.

———— and J. A. Black. 1982. "Land Use-Transport Changes and Global Restructuring in Sydney since the 1970s: The Container Issue." In R. V. Cardew, J. V. Langdale, and D. C. Rich, eds., *Why Cities Change: Urban Development and Economic Change in Sydney*. Sydney: Allen and Unwin.

Roberts, Bryan, Ruth Finnegan, and Duncan Gallie, eds. 1985. *New Approaches to Economic Life/Economic Restructuring: Unemployment and the Social Division of Labor*. Manchester: Manchester University Press.

Roberts, Sam. 1987. "If Companies Move to Suburbs, It Still Hurts." *New York Times*, May 28, B1.

Rodriguez, Nestor P., and J. R. Feagin. 1986. "Urban Specialization in the World System." *Urban Affairs Quarterly* 22(2): 187–220.

Rose, D. 1984. "Rethinking Gentrification: Beyond the Uneven Development of Marxist Theory." *Environment and Planning D: Society and Space* 2(1): 47–74.

Rosenberg, Terry J. 1989. "Poverty in New York City, 1985–1988: The Crisis Continues." Working Paper prepared by the Community Service Society of New York.

Ross, R. and K. Trachte. 1983. "Global Cities and Global Classes: The Peripheralization of Labor in New York City." *Review*, vol. 6, no. 3: 393–431.

Rossi, Frank A. 1986. "Government Impediments to Trade in Accounting Services." *University of Chicago Legal Forum* 1(1): 135–68.

Roulleau-Berger, Laurence. 1999. *Le Travail en Friche*. La Tour d'Aigues: Editions de l'Aube.

Ryu, Ohtomo. 1988. "Foreign Employment III: 'Modern Paradise': Japan for the Third World Countries; Report on Illegal Aliens." *Toyo Keizai Weekly Magazine*, March 12: 15–17.

Sachar, A. 1990. "The global economy and world cities." In A. Sachar and S. Oberg, eds., *The World Economy and the Spatial Organization of Power*. Aldershot: Avenbury.

Safa, Helen I. 1981. "Runaway Shops and Female Employment: The Search for Cheap Labor." *Signs* 7 (Winter): 418–33.

Saito, A. 1998. "Global City Strategy: A Case Study of Tokyo Waterfront Sub-center

Development." A revised version of paper presented at Hiroshima Conference "City, State and Region in a Global Order: Toward the 21st Century." December 19–20, Hiroshima International Conference Center, Hiroshima, Japan.

———. 2001a. "The Politics of Urban Development in a Global City: Tokyo and the Waterfront Sub-Centre Project." (Unpublished Dissertation, Department of Urban and Public Planning, London School of Economics).

———. 2001b. "A Global City in a Developmental State: Urban Planning in Tokyo." In Thornley, A. and Rydin, Y., eds., *Planning in a Globalised World*. Ashgate: Aldershot.

Sakiyama, K. 1981. "Urbanization and Urban Problems: On the Decline of Metropolis." In K. Sakiyama and K. Yoshioka, eds., *Decline and Redevelopment of Metropolis*. Tokyo: Tokyo University Press.

Salomon Brothers, Inc. Various years. *Prospects for Financial Markets*. U.S. ed. Bond market research.

Sapir, Andre, and Ernst Lutz. 1981. "Trade in Services: Economic Determinants and Development Related Issues." World Bank Staff Working Paper, no. 480.

Salzinger, Leslie. 1995. "A Maid by Any Other Name: The Transformation of "Dirty Work" by Central American Immigrants." In Burawoy, M. et al., eds., *Ethnography Unbound: Power and Resistance in the Modern Metropolis*. Berkeley: University of California Press.

Santos, Milton, Maria Adelia A. De Souze, and Maria Laura Silveira, eds., 1994. *Territorio Globalizacao e Fragmentacao*. Sao Paulo: Editorial Hucitec.

Sassen, Saskia. 1982. "Recomposition and Peripheralization at the Core." *Contemporary Marxism* 5: 88–100. (Reisssued in S. Jonas and M. Dixon, eds., *The New Nomads: Immigration and Changes in the New International Division of Labor*. San Francisco: Synthesis Publications.

———. 1988. *The Mobility of Labor and Capital: A Study in International Investment and Labor Flow*. London: Cambridge University Press.

———. 1990. "The Interdependence of Cities." In *The Committee on Urban Studies Report for 1989*. Report prepared for the UNESCO Committee on Urban Studies. Submitted to UNESCO, Paris.

———. 1995. "Immigration and Local Labor Markets" in A. Portes, ed., *The economic sociology of immigration: essays on networks, ethnicity, and entrepreneurship*. New York: Russell Sage Foundation.

———. 1999. "Making the global economy run: the role of national states and private agents." *International Social Science Journal*, September 1999, vol. LI, no. 3.

———. 2001. "Cities in a World Economy: Theoretical and Empirical Elements." In *Handbook on Urban Studies*. Sage Publications, Forthcoming.

Sassen, S. and William Testa (forthcoming). "Chicago As a Global City." University of Chicago Department of Sociology and the Federal Reserve Bank of Chicago.

———. 1996. *Losing Control? Sovereignty in an Age of Globalization*. The 1995 Columbia University Leonard Hastings Schoff Memorial Lectures. New York: Columbia University Press.

———. 1998. *Globalization and Its Discontents. Essays on the Mobility of People and Money*. New York: New Press.

Sassen, S. and William Testa (forthcoming). 1999a. "Global Financial Centers." *Foreign Affairs*, vol. 78, no. 1: 75–87.

———. 1999b. *Guests and Aliens.* New York: New Press.

——— ed. 2000. *Cities and Their Cross-Border Networks.* New York and London: Routledge.

———. 2001. *Cities in a World Economy.* Second ed. Thousand Oaks, Calif.: Pine Forge Press.

———. 2002. *Denationalization: Rights, Obligations, and Authority in a Global Age.* (Forthcoming).

Sassen-Koob, Saskia. 1980. "Immigrants and Minority Workers in the Organization of the Labor Process." *Journal of Ethnic Studies* 8 (Spring): 1–34.

———. 1982. "Recomposition and Peripheralization at the Core." In M. Dixon, S. Jonas, and D. McCaughey, eds., *The New Nomads: Immigration and the New International Division of Labor.* San Francisco: Synthesis Publications.

———. 1984. "The New Labor Demand in Global Cities." In M. P. Smith, ed., *Cities in Transformation,* 139–71. Beverly Hills, Calif.: Sage.

———. 1986. "New York City: Economic Restructuring and Immigration." *Development and Change* 17:85–119.

———. 1989. "New York City's Informal Economy." In A. Portes et al., eds., *The Informal Economy: Studies in Advanced and Less Developed Countries.* Baltimore: Johns Hopkins University Press.

Sassen-Koob, Saskia, and Catherine Benamou. 1985. "Hispanic Women in the Garment and Electronics Industries in the New York Metropolitan Area." Research progress report prepared for the Revson Foundation, New York.

Sassen-Koob, Saskia, and W. Grover. 1986. "Unregistered Work in the New York Metropolitan Area." Working Paper, Columbia University, Program in Urban Planning.

Sauvant, Karl. 1986. *International Trade in Services: The Politics of Transborder Data Flows.* Boulder, Colo., and London: Westview Press.

Sauvant, Karl, and Zbigniew Zimny. 1985 "FDI and TNCs in Services." *CTC Reporter,* no. 2: 24–28.

Savage, Mike, Peter Dinkins, and Tony Fielding. 1988. "Some Social and Political Implications of the Contemporary Fragmentation of the 'Service Class' in Britain." *International Journal of Urban and Regional Research* 12(3): 455–76.

Savitch, H. 1987. "Post-Industrial Planning in New York, Paris, London." *Journal of the American Planning Association* 53(1): 80–144.

———. 1988. *Post-Industrial Cities.* Princeton, N.J.: Princeton University Press.

Savitch, H.V. 1996. "Cities in a Global Era: A New Paradigm for the Next Millenium." In Cohen et al., eds., *Preparing for the Urban Future: Global Pressures and Local Forces.* Washington, D.C.: Woodrow Wilson Center Press and Johns Hopkins Univeristy.

Sazanami, Yoko. 1988. "Japan's Trade and Investment in Finance, Information, Communications, and Business Services." In C. H. Lee and S. Naya, eds., *Trade and Investment in Services in the Asia-Pacific Region.* Center for International Studies, Inha University, South Korea.

Scharenberg, A. 2000. *Berlin: Global City oder Konkursmasse?* Berlin: Karl Dietz Verlag.

Scherer, F. M. 1980. *Industrial Market Structure and Economic Performance.* Chicago: Rand MacNally.

Schiffer, Sueli Ramos. 2000. "São Paulo." In Sassen, S., ed., *Cities and Their Crossborder Networks.* New York and London: Routledge.

Schnorbus, R. and William Strauss. 1996. "The U.S. auto outlook—A global perspective." *Federal Reserve Bank of Chicago, Chicago Fed Letter,* August, no. 108.

Schoenberger, Erica. 1985. "Foreign Manufacturing Investment in the United States: Competitive Strategies and International Location." *Economic Geography* 61(3): 241–59.

———. 1997. *The Cultural Crisis of the Firm.* Oxford: Blackwell.

Schoer, K. 1987. "Part-Time Employment: Britain and West Germany." *Cambridge Journal of Economics* 11(1): 83–94.

Schwartz, Robert 1988. *Equity Markets.* New York: Harper and Row.

Scott, A. J. 1993. *Technopolis: High-Technology Industry and Regional Development in Southern California.* Berkeley: University of California Press.

Scott, Allen J. 1986. "Industrialization and Urbanization: A Geographical Agenda." *Annual of the Association of American Geographers* 76:25–37.

———, ed. 2000. *Global City-Regions: Trends, Theory, Policy.* Oxford: Oxford University Press.

———. 1988. *Metropolis. From the Division of Labor to Urban Form.* Berkeley: University of California Press.

——— and Michael Storper, eds. 1986. *Production, Work, Territory.* Boston: Allen and Unwin.

Sekio, Sugioka. 1987. *Internationalization and Regional Structure.* Chiba, Japan: Chiba University.

Shah, S. 1975. *Immigrants and Employment in the Clothing Industry—the Rag Trade In London's East End.* London: Runnymede Trust.

Shaiken, Harley. 1985. *Work Transformed: Automation and Labor in the Computer Age.* New York: Holt, Rinehart and Winston.

Shapira, Philip. 1984. "The Crumbling of Smokestack California: A Case Study in Industrial Restructuring and the Reorganization of Work." Institute of Urban and Regional Development Working Paper, no. 437. Berkeley, Calif.

——— and Plant Closure Project. 1983. *Shutdowns and Job Losses in California: The Need for New National Priorities.* Testimony prepared for the Subcommittee on Labor Management Relations, Subcommittee on Employment Opportunities, U.S. House of Representatives, Hearing on H.R. 2847, Los Angeles, Calif., July 8.

Sheard, P. 1982. "Auto-Production Systems in Japan: Some Organisational and Locational Features." *Australian Geographical Studies* 21: 49–68.

Sheets, R. G., S. Nord, and J. J. Phelps. 1987. *The Impact of Service Industries on Underemployment in Metropolitan Economies.* Lexington, Mass.: D. C. Heath and Company.

Shelp, Ronald Kent. 1981. *Beyond Industrialization: Ascendancy of the Global Service Economy.* New York: Praeger.

Shibata, Tokue. 1988. "The Post-War Japanese Economy and Its Infrastructure." Typescript. Tokyo Keizai University.

Short, John R. and Y. Kim. 1999. *Globalization and the City*. Essex: Longman.

Shrkoy, M. 1994. "London's Ethnic Minorities: One City Many Communities. An Analysis of 1991 Census Results." London: London Research Centre.

Silber, William. 1983. "The Process of Financial Innovation." *American Economic Review* 73(2): 89–95.

Singelmann, J. 1974. "The Sectoral Transformation of the Labor Force in Seven Industrialized Countries, 1920–1960." Ph.D. diss., University of Texas.

———. 1978. *From Agriculture to Services: The Transformation of Industrial Employment*. Beverly Hills and London: Sage.

——— and H. L. Browning. 1980. "Industrial Transformation and Occupational Change in the U.S., 1960–70." *Social Forces* 59: 246–64.

Sinkey, Joseph F. 1979. *Problem and Failed Institutions in the Commercial Bank Industry*. Vol. 4 of *Contemporary Studies in Economic and Financial Analysis*. Greenwich, Conn.: Jai Press.

Skeldon, R. 1997. "Hong Kong: Colonial City to Global City to Provincial City?" *Cities* 14, 5: 265–71.

Sklair, Leslie. 1985. "Shenzhen: A Chinese 'Development Zone' in Global Perspective." *Development and Change* 16: 571–602.

Skocpol, Theda. 1985. "Bringing the State Back In: Strategies of Analysis in Current Research." In Peter Evans, Dietrich Rueschemeyer, and Theda Skocpol, eds., *Bringing the State Back In*. New York: Cambridge University Press.

Smith, Beverly. 1986. "Democracy Derailed: Citizens' Movements in Historical Perspective." In Gavan McCormack and Yoshio Sugimoto, eds., *Democracy in Contemporary Japan*. New York: M. E. Sharpe.

Smith, Carol A. 1985. "Theories and Measures of Urban Primacy: A Critique." In M. Timberlake, ed., *Urbanization in the World-Economy*. New York: Academic Press.

Smith, D. and Timberlake, M. 2001. "Cities in Global Matrices." In Sassen, S., ed., *Global Networks/City Links*. New York and London: Routledge.

Smith, M. P. 1987. "Global Capital Restructuring and Local Political Crises in U.S. Cities." In J. Henderson and M. Castells, eds., *Global Restructuring and Territorial Development*. London: Sage.

———. 1988. *City, State and Market: The Political Economy of Urban Society*. New York: Basil Blackwell.

———. 1998. "The Global City: Whose Social Construct Is It Anyway?" Urban Affairs Review, vol. 33, no. 4, March 482–88.

——— and J. R. Feagin. 1987. *The Capitalist City: Global Restructuring and Community Politics*. Oxford: Basil Blackwell.

Smith, N. 1982. "Gentrification and Uneven Development." *Economic Geography* 58(2): 24–35.

———. 1984. *Uneven Development: Nature, Capital and the Production of Space*. New York: Basil Blackwell.

———. 1987. "Of Yuppies and Housing: Gentrification, Social Restructuring, and the Urban Dream." *Environment and Planning D: Society and Space* 5: 151–72.

———. 1996. *The New Urban Frontier*. London: Routledge.

——— and P. Williams. 1986. *Gentrification of the City*. Boston: Allen and Unwin.

Smith, Paul F. 1982. "Structural Disequilibrium and the Banking Act of 1980." *Journal of Finance* (May): 385–98.

Smith, Robert C. 1997. "Transnational Migration, Assimilation and Political Community." In M. Crahan and A. Vourvoulias-Bush. eds., *The City and the World.* New York: Council on Foreign Relations.

Soja, Edward W. 1989. *Postmodern Geographies: The Reassertion of Space in Critical Social Theory.* London: Verso.

————, R. Morales, and G. Wolff. 1983. "Urban Restructuring: An Analysis of Social and Spatial Change in Los Angeles." *Economic Geography* 59(2): 195–230.

Spitznas, Thomas. 1981. "Estimating the Size of the Underground Economy in New York City." *The Regional Economic Digest* (semiannual publication of the New York Regional Economists' Society) 1(1): 1–3.

Squires, G., L. Bennett, K. McCourt, and P. Nyden. 1987. *Chicago: Race, Class, and the Response to Urban Decline.* Philadelphia: Temple University Press.

Stanback, Thomas M., Jr., 1979. *Understanding the Service Economy.* Baltimore: Johns Hopkins University Press.

———— and Thierry J. Noyelle. 1982. *Cities in Transition: Changing Job Structures in Atlanta, Denver, Buffalo, Phoenix, Columbus (Ohio), Nashville, Charlotte.* Totowa, N.J.: Allanheld, Osmun.

————, Peter J. Bearse, Thierry J. Noyelle, and Robert Karasek. 1981. *Services: The New Economy.* Totowa, N.J.: Allanheld, Osmun.

Standing, Guy. 1989. "The 'British Experiment': Structural Adjustment or Accelerated Decline?" In A. Portes et al., eds., *The Informal Economy: Studies in Advanced and Less Developed Countries.* Baltimore: Johns Hopkins University Press.

Stegman, M. 1985. *Housing in New York: Study of a City, 1984.* New York: Department of Housing Preservation and Development, New York City.

————. 1988. *Housing and Vacancy Report, New York City, 1987.* New York: Department of Housing Preservation and Development, New York City.

Stephens, J. D., and B. P. Holly. 1981. "City System Behaviour and Corporate Influence: The Headquarters Locations of U.S. Industrial Firms, 1955–75." *Urban Studies* 18:285–300.

Stepick, Alex. 1989. "Miami's Two Informal Sectors." In A. Portes et al., eds., *The Informal Economy: Studies in Advanced and Less Developed Countries.* Baltimore: Johns Hopkins University Press.

Steven, Rob. 1983. *Classes in Contemporary Japan.* Cambridge: Cambridge University Press.

Stigler, George. 1951. "The Division of Labor Is Limited by the Extent of the Market." *Journal of Political Economy* 59(3): 185–93.

Stoffaës, C. 1981. "L'emploi et la révolution informationnelle." *Informatisation et Emploi, Menace ou Mutation?* Paris: La Documentation Française.

Stone, Charles F., and Isabel V. Sawhill. 1986. *Labor Market Implications of the Growing Internationalization of the U.S. Economy.* National Commission for Employment Policy Research Report, no. RR8620. Washington, D.C.

Storper, Michael, and David Walker. 1983. "The Labor Theory of Location." *International Journal of Urban and Regional Research* 7(1): 1–41.

Stren, Richard. 1996. "The Studies of Cities: Popular Perceptions, Academic Disciplines, and Emerging Agendas." In Cohen et al., eds., *Preparing for the Urban Future: Global Pressures and Local Forces*. Washington, D.C.: Woodrow Wilson Center Press and Johns Hopkins University.

Strober, Myra H., and Carolyn L. Arnold. 1987. "Integrated Circuits/Segregated Labor: Women in Computer-Related Occupations and High-Tech Industries." In Heidi I. Hartmann, ed., *Computer Chips and Paper Clips*. Washington, D.C.: National Academy Press.

Stuart, A. 1989. *The Social and Geographical Mobility of South Asians and Caribbeans in Middle-Age and Later Working Life*. LS Working Paper, no. 61, City University, London.

Sum, Ngai-Ling. 1999. "Rethinking Globalisation: Re-articulating the Spatial Scale and Temporal Horizons of Trans-border Spaces." In Olds, K. et al., eds., *Globalization and the Asian Pacific: Contested Territories*. London: Routledge.

Survey of Current Business, International Investment Division. 1981a. "U.S. Business Enterprises Acquired or Established by Foreign Direct Investors in 1979." *Survey of Current Business* 61(1): 28–39.

———. 1981b. "1977 Benchmark Survey of U.S. Direct Investment Abroad." *Survey of Current Business* 61(4): 29–37.

———. 1984. "Plant and Equipment Expenditures, First and Second Quarters and Second Half of 1984." *Survey of Current Business* 64(3): 26–31.

———. 1985a. "Foreign Direct Investment in the United States: Country and Industry Detail for Position and Balance of Payments Flows, 1984." *Survey of Current Business* 65(8): 47–66.

———. 1985b. "U.S. Direct Investment Abroad: Country and Industry Detail for Position and Balance of Payments Flows, 1984." *Survey of Current Business* 65(8): 30–46.

———. 1986a. "U.S. Direct Investment Abroad: Detail for Position and Balance of Payments Flows, 1985." *Survey of Current Business* 66(8): 40–73.

———. 1986b. "Foreign Direct Investment in the U.S.: Detail for Position and Balance of Payments Flows, 1985." *Survey of Current Business* 66(8): 74–88.

———. 1987. "U.S. Sales of Services to Foreigners." *Survey of Current Business* 67(1): 22–39.

———. 1988a. "Foreign Direct Investment in the United States: Detail for Position and Balance of Payments Flows, 1987." *Survey of Current Business* 68(8): 69–83.

———. 1988b. "International Services: New Information on U.S. Transactions with Unaffiliated Foreigners." *Survey of Current Business* 68(10): 27–34.

———. 1988c. "U.S. Direct Investment Abroad: Detail for Position and Balance of Payments Flows, 1987." *Survey of Current Business* 68(8): 42–68.

———. 1989a. "The International Investment Position of the U.S. in 1988." *Survey of Current Business* 69(6): 41–49.

———. 1989b. "U.S. Direct Investment Abroad: Detail for Position and Balance of Payments Flows, 1988." *Survey of Current Business* 69(8): 47–61.

———. 1989c. "Foreign Direct Investment in the U.S.: Detail for Position and Balance of Payments Flows, 1988." *Survey of Current Business* 69(8): 62–88.

———. 1998a. "United States Direct Investment Abroad." 79 (10): 117–156.

————. 1998b. "Annual NIPA Revision: Newly Available tables." 78(10): 5–15.

————. 1998c. "Foreign Direct Investment in the United States. Detail for Historical-Cost Position and Related Capital Flows 1997." 78(9): 74–110.

————. 1999. "U.S. International Services: Cross-Border Trade in 1998 and Sales Through Affiliates in 1997." 80 (10): 48–95.

Susser, I. 1982. *Norman Street, Poverty and Politics in an Urban Neighborhood.* New York: Oxford University Press.

————. 1988. "Households, Social Reproduction and the Changing Economy of New York City." Paper prepared for a meeting of the Dual City Working Group held in New York City, November 11–12. New York: Committee on New York City, Social Science Research Council.

and Reform in Japan and the United States." In H. Patrick and R. Tachi, eds., *Japan and the United States Today: Exchange Rates, Macroeconomic Policies, and Financial Market Innovations.* New York: Columbia University Press.

Suzuki, Y., and H. Yomo, eds. 1986. *Financial Innovation and Monetary Policy: Asia and the West.* Proceedings of the Second International Conference. Tokyo: University of Tokyo Press.

Tabak, F. and Michaeline A. Chrichlow, eds. 2000. *Informalization: Process and structure.* Baltimore, Md: The Johns Hopkins University Press.

Tachabanaki, T. and Yagi, T. 1995. "Distribution of Economic Well Being in Japan: Towards a More Equal Society." In Peter Gottschalk, Biorn, A. Gustafsson, and Edward Palmer, eds., *The Distribution of Economic Welfare in the 1990s.* Cambridge: Cambridge University Press.

Tanzi, Vito. 1982. *The Underground Economy in the United States and Abroad.* Lexington, Mass.: D. C. Heath.

Tauchen, H., and A. D. Witte. 1983. "An Equilibrium Model of Office Location Contact Patterns." *Environment and Planning A* 15: 1311–26.

Taylor, Peter J. 2000. "World Cities and territorial states under conditions of contemporary globalization." *Political Geography* 19(5): 5–32.

Taylor-Gooby, P. 1989. *Polarization, Privatization and Attitudes to Poverty.* Mimeo. University of Kent at Canterbury, Social Policy Department.

Teranishi, K. 1990. "Tokyo Rinkaibu Kaihatu No Kadai To Tenbo" (Problem and Prospect of Waterfront Development in Tokyo). *Tokyo Kou,* 172: 1–19.

Teranishi, S. 1991. "Sekai Toshi To Tokyo Mondai (Global City and Tokyo Problem)." *Keizaigaku Kenkyu,* vol. 32: 161–213.

Terasaka, Akinobu et al. 1988. "The Transformation of Regional Systems in an Information-Oriented Society." *Geographical Review of Japan* 61(1): 159–73.

Tetsu, Naito. 1988. "Foreign Employment II: Demand-Supply Theory No Longer Applies; Receiving of Unskilled Laborforce." *Toyo Keizai Weekly Magazine* 12: 12–14.

The Guardian. 1993. "European Federation for Retirement Provision." October 5, 1993.

Thomas, Margaret. 1983. "The Leading Euromarket Law Firms in Hong Kong and Singapore." *International Financial Law Review* (June): 4–8.

Thomson Financial. 1999. *International Target Cities Report.* New York: Thomson Financial Investor Relations.

Thrift, N. 1987. "The Fixers: The Urban Geography of International Commercial Capital." In J. Henderson and M. Castells, eds., *Global Restructuring and Territorial Development*. London: Sage.

———. 1994. "On the Social and Cultural Determinants of International Financial Centres: the Case of the City of London." In Corbridge, S. et al., eds., *Money, Power and Space*. Oxford and Cambridge: Blackwell.

——— and P. Williams, eds. 1987. *Class and Space*. London: Macmillan.

Thurow, Lester C. 1980. *The Zero-Sum Society*. New York: Basic Books.

———. 1989. "Regional Transformation and Service Activities." In Lloyd Rodwin and Hidehiko Sazanami, eds., *Deindustrialization and Regional Economic Transformation*. Boston: Unwin Hyman.

Tiebout, C. 1957. "Location Theory, Empirical Evidence, and Economic Evolution." *Papers and Proceedings of the Regional Science Association* 3: 74–86.

Tienda, Marta, Leif Jensen, and Robert L. Bach. 1984. "Immigration, Gender and the Process of Occupational Change in the U.S., 1970–1980." *International Migration Review* 17(4): 1021–24.

Timberlake, Michael, ed. 1985. *Urbanization in the World-Economy*. Orlando, Fla.: Academic Press.

TMG. 2000. *Statistical Yearbook of Economy and Labour*. Tokyo: TMG; Bureau of Labor and Economic Affairs.

TMG. 2001. *White Paper on Homelessness in Tokyo*. Tokyo: TMG; (March).

Tobier, Emanuel. 1984. *The Changing Face of Poverty: Trends in New York City's Population in Poverty, 1960–1990*. New York: Community Service Society of New York.

———. 1990. "The Homeless." In C. Brecher and R. Horton, eds., *Setting Municipal Priorities 1991*. New York: New York University Press.

Tokyo Department of City Planning. 1988. *Report 1: The Problem of Foreign Labor—Opinions of Ministries*. Tokyo: Department of City Planning.

Tokyo Keizai Data Bank. 1999. *Nihon no Kaisha (74,000 Nenban Companies in Japan Yearbook)*. Tokyo Keizani Shinposha: Tokyo.

Tokyo Metropolitan Government, 1983. *Survey of Tokyo Daytime Population*. Tokyo: TMG.

———. 1984. *Plain Talk About Tokyo*, 2d ed.

———. 1986. *Tokyo Statistical Yearbook*.

———. 1988. *Trends of Labor and Wages in Tokyo-to*, April 1988.

———. 1983. *Survey of Tokyo Daytime Population*.

———. 1984a. *Long-Term Plan for Tokyo Metropolis*.

———. 1984b. *Plain Talk about Tokyo, 1984*. TMG Municipal Library Publication.

———. 1985. *Report on Land-Related Data, 1984*.

———. 1986. "Distribution of Tokyo's Fashion Industries." Unpublished report.

———. 1987a. *Tokyo Statistical Yearbook 1985*.

———. 1987b. *Talk about Tokyo, 1987*.

———. 1987c. *Tokyo Emergency Land Use Report*, 1–5. October 15.

———. 1988a. *Statistical Annual Report on Metropolitan Citizens' Incomes*.

———. 1988b. *Trends of Labor and Wages in Tokyo-to, Monthly Report*. April.

———. 1988c. "Land Value Shift December 1986–December 1987." Unpublished report.

——. 1997. *Tokyo Statistical Yearbook.*

——. Various years. *Monthly Labor Survey.*

Tokyo Stock Exchange. 1988. *Tokyo Stock Exchange 1988 Fact Book.* Tokyo: Tokyo Stock Exchange.

Touraine, Alain. 1969. *La Société post-industrielle.* Paris: Denoel.

Townsend, P. 1979. *Poverty in the United Kingdom.* Berkeley: University of California Press.

——. 1985. "A Sociological Approach to the Measurement of Poverty—A Rejoinder to Professor Amartya Sen. *Oxford Economic Papers* 37(4): 659–68.

——, with P. Corrigan and U. Kowarzik 1987. *Poverty and Labour in London—Interim Report of a Centenary Survey.* London: Low Pay Unit.

Toyoshima, Toshihiro. 1988. *Growing Foreign Investors' Activities and the Future of Internationalization.* Report no. 12. Tokyo: Japan Development Bank.

Trachte, K., and R. Ross. 1985. "The Crisis of Detroit and the Emergence of Global Capitalism." *International Journal of Urban and Regional Research* 9: 216–17.

Tsuda, T. 1999. "The Permanence of "Temporary" Migration: The "Structural Embeddedness" of Japanese-Brazilian Immigrant Workers in Japan." *The Journal of Asian Studies,* vol. 58, no. 3: 687–722.

Tucker, K. A., and Mark Sundberg. 1988. *International Trade in Services.* London and New York: Routledge.

Tucker, K. A., M. Sundberg, and G. Seow. 1983. "Services in ASEAN-Australian Trade." In *ASEAN-Australian Economic Papers,* no 2. Kuala Lumpur and Canberra.

United Kingdom Central Statistical Office. 1986. *Regional Trends.* London: HMSO.

——. Various years. *Annual Abstract of Statistics.*

United Kingdom Department of Employment. 1982. *Census of Employment, 1981.* London: HMSO.

——. 1984. *New Earnings Survey.*

——. 1985. *Annual Family Expenditure Survey, 1985.*

——. 1986. *Employment Gazette, 1986.*

——. 1987a. "Census of Employment, 1984." *Employment Gazette,* January.

——. 1987b. *Employment Gazette.* Historical Supplement no. 2, October.

——. 1987c. *New Earnings Survey.*

——. 1988. "Ethnic Origins in the Labour Market." *Employment Gazette,* March: 164–77.

——. Various years. *Annual Family Expenditure Survey.*

United Kingdom Inner London Education Authority. 1987. *The London Labor Market-Facts and Figures.* May.

United Kingdom Office of Population and Surveys. 1963. *Census 1961, England and Wales.* London: HMSO.

——. 1973. *Census 1971, England and Wales.*

——. 1983. *Census 1981, England and Wales.*

United Kingdom, Office for National Statistics. 1990. *New Earnings Survey.*

——. 1995. *Annual Employment Survey.*

——. 1996. *Annual Employment Survey.*

United Kingdom, Office for National Statistics. 1996. *Input-Output Tables, Demand for Products.*

———. 1998. *Annual Employment Survey.* Results by Local Authority District/Unitary Authority.

———. 1998. *Labour Market Trends.* Vol. 106. No. 12.

———. 1999. *Earnings and Productivity Division*, UK Labour.

———. 1999. *Focus London '99.*

———. 1999. *Key Statistics for Local Authority and Workplace and Transport to Work Reports.*

———. 1999. *Labour Market Trends.*

———. 1999. *New Earnings Survey, Parts A–G.* (various issues: 1986, 1987, 1990, 1995, 1997).

———. 2000. *Labour Market Trends.* Vol. 108. No. 6.

United Kingdom, Office of Population and Surveys, 1973. Census 1971, *England and Wales.*

———. 1981. *Workplace and Transport to Work Report.*

———. 1983. *Census 1981, England and Wales.*

———. 1991. *Key Statistics for Local Authority and Workplace and Transport to Work.*

United Kingdom Statistics Bureau of the Management and Coordination Agency. 1998. *Labour Force Survey.*

United Kingdom. Department of Employment. 1982. *Census of Employment, 1981.* London: HMSO.

———. 1984. *Census of Unemployment, 1984.*

———. 1987. *Employment Gazette, January 1987.*

———. 1991. *Employment Gazette, February 1991*, vol. 95, no. 10.

United Nations Centre on Transnational Corporations. 1979. *Transnational Corporations in World Development: A Re-Examination.* New York: UN Centre on Transnational Corporations.

———. 1981. *Transnational Banks: Operations, Strategies, and Their Effects in Developing Countries.*

———. 1985. *Trends and Issues in Foreign Direct Investment and Related Flows.*

———. 1989a. *Transnational Service Corporations and Developing Countries: Impact and Policy Issues.*

———. 1989b. *Transnational Corporations and International Economic Relations: Recent Developments and Selected Issues.*

———. 1989c. *Transnational Corporations and the Growth of Services: Some Conceptual and Theoretical Issues.*

———. 1989d. *Foreign Direct Investment and Transnational Corporations in Services.*

United Nations Conference on Trade and Development (UNCTAD). 1994. *World Investment Report 1994: Transnational Corporations, Employment and the Workplace.* New York: UNCTAD.

———. 1996. *World Investment Report 1996: Investment, Trade and International Policy Arrangements.* New York: UNCTAD.

———. 1997. *World Investment Report: Transnational Corporations, Market Structure, and Competition Policy.* New York: UNCTAD.

———. 1998. *World Investment Report: Trends and Determinants.*

——. 1999. *World Investment Report, Foreign Direct Investment and the Challenge of Development.*

United Nations Conference on Trade and Development and United Nations Economic Commission for Europe. 1998. "The Russian Crisis of 1998." Third World Network website: *http://www.twnside.org.sg/title/1998-cn.htm.*

United Nations Department of Economic and Social Affairs. 1996. *Urban Agglomerations.* New York: UN.

——. 1998. *World Economic and Social Survey 1998: Trends and Policies in the World Economy.* New York: UN.

United States Congress. 1978. Senate Committee on Banking, Housing and Urban Affairs. *International Banking Act of 1978.* Washington, D.C.: GPO

——. 1981. House Committee on Banking, Finance and Urban Affairs. *Financial Institutions in a Revolutionary Era.* 97th Cong., 1st sess. Committee Print 97–98. Washington, D.C.: GPO.

——. 1982. Senate Committee on Banking, Housing and Urban Affairs. *Foreign Barriers to U.S. Trade: Service Exports.* Washington, D.C.: GPO.

——. 1985. Office of Technology Assessment (OTA). *Automation of America's Offices.* OTA-CIT-287.

——. 1986. Office of Technology Assessment. *Trade in Service Export and Foreign Revenues, Special Report.* OTA-ITE-316, September.

United States Congressional Budget Office. 1987. *Contract Out: Potential for Reducing Federal Costs.* Washington, D.C.: GPO, June.

United States Department of Commerce, Bureau of the Census. 1977–1987. *County Business Patterns,* issues for the United States, California, Illinois, Michigan, Massachusetts, New York, and Texas for 1977, 1980, 1981, 1982, 1984, 1985, 1986, and 1987.

——. 1981. *1980 Census of Population, Supplementary Report.*

——. 1982a. *1980 Census of Population and Housing Supplementary Report: Provisional Estimates of Social, Economic, and Housing Characteristics.*

——. 1982b. *Annual Housing Survey, 1976 (United States): SMSA Files.* Ann Arbor: Inter-university Consortium for Political and Social Research.

——. 1983. *Statistical Abstracts of the United States, 1983.*

——. 1984. *Annual Housing Survey, 1983 (United States): SMSA Files.* Ann Arbor: Inter-university Consortium for Political and Social Research.

——. 1984. *Place of Work.*

——. Various years a. *Statistical Abstracts of the United States,* various issues.

——. Various years b. *Microdata from the Survey of Income and Education.* Data Access Description no. 42.

United States Department of Commerce, Census Bureau. *County Business Patterns.* U.S. Census Bureau website: *www.census.gov.*

——. issues for the United States, 1983, 1987, 1989, 1995, 1998.

——. issues for the U.S. and New York, 1977, 1981, 1983, 1984, 1985, 1995, 1996, 1997, 1998.

United States Department of Commerce, International Trade Administration. 1970. *Economic Factors Affecting the Use of Items 807.00 and 806.30 of the Tariff Schedules of the United States.* Washington, D.C.: International Trade Administration. *See* United States International Trade Administration.

United States Department of Commerce, International Trade Administration. 1980a. *Current Developments in the U.S. International Service Industries.*

————. 1980b. *Import Trends in TSUS Items 806.30 and 807.00.*

————. 1980c. *Selected Data on U.S. Investment Abroad, 1966–1978.*

————. 1980d. *Market Share Reports.*

————. 1982. *Foreign Economic Trends and Their Implications*, various issues.

————. 1984. *International Direct Investment: Global Trends and the U.S. Role.*

————. 1988. *U.S. Industrial Outlook: Commercial Banking.* (Cited as U.S. Industrial Outlook)

United States Department of Commerce, Office of the U.S. Trade Representative 1983. *U.S. National Study on Trade in Services.* Washington, D.C. GPO.

United States Department of Labor. 1997. Occupational Safety and Health Administration, SIC Search can be found at http://www.osha.gov/oshstats/sicser.html.

United States Department of Labor, Bureau of Labor Statistics. 1979. *Employment and Earnings, for States and Areas, 1939–1978.*

————. 1982a. *Area Wage Survey, New York, 1981.*

————. 1982b. *Geographic Profiles of Employment and Unemployment, 1981.*

————. 1984. *Occupational Employment in Selected Services.*

————. 1985. *Geographic Profiles of Employment and Unemployment, 1984.*

————. 1986a. *Geographic Profiles of Employment and Unemployment, 1985.*

————. 1986b. *National Survey of Professional, Administrative, Technical, and Clerical Pay, March 1986.*

————. 1988. *Area Wage Survey, New York, 1987.*

————. 1989. *The 1989 Mid-Year Report.* New York: BLS, Middle Atlantic Region.

————. 1990. *Employment and Earnings for States and Areas.* Bulletin 1370–24.

————. Various years. *News.* Middle Atlantic Region.

United States Immigration and Naturalization Service, 1972. *Annual Report.* Washington, D.C.: GPO.

————. 1981. *Annual Report.*

————. 1985. *Annual Report.*

————. Document Service. United States Department of Commerce, International Trade Administration.

United Sates International Trade Commission. 2001. *Harmonized Tariff System 9802.* Washington, D.C.: Department of Commerce.

United States Office of Trade Representative. *See* United States Department of Commerce, Office of the U.S. Trade Representative.

United States Office of Management and Budget. 1972. *Standard Industrial Classification Manual*, 278–90.

United States President's Commission for a National Agenda for the Eighties. 1980. *Urban America in the Eighties.* Washington, D.C.: GPO.

United States, Bureau of Labor Statistics. 1998. *Occupational Employment Statistics Survey.* Department of Labor website: *http://stats.bls.gov/oeshome.htm.*

————. 1983. *Survey of Current Business*, September. Washington, D.C.: U.S. Department of Commerce.

————. 1989. *Survey of Current Business.* October.

————. 1999. *Survey of Current Business.* September.

Veltz, Pierre. 1996. *Mondialisation Villes et Territoires: L'Economie d'Archipel.* Paris: Presses Universitaires de France.

Vernon, Raymond. 1966. "International Investment and International Trade in the Product Cycle." *Quarterly Journal of Economics* 80: 190–207.

———. 1979. "The Product Cycle Hypothesis in a New International Environment." *Oxford Bulletin of Economics and Statistics* 41(4): 255–67.

Waite, Donald. 1982. "Deregulation and the Banking Industry." *Bankers Magazine*, January–February: 26–35.

Wall Street Journal. 1986. "Global Finance and Investment." Annual Special Report. *Wall Street Journal*, September 29.

———. 1987. "Global Finance and Investment." Annual Special Report. *Wall Street Journal*, September 18.

———. 1987. "Global Finance and Investment—Annual Special Report," September 29.

———. 1988. "Global Finance and Investment." Annual Special Report. *Wall Street Journal*, September 23.

———. 1989. "World Business." *Wall Street Journal*, September 22.

———. 1998. "Global Finance and Investment." Annual Special Report," September 28.

Walker, Richard. 1996. "Another round of globalization in San Francisco." *Urban Geography* 17 (1): 60–94.

Walter, Ingo. 1985. *Barriers to Trade in Banking and Financial Services*. London: Policy Research Center.

———. 1988. *Global Competition In Financial Services*. Cambridge, Mass.: Ballinger-Harper and Row.

Walters, Pamela Barnhouse. 1985. "Systems of Cities and Urban Primacy: Problems of Definition and Measurement." In M. Timberlake, ed., *Urbanization in the World-Economy*. Orlando, Fla.: Academic Press.

Walton, John. 1982. "The international economy and peripheral urbanization." In I. Norman and S. Fainstein, eds., *Urban Policy Under Capitalism*, op. cit.

Ward, Kathryn B. 1985. "Women and Urbanization in the World-System." In M. Timberlake, ed., *Urbanization in the World-Economy*. Orlando, Fla.: Academic Press.

Warf, B. 1991. "The internationalization of New York Services." In P. W. Daniels ed., *Services and Metropolitan Development: International Perspectives*. London: Routledge.

———. 1994. "Vicious Circle: Financial Markets and Commercial Real Estate in the United States." In Corbridge et al., op. cit.

——— and R. Erickson. 1996. "Introduction: Globalization and the U.S. City System." *Urban Geography* 17(1): 1–4.

Weber, A. 1909. *Theory of the Location of Industries*. Chicago: University of Chicago Press.

Wegener, M. 1995. "The changing urban hierarchy in Europe." In J. Brotchie et al., eds., *Cities in Competition: Productive and Sustainable Cities for the 21ˢᵗ Century*. Melbourne: Longman Australia.

Weitzman, Phillip. 1989. "Worlds Apart: Housing, Race/Ethnicity and Income in New York City, 1978–1987." Working Paper prepared by the Community Service Society of New York.

Weiwel, W. 1988. *The State of the economy and economic development in the Chicago metropolitan region*. Chicago: Metropolitan Planning Council.

Westaway, J. 1974. "The spatial hierarchy of business organization and its implications for the British urban system." *Regional Studies*, vol. 8, no. 11: 145–155.

Wheeler, J., Y. Aoyama, and B. Warf, eds. 1999. *Cities in the telecommunications age: the fracturing of geographies*. New York: Routledge.

Whichard, Obie G. 1981. "Trends in the U.S. Direct Investment Position Abroad, 1950–1979." *Survey of Current Business* 61(2): 39–56.

White, James Wilson. 1976. "Social Change and Community Involvement in Metropolitan Japan." In J. W. White and F. Munger, eds., *Social Change and Community Politics in Urban Japan*. Chapel Hill: University of North Carolina, Institute for Research in Social Sciences.

———. 1998. "Old wine, cracked bottle? Tokyo, Paris, and the Global City Hypothesis." *Urban Affairs Review* 33: 451–477.

———, ed. 1979. *The Urban Impact of Internal Migration*. Chapel Hill: University of North Carolina, Institute for Research in Social Sciences.

Whittemore, F. 1987. "Internationalization of Investment Banking." In H. Patrick and R. Tachi, eds., *Japan and the United States Today: Exchange Rates, Macroeconomic Policies, and Financial Market Innovations*. New York: Columbia University Press.

Williams, C. C. 1997. *Consumer Services and Economic Development*. London: Routledge.

Williamson, B. 1980. *The Banking and Insurance Industries in London*. Greater London Council Central Policy Unit.

Williamson, Oliver. 1978. *Markets and Hierarchies: Analysis and Antitrust Implications*. West Drayton, Middlesex: Collier Macmillan.

———. 1980. "Transaction Costs Economics: The Governance of Contractual Relations." *Journal of Law and Economics* 22(2): 233–61.

Wilson, P.E.B., and J. Stanworth. 1985. *Black Business in Brent*. London: Small Business Research Trust.

Wilson, W. J. 1987. *The Truly Disadvantaged: The Inner City, the Underclass and Public Policy*. Chicago: University of Chicago Press.

Winder, Robert. 1986. "France: Le Big Bang." *Euromoney*, January supplement, *Euromarkets 1986: Rough Ride Ahead*, 44–58.

Wood, P. and P. N. O'Farrell. 1999. "Formations of Strategic Alliances in Business Services: Towards a new client-oriented conceptual framework." *Services Industries Journal* 19: 133–151.

Wood, P. A. 1984. "The Regional Significance of Manufacturing-Service Sector Links: Some Thoughts on the Revival of London's Docklands." In B. M. Barr and N. M. Waters, eds., *Regional Diversification and Structural Change*. BC Geographical Series. Vancouver: Tantalus Research.

———. 1987. "Producer Services and Economic Change: U.K. Reflections on Canadian Evidence." In K. Chapman and G. Humphry, eds., *Technological Change and Industrial Policy*. London: Blackwell.

———. 1996. "Business services, the management of change and regional development in the UK: a corporate client perspective." In *Trans-Institutional British Geography*, vol. 21: pp. 649–665.

———. 2000. "Change, culture and the role of consultancies in corporate restructuring: Regional implications in the UK." Paper presented to international workshop: *The Firm in Ecological Geography*, University of Portsmith, March 9–11, 2000.

Wood, P. A., J. Bryson, and D. Keeble. 1993. "Regional patterns of small firm development in the business services: evidence from the UK." *Environment and Planning*, vol. 25: 677–700.

Wood, P. R. 1997. *Maps of World Financial Law*. London: Allen & Overy.

World Bank. 1980. *World Tables, 1980*. Baltimore: John Hopkins University Press.

———. 1988. *World Development Report, 1988*. Washington, D.C.: World Bank.

———. 1998. *World Development Report, 1998*. Washington, D.C.: World Bank.

———. 2000. *Global Economic Prospects 2000*.

Yamaguchi Fighting Group and Supporting Group. 1988. "Show The Anger!" July 10. Pamphlet. Japan.

Yamaguchi, Takashi. 1979. "Japan's Urban System—An Overview." *Proceedings, Department of Humanities, University of Tokyo* 69: 1–15.

Yeung, Yue-man. 1996. "An Asian Perspective on the Global City." *International Social Science Journal* 147: 25–32.

Yoshihara, Kunio. 1982. *Shogo Shosha: The Vanguard of the Japanese Economy*. New York: Oxford University Press.

Zach, C. 1995. "Exporting English Know-How." In *International Financial Law Review* December: 31–34.

Zaloom, Caitlin. 2001. "Risk, Reason, and Technology: Trading futures in the Pits and on the Screen." (Unpublished Dissertation, Department of Anthropology, University of California Berkeley).

Zukin, S. 1982. *Loft Living, Culture and Capital in Urban Change*. Baltimore: Johns Hopkins University Press.

Index

Page references followed by *t* indicate tables.

Abercrombie's Greater London Plan (1944), 258

Abu-Lughod, Janet, 157, 160

accounting services: declining representation in cities of, 169; development/growth of, 98–99; networks of, 105; SMEs, 145–46

advertising services: declining representation in cities of, 169; networks of, 105

African Americans: New York social geography and, 265; as part of NYC workforce, 306. *See also* minority groups

agglomeration economy: capital mobility and, 24–32; of large urban centers, 104–5; location growth and, 101–10; new coordination of, 5, 33–34; of new production types, 24; telecommunication/information technologies and, 19, 34–35

Allen, J., 143

American Stock Exchange, 121

America's Global Cities (Abu-Lughod), 157

apparel industry: informal economy of NYC, 296, 298; Japanese, 219; London, 301

Asian workforce (London), 308–14

Atlanta, location quotients for, 151*t*

Attali, Jacques, 95

auto manufacturing decentralization, 27–28

backbone capacity, 115–16*t*

Balance of Payments Manual (IMF), 38

banking industry. *See* transnational banks

basic vs. nonbasic industries model, 253

Bell, Daniel, 5, 9, 93, 94, 253

Black workforce (London), 308–14

blue-collar jobs: in London, 275; in Manhattan, 266

Bluestone, Barry, 226, 245

Blumenfeld, H., 253

Boston: location quotients for, 151*t*; producer services earnings in, 247

Bretton Woods agreement (1945), 3, 24, 188

Brint, Steven, 264, 265, 271

British Telecom, 71

Bryson, J. R., 107, 145, 146

Buck, N., 211

Budd, Leslie, 113, 114

Bureau of Economic Analysis of the Department of Commerce (U.S.), 38

Cambridge (UK), 103

Canadian earnings distributions, 224

capital mobility: agglomeration economy and, 24–32; components of, 23–24, 172–73; impact on domestic autonomy by, 79, 83; labor market formation and, 32–34; locational dimensions of, 23, 172; transnationalization of corporate ownership and, 26–28*t*.. *See also* currency

Castells, Manuel, 95, 96, 109, 349

casual labor market. *See* informal/casual labor market

CBD employment (Japan), 220–21

central functions, 120–21, 171

centralization: decline in UK firm, 106–7; spatial dispersion of economic activities and, 19; spatial dispersion of financial, 122–25. *See also* location patterns

Chicago: business/engineering/management services employment in, 228*t*; comparing FIRE sector of NY and, 155–56*t*, 161*t*; comparing selected employment in NY and, 156*t*; comparison of law firms in LA/NY and, 154–55; declining share of global futures market, 160–61; IT employment in, 158*t*–59*t*; location quotients for, 151*t*, 152*t*–53*t*; ongoing transformation of, 157, 160–62; producer services earnings in, 247; share of producer services employment in, 148–49*t*

Chicago Board Options Exchange, 121

Christaller, Walter, 101
cities: concentration of high-income work-
    ers in, 286; consequences of global
    economy for, 343–44; de-nationalized
    financial center function of, 87–88; dis-
    tinction between global city and, 350–
    51; division of functions vs. competition
    between, 357–58; earnings inequality
    between, 221–29; earnings inequality
    between global cities and, 246–49;
    identification/measurement as global,
    354–55; impact of economy transforma-
    tion on, 128; institutional investment in
    equities by region for, 178t; literature on
    conditions for growth of, 127–28; new
    four functions of, 3–4; ranked by insti-
    tutional equity holdings, 177t; ranked by
    insurer assets, 186t; role in globalization
    of manufacturing by, 344; social geogra-
    phy patterns of, 256–62; top-ranked
    headquarters rankings of, 108, 109t. See
    also global city model; social order
City of London: employment distribution
    by industry in, 213t–14; foreign owner-
    ship of real estate in, 194t; property
    market of, 192–94; real estate
    ownership/occupation in, 194t; salaries
    of professionals in, 271; urban decline
    of, 259. See also London
Clark, Colin, 93
class polarization. See spatial/class
    polarization
clerical jobs: decline of Manhattan, 262–
    63; in London, 275
Cleveland, producer services earnings in,
    247
Coe, N., 145
Cohen, Stephen S., 334
The Coming of Post-Industrial Society
    (Bell), 9
competition: city division of functions vs.,
    357–58; financial system collaboration
    and, 174; global city-region construct of,
    352–53; specialization due to growing,
    100
concentration. See locational concentration
consumer services: industrialization of,
    29–30; population distribution and,
    101
consumption structure: economic inequal-
    ity impact on, 284–88; high-income

workers and, 285–86; technology and
    separation of production and, 105–6
corporations. See TNCs (transnational
    corporations)
credit rating services: agencies, 121n.15;
    NYC collection and, 153
Cross, M., 236, 245
cross-border transactions. See international
    transactions
Crozier, Michel, 93
currency: key international, 187–90; re-
    valuation of yen, 279n.17. See also capi-
    tal mobility

Daniels, P. W., 101, 107, 145, 146
datums, 120
debt: financing instruments of, 73t, 83–84;
    financing of, 11, 68–74t; leading curren-
    cies of international, 189t
decentralization: of auto manufacturing,
    27–28; impact on employment by, 25
DeFreitas, Gregory, 308
deinstitutionalization, 268
Delaunay, Jean Claude, 94, 95
deprivation index (1984), 277
deregulation: financial market integration
    following, 118, 119; global market
    formation due to, 92; producer/
    manufacturing services role by, 91–92;
    specialization due to, 100–101; of To-
    kyo financial system, 174
Detroit: location quotients for, 151t; pro-
    ducer services earnings in, 247
developed countries: FDI in developing
    (1960–1998) from, 39t, 44t; immigra-
    tion and informal economy of, 291;
    world services trade by, 49–55, 50t–52t,
    53t, 54t, 55t
developing countries: external debt/debt
    service (1991–1999) in, 75t; FDI
    (1960–1998) from developed to, 39t,
    44t; Japanese offshore production in,
    219; literature on informal sector of,
    290–91; world services trade by, 50t–
    52t
dispersion. See spatial dispersion of eco-
    nomic activities
Djellal, F., 116
Drennan, Matthew P., 246, 247, 249
Dunford, Mick, 278
Dutka, A. B., 105

E*Trade, 120
earnings: distribution in selected OECD
countries, 222*t*; of female/youth vs.
white males, 224, 226; growth in NY,
229*t*–34; growth in U.S., 229*t*; hourly
wages of NYC, 231*t*–32, 233*t*, 234; institutionalization of family wage, 291–
92; link between technology-induced
skill demand and, 225; of London
professionals/managers, 271; NYC median occupation/industry hourly wage,
231*t*; overview of London and UK,
234–40*t*, 236*t*, 237*t*, 238*t*, 239*t*, 241*t*;
overview of Tokyo employment, 240–
44, 242*t*; underground economy unregistered, 294. *See also* income levels; low-
wage jobs
earnings inequality: among OECD countries, 233; between cities, 221–29; earnings polarization distinguished from,
244–46; gender differences and, 224,
226, 238*t*, 239*t*, 241–44*t*; in global
cities vs. other cities, 246–49; issue of
interpretation in, 363; low-wage jobs
and, 224–25; New York social geography and, 265–66; studies on issues of,
244–49; in U.S./NYC/NY state, 230*t*
economic activities: immigrant community,
296; immigrants and expansion of informal, 290–91; performed in situ, 33; theoretical models on, 252–55. *See also*
spatial dispersion of economic activities;
underground economy
economic decline areas. *See* urban decline
economic development theory, 252–53
economic growth: centralizing functions of
telecommunications and, 336–37;
informalization/casualization of work
and, 288; low-wage job expansion as
function of, 9–10; new trends in, 255–
56; social orders from different types of,
255; specialization and, 96–101; theoretical models on, 252–55
economic order: basic vs. nonbasic industries model on, 253; economic development theory on, 252–53; from different
types of economic growth, 255; immigration in social geography and restructured, 321–23; postindustrial model on,
253–54; understanding global city, 5.
See also world economy

economic theoretical models, 252–55
electronic trading, 174–75
electronics firm organizations: three types
of, 104; vertical integration/
disintegration debate and, 102–4
Elliott, James R., 248, 249
"emerging market" (1990s), 69
The Employers Survey (1997), 114–15
employment: in business/engineering/
management services, 228*t*; growth of
UK information technology, 146–48;
high-income gentrification and, 285;
higher percentage of producer service,
130–31*t*; of immigrant workers, 33; impact of manufacturing decentralization
on, 25; law firms with outside country,
35*t*; low-wage, 9–10, 224–29, 248–49;
NY minority groups and low rates of,
270; producer service share of, 131*t*,
132*t*, 133*t*–34*t*, 135*t*–36*t*; rates of
NYC, 307*t*; types of underground economy, 299; UK/Japan/U.S. cities and
share of national, 141*t*–42*t*; in UK/
London by ethnic origin, 313*t*. *See also*
FIRE sector employment; labor market;
part-time employment; work structure
Euro, 188
Europe: locational patterns hypotheses applied to, 101–2; new forms of centrality
in, 124–25; property market in, 191*t*.
See also Germany; United Kingdom
Eurozone, 20

Fallick, B., 228
Family Expenditure Survey (UK), 273
family wage: changes in NYC metro area,
308*t*; institutionalization of, 291–92;
service industries and erosion of, 292.
See also earnings; income levels
FDI (foreign direct investment): as capital
relocation indicator, 37; changes in
global pattern of, 43; changes in sectoral
distribution of, 43; in context of cross-
border trade, 48–49, 52–53, 55–56;
from developed to developing countries
(1960–1998), 39*t*, 44*t*; distinguished
from other kinds of investment, 38; flow
by region (1986–1997) of, 39*t*; flow in
nine industrialized countries (1991–
1997), 40*t*; major patterns of, 37–43; in
producer services, 58–63; in service sec-

FDI (foreign direct investment) (*cont.*) tors, 56–58; U.S. services abroad, 60*t*. *See also* IMF (International Monetary Fund)

Fielding, A., 278

financial centers: backbone capacity of, 115–16*t*; cross-border networks of, 121–22; gateway functions of, 173–74; global cities as, 5, 12; growing importance of, 127; new forms of centrality and, 122–25; summary on order of, 355–58; trend towards consolidation of, 120–22. *See also* transnational banks

financial crises (1980s/1990s): indicators/consequences of major, 80*t*–82*t*; Mexican crisis (1994–1995), 67, 80*t*, 173; New York City crisis (1987), 80*t*; Russian default (1998), 21, 67, 82*t*; southeast Asian crisis (1997), 21, 78–79, 81*t*, 83; Third World debt crisis (1982), 31, 67, 72

financial industry: cross-border networks of, 121–22; economies of scale/scope in, 114; explanation for growth of, 10–13, 65–84; global city character and emerging, 6, 19; history of postwar growth in, 66–68; impact of financial crises on, 21, 31, 67, 72, 78–83; impact of international transactions on, 19–21; integration following deregulation of, 118, 119; international property market role by, 193–95; overview of analysis of, 355–58; security firms, 184*t*; spatial organization of, 110–22; U.S./Japanese budget deficits and growth of, 335–36. *See also* international financial transactions; transnational banks

financing instruments: development/utility of, 83–84; international capital market activity by, 73*t*; international capital market major, 73*t*

financing services: activity complex structure of, 114; expanding demand for specialized, 11; formation of international equity markets, 68–71; instruments used in, 73*t*, 83–84; organized around lenders and borrowers, 113–14; securitization, 71–74*t*; urbanization and localization economies of, 114–15

FIRE sector employment: comparing Chicago and NY, 155–56*t*; comparing NY

and Manhattan, 208–9, 232, 263; increase of NY (1950–1987), 206; limited growth of Tokyo, 215, 220; location quotients in NY/Chicago/LA of, 161*t*; locations of, 131; low-wage jobs in, 227; New York City's share of, 137–40, 139*t*, 149, 207; as percentage of London employment, 270–71

Firestone, 27

Fordism model, 253, 361

Fothergill, S., 211

Fourth Plan (Japan), 278

Frankfurt: growth as financial center, 174; property market in, 191*t*; TNCs headquarters in, 108

Friedmann, John, 171, 349

Fuchs, Victor, 93, 94

Gadrey, Jean, 94, 95

Galbraith, J. K., 93, 94

garment industry: London, 301; New York City, 296, 298

Garnick, D. H., 246

gateway functions (financial centers), 173–74

GATS (General Agreement on Trade in Services), 34, 46, 105

GATT (General Agreement on Tariffs and Trade), 46

GDP (gross domestic product): cross-border transactions percentage of, 118–19*t*; growing differentials in UK/London, 278; percentage of foreign investments in Japanese, 166

gender differences: in earnings, 224, 226; of Japanese professionals, 280; in London's minority workforce, 311; of Manhattan mangers/professionals, 263–64; part-time employment and, 289–90; in Tokyo employment earnings, 241–44*t*; UK/London weekly earnings and, 238*t*, 239*t*

General Household Survey data, 236

gentrification: described, 261; difference of new form of, 323; informal labor market and high-income, 296–97; labor intensive high-income, 285; in London, 273; in Manhattan, 266–67; in Tokyo, 279

Germany: export of producer services by, 59*t*; FDI patterns in, 40*t*–41*t*, 58; financial assets (1990–1997) of, 77*t*

global capital markets. *See* international capital markets

global city model: appearance of new, 4; competition vs. division of functions in, 357–58; debate over critiques of, 346–55; distinction between city and, 350–51; earnings inequality in cities vs., 246–49; economic polarization of, 9–10; financial industry transformation impact on, 6, 19; identification/measurement of, 354–55; incorporation of immigrants in, 322; new forms of centrality in, 122–25; as production service sites, 5–6, 359–61; relationship between nation-states and, 7, 8–9, 358; social connectivity/central functions of, 120–21; understanding economic order within, 5; world economy role by, 4–5. *See also* new urban regime

global city-region: competition structure in, 352–53; implications of, 350, 351–52

global control capability, 6–7

global futures market (Chicago), 160–61

global urban centers: agglomeration economy of, 104–5; impact of international services/finance on, 7–8; international property market of, 190–95; locational patterns of ITC firms in, 116; low-wage employment and hierarchy of, 248–49; rebuilding of, 124n.17, 191–92, 195; space economy of producer services and hierarchy of, 140–57

global urban systems: comparison of UK/U.S./Japanese, 129, 195–96; as coterminous with nation-states, 171; creation of new regime of, 329–44; developing networked system connecting, 172–75; expansion and concentration in, 175–87; globalization of economic activity and, 333; literature on city growth and, 127–28; low-wage employment and, 248–49; role of key currencies in, 187–90; space economy of producer services and, 149–57

globalization: critique on homogenization of, 346–47; introducing place-ness into notion of, 350; new territorialization of, 345; role of cities in manufacturing, 344; urban systems and economic activity, 333. *See also* global city model; transnationalism; world economy

gold standard (prewar), 76–78

Gordon, I., 137, 211, 226

Gottschalk, P., 223

Great Britain. *See* United Kingdom

Greater London Council (UK), 300

Green Belt (London), 258

Greenfield, H. I., 96, 99

Gudgin, G., 211

Hall, Peter, 171

Hamnett, C., 236, 245

Hanseatic League, 4, 170

Harris, Richard, 261

Harrison, Bennett, 226, 245

Harvey, David, 350

high-level workers. *See* professionals/managers

Hill, T. P., 93

Hispanics: New York social geography and, 264–65; as part of NYC workforce, 306. *See also* minority groups

Hitachi, 27

homeless: Manhattan, 268–69; Tokyo, 281

homework: London, 301; New York City, 298

Hong Kong, 174

Hoover, Edgad M., 205

hourly wages (NCY occupation/industry), 231t–32, 233t, 234

housing: City of London ownership/occupation of, 194t; difficulties of securing Tokyo, 280–81; gentrification of Manhattan, 266, 267, 269–70; high-income gentrification renovation of, 285; informal labor market and gentrification of, 296–97; London IT workers and patterns of, 273–75; rising prices of London, 273; Tokyo's inner-city decline in, 283

Houston location quotients, 151t

Howell, D. R., 225

Hurstfield, Jennifer, 302

IMF (International Monetary Fund): bailouts by, 79; FDI guidelines by, 37–38. *See also* FDI (foreign direct investment)

immigrant workers/communities: economic restructuring/social geography and, 321–23; incorporated into global cities, 322; informal economy and, 295–96; Japan and new illegal, 314–21; Japa-

immigrant workers/communities (*cont.*)
    nese daily laborers from, 304–5; Japa-
    nese government policies on, 318–20;
    London workforce of, 308–14; neigh-
    borhood subeconomy of, 296; NYC's
    minority and, 306–8; role in global la-
    bor market by, 305–6. *See also* migration
    patterns; minority groups
income levels: changes in average NYC
    family, 308*t*; consumption patterns and,
    285–86; from London employment,
    234–40*t*, 236*t*, 237*t*, 238*t*, 239*t*, 241*t*;
    of London IT workers, 273–75; of Lon-
    don professionals/managers, 272–73; of
    London's ethnic group, 312–13*t*; Man-
    hattan declines in household, 267–68;
    service job concentration and high,
    269*11*; social inequality reflected by
    London's, 277–78. *See also* earnings
industrialized countries. *See* developed
    countries
industry: substantive nature of, 358; theo-
    retical perspectives on social order and,
    252–56. *See also* financial industry; ser-
    vice sector
industry (Japan): apparel and textile, 219;
    changes in employment by, 133*t*; em-
    ployment distribution by, 221*t*; location
    quotients of, 164*t*; promotion of Osaka,
    217; Tokyo employment changes by,
    133*t*, 222*t*; Tokyo employment distribu-
    tion of manufacturing/service, 203*t*
industry (UK): Cambridge organization of,
    103; changes in London employment by,
    133*t*, 211–12*t*; City of London employ-
    ment distribution by, 213*t*–14; employ-
    ment changes by, 133*t*; employment
    distribution by, 213*t*–14; London
    employment distribution by
    manufacturing/service, 203*t*, 213*t*–14
industry (U.S.): change in Manhattan em-
    ployment by, 207*t*; employment changes
    by, 132*t*; Manhattan employment distri-
    bution by, 208*t*; NCY hourly wage by,
    231*t*–32, 233*t*, 234; NYC employment
    change by, 132*t*; NYC hourly wages by,
    231*t*–32, 233*t*, 234; NYC median
    hourly wage by, 231*t*; Silicon Valley or-
    ganization of, 103
informal/casual labor market: in London,
    300–302; in New York, 294–300; over-

view of expanding, 289–94; in Tokyo,
    302–5. *See also* underground economy
information, 120–21
information society notion, 95
insurance services assets, 186*t*
international capital markets: compared to
    prewar gold standard, 76–78; current
    state of, 74–78; financing instruments
    used by, 73*t*; main borrowers (1984–
    1997) by, 74*t*
international currency, 187–90
international equity markets, 68–71
international financial transactions: cross-
    border networks and, 121–22; emerging
    patterns of, 21; impact on financial in-
    dustry by, 19–21; limitations/durability
    of, 20; networked systems for, 172–75;
    as percentage of GDP, 118–19*t*; types of
    complexity created by, 173. *See also* fi-
    nancial industry; transnationalism
international property market, 190–95
international transactions: characteristics of
    service sector in, 45–48; defining nature
    of service, 48–49, 52–53, 55–56; forma-
    tion of equity market, 68–71; leading
    currencies in, 187–90; mergers and ac-
    quisitions (M&As), 43, 44*t*, 45*t*, 67. *See
    also* transnationalism
interpretation/evaluation/judgment, 120–
    21
IT (information technology): Chicago/
    NY/LA employment in, 158*t*–59*t*;
    growing London region, 146–48; im-
    pact on agglomeration by, 19; impact on
    service demands by, 95–96; income/
    residential patterns of London, 273–
    75
ITC (information technology consultancy)
    firms, 116
Iyotani, Toshio, 320

Japan: auto manufacturing restructuring
    by, 27–28; bank foreign liabilities/assets
    in U.S./UK and, 185*t*; comparing loca-
    tional concentration of UK/U.S. and,
    148–57, 167–70; comparison of urban
    systems of UK/U.S. and, 129, 195–96;
    equity market expansion by, 70–71; ex-
    port of producer services by, 59*t*; FDI
    patterns in, 40*t*–44*t*; FDI in U.S. service
    sector by, 56–57*t*; financial assets

(1990–1997) of, 77*t*; financial industry growth and budget deficits of, 335–36; funds raised through bonds by, 75*t*; global role by yen currency of, 188–89; government policies on immigrant workforce in, 318–20; investment in telecommunications by, 336–37; labor migration to, 33–34; location quotients of financial/service industries in, 164*t*; new illegal immigration to, 314–21; population growth of foreigners in, 317*t*; potential world share of producer services by, 179; service sector trade by U.S. vs., 55*t*–56; stock market capitalization in, 69–70; three non-Japanese nationality groups in, 315*t*–16*t*; U.S. services trade with, 61*t*; world services trade by, 49–55, 50*t*–52*t*, 53*t*, 54*t*, 55*t*; yen revaluation of, 279n.17. *See also* Tokyo

Japanese employment: changes by industry, 133*t*; distribution (1975–1995) of, 220*t*; employment distribution by industry, 221*t*; national share of major cities of, 142*t*; new illegal immigration and, 314–21; selected cities' producer services, 162*t*–67; share of selected producer services, 134*t*

Japanese hiring halls, 303–4

Japanese "intelligent buildings," 336–37

Kanto industrial area, 217–18

Katouzian, Homa, 96

Kawasaki industrial complex, 217

key international currency, 187–90

Klosterman, R. C., 245

Labor Force Survey (1981), 310

labor market: basic vs. nonbasic industries model on, 253; capital mobility and formation of, 32–34; causal and informal, 289–305; economic development theory on, 253–54; Fordism, 253, 361; forms of production in, 287–88; illegal immigration and segmentation of Japanese, 320–21; male-dominated "labor aristocracy" in, 291–92; migration of Japanese, 33–34; patterns of Tokyo population migration, 215–16, 259–60; postindustrial model on, 253–54; race/nationality in the, 305–23; social geog-

raphy component of, 256–62. *See also* employment; work structure

law firms: comparison of NY/LA/Chicago, 154–55; decline of representation in cities of, 169; with foreign branches, 154*t*; outside home country lawyers rankings of, 35*t*

Levitt, Theodore, 29

Levy, Frank, 224

locational concentration: comparing UK/U.S./Japan's, 148–57; global urban system expansion and, 175–87; growing UK IT employment, 146–48; of producer services, 104–5; of UK producer service employment, 137

locational patterns: of domestic financial services, 113–17; of ITC firms, 116; of Japanese producer services, 162*t*–67; literature on, 101–2; summary of U.S./UK/Japanese producer services and, 167–70; trends in producer service, 130–40; vertical integration/disintegration debate on, 102–4. *See also* capital mobility; spatial dispersion of economic activities; spatial organization of finance services

Logan, John, 265

London: banks located in, 183–84, 183*t*; concentrated poverty/disadvantaged areas of, 275–78; deprivation index (1984) on areas of, 277; economic history since 1960 of, 209–14; as financial center, 5, 12; loss of manufacturing services in, 209–11; producer services concentrated around, 106–7, 137; producer services location quotients in, 1, 135*t*, 136*t*; as production site, 6; property market in, 190, 191*t*, 193; real estate ownership in, 194*t*; rising housing prices in, 273; security firms in, 184*t*; share of FIRE/business services in, 138–40, 139*t*; social geography of, 270–78; spatial structure of financial services in, 113; TNCs headquarters in, 108, 109*t*; unemployment rates in, 301–2; urban development in NYC/London and, 257–60. *See also* City of London; United Kingdom

London employment: Black/Asian workforce and, 308–14; changes by industry, 133*t*, 211–12*t*; distribution of

London employment (*cont.*)
manufacturing/service industries, 203*t*,
213*t*–14; earnings/income from, 234–
40*t*, 236*t*, 237*t*, 238*t*, 239*t*, 241*t*; Employers Survey (1997) findings on, 114–
15; growth of IT, 146–48; income levels
of IT, 273–75; informal labor market of,
300–302; national share of, 141*t*–45;
part-time, 300–301; percentage of
FIRE, 270–71; population and 1977,
1985, 1998, 201–2*t*; of professionals/
managers, 271–72; share of selected
producer services, 134*t*, 135*t*

Los Angeles: business/engineering/
management services employment in,
228*t*; comparison of law firms in LA/
Chicago and, 154–55; FIRE location
quotients in, 161*t*; IT employment in,
158*t*–59*t*; location quotients for, 151*t*,
152*t*–53*t*

Low Pay Unit (UK), 300

low-wage jobs: debate over increasing
trends in, 226–29; expansion as function
of economic growth, 9–10; generated by
producer services, 286–88; growing
earnings inequality and, 224–25; OECD
and inequality of, 227–28; urban hierarchy linked to, 248–49. *See also* earnings; employment

M&As (mergers and acquisitions): increases of TNCs due to, 107; increasing
rate of international, 43, 44*t*, 45*t*, 67

McDowell, Linda, 272

Machimura, Takashi, 243, 244

Machlup, F., 95

male "labor aristocracy," 291–92

Manhattan: gender differences among professionals of, 263–64; gentrification of,
266, 267, 269–70; homeless in, 268–
69; location quotient of blue-collar jobs,
266; residential patterns of, 263. *See also*
New York City

Manhattan employment: change by industry, 207*t*; comparing FIRE NY employment, 208–9, 232, 263; decline of
clerical, 262–63; employment distribution by industry, 208*t*. *See also* New York
City employment

manufacturing services: Chicago's loss of,
157; decentralizaton (1980s) of, 25–26;

deregulation role in, 91–92; growth and
specialization of, 96–101; hourly wages
for NCY, 231*t*; immigrant communities
and, 296; informal labor market and
NYC, 297; location patterns of, 106–7;
loss of London, 209–11; New York City
employment in, 204–9; producer services and internationalization of, 48–49,
334–35; recomposition of Tokyo's,
216–21; role of cities in globalization of,
344; transnationalization of corporate,
26–28*t*

Marshall, J. N., 96, 106, 143, 144

Marx, Karl, 33

Mexican crisis (1994–1995), 67, 80*t*,
173

migration patterns: expansion of informal
economy and, 291; Japanese labor force
and, 33–34; suburbanization, 259–60,
262–63; Tokyo labor market and, 215–
16, 259–60. *See also* immigrant
workers/communities

minority groups: London's concentration
of, 275–76, 308–14; Manhattan professionals and, 264–65; New York social
geography and, 265; NYC's workforce
of immigrants and, 306–8; population
projections for London's, 312*t*; three nationality groups of Japanese, 315*t*–16*t*;
Tokyo's social disadvantage and, 283–
84; unemployment rates of New York,
270, 307*t*–8. *See also* immigrant
workers/communities; racial/ethnicity
differences

Mollenkopf, John, 154

monthly earnings (Tokyo), 241–44, 242*t*

Moody's Industrials, 205, 206

moral hazard problem, 79

Moses, Robert, 258

Moulaert, F., 116

Murata, Kiyoji, 218

Murnane, R., 224

NAFTA, 34, 105

Nagoya, 162*t*, 164*t*, 166, 167

Nakabayashi, Itsuki, 282, 283, 284

NASDAQ, 120, 121–22, 175, 176

Nasdaq Japan, 122

nation-states: relationship between global
cities and, 7, 8–9, 358; urban systems as
coterminous with, 171

National Association of Securities Dealers, 121

National Capital Region Development Plan of 1963 (Tokyo), 258

National Capital Region Development Plan of 1968 (Tokyo), 258–59

National Economic Development Office (NEDO), 290

National Land Agency survey (Tokyo), 166

National Steel Corporation, 27

networks: accounting and advertising services, 105; cross-border financial center, 121–22; development of global urban, 172–75. *See also* telecommunications technology

New Earnings Survey data (UK), 234, 235, 237

The New Industrial State (Galbraith), 93

new urban regime: conditions leading to, 329–34; consequences for cities of, 343–44; examining durability of, 334–37; impact on social order by, 337–43. *See also* global city model

New York City: backbone capacity of, 115–16*t*; banks located in, 183–84, 183*t*; comparison of law firms in LA/Chicago and, 154–55; economic history since 1960 of, 204–9; as financial center, 5, 12; four classifications of professionals/managers, 264–65; growth in earnings in, 229*t*–34; location quotients for, 151*t*, 152*t*–53*t*; migration to suburbs from, 259; producer services location quotients in, 135*t*, 136*t*; as production site, 6; property market in, 190, 191*t*; security firms in, 184*t*; social geography of, 262–70; TNCs headquarters in, 108, 109*t*; urban development in London/Tokyo and, 257–60. *See also* Manhattan; United States

New York City crisis (1987), 80*t*

New York City employment: business/engineering/management services, 228*t*; changes by industry in, 132*t*; comparing Manhattan and, 208–9, 232; comparing selected Chicago and, 156*t*; history since 1960 of, 204–9; hourly wages by occupation/industry, 231*t*–32, 233*t*, 234; informalization of, 294–300; IT in, 158*t*–59*t*; rates of underemployment and, 307*t*; share of FIRE/business,

137–40, 139*t*, 149, 161*t*, 207; share of selected producer services, 134*t*, 135*t*. *See also* Manhattan employment

New York State employment, 230*t*

Noyelle, Thierry, 105, 248

occupation: NYC hourly wages by, 231*t*–32, 233*t*, 234; UK/London weekly earnings by, 238*t*, 239*t*. *See also* professionals/managers

October crash (1987), 67–68

OECD countries: benchmark definition of FDI by, 38; earnings distributions in selected, 222*t*; earnings inequality among, 223; institutional low-wage limitations in, 227–28; part-time employment in, 290

office work dispersal patterns, 28–29

OPEC cartel prices, 66–67

Osaka, 162*t*, 164*t*, 165, 166, 182, 217

Pacific Exchange, 121

Parker, A. J., 95

Parr, J., 113, 114

part-time employment: growth of service jobs and, 289–90, 291–92, 293; of Japanese female professionals, 280; in London, 300–302; Tokyo's daily laborers as, 302–5; United States legislation on, 302

place-ness notion, 350

population distribution: consumer services and, 101; deprivation index (1984) on London's, 277; Japanese labor force and migration of, 33–34; of non-Japanese minority groups, 315*t*–16*t*, 317*t*; projections of London's ethnic group, 312*t*; suburbanization migration and, 259–60, 262–63; Tokyo labor market and migration, 215–16, 259–60

Porat, Marc U., 95

postindustrial model, 253–54

producer services: capital mobility and increased, 24; central places and specialization of, 101–2; changing modes and demands of, 95; defining, 91; deregulation role in, 91–92; economy supply capacity of, 90–91; eight top exporters of, 59*t*; employment share of, 131*t*, 132*t*, 133*t*–34*t*, 135*t*–36*t*; explanation for rapid growth of, 10–13; global city as

producer services (*cont.*)
sites for, 5–6, 359–61; growth and specialization of, 96–101; increase of To-kyo, 219–21; international transactions/ FDI in, 58–63; internationalization of manufacturing and, 48–49, 334–35; labor market and reorganization of, 32–34; location trends for, 130–40; locational concentration of, 104–5; low-wage/high-income employment generated by, 286–88; spatial/concentration patterns of, 167–70, 330–33, 359–61; TNCs and growth of, 97–100; UK regionalized mode of, 143–44
professionals/managers: consumption patterns of high-income, 285–86; four category classifications of, 264–65; gender differences in Manhattan, 263–64; growing need for Japanese, 280; London, 271–73; producer services generating demand for, 286–88. *See also* occupation; workers
Promotion of Replacement of Industry Act of 1952 (Japan), 217
property market: international, 190–95; Manhattan low-rent housing, 267–68, 269. *See also* housing; real estate ownership
Public Use Microdata Samples (PUMS), 248

racial/ethnicity differences: labor market and, 305–23; in London income levels, 312–13*t*; of Manhattan professionals, 264–65; New York social geography and, 265. *See also* minority groups
real estate ownership, 193–95, 194*t. See also* housing; property market
Restriction of Industry and Others Act of 1959 (Japan), 217
Rimmer, P. J., 166, 179
risk management, 121n.16
Russian crisis (1998), 21, 67, 82*t*

San Francisco, location quotients for, 151*t*
Sassen, Saskia, 34
Scott, Allen J., 352
securitization of finance, 71–74*t*
security firms, 184*t*
service sector: changing FDI in, 43; characteristics of cross-border, 45–48; com-parison of Japan/U.S. trade in, 55*t*–56; defining cross-border trade in, 48–49, 52–53, 55–56; demand induced/supply critical, 96; FDI in, 56–58; growth and specialization of, 96–101; impact of information technology on, 95–96; international transactions in, 44–48; part-time jobs and growth of, 289–90; production mode changes and, 95; Stigler's classic study on, 99; traditional scholarship on, 92–95; transformed work structure and demands on, 94–95; U.S./Japanese investment in, 56–57*t. See also* manufacturing services; producer services
"Silicon Valley" (U.S.), 103
Singelmann, J., 94
Smeeding, T., 223
SMEs (small-medium-sized enterprises), 145–46
Smith, N., 261
social connectivity, 120–21
social geography: comparing Tokyo's with NY/London, 278, 279, 280; immigration in economic restructuring and, 321–23; of London and region, 270–78; overview of New York's, 262–70; overview of Tokyo's, 278–81; patterns of city, 256–62; of Tokyo's inner city, 281–84
social order: casual/informal labor markets and, 289–305; consumption and inequality of, 284–88; consumption structure and, 284–88; new industrial complex transformation of, 337–43; overview of spatial polarization and, 361–63; race/nationality in labor market and, 305–23; social geography component of, 256–84
southeast Asian crisis (1997), 21, 78–79, 81*t*, 83
spatial dispersion of economic activities: centralization due to, 19; impact of technology on, 108–10; labor market reformation from, 32–34; of manufacturing, 25–28; of office work organization, 28–29; of production, 167–70, 330–33, 359–61; as redeployment of growth poles, 30; of retailing of consumer services, 29–30. *See also* economic activities; locational patterns

spatial organization of finance services: digital era, 117–22; domestic location patterns of, 113–17; new forms of centrality and, 122–25; transformation and emerging, 110–12

spatial/class polarization: casual/informal labor markets and, 289–305; consumption structure and, 284–88; NY/London/Tokyo social geography and, 262–84; overview of critiques on, 361–63; race/nationality in labor market and, 305–23; social geography component of, 256–62

specialized services: central places and increase of, 102; classic Stigler study on, 99; expanding demand for, 11–12; growth of service sector and, 96–101

Stanback, Thomas M., Jr., 99, 248

state. *See* nation-states

Stigler, George, 99

Stock Exchange Year Book, 98

stock markets: capitalization in, 69–70; capitalization in leading, 176*t*; electronic trading of, 174–75; "emerging" (1990s), 69; foreign listings in major, 177*t*; Tokyo's, 175n.1–176

Stoffaes, C., 95

Storper, Michael, 23

suburbanization migration, 259–60, 262–63

supply critical services, 96

sweat work: London, 301; New York City, 298

Taylor, Peter J., 90

technology: impact on spatial organization of economy, 108–10; link unequal earnings and skills in, 225; production/consumption separation and, 105–6; spatial organization of finance and digital, 117–22. *See also* IT (information technology)

telecommunication technology: economic growth and centralizing functions of, 336–37; impact on agglomeration by, 19, 34–35; impact on Tokyo office density, 166; production/consumption separation and, 105–6; transborder data flows facilitated by, 47

Terasaka, Akinobu, 165, 166

textile industry: Japan, 219; London, 310

Third World debt crisis (1982), 31, 67, 72. *See also* developing countries

Thomson Financial, 176–77

Thrift, N., 272

Tiebout, C., 253

TNCs (transnational corporations): agglomeration and locational patterns of, 101–10; capital mobility and ownership of, 26–28*t*; foreign affiliates of domestic, 47–48; growth of producer services and, 97–100; headquarter locations of major, 108, 109*t*; international delivery of services role by, 29; M&As of, 43, 44*t*, 45*t*, 67; parent/foreign affiliates (1990–1998) of, 62*t*–63

Tokyo: banks located in, 183–84, 183*t*; changing transnational control areas of, 187; deregulation and available capital in, 174; economic history since 1960 of, 214–21; as financial center, 5, 12; as global banking center, 182; impact of telecommunications capability on, 166; inner city of, 281–84; labor market and population patterns, 215–16, 259–60; location quotients of financial/service industries in, 164*t*; producer services location quotients in, 136*t*, 162*t*–67; as production site, 6; property market in, 190, 191*t*; re-positioned as capital exporter, 21; recomposition of manufacturing services in, 216–21; security firms in, 184*t*; share of FIRE/business services in, 138–40, 139*t*; social geography of, 278–81; TNCs headquarters in, 108, 109*t*; urban development in NYC/London and, 257–60. *See also* Japan

Tokyo employment: changes by industry, 133*t*, 222*t*; distribution by industry, 220–21*t*; distribution of manufacturing/service industries, 203*t*; earnings of, 240–44, 242*t*; impact of population patterns on, 215–16; of part-time daily laborers, 302–5; population and 1977, 1985, 1998, 201–2*t*; share of selected producer services, 134*t*

Tokyo Metropolitan Region, 278

Tokyo's stock market, 175n.1–176

Touraine, Alain, 93

Townsend, A., 145

transnational banks: capital mobility impact on U.S., 24–25; declining representation

transnational banks (*cont.*)
in cities of, 169; global ranking of largest centers of, 179, 180*t*–81*t*, 182; historic financial dominance by, 7; in NY/London/Tokyo, 182–84, 183*t*; postwar development of, 66–68; transition of U.S., 3; U.S. location quotients for, 150, 151*t*–52*t*; U.S./UK/Japan foreign liabilities/assets of, 185*t*. *See also* financial industry

transnationalism: of capital markets, 74–78; changing areas of Tokyo, 187; of equity markets, 68–71; impact on cities of, 128; process of ownership and acquisitions, 196; of producer and manufacturing services, 48–49, 334–35; of property market, 190–95. *See also* globalization

Tsuda, T., 316

UN Centre on Transnational Corporations, 46

underground economy: described, 290–91; patterns of New York, 294–300; types of firms involved with, 298–99; types of jobs as part of, 299; unregistered income of, 294. *See also* informal/casual labor market

unemployment rates: of London, 301–2; of NY minority groups, 270, 307*t*–8

"Union of Daily Workers" (Japan), 304–5

United Kingdom: bank foreign liabilities/assets in U.S./Japan and, 185*t*; comparing locational concentration of U.S./Japan and, 148–57, 167–70; comparison of urban systems of U.S./Japanese and, 129, 195–96; concentration of producer service employment in, 137; earnings of London and, 234–40*t*, 236*t*, 237*t*, 238*t*, 239*t*, 241*t*; employment by ethnic origin in, 313*t*; employment changes by industry, 133*t*; employment distribution by industry in, 213*t*–14; employment share of selected producer services, 134*t*; equity market expansion by, 70–71; export of producer services by, 59*t*; FDI patterns in, 40*t*–44*t*, 58; financial assets (1990–1997) of, 77*t*; funds raised through bonds by, 75*t*; growth of accounting services in, 98; growth of IT employment in, 146–48; international equity market and, 70–71;

national employment share of major cities in, 141*t*; stock market capitalization in, 69–70; U.S. services trade with, 61*t*; world services trade by, 50*t*. *See also* London

United States: bank foreign liabilities/assets in UK/Japan and, 185*t*; business/engineering/management services employment in, 228*t*; comparing locational concentration of UK/Japan and, 148–57, 167–70; comparison of urban systems of UK/Japanese and, 129, 195–96; employment changes by industry in, 132*t*; employment share of selected producer services, 134*t*; equity market expansion by, 70–71; export of producer services by, 59*t*; FDI flows in services abroad by, 60*t*; FDI in Japanese service sector by, 56–57*t*; FDI patterns in, 40*t*–44*t*; financial assets (1990–1997) of, 77*t*; financial industry growth and budget deficits of, 335–36; funds raised through bonds by, 75*t*; growth in earnings in, 229*t*; growth in employment/producer service employment in, 131*t*; immigration in economic restructuring/social geography of, 321–22; Japanese-affiliated manufacturing plants in, 27; legislation on part-time workers, 302; national employment share of major cities of, 142*t*; rebuilding of neglected urban areas in, 124n.17, 191–92, 195; service sector trade by Japan vs., 55*t*–56; services trade with Japan, UK by, 61*t*; stock market capitalization in, 69–70; unequal earnings distributions in, 223–26; world services trade by, 49–55, 50*t*–52*t*, 53*t*, 54*t*, 55*t*. *See also* New York City

urban decline: City of London, 259; conditions contributing to, 13; of London areas, 273; Tokyo's inner city, 282–84

urban development: comparison of London/Tokyo/NYC, 257–60; locational concentration and global, 175–87

urban hierarchies. *See* global urban systems

urban redevelopment: in central Tokyo, 279; of London areas, 273; Manhattan,

266, 267, 269–70; projects of, 124n.17, 191–92, 195. *See also* gentrification
U.S. transnational banks: capital mobility impact on, 24–25; transition of, 3
utility, 84

Vernon, Raymond, 205

wages. *See* earnings; income levels
Walker, David, 23
Weber, Max, 4, 5
weekly earnings (London/UK), 236*t*, 237*t*, 238*t*, 239*t*, 240*t*
Williams, P., 261, 272
Wolff, Goetz, 171, 349
women. *See* gender differences
Wood, Peter, 143
work structure: consumption patterns and high-income, 285–86; economic growth and informalization/casualization of, 288; flexible arrangements of, 289; informationalization of NYC, 294–300; institutionalized family wage and gender-based, 291–92; overview of casual/informal, 289–94; service demands and transformed, 95–96. *See also* employment; labor market

workers: capital mobility and new mobility of, 33–34; changing availability of Tokyo's, 215–16; dispersion impact on empowerment of, 32–33; earnings of female/youth vs. white male, 224, 226; employment of immigrant, 33; impact of manufacturing decentralization on, 25; professional/managerial, 263–65, 271–73, 280, 285–88. *See also* earnings; employment; immigrant workers/communities
The World Cities (Hall), 171
"world city" concept, 349
world economy: impact of increased capital mobility on, 24; international transactions and conditions of, 19–20; material practices characterizing, 25–32; role of global cities in, 4–5; services trade in, 49–55, 50*t*–52*t*, 53*t*, 54*t*, 55*t*; spatial/integrated duality of, 3; technology impact on spatial organization of, 108–10. *See also* globalization

yen revaluation, 279n.17
Young, K., 211

Zysman, John, 334